THE VERNEYS

By the same author

Historic Houses of the National Trust
Country Houses from the Air
Life in the English Country Cottage
Visions of Power: Ambition and Architecture
The Polite Tourist: A History of Country House Visiting
The Arts & Crafts House
His Invention So Fertile: A Life of Christopher Wren
By Permission of Heaven: The Story of the Great Fire of London

THE VERNEYS

A true story of love, war and madness in
seventeenth-century England

Adrian Tinniswood

Jonathan Cape
London

Published by Jonathan Cape in 2007

2 4 6 8 10 9 7 5 3 1

First published in Great Britain in 2007 by
Jonathan Cape
Random House, 20 Vauxhall Bridge Road,
London SW1V 2SA

www.randomhouse.co.uk

Addresses for companies within The Random House Group Limited
can be found at www.randomhouse.co.uk/offices.htm

The Random House Group Limited Reg. No. 954009

A CIP catalogue record for this book is available from the British Library

ISBN 9780224072557

The Random House Group Limited makes every effort to ensure that
the papers used in its books are made from trees that have been legally
sourced from well-managed and credibly certified forests.
Our paper procurement policy can be found at
www.randomhouse.co.uk/paper.htm

Typeset by Palimpsest Book Production Limited,
Grangemouth, Stirlingshire
Printed and bound in Great Britain by
William Clowes Ltd, Beccles, Suffolk

To Bridgefort
For making me welcome

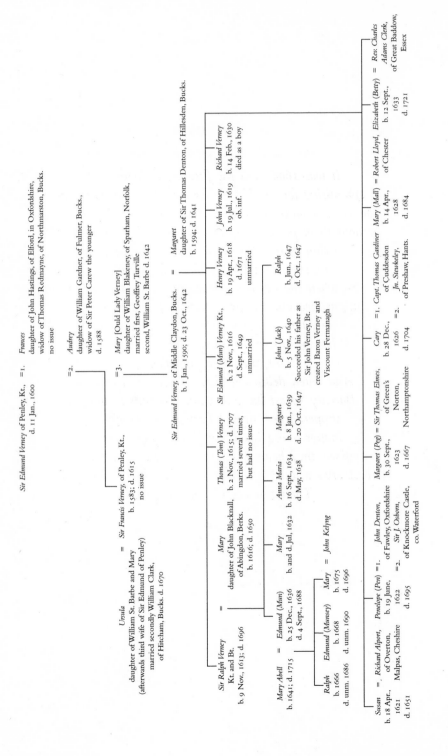

Sir Edmund Verney of Penley, Kt., d. 11 Jan., 1600
=1. Frances daughter of John Hastings, of Elford, in Oxfordshire, widow of Thomas Redmayne, of Northmarston, Bucks. no issue
=2. Audrey daughter of William Gardner, of Fulmer, Bucks., widow of Sir Peter Carew the younger d. 1588
=3. Mary [Ould Lady Verney] daughter of William Blakeney, of Sparham, Norfolk, married first, Geoffrey Turville second, William St. Barbe d. 1642

Ursula daughter of William St. Barbe and Mary (afterwards third wife of Sir Edmund of Penley) married secondly William Clark, of Hitcham, Bucks. d. 1670 = Sir Francis Verney, of Penley, Kt., b. 1583; d. 1615 no issue

Sir Edmund Verney, of Middle Claydon, Bucks., b. 1 Jan., 1590; d. 23 Oct., 1642 = Margaret daughter of Sir Thomas Denton, of Hillesden, Bucks. b. 1594; d. 1641

Sir Ralph Verney Kt. and Bt. b. 9 Nov., 1613; d. 1696 = Mary daughter of John Blacknall, of Abingdon, Berks. b. 1616; d. 1650

Thomas (Tom) Verney b. 2 Nov., 1615; d. 1707 married several times, but had no issue

Sir Edmund (Mun) Verney Kt., b. 2 Nov., 1616 d. Sept., 1649 unmarried

Henry Verney b. 19 Apr., 1618 d. 1671 unmarried

John Verney b. 19 Jul., 1619 ob. inf.

Richard Verney b. 14 Feb., 1630 died as a boy

Margaret (Peg) = Sir Thomas Elmes, of Green's Norton, Northamptonshire b. 30 Sept., 1623 d. 1667

Cary =1. Capt. Thomas Gardiner of Cuddesdon =2. Jn. Steukeley, of Preshaw, Hants. b. 28 Dec., 1626 d. 1704

Mary (Mall) = Robert Lloyd, of Chester b. 14 Apr., 1628 d. 1684

Elizabeth (Betty) = Rev. Charles Adams Clerk, of Great Baddow, Essex b. 12 Sept., 1633 d. 1721

Edmund (Mun) b. 25 Dec., 1636 d. 4 Sept., 1688 = Mary Abell b. 1641; d. 1715

Mary b. and d. Jul., 1632

Anna Maria b. 16 Sept., 1634 d. May, 1638

Margaret b. 8 Jan., 1639 d. 20 Oct., 1647

John (Jack) b. 5 Nov., 1640 Succeeded his father as Sir John Verney, Bt. created Baron Verney and Viscount Fermanagh

Ralph b. Jun., 1647 d. Oct., 1647

Mary = John Kelyng b. 1675 d. 1696

Edmund (Mundey) b. 1668 d. unm. 1690

Ralph b. 1666 d. unm. 1686

Susan = Richard Alport, of Overton, Malpas, Cheshire b. 18 Apr., 1621 d. 1651

Penelope (Pen) =1. John Denton, of Fawley, Oxfordshire =2. Sir J. Osborn, of Knockmore Castle, co. Waterford b. 19 June, 1622 d. 1695

*It was 1608, and the future was looking
promising for the Verney family. Over the past
100 years a mixture of luck and good judgement had
brought them prosperity and security, and transformed
a clan of country squires into influential
courtiers and large-scale landowners.
So when the head of the family suddenly sold
up, walked out on his teenage wife and moved
to Morocco, the Verneys were shaken.
When he turned to piracy and converted to
Islam, they were appalled.
And when death ended his short career as a
Barbary Coast buccaneer, and his turban and
slippers were shipped back to the family
manor house in a tiny Buckinghamshire
village, they heaved a sigh of relief and settled
back into a quiet life of farming and local politics.
Their troubles had just begun.*

Contents

List of Illustrations

All illustrations marked ★ are © Sir Edmund Verney, Bt and the Claydon House Trust (Photograph: Photographic Survey, Courtauld Institute of Art). Those marked ★★ are © Sir Edmund Verney, Bt and the Claydon House Trust (Photograph: Conway Library, Courtauld Institute of Art, London).

Ralph Verney's six sisters*; **20.** William Denton (1605–91)*; **21.** Sir Roger Burgoyne (1618–77)*; **22.** Anne Hobart, one of the Verneys' Irish cousins*; **23.** Mun Verney (1636–88)*; **24.** Jack Verney (1640–1717) by Soest*; **25.** Aleppo in Syria; **26.** The inside view of the Royal Exchange by Wenceslaus Hollar (British Museum, London, UK/The Bridgeman Art Library); **27.** Jack the prosperous London businessman*; **28.** Elizabeth Palmer (1664–86), 1st wife of Jack Verney*; **29.** Mary Lawley (1661–94), 2nd wife of Jack Verney*; **30.** Elizabeth Baker (1678–1736), 3rd wife of Jack Verney*; **31.** Sir Ralph Verney by Sir Peter Lely*; **32.** Letter from Jack Verney to Sir Ralph Verney, 20 July 1659 (© Sir Edmund Verney, Bt and the Claydon House Trust); **33.** The Verney monument in the Church of All Saints, Middle Claydon**

Introduction

To know the Verney family is to understand seventeenth-century England.

When you consider what a turbulent and intricate period the seventeenth century was, that's quite an achievement. In a terrifying rite of passage, the English went to war with the Scots. They went to war with the Irish. Then, in a bloody and miserable conflict of ideologies, they went to war with each other. They struggled with plague and famine and fire and revolution; they won and lost a republic. They tried to blow up one king; they killed another and turned out a third.

The Verneys lived through all of these events. And because of a remarkable survival, we know them better than we know any other Stuart family. In 1827 a young Guards officer named Sir Harry Calvert inherited the Verney estate at Claydon House in Buckinghamshire from a distant cousin. He assumed the surname of Verney by royal licence and, after some romantic adventures in South America which included hunting with Indians, crossing the Andes, putting down a rising in Santiago and sailing round Cape Horn, he took up his inheritance and settled down to the life of a country squire.

Claydon had recently gone through an unhappy time. It was massively and badly remodelled between 1757 and 1771 by Ralph, Earl Verney, a flamboyant character who went everywhere attended by a pair of black footmen who heralded his presence by 'perpetually making a noise' on silver French horns. Described as 'lavish in his personal expenses, and fond of show',[1] the Earl coupled expensive habits with a series of disastrous investments, an unhappy combination which lost him his fortune. As his debts spiralled out of control, he sold off the family silver and plate and his wife's jewels. The best of the Claydon furniture was auctioned at Christie's; and the Earl himself fled to France to escape his creditors.

After his death in 1791, his prim spinster niece Mary pulled down two-thirds of the house and sold land to pay off mortgages and debts which amounted to more than £100,000. When Mary died in 1810, the last of the direct line, Claydon went to her half-sister, who lived in decayed grandeur in the south wing, all that remained of Earl Verney's vast mansion.

So Sir Harry inherited a place with a long pedigree – the Verneys had owned Claydon since the 1460s – and an uncertain future. Although no longer encumbered with debt, the estate had been neglected for decades, and the house itself was dilapidated and sparsely furnished. There were serious structural weaknesses, which were the legacy of Earl Verney's remodelling work, and family portraits by Van Dyck and Lely and Cornelius Jansen lay stacked in outhouses – 'one of them fastened over a hole to keep out rats'.[2]

As he took stock of his inheritance, Sir Harry discovered a wainscoted gallery at the top of the house. It was 40 feet long, and crammed to overflowing with more than 100,000 family and estate papers. They were bundled up in heaps on the floor, stacked against the walls, laid out on the trestle tables which filled the room. There were playbills and rent rolls, newsletters and notebooks, medieval charters and Georgian verse. And there was an enormous amount of personal correspondence, which had been kept, it seemed, for no other reason than because it was there. (One bundle carried the label 'Private letters of no interest'.) The documents ranged in date from the fourteenth century to the eighteenth; the seventeenth century was particularly well represented, with more than 30,000 private letters.

In fact, when he opened the door to that dusty old gallery, Sir Harry stumbled upon the largest and most continuous private collection of seventeenth-century correspondence in Britain – perhaps even in the Western world.

And what a story it told! The lives of this apparently ordinary family of Buckinghamshire gentry were recorded in the most intimate detail. The Verneys not only married and died and entertained and squabbled, and did all the things that gentry families were meant to do. They fought in France and the Netherlands; they travelled to the plantations of Barbados and the forests of Virginia; they took refuge in the desert fortresses of North Africa and traded in the souks of the Levant. Some of them looked on, appalled, at the brutalities of war; others were the perpetrators. Some were kind and highly principled; others were cheats and robbers. Some married for money; others died for love. And everything from petty victories and dreadful tragedies to the books they read and the food they ate was recorded in these letters.

The Verney responsible for amassing this collection was Sir Ralph (1613–96) who, as head of the clan, presided over Claydon's fluctuating fortunes for more than fifty years. Earlier Verneys wrote and received letters, signed leases and agreed contracts; and some of them survived. But Sir Ralph Verney kept everything: not only the leases and deeds and inventories which one might expect to see in the muniment room of a country house, but intimate personal letters from his wife and children, his parents, his nine siblings and their families, his aunts and uncles and friends and neighbours. And because he invariably kept the drafts of his replies, and even his rough jottings, he bequeathed to posterity a peculiarly *complete* correspondence. This he methodically organised, making a note of the subject of each letter, who it was from and the date he received it. A scribbled invitation to dinner from a neighbour in the next village, a love letter from his wife in London, a desperate plea for money from a brother in the West Indies – all were carefully saved, endorsed in his precise and spidery hand and put away for posterity to read.

Sir Ralph Verney's son John (1640–1717) continued this tradition of hoarding every scrap of paper that came across his desk. More than 7000 letters survive from the last twenty-five years of John's life, 1450 of which he wrote himself. He also read and annotated the earlier correspondence, occasionally jotting down the date of a birth, a marriage or a death: no doubt his elevation to the peerage in 1703 as Viscount Fermanagh increased his interest in the family pedigree. Subsequent generations of Verneys either added to the collection, or at least, did it no harm.

This was the treasure trove which Sir Harry discovered in the gallery at Claydon. News of his find soon began to circulate among scholars and antiquaries; and in the early 1840s John Bruce, a vice-president of the Society of Antiquaries, edited the pencil notes that Sir Ralph Verney had taken as an MP in the Long Parliament between 1640 and 1642. The sixty-eight sheets of foolscap were transcribed and published as *Notes of Proceedings in the Long Parliament* in 1845 by the Camden Society, which had been founded seven years earlier with the object of publishing manuscripts and reprinting 'works of sufficient rarity and importance to make reprints desirable'. Sir Harry Verney, whom Bruce congratulated on his 'love and zeal for historical truth', was elected to the Society's Council in the same year.[3]

In 1853 Bruce edited *The Letters and Papers of the Verney Family Down to the End of the Year 1639*, again for the Camden Society. It was a brave move, since the idea that history could deal with the everyday lives of families, even well-connected gentry families like the Verneys, was still regarded with mistrust. In his introduction, Bruce made the case for the Verneys in words which were way ahead of their time:

> It is an erroneous, although among antiquaries by no means an uncommon, notion that unofficial papers are only of importance when they can be connected with the most interesting events or the most noble families. I should contend, on the contrary, that the value of such papers is to be estimated by the degree in which they give an insight into the feelings and opinions, the real inner life, and not the mere outside appearance, of the men and women, whatever their station, to whom they relate.[4]

Bruce had always intended to carry the story of this 'real inner life' beyond 1639, but he put it off while he worked on other projects, and his sudden death in 1869 brought his plans to an abrupt halt. Some years later, an historian named Alfred Horwood went through the Claydon material on behalf of the Royal

Commission on Historical Manuscripts, which had been set up by royal warrant to report on collections of papers of value for the study of British history in private and institutional hands. The RCHM's 7th Report, which appeared in 1879, contained the results of Horwood's visits to Claydon, in the form of seventy-six pages of abstracts and extracts. He took a delight in everything, but, as Bruce had warned, the focus was firmly on the light that the Verneys could shed on national events rather than on their own lives. 'The letters give much court and town news,' said Horwood, singling out for particular comment 'an account of the last moments of the life of the Duchess of York in 1671, and of the proceedings of the Ecclesiastical Commission against the Bishop of London in 1686'.[5]

Late Victorian Britain saw a resurgence of interest in the seventeenth century, and between them John Bruce and Alfred Horwood managed to bring the Verney Papers to the attention of eminent Victorian historians such as S. R. Gardiner and C. H. Firth, both of whom used them to supply valuable political information about the period and, in Firth's words, 'to illustrate the manner in which contemporaries regarded the events of the great civil war, and to show how the revolutions of the times affected the lives of those who passed through them'.[6]

But it was an amateur historian who really established the Verneys as characters worthy of study in their own right. In June 1858 Sir Harry Verney, whose wife Eliza had died the previous year, married for a second time. His bride was thirty-nine-year-old Frances Parthenope Nightingale, the older sister of Florence.[7] Parthe, as she was known, had a complicated relationship with Florence (as did Sir Harry, who only proposed to Parthe after Florence turned him down). She was neurotic and obsessive about her sister, scandalised when she decided to go into nursing but eager to bask in reflected glory when she returned from the Crimea as a national celebrity. While Florence Nightingale's hagiographers were happy to paint a bleak picture of Parthe's character – 'the elder, the plainer, the less intelligent, the less remarkable'[8] – they tended to overlook her better qualities. She was a good wife and mother to Sir Harry and his seven children. She was an observant social commentator, publishing novels and short stories exploring the plight of working-class communities, and a host of earnest essays on subjects as diverse as 'Class Morality', 'Dreams, Visions and Ecstasies', 'Sentimental Religion' and 'The Miseries of War'. And she fell in love with Sir Ralph and John and all the other seventeenth-century Verneys whose lives were recorded in such meticulous detail in the bundles of letters in the Claydon muniment room.

Between them, Bruce and Horwood had made a start on organising the Verney Papers, but the process was nowhere near complete. Parthe went through the letters systematically, focusing particularly on the family's exploits around the time of the English Civil War. She rescued the portraits from their outhouses and put names to them; and in 1885 she published a short article on the history of Claydon.

This was the prelude to a much more substantial work. With the help of her daughter-in-law Margaret Maria Verney and two young friends, Catherine and Frederica Spring Rice, Parthe spent much of the 1880s compiling material for what was to become a minor classic – her two-volume *Memoirs of the Verney Family during the Civil War*. The task was especially hard because she suffered from rheumatoid arthritis, and by the end of the decade she was so crippled that she could not hold one of the precious letters in her hands, or even turn the pages of a book.

Nevertheless, Parthe managed to finish the first volume of the *Memoirs* by September 1889, when she presented the manuscript to 'my dear Harry' as a gift for his eighty-eighth birthday. She was still working on the second volume when she died at Claydon on 12 May 1890: it was completed from her notes by her daughter-in-law and the work was published two years later, with Margaret Maria adding *Memoirs of the Verney Family during the Commonwealth, 1650–1660* and *Memoirs of the Verney Family from the Restoration to the Revolution, 1660–1696* in 1894 and 1899. Margaret produced an abridged edition of the *Memoirs* in 1904; and just before her own death in 1930 she edited two volumes of eighteenth-century Verney correspondence.

The *Memoirs* are products of their age, sometimes reticent, sometimes overeager to turn the Verneys' story into a seventeenth-century version of *The Forsyte Saga*. But because of the dedication of these two women, the Verneys have become the stuff of legend.

★   ★   ★

Any collection of letters has one pre-requisite which historians often neglect – a reliable postal service. The medium may not be the message, exactly; but without the expectation that a letter will be read, correspondence wouldn't get very far.

Postal services in the seventeenth century were organised and reliable. When Sir Edmund Verney was with the King's army at Newcastle in the spring of 1639, his letters usually reached his son Ralph in London within two or three days, covering a distance of about 300 miles at an average speed of between four and seven miles an hour. The post between the family's London lodgings in Covent Garden and their country house at Claydon sixty miles away was almost as efficient, with letters arriving within one or two days of being written.

The fast delivery times between London and Newcastle were because Newcastle was one of the stops on the Great North Road, one of the five postal routes out of London which had begun the previous century as governmental lines of communication with Scotland, Ireland and Europe. The English section of the Great North Road ended at Berwick-on-Tweed, from where post was taken on to its northern terminus at Edinburgh. The West Road stretched down to Plymouth and on to Falmouth in Cornwall, the last port of call for the Americas and the Mediterranean. The Kentish Road to Dover and Deal was the quickest route to the Continent; the road to Milford Haven in Wales went via Bristol and Cardiff, and from Milford Haven ships sailed for Waterford; and the so-called Chester Road actually went beyond Chester to Holyhead, the main port for goods bound for Dublin. A sixth post to Yarmouth on the east coast was established in 1653 to serve Holland and the Low Countries.

All these routes were divided into stages of anywhere between ten and twenty-five miles (the average was around fifteen miles), so that each stage could be ridden hard and a fresh horse provided by the postmaster at the end of the stage for the next. Those who, like the Verneys, lived some distance from a staging post, would either use their servants to deliver letters to the postmaster or would send them with carriers and waggoners.

Postage was collected on delivery rather than being pre-paid as it is today. It varied a little in the course of the century, but for most of the period the Inland Office, which was the department of the Post Office which dealt with England and Wales, charged 2d. to carry a single sheet up to eighty miles; and 3d. to carry it beyond that. There was a further charge if the letter went to Scotland or Ireland. The Foreign Office, which was a separate department, charged 6d. for letters to northern France, 8d. to Hamburg, Cologne and Frankfurt, and 9d. to Paris, Venice, Rome, Geneva and Naples. A letter to the Levant cost a shilling.

Two sheets were charged at double the rate, which is why most of the Verney letters were written on one side of a single folded piece of paper. An envelope wasn't used, since it counted as a second sheet, except in the case of letters sent to the Levant, a journey so long and arduous that some kind of protective covering was considered essential. (Letters to and from John Verney, who lived in Aleppo for eleven years in the 1660s and 1670s, commonly took between three and six months to reach their destination. Many just disappeared.)

Addresses varied widely in their precision, their formality and their flamboyance. There were no street numbers, so correspondents were sometimes quite eloquent in their descriptions. 'To his much honoured father Sir Edmund Verney knight marshal of England at his house in the Covent Garden present these with care' is one example; 'To his assured loving brother Mr Ralph Verney Esqr. at the Pyatzo in the Covent Garden' is another. But letter writers often relied heavily on the fact that the recipient would be known in the neighbourhood. 'For Ralph Verney Esqr. in Covent Garden this' is a more typical address. One writer of a love letter simply put 'To the fair hands of Mrs Ann Temple'.[9] Letters were routinely sealed with wax, to prevent tampering – or at least to show when it had occurred. Everyone in the seventeenth century assumed that the Post Office opened the mail, and they were quite right. During the 1650s, for example, Cromwell's Secretary of State, John Thurloe, employed a team of men to intercept and examine mail in a secret room next door to the Foreign Office. Every post night around eleven o'clock one of Thurloe's agents 'went into that room privately'.[10] Decades later the inventor and mathematician Samuel Morland, who worked as an intelligence gatherer for Thurloe, claimed that during the Commonwealth he had devised all sorts of machines for opening and resealing letters so that no one would notice, for copying seals, transcribing letters at speed and forging handwriting.

None of the Verneys went in for the kind of seditious material which the authorities were looking for when they intercepted the mail. But they were still quite careful. Sir Ralph Verney's eldest son, Edmund, habitually wrote to his father in French, so that his letters couldn't be read by curious postboys. And when Sir Ralph and his family were in exile in France during the 1640s they devised a system of code-words for friends and relations. Sir Ralph's friend Sir Roger Burgoyne even resorted to a simple alpha-numeric code whenever he mentioned the name of a government official.

When sender and recipient were both living in the country and weren't too far apart, the Verneys and their kin made use of servants, waggoners, even the local clergy, to carry their letters for them. The situation was slightly different in London, where many of them lived for much of the year. Until 1680 there was no postal service within London itself, and correspondents had to rely on servants or porters to fetch and carry their messages. Then a merchant named William Dockwra set up a service for the 'conveying of letters or pacquets under a pound weight, to and from all parts within the cities of London and Westminster and the out parishes . . . for one penny'.[11] Dockwra's penny post was halted two years later on the grounds that it infringed the Post Office's monopoly (which belonged to the Duke of York and brought him tens of thousands of pounds every year). But it was promptly adopted as an official government service, so the Verneys and their friends and relations in London could send messages to each other cheaply and expect them to be delivered within the hour. In practice, though, it was more convenient to send a page or footman round to someone's house with a message, since they could wait for a reply and bring it straight home.

A letter, said *The Ladies' Dictionary* in 1694, 'is or ought to be the express image of the mind, represented in writing to a friend at a distance; wherein is declared what he or she would do or have done'.[12] 'The familiar speech of the absent' was how the Elizabethan writer Angel Day defined it.[13] Taken in isolation, each and every one of the thousands of Verney letters offers a glimpse into the mind of the writer – but it also establishes a three-cornered relationship between that writer, the original recipient and the twenty-first century reader. The seventeenth century produced some of the best-known personal narratives in British history. One thinks of Samuel Pepys and his impressionistic descriptions of national disasters like the Plague and the Fire of London, his terribly honest accounts of more personal disasters like his affairs and jealousies and squabbles with his wife. One thinks of the diaries of John Evelyn and Lady Anne Clifford, of Robert Hooke and Anthony à Wood. The urge to record the everyday and turn it into a testament was a powerful force in Stuart England.

But a diary is always a monologue. Events are given a particular spin, made to conform to a single world view, often rewritten long afterwards with the raw emotion filtered out. The Verneys' story is a series of conversations, with all that that implies. The letter writers make mistakes, and jump to conclusions. They vent their anger and then regret it. They are hopelessly indiscreet one minute, furtive the next. They say hurtful things, and then can't understand the hurt they cause.

And they lay themselves bare. An impoverished aunt pleads for money to pay her gambling debts; a defiant sister refuses to give up the father of her bastard child; a mother weeps for her dead baby, and a desperate husband refuses to admit to himself that his wife is going to die. Amidst all the light which the Verneys' story sheds on life in seventeenth-century England, this haunting vulnerability is a shadow which lingers. We know the Verneys almost too well, and it is impossible not to care.

Part 1
Edmund and Ralph

1

Francis Turns Turk

$\mathcal{S}$ ir Francis Verney lay on his bed in the great hall of the sick at Messina. He was thirty-one years old. He was a long way from home. And he was dying.

The weather-beaten Scot who stood at his side gazed down at him with a mixture of pity and curiosity. William Lithgow knew that if only a tithe of the stories told about Sir Francis were true, he had seen more of death than most men. One of the most feared pirates on the Barbary Coast, he was said to have seen dear friends fall at his side with Berber arrows in their backs as they rode like devils through the deserts of Morocco; to have laughed as his crew of Moors and renegades bound weeping children together back-to-back and tumbled them into the waters of the Mediterranean. This 'sometimes great English gallant', as Lithgow described him,[1] must have killed more people with his own hands than he cared to remember.

Now it was Verney's turn, and he was to die not on the gallows, as his family had expected, nor in some skirmish with terrified villagers during a raiding party for slaves, but in a hospital bed, poor and friendless. And as one whose pragmatism in spiritual matters had taken him from Puritanism to Roman Catholicism by way of Islam, the destination of Sir Francis Verney's soul was, to say the least, uncertain.

Lithgow had met the notorious buccaneer in Palermo six weeks earlier, and both had subsequently travelled the 180 miles along the Sicilian coast to Messina. The Scot was a professional traveller, whose peregrinations had already taken him right across Europe and all round the Mediterranean basin; he had come to Messina in search of safe passage to Naples on the next stage of his journey. Verney, whose career as a pirate had ended several years previously, was now a common soldier looking for employment. He was probably drawn by the great fair held in Messina every August, where raw silk was bought and sold and despatched all over the Aegean and the Levant, and where a mercenary's services might well be required as escort.

Lithgow already knew something of Sir Francis's chequered background, hence his description of him as a 'sometimes great English gallant'. He knew the man had spent his inheritance, fled from England, taken to piracy and turned Turk in Tunis. In any case, the little bundle of belongings which lay beside the dying man's bed was testament to his culturally diverse past. They included a turban, some slippers and a couple of long silk tunics like those worn by Ottoman janissaries. But there was also a staff inlaid with crosses, of the sort carried by Christian pilgrims to Jerusalem.

Sir Francis Verney died on 6 September 1615, a day or two after Lithgow came to see him in the hospital of La Pietà at Messina. His end left the traveller both fascinated and moved. Paying for his fellow-countryman's burial and 'bewailing sorrowfully the miserable mutability of fortune', the Scot wondered what it was that made a young English squire abandon his country and renounce his faith.[2] What turned him into one of the most feared renegade corsairs on the Barbary Coast? And what brought him to Sicily and left him to die, as Lithgow said later, 'in the extremest calamity of extremest miseries'?[3]

The Verneys were a wealthy gentry family with a long lineage and a habit of backing the wrong side. In the fifteenth century Sir Ralph Verney, the head of the family and a Lord Mayor of London, supported the Yorkists in the Wars of the Roses. In the sixteenth century two of his great-great-grandsons nearly lost their heads over their roles in the most desperate of the various hare-brained schemes to overthrow Mary Tudor, Henry Dudley's 1555 plot to rob the Exchequer and use the money to gather an army of disaffected Protestants on the Isle of Wight.

But the Verneys managed to combine their penchant for lost causes with some astute political matches. The Yorkist Sir Ralph, for example, married his eldest son to the daughter of a prominent Lancastrian. His second son married Eleanor Pole, a lady-in-waiting to Elizabeth of York – and a cousin to her husband, Henry VII. As a result (and in spite of the flirtation with treason during the 1550s), the family managed to thrive for most of the sixteenth century. A Verney attended Catherine of Aragon at the Field of Cloth of God; another was present at the christening of Edward VI, and was a member of the reception committee which greeted Anne of Cleves when she arrived in England at the end of 1539 for her brief marriage to Henry VIII. Never at the centre of power, the Verneys could usually be found hovering on the edges of one important royal circle or another.

By 1558, when Francis's father Sir Edmund inherited the Verney estates, the family had managed to acquire a substantial amount of property spread across Buckinghamshire and Hertfordshire. Their principal seat was Pendley, just on the Hertfordshire side of the border between the two counties. There was only a manor house – the village of Pendley had been deserted after one of Sir Edmund's forebears enclosed the park in the fifteenth century, and the family now buried their dead in the nearby church of Aldbury. In Hertfordshire they also held the manor of Bunstrux (which has long since been swallowed up by Tring); but most of their property lay in Buckinghamshire, and included the manors of Quainton, Dinton, Mursley – and Middle Claydon, where there was a substantial stone house. This was currently let to the Giffard family, who had rebuilt it back in the 1530s on condition that they were given a 100-year lease. One of Sir Edmund's brothers, Urian, was married to Lettice Giffard, whose father Sir George lived at Claydon.

Sir Edmund Verney married three widows in succession. Frances Hastings died before she could bear him any children, although she brought with her a son by her first husband, Thomas Redmayne of North Marston in Buckinghamshire. The second widow was Audrey, daughter of a Buckinghamshire squire named William Gardner and the widow of Sir Peter Carew, son of the Dean of the Queen's Chapel. She had no children by Carew, but she did have one by Sir Edmund – this was the piratical Francis, who was born in 1583. Five years later Audrey died, and Sir Edmund married his third widow. It was also a third wedding for his wife: Mary Blakeney had already been married to Geoffrey Turville of New Hall Park in Leicestershire, and William St Barbe of Ashington in Somerset. She had children by her first two husbands, and promptly produced a son for her third. Francis's half-brother Edmund was born on New Year's Day, 1590.

This was the reality of family life in Elizabethan England. Social historians talk fondly of the extended Tudor family, in which children were brought up by grandparents and aunts, and the ties of blood and marriage extended far beyond the confines of the home. But it is hard for us to appreciate just how far they *did* extend. By the time he was six years old, Francis had a half-brother and an indeterminate number of stepbrothers and stepsisters, Redmaynes and Turvilles and St Barbes. As a result of his father's marriages he was connected to seven different families: the Hastings and Redmaynes through Sir Edmund's first wife; the Gardners and Carews through his second; and the Blakeneys, Turvilles and St Barbes through his third and last. And lest we think these were relationships in name only, it is worth noticing that a hundred years later Sir Edmund's grandchildren and great-grandchildren were still in regular contact with their Turville and St Barbe cousins.

Sir Edmund Verney died on 11 January 1600 in the Stone House at Chalfont St Giles, which he probably acquired through his marriage to Audrey Gardner. And that's when Francis's troubles really began. Primogeniture was a powerful moral imperative in late Elizabethan England; and the consolidation of family estates under the ownership of a single heir was the norm. But unusually for someone of his class and background, Sir Edmund had gone to great lengths to make sure that his last wife Mary and their ten-year-old son Edmund would be provided for at his death.

By the terms of his will parts of the estate went straight to Francis. These included the manors of Pendley and Bunstrux and another manor at Fleet Marston, a Buckinghamshire village where the Verneys had held land since the thirteenth century. The manors of Quainton and Dinton, which were traditionally reserved for the use of Verney widows, were left to Mary for life as her widow's jointure, with Francis inheriting them when she died. And Mursley, Middle Claydon and the Stone House at Chalfont were settled on her until her son Edmund reached the age of twenty-one, when they passed to him.

This represented quite a break with common use and practice; and, because it effectively broke several entails, Sir Edmund had to obtain a private Act of Parliament, which he duly steered through the Commons and the Lords in 1598.

To complicate matters further, in 1599 Sir Edmund and Lady Mary decided to cement their families' fortunes by marrying Francis to his stepsister, Ursula St Barbe. Lady Mary's daughter by her second marriage was twelve at the time; Francis was fourteen. The intention behind this was obviously to protect Lady Mary's interests and those of her daughter. The practical effect was to make Francis, who was still only fifteen when his father died, feel that his stepmother had taken charge of his birthright.

We don't know much about Francis's early life – only that he went up to Trinity College, Oxford, in September 1600 when he was fifteen; that he left without taking a degree; and that by 1604 he was living in a rather shady neighbourhood just off Fleet Street, rather than in his stepmother's house in Drury Lane. There was nothing unusual in any of this: in seventeenth-century Oxford, around one in eight students were fifteen or younger when they matriculated; fewer than half actually bothered to graduate; and when the sons of gentlemen left university, they often made straight for the alehouses and whorehouses of London. Country life and estate management could wait.

However, Francis led a wilder life than some in the warren of tenements and courts outside the walls of the City of London. One of his servants, Richard Gygges, was killed in a fight. Francis himself got into serious debt, and the friends who had guaranteed that debt began to press him for their money. In March 1605, while he was still only twenty, he asked James I's Secretary of State, Robert Cecil, for permission to fell some timber which, he said, was growing on his own land and which would be his by

right in a matter of months when he came of age. The reason
for the urgency was that he needed to raise cash 'for the discharge
of divers gentlemen that stood engaged as sureties for him'.[4]

In his capacity as Master of the Court of Wards Cecil cheerfully gave his blessing to the scheme. However, Francis had omitted
to mention that access to the wood was over land which was part
of his stepmother's jointure, and which she had rented out for
grazing and as a coney warren. Deciding that Cecil's approval was
all he needed, he immediately set about felling the timber. Within
days, Lady Mary was in London with her lawyer, waving a letter
for Cecil to sign which would confirm her own rights and put
a stop to the felling operation. Her stepson had spoiled her pasture
'with carrying of the wood', she maintained, and destroyed the
rabbit warren, 'which she has let out at a good round rent'.[5] If
Cecil was in any doubt as to who was in the wrong, Lady Mary's
lawyer invited him to consult the Attorney of the Wards, Sir
Thomas Hesketh, who was well acquainted with the matter.

This dispute over a churned-up field and some nervous rabbits
signalled the start of a bitter legal battle between Francis and his
stepmother (and mother-in-law – Ursula, his wife and stepsister,
doesn't figure in the story at all, and one can only wonder where
her allegiances lay). Pasture, rabbits and family loyalties all took
second place to the main issue, which was now about the fair-
ness of Sir Edmund's will – about who should control the Verney
estates, in other words.

On 5 March 1606, by which time Francis had reached his
majority, the dispute reached the House of Commons, when MPs
were asked to repeal the Act 'for Confirmation of the Jointure of
the Lady Verney, Wife of Sir Edmund Verney Knight', which had
been passed seven years earlier. The bill passed its first reading, and
on Wednesday 26 March lawyers for Francis and his stepmother
appeared before the House to put their respective cases. Francis's
counsel, a Mr Wincall, pressed hard for the justice of his client's
cause, and there was 'much dispute, and argument'; but Lady Mary's
counsel, Randall Carew, proved the more persuasive. He pointed
out that Sir Edmund Verney had personally steered the original
bill through Parliament, and had 'laboured divers friends in it'. But
the most telling argument was that if Francis had his way, it would
sink a whole raft of leases and land transfers which had gone

through on the strength of it, causing 'the overthrow of many purchasers, sixty at least'. His attempt to repeal his father's Act was rejected at the second reading.[6]

Magnanimous in victory and anxious to patch up her differences with Francis, Lady Mary gave up her claim to Quainton that summer. But the rental income from an 800-acre estate wasn't enough for the young man. In 1607 he sold Quainton for £500, presumably to settle his outstanding debts. Then he sold Fleet Marston. Then he sold Pendley itself – the land, the house and all the furniture – and took himself off to the Holy Land. The pilgrimage to Jerusalem apparently gave him a brief taste of piety, since when he stopped off in Paris on his way home, the English ambassador Sir George Carew noted approvingly that he 'frequented the exercises of our religion at my house'.[7] But his religious principles didn't extend to forgiving Lady Mary. He spent the summer and autumn of 1608 winding up what was left of his business affairs, and then sailed away from his wife, his step-mother and his country. He never saw any of them again.

According to family tradition, Francis headed down to seek his fortune in North Africa. There is no hard evidence to support the idea, but it is not as far-fetched as it might seem. In the early years of the seventeenth century a force of around 200 Englishmen was fighting in the service of Moulay Zhadane, one of several claimants competing for the throne of Morocco. Through his uncle's marriage to Lettice Giffard, Francis was related to their commander, Captain John Giffard, whose family leased Middle Claydon from the Verneys. Captain John was a favourite with Moulay Zhadane, who paid him 25s. a day and 'bestowed upon him a rich sword, valued at a thousand marks, and a scarlet cloak richly embroidered with pearl', which had originally been sent as a gift from Queen Elizabeth to Moulay Zhadane's father.[8] His second-in-command was 'his near and very dear kinsman', Philip Giffard.[9] Both men were later killed in a desert skirmish with Moors opposed to Moulay Zhadane. Yet another Giffard was the Barbary Coast pirate Richard Giffard. The captain of the aptly named *Fortune*, he caused a considerable stir in 1606 when he set fire to a prize at Algiers because no one would offer him a fair price for it. Since the harbour was filled with Algerian ships at the time, he was not popular.

Whether or not Francis was drawn to North Africa by the prospect of joining up with any of the Buckinghamshire Giffards is a moot point. What is clear, however, is that within less than a year of his leaving England he was operating as a pirate himself. In 1609 Francis Cottington, who was attached to the English embassy in Madrid, reported that he had captured three or four Poole ships and one from Plymouth, which implies that he was active along the south coast. And in October of the same year a newsletter written in London passed on the rumour that 'Sir Francis Verney, who is become a strong pirate upon the Barbary coast, hath seized the provision of wine coming for the King from Bordeaux'.[10] This was confirmed six weeks later, 'and he is said to have taken a much richer prize'.[11] King James was so concerned at Francis's activities that he despatched a ship of war to escort a convoy of merchant vessels en route for Aleppo in the Levant. Around the same time, Francis was mentioned as one of the four leaders of the Tunisian pirate fleet, along with John Ward, Richard Bishop and 'Black' Osman, captain of janissaries at Tunis.

These are all the details we have of Francis Verney's swift and dramatic transition from discontented Buckinghamshire squire to feared Barbary corsair. But we do know that he wasn't alone. Many of the pirates who operated out of the three major centres of piracy in North Africa – Algiers, Tunis and Tripoli – were Europeans. In 1581, for example, twenty-three out of thirty-five Algerian captains were European renegades. Another was the son of a renegade, and another was a Jew.

Most of these men were professional sailors with criminal pasts, fugitives from their own countries or opportunists who had committed perhaps a single act of piracy, and then fled to the safety of the Mediterranean where they were out of reach of the law. John Ward, one of Francis's fellow-corsairs at Tunis, was raised as a Kentish fisherman before joining the navy, when he succumbed to temptation and stole a succession of ships, each larger and richer than the last. By the time Francis joined him he was in command of a 200-ton flyboat named the *Gift*, which was armed with thirty cannon and manned by a motley crew of Englishmen, Dutchmen, Spaniards and Turks. Richard Bishop, who came from Yarmouth, was his first lieutenant; John Smith of Plymouth, one of the most proficient engineers in Europe, was his gunner.

What *was* unusual – and what remains hard to explain today – is Francis's lack of naval experience. Like Ward and Bishop, the vast majority of the European corsairs came from seafaring backgrounds. Yet as far as we know, Francis had no experience at all of life at sea, unless one counts his being a passenger on one of the merchant vessels which traded with the Levant when he travelled to Palestine in 1608.

However, these were boom years for the Barbary Coast corsair, and John Ward was partly responsible for the boom. Until the beginning of the seventeenth century the galley was still the commonest seagoing vessel in the southern Mediterranean. Basically unchanged since the time of the Romans, it needed anywhere between fifty and 200 slaves to act as oarsmen, depending on the vessel's size. But in about 1606 Ward introduced the Tunisians to the concept of the square-rigged sailing ship of the type then used in the Atlantic; a renegade Dutch sea captain named Simon Danser performed the same service for the Algerians at about the same time. The effect was dramatic: corsairs no longer had to confine their activities to coastal waters, and the entire Mediterranean basin – not to mention the British Isles and most of the Atlantic seaboard – was suddenly available to them.

The Algerians established a base on the Cape Verde Islands off the West African coast, from where they preyed on Atlantic shipping; in 1617 they sacked Madeira, taking 1200 prisoners. Ireland and the south-west of England were subject to raids, and within a decade the corsairs were operating as far north as Iceland and the Newfoundland Banks. Fishing boats with neither man nor tackle on them were sometimes found drifting off the coast of Cornwall or Devon, the only evidence that their crews had met a pirate ship. Sir Richard Moryson, vice-president of Munster, once arrived in Youghal on the coast of Co. Cork to find the harbour filled with eleven corsair ships and around 1000 men; he wisely decided that discretion was the better part and quietly withdrew. (According to one reformed pirate, Sir Henry Mainwaring, his comrades often found a warm welcome in Ireland, where 'they have all commodities and conveniences that all other places do afford them', including 'good store of English, Scottish and Irish wenches, which resort unto them'.[12])

The relationship between the corsairs, the Moslem governors

of their bases in North Africa and their Christian quarry was complicated. Tunis, Algiers and Tripoli were nominally part of the Ottoman Empire; however, their pashas ruled as independent warlords, and although Ahmed I (sultan from 1603 to 1617) made occasional attempts to rein in their piratical activities, by and large they ignored him and did things their own way. They provided safe haven for the corsairs, and markets for their prizes – indeed, their percentage of the prize money was often the main source of public finances. They offered access to the caravan routes travelling eastward to the Levant, so that both captured goods and fresh slaves commanded decent prices. The goods were often bought up by Jewish merchants who prospered in such dynamic commercial environments, and sold them back to dealers in Europe. It is perfectly possible that the consignment of Bordeaux wine which Francis Verney diverted en route to the court of James I might eventually have found its way to its intended destination. The trading was a two-way process: the cannon, powder and shot which corsairs used to subdue their victims was sometimes captured, but more often bought in European markets.

Slaves were a valuable commodity, and it was rare for prisoners to be killed without good cause. That was small consolation to the victims, who were routinely ill-treated and tortured when they were first captured – to break their wills, to force them to give information about wealthy passengers and valuables which might be hidden aboard, and to add a sense of urgency to their letters home, so that relatives would make haste to produce a ransom. 'My patroon [slave-master] made me work at a mill like a horse from morning until night,' wrote one young man to his father in England, 'with chains upon my legs, of 36 pounds weights apiece, my meat nothing but a little coarse bread and water, my lodging in a dungeon underground, where some 150 or 200 of us lay altogether, having no comfort of the light but a little hole, and being so full of vermin for want of shift and not being allowed time for to pick myself that I am almost eaten up with them, and every day beaten to make me either turn Turk or come to my ransom.'[13] Those prisoners who weren't ransomed were sold as galley slaves or domestic workers, or 'suffered to work upon any manner of trade or occupation wherein we were in any way expert', as a freed English slave recalled in the 1590s.[14] Some were treated badly, others quite well. Apostasy loomed large in contemporary anti-Islamic European propaganda, along with the barbarity and cruelty of the 'Mahometans', but in reality there was no particular pressure put upon captives to convert to Islam, if only because those who did automatically became free men and thus lost their value to their captors. Of course, this was in itself a powerful incentive to change one's religion.

As far as Christian Europe was concerned, those who did turn Turk were lost forever. The corsairs who embraced Islam acquired an ideological basis for their activities, since the Barbary states viewed attacks on Christian shipping as part of a larger *jehad* against the infidel. There seems little doubt that Francis converted – his contemporaries certainly thought so, and, if they are right, he was following the example of large numbers of prominent European commanders who made their careers on the Barbary Coast. (It says a great deal about Victorian mores that neither John Bruce, who first described Francis's career in 1853, nor Frances Parthenope Verney, who wrote the two-volume *Memoirs of the Verney Family* in the 1890s, could even countenance the possibility of his committing what Bruce called 'the unnecessary and improbable offence of becoming a renegado'.[15] A pirate in the family was wrong but romantic; an apostate was beyond the pale.) John Ward was one such renegado: William Lithgow met him in Tunis in 1615, just before his encounter with the dying Francis in Messina, and spoke of how Ward had 'turned Turk and builded there a fair palace beautified with rich marble and alabaster stones, with whom I found domestic some fifteen circumcised English runagates'.[16] A few years later another Englishman in Tunis commented that Ward wore Turkish dress and drank only water, no wine.

Sadly, there are no such glimpses into Sir Francis Verney's domestic arrangements in Tunis. What we do know is that his fall from grace as a corsair was as dramatic as his meteoric rise. William Lithgow was told (by whom, he doesn't say) that he was 'taken at sea by the Sicilian galleys, in one of which he was two years a slave'.[17] His capture must have taken place between 1610 and 1613, and compared to the life of a sea rover his time as a galley slave will have been desperately grim. Galley slaves were badly treated on Moslem vessels, but there was general agreement that conditions were even worse aboard French, Spanish and Italian galleys. His deliverance from captivity came about through the intervention of an English Jesuit who, again according to Lithgow, redeemed him after he promised to convert back to Christianity. The redemption of captives was a favourite subject for philanthropy in the seventeenth century, although it usually focused on Europeans held by Arabs. It is not clear if the Jesuit required Francis to embrace his own brand of Christianity, although it seems likely. The English sailor Richard Hasleton, who was rescued from Algerian slavers by a Genoese galley in the 1590s, was mercilessly starved, flogged and racked by his saviours because he refused to accept the Catholic faith. Ironically, Francis's Protestant family back in England would have regarded his conversion to Catholicism as barely preferable to Islam.

A free man in Sicily, but with no money, no friends, no status and nowhere left to run, Francis enlisted as a common soldier in Palermo in the service of the Duke of Sona, the Spanish viceroy. The news of his end in the hospital of La Pietà at Messina was sent home by an English merchant, John Watchin, along with his turban, slippers, silk tunics, pilgrim's staff and a formal death certificate. No doubt it was greeted with some relief. However, when Ursula Verney remarried in 1619, she found that her dead husband's reputation pursued her. She was described by a contemporary gossip as 'widow to him that turned Turk', while her new father-in-law, a Buckinghamshire landowner named Sir William Clarke, promptly threatened to disinherit his son 'and hath vowed they shall never come within his doors'.[18]

Ursula's mother, Lady Mary, did not remarry. Three husbands were quite enough; and in any case, she had acquired a taste for power which was hard to relinquish. She continued to live in her house at Drury Lane, making desultory efforts to find a country estate to replace Quainton; making matches for her Turville and St Barbe daughters; and making sure that Edmund, her son by Sir Edmund Verney, was given a good start in life.

By the time his half-brother died in Messina in 1615, Edmund was twenty-five, knighted and married, with a twenty-month-old son and another child on the way. That makes him sound like a dreary stay-at-home in comparison with his renegade sibling, but nothing could be further from the truth. After a spell at St Alban's Hall, Oxford, where his mother enrolled him in March 1604 when he was just fourteen, he completed his education by travelling in Europe throughout his late teens, going first to the Netherlands with the soldier and courtier Sir George Goring 'to see the Low-Country wars';[19] then to the court of Henry IV of France and eventually to Italy, in company with the great Jacobean diplomat Sir Henry Wootton, ambassador at Venice.

Such an itinerary would be conventional enough for the Grand Tourists of the eighteenth century. In the early seventeenth, it was still a novelty. But the mixture of diplomatic and cultural experiences was good preparation for the next stage in Edmund's career. In June 1610, before the Lords and Commons assembled in Westminster Hall, James I proclaimed that his eldest son, Henry, was Prince of Wales. At the same time Prince Henry, who at sixteen was four years Edmund's junior, was given his own revenue, his own palaces at Richmond and St James's, and his own household of 400 courtiers and officials. Some were middle-aged men who had been with him since childhood: his tutor Adam Newton, who was made Secretary; the Puritan Sir David Murray, erstwhile Keeper of the Privy Purse and now given the post of Groom of the Stole and Gentleman of the Robes; and Sir Thomas Chaloner, Henry's governor since 1603, who became Chamberlain. Others were new to Henry and indeed, to life at court – active, physical types, men with military experience in Europe, or at least with some prowess in the tiltyard. One of these 'young and sprightly blossoms', as a contemporary described them, was Edmund Verney.[20] In 1610 he was made Chief Sewer in charge of the service of the table in Prince Henry's household, with an annual stipend of £20.

There are several possible explanations for Edmund's entrance into court life. Sir Thomas Chaloner was a neighbour in Buckinghamshire – his family had a seat at Steeple Claydon, next door to the Middle Claydon estate leased to the Giffards and close by most of the other surviving Verney holdings in the county. In seventeenth-century England, local connections were supremely important.

So were family connections; and Edmund had an uncle, another Francis Verney, who was a falconer in Prince Henry's household. Then there was the redoubtable Lady Mary. Edmund's mother was on good terms with Anne of Denmark, and while it is true that Anne didn't get on particularly well with the Prince – she tended to favour her younger son, Charles – she was currently doing her best to be nice to him, having realised rather belatedly that if James I died before her, a hostile Henry IX could wreak havoc with her extravagant lifestyle. It may well be that Lady Mary asked the Queen to further Edmund's interest with the Prince.

Edmund also had friends in Henry's household – Sir George Goring, with whom he had toured the Low Countries, was one of the Gentlemen of the Privy Chamber. But his background and experience counted as much as his connections. The Prince had a high regard for Italy and France – a picture of Henry IV of France was one of only two portraits to hang in his gallery at St James's Palace (the other was Maurice of Nassau), and when the French King was assassinated in 1609 Henry was so upset that he took to his bed, crying 'My second father is dead'. He tended to favour those with experience of foreign travel, and a surprisingly high proportion of his officials had spent time in Europe. Even more important was Edmund's Protestant pedigree: it was said that of the 400 nobles and gentlemen in the Prince of Wales's household, 'there was not one known or suspected Papist'.[21] This was in marked contrast to the court of his father, who tolerated Catholics so long as they were discreet; and that of his mother, who was herself a covert Papist.

Prince Henry's household was thus a strange and seductive mixture of earnest Protestantism and Renaissance charisma. Bacon wrote respectfully of how the Prince was 'wonderfully patient in hearing . . . so that his mind seldom wandered from the subject, or seemed fatigued, but he applied himself wholly to what was said or done.'[22] The Venetian theologian Paolo Sarpi described how 'from all sides, one hears about the great *virtu* of the Prince, son to the King of England'.[23] He was an expert horseman, building the first riding school in England at St James's Palace, and employing Henry IV's riding master, Monsieur St Antoine, to teach him the highly mannered equine ballets which were then fashionable in France and Italy. To quote Bacon again, 'he was much devoted to the magnificence of buildings and works of all kinds . . . and was a lover both of antiquity and arts'.[24] And he was a fervent champion of militant Protestantism at home and abroad. When the old courtier Sir John Harington told him that 'Henry the Eighth pull'd down Monks and their cells,/Henry the Ninth should pull down Bishops and their Bells', he was saying no more than everyone knew.[25] Prince Henry hated Catholicism and all aspects of Anglicanism which leaned towards ritual. Sir John Holles, Comptroller of the Prince's Household, later commented that 'for our home preservation he held up religion and held in the presumptious [*sic*] papist . . .' – an attitude which Edmund Verney both applauded and endorsed until the day he died.[26]

Edmund's master was serious and highly principled, and he expected his household to follow his example and to observe standards of decorum which would have been incomprehensible to members of his father's drunken and raucous court. He was also a connoisseur, exhibiting a taste which was considerably more sophisticated than that shown by either James I or the Tudors who preceded him. He acquired bronzes by Giovanni Bologna, paintings by Tintoretto and Holbein, books and antique coins and medals, seeking quite deliberately to emulate the great Renaissance princes. Ottaviano Lotti, representative in England of Grand Duke Cosimo II de' Medici, recalled how, during a visit to Richmond Palace, Henry quizzed him carefully about the decoration of the Grand Duke's galleries and the nature of his collections. The Prince patronised designers and artists of the calibre of Inigo Jones, the Huguenot miniaturist Isaac Oliver, the French garden designer Salomon de Caux and the Florentine Constantino de' Servi, who produced dramatic plans for remodelling Richmond Palace.

And like a true Renaissance prince, he was eager for a life of action, in sharp contrast to his father, who would go to any lengths to avoid confrontation. He cherished dreams of leading a Protestant coalition in an anti-Hapsburg crusade to topple Catholicism in northern Europe. After James I remonstrated with him for failing to be more interested in scholarship and said that if he did not take his learning more seriously his younger brother Charles would reign in his place, he declared, 'I know what becomes a Prince. It is not necessary for me to be a professor, but a soldier and a man of the world. If my brother is as learned as they say, we'll make him Archbishop of Canterbury.'[27]

But this hero, this warrior-prince, this embodiment of 'deep knowledge, greatness, long life, policy, courage, zeal, fortune, awful majesty',[28] had no chance to fulfil his promise. In October 1612 he fell sick with typhoid fever, which grew worse until he was forced to take to his bed. On Sunday 1 November he was visited by his distraught family; in a poignant gesture, the eleven-year-old Prince Charles pressed a little bronze horse by Giovanni Bologna into the hand of his desperately ill brother. Five days later Henry was dead.

Prince Henry's death meant the dissolution of his household, after only seventeen months. It also ensured his reputation as the best king that England never had: 'Our rising sun is set ere scarce he had shone,' wrote the Earl of Dorset two weeks later, '. . . all our glory lies buried'.[29] And the impact of Henry's court on Edmund Verney lasted for the rest of his life. For one thing, his brief experience of life in a royal household so impressed him that he went on to serve the Prince's brother, Charles, and remained a courtier until the day he died. Although he never became a dedicated virtuoso in the same way as the Earl of Arundel or the other members of the Whitehall Group which gathered around Charles I in the 1620s, he would commission portraits from the best painters of his day, including Daniel Mytens (*c.* 1540–*c.* 1647) and Sir Anthony Van Dyck (1599–1641). Perhaps most significantly of all, he absorbed the sense of militant Protestant chivalry which informed everything that Prince Henry did. He became the archetypal Protestant knight, imbued with a moral and religious Puritanism, an enormously powerful sense of honour and an equally powerful loathing for Roman Catholicism.

Edmund's time in Prince Henry's household also made him a knight in the more literal sense, in that he was knighted at the Palace of Whitehall in January 1611, shortly after his twenty-first birthday. That same year he sailed to Spain in the train of Sir John Digby, James I's new ambassador to Madrid, who was charged with the task of finding out if Philip III of Spain might accept Prince Henry as a husband for one of his two daughters. Marriage to a Catholic Hapsburg was an appalling prospect for the Prince, but entirely in accordance with his father's efforts to steer a middle way through the religious minefield that was Europe in the 1610s.

James's matrimonial plans for both Henry and his daughter Princess Elizabeth were disarmingly simple – one should marry into a Catholic royal family and the other into a Protestant, and it didn't really matter who went where.

Fortunately for Henry, the scheme fell through. According to the English history books, Philip was only prepared to offer his second daughter Maria, rather than the ten-year-old Infanta, Anne of Austria; James took umbrage at this and decided to look else-where for a daughter-in-law. The Spanish tell a slightly different story, saying that Philip would not consent to either daughter marrying Prince Henry because the boy refused to accept the Catholic faith.

Whatever the reason, Sir Edmund was back in England by the autumn of 1611, leaving behind the luxurious mansion by the Prado – 'the fairest and pleasantest house in Madrid' – where the embassy had lodged.[30] He found his formidable mother making plans for his own marriage. Her target was Margaret Denton, whose family lived in a substantial country house at Hillesden, a hamlet which lay halfway between Buckingham and Middle Claydon, and about four miles from each. Margaret, who was Sir Thomas Denton's eldest child, was seventeen or eighteen and could bring with her a hefty dowry of £2300, which would go some way to repairing the damage done to the family fortunes when Sir Francis sold up and left the country.

The negotiations were delicate and protracted. Sir Edmund was a promising young courtier from a good upper-gentry family with a respectable pedigree (as long as one could overlook his brother). But he was several rungs below the Dentons on the social ladder. They were a powerful and well-connected force in Buckinghamshire. Sir Thomas had served as High Sheriff for the county in 1597, and sat as an MP in the parliament summoned by James I when he succeeded to the throne in 1603. His wife Susan was one of the Temples of Stowe.

The Dentons certainly didn't dismiss out of hand the prospect of their daughter marrying Sir Edmund: quite apart from anything else, they had eleven other children to dispose of. But their man of business made it plain that the Verneys were going to have to come up with a settlement which was large enough to smooth over any inequalities of rank. In fact they were going to have to show that Margaret would be provided with a jointure of £400 a year if her husband predeceased her. The estate at Mursley which Sir Edmund had inherited when he turned twenty-one brought in only half that amount, so this was something of a problem.

After the two families met at Hillesden to discuss a way forward, Lady Mary came up with a plan. She relinquished a debt owed to her of £1000 in return for an annuity for life of £100, enabling Sir Edmund to buy enough property to make up some of the deficit. Sir Thomas Denton eventually agreed to settle for less than the £400 he had asked for, and also offered the young couple four years' free board at Hillesden. If Prince Henry's death cast a shadow over Edmund's career prospects, it did nothing to prevent the wedding, which took place at Hillesden on 14 December 1612, exactly one week after the Prince's state funeral at Westminster Abbey.

For the next eight years Sir Edmund divided his time between his parents-in-laws' house, his mother's house in Drury Lane and lodgings at St James's Palace, where he was serving as one of the Gentlemen of the Privy Chamber to Prince Charles. Margaret tended to remain with her family at Hillesden. Their first child, Ralph, was born there on 9 November 1613, the prompt arrival of a male heir meeting with general rejoicing. Hillesden was also the venue for the delivery of the Verneys' next seven children, who arrived at alarmingly short intervals: Thomas on 2 November 1615; Edmund on 2 November 1616; Henry on 19 April 1618; John on 19 July 1619; Susan on 18 April 1621; Penelope on 7 June 1622; and Margaret on 30 September 1623. All except John survived into adulthood, which was something of a feat in the seventeenth century. There must have been times when Hillesden was more like a nursery than a country house – five of the Dentons' own children were under ten when Ralph was born, and his youngest aunt was only a year older than him.

That was one reason why Sir Edmund decided to establish the prolific Verneys in a country house of their own, although Margaret continued to go home to her mother at Hillesden for her confinements. Claydon was the obvious choice. It was close to Hillesden; it was within a day's ride of London; and it was an attractive and substantial house, having been rebuilt towards the end of the fifteenth century, and then remodelled quite drastically by the

Giffards in the sixteenth. By 1620, when Sir Edmund bought out the remaining fifteen years of the Giffard lease, it was a typical product of its time – neither the 'proud ambitious heap' which contemporaries loathed and envied in equal measure, nor a rambling and laughably old-fashioned medieval manor house of the kind which were currently being pulled down and replaced by proud ambitious heaps all over the country. Two pencil drawings from the seventeenth century show a three-storey redbrick building on an H footprint, with tall chimney stacks and a determined symmetry. Crow-stepped gables hover uncertainly over elegant broken pediments and urns; fashionable balustraded balconies nestle within deeply projecting wings; and the overall effect is of a series of well-intentioned facelifts which enrich Claydon's sense of continuity rather than disrupting it.

It is unlikely that Edmund and Margaret shared such romantic views of organic architectural growth. Modernity was everything to the Jacobeans, and those who believed with Francis Bacon that 'it is a reverend thing to see an ancient castle or building not in decay' were few and far between.[31] Sir Edmund needed a country seat, not only to accommodate his growing family, but also to confirm his growing prestige as a royal courtier. Claydon was conveniently located and conveniently large, and that was reason enough for them to move in – the first Verneys actually to live there since the family purchased the manor of Middle Claydon back in 1463. At £3639, the cost of buying out the lease was not so convenient, and Sir Edmund had to borrow heavily to raise the cash.* But he had hopes of preferment and his master Prince Charles had agreed to compensate him for various debts he had incurred in royal service. In fact he had promised to pay £4000 in four annual instalments, and he did indeed hand over the first thousand pounds. However, Sir Edmund's touching faith in his prince's word proved unduly optimistic. Charles never did stump up the money, and Sir Edmund remained in debt for the rest of his life.

---

* According to John Broad, whose *Transforming English Rural Society: The Verneys and the Claydons, 1600–1820* is a masterly analysis of the family's changing financial fortunes, Sir Edmund probably borrowed the money from Toby Palavacino, heir to the Italian banking family.

2

Venturous Knights

There is only one picture of Sir Edmund Verney's wife Margaret: it is by an unknown artist and was probably painted some time in the 1620s or 1630s. She looks tired, as well she might. Having given birth to eight children by the age of twenty-seven, she produced four more between 1623 and 1633: Cary, Mary, Richard (who died young) and Elizabeth. She also looks slightly unkempt: her high, square forehead is framed with hair which falls in unfashionably long strands across her shoulders and down her back. This, and the fact that she wears a lace-trimmed day smock, suggest a degree of informality unusual in Caroline portraits.

Margaret looks out just over the viewer's shoulder, lost in her own thoughts, while her right hand rests lightly on some flowers lying on a table. A heavy locket or pomander with a single pendant pearl hangs around her neck – perhaps a reference to her name, which derives from the Greek word for 'pearl' – and she leans her head against her raised left hand. The bare forearm comes as a shock. It is misshapen and covered in ugly blotches, so that it dominates the portrait. In contrast to the smooth white face and exposed right arm, the skin is a 'mass of scar tissue.

The presence of these scars is something of a mystery. We don't know how Margaret came by them, only that she was sensitive about other people seeing them. When she made her will, for instance, she went to great lengths to ensure they wouldn't be exposed to public view, even in death. So why display them so obviously here? The picture is clearly more allegory than conventional portrait, but what does it represent – the transience of beauty? The mutability of human flesh?

Two likenesses of Margaret's husband, both painted around the 1620s, suggest that Sir Edmund managed to carry his cares more lightly – or that the courtier's life was less onerous than his wife's. One portrait shows a dashing young man with moustaches, a pointed beard and an earring, sporting a rich lace collar and a crimson sash. However, a note on the back of the canvas says not only that it was painted in Spain, but that it is 'very unlike'.

The figure who gazes out from the second portrait looks the very archetype of the Stuart courtier, from the tips of his fingers which rest lightly on a gold cane, to his feet encased in their spurred loose boots of Spanish leather. In fact he is so romantic, so dashing, that for most of the nineteenth and twentieth centuries he was thought to be Sir Francis, the Barbary buccaneer. But the style of costume and the age of the subject, who is obviously in his thirties at least, don't add up. It's now generally accepted that the portrait is by or after Daniel Mytens, who was court portrait painter to James I and one of the Prince of Wales's picture drawers; and that it shows Sir Edmund in the 1620s rather than Sir Francis in the early 1600s. If that is the case, then Sir Edmund in his thirty-something prime was a very handsome man indeed – tall, proud and every inch the urbane cavalier.

His master, the Prince of Wales, was proud, but he was hardly tall and hardly urbane. Charles was 5 foot 4 inches and bow-legged, with a pronounced stammer which he attempted – and failed – to cure by talking to himself with his mouth full of pebbles. Reserved, inclined to outbursts of petulance and singularly lacking in personal charm, he was a poor substitute for his dead brother, something of which he was made painfully aware throughout his adolescence. When he was created Prince of Wales in November 1616, a few days before his sixteenth birthday, his mother refused to attend because she couldn't bear the way in which the ceremony was dredging up memories of her dead son.

But if Charles's court had none of the charisma of Prince Henry's, it was still a court. And being a courtier suited Sir Edmund. It offered him status with his neighbours and enabled him to stand on more equal terms with his wife's family; and – a not unrelated point – as a Gentleman of the Privy Chamber to the Prince of Wales, he had easy access to the small group of men who ruled the country.* He may have been a small fish in comparison to the influential nobles gathered round the throne; but the mere fact that he could claim acquaintance with them made him a big fish in Buckinghamshire.

Nor should we underestimate the powerful attraction of the sheer glamour which surrounded the Stuart court. Like his master, Sir Edmund viewed with distaste the drunken horseplay that characterised James I's court, the rather public way in which the King displayed his homosexual proclivities. But after 1616, when as Prince of Wales Charles began to play a more prominent role, even a minor courtier like Sir Edmund was drawn into the royal circle – not as a participant, but certainly as an onlooker at the increasingly elaborate entertainments, the rites of kingship through which James sought to define himself. In masques with titles such as *The Golden Age Restor'd, Time Vindicated, The Fortunate Isles and their Union*, the masquers (who included Prince Charles himself on occasion) celebrated royalty and the peace and prosperity which the Stuarts – by their own account, at least – continued to bring to England. James encouraged his subjects to regard him as rather more than mortal:

> Kings are justly called gods [he said in 1609], for that they exercise a manner or resemblance of divine power upon earth. For if you will consider the attributes to God, you shall see how they agree in the person of a King. God hath power to create, or destroy, make, or unmake at his pleasure, to give life,

---

* To give some idea of just how small that group was, there were somewhere in the region of 115 peers by the end of James I's reign, and 179 by the end of Charles I's. James and Charles I between them created about 3400 knights, of whom Sir Edmund was one.

or send death, to judge all, to be judged nor accomptable to none. To raise low things, and to make high things low at his pleasure, and to God are both soul and body due. And the like power have kings.[1]

No matter what Sir Edmund might have thought of James as a man, his experience of the court taught him to push those thoughts to one side and focus on James as King, exercising divine power on earth. And even one as puritanically inclined as he was could hardly fail to enjoy being at the heart of things. When his master attended Parliament for the first time as Prince of Wales in 1621, riding in a vast procession of messengers and trumpeters and heralds, bishops and nobles, wearing his cap and coronet and accompanying the King, the sense of being at the heart of so much theatricality and pomp could hardly fail to impress. Charles had a chamber specially prepared for him in the Palace of Westminster, and right at the start of the 1621 session 'with a fair retinue and his guard went on foot . . . through King Street and Westminster Hall to the higher house of Parliament, meaning he says to sit often there with the Lords'.[2] It seems highly likely that Sir Edmund formed part of this 'fair retinue'.

And he learned to be keenly aware of the factionalism which was the lifeblood of the court. Throughout his reign James I adored the company of attractive young men. By 1621 his favourite was the charming and beautiful George Villiers, second son of a poor Leicestershire squire who, having attracted the King's attention in 1614, began an ascent which Clarendon would later describe as 'so quick, that it seemed rather a flight than a growth'.[3] James christened him 'Steenie', an allusion to St Stephen, who is described in the New Testament (Acts 6:15) as having the face of an angel. He was made a Gentleman of the Bedchamber in 1615; Master of the Horse and Viscount Villiers in 1616; Master of the Wardrobe and Earl of Buckingham in 1617; and Marquis of Buckingham in 1618. Although Prince Charles initially resented Buckingham's intimacy with his father, Steenie managed to win him round; and as he did, Sir Edmund saw that establishing ties with the favourite could bring material and political benefits. During a royal progress in the summer of 1622, he approached the Marquis at Newmarket and asked outright for the lieutenancy of Whaddon Chase, a medieval hunting forest to the east of Buckingham. Steenie was Keeper of the Chase, and his response – given via one of his servants, Sir Richard Graham – is a perfect example of the way in which favours were granted and political ties forged in Stuart England. Graham began by reminding Sir Edmund of the intense competition for the lieutenancy. 'There hath been many suitors for the said place to my lord,' he wrote; 'and Mr Waterhouse hath been a very earnest suitor.'[4] Then came a little flattery: 'My lord did forbear to give him [i.e., Mr Waterhouse] or any other any answer, because he thought you had a mind to it.' And finally, the decision:'He wishes that the employment be worth your deserving, and grants you the lieutenancy with all his heart.'

Or almost finally. The lieutenancy of the Chase provided Sir Edmund with social cachet, but it was just as important that it provide him with a supply of venison which he could distribute to friends and relations, extending his own web of obligations and favours. Buckingham was happy to appear not only obliging, but generous. 'For the venison you desired me to procure you, I did acquaint my lord, and his lordship saith, he will not limit you by the allowance of a warrant, but gives you free leave to kill what you will, both in the park and the chase. You need not be sparing to pleasure yourself and your friends also . . .'[5]

The lieutenancy of Whaddon Chase gave Sir Edmund status among his Buckinghamshire neighbours, and a supply of venison with which, by giving presents of the occasional haunch or umble pie, he could remind them of that status and establish their debt to him for favours received. He in turn was now obligated to the Marquis of Buckingham and simultaneously assured of Buckingham's goodwill towards him.

In the spring of 1623 Sir Edmund went back to Spain, twelve years after his last visit. Once again, the purpose of the trip was to secure a Spanish bride for a prince. James I had never given up his hopes of marrying one of his children to a Protestant ruler and another to a Catholic. Princess Elizabeth had been married in 1613 to the fiercely Protestant Frederick V, Elector Palatine of the Rhine and later King of Bohemia; so Prince Charles was destined for a match with a Catholic bride. Between 1614 and 1618 Sir John Digby, who was still James I's ambassador to Madrid, tried to negotiate for the hand of the Infanta Maria. Nothing came of this, largely because Spain demanded concessions for English Catholics to which the King dared not agree; but Digby was ordered to take up the idea again in 1621, when the pious Philip III died unexpectedly and was succeeded by his eighteen-year-old son Philip IV. There was now a particularly pressing reason for trying to reconcile Protestants and Catholics in Europe: in 1620, as what would become the Thirty Years War lumbered into life, Frederick V was decisively defeated by a Catholic force under the Emperor Ferdinand at the Battle of the White Mountain, and James I's son-in-law lost his crown, his kingdom and his palatinate. A union between the Infanta Maria and Prince Charles might encourage the King of Spain to resolve the difficulties of Frederick and Elizabeth; this would in turn help James I to calm popular and increasingly vociferous demands at home that he should be sending a Protestant army to restore his son-in-law's fortunes.

At first, the negotiations seemed to go well. There were hints from Madrid that Spain was softening its hard line on religion, and by 1622 Charles was taking Spanish lessons so that he could talk to his future bride. In January 1623 the Spanish ambassador, Count Gondomar, let it be known that if the Prince were to travel to Madrid to press his suit in person, he could be sure of a warm reception.

Charles had spent the past eleven years being the runner-up in a contest with his dead brother. Henry was the knight-errant, the romantic hero, the man of action. Now there was an opportunity for Charles to play the chivalrous knight, to show the nation – and his parents – that he too could cut some figure in the world. Having secured the reluctant agreement of his father, the Prince set off for Spain on 18 February accompanied by the Marquis of Buckingham – a pair of 'sweet boys, and dear venturous knights', as the King called them, 'worthy to be put in a new romance'.[6] With only two courtiers as travelling companions – Endymion Porter, who had been brought up in Spain, and the Prince's secretary Sir Francis Cottington, who was described by a contemporary as 'an Hispaniolized Englishman'[7] – they went incognito, wearing false beards and travelling under the names of Tom Smith and John Smith.

After a six-hour Channel crossing, during which both the

venturous knights were seasick, they travelled overland down
through France and into Spain, eventually leaving their companions behind. On the evening of 17 March the pair arrived at the
English ambassador's lodgings in Madrid, the House of the Seven
Chimneys off the Calle de Alcala. Buckingham went in and
announced to an astonished and appalled Sir John Digby that the
young man holding the horses at the door was the Prince of Wales.[*]

Sir Edmund Verney's role in this bizarre business began a few
weeks later. King James, having allowed his son to undertake
what he fondly described as 'this knight-errant pilgrimage',[8] had
managed at one fell swoop to upset Digby's marriage negotiations, which were at an extremely delicate stage; to place the heir
to the throne of England in the hands of a traditional enemy;
and to alienate the Puritan faction at home, which was convinced
that once the Jesuits got their hooks into Charles, he was bound
to convert to Catholicism. 'They err who think there is any thing
to be had from a Papist for love rather than for fear,' wrote one
pamphleteer; 'or that Spain will ever desist from aspiring to the
universal Monarchy of Christendom.'[9] Now James decided it was
time to despatch a party of Charles's household servants, so that
his son would at least be equipped to behave like a prince while
he stayed in Madrid. On 3 April sixty members of the household boarded the *Adventure* at Portsmouth, under the command
of Charles's master of horse, Lord Andover. They included Sir
Spencer Compton, the Master of the Ward; Sir Robert Carey,
the Prince's Chamberlain; his Comptroller, five Grooms of the
Bedchamber, two Gentlemen Ushers of the Presence, two Anglican
chaplains, three pages – and eight Gentlemen of the Privy
Chamber, one of whom was Sir Edmund Verney.

After a rough voyage the *Adventure* anchored off Santander on
the north coast of Spain on 11 April. Sir Edmund and the others
went ashore and were dismayed to find the town 'a very poor
thing, having neither glass windows nor chimneys'.[10] Nevertheless
they spent a week there, recuperating from the Bay of Biscay,
waiting for the arrival of mules to carry them to Madrid and

---

[*]To be accurate, Digby was now the Earl of Bristol, having been elevated to the
peerage the previous year. (And while we're on the subject of titles, the Marquis
of Buckingham heard while in Madrid that King James had given him a dukedom.)

generally engaging in what has, from time immemorial, been the favourite pastime of Englishmen abroad – feeling superior to foreigners. The women of Santander were fat and ugly; the men were lazy and haughty; everybody was superstitious and idolatrous. 'Upon holy days,' wrote Sir Richard Wynn, one of Sir Edmund's fellow Gentlemen of the Privy Chamber, 'all these people do but go from one cross to another shrine, with their beads in their hands, praying in a language they understand not, and adoring of dumb images.'[11]

The mules finally arrived, and very soon Sir Edmund and his friends began to think Santander was not such a bad place after all. The 240-mile route to Madrid wound over precipitous tracks and mountain paths, over snow-capped hills through burning hot scrubland – 'the most wicked ways and country that ever Christians passed'.[12] And this was only the first day; there was worse to come. The midday meal was taken at a plank rather than a table, with no cloth or napkins; it consisted of a few eggs and a goat which had been 'held above the fire until it was burnt black'.[13] When the happy band reached their inn that night, 'a long room, so much decayed, that we expected hourly when it would fall upon us',[14] they found no stools to sit on while they ate their supper, no glass in the windows, no beds to sleep on. What they did find was a letter from the Prince of Wales telling them all to go home.

This plunged the entire party into confusion. They were unsure whether the letter was a Jesuitical ploy or a genuine royal command. 'It struck such a general sadness in us all,' wrote Wynn, 'that for half an hour there passed not a word between us, some troubled with their return, others with the fear of the ill success of our master's business, and some with the doubt of his safety.'[15] After some heated discussion, most of the party opted to return to Santander and the *Adventure*. (No doubt the prospect of avoiding another ten days or so on the back of a mule played some part in their decision.) Sir Robert Carey and Sir Spencer Compton decided to travel on to Madrid to make sure their master was safe, while Sir Edmund and five others agreed that another voyage through the Bay of Biscay was not for them: they would carry on by mule to Burgos, ninety-odd miles south of Santander, and then ride post through France to make a much shorter Channel crossing.

But by the time Sir Edmund reached Burgos – 'the most nasty and beastly town kept in the world'[16] – the situation had become even more complicated for the Englishmen. Sir Spencer Compton fell sick and couldn't carry on. Sir Edmund and his group were told to stay where they were. Sir Richard Wynn and one of the Gentlemen Ushers were ordered to Madrid. Eleven other members of the household and their servants were ordered back to England as quickly as possible; the *Adventure* was commanded to remain at anchor off Santander.

At this point everyone, no matter where they were on the route, seems to have decided to head for Madrid, where at least they could hope for some clear instructions. They rode on pack mules which had neither saddles nor bridles, and which did not take kindly to being jabbed with spurs. Not surprisingly, the courtiers fell off quite a lot.

Travel was notoriously difficult in a country where, in the words of one seventeenth-century travel guide, 'the warm sun . . . is somewhat too liberal of his beams'.[17] Sir Charles Cornwallis, Digby's predecessor as ambassador, never veered from his conviction that the country was 'one of the most confused and disordered in Christendom',[18] and *he* travelled by litter, with a train of one thousand mules, civic receptions in every town and village along the way and Moorish dancers to entertain him each night. Sir Edmund and his companions had no such luxury. Tired and bruised, they rode into Madrid on 29 April 1623.

In the meantime the Spanish court had been giving a warm welcome to Prince Charles, convinced as they were by his unorthodox visit that he must be ready to convert to Catholicism in order to win his bride. Philip had agreed to an informal meeting with Charles as soon as he heard the news of his arrival, although informality is a relative term. Buckingham wrote to James I that 'we had a private visit of the King, the Queen, the Infanta, Don Carlos, and the Cardinal, in the sight of all the world, and I may call it a private obligation hidden from nobody; for there was the Pope's nuncio, the Emperor's ambassador, the French, and all the streets filled with guards and other people'.[19] The best of the nobility went before the King's coach, and all the ladies of the court came after it, while the entire procession rode up and down past the Prince's coach three times – all the while pretending not to notice it, because Charles had not yet officially arrived in Madrid.

His official arrival took place in the pouring rain on Monday 27 March. But the Spanish did not allow the weather to cast a cloud over the spectacle. A magnificent procession wound its way from the monastery of San Jeronimo to the royal palace, with Philip dressed in gold and Prince Charles in rather more subdued clothes 'in the English manner', but still creating quite a stir. 'He is a fine, handsome youth of about twenty-two,' wrote one eyewitness, 'with a long face, rather sunburnt from the journey, and his beard is just beginning to show.'[20] There were bullfights, dances, illuminations and fireworks; the King ordered the release of a large number of convicts in the Prince's honour, and relaxed a series of restrictions on the use of coaches and fine clothes which had been introduced the month before as an economy measure. The Queen presented Charles with some elaborate gifts, including perfume and underclothes. (It had been a long journey after all, and the Prince had travelled light . . .)

When Sir Edmund Verney and the rest of the English courtiers straggled into Madrid a month later they found they had missed all the celebrations. Charles seemed optimistic enough about the marriage negotiations: he had not had much chance to talk with the Infanta, but letters were passing to and fro between him and the Pope, who was prepared to grant a dispensation in return for various concessions to English Catholics. Back home, King James ordered his Surveyor of Works, Inigo Jones, to fit out Catholic chapels at St James's and Somerset House, ready for the use of Maria and her attendants. Jones was told 'to have them done out of hand, and yet with great state and costliness';[21] the plans were sent back to Spain for approval, and with great ceremony on 16 May the Spanish ambassador, Don Carlos Coloma, laid the first stone of the chapel at St James's Palace.

In Madrid, Charles and Buckingham had both taken to wearing Spanish clothes – 'such an attire as will make the handsomest man living look like another thing,' wrote one of Sir Edmund's companions.[22] But if the Prince's sartorial taste didn't impress his household officers, nor did his domestic arrangements. He had been given a small set of lodgings at the royal palace, with a little garden 'so nasty and ill favouredly kept, that a farmer in England

would be ashamed of such another'.[23] Worse, there was no room
at the palace for the newcomers. They made rather desperate
attempts to find their own lodgings, with the Spanish charging
an exorbitant forty shillings a week for the cheapest chamber,
until eventually space was found for them at a mansion on the
other side of the city. After some desultory sightseeing, most of
them sat around playing cards and waiting for a summons from
their master, 'for to say truth, there was nothing to be done else'.[24]
Sir Edmund and another of the Gentlemen of the Privy Chamber,
Sir William Howard, were more enterprising than the rest, and
seem to have secured lodgings away from the others and close
to Prince Charles. But there was an undercurrent of resentment.
Most of the Prince's senior officers were deliberately kept away
from him. The two Anglican chaplains, whose role was to set up
a prayer room for him at the royal palace, were told they would
be thrown out if they even set foot in the place. After a week
of this, the Prince ordered his servants to go home. It is hard to
gauge the reasoning behind his decision, but the fact that there
was some trouble between the English courtiers and the Spanish,
and that they were proving an expensive luxury without adding
much to his status or wellbeing, probably had a lot to do with
it. Keeping on a few personal attendants and four Gentlemen of
the Privy Chamber, he packed the rest off to Santander, the
Adventure and the Bay of Biscay. Those who couldn't face another
voyage like the one which had brought them to Spain were given
permission to travel overland through France.

   Sir Edmund was one of the handful of courtiers whom Charles
kept by him. He stayed in Madrid for another four months, watching
his master grow more and more frustrated at his lack of progress
with the Infanta. At one point the Prince actually scaled a garden
wall in the Casa del Campo in an effort to woo his princess,
without much success. For her part, Maria seems to have blown
hot and cold about the match. One minute she was flirting coquet-
tishly as Charles gazed at her adoringly for half an hour on end;
the next she was declaring that she would rather become a nun
than marry a heretic. Her confessors, meanwhile, did their best to
confirm her in her pious resolve. 'What a comfortable bedfellow
you will have,' they whispered to her. 'He who lies by your side,
and will be the father of your children, is certain to go to Hell.'[25]

In the end, though, the Infanta's personal views and even the advice of her priests didn't really count for much.* The Anglo-Spanish marriage was a matter of policy: Charles had to extract a promise from Philip to help restore Frederick to the throne of Bohemia. He was also determined not to go home without his bride, believing that the Spanish were quite capable of reneging on the deal the moment he quit the country, which would leave him looking very stupid indeed. For their part, Philip and his chief minister, the Count of Olivares, pushed hard for a whole raft of concessions: the suspension or repeal of the penal laws against English Catholics; freedom of religion for Maria and her household; her right to control the upbringing of any children of the marriage. Olivares offered little room for compromise – it was as if he was putting obstacles in the way of the match rather than trying to reach agreement.

And so he was. Unlike Philip and Count Gondomar, who had been recalled to Madrid to help with negotiations, Olivares did not think the marriage was necessary for good Anglo-Spanish relations. Moreover, he knew that in reality Philip was in no position to help Charles's sister and brother-in-law to regain their kingdom. There was a moment of embarrassment in July when an impatient Charles suddenly caved in and agreed to all the Spanish terms – as long as the marriage took place by Christmas. In September he took an oath to observe the marriage articles; there was general rejoicing in Madrid, with fireworks and bonfires in the streets; and Maria, who was now being called the *Princesa de Inglaterra*, began daily English lessons with an ex-embassy chaplain who had converted to Rome.

But Olivares continued to make life difficult, declaring that the Princesa would not be travelling to Inglaterra until official papal approval of the marriage arrived the following spring. By now all kinds of tensions were starting to show. The stalemate resulted in

---

* Although Charles clearly thought they counted for something, since he demanded security from the Spanish government against the possibility that Maria would enter a convent at the last minute, 'and all the world will justly condemn me for a rash-headed fool, not to foresee and prevent this in time' (Charles to the Earl of Bristol in Sir Charles Petrie (ed.), *The Letters, Speeches and Proclamations of King Charles I*, 31).

personal hostility between Buckingham and Olivares. Rumours
went round Madrid that the Prince's courtiers were trying to
subvert faithful Spaniards from their religion. For their part, most
of the English viewed the Spanish in general as thieves and liars,
and the army of priests and theologians who hovered around the
royal palace as worse than that. Sir Edmund Verney in particular
was unable to share Charles's easy toleration of Catholicism and,
not for the last time, he found himself having to place loyalty to
his master above his own strongly held personal convictions. When
the Prince's 'Hispaniolized' secretary, Sir Francis Cottington, fell
sick and converted to Catholicism on what he assumed to be his
deathbed, it seemed as though Rome were exerting a malign
influence over the expedition, a view which was only partly miti-
gated by the way in which Cottington recovered and diplomatically declared himself to be a Protestant again. (He made quite
a habit of switching faiths in the course of a long diplomatic
career, eventually dying a Catholic at Valladolid in 1652.)

In August 1623, when temperatures in Madrid rose into the
eighties, Buckingham caught a cold 'and a little fit of an ague'.[26]
He was bled and made a swift recovery, but the sickness spread
through the Prince of Wales's household. One of Charles's pages,
a twenty-year-old named Thomas Washington, came down with
a much more serious bout of fever and seemed likely to die.

While Washington lay sick and delirious in his chamber, he
was visited by an English priest named Ballard, who saw an opportunity to save a soul and spelled out in lurid detail what lay in
store if he died a heretic. As he was going downstairs after the
sick visit, Ballard met Sir Edmund Verney, who demanded to
know what the priest was doing in Washington's lodging. Sir
Edmund was a Puritan at heart. He did not like Roman
Catholicism, he did not trust Roman Catholics, and he thought
– along with rather too many of his fellow-countrymen – that
Catholic priests were duplicitous, untrustworthy and lacking in
integrity. The two men began arguing over the propriety of
Ballard's attempt to convert the dying boy. They soon fell 'from
words to blows', in the words of one contemporary, and in the
tussle Sir Edmund punched Ballard in the face.[27]

It isn't clear what happened next, but it seems that they were
dragged apart and Verney was hit by a Spanish guard in the

process. Certainly when the Spaniards made an official complaint to Charles about his behaviour, the Prince countered with a complaint of his own that one of his Gentlemen of the Privy Chamber had been assaulted.

Poor Thomas Washington died a couple of days later on 15 August, his Protestant soul still safe from popery, and his body was buried in the back garden of Digby's residence by the Calle de Alcala.* But the brawl was the culmination of several months of bickering and jostling between English and Spanish courtiers and, although Count Gondomar intervened to smooth things over, Philip let Charles know that if he intended to stay in Madrid much longer it might be as well to send Sir Edmund and the rest of his courtiers home.

He needn't have bothered. It was finally dawning on Charles and Buckingham that Olivares would never let the Infanta out of Spain. When he told them that the only way to restore Frederick and Elizabeth to their lands was for their infant son to marry the Holy Roman Emperor's daughter and be raised a Catholic at the Imperial Court, Charles decided to cut his losses and head for home. On the surface, relations remained cordial, with Charles looking forward to marrying Maria by proxy in November, and distributing farewell gifts to all and sundry – so many, in fact, that in spite of having begged a fresh supply of jewels from his father several months earlier, he ran out and had to borrow a diamond cross from Sir Edmund to give to Don Maria de Lande. On 12 September, after a tour of the Escorial, which they agreed was the eighth wonder of the world (and where Velázquez drew the Prince's portrait), Charles and his retinue took their leave of Philip and the royal family and rode to Santander, where they took ship for England, arriving in Portsmouth on 5 October. The following month the Prince cancelled the proxy wedding until his brother-in-law was restored to his palatinate, knowing full well that this was not going to happen.

The expedition had been a disaster. Not only had Charles

* Nineteenth-century sources state that Washington was a Buckinghamshire boy, hence Sir Edmund's concern for a neighbour in distress. He was in fact from Sulgrave Manor in Northamptonshire, and the great-great-great-uncle of the first President of the United States.

failed to bring home his bride, he had made a fool of himself in the process and tarnished his credentials as a hero of Protestantism. Moreover, he and his father completely misjudged the depth of anti-Catholic and anti-Spanish feeling at home. There were scenes of wild rejoicing at Portsmouth when he landed without Maria, and the young diarist Simonds D'Ewes noted with satisfaction that 335 bonfires were lit between Temple Bar and Whitehall (a distance of just under a mile) to celebrate the collapse of the Spanish match. The following summer Thomas Middleton's *A Game at Chess* was put on at the Globe, satirising Gondomar as the Black Knight bent on world domination and thwarted by Charles and Buckingham as the White Knight and the White Duke. The players managed to acquire Gondomar's litter to add a touch of authenticity, and around one-tenth of the population of London flocked to see the play before complaints from the Spanish ambassador caused the authorities to shut it down.

Hardly an expert at handling rejection, Prince Charles moved quickly into a marriage contract with the daughter of the King of France, Henrietta Maria; and almost as quickly into war with Spain. Buoyed up by popular anti-Spanish sentiments at home, and eager to avenge his humiliating expedition to Madrid, he and Buckingham pushed James I into marginalising the pro-Spanish faction at court and summoning a Parliament which would vote for a war chest. Although he was only fifty-seven when his son came home from Madrid, James was infirm way beyond his years, and pathetically unable to stand up to either his son or his favourite. 'I had rather live banished in any part of the world with you, than live a sorrowful widow-life without you,' he told Buckingham. 'God bless you, my sweet child and wife, and grant that ye may ever be a comfort to your dear Dad and husband.'[28] He died in March 1625, taking with him what little moderating influence he had on Charles and Buckingham.

The consequences of the Spanish expedition for Sir Edmund were far-reaching. What he saw of Spanish political and religious life confirmed him in his loathing for Catholicism and his mistrust of Hapsburg Europe – one reason why, in the Parliament which James reluctantly called for the spring of 1624, he was returned as MP for the borough of Buckingham. His particular branch of the family had not sat in the Commons for more than seventy years.

The escapade in Madrid also brought him closer to Prince Charles, and reinforced the young courtier's conviction that in all honour his place was by the Prince's side, right or wrong. Charles was not particularly astute when it came to choosing his personal servants and advisers, but he did recognise a loyal friend and servant in Sir Edmund. Soon after coming to the throne he confirmed for life a pension of £200 a year which Sir Edmund had previously had (on those occasions when it was actually paid) at the pleasure of the Prince of Wales. Then on 16 February 1626 Charles appointed him knight-marshal of the King's household, a post which brought with it a second pension of £200 a year, an additional salary of 10s. a day, and a further £80 or £90 as Gaoler of the Marshalsea, an office which came with the knight-marshalship.

Although usually drawn from the kind of gentry background to which Sir Edmund belonged, rather than the nobility, the marshal of the household was an important figure, with an honourable and ancient pedigree dating back to the early Middle Ages. Starting out as a minor domestic servant, he had evolved into the head of palace security, a sort of royal policeman. By the time Sir Edmund was granted the post, the marshal's role was to control members of the King's household, who, because they *were* members of that household, had special privileges and status which could place them beyond the reach of the common law.

The knight-marshal's jurisdiction had once radiated outward for twelve miles from the monarch's person, the 'verge' within which members of the royal household were exempt from prosecution by the normal courts. So when medieval kings or queens went on progress, the marshal could apprehend wrongdoers within twelve miles round about. During the Middle Ages the Court of the Marshalsea, which was presided over jointly by the marshal and the steward of the household, had steadily extended its jurisdiction until it covered cases where an offence had taken place within the verge, no matter whether either plaintiff or defendant were royal servants. In December 1316, for instance, Sybil de la Haghe asked the court to exact £20 damages from Richard of Cotgrave, who had knocked out five of her teeth the previous week within the verge (which was then in Nottinghamshire, because that was where the King happened to be). He was found guilty, fined twenty marks (a mark was £0.66) and committed to the marshal's charge for a week until he paid up. The marshal usually received a fee of one mark from his prisoners, and in Cotgrave's case, at least, the clerks received four marks as their share of the fine – a healthy 20 per cent.

Sir Edmund's sphere of influence was less ambulatory than that of his predecessors – by the early seventeenth century the verge was fixed at a twelve-mile radius from Westminster, rather than from the monarch's person wherever he or she happened to be – but he was still able to arrest any member of the royal household and bring them before the Marshalsea Court which sat every Friday to hear complaints and grievances by or against the King's men; and if found guilty, transgressors were liable to be consigned to imprisonment in the Marshalsea, the notorious gaol on the south bank of the Thames in Southwark. The Marshalsea also housed highborn debtors, prisoners of conscience – anyone, in fact, who was considered too distinguished to be thrown into Newgate or the house of correction at Bridewell, but who did not quite possess the necessary social credentials to enter the Tower of London.

It is hardly surprising that throughout the Middle Ages the marshal was a deeply unpopular character. He and his officers were regularly accused of extortionate practices, of taking bribes, of unlawful imprisonment and generally of overreaching their authority. The Marshalsea was one of the targets of Wat Tyler's Rebellion in 1381; four centuries later it was vilified as 'An old pile most dreadful to the view/Dismal as wormwood or repenting rue'.[29] Because the Court of the Marshalsea tended to exact justice more rapidly than other courts, it was popular with plaintiffs, and by the fifteenth century it was hearing cases of contract where neither party was a servant of the crown, justifying this extension of its jurisdiction by the simple expedient of insisting that both parties were members of the royal household and ignoring any claims to the contrary. Unhappy that the Marshalsea was taking away their business, the Courts of the King's Bench and the Common Pleas persuaded Parliament to enforce the ancient rule that the Marshalsea should deal with royal servants only; but there were constant battles over jurisdiction right into the seventeenth century. Eventually, after a series of cases in which the marshal's men gaoled officers of other courts for making arrests within the verge and were themselves found guilty of false imprisonment, assault, battery and wounding as a result, James I was forced to reform the Court of the Marshalsea. He accepted that it was a court solely for his own household; but at the same time he set up a second tribunal, the Court of the Verge, which had the jurisdiction which the Marshalsea had lost, and which was presided over by the marshal and the steward. Just before James died, the Verge was limited to hearing cases where damages were less than five pounds; but everyone regarded the two courts as identical, and even when they were merged in 1630 to form the Palace Court, 'a court of record for the Palace of Westminster and twelve miles about the same, by the name of the King's Court of his Palace of Westminster, for all personal pleas and actions', everyone continued to refer to it as the Marshalsea.[30]

Sir Edmund Verney was appointed knight-marshal of the household at the beginning of 1626, a time when his role as judge in the Courts of the Marshalsea and the Verge was the subject of some severe scrutiny by other courts. But he also had another and arguably more difficult job as marshal — that of keeping order within the sprawling precincts of the Palace of Whitehall, the primary residence of the Kings and Queens of England ever since 1529, when Henry VIII appropriated the Westminster residence of the Archbishop of York from Cardinal Wolsey. Officially named 'the new Palace of Westminster', York Place was already being called 'Whitehall' in 1530, a reference to the white stonework of Wolsey's great hall. This vast complex of lodgings and domestic offices, with its own tennis court and cockpit, its own tiltyard and gardens, even its own builder's yard, dock and granary, stretched for a good 600 yards along the Thames between Westminster Abbey and Charing Cross. Much of it was hopelessly old-fashioned and shapeless. 'Nothing but a heap of houses erected at divers times'[31] was the verdict of one foreign observer. 'An assemblage of several houses, badly built, at different times,' said another, with 'nothing in its exterior from which you could suppose it to be the habitation of the king.'[32] But that wasn't altogether fair. Rising up in the midst of this badly built assemblage was Inigo Jones's stunning Banqueting House of 1619–22, the finest classical building in Britain and a stark and elegant contrast to the muddle of red, black and white painted structures that surrounded it. And less contemporary, but just as impressive in their own way, were the two gatehouses which spanned the highway running through the middle of the palace complex: the castellated Holbein Gate with its terracotta roundels depicting Roman emperors, a reminder of royal authority; and the more classical King Street Gate, capped with two rather lovely cupolas and covered with pediments, busts and signs of the zodiac.

The road spanned by these two gates was one of Sir Edmund's more difficult security problems. By modern-day standards, Whitehall was astonishingly open. There was a more or less permanent market at the entrance, and several stalls inside the walls; people wandered through the courtyards without a thought for security; and beggars and whores hung around doorways and quasi-public areas, confident that there was easy money to be made from the constant stream of courtiers who came and went. One of Sir Edmund's jobs was periodically to sweep through the public parts of the palace, paying special attention to 'the exclusion of boys and vile persons, and punishment of vagabonds and mighty beggars, not permitting any of them to remain in, about, or near unto the Court'. He was also told to ensure that 'all such unthrifty and common women, as follow the Court, may be likewise, from time to time, openly punished, banished, and excluded'.[33] Every courtier and official lodging at Whitehall had to provide Sir Edmund with a list of their servants; anyone that he, his deputy or his officers found in the palace but not on the list was liable to be fined or imprisoned.

It was not only the uninvited who caused a problem at Whitehall. At any one time there were between 1500 and 2000 people living in the precincts of the palace, from senior officials like the Secretary of State, the Lord Chamberlain and the Earl Marshal (Thomas Howard, Earl of Arundel, who was Sir Edmund's immediate superior), to embroiderers and haberdashers, stocking menders and tapsters. There were twelve laundresses, eighteen laundry maids and an unspecified number of 'men washers' – and that was only after James I had issued a decree limiting 'the great and excessive number' because of the 'many abuses and disorders' which they committed.[34] It was the knight-marshal's job to make sure that these people behaved themselves – not only the laundry maids and stocking menders, but the courtiers and other officials.

This obviously required a degree of tact: the law was the law, but the consequences of arresting, say, one of Buckingham's servants for debt and throwing him into the Marshalsea might be much more complicated than apprehending one of the Whitehall tapsters. A pragmatic approach to wrongdoing was a vital part of being a successful knight-marshal of the household.

In spite of the reforms which took place in the reign of James I there were — as with most positions in the royal household — opportunities for making extra money. Just how much is hard to say, although the fact that Sir Edmund's predecessor had purchased the post of knight-marshal for £3000 implies that it was quite a lot. By way of comparison Sir John Finet, who became the King's master of ceremonies in 1627, also earned an official stipend of £200. On top of this he received an annual allowance which varied from £134 to £334, and gifts and gratuities of anything up to £402. Taken together, Finet's stipend, allowances and gratuities averaged around £600, and in a good year they amounted to more than £800. Sir Edmund had £400 in pensions, his salary of £182 10s., his £80-odd as Gaoler of the Marshalsea, the fees he took for presiding at the Marshalsea Court and those demanded from the hapless occupants of his gaol; so the knight-marshal's income probably exceeded this figure. And that wasn't all. Sir Edmund also took in as much again in rental income from Claydon and various other bits and pieces of land in Buckinghamshire, Oxfordshire and Berkshire. In theory he was a wealthy man.

But not in practice. Keeping up Claydon cost money, and he had to pay for his board at his mother's Drury Lane house. Court life, with its complicated etiquette of favours and obligations, was expensive. His pensions were paid at irregular intervals. There were certain fixed commitments — a widow's jointure of £200 a year for his mother, for example, and another of £50 a year for his sister-in-law, Ursula. He had to service the debts he had incurred on the purchase of Claydon, and there was no prospect of Charles I coming up with the £3000 he had promised. By the time Charles came to the throne Sir Edmund had already been forced to sell off all his Mursley lands, piece by piece; they raised a total of £2885.

Then there was the family to provide for. It was taken for granted, of course, that the eldest boy, Ralph, would get more or less everything when his father died. The other three sons, Tom, Edmund and Henry, could make their own way, although they might receive small annuities from the Verney estate. The girls were a different matter. When Sir Edmund was appointed knight-marshal, he and Lady Margaret had four daughters, and two more came along over the next seven years. At some point in the future husbands would have to be found for each of them, and Sir Edmund reckoned that this would involve dowries of £1000 apiece, and some careful forward planning. Susan, the eldest girl, would be twelve – and thus old enough to be married – in 1633, with Penelope following her the next year, and Margaret the year after that.

The time-honoured route to long-term financial solvency was to marry one's eldest son to an heiress. Puritan preachers consistently condemned this practice from the pulpit. 'A wife and a discreet woman is better than wealth; her price is far above pearls,' declared Thomas Gataker in a wedding sermon preached in 1623. 'For house and possessions are the inheritance of the fathers; but a prudent wife is of the Lord.'[35] Robert Wilkinson made a similar point in a sermon of 1607. Taking his text from Proverbs 31: 14 – 'She is like the merchants' ships; she bringeth her food from afar' – Wilkinson railed against the habit of choosing a wife for the size of her dowry, 'for the worst wives have many times the best portions; and the best wives . . . have oft times none at all'.[36] Men in search of a bride now behaved like Judas when he betrayed Christ, asking only 'What will you give?'

Prospective bridegrooms and their fathers were less apt to take the moral high ground. Even Reverend Gataker had to admit that wealth in a wife might be construed as God's blessing and that, all other things being equal, it needn't exactly be a bar to matrimony. But heiresses were not so easy to find. So when at the end of 1626 Sir Edmund heard that a particularly wealthy example was about to come on to the market, he seized his chance. The fact that she was an orphan, and that her guardianship might be bought for £1000, simplified matters. The fact that she was only ten years old was neither here nor there.

3
Sufficient Intellectuals

ary Blacknall came from Abingdon in Oxfordshire.
Born on St Valentine's Day 1616, she was the
youngest daughter of one of the wealthiest men
in the town; and when her father and mother died on the same
day, 21 August 1625, she and her sister Jane were made wards of
the crown.* Her maternal grandfather and three uncles petitioned

---

* The Blacknalls may have fallen victim to the plague, which swept through
Abingdon in 1625. An epitaph in St Nicholas' church, although put up several
decades after their deaths, still resonates with a thoroughly Jacobean relish:

> When once they lived on earth, one bed did hold
> Their bodies, which one minute turn'd to mould;
> Being dead, one grave is trusted with that prize
> Until the trump doth sound and all must rise;
> Here death's stroke, even, did not part this pair,
> But by his stroke they more united were;
> And what they left behind you plainly see,
> One only daughter and their charity . . .

the Court of Wards and Liveries for leases over the Blacknall lands and custody of Mary and her sister Jane. They offered £2000 for the lease, the custody and the right of choosing husbands for the two girls; and between them they paid half of this fine straight to the crown, entering into a bond for the rest.

Mary's older sister followed her parents to the grave in September 1626, leaving the little girl as sole heiress to the Blacknall estates. By now she was living with an aunt and uncle, Anne and Richard Lybbe, at Hardwick Court, an imposing Tudor manor house on the border between Oxfordshire and Berkshire; and although by the terms of their agreement with the Court of Wards her guardians were supposed to keep her unmarried until she was at least fourteen, the prospect of acquiring an heiress proved just too tempting for the Lybbes. Within a couple of months of Jane Blacknall's death they had persuaded Mary's grand-father and a second uncle, Anthony Blagrove, to agree to Mary marrying their son; and they pressed ahead with the wedding plans as quickly as they could.

But they weren't quick enough. Mary's third uncle, Charles Wiseman, was not at all comfortable with the way things were going. He refused to give his approval for the marriage and complained directly to the Court of Wards, with dramatic results. The Lybbes were immediately commanded by the King, 'all excuses and delays set apart', to surrender Mary to Sir John Denham, Lord Chief Baron of the Exchequer. Denham had a country house some thirty miles away at Boarstall in Buckinghamshire, and the child was to be left there with Lady Denham 'to be by her brought up, amongst her own daughters, unmarried, unaffyed [i.e. unaffianced], and uncontracted'. Lybbe was told that if he failed to hand Mary over, he and her other guardians would be fined £5000. The Sheriff of Berkshire was ordered to ride over to Hardwick to enforce the injunction; if the Lybbes refused to comply, he was to 'forthwith take and seize the body of our said ward, and safely to deliver her into the custody of the said Sir John Denham, or his lady in his absence ... not failing the accomplishment hereof, as you will answer to the contrary at your peril'.[1]

Mary never reached Sir John Denham's house. The Lybbes decided that if their son couldn't have her, she should be offered to the highest bidder. At this point Sir Edmund Verney arrived on the scene, although hardly as a knight in shining armour. He and another aspiring father-in-law, Sir Richard Harrison of Whistley in Berkshire, were both invited to express an interest in Mary's future; and Sir Edmund came up with the better offer, agreeing to indemnify Mary's guardians against any action by Sir John Denham and to pay the outstanding £1000 which they owed to the Court of Wards and Liveries. He may also have hinted that the guardians would receive a cut of the inheritance at a later date – Anthony Blagrove was certainly under that impression. Sir Edmund had to borrow to finance the arrangement, but since Mary's inheritance amounted to around £16,000, it was worth it.

The guardians assigned him the wardship and agreed to deliver up the girl within a week. Uncle Wiseman, who was alone in maintaining an altruistic interest in his niece's welfare, imposed a condition that there should be no early marriage to a Verney, any more than there would have been to a Lybbe. Mary should be 'allowed to make her choice at years competent'.[2]

In reality, Mary Blacknall had no choice. All along, Sir Edmund's objective in acquiring her wardship was to marry her and her £16,000 to his son Ralph. Still the Lybbes were reluctant to hand her over, and she was living with them in 1628, in spite of their agreement with the Verneys. They were supported by Uncle Blagrove, who, having assumed that Sir Edmund would offer him a share of Mary's estate, was aggrieved when he didn't. Sir Edmund was eventually forced to complain to the Court of Wards, claiming he was being obstructed because he would not allow the Blagroves any part of Mary's inheritance.

The court gave a judgement in Sir Edmund's favour, and Mary Blacknall was married to Ralph Verney at Middle Claydon on 31 May 1629. She was thirteen years old; her husband was fifteen.

Her new mother-in-law wrote to Aunt Wiseman with the news. 'Your niece and my son are now married,' she said. Mary 'desired so much to have it privately done as we had very few present at it; but now it is past I hope we shall see Mr Wiseman and your-self here'.[3] At the same time Mary also wrote: 'I think it fit to acquaint you that now I am married, in which state I hope God will give me his blessings and make it happy to me.' She too was keen to placate the Wisemans over their not being invited to the wedding. 'Sir Edmund and my lady would have had you at the marriage,' she said; 'but I prayed them it might be privately done, and so it was.' There is something faintly unsettling about the fact that the first drafts of both these letters were written by Sir Edmund for his wife and daughter-in-law to copy out.

Mrs Wiseman was a little anxious, not so much at the tone of the letters as at the suddenness of the marriage. She wrote back to complain that Sir Edmund had not yet settled his estate on Ralph 'according to his promise', something which usually happened before the marriage of an heir. And she expressed surprise that Mary should enter into a match without consulting them first. 'Your uncle and I ever intended this match,' she told the girl, 'but always desired that you would do nothing without our advice, which would have been the better for you both.' Apparently the Lybbes were furious: 'Your Aunt Lybbe saith that she hopeth that I shall repent the match as much as any thing that I ever did.'[4]

The young couple were kept from having sexual relations until well after Mary's fourteenth birthday in February 1630. The bride spent some of the time at Hillesden, and she may have made an extended visit to the Wisemans, who lived down at Steventon in Berkshire. The groom went up to Oxford soon after the wedding.

There was some urgency, however. The point of the match – apart from Sir Edmund's desire to get his hands on the Blacknall estates – was for his heir to father an heir of his own, thus securing the future of the Verney fortunes. So the marriage was consummated in the summer of 1631, giving rise to a barrage of excruciating comments from Ralph's Oxford tutor about 'Hymen's delights' and the need for him to keep his mind on his studies – 'the sweetness of a kiss will relish better after the harshness of a syllogism'.[5] Mary became pregnant in the autumn, and on 21 July 1632 she gave birth to a girl, the first of seven children she bore Ralph over the next fifteen years. The baby, also called Mary, was baptised the same day. She died the next.

Ralph had followed in his father's footsteps by going up to Magdalen Hall in 1629, and he followed in them again a couple of years later by coming down without taking a degree.* Magdalen, which with nearly 300 students was one of the largest of the colleges and halls, had a good reputation among puritanically inclined gentlemen: its principal, John Wilkinson, was one of those who set his face firmly against the ceremonialism in matters of religion which was then creeping into the university.

There were family connections, as well. Magdalen had been the starting point for the distinguished academic career of Ralph's uncle, William Denton, who graduated MA in 1627 and was currently studying in Oxford to be a physician. (He received his BM, his DM, and his licence to practise in 1634.) As the heir of a landed family, Ralph had no need of a career – or to be more accurate, his career was already mapped out for him. But the fact that 'Uncle Doctor', as the family called William Denton, would be on hand to mentor him, coupled with Magdalen's puritan bent, helped Sir Edmund to decide it was the right place for his eldest son to gain an education.

As important as the choice of hall or college was the choice of personal tutor. A boy's tutor supervised not only his instruction, but his conduct and finances, even his religious observance. He directed his studies, and taught him in his own room, supplementing the formal lectures which were supposed to be at the core of the syllabus, and often providing him with manuscript notes – either of his own devising, or else acquired from others along the way – to help with digesting the prescribed texts. A good tutor could have a tremendous effect on his pupil's development, social as well as academic. 'I know it is not your intent to have him earn his bread by his books,' one tutor wrote to the father of a gentleman student in the 1620s. 'When you left him here I took upon me the charge of a gentleman, I shall blush to return him to you again a mere scholar.'[6]

Ralph Verney's tutor, the Rev. John Crowther, was decent and solid, but he wasn't what you'd call an inspiring teacher. Seven

---

* There is some uncertainty over Ralph's stay in Oxford. He doesn't appear in the University Registers, although it is quite clear from the Verney Papers that he was at Magdalen Hall in the late summer of 1631, and that he left soon afterwards. Since a two-year stay was the norm for those students who weren't taking a degree, 1629 seems a fair guess for the start of his academic career.

years older than his charge, he had graduated MA from Magdalen Hall in the summer of 1628, so Ralph was probably one of his first students.* He was also one of his last. In 1632, the year after Ralph left Oxford, Crowther was begging Sir Edmund to find him a place in the household of any nobleman or gentleman 'who hath preferment in his gift', or with an embassy overseas, or with 'any regiment of soldiers'.[7] Anywhere, in fact, that didn't involve him in teaching students. Sir Edmund duly obliged, and found Crowther a place as chaplain to one of his Denton sisters-in-law.

We can be sure that Ralph wasn't the cause of Crowther's flight from Oxford. A serious, rather lugubrious young man with a long face and a long nose, he may not have stretched for the glittering prizes, but he gave his tutor little trouble, and he seems to have been careful in his studies, as he was careful in his life. The typical daily routine for an undergraduate in term time involved rising at five, prayers at six, followed by Bible reading and private study and then a session with one's tutor between eight and nine. William Trumbull, who entered Magdalen College (not to be confused with Magdalen Hall, which lay next door) in 1622, described how he would read Diogenes Laertius on the *Lives of the Philosophers* with his tutor, before attending the formal disputations in the schools from half past nine to eleven o'clock. After dinner he read from the Roman historian Florus, and after supper he went over his day's studies and read the Bible again before going to bed at ten.[8] But Trumbull was a committed scholar, one of the select group of Oxford students in the seventeenth century who actually left with a degree. At the other end of the spectrum there were plenty of young men who could feel a kinship with Thomas Hood when he proudly claimed, 'I came illiterate and so departed. I neither studied nor learnt anything.'[9]

Like the majority of students, Ralph fell somewhere between these two extremes. Crowther was at pains to point out that God had given him 'sufficient intellectuals'. He was also keen to impress upon the boy that an education was an important part of being a gentleman: 'You know what honour to his family,' he wrote in

---

* One-third of students were assigned to a tutor who was under twenty-five years old; another one-third had tutors aged between twenty-five and twenty-nine. Fewer than one in ten studied with a tutor who was over forty.

November 1631, 'what a credit to himself (to let go religious motives), doth a gentleman purchase, who hath not only the outward gifts of fortune, but is fraught with the diviner perfection of mind.'[10] By no means everyone subscribed to the idea that a knowledge of Greek and Latin, logic and philosophy were essential if a young man was to play a full part in gentry society; but it was rapidly gaining ground during the early seventeenth century, and the undergraduate curriculum at Oxford was designed to provide the sons of the gentry and nobility with a good grasp of the basics. Even during vacations, Crowther bombarded Ralph with homilies and homework. Enclosing a set of notes on astronomy for him to read in conjunction with his set texts, he wrote, 'I desire, till you hear from me again, that you only study your logic and astronomy notes. I hope you may dispense with your pleasures to spend three or four hours a day in the study of these.'[11] History and geography were also important. Ralph was told to compile a 'genealogy of the kings', and gently reproved when Crowther checked it and found it to be 'somewhat imperfect and also false in many places'.[12] The tutor even offered to come over to Claydon at Christmas for a week or two to coach Ralph in geography, a subject 'I know you'll account most necessary and willingly embrace'.[13] History doesn't record what Ralph thought of the idea, but three months later, after he had come down from Oxford, Crowther was urging him to read Edward Grimstone's *Estates, Empires, and Principalities of the World* (1615) and W. Shute's *General History of the Magnificent State of Venice* (1612). Was this an indication of the boy's abiding interest in geography, or simply of his continuing failure to 'willingly embrace' the subject?

Ralph's best friend at Oxford was an Irishman, James Dillon, the eldest son of the Earl of Roscommon. The Verneys already had a number of Irish relations through Sir Edmund's half-sister Alice Turville. Alice had married Sir John Leeke, who lived in Co. Cork as a tenant of the Earl of Barrymore: one of their daughters, Dorothy, was living at Claydon as a kind of gentlewoman-companion to Lady Margaret; another, Anne, had married a young English lawyer named Nathaniel Hobart, and the Verneys and the Hobarts saw a lot of each other in London. Ralph stayed with them sometimes, and when Sir Edmund decided in the summer of 1634 to lease two houses in the Earl of Bedford's new

Piazza at Covent Garden, he offset the cost – £160 a year – by subletting rooms to Nat Hobart.

James Dillon had a place in this genealogical melange. His mother Margaret was a daughter of the Earl of Barrymore, and hence a connection of the Leekes. The Dillons were recent converts to Protestantism, an apostasy which had earned them an Irish peerage and an entrée into English society; and James, having been reclaimed from the superstition of the Romish church by no less a figure than James Ussher, the vigorously anti-Catholic Archbishop of Armagh, went up to Exeter College in 1628. He was godfather to Ralph and Mary's first short-lived child, and if his letters are anything to go by, he flirted incorrigibly with Doll Leeke and Mary Verney – 'the two souls that give life to the company wherein they are'[14] – and also with just about every female member of the Verney clan. By a bizarre conceit Doll became 'the pretty plum rogue, my brother' in their correspondence; Ralph was 'dear servant'; and Dillon himself was variously addressed as Ralph's 'most affectionate and obliged mistress' and 'Gillian Bogland'.

In 1633 Ralph accompanied his father up to Edinburgh for the long-delayed Scottish coronation of Charles I. (Sir Edmund fell off his horse on the way north and hurt himself so badly that his family heard rumours that he had been killed: he was well enough to carry on, in fact, but he suffered from painful bouts of sciatica for years afterwards, and made regular trips to Bath to take the waters.) The expedition was a rare event for Ralph. His experience of national events was generally at second hand, and his requests for news from Dillon, who had gone into service with Thomas Wentworth, Lord Deputy of Ireland, show a certain wry wistfulness:

We country clowns hear various reports of Mr Prynne's censure. [The Puritan pamphleteer William Prynne was accused of sedition for describing woman actors as 'notorious whores', just as Henrietta Maria was rehearsing an appearance in a court masque.] Some say he is to lose his hand and ears, others say his hand only; a third sort there are that say neither hand nor ears, but he must pay £6000 and endure perpetual imprisonment. I know none can relate the truth of this better than yourself, for you love not pleasing amatory dreams in a morning slumber, nor lazy stretchings on a downy bed; no, your spirit scorns such soft contents. I dare say you rise early every star chamber day to hear the sage censures of the grave counsellors; to you therefore I fly for information . . .'[15]

Dillon duly reported back that the Star Chamber had decided Prynne was to lose his ears, pay a fine of £4000 and suffer 'perpetual imprisonment'. (He was wrong – the dissident was fined £5000.) Another time he told Ralph that the imperial military commander Albrecht von Wallenstein had been murdered by command of the emperor; that French and Dutch fleets were nearing the English coast; that 'the great Turk sends for his edicts through the world to call the Jews back to their Palestine, and the building of their new Jerusalem'.[16] In return, Ralph's news was rather more prosaic: 'I am now going to meet some of my neighbours a duck hunting, I am told they have excellent dogs, therefore excuse my haste.'[17]

Although Ralph travelled regularly between his father's London house and Claydon, from the moment he came down from Oxford Sir Edmund began to groom him in the business of estate management. The Claydon bailiffs, John Roades and his son William, were responsible for running the estate; and although Sir Edmund spent most of his time at court, he took an astonishingly detailed interest in everything from land exchanges and the renewal of leases to the sale of sheep from the home farm and the right moment to plough the fields. 'The gardener shall pleach no hedge this year . . . ,' he told Ralph. 'If you find him fiddle about his work, agree with him by the great [i.e. a contract for the whole job] for truly I will no longer endure his day work; it is intolerable to bear with his knavery.' On another occasion: 'I think it will do the colts no hurt to play abroad in the heat of the day, but I hear the pied colt got his mischance by a stroke of one of the cart horses, and that must be by carelessness of servants.'[18]

Inevitably Ralph became pig-in-the-middle, forever relaying requests from the bailiffs to his father, and questions and commands from his father to the bailiffs. When Sir Edmund's hounds misbehaved, he berated Ralph over his reluctance to play a full part in the management of the estate: 'I know you can accuse them only by hearsay, for you will not take the pains to inform your-self by taking a view of their behaviour.'[19] But Ralph didn't really have much choice: he had a little experience, a little authority, and a father who was eager for him to shoulder the burden of running the estate but who wasn't prepared to relinquish his own hold on it.

Around the middle of the 1630s, Sir Edmund stopped grooming Ralph and began to rely on him for the day-to-day management of the family fortunes. Exactly when this happened is hard to say; but the moment when Ralph discovered the role his father prescribed for him is easier to pinpoint. In March 1636 he confessed to Sir Edmund that he yearned for adventure. Charles I was sending Thomas Arundel – the Earl-Marshal of England and thus Sir Edmund's direct boss – on an embassy to the Holy Roman Emperor Ferdinand II at Vienna; and Ralph wanted to go with him. Could his father arrange it?

Sir Edmund's reply was a clever piece of prevarication. 'No man would be gladder of such an opportunity to let you see something abroad, than I should be,' he wrote. But Arundel wasn't even taking young noblemen with him; he was leaving in days, so there was no time for Ralph to prepare for such a journey. And most importantly of all, 'you know I cannot settle my busi-ness without you'.[20]

Ralph was only twenty-two. He had a wife just out of her teens, an eighteen-month-old daughter (Anna Maria had been born in September 1634) and, although he didn't yet know it, another child on the way: the longed-for son and heir was born on Christmas Day 1636, and named Edmund after his grandfather. Even for the seventeenth century, the poor lad was very young to be lumbered with all the cares of managing an estate and a family. But for an absentee father who didn't enjoy the tiresome business of gath-ering rents and buying horses, Ralph was a godsend; and his father was cheerful but firm about his son's dreams of adventure. 'Now I think your journey is at an end, and so with my love to my daughter, I remain your loving father.'[21] That was that.

In other families, some of the day-to-day burden of estate management might have devolved on to the second son. But not in the Verney household. Not to put too fine a point on it, brother Thomas was no good. Two years younger than Ralph, he was the despair of his family, by turns callous, dissembling, whining, violent and dishonest.

The trouble started in 1634, soon after Tom left school in Gloucester. He launched into negotiations for an unsuitable marriage without consulting his father or asking his permission. Sir Edmund was really angry – marriages, even those of younger sons, involved money and honour, and their planning was not to be left to children. Tom's response was simply to shrug his shoulders; but within a couple of weeks he was forced to take the matter rather more seriously, because Sir Edmund and Lady Margaret decided to pack him off to Virginia.

The first permanent English colony in North America was still quite a novelty in 1634. It had been founded only twenty-six years earlier, on 14 May 1607, when a party of 104 men – mostly gentry, but including a dozen labourers, four carpenters, a blacksmith, a bricklayer, a mason, a barber, a tailor, a surgeon and a drummer – established the settlement of Jamestown on the banks of the James River sixty miles from the mouth of the Chesapeake Bay. The place was presented – especially in the promotional literature which aimed to lure fresh colonists – as a veritable utopia. The horses were braver and more beautiful than those in England. The earth was so extraordinarily rich that does in the teeming forests gave birth to two or even three fawns at a time. 'The mildness of the air, the fertility of the soil, and situation of the rivers are so propitious to the nature and use of man, as no place is more convenient for pleasure, profit, and man's sustenance, under that latitude or climate.'[22] In reality, harsh winters, periodic attacks by the Powhatans and the colony's inability to support the vast numbers of settlers who were shipped in by the Virginia Company in the early years resulted in a terrifyingly high death rate. In 1618 the population of the colony was a thousand; six years later, after the arrival of perhaps as many as 4000 Englishmen and women, it was about 1500.

In 1624 the charter of the Virginia Company was revoked, and the government of the colony was taken over by the crown. Slowly but surely it began to prosper, with tobacco as the staple export. Prices rose and fell, from three shillings a pound down to a penny a pound and back up again, but by 1633 the economy was doing well enough for a visiting Dutch sea captain to remark on the tobacco planters' extravagant habit of playing cards, using their servants as stakes.

The colony quickly became a recognised means for 'parents to disburden themselves of lascivious sons, masters of bad servants and wives of ill husbands', much to the exasperation of the more upright settlers, who complained that 'to dog the business with such an idle crew' was hardly helpful.[23] On the other hand, it was acknowledged (in England, at least, if not in Virginia) that when young men who were addicted to ease and idleness and carnal pleasures found 'that they must labour or else not eat, and be tied within the bounds of sharp laws, and severe discipline', it could be the making of them.[24] This held an obvious appeal for the parents of disobedient children.

Sir Edmund left it to his wife to organise Tom's voyage, and she in turn approached a merchant with experience in arranging passages for budding New World colonists. John Sadler of Bucklersbury was a major developer of lands in Virginia; the previous May, for example, he and two fellow-London merchants acquired Martin's Brandon, a 4450-acre plantation on the James River. There is no evidence that Sadler ever visited Virginia himself, but he was well placed to advise Lady Mary on what Tom would require out there.

The basics included at least three indentured servants, one of whom should be a cooper. Sadler could provide servants at a day's notice, although he suggested Tom bring the cooper with him from Buckinghamshire, since they were harder to find in London. Each servant would cost £12, including passage and clothing. Once arrived in Virginia, he could hire them out while he took stock of the colony. If he decided to stay, they would be seasoned, and 'enabled to direct such others as shall be sent unto him'.[25] If he didn't like the place, he could sell them, along with all his other chattels: the colonists were so desperate for English goods that he was bound to make a 50 per cent profit on everything he took out with him (including the servants).

There was no shortage of food in the colony, said Sadler, mindful of the terrible stories of the 'starving time' which had reached England back in the early days of the Jamestown settlement. But household goods and linen were definitely in short supply. Tom would need to take his own bedding: a feather bed, bolster, pillow, blankets, rug, curtains and three pairs of sheets. He should also have plenty of items for sale, so that he could buy enough corn to supply himself, the men he took with him, and any additional servants he might send for once he was established. It was a frequent complaint in Virginia that settlers were arriving without the means to support themselves: 'If such numbers of people come upon me unexpected,' wrote the Governor in 1620, 'and that an unhealthful season and too late to set corn I cannot then be able to feed them out of others' labours.'[26]

And having just assured Lady Mary that most households 'are so well provided as to entertain a stranger with all things necessary for the belly', Sadler went on to admit that a scarcity of corn was still not unknown. It 'sometimes doth so fall out through the covetousness of the planters, that strive to plant much tobacco and little corn, so that want comes upon some of them before they are aware of it'.[27] The broker already had flour, spirits, grocery wares and fowling pieces, and could get together the rest of Tom's equipment at half a day's notice. The entire charges for the venture would come to around £68, or £56 if Tom took two servants with him instead of three.

Sadler urged Lady Margaret to move quickly; the *Merchant's Hope*, a vessel owned by William Barker, one of his business associates, was at anchor in the Thames and making ready to sail. Because of 'the intimacy I have with the owners of the ship' he could guarantee Tom a comfortable berth in 'the great cabin'.[28]

Lady Margaret took her cue from Sadler. On 1 August, the day after his letter arrived, she wrote back:

For his necessary provisions, I . . . have sent up a man furnished with such a proportion of money as you have writ for, and have made what haste I could to convey him [i.e. Tom] unto you, that he might not lose the benefit and accommodation of that ship which you write unto me is now going, where in you had provided him so good a cabin, and have also sent his other necessaries of wearing apparel and linen, and I hope completely for such an employment and journey. And if there be any thing wanting, I have given this my servant power to treat with you about it.[29]

Two days later, on 3 August, Tom was with Sadler in London, and on 8 August he and his goods were being stowed aboard the *Merchant's Hope*. Either Sadler had been unduly optimistic about the costs of the expedition, or Lady Margaret had decided her son wasn't going to suffer from being underequipped: the 'goods, provisions and servants, with the charges arising upon the same' amounted to £117 13s. 6d. – more than twice the merchant's estimate. In a stark reminder of the risks attached to Tom's journey, a signed note gave one William Webster the authority to sell and dispose of all the boy's possessions and return the money to Sir Edmund if he died.*

The transatlantic sea routes between England and America were busy in the 1630s. In one year alone – 1635 – at least twenty vessels left London bound for Virginia, eighteen more went to New England and a further fifteen went to Barbados, St Christopher and Bermuda. The *Merchant's Hope* made regular crossings, carrying around seventy-five passengers, both men and women. A surviving passenger list of 31 July 1635 contains the name of sixty-four men and eleven women, their ages ranging from fourteen to fifty-one: most were around Tom's age, in their late teens or early twenties.

The 3700-mile voyage to Virginia could take anything up to two months, depending on wind, weather and the navigational abilities of the vessel's master. The *Merchant's Hope* would sail out of the Thames estuary, past Gravesend, then around the southeast corner of England and into the Downs off the Kent coast, where she might take on further passengers. It was common for vessels bound for the Americas to make one last stop for supplies at one of the western ports – Dartmouth or Falmouth – before leaving Europe behind and launching out into the ocean.

Crossing the Atlantic in a ship which was maybe 100 feet long at the waterline by 35 feet across the beam was not usually a happy experience, even for someone who had a privileged berth in the 'great cabin'. Wormwood conserve was recognised as a palliative for seasickness, as were sugar-paste pills with cinnamon,

* A William Webster is among those named in the Virginia Company's Second Charter of 1609. Sir Thomas Denton, Sir Edmund's father-in-law, is named in the Third Charter of 1612. Both men ventured £37 10s. in the Company.

ginger and musk. Captain John Smith, giving advice to inexperienced planters who were preparing for their voyage to Virginia, was at pains to warn them that the master of their vessel might not care too much whether they lived or died, 'for a common sailor regards not a landsman, especially a poor passenger, as I have seen too often approved by lamentable experience'.[30] In 1620 the *Mayflower* was blessed with just such a crew: one 'proud and very profane' young mariner was always sneering at the passengers' seasickness, and telling them how 'he hoped to cast half of them over board before they came to their journey's end, and to make merry with what they had'. It was some consolation to the God-fearing Puritans when he died in the mid-Atlantic, 'and so was himself the first that was thrown overboard'.[31]

Tom reached Virginia in late September or early October 1634, with his indentured servants, his flour and corn and fowling pieces. He passed his nineteenth birthday there, taking stock and getting to know a world which was both alien and familiar. There were forests of oak, ash and elm inhabited by deer which looked just like the deer on Whaddon Chase; in winter there were swans and cranes, herons, geese, ducks and pigeons. But there were also birds of 'some other strange kinds, to us unknown by name'.[32] There were beavers and bears, neither of which Tom would have seen outside of chapbooks, and opossums, which carried their young in bags under their bellies; and strange squirrels which had skin between their front and back legs. When they stretched that skin it formed wings, so that when they jumped from branch to branch 'they have been seen to fly 30 or 40 yards'.[33] Then there were the native Americans, 'savages', with bows and arrows and barbarous ways, who sacrificed children, occasionally attacked colonists, and worshipped strange gods. 'All things that are able to do them hurt beyond their prevention,' wrote one of the early settlers, 'they adore with their kind of divine worship; as the fire, water, lightning, thunder, our ordnance, pieces, horses, &c. But their chief God they worship is the Devil.'[34]

Virginia really was a land of opportunity in the 1630s. A young man possessed of good business sense, good connections and good muscles could grow wealthy. A cowherd might go to church wearing silk; 'a wife of one that in England had professed the black art, not of a scholar but of a collier of Croydon, wears her rough beaver hat with a fair pearl hat band'.[35] The colony could have been the making of Tom or, with its lurking perils and hard labour, it could have been the death of him.

In the event, he was neither killed nor cured. A single winter in Virginia proved to be too much and the following spring he took ship back to England, to the exasperation of his father – and his elder brother Ralph, to whom Tom increasingly looked for help in pleading his case with his parents.

Sir Edmund's reaction to Tom's speedy return from America was to pack him off to sea, and by June 1635 he was serving aboard one of the King's ships in the Channel, asking Ralph to 'speak for me to my mother, for travellers ever want money'.[36] His naval career lasted all of two months, and in August he announced that he was off to seek his fortune soldiering in Flanders. Could Ralph 'speak to my friends for a little money to carry me over thither'?[37] Two months after *that* he was back in England, flat broke and in the Marshalsea – it isn't clear if he was hiding from his creditors or if they had put him there. Either way, his father was certainly very angry indeed. He forbade anyone to lend the boy money or buy him clothes without his permission, inspiring Tom to a series of grovelling apologies. 'Let these lines (dear father) stir you to have pity, and compassion upon me,' he wrote on 11 October, 'that I may receive but one smiling and merry countenance from you, where I have formerly an angry, and frowning countenance. Then shall you see every day an amendment in me.'[38] Eleven days later, after Ralph had tried to intercede for him, that amendment had apparently taken place. He was now a reformed character, he said: 'Let me once again upon my bended knees crave at your merciful hands pardon, and forgiveness, for that ill misspent life, which I have formerly led.'[39]

Next, Tom enlisted with an English regiment in France (borrowing the money for his equipment from Ralph). Within weeks he was back in London, to find that his family assumed he had run away from the army. Considering his past record, one could hardly blame them, but Tom was filled with righteous indignation. He was merely delivering some letters from his colonel to friends in England, he insisted. If everyone had such an ill opinion of him, then 'this is the last you shall receive from me as long as I have being'.[40]

It was not the last. In May 1636 he was back in France and writing to Ralph for a loan of £20. Although not yet twenty-one, he was learning how to use his brother's sense of honour as leverage and the Verney name as an instrument of blackmail. He had borrowed from someone in Paris who knew the Verneys, he said: 'You are of so good and so loving a nature that you will scorn to see your brother disgraced for so small a sum.'[41] When the money wasn't forthcoming, he repeated his request: 'my honour and fortune [and by implication, the honour of the family] lies engaged for it'.[42]

Back in England and back in the Marshalsea, Tom told Ralph that 'before I will borrow I will starve'.[43] Then he asked for a loan of twenty shillings. He continued to get into trouble over money, continued to hope that there was a pot of gold waiting at the end of the next rainbow. In 1637 he went to Stockholm, looking for preferment in a well-known infantry regiment which the Englishman George Fleetwood had raised to serve the King of Sweden. Nothing came of it, since Fleetwood had recently lost four companies in action and now complained of having more officers than he had soldiers. But the escapade inevitably involved Tom in more expense, and more letters home. 'Everything is so extreme dear that it would grieve anyone to see it,' he told his father, 'as you shall see by that little bill I have enclosed.'[44] Early in 1638 he was in London again, and involved in a duel with a gentleman 'about some words which passed between him and myself'.[45] That summer his father's patience ran out. Sir Edmund refused to help Tom with any more money or even to see him. The boy was exiled to Claydon, where the servants both there and at Hillesden were told that under no circumstances were they to lend him any money. Sir Edmund even ordered them not to provide Tom with a horse – not because he would use it to escape but because he would sell it. When his latest dreams of making his fortune in Europe or the New World were ignored, he blustered and whined. 'My mother hath given an express command to let me have nothing but a dons lace shirt to keep me from lice, which is extremity itself, and not the way to make me lead a reformed life.'[46] Eventually he threatened suicide, saying that 'rather than lead this hellish life, I will take a rope and make an end of myself, and then neither father, mother, brother, nor sister, nor any friends else shall take any more care of me'.[47] No one took him seriously.

One of the interesting features of Tom's bad behaviour is the deft way in which he adopted different voices towards his father and his brother. Ralph was the conduit to his father's purse, but Tom could afford to abuse him, to play on his affections and his sense of family honour, to flatter him shamelessly and to rant and rave at his failure to help him. As the second son, Tom had stood a good chance of inheriting the family estates for a time: Ralph and Mary's short-lived first child of 1632 had been followed by a stillborn baby in 1633, and then by the birth of Anna Maria. (James Dillon stood godfather to her.) The safe arrival on Christmas Day 1636 of their first son, Edmund, may not exactly have put paid to Tom's hopes of inheriting, but it certainly lengthened the odds. From then on his dealings with Ralph were more resentful, more obviously manipulative.

He could not afford to alienate Sir Edmund, though. Tom's father had a financial hold over him, as he did over the entire family – with the exceptions of Ralph, whose marriage to Mary Blacknall had guaranteed him a separate income, and Lady Margaret, who had money of her own. But his control went much further than that. The entire Verney family, even the delinquent Tom, was frightened of Sir Edmund's displeasure, and ready to obey him in everything. This was partly due to the force of the man's character, which was considerable, but it was also the result of a puritan culture which promoted the father as arbiter and emphasised filial duty and obligation: 'Children are not to follow their own will, or to be led by themselves in anything; but to be ordered and guided by their parents in all their ways.'[48] 'It is better thy child be whipped, than damned; and let not thy child's weeping and crying under the rod move thee to withhold due correction.'[49] For all his many faults and manipulative ways, Tom was constantly asking not only his father's forgiveness for his sins, but also his permission – to stay in Stockholm, to emigrate to New England. Even when he was stuck at Claydon and telling Ralph that he was about to hang himself, he was careful to tell their father how grateful he was 'that you are pleased to harbour me under your roof'.[50]

'It is a very great calamity to godly parents to have wicked and ungodly children,' declared a seventeenth-century minister in a sermon entitled *Parents' Groans over their Wicked Children*.[51] For a time, it looked as though Sir Edmund's third son and namesake was going the same way as Tom. Mun (as he was known) followed Tom to school at Gloucester, transferring to Winchester when he was fifteen or sixteen. Already he was getting into trouble, and trying to excuse his behaviour to his father by blaming the company he kept. In January 1636, at the relatively advanced age of nineteen, he was sent to Magdalen Hall, where he singularly failed to shine. In fact during the eighteen months he spent at Oxford he progressed from fretting that the authorities might make him get a haircut – 'the principal protested that after this day he would turn out of his house whomsoever he found with hair longer than the tips of his ears,' he told Ralph, begging his brother to take him away from college until the principal calmed down – to cutting classes.[52] By Christmas his young tutor, Henry Wilkinson, an earnest Buckinghamshire-born Puritan, was tactfully informing Ralph (rather than Sir Edmund) that Mun 'doth not carry himself so ingeniously as he ought in any respect'.[53] He meant by this that the boy was missing his lectures, and not turning up for prayers in hall, which were compulsory. Wilkinson hinted that there was more which he could only communicate by word of mouth, and suggested that he and Ralph meet privately to discuss Mun's behaviour.

Ralph either wouldn't or couldn't keep quiet about Mun's transgressions, which seem to have involved running up debts with half the tapsters of Oxford. Their mother found out, and although Mun promised to turn over a new leaf, she informed her husband. Their son hadn't paid Wilkinson for his tutoring; he hadn't paid for his diet, or for his books, or for his laundry. And although he was his father's pet – the two men had just the same good-natured irresponsibility – Sir Edmund reacted very badly indeed. He neither ranted nor raved nor threatened punishment; he simply used every parent's trump card, and told Mun he was disappointed:

Son – and now I have said that, my griefs grow high upon me; for you were a son in whom I took delight; a son that I had a particular affection for above some others, and above most of my children. But God has in you punished me for that partiality . . . you are now grown so lewd and false that I blush to think you mine . . . I find by your mother that you are run in debt both to your tutor and to divers others, and I perceive by her

importunity that if I would pay these debts you have now promised a great amendment and I find you have fooled her into a
belief of it. But Sir, let me tell you . . . as you have left yourself
and me for your mean company, so I can leave you to them
without any farther care of you. I will say no more, but that by
your being my unworthy son, I am made your unhappy father.[54]

It worked. Mun begged to be taken away from Oxford, saying this
was the only way to break with his bad ways; and in July 1637 he
was placed with Ralph's old tutor, John Crowther, who was now –
after some more intervention by Sir Edmund – the vicar of Newton
Blossomville, a little village on the border with Bedfordshire about
twenty miles north-east of Buckingham. Crowther quickly discovered that Mun had learned nothing at Oxford: he 'understands not
the very first grounds of logic, or any other university learning,
and hath no books to initiate him in it'.[55] But Sir Edmund showed
every confidence in the clergyman, warning him only to keep the
boy away from the sons of the nobility who lived in the neighbourhood, in case he fell into temptation. 'I shall not despair that
I may again love him,' said Sir Edmund.[56]

Things didn't go as well as he hoped. Mun wrote his last Latin
exercise for his tutor less than a month after arriving at Newton
Blossomville: it was Crowther's will, dictated as the man lay on
his deathbed. ('He entreated me to write it in Latin because his
wife should not understand it.'[57]) Mun was left to wind up his
tutor's affairs, to look after the grieving widow and, presumably,
to acquaint her with the details of her late husband's will, which
were unexceptionable. He checked through Crowther's sermons
for any seditious material, and negotiated on Mrs Crowther's
behalf with the parson's successor, John Barton, who wasn't
inclined to observe any of the usual niceties: less than a week
after her husband's funeral he was threatening the widow with
legal action over some corn she had sold to a neighbour, and
refusing to buy anything from her unless he could have it for
half its value. He 'useth her not very kindly,' observed Mun.*

---

* Mun Verney to Ralph Verney, 25 August 1637; M636/3. Barton was domestic
chaplain to the Earl of Peterborough, whose family were lords of the manor of
Newton Blossomville.

Ironically, Crowther's sudden death proved to be rather a good thing for Mun. He behaved well, handling the responsibility and exhibiting a degree of sympathy and kindness to others which was notably lacking in the vicious Tom and the stiff and already rather pompous Ralph. When he moved on to stay with the Dentons at Hillesden that autumn while Sir Edmund decided his career, there was no more talk of an unhappy father.

Henry, the fourth Verney boy, was sent to Paris when he was sixteen or seventeen to finish his education; he was there in 1635, an unenthusiastic and – by his own account – unaccomplished linguist. Sir Edmund intended him for the army, a career which had considerable potential in the context of the European wars. Henry was detached, almost bewildered, at the prospect. On his nineteenth birthday he freely admitted to Ralph that he wasn't particularly enamoured of the soldier's life – 'I tell you truly I do not like of it' – but it wasn't the danger or the privations which distressed him. It was the frustrating way the war had of distracting him from his true vocation, which was horseracing. 'It is not the firing of the bullet that fears me at all,' he told his brother; 'but the true reason is that I have always given myself so far to the sports and pleasure of the world that I cannot give my mind to this course of life.'[58] He did manage to give his mind to some action, taking part in the Siege of Breda when it was recaptured in October 1637 by Frederick Henry, Prince of Orange, after being occupied by Spanish troops for twelve years. But once Breda was taken and Henry settled into his role as a member of the garrison, his thoughts immediately turned back to his first passion. He was at pains to reassure his father that he took life more seriously now, and that although he still loved racing he was resolved to leave it behind him. In the next breath he was proudly informing his family that he had just won £50 in a race with a Dutchman. As Mun rather wryly commented, 'I do not at all wonder at brother Henry liking a soldier's life, since he can follow that and horse matches too.'[59]

4

I Will Provide

The movements of the six Verney girls in the 1630s are more difficult to disentangle than those of their brothers, and as a result their distinct personalities take longer to emerge. They were that much younger, of course: when seventeen-year-old Henry, the youngest boy, was sent to Paris in 1635, the eldest girl, Susan, was only thirteen; Penelope was twelve; Margaret was eleven; Cary was nine, Mary was seven and Elizabeth was only two. Then again, we have less evidence of their early lives for the simple reason that they weren't packed off to school, to university or to exotic foreign locations, and so they didn't write home as the boys did.

We don't know what Sir Edmund and Lady Margaret thought about the education of girls, but if Ralph's views are anything to go by it wasn't much. He didn't believe there was any point in girls being taught Latin, Hebrew or Greek, and he later informed Nancy Denton, a god-daughter who aspired to learning, that 'a Bible (with the Common Prayer) and a good plain catechism in your mother tongue being well read and practised, is well worth all the rest and much more suitable to your sex'.[1]

French could be a useful accomplishment, since the language afforded so many suitable books – not only romances, plays and poetry, but collections of recipes, gardening books and 'all manner of good housewifery'. But under no circumstances should a young woman be taught shorthand (something which had grown quite fashionable since the publication in 1602 of John Willis's *Art of Stenography*) since it only encouraged the deplorable habit of taking down notes on the sermon every Sunday. 'Had St Paul lived in our times I am most confident he would have fixed a shame upon our women for writing (as well as for their speaking) in the church.'[2]

'Teach her to live under obedience,' Ralph told Nancy's father, his friend and uncle William Denton; 'and whilst she is unmarried, if she would learn anything, let her ask you, and afterwards her husband, at home'.[3] On another occasion he commented that his own little girl was rather backward, but 'I doubt not she will be scholar enough for a woman'.*

Ralph's attitude was not universal – fortunately for Nancy Denton, her own father held much more advanced views on the education of women – but it was typical, and one finds similar advice scattered throughout seventeenth-century manuals and conduct-books. 'I desire her bringing up may be learning the Bible . . . , good housewifery, writing, and good works,' wrote Elizabeth Jocelin in *The Mother's Legacy to her Unborn Child* (1624): 'other learning a woman needs not'.[4] She did, however, require other skills if she was going to attract a husband, which was the only career path open to girls like the Verney sisters. Robert Burton remarked how it was part of a gentlewoman's upbringing 'to sing, dance, and play on the lute, or some such instrument, before she can say her paternoster, or Ten Commandments. 'Tis the next way, their parents think, to get them husbands.'[5] And Thomas Middleton expressed the same sentiment rather more vividly at the beginning of the century, when he laughed at

Memoirs of the Verney Family (1907) I, 500. Ralph wasn't consistent: another time he expressed the wish that the same daughter, Peg, should learn Latin; but this was after the Civil War, when his family was facing an uncertain future. If Peg had enough Latin to understand a doctor's bill and to write one, that might see her married without his having to provide a dowry.

young women who saw music as a means to catch a husband: 'the voice between her lips, and the viol between her legs, she'll be fit for a consort very speedily'.[6]

The Verney girls learned to dance, to sing and to play instruments – as did the rest of the family. Their sister-in-law Mary regularly accompanied herself on a guitar of ebony inlaid with pearl; even Ralph played the theorboe, a kind of large lute. The girls learned needlework and embroidery. They were all literate, although, like most Stuart gentlewomen, their lack of formal education showed in the fact that they were generally less accomplished at their letters than their brothers, adopting a phonetic system of spelling. Describing one of her first suitors to her brother in 1643, for example, Pen Verney wrote that 'hee would meany times com and site with mee, or call me to goo a walking with him to or thre ouers together'.[7] Four years later her sister Mall told Mary Verney how she had teased Mun: 'Just now my wicked brother Mun is com to us, but wee have all moust scrat out his very eyes out of his balle pate . . . he toock gidy & blushed to see as I laft att him . . .'[8]

The sisters were raised in a world dominated by powerful matriarchs. Their mother, Lady Margaret, played an active part in the management of the family which went far beyond 'good housewifery': it was she, remember, who made the arrangements for Tom's brief foray to Virginia and who liaised directly with the agent in London. And in many ways her life was conducted apart from her husband; she rarely if ever attended court herself, preferring to spend her time at Hillesden and Claydon, and Sir Edmund maintained a definite degree of separation between his roles as courtier and as husband and country landowner. Yet in spite of the long periods which the couple spent apart – or perhaps because of them – they had a good marriage, even by the less exacting standards of the seventeenth century. Twelve children in twenty years are proof enough of that, and the letters they exchanged are warm and unaffected. Sir Edmund occasionally ran errands for his 'Good Puss' – in 1636, for example, when there was plague in the capital, he asked for a list of 'what you shall necessarily want, as gloves and such things', and said he would provide them for her – and she in turn didn't scruple to ask him to use his influence at court. 'Good Puss,' he wrote in reply to one such request, 'for those people you write about to have cure for the King's Evil, I will have all the care of them I can.' Unfortunately touching the scrofulous was not something that Charles particularly relished, and the medieval ritual was strictly rationed. 'Till Good Friday he will heal none. I believe he will heal that day, and in Easter holidays.'[9]

In fact between 1625 and 1639 Charles issued at least twenty proclamations prohibiting or limiting the activities of scrofulous petitioners; by 1638, they had to produce a certificate from their local parish priest and statements 'by one physician and one surgeon at least' that they did indeed suffer from the King's Evil. Charles's belief in the mystical power of monarchy might have conquered his innate distaste, except for the suspicion among his ministers that the poor were drawn less by the prospect of a miraculous cure, and more by the gold coin which he gave to every sufferer he touched.

The girls' Verney grandmother – Lady Mary, the stepmother and mother-in-law who had fallen out with Sir Francis back in 1604 – spent most of her time in London, where she shared the Covent Garden house with her son and issued peremptory commands to her grandchildren. On one occasion the ninety-year-old commanded Mun to check on the state of the Verney vault at Aldbury, where her last husband had been buried nearly four decades earlier. The local clergyman reassured Mun that it was in as good a state as when his grandfather was buried in it, and threw in the comforting thought that he would provide an excellent funeral sermon for Lady Mary at a week's notice. 'I durst not acquaint my grandmother,' said Mun.[10]

Rather more of a presence in the girls' lives was their maternal grandmother, Lady Susan Denton, who had been a widow since 1633 and who presided over the household at Hillesden.* Both there and at Claydon they also came into regular contact with

---

* Ralph had informed James Dillon of Sir Thomas Denton's death thus: 'The great God in whose hand is the soul of every living thing hath by death taken my grandfather into an endless life.' Dillon responded by sending a copy of Edward Brerewood's *Elementa Logicae* and a textbook on rhetoric. Judging from Ralph's letter, he didn't need much coaching in the art of rhetoric. Ralph Verney to James Dillon, 27 September 1633; M636/2.

the army of aunts and female cousins who formed the larger part of the Denton–Verney tribe. Some were well off with good marriages, like Aunt Isham, their mother's sister Elizabeth, who was married to Thomas Isham of Pytchley in Northamptonshire, but who like Margaret Verney spent long periods at Hillesden, where she acted as companion to and calming influence over the imperious and impatient Lady Susan. Others, like Doll Leeke, were poor relations, spinsters whose twilight existence of dependency and hovering deference served to remind the girls what lay in store for them if they failed to find husbands.

Perhaps the Verney girls' most influential role model was their sister-in-law. Close to them in age, and raised with them since early adolescence, Mary was like a sister. Indeed, they called her 'Sister' without affectation, just as Sir Edmund and Lady Margaret called her 'Daughter'. But as wife to the eldest son and heir and, after 1636, mother to *his* son and heir, she held a position in the household which they did not. In the natural scheme of things Mary would eventually run the Claydon household. She would be able to grant small favours and she would be well placed to exclude those who displeased her. Meanwhile, Sir Edmund treated her with more affection than he did his own daughters, calling her his 'dear heart', and signing himself in his letters her 'loving father and faithful friend'.[11] The Verney boys made sure they kept on her good side (apart from Tom, whose inability to appreciate just where he stood in the pecking order was half of his problem). She was a conduit to Ralph, who was in turn a conduit to their father in the important and regular business of begging him for money, and who would eventually have complete control over the family finances. It made sense to have her as a friend.

It is a testament to Mary's character that she never let this power go to her head. I suppose one could argue that since she was living with her in-laws it was in her interest to be nice to them. But she was kind to and patient with the sisters, as she was with her importunate brothers-in-law, and she never abused her position. She only ever gave them a slap — and then it was always a verbal slap — if she thought they were exploiting Ralph, or being disrespectful to him. The sisters might never be able to aspire to Mary's status, which had arrived on the back of a huge inheritance of her own, but she was a constant reminder of the advantages which could accrue to a young girl who made the right match.

In the third week of May 1638 Anna Maria Verney fell sick. Ralph was away from home. By midnight on 18 May it was obvious to her mother and grandfather that the three-year-old was going to die, and at one o'clock the following morning Sir Edmund sat down at his writing table to break the news to his son: 'Ralph, your sweet child is going apace to a better world; she has but a short time to stay with us.'[12]

Ralph and Mary had already lost their first two children; even for an age in which a quarter of infants died before their tenth birthday, the death of a third was a hard thing for the family to bear. Sir Edmund urged Ralph to come home quickly for his wife's sake; and, adopting a conventional approach to infant death, he reminded him that it would be wrong to question divine goodness: 'I hope you have such a sense of God's blessings to you as you will not repine at his decrees.'[13] In much the same way, the Puritan Nehemiah Wallington was reproved by his wife Grace when their own three-year-old child died in 1625: 'Husband, I am persuaded you offend God in grieving for his child so much. Do but consider what a deal of grief and care we are rid of, and what a deal of trouble and sorrow she is gone out of; and what abundance of joy she is gone into.'[14]

Anna Maria was buried three days later. Everyone was upset – the death of a child was a dreadful thing – but everyone also knew the brutal truth was that it could have been worse. It could have been Anna Maria's brother Edmund. It could have been Ralph himself. Either event would have brought the Verneys a step closer to the awful prospect of Tom as heir to the family estates. In the same letter in which he informed Ralph of the little girl's impending death, Sir Edmund urged his son to have a care for his own health – 'for this is a dangerous year for heats and colds' – and not to hurry home, in case he made himself ill. 'That may give an end to all our comforts.'[15]

Soon after Anna Maria's death, little Edmund went to live with his great-grandmother at Hillesden. Lady Susan was indisputably the matriarch of the Verney clan as well as the Dentons. Ralph, rather than her own eldest son Alexander, acted as her business manager; her daughter, Lady Margaret, still spent part of every year with her; and most of the Verney girls (and their brothers, come to that) had extended stays at Hillesden at one time or another. In the autumn of 1638, for example, Susan Verney was exiled to her grandmother's house, or took refuge there, after she upset her parents. We don't know exactly what it was that the teenager did wrong, but her parents' disfavour made her thoroughly unhappy and her brother Mun – also living with the Dentons at the time – tried to patch things up, telling Ralph that 'shame and a kind of amazed fear hath deterred her from so plain an opening of her misery to them [i.e. their parents] as she hath done to me'.[16]

Sir Edmund spent most of his time in London. He was able to keep court and country separate because Ralph was there to act as intermediary, supervising the work of William Roades (who, as well as being the family's steward, was also a tenant farmer and as such occupied the role of village elder as much as that of Verney servant). It was Ralph who managed the estate. Nevertheless, the knight-marshal ruled from a distance with an iron rod and an eye for detail, and questions about virtually everything continued to be referred to him for a decision. The cost of building a new house for a tenant had to be offset by increasing the rent; the negotiation of a new lease must meet with his approval. When in response to government concerns the parish constable at Claydon prepared a statement about recent enclosures and showed it to Ralph, Ralph sent it straight to his father. And Sir Edmund rewrote it, stretching the truth to present himself in a much more favourable light. 'Let the return be made according to this direction,' he told Ralph, 'and let [the constable] make no other.'[17]

With his father's guidance, Ralph managed the Verney estates well, consolidating the property and pursuing a policy of enclosing open fields and wastes. But Sir Edmund still lived well beyond his means, and he was forever on the watch for the kind of get-rich-quick scheme which promised to catapult him out of debt and rain down ample dowries for his daughters. One option, much favoured by his contemporaries, was to acquire a monopoly of some kind from the King: Sir Edmund's predecessor as knight-marshal, Sir Edward Zouch, had done quite well out of a patent for glass-making in 1613, and as a young man Sir Edmund himself had already invested – with rather less success – in a share of a patent for sorting, or 'garbling', tobacco. When the tobacco-garbling patent did begin to yield good profits in the later 1630s, it was promptly taken back by the Lord High Treasurer. This was a problem with patents: they were understandably unpopular with traders and manufacturers who had to pay out on them, and they were liable to be rescinded if they were too successful. At one stage Sir Edmund was considering a share in another patent, 'for the supply of turf to be taken from the waste places of his Majesty's dominions'; at another he was involved in a questionable and unsuccessful attempt by the Earl of Carlisle to obtain lands in Co. Wicklow.

In 1636 he put money into an ambitious project to drain 95,000 acres of fenland around the Nene, the Ouse, the Welland and the Isle of Ely. A company set up by his Covent Garden landlord, the 4th Earl of Bedford, raised £100,000 and employed the celebrated Dutch embankment engineer Cornelius Vermuyden. The plan was that when the reclaimed land soared in value, Bedford would receive 40,000 acres; Charles I, who had contributed £20,000, would get 12,000 acres; and the rest would be divided between the other investors. Sir Edmund put in £600, and persuaded Ralph to come in with him. 'I will provide to make good your part of the bargain in your absence,' he wrote. 'I am confident you will have a good bargain of it.'[18] Nat Hobart, the young lawyer friend of the Verneys who was married to Ralph's cousin Anne Leeke, also put up a stake.

The project failed to thrive, not least because even Vermuyden couldn't get to grips with the complexities of draining such vast areas of flat land. And 'in the prosecution of this work', to quote the anonymous author of *A Narrative of the Draining of the Great Level of the Fens*, 'the adventurers . . . exhausted their estates, some to their ruin, but all to very great loss'.[19] When the money ran out, a levy was imposed on the shareholders: Sir Edmund and his son were able to pay, but poor Nat Hobart had to hide from his creditors in the Verneys' Covent Garden house. 'The fens have near drowned him,' said his father-in-law, Sir John Leeke, suggesting that he escape to Ireland. 'Poor Nan [Nat's wife] will be loth to have him from her arms, but it would break her heart to have him in restraint.'[20]

Sir Edmund was unlucky or rash in all his get-rich-quick schemes, and they seemed to have cost him more than he ever made out of them. He muddled along until 1638, when his precarious finances reached crisis point and he was forced to borrow £1000 from one of his wife's sisters, and to mortgage Claydon for £3250 to Frank Drake, who was the husband of one of her nieces. Even this wasn't enough to keep him afloat, and the following year he made a deal with Ralph. In return for taking over annuity payments for his Verney grandmother and aunt, and giving his father £4000 in cash, Ralph received the rental income from parts of the Claydon estates. He raised the money by selling off some of the Blacknall lands which had come to him when he married Mary.

Sir Edmund's most dramatic attempt to save his failing fortunes involved him in swapping his £182-a-year salary as knight-marshal, *and* one of the £200 pensions awarded him by Charles I, for a claim on the alnage. Dating back to at least the fourteenth century, the alnage started life as a form of quality control on the woollen industry; government-appointed inspectors, or alnagers, were supposed to check all cloths and fix a seal of approval to those bales which reached a specified standard. Since a fee was payable, this soon became a straightforward tax on cloth, and by the seventeenth century clothiers were buying seals from the alnager, who no longer made any pretence of checking the product. Revenue varied, but at a farthing a seal it was a lucrative business, both for its farmers and for the Exchequer. In exchange for giving up his marshal's salary and pension, and also waiving a claim for £1500 which King Charles owed him, Sir Edmund acquired a twenty-one-year charge of £400 per annum on the alnage.

On the surface that might not seem so clever. Over the entire period of the charge he was, after all, giving up an income of £8022 plus the King's £1500 – a total of £9522 – in return for £8400 from the alnage. But the alnage was a much safer bet than royal favour and royal promises, both of which were subject to political machinations, the immediate needs of the Exchequer and the King's whims. Those who had a charge on the alnage were given priority over the Exchequer, so that they received their money before the farmers handed over their receipts. It was a foolproof way of maintaining a steady stream of income, and Sir Edmund directed that stream straight into a trust, which he intended to use for two different purposes: as security to raise his daughters' dowries and small annuities for his three younger sons; and as a fund on which he could draw to pay off his debts. It would have been a good idea, if he hadn't continued to live well beyond his means. Within four years those debts had grown again to more than £8500 – something approaching three times his gross annual income.

Part of the problem was the expense involved in being a member of the King's court. When Sir Edmund attended Charles I to Edinburgh in 1633 for his Scottish coronation, for example, his wardrobe cost a small fortune. A purple satin suit, a waistcoat and cap of cloth-of-gold, riding gear of soft Cordovan leather and a mountain of lace trimming did not come cheap.

A very special occasion, of course: but there were rather a lot of special occasions for the servants of a monarch who revelled in majesty. Charles I's court glittered. Visitors to Whitehall marvelled at the Titians and Raphaels, the Leonardos and Dürers – all part of a royal collection which outshone those of every other European monarch outside Italy. The entertainments put on by the King and Queen were legendary, the pageantry of their state receptions was awesome to see.

Take just one example, the visit of Indah ben Abdullah, ambassador extraordinary from the Sultan of Morocco, who arrived in England in October 1637 to negotiate trade agreements. He brought with him as presents for the King four hawks, four Barbary horses valued at £300 or £400 each, two saddles 'with the bridles and stirrups plated over with massive gold of rare workmanship',[21] and sixteen freed English slaves. After being received at Greenwich in the King's barge, he was escorted by fifteen Gentlemen of the Privy Chamber to Tower Wharf, the point at which the public entry of an ambassador into London usually began. From there, Indah ben Abdullah was led to his lodgings, a private house in Wood Street, by a torch-lit procession of aldermen in their scarlet gowns and gold chains of office, 'all on horseback, riding two and two before him'. Once he was settled, he and his retinue of twenty-eight rode 'with a slow pace along the streets' to meet the King.* Seven trumpeters on horseback preceded him; then came the four Barbary horses, each led by a Moor in red livery, then the freed slaves. There were civic dignitaries 'richly clothed, having great plumes on their hats'; ten Gentlemen of the Privy Chamber (there should have been twelve, but two didn't turn up); the ambassador himself, on horseback and accompanied by the Earl of Shrewsbury, and with a servant carrying his scimitar and another his slippers, four footmen in blue livery and eight of his own men 'in their country habits on horseback'; and four hundred part-time soldiers drawn from the four regiments of the London trained bands, the local militia. Sir Edmund's deputies and the Lord Chamberlain's men could hardly contain the crowds which pressed in around Whitehall as the ambassador was conducted into the King's presence, where he spoke briefly to Charles and Henrietta Maria (in Arabic, which was translated by an English merchant he had brought with him). After a short interval, Charles went with Indah ben Abdullah across the Whitehall tiltyard and into St James's Park, 'there to receive the present of horses, which led forth, one by one, before his majesty were by him severally viewed, as were, after them, the captives'.† Determined not to appear less magnanimous than the Sultan of Morocco, Charles made sure that when the ambassador left England some months later he took with him an equally impressive collection of gifts: a coach, lined with crimson velvet, gilded and painted with flowers; five horses to pull it, plus another six or seven horses; an array of textiles, including 'many whole pieces of the purest fine Hollands and Cambricks'; 100 lances; and copies of Van Dyck's portraits of the King and Queen.

---

* There was a gap of eighteen days between the ambassador's arrival in the City and his audience with the King, because he was sick with a fever. Charles paid his expenses for this period, which came to a hefty £450.

† Albert J. Loomie (ed.), *Ceremonies of Charles I: The Note Books of John Finet 1628–1641*, 234. The hawks had been handed over four or five days earlier, because they were failing to thrive in the Wood Street lodgings. One can't help wondering where the freed slaves had been kept in the meantime.

Charles and Henrietta Maria excelled at theatricality and grand gestures. During the Moroccan ambassador's stay he attended a Twelfth Night masque, William Davenant's *Britannia Triumphans*, which was held in the recently completed Masking House at Whitehall. With sets by Inigo Jones, this allegory of heroic virtue and Britain's largely illusory naval might was a spectacular piece of stagecraft, judging from the published stage directions:

> . . . the scene changes, and in the farthest part the sea was seen, terminating the sight with the horizon; on the one side was a haven, with a citadel, and on the other broken grounds and rocks; from whence the sea-nymph Galatea came waving forth, riding on the back of a dolphin, in a loose snow-white garment, about her neck chains of pearl, and her arms adorn'd with bracelets of the same; her fair hair dishevelled and mixed with silver, and in some part covered with a veil which she with one hand graciously held up. Being arrived to the midst of the sea, the dolphin stayed, and she sung with a chorus of music . . .*

There was an intense political programme at the heart of court life. The masques, the magnificent hospitality, the public displays, were designed to confirm the King's status and to emphasise the God-given nature of kingship. Charles and Henrietta Maria had always been keenly aware of the political potential of public spectacle; but since 1629, when the King dissolved Parliament after the Commons dared to question his authority and his decidedly un-Protestant inclinations in religious matters, his use of the Whitehall court as an instrument of statecraft had assumed

---

* Inigo Jones and William Davenant, *Britannia Triumphans* (1637 [i.e., 1638]), 24. The best part of *Britannia Triumphans* is the wonderfully inappropriate 'Valediction' with which Davenant closes, a hymn of praise to Charles I's sexual prowess:

> To wish unto our Royal Lover more
> Of youthful blessings than he had before,
> Were but to tempt old Nature 'bove her might,
> Since all the Odour, Music, Beauteous Fire,
> We in the spring, the spheres, the stars, admire
> Is his renewed, and bettered every night!

a new importance. Dispensing with what he called 'the unduti-
ful and seditious' Commons – and with the Lords as well –
Charles ruled by royal prerogative, financing his government by
a series of measures which ranged from conventional customs
duties to the decidedly less conventional enforcement of ancient
forest laws and the redefinition of vast tracts of private land as
royal forest, which enabled the Crown to fine those who had
'trespassed' upon them. The King's most notorious means of
raising income without recourse to Parliament was, of course,
the ship money, an old levy which had traditionally been imposed
on coastal towns to provide ships for the navy which would
protect their commerce, but which was extended to include first
the City of London and then all inland counties.

There was plenty of opposition to the Personal Rule, much
of it coming from gentry families like the Verneys. It was
compounded by rising disquiet about the way in which Charles
was upholding the position of the Anglican hierarchy against a
hostile Puritan gentry, creating a link between Crown and bishops
which was so strong that, in the words of the twentieth-century
historian Godfrey Davies, 'any opposition to the church was
regarded as sedition at court and any criticism of the monarchy
was denounced as blasphemy in the pulpit'.[22] Urged on both by
his Catholic queen and by his fervently anti-Puritan Archbishop,
William Laud – 'a little low red-faced man of mean parentage',
in the opinion of Simonds D'Ewes[23] – Charles sanctioned an
increasingly repressive attitude towards nonconformity in religion.
Preaching licences were given only to ritualists. Congregations
accustomed to receiving communion in their pews or at an
ordinary table standing in the middle of the nave were ordered
to kneel at the rail of an altar which was firmly placed against
the east wall of the chancel. That altar became an object of
veneration, 'the greatest place of God's residence upon earth', in
Laud's words, 'yea, greater than the pulpit.'[24] To Protestants like
Sir Edmund and his Buckinghamshire neighbours, this all stank
of popery.

Charles used the court at Whitehall to confirm his authority,
to counter criticism of his behaviour, to validate his ideology.
The reason that *Britannia Triumphans* dealt with Britain's mastery
of the seas was because it was a thinly veiled justification of ship

money. And it was no coincidence that one of its scenes showed a horrid hell populated by mutinous citizens; or that in another, Fame hailed the King as the nation's saviour: 'O thou, our cheerful morning rise/And straight those misty clouds of error clear,/ Which long have overcast our eyes,/And else will darken all this Hemisphere . . .'[25] Indeed, the very fact that it was being staged in the new Masking House at Whitehall was itself a direct result of Charles I's myth-making: Inigo Jones's Banqueting House, which had been the venue for court masques since 1622, was now out of bounds to the masquers because the King feared its brand-new Rubens ceiling 'might suffer by the smoke of many lights'.[26] That ceiling, commissioned by Charles as he embarked on the Personal Rule and installed over the winter of 1635–6, was a masterly paean to kingship and the benefits of Stuart rule. In one panel, Hercules as the personification of Heroic Virtue gives a savage beating to Rebellion; in another, Wise Government holds a bridle over Intemperate Discord. A cherubic infant Charles I is held aloft by England and Scotland in one canvas, while Wisdom holds the joined crowns of the two nations over his head. Other canvases praise the peaceful government of James I (and by extension, that of his son); and the divine nature of kingship, with James being carried up on the back of an eagle to join the gods in heaven. Those ambassadors and other dignitaries who were ushered into the Banqueting House in the later 1630s to be presented to the King, or who clustered in its galleries watching him presiding over the annual dinner for his Knights of the Garter, could have no illusions about the ideological message. The Stuarts had ushered in a golden, God-given age of peace and plenty. The King, and only the King, knew what was best for his subjects.

Sir Edmund responded to the elaborate mythology of monarchy which Charles constructed around himself with conflicting emotions. He found himself torn between his personal loyalty to the monarch, on whom he depended and whom he had served for a quarter of a century, and his unease at the Crown's assumption of absolute power. In matters of religion he was temperamentally opposed to the Catholic-leaning ritualism favoured by Charles and Archbishop Laud.

But Puritanism came in many different colours. (They weren't all shades of black, either – Sir Edmund's purple satin suit and waistcoat of cloth-of-gold should dispel any last lingering doubts about that.) At one extreme there were fanatics whose Protestantism bordered on the dysfunctional, like William Prynne, who believed that the bishops were intent on stamping out all orthodox sincere preachers and bringing in popery, superstition and idolatry, and who worked himself into a frenzy of righteous indignation because 'our theatrical amorous mixed lascivious dancing is sinful and unchristian',[27] a symptom of 'this effeminate, unchaste lascivious age wherein we live'.[28] At the other end of the spectrum there were country gentry like the Dentons and the Temples, who were quite capable of correcting with a sharp word any Arminian errors which a ritualistic rector might commit during Sunday service; who resented the ship money not only because they thought it an attack on their traditional liberties, but also because they had to pay it; who were really rather partial to amorous mixed lascivious dancing. *Their* Puritanism, like their politics, had less to do with Protestant zealotry, and more to do with a deep hatred of Roman Catholicism and Catholic Europe, which had its roots in the Marian persecutions and Hispanophobia of the sixteenth century.

Sir Edmund's Puritanism was not that of 'phanatickes' like William Prynne. He was suspicious of the bishops' attempts to impose their particular brand of uniformity of worship, and he initially refused to install altar rails at Claydon, receiving a reprimand for his slackness. But he was a pragmatist, and the rails were in place by 1634. The issue was worth his making a point; it wasn't worth more than that. In much the same way he disapproved of the King's arbitrary attitude towards taxation. But when his Buckinghamshire neighbours organised resistance to the ship-money levy, he kept out of their quarrel, even when his brother-in-law Sir Alexander Denton and his kinsman, Sir Peter Temple of Stowe, got into trouble for dragging their feet over the collection of the tax. (Sir Peter was summoned before Council to explain his negligence, and Sir Alexander was placed in the custody of government agents to ensure that he collected more than £700 in arrears.)

This was partly the result of his position at court, which meant that he had to be more circumspect than country gentry like

Denton and Temple. But it was more than that. The bonds which tied Sir Edmund to his royal master involved more than expediency. There was loyalty and fidelity, good name and reputation – those values which a Stuart courtier characterised by the word 'honour'. For all his easy-going and distinctly generous brand of Puritanism, his flexible approach to politics and religion, such things mattered to him – not in a high-flown, literary way, but as a basic tenet of faith. Loyalty to the King right or wrong for Sir Edmund Verney was a moral imperative, a commandment: 'As we are required to honor the fathers of private families, so much more the father of our country and the whole kingdom.'[29]

In the light of what was to come, this is an important point. Sir Edmund saw no contradiction in disagreeing with his sovereign's policy and still remaining absolutely faithful to that sovereign. 'Neither suppose crimes in Princes, as tyranny, infidelity, heresy, apostasy . . . nothing can free subjects from their fidelity and allegiance unto their Prince.'[30]

This was not hypocrisy or blindness. This was not self-interest. This was honour.

5

A Little Fading Honour

On 7 February 1639 a messenger arrived at the Verneys'
Covent Garden house with a summons from the Palace
of Whitehall. The Earl of Pembroke in his capacity as
Lord Chamberlain informed Sir Edmund Verney that King Charles
had 'resolved upon a royal journey to York' and that, as a Gentleman
of the Privy Chamber, Sir Edmund's presence was required in that
city by 1 April next. He was to appear in York 'in russet arms, with
gilded studs or nails, and befittingly horsed'; and his servants should
be equipped and armed, 'after the manner of a hargobusier'. If for
any reason he was unable to comply with the King's command,
then he must send 'some gentleman of quality' to deputise for him.[1]

Sir Edmund was not very well. He was suffering from gout
and plagued with sciatica, which had made him noticeably
depressed over Christmas. Moreover, he was right in the middle
of another scheme to solve all his money worries at a stroke, by
pushing through a patent to license all hackney carriages in
London. If it succeeded, the advantage to the coachmen was a
regulated trade without interlopers; the advantage to Sir Edmund
was a steady stream of licence fees.

And on top of all this, he was at the heart of some extremely delicate negotiations over a possible husband for his sister-in-law. Lady Margaret Verney's youngest sister – who rather confusingly was also called Margaret – was eighteen years her junior, and only a year older than Ralph. As a teenager she had been married off to a wealthy but wild landowner, John Pulteney of Misterton in Leicestershire, who under her influence 'had been led away from dissipations in which he had been accustomed to indulge', as one Victorian historian rather sweetly put it.[2] The Pulteneys were useful to the Verneys. It was they who had found Ralph's Oxford tutor John Crowther a curacy when he decided he couldn't face teaching any more; and they eased some of the pressure on Sir Edmund's domestic finances by taking in Peg, his third daughter (and Margaret Pulteney's god-daughter), when she was barely in her teens.

John Pulteney's rejection of dissipation and indulgence didn't happen quickly enough to prevent him from dying young in May 1637, and Aunt Pulteney was left a rich, childless and highly eligible widow, while she was still only twenty-five.

A widow had much more freedom to choose a husband than she had as a spinster; but in view of Aunt Pulteney's enviable financial position, her Denton kin thought it best to involve the well-connected Verneys. Throughout 1638, suitors were considered and discarded. Sir John Paulet's estate didn't lie in Buckinghamshire, which was enough for the widow's mother, the formidable Lady Susan Denton, to dismiss him as unsuitable. Lord Deincourt was rich enough – and ardent enough, to judge from his love letters. 'The torments which I now suffer for your beauty are insupportable,' he wrote. 'Since the happy hour when first I see you my heart hath still been contemplating upon your beauties, and the only joy of my life consisteth in the remembrance of you and your rare virtues'.[3] But Margaret Pulteney found him repulsive and was determined that, no matter what pressure was brought to bear on her, she would only marry someone she liked. 'This liberty I will take to myself, that is, to make choice of one as I affect. As for him [Lord Deincourt], I find I cannot.'[4]

By the beginning of 1639 there were two contenders in the race. One is simply referred to by all concerned as 'Lord Charles'. We don't know his identity, but we do know that he had powerful friends – the Earl of Pembroke was championing his cause, and the Lord Chamberlain's opinion mattered with both the Verneys and the Dentons. The other suitor was Lord Howard of Escrick, the youngest son of the Earl of Suffolk. He had good connections, and huge estates in Yorkshire and Essex. He also had five children by his late wife, a point which led Lady Susan into agonies of indecision: the Howards were a great family, but five children were too much of a commitment for her daughter. What chance would any offspring of the marriage stand, when they came so far down the pecking order? 'I should never venture upon so many children as five,' she told Ralph; even so, 'I will neither write anything against this match, nor with it.'[5]

Sir Edmund and Ralph were both at the centre of the negotiations. Margaret regularly confided in Ralph, while Lady Denton and the Lord Chamberlain were keen for Sir Edmund to use his influence with the young widow. In the end, everyone agreed there should be a cooling-off period, after which Aunt Pulteney would decide between Lord Charles and Lord Howard. Everyone but Margaret Pulteney, that is.

Given the gout and sciatica, the precarious state of his business enterprises, the complicated state of his family interests, Sir Edmund might have been forgiven for sending a deputy to attend the King in York. And if the journey north had been nothing more than a royal progress, perhaps he would have done just that. But Charles I was not in York for a holiday. He was there to muster an expeditionary force, and then to march on Scotland.

Although the King was a Scot himself – he was born at Dunfermline on 19 November 1600 – he had had a rather long-distance relationship with his native kingdom since moving to England in 1604, the year after his father James VI succeeded to the English throne as James I. In fact after he left, he had only ever visited the country on two occasions, one of which was for his coronation. It says a lot about his priorities that, although he was crowned King of England at Westminster in 1626, the Scots had to wait another seven years before he got round to a coronation in Edinburgh.

That didn't mean Charles was prepared to let Scotland go its own way. His determination to enforce religious uniformity across the churches of his kingdoms had led in 1637 to a riot in St

Giles' Cathedral, Edinburgh. When the Dean attempted to read from a new prayer book which had been imposed without consultation and which seemed – to the hard-line Presbyterian Scots, at least – to stink of ritual and Roman Catholicism, they reacted vigorously: 'a noise and clamour was raised throughout the church, that no voice could be heard distinctly, and then a shower of stones and sticks and cudgels were thrown at the dean's head'.[6] The following year thousands of Scots signed the National Covenant, demanding the abolition of bishops, rejecting the King's attempts at innovation in matters of religion and calling for a free Parliament and a free General Assembly.

Charles reacted by buying guns in the Low Countries, fortifying the garrison towns of Carlisle and Berwick-on-Tweed on the Borders and mobilising local militias. At the same time, the Covenanters quietly prepared for war, and during the winter of 1638–9 Scottish mercenaries serving in Europe began to drift home. They included the brilliant Alexander Leslie, a field marshal in the Swedish army, who became commander-in-chief of the Scots forces: 'he took up the trade of killing men abroad, and now is returned to kill, for Christ's sake, men at home'.[7]

Charles was careful not to advertise his intentions. But over the winter he hatched a plan with his closest advisers for a three-pronged assault on Scotland. A fleet commanded by the Marquis of Hamilton would sail from Hull to land an army of 5000 men on the east coast of Scotland, who would rendezvous with forces from the Royalist garrison at Aberdeen. Another fleet would take an army under the command of the Earl of Antrim from Ulster to the west coast, to reinforce the garrison at Dumbarton Castle. Charles himself would march the main army from York up into the Lowlands, where they would rendezvous with Royalists holding Edinburgh and Dalkeith castles against the Covenanters. His general-in-chief was the Earl of Arundel, memorably described by Clarendon as 'a man who had nothing martial about him but his presence and his looks', but who was chosen for his negative qualities: 'he did not love the Scots; he did not love the puritans; which good qualifications were allayed by another negative, he did love nobody else'.[8] More qualified men in the King's court were jealous of Arundel's preferment, while the fact that he was a Roman Catholic only confirmed suspicions that the

Covenanters were right, and the King was indeed sympathetic to popery.

War was in the air. Young Edmund, Ralph's brother, volunteered for the King, and rode north, half-hoping, half-fearing that one side or the other would back down. 'But if it should come to blows, yet why should not I think of escaping as well as any other?'[9] Sir Edmund's brother-in-law William Denton, who had been appointed as one of Charles's physicians in 1636, was ordered up to York. Sir Edmund himself was ideologically inclined towards the Covenanters' views on the need to keep Protestantism free from innovation, superstition and bishops. But his private beliefs were of no account when it came to his public duty: no matter how much he might disagree with the King's policy for Scotland, he was the King's servant. So he packed up his arms and armour along with his gout and his sciatica and set out on the 200-mile trek northwards to York, under no illusions about the purpose of his journey, or the possible outcome.

During his absence in the north, Ralph was left in charge – in charge of the estate, in charge of his brothers and sisters, in charge of the business with the hackney carriages, in charge of Margaret Pulteney's marriage plans. And Sir Edmund made his will before he went. Ralph was sole executor, his father 'having had experience of his fidelity unto me and of his love for his brothers and sisters'.[10]

Ralph and Sir Edmund were so different. The father was a soldier, a man of action, an Elizabethan adventurer. The son was a broker, a worrier, a country gentleman who wanted nothing so much as a quiet life. But for two men who by nature were reserved and aloof in their dealings with others, the love between them was fierce. Both were distraught at parting, perhaps for ever, and Sir Edmund's first thought when he arrived in York was to write a tender letter to his eldest son:

Good Ralph
Since Prince Henry's death I never knew so much grief as to part from you; and truly, because I saw you equally afflicted with it, my sorrow was the greater. But Ralph, we cannot live always together. It cannot be long ere by course of nature we must be severed, and if that time be prevented by accident, yet

we must resolve to bear it with that patience and courage as becomes men and Christians; and so the great God of heaven send us well to meet again, either in this world or in the next.[11]

'Since Prince Henry's death': the death of Henry Frederick, Prince of Wales, had been a defining moment in Sir Edmund's life, the pain and grief still vivid in his heart twenty-seven years later. Perhaps it also shaped the course of British history. Perhaps Prince Henry would have avoided the errors of judgement that Charles was making – errors which were leading him down a road which would end on a scaffold in Whitehall.

Things were not going well for the King. Sir Edmund arrived in the King's camp to find that the garrisons at Edinburgh and Dumbarton had handed over their castles to the Covenanters, without putting up any resistance at all. The Earl of Traquair, who had promised to hold Dalkeith Castle for the King, had second thoughts and gave it up without a shot being fired, leaving behind a large quantity of arms and ammunition and the royal crown and sceptre of Scotland, which were carried off to Edinburgh 'in great joy and triumph'.[12] At Aberdeen, Charles had relied on the loyal Marquis of Huntley, who was now persuaded by General Leslie to surrender the castle and disband his 5000-strong Royalist force 'without so much as a bloody nose', said Sir Edmund. 'The king has been basely betrayed.'[13]

A major part of the Royalist strategy had been shock and awe. Charles was convinced that when the Covenanters realised what a mighty force was converging on them from all sides, resistance would collapse and their leaders would rush to negotiate. The fall of the four Royalist castles meant that shock and awe were in short supply, and the only course left to the King and his commanders was for the main army assembling in the north of England to march on Edinburgh. Sir Edmund was convinced that there would be war before the summer was out. 'Now all Scotland is gone,' he told Ralph. 'I would it were under the sea, for it will ask a great time, and cost much blood, to reduce them again.'[14] He asked his son to say nothing to the women in case the news frightened them.

Sir Edmund was having rather a miserable time of it in York. His gout was hurting so much that he begged Lady Margaret to send up some medication he'd left with her. His servant Peter had walked out on him and gone back to London. And although he had sent his arms and armour up by carrier, there was no sign of them and no news of what had happened to them.

In the middle of all these troubles, Ralph received some dreadful news about his Aunt Pulteney. 'Oh Sir,' he wrote to his father, 'She is married, she is married!'[15] To a Roman Catholic.

Without consulting a soul, Aunt Pulteney had turned her back on Lord Howard and Lord Charles, ignored her family's best interests and chosen a husband for herself. That was bad enough, but to pillars of the Protestant establishment like the Verneys, the fact that he was a Catholic was about as bad as Uncle Francis turning Turk. Worse, even – at least the piratical Francis had had the grace to commit his awful act of apostasy in North Africa, out of sight and out of mind. It wouldn't be long before everyone knew about Margaret Pulteney's marriage – and that included her hopeful suitors, the Lord Chamberlain and the court. It included her formidable mother, Lady Susan.

In other respects Margaret's new husband, William Eure, was acceptable enough. He was the younger son of a lord, and a professional soldier with an income of about a thousand a year. But he was a Catholic, and no one could forgive him for that. In York, Sir Edmund was appalled when the news came; his hands started to shake, and for the rest of the day he could hardly hold anything steady. Then, because there was some confusion as to whether the woman was actually *married* to Eure or only betrothed, he marshalled the family into action. He wrote to Margaret in an effort to persuade her to change her mind. He wrote to Ralph's wife, begging her to use all her influence with her aunt: 'I fear she will do a foolish and a wicked thing,' he confided.[16] And he wrote to poor Ralph, who was feeling thoroughly miserable at the thought that he had let his father down. Margaret must be packed off to Hillesden while Ralph and his wife tried to talk her out of the marriage; at the same time, the news must be kept from Lady Susan; and it must at all costs be kept from her two suitors and the Lord Chamberlain, who were up in the north with Sir Edmund.

This wasn't as easy as it might have been, since Colonel Eure was on his way to join the army at York. What if he talked? Sir Edmund bumped into him towards the end of April and, noticing that he was dressed in his buff coat as though he was preparing to go into action, commented hopefully that 'if he does, some lucky bullet may free her of this misfortune'.[17]

Ralph did as he was told, although within a few days the rumours were starting to spread in London and York. Lord Charles and Lord Howard heard that Colonel Eure had an interest in the object of their desire; so did the Lord Chamberlain, who wrote directly to Margaret Pulteney, enclosing a love letter from Howard. Sir Edmund told Ralph his aunt should neither confirm nor deny the stories, and Ralph dutifully wrote out a noncommittal reply for Margaret to send to the Lord Chamberlain, in which she hinted fairly broadly that Lord Howard was out of luck. But this only intensified the speculation, since everyone assumed Lord Charles was now the frontrunner.

Lady Margaret Verney reprimanded her sister because she'd heard the couple had been seen in bed together and were married. She was sure there must be some mistake, she said, not altogether convincingly; the widow couldn't be so immodest. The widow responded with the logical comment that if she was married to Eure, what was immodest about them being in bed together?

The scandal rumbled on, with Sir Edmund and Ralph doing everything they could to preserve their relative's good name and their family's reputation. Throughout the whole affair Margaret Pulteney showed tremendous strength of character. 'The town makes havoc of my good name,' she confided in Ralph: 'But let them devise their worst. I defy them all. None in the world can call me to an account for my actions for I am not in any one's tuition – as I have sent your mother word.'[18]

Meanwhile, Sir Edmund continued to rage in his lodgings, mad with grief and anger and desperately thinking up ways to retrieve the situation. If his sister-in-law was really determined to marry Eure, his fall-back strategy was for the man to stay out of the way over the summer while she gently rid herself of her two noble suitors, and then for the couple to wed very quietly in the autumn. So when Margaret told him the business was past recall, he feared the worst. A Christmas baby hard on the heels of an autumn wedding would be rather hard to explain. 'Hereafter I must love my friends less, that I may digest their misfortunes better,' he told Ralph. 'This woman lay so near my heart that I shall find her folly there whilst I have an hour to live.'[19]

While Sir Edmund agonised over Margaret Pulteney's betrayal and dreamed of putting a bullet in William Eure's back, the war effort was slowly getting into its stride. King Charles hoped that his loyal nobles would arrive at York with companies of fully equipped followers, in the manner of medieval warlords responding to their King's general muster. He was disappointed, and it took most of April for a force of around 15,000 men to gather in billets outside the city 'which was done to avoid disorder which common soldiers are apt to occasion in great towns where there is such means to licentiousness'.[20] Most were part-timers from the county militias and they were woefully underequipped. During the early part of April there was also a shortage of officers, caused (according to rumour) by Charles I's reluctance to mobilise them – and thus to pay them – until and unless it was absolutely necessary. But as the spring wore on, more men turned up, regular drills were held and arms and munitions began to arrive. Stories flew round the camp. The Marquis of Huntley had deserted the Royalist cause and signed the Covenant, said some; he had only done so with the consent of the King, said others, and was acting as a double agent. 'This is a time for stratagems,' wrote one young soldier, 'and that fills us all with strange conceits'.[21] The Earl of Arundel ordered a printer and press to be sent up from London by wagon, 'to set out his Majesty's daily commands for his court or army'.[22] An English ambassador signed a contract with Hamburg arms dealers for 3000 muskets, 700 pairs of pistols and a quantity of pikes and breastplates.

Sir Edmund was still anxious about his own equipment. His armour had gone to London by mistake; from there Ralph had it sent to Newcastle, the next stop for the King's forces on their inexorable march northwards. But an outbreak of plague in the town delayed the army's progress, and by the end of April Sir Edmund was with the court at Durham, and still without his armour. However, he had already seen enough to realise that this would be a modern war; when he finally went into action his old helmet would be more of a hindrance than a help, as would the heavy cuirass that he had intended to wear. So he decided to have nothing more than light breastplate, backplate and long gauntlet. The trouble was, the elusive consignment of armour didn't include a long gauntlet, so he wrote to Ralph to have his armourer make one up 'with all the speed he can possibly'. He also told his son that if he had 'a pot for the head that were pistol proof, it may be I would use it, if it were light'.[23] As soon as the things were ready they should be sent by sea to the mayor's house at Newcastle, to await his arrival there.

In the meantime, the unwarlike Ralph suggested rather hesitantly that perhaps he should arm himself and head for the Borders to take his place in the King's army? Writing to his father of his preparations for war, he confessed he was not at all looking forward to the journey, nor did he think Sir Edmund's affairs were in such a state as he could comfortably leave them; but then he thought better and rewrote the letter with these lines omitted.

Ralph wasn't the only Englishman who was reluctant to fight the Scots. Some courtiers pleaded ill health, others old age. Professional officers and artillerymen refused to budge until their rates of pay had been fixed. An engineer named De Bois demanded twenty pounds to pay for his passage to Newcastle. More highly principled noncombatants shared Sir Edmund's misgivings about the rightness of the King's cause, but not his fierce and determined loyalty. Charles I had not called a parliament for ten years, and the fact that he didn't call one now, when he was about to embark on a war, went against all precedent.

Nor was it just the arbitrary nature of his actions which was causing men to question his authority; there was also a hint of duplicity. When he called the muster at York, he was careful to maintain the fiction that he only wanted to defend the borders of his kingdom and repel the Scots if they crossed into England; there was no talk of invading Scotland. Indeed, the feudal call to arms specifically excluded intervening in another kingdom's affairs: the nobility's military obligations were based on an early fifteenth-century statute which declared that 'no man be compelled to go out of his shire, but where necessity requireth, and sudden coming of strange enemies into the realm; and then it shall be done as hath been used in times past for the defence of the realm'.[24] Mindful of his shaky legal position, Charles gathered his nobles together at York on 21 April 1639 and asked them to take a new, more flexible military oath.

Two refused. Lord Saye and Sele and Lord Brooke were both willing to defend the kingdom and willing to take the traditional oath of allegiance. That ought to be enough, they said. Lord Brooke went further, arguing that if the Covenanters were such a danger to the realm, the King should summon a parliament to provide properly for the coming war.

Charles reacted by putting them under house arrest in York and then, when they continued to argue their case rather too eloquently, by sending them home. Sir Edmund was incensed, particularly by the treatment of the elderly Lord Saye. 'There was never so weak a thing done as the commitment of that man,' he told Ralph.[25]

Sir Edmund had an astute grasp of how the crisis was playing out. The Royalist army was weak, and if the King was forced to fight in the early summer, 'we shall have our throats cut'. But there wasn't enough money to sustain a long campaign, and so it was obvious that Charles had no choice but to press ahead to the border. His commander-in-chief, the Earl of Arundel, was constantly pushing him to fight; so were the other Catholics in the army – a point which made Sir Edmund deeply suspicious.

He was tired, and although he never wavered in his resolve to stand by the King and do the right thing, he was miserable at the thought of so much bloodshed with so little prospect of success. 'For my own part, I have lived till pain and trouble has made me weary to do so, and the worst that can come shall not be unwelcome to me; but it is a pity to see what men are like to be slaughtered here, unless it shall please God to put it in the King's heart to increase his army, or stay till these may know what they do, for as yet they are as like to kill their fellows as the enemy.'[26]

But while he might be prepared for the worst, he was still eager to have his long gauntlet; he begged Ralph to send it as soon as possible. He also told him to burn the letter which contained such defeatist sentiments. (Ralph kept it.)

The King arrived in Newcastle on 6 May, and Sir Edmund was by his side. His son, young Mun, was already there, but sick with a fever and quartered a few miles out of the town. Ague was moving swiftly through the army; so was smallpox, which had decimated several regiments over the past couple of weeks. The knight-marshal continued as pessimistic as ever: 'Our men are very raw, our arms of all sorts nought, our vittle scarce, and provision for horses worse . . . Commend me to all my friends, and so God send us well to meet either in this world or in the next.'[27] He finally managed to rendezvous with his armour, and found that there was a long gauntlet included with it all the time. But the helmet which he didn't intend to use was much too small – only a madman could have thought it would fit – and so he wrote again to Ralph asking him to check that the armourer who was making his pistol-proof pot had the right measurements. 'If the pot I expect daily from him be so too, I am undone,' he complained. 'This will come upon no part of my head, it is so very little.'[28]

The main army was now only forty miles from the Scottish border. Charles I offered a pardon to any Covenanters who would 'cease to be obstinate'; they answered politely but firmly that they had done nothing to be pardoned for, and asked the King for reassurance about their 'fears of innovations in religion'.[29] This only made him crosser than ever, and more adamant that his Scottish subjects must be brought to heel. An English force under the Earl of Essex had secured Berwick-on-Tweed in March, forestalling a pre-emptive strike by Leslie's Covenanters. Now the Earl of Holland, who was in command of the King's cavalry, was ordered to take some men and cross the border. Sir Edmund volunteered to go with him.

He did his best to keep the mission from his family, but he made the mistake of confiding in Nat Hobart, who couldn't keep his mouth shut and told Ralph.

Ralph immediately fired off a passionate plea to William Denton, begging the doctor to try and try again to persuade his brother-in-law against leaving the King's camp. 'If my father goes to the Borders, he is lost; I know his courage will be his destruction. No man did ever so wilfully ruin himself, and his posterity. God forgive him, and grant me patience. Certainly his heart is more than stone.'[30] At the same time he wrote Sir Edmund a letter so full of anger, pain and fear that it sounds for all the world like a desperately worried father rather than a dutiful son:

You may easily guess how this afflicts me, for if you go (knowing your forwardness) I shall never think to see you more, but with grief confess that never man did more wilfully cast away himself. Till now I never had the least reason to suspect your affection, but when I see you thus hastily run to your own ruin, and as it were, purposely to lose that life that is so much dearer to me then my own, how can I think you love me? Hath the vain hope of a little fading honour swallowed up all your good nature? Are your compassions quite shut up? Will neither the numberless sighs of your dearest friends, nor the incessant cries of your forlorn widow, nor the mournful groans of your father-less brood, prevail to stay you? Are you so absolutely resolved by this one act to blot all your former? And (by needless hazarding yourself) expose your wife and children to perpetual misery, and entail afflictions upon your whole posterity?[31]

A little fading honour? 'Mine honour is my life; both grow in one:/Take honour from me, and my life is done', as the Duke of Norfolk says in *Richard II*. Sir Edmund came from a genera-tion of courtiers which didn't just pay lip service to such senti-ments; a generation for whom reputation really *was* more important than friends and family – more important than life itself. And we shouldn't forget how the juggernaut of war has its own momentum, which inspires excitement and exhilaration as well as fear and disgust. Sir Edmund was learning to enjoy war.

Poor Ralph! There he was, stuck in London trying to manage his father's business affairs, mediating between his wayward aunt and his bad-tempered grandmother, negotiating with hackney coachmen over the patent. Trying to gain his father's approval. His three brothers followed their dangerous but undeniably exciting lives, Henry with the garrison at Breda, Mun with the King's army in the north, Tom – who had just been packed off back to the New World – on a plantation in Barbados. And this was how Sir Edmund rewarded him, by rushing towards a hero's death in Scotland. Conventional roles were turned upside down as he talked of responsibilities and consideration for others, like an anxious parent chiding an inconsiderate teenager.*

As soon as he received Ralph's letter, Sir Edmund wrote straight back, doing his best to reassure his son. There was not much risk involved in Holland's expedition, he said, which had in any case moved on to become a general mobilisation, with the entire army

---

* The Verneys' Victorian biographers note, quite rightly, that 'Sir Edmund was very much the younger man of the two, and continued so to the end of his life' (*Memoirs of the Verney Family* (1907), I, 77).

heading for Scotland. It was only because he knew everyone at home would leap to the wrong conclusion that he had avoided mentioning the idea. He was also careful to say how much he appreciated his son's concern and good advice, and to emphasise that he would never deliberately place himself at risk. But then came the reminder of what honour demanded. 'Nor will I think you could wish me to leave anything undone when it falls to my turn to be in action.'[32]

There had already been a number of fatalities, accidental and otherwise. Infantry companies on their way north from Essex killed a pregnant woman as they looted houses on their route. A young cavalryman named Thomas Dawney got drunk in York and tried to show off his horsemanship; his mount fell on top of him and he was so badly hurt that he died the next day. And when soldiers from Sir Jacob Astley's regiment stole cattle from a farm outside Newcastle, the owner complained and they were reprimanded – which so incensed one of the offenders that he set fire to the man's hay. The soldier was hanged from a newly erected roadside gibbet, so that as his comrades passed on their way to the border they could see his dangling corpse and the inscription nailed to his gallows: 'for wilful and malicious burning of a stack of hay'.[33]

Vandalism and casual violence were a normal part of preparing for war in the seventeenth century. But on 19 May, the day after Ralph received his father's reassuring letter, the violence took a more dramatic turn. Lieutenant General George Goring's regiment of horse arrived at its quarters in Wark on the border, and a young colonel named Garrald set out to ride across the Tweed on an unauthorised one-man reconnaissance mission. Some townsfolk saw him go and, realising the risk he was running, went to warn Charles Price, a captain in Garrald's regiment. Price sent two riders to bring him back; when they failed to return, he mounted up and went in search of them himself, taking eight or ten soldiers with him.

Captain Price met up with Garrald and his two escorts just inside the Scottish border and the party turned for home, but before they reached the Tweed they caught sight of a group of thirty Scottish cavalrymen riding hard towards them. Price decided to stand his ground, and waited for the Covenanters to close with them. The two sides faced each other, weapons cocked, and exchanged rather tense pleasantries. Price, who was outnumbered two to one, did his best to defuse the situation. He asked politely if the Scots were friends to their King, and when they said they were, he suggested that everyone should lower their guns. They refused. So then he proposed that the two parties should doff their hats to each other and ride back to their respective camps. Suddenly, without warning, a Scottish trooper fired his musket right at Price's corporal. The shot broke the man's arm and pierced his buff coat, wounding him in the body. An English trooper immediately shot the Scotsman dead.

This might have been the signal for a bloodbath, with both sides blasting away at each other from close range. But neither wanted to fight, and the sudden violence – the powder smoke and blood and screaming – stopped as soon as it had begun. English and Scots both simply picked up their casualties and rode home. When Lord Holland heard about the incident he wrote to his Scottish counterpart, the Earl of Home, to apologise and to promise that Garrald would be punished for crossing into Scotland without permission. The Earl responded by suggesting that the English should stay away from the border, otherwise such accidents were bound to happen.

Sir Edmund was still in Newcastle with the King. News of the shooting reached him in less than forty-eight hours. 'This is the first blood that has been drawn in this business,' he told Ralph. 'If more must be lost in this unhappy quarrel, I pray God it may be at the same rate.'[34]

The knight-marshal was just about to set off for the border himself. In the end he didn't go with Lord Holland's horse, not because Ralph's pleas and Dr Denton's stern words had any effect, but simply because the King ordered his Gentlemen of the Privy Chamber to remain with him at Newcastle. Now he was going to supervise the erection of the royal pavilion at the forward camp, which was being set up a couple of miles outside Berwick-on-Tweed. The pistol-proof pot still hadn't turned up, and Ralph got the blame. He had told his son to check it was big enough. Ralph had, and it wasn't, so it went back to the armourer. Now Sir Edmund reprimanded him: 'I am very sorry you were so curious to try the pot, for an ill one had been better than none. I doubt it may come too late now.'[35]

As he rode north to Berwick, the afternoon grew heavy and dark and an eclipse of the sun filled the whole army with a sense of foreboding. 'There wanted not those who construed this eclipse as an ominous presage of bad success to the King's affairs.'[36]

The army, grown by now to 15,000 foot soldiers and 3000 horse, entrenched itself beside the banks of the Tweed and waited. Morale was low, food was scarce, the locals were quietly hostile to the King and for the Covenant, the nights were bitterly cold and smallpox was ripping through the tents. The Lord Chamberlain came down with an ague – Dr Denton was treating him at Chillingham, twenty miles south of Berwick – and Sir Edmund's pot still hadn't arrived. The King had issued a proclamation from York back in April, promising pardon to the rebels if they abandoned their fight. Now Lord General Arundel and the Earl of Holland left camp at one in the morning on 1 June 1639 with several hundred cavalry, riding into the Scottish town of Dunse and having the proclamation read by the sheriff of the county at the market cross.

It was hardly a conciliatory gesture. Although the King declared himself to be a defender of the true Protestant religion, and promised he would never permit 'any innovation of religion to creep into this or any other of our kingdoms', he also swore that if any of the rebels saw fit to continue their insolence, 'we shall be forced to have recourse to some more sharp and quick way to cure their obstinacy and rebellion by the sword of justice'.[37] (In an early draft of the proclamation, he placed a price on the heads of the rebels – £1000 for every earl, £600 for a lord and £500 apiece for Leslie and Hamilton – but he seems to have thought better of this before the document was printed.) The Scots were also warned that if they ventured within ten miles of the border this would be interpreted as an invasion of England, in which case the King's army was expressly commanded to proceed against them as rebels, 'to set upon and destroy them'.[38]

The proclamation wasn't intended to placate the rebels. Arundel and Holland hoped to surprise General Leslie's troops, although news of their impending visit went before them and when they arrived at Dunse there was no sign of any Scottish force. There were only women there who, when asked what had become of their husbands, seemed to forget they had any. They begged Holland 'for God's cause not to burn their houses, kill their children, nor bring in popery, as Leslie told them the King meant to do'.[39] Reassured by the English officers, they set to make the best of the temporary occupation, selling wine, milk, cakes and trinkets to the troops.

The only real consequence of Holland's foray was a row with William Cavendish, Earl of Newcastle, who considered it an insult that Holland had told his troop of mercenaries to bring up the rear. Weeks later he challenged Holland to a duel; Charles had his commander of horse placed under arrest to stop it; and Sir Edmund, whom Holland had named as his second, had to turn up on the field alone to explain to Newcastle why his adversary wasn't there.

Three days after Dunse, Sir Edmund rode out with the Earl of Holland on another expedition, *still* missing his pistol-proof pot. This time Holland took about 1000 cavalry and 3000 infantry to Kelso, having heard that a small force of Covenanters was digging in outside the town. His orders were to drive them away.

Kelso was more than ten miles from the English camp and after the bitter cold nights of late May, the weather was now blisteringly hot − so hot, in fact, that the infantry couldn't keep up with the horse. Foot soldiers were collapsing in the road; others were so thirsty they refused to march, and simply lay down like animals to lap from pools of stagnant ditchwater.

The result was that when Sir Edmund arrived at Kelso with the Earl of Holland and the rest of the cavalry, the English muskets and pikes had fallen miles behind. A small party of Scottish pikemen watched from a piece of rising ground outside the town as the horsemen approached, and then ran away, down the hill to their trenches. When the English cavalry chased them, they found that they had been lured into an ambush. The Tweed was on their left, and a treacherous marsh on their right: in front of them rose up 'a sudden and unexpected number of flying colours before us, issuing out of the trenches and from the town behind'.[40] Covenanter foot and horse moved to outflank them and cut off their retreat. Holland and the other commanders drew their swords and cantered steadily into this valley of death, ready to order a charge. But more and more Scots appeared in battle formation, and through their telescopes the English officers could see huge clouds of dust stirring on the hills in the distance, as if an even greater force were closing in on them.

'Pistols and carbines were all cocked, swords drawn, and trumpets going to mouth', according to William Denton, when Holland decided discretion might be the better part of valour.[41] Convinced that his troops were outnumbered ten to one, he cancelled the order to charge and coolly sent a herald to ask the Covenanters what they were doing in such numbers so close to the border with England? Quite naturally, General Leslie responded by asking the messenger how it was that a thousand English cavalrymen found themselves in Scotland. Wouldn't it perhaps be better if they left? Holland decided it would, and the English army retreated back across the border.

Sir Edmund was disgusted – not so much with the Earl's reluctance to fight (although he was certainly frustrated that 'we had not one blow'[42]) – but with the whole conduct of the war. English intelligence was flawed, he said; the war effort was under financed; the King was mistaken in believing that the Covenanters could be bullied into submission. There was much more solidarity among the Scots than Charles's advisers realised; and Leslie's army was much bigger than they knew. (He was actually mistaken on this last point: Leslie brilliantly manoeuvred his forces at Kelso to make them seem greater than they were, and drove herds of cattle across the hills to stir up the dust clouds which intimidated the Earl of Holland.) The knight-marshal thought the Scots insufferably proud and insolent, enough to make the heart of every loyal Englishman break with rage. So why was no one actually *doing* anything?

The truth was that Charles I was dithering. His advisers couldn't agree on what to do next, and several of his senior and middle-ranking commanders were not only unenthusiastic about an invasion, but also in private agreement with the Covenanters about Charles's motives in seeking to impose a uniform liturgy on both kingdoms. They kept their own counsel on the matter, but it was slowly dawning on the King that his nobles were divided about the righteousness of their cause.

In the meantime, discipline was breaking down in the camp. Over the past few days nervousness, carelessness and drunkenness had led to an alarming number of incidents involving firearms. One of the Earl of Holland's troopers accidentally discharged his pistol and blew out the brains of a 'young gent of quality of Lincolnshire'.[43] The Earl of Westmorland's brother was woken in the night when three shots went through his tent and pierced his bed curtains. A stray bullet even ripped through the King's own pavilion.

Arundel doubled the sentries around the perimeter of the camp and a round-the-clock watch was put on the King's privy chamber, with pairs of guards ordered to stand with pistols 'ready spanned and cocked'.[44] There was also a risk to the King from Scottish snipers. For some reason Sir Edmund had allowed the royal tent to be pitched by the river. There were no earthworks to defend it, and it lay within musket shot of a commanding hill on the Scottish side of the Tweed. And there was just as much unease at the realisation that the entire camp was vulnerable if the Covenanters managed to position their artillery on that hill. If they launched a cavalry charge, the river at this point was fordable by forty horses abreast. 'We are like to have the worst of the war,' Sir Edmund told his son at the beginning of June. 'When my pot is done let it be quilted and lined and sent to me, for here is no hope at all of peace.'[45]

At six on the morning of 4 June 1639 the alarm was raised in the camp. Far from heeding the English warning about keeping out of the ten-mile buffer zone between the two kingdoms, Leslie and his Covenanter army were in sight. In fact they had pitched camp on the heights of Duns Law, only five miles away across the Tweed, and there were hordes of them. Sir Edmund reckoned on 15,000, with another 30,000 on their way. A few hours later, a startled Charles I emerged from his pavilion and surveyed the sea of tents and fires through his perspective glass: it seemed inevitable that the Scots were only waiting for Leslie's order before they swept across the river and overran the English camp.

Ever a master of dramatic effect, the King simply shrugged and said to one of his attendants that there weren't all that many Scots. Then he went back to his tent and sat down to dinner. His courtiers were astounded. Everyone else stood to arms and waited.

Nothing happened, for the simple reason that the Covenanters hadn't come to fight. General Leslie had actually moved to the banks of the Tweed with the intention of deterring the English from making another incursion like the foray to Kelso. He well knew that while the Covenanters' anti-Catholic stance had some support south of the border, if he invaded he would only succeed in creating a united front among the English. Moreover, Leslie's army was in a much weaker state than English intelligence had suggested. It consisted of no more than 16,000 men in total, slightly fewer than the King's forces. They were just as badly provisioned and equipped as the English, and Leslie was facing the prospect of having to fight on two fronts, since a week or so earlier the Gordon clan had risen against the Covenanters in Aberdeenshire and retaken Aberdeen.

Charles I and his commanders didn't know this. They were convinced that if the Scots decided to cross the river, nothing could stop them. 'Our army is very weak, and our supplies come slowly to us, neither are those men we have well ordered,' Sir Edmund reported to Ralph. At the same time he was worried that the Covenanters would demand more than the King could possibly agree to, 'and then we shall have a filthy business of it'.[46]

After a standoff which lasted for two days, there was an exchange of messengers. Then the Earl of Dunfermline arrived in the Royalist camp and suggested that all the Covenanters wanted was for the King to listen sympathetically to their grievances. Still Charles refused to negotiate, insisting that the Covenanters must first hear his proclamation of 25 April. This was a face-saving gesture – the King can't really have believed he had only to remind the Scots of their obligations to the Crown for them to change their minds and go home (although an ability to empathise with his subjects was never one of his strong points). Because the Covenanters were eager to speak with English courtiers known to be sympathetic towards their brand of Protestantism, the King sent Sir Edmund Verney across the Tweed to open the negotiations.

Sir Edmund explained to the Scottish commanders that if they wanted a treaty they would have to listen to the York proclamation. They entertained him courteously enough, while they sent to Edinburgh to consult with their comrades. Then they agreed it could be read to a group of officers, although not to the whole Scottish army. This was duly done in Sir Edmund's presence and, with the formalities out of the way, he got down to the matter of arranging a peace conference. Six senior Covenanters were to be granted safe passage to the English camp, where they would sit down in the Lord General's tent to parley with six English nobles, who would include the Earls of Arundel, Essex and Holland.

The details of the meeting still had to be ironed out when Sir Edmund returned to the King's camp late in the afternoon of 7 June; but he was uncharacteristically pleased with himself at how things had gone. 'I dare boldly say I handled the business so that I begat this treaty; otherwise we had, I doubt, been at blows.'[47]

Sir Edmund wasn't party to the actual peace negotiations, which began at ten o'clock on the morning of 11 June. Contrary to their agreement, the King put in a surprise appearance, sweeping into Arundel's tent without warning just as the two sides were sitting down. The Covenanters had their backs to the entrance, so they didn't even notice his arrival until he sat down at the table. Charles really was a master of the gesture. He justified his presence by saying the Scots had often complained that he wouldn't hear their grievances, so here he was to listen. According to a Royalist who was in the camp (but not in the tent) this speech was accompanied with 'many expressions of greatness and majesty, yet mixed with admirable demonstrations of reason, justice, grace, and goodness'.[48] A less charitable interpretation might be that the King was trying to bully the Scots into submission.

By the end of the meeting, after which both sides sat down to dinner with the Lord General, it was still touch and go whether there would be war or not. The English were a good deal less worried about the Covenanter forces, which were much less impressive than they had feared. As the first day of the peace conference came to an end, Sir Edmund reported to Ralph with more confidence than he had shown for most of the campaign:

> The Scots have a good army, but far short of what they have bragged on; truly I think we shall have the better army, for now our supplies are come to us, we shall be able to make really 13,000 foot and 2,200 horse. They will have more foot, but are weak in horse, nor are they so well armed as we, so that I think they will hardly be drawn to meet us in open field, and we have 2,000 foot more ready at a day's warning.[49]

There was still pressure on Charles to reach a negotiated settlement with the Scots. On the night that Leslie's army appeared at Duns Law, the Earl of Bristol, who had already provoked a row by arguing that the King should stay safely in Newcastle rather than parading himself on the border, complained to his sovereign about the way the clergy in the camp were conducting themselves. Then he told him – in public – that most of the nobles and privy counsellors present were ready to petition him for a parliament. Charles did his best to limit the damage by saying he would discuss this with Bristol in private (which he did, for a whole hour), and other members of the court were swift to disown the Earl. But there was no doubt the King's camp was in disarray. A temporary peace would allow Charles to retrench, to refinance, to mobilise a more efficient army – and then to put down the Covenanters with a sharper, stronger sword of justice.

For their part, the Scots were just as keen to buy time, for much the same reasons. Leslie didn't want to be seen as the aggressor, but he knew he couldn't sustain an army in such a state of readiness for any length of time. The Covenanters asked for a general assembly of the Kirk in Glasgow to establish their religious freedoms, and a parliament in Edinburgh to ratify its decisions. The Royalist commissioners demanded that the Scots give up all the King's castles in Scotland and release all prisoners. Both armies were to withdraw and disband. The precise terms of the peace were left rather vague, a situation which suited both sides.

By 15 June Sir Edmund was confident of the outcome of the negotiations: 'I believe there is no more doubt now but that we shall have peace.'[50] He was right, and although neither side really believed it would be a lasting peace, they were happy enough to return home and prepare for their next encounter. With an eye to making a profit from the demobilisation, Sir Edmund bought fifty horses from the army which he planned to graze at Claydon until he could sell them at a good price. His precious pistol-proof pot still hadn't arrived, but now he didn't care. 'I will keep it to boil my porridge in,' he said.[51]

6

The Best of Men

*M*argaret Pulteney broke the news of her marriage to her mother at the end of May 1639, and Lady Susan was devastated. 'Your mother writes me word about a samite gown,' she told Ralph. 'I remember I did heretofore think of such a thing, but now I pray tell her, if she would provide me sackcloth and line it with ashes'.[1]

It was, of course, William Eure's religion that distressed her. 'That is such a cut to me that yet hath almost killed me,'[2] she said. And although initially it was the bride who bore the brunt of her anger, as the weeks went by the old lady turned on Ralph, blaming him first for being foolish and not realising what was going on between her daughter and Eure until it was too late; and then for duplicity and treachery in actively encouraging the match behind her back. The Verneys were the talk of town and country for the way the couple had fooled them, she said; but *some* of them had known what was going on all the time, and they had done nothing to stop it.

Ralph was hurt. He told his grandmother that she shouldn't jump to conclusions without knowing all the facts. 'Justice will first hear, and then determine, but you go a contrary way, with this whole house in general, in particular with me.'³ But he remained polite, and made the due allowances for her age and position in the family.

In the middle of June a suspicious Sir Edmund wrote from Berwick to ask Margaret exactly who had performed her wedding ceremony. She didn't dare tell him herself, and persuaded her nephew to break the bad news. 'The unhappy woman was married by a popish priest,' said Ralph. 'She (being, as I suppose, ashamed of so foul an act) desired me to inform you of it.'⁴ She hadn't told anyone else. The enormity of her action made Ralph even more sensitive about accusations of neglect or complicity. So when he went to Hillesden to see his three-year-old son Edmund and found Lady Susan turning on him with renewed fury and laying the blame for the whole business on him and his mother, it was too much.

The old lady got more than she bargained for. After the reasoned arguments and icy politeness of the past month or so, Ralph's temper suddenly snapped and, in front of Aunt Isham, he told his grandmother exactly what he thought of her. He would never behave dishonourably; and if she believed he had, then 'she might do well never to employ those that had dealt treacherously with her'.⁵ She shouted that her children were all fools, and Ralph responded to this insult thrown at his mother by saying that by casting such false aspersions on her own children 'she did but defile her own nest'. The fight ended with Ralph saying that he knew he was innocent of any dishonourable conduct, so her harsh words meant nothing to him – except that he had thought she loved him. Obviously he was mistaken.

Ralph can't be blamed for lashing out – Lady Susan was enough to try the patience of a saint. But his reaction owed less to his grandmother's discourtesy and more to his own self-doubt and her refusal to give him his due as putative head of the Verney clan. His father's readiness to leave the running of the family to him left him with the worst of both worlds. He had responsibility without power; everyone made demands of him, but no one showed him much respect.

And, always an inveterate worrier, the events of the past few months had given Ralph rather too much to worry about. Dr

Denton was feeding him with dire warnings about his father's recklessness on the border. He had been keen to tell the young man that Sir Edmund was rashly exposing himself to risk with Lord Holland; and that if the Berwick negotiations failed, he 'will be in almost every danger, and now no persuasions can remove him'.[6] In fact Denton seemed to take a mischievous delight to scaring Ralph half to death, and now he wrote to let him know that some unpleasant stories were circulating in the camp about the retreat from Kelso. A man named Cunningham had told Henrietta Maria that Holland's cavalry had run away from Leslie's troops: for this slur on his honour Sir Edmund intended to offer Cunningham an opportunity to fight. 'Make what use of it [i.e. this information] you please,' he told Ralph, 'but not a word as from me.'[7] Nothing came of it, but the prospect of his father engaging in a duel made Ralph more fretful still.

Tom Verney, meanwhile, was in Barbados. His father had packed him off to the West Indies at the beginning of 1639 on the recommendation of the Earl of Warwick, in the hope that he might finally make something of himself, or at least keep out of gaol. Sir Edmund arranged for him to live temporarily on the estate of Captain James Futter, deputy governor of Barbados, Warwick's agent and one of the first settlers on the island. He was its most accomplished planter, according to contemporaries. Sir Edmund's idea was that Futter would teach Tom the practical side of cotton-farming and help the boy to establish himself with a small plantation of his own.

When Tom arrived on Barbados in 1639 it was only thirteen years since the *William and John* had landed the first forty English settlers and their eight black servants, but the colony already had a troubled and complicated history. The *William and John* expedition was financed by a London merchant, Sir William Courteen, under the patronage of the Earl of Marlborough, Lord High Treasurer; Marlborough had secured a patent for the island from James I shortly before the latter's death in March 1625. Unfortunately, James I had also granted *all* the Caribbean islands – including Barbados – to his old friend James Hay, Earl of Carlisle, who intended to administer them as a palatinate which he named 'Carliola'. Marlborough and Carlisle went to law over the island and, although Marlborough gave up his claim after Carlisle agreed to compensate him and his heirs with a perpetual annuity of £300, Sir William Courteen received no such compensation and continued to pursue his own claim. This time he enlisted the help of the Earl of Pembroke, who – while Carlisle was on a diplomatic mission to Lorraine, Piedmont and Venice – managed to persuade Charles I to grant Barbados to *him*. The King changed his mind again when Carlisle came home and complained, but the upshot was that, realising how tenuous was his hold on this particular corner of Carliola, Carlisle swiftly leased 10,000 acres (one-tenth of the island) to a group of London merchants and authorised them to establish their own settlement.

By 1628 the original Courteen colony, which had established itself at Jamestown, was in direct competition and occasional conflict with the new Carlisle colony, which had settled in swampy land four miles south at what is now Bridgetown. In January 1629 a ship arrived with a commission from the Earl of Pembroke, appointing his representative John Powell as governor of Barbados; Powell had the leaders of the Carlisle colony sent back to England in irons. Then, three months later, another vessel arrived, containing a governor appointed by the Earl of Carlisle; Powell was lured on board, clapped in irons and himself shipped back to England. After a pitched battle between the two factions, peace was finally established in 1629 and a Carlisle appointee, Sir William Tufton, became governor that December, only to be deposed less than seven months later. During a drought and famine Tufton accused his successor, Captain Henry Hawley, of keeping relief supplies for his own use; Hawley had Tufton shot for treason. (One of the judges in the case was shot a couple of years later, having been convicted of murdering another colonist.) In 1636 Hawley resolved with his Council that blacks and Indians brought to Barbados for sale should serve for life rather than the fixed period of between three and seven years which was customary with indentured white servants. He thus established a legal framework for slavery which would last for 200 years, although until the mid-1640s plantation owners continued to rely on bonded whites.

When Tom arrived in Barbados he thanked God that the rule of law was 'indifferent good', although with his track record 'indifferent' was probably more appealing to him than 'good'. He also commented on its inconsistency: 'it would be far better were it not for some justices that doth make laws one court, and break them the next'.[8] At the time, Captain Hawley's position as governor was hanging in the balance. He had been busy doling out grants of land – more than 17,000 acres in 237 parcels over the past couple of years – but the proceeds hadn't found their way back to the Carlisle family. Around the time of Tom's arrival they sent out Major Henry Hunks to arrest Hawley for embezzlement and to take his place as governor, but Hawley refused to budge and Hunks had to withdraw to Antigua to ponder his next move.

These uncertainties meant nothing to Tom. He had been packed off to Barbados to make his fortune, and that was exactly what he intended to do. So with Captain Futter's help he bought 100 acres of land from Hawley, and within weeks of his arrival he was working out how to convert this potential cotton plantation into gold as quickly and as painlessly as possible. The creation of a properly equipped labour force was the answer and, predictably, the money and supplies his father had given him were nowhere near enough to achieve this. He immediately wrote home for more.

Careful to keep on the right side of his father, he prefaced his list of wants with a 'true relation of the country' which Sir Edmund had asked for when he parted from his errant son.[9] The Barbados climate, especially in the early months of the year, was in pleasant contrast to the Buckinghamshire winter, with daytime temperatures in the high seventies, cooling breezes and little in the way of rainfall. Tom began by noting that his new home was 'the best and healthfullest in all the western islands' – but the quality of churchmanship was not quite up to the standard he would have wished for. (He invariably resorted to piety when he was trying to wheedle money or favours from his family.) However, if the Earl of Warwick, who was currently trying to buy Barbados from the heirs of the recently deceased Earl of Carlisle, were to take control, he was hopeful that 'we shall have better orders in the island than we have hitherto had'.[10] There were in fact already four Anglican churches on the island, although these were hard pressed to cater for a population which had risen to about 6000. But then not all of that population were interested in attending

Anglican services: the growing community of indentured servants included large numbers of English and Irish Catholics and, attracted by the relaxed religious atmosphere, several of the more radical Protestant sects also found their way to the island, including the communistic Familists and the antinomian Ranters. The Reverend James Parker, who arrived in 1646, was shocked at the way in which everyone was allowed to follow their own conscience in matters of religion, a lax approach which had led to a prolifera- tion of sects happy to deny the ordinances of the Anglican Church.

Rumours of religious unorthodoxy had reached England by 1639, and Tom may well have been playing up to his father's strictly conventional views on any kind of dissent. Once he had dealt with the colony's spiritual wants, he turned to a discussion of how its physical needs were supplied. The oranges and lemons were bigger and better than anything he had ever seen. 'Another fruit here is your limes, which is much about the bigness of a crab[apple], and far sourer.'[11] Then there were guavas, cinnamon, ginger and cabbages which grew on 100-foot-high trees (palm cabbages, or *acai*). The settlers made bread and beer from cassava root: the one was 'very fine and white, although not so tooth- some as ours'; the other was 'as strong as our ten shilling beer in England'.[12]

Plantains were good eaten raw, stewed, baked, fried or pulped into 'a very fine cool drink . . . very pleasant for the palate'.[13] Mobby, a drink brewed from pressed sweet potatoes, was also popular; indeed, Tom thought the sweet potato was the best provi- sion the island had to offer, since after only a month of two of exposure to its delights, servants wanted nothing else to eat and drink but sweet potatoes and mobby. But he reserved his greatest praise for the queen pineapple, so delicious that James I swore it was the apple with which Eve tempted Adam. Tom was quite overcome by its 'luscious' taste: 'I might speak much more of this pine, but whilst I am a-writing the description of it makes me long after it . . .'[14]

The serpents in Tom's own Eden were the land crabs, which were everywhere; and the drunks, which were almost as common, so that 'I have seen upon a Sabbath day, as I have been walking to church, first one, presently after another, lie in the highway so drunk that [land crabs] have bit off some of their fingers, some their toes, nay, and hath killed some before they have wakened'.[15] Too much cassava beer, presumably.

Tom's capacity for deception – and self-deception – was quite remarkable. He ended his letter to his father by assuring him that his report was evidence of his reformed ways, and that it had 'cost me many a weary step and watchful night'.[16] At the same time he wrote to his mother that he was leading a new life. But as always, these protestations were the prelude to a list of demands. Tom wanted men to work his plantation; he wanted four cases of spirits to fortify them on their voyage and after they arrived ('for my own part I cannot drink none'); he wanted beef and oil and sugar; he wanted twenty cheeses, and household stuff, and pewter and linen. Two hundred pounds would pay for the men and their passage, and 'after one year's time I shall be able (by the grace of God) to return the principal with use'.[17] As for the rest, he relied on his parents' generosity.

That generosity was slow in coming because, by the time the letter arrived, Sir Edmund had set out for Scotland. Three months later Tom tried again, this time enclosing a testimonial from James Futter, which assured his father that he was 'an extraordinary good husband, and careful'; [18] and a letter to Ralph, begging his brother to put in a good word for him, and to 'encourage my father in the disbursing of the money for me'.[19] It transpired that he had bought his plantation on credit, and unless he could turn a profit quite quickly, he was likely to lose it 'and undergo much disgrace by it'.[20]

His most pressing need was for manpower. When Courteen's colonists arrived on Barbados there was no indigenous population, and throughout the 1630s the settlers relied heavily on the use of indentured servants. Tom asked his father to supply twenty able men for his plantation, of whom at least six should be skilled artisans – two carpenters, two sawyers, a weaver and a tailor. They would need suitable clothing and arms – a musket, sword, belt and pair of bandoliers each, with a hundred pounds' weight of powder. Sir Edmund was asked to provide twelve dozen pairs of drawers, twelve dozen shirts, twelve dozen shoes, six dozen neck-cloths, six dozen coarse linen stockings, and six dozen of the ubiquitous knitted Monmouth caps, normal headgear for labourers and sailors in the seventeenth century (and recommended wear for settlers in the Americas since at least 1607). Tom told his mother he was building a 'sorry cottage' to house his labour force,[21] and of course he needed somewhere rather less sorry for himself, so he asked for 'nails of all sorts to build with', 30,000 in all. The men needed thread to mend their clothes and twine to mend their shoes; coarse bed tick and lines for their hammocks; hoes, bills, spades, axes and pickaxes for cultivating the land. Tom himself would like two more suits, some soap, wax lights and foodstuffs. And his original request for four cases of strong waters now went up to six, so that the men could drink a dram each morning. 'For my part I drink none.'[22]

Sir Edmund read Tom's new list in July. The King was still at Berwick, but Sir Edmund's sciatica was so bad that he obtained permission to travel to Bath for treatment. He stopped off at Hillesden on the way to make peace with Lady Susan, and then went on to London, where he met up with Ralph and found Tom's letter. Experience had taught him to be extremely cautious where his second son was concerned: in reply he pleaded that since he was about to go back to Scotland, he didn't have the time to give proper consideration to Tom's letter. He asked Ralph to gather some servants in time for the next ship sailing for the Caribbean, but not as many as Tom wanted. And he made it crystal clear that he wasn't about to trust the boy with hundreds of pounds' worth of men and provisions until he had done something to earn that trust:

> Enable yourself to know what is fit for plantation, and let me alone to assist you, if you prove industrious and careful of my directions, so that I may put a trust and confidence in you, which as yet I dare not do, because I have found you false of your word, and careless of all I have said to you. I doubt not then, but, with your own help, to make you a fortune; but if you continue in your old courses I will certainly forsake you.[23]

His lack of faith in Tom's reformation turned out to be quite justified.

Ralph went to Bath with his father in July 1639. But mindful of his duties, Sir Edmund trekked all the way back to Berwick, arriving just in time to discover that the King had decided to return to London to plot a second campaign against the Scots.

All through the summer and autumn of that year Ralph was shouldering more and more of the responsibility for servicing and policing the extended Verney clan, a role his father cheerfully delegated to him, just as he had to Ralph's mother in the 1620s. He advised the Verney and Denton matrons on business matters and shopped for their luxury goods; he called the younger members to order; and he was above all else an intermediary, channelling a stream of requests for favours or money from relations to Sir Edmund, and relaying his answers back to them. This gave him a great deal of power within the clan, of course, but it also left him open to constant sniping and complaints. His three brothers were the worst, perhaps because, although they depended on him to extract money from their father, they were less inclined to show him respect than other members of the family. So although Ralph did his best to round up servants for Tom's plantation, Tom blamed him when Sir Edmund refused to supply everything the novice planter demanded. Henry blamed him when their father declined to indulge his passion for horseracing by sending a fast mount over to Breda. *Everyone* blamed him when their letters home weren't answered: Tom rather pointedly quoted the saying 'Out of sight, out of mind'; Henry moaned that no one was writing to him. Mun, whose experiences in the Scottish campaign had convinced him his future lay in a military career, went to Flanders as an ensign in the summer of 1639, where he too complained about Ralph's neglect, pointing out at Christmas that he had written twelve letters to his brother's paltry three.

Along with the complaints came the requests. Could Ralph send Henry a decent bridle? (He did, and Henry won £50 in a six-mile race against a Dutchman.) And some coarse cloth and baize to make a winter suit? And could he persuade their father to give him a loan? Mun wanted a long grey baize-lined cloak for the winter, and some books to read. He also asked Ralph to pay some of his debts: before he sent out for Flanders the boy had done his best to pay off various Oxford tradesmen to whom he still owed money from his student days. But he hadn't been able to find one of his biggest creditors, and had had to come away without stumping up the £17 or £20 he owed him. 'I think that I had most of this money out of the poor man's purse, and truly I do think that I am bound both in honesty and conscience to pay him. Therefore . . . I pray will you do me favour to let it be sent him; I know no other name of his but Matthew; he was in my time tapster in the Greyhound, but since he is gone from thence, but lives in Oxford still; the people of the Greyhound can direct anyone that you shall appoint to enquire after him to the place where he lives . . .'[24]

Ralph was also still having to deal with the fallout from Margaret Pulteney's marriage. After his frank exchange of views with Lady Susan Denton in June 1639, Aunt Isham had done her best to play the peacemaker, pointing out that his grandmother was old. He shouldn't take her words too seriously. She also reported that Lady Susan was upset because she thought Ralph was going to take his son away from Hillesden, where he had been living now for nearly a year. If she was trying to stir up sympathy for Lady Susan, she rather spoiled the effect by telling him that the old woman wouldn't give the little boy up until Sir Edmund came home from the war and discussed the matter with her – a subtle reminder, if Ralph needed one, that he was not yet head of the family and that decisions about the future of the Verney heir were much too important to be left to the child's parents. But Lady Susan was well aware of how much she depended on her grandson to conduct her affairs. After Sir Edmund called in to see her on his way back from Berwick at the end of June she wrote Ralph a business letter which, if not exactly conciliatory, at least made no reference to sackcloth and ashes or betrayal. She was also doing her best to be nice to Colonel Eure; Aunt Isham noted with some surprise that the old lady 'shows him more respect than I thought she would a' done'.[25]

Ralph and Mary did take their son away from Hillesden to live with them in Covent Garden for the autumn and winter, although it is hard to tell if this was because of Ralph's quarrel with Lady Susan or simply because he felt it was time the boy took his place in the London household. Little Edmund, who now had a sister again – Margaret was born in January 1639 – was a quiet, withdrawn boy, much happier in the familiar surroundings of his great-grandmother's country house at Hillesden than he was living with his own parents. In an extended seventeenth-century family this wasn't so unusual, but his extreme shyness worried Ralph and Mary. It worried Sir Edmund, too: the whole future of the Verney fortunes rested on this two-year-old's tiny shoulders, and the slightest deviation from the social norm was a cause for concern. The accepted course was to beat some manners into him; but as soon as Lady Susan heard that the Covent Garden household was unimpressed with her charge, she became upset and angry that the grown-ups might not appreciate how sensitive he was. 'If you do go a violent way with him, you will be the first that will rue it,' she warned Ralph, 'for I verily believe he will receive injury by it . . . I had intelligence your father was troubled to see him so strange [used here in the archaic sense of 'reserved, distant']. I pray tell him from me I thought he had had more wit . . . Be sure that [the boy] be not frighted by no means: he is of a gentle sweet nature, soon corrected.'[26] Lady Susan's penchant for straight talking, and her readiness to tell her relatives their faults – 'I love to deal above ground', she once said[27] – meant that she was never an easy person to get along with. But she had a real soft spot for Ralph's son, talking proudly of how the right mix of love and fear was turning him into a little courtier who could greet his Denton aunts with 'Good morrow, lady', and 'Bless me, lady'. Ralph's brother Mun was just as enchanted with his namesake nephew: 'that sweet promising countenance of your pretty son is able to inspire even the ignorant with such a prophesying spirit,' he told Ralph; 'there's not that lineament either in his face or body but prognosticates more for itself than I can do for it'.[28]

In August 1639 word reached Ralph that his sister Peg had made some disparaging remarks about Aunt Margaret Eure and her new husband. Peg, who was not quite sixteen, was Margaret's god-daughter; for some time she had been lodging under her aunt's roof and, until the marriage, she had been her favourite. The girl was finding it hard to accept that William Eure was now the centre of attention, and she wasn't particularly discreet about her feelings. Ralph wasn't sure what it was she'd said about the Eures, and she wasn't about to tell him. All she admitted to was that the only person with whom she might have discussed her aunt's marriage was her brother Mun, and that she had now learned her lesson about trusting brothers to keep their mouths shut.

Ralph claimed, not altogether convincingly, that he couldn't believe her 'so indiscreet as to speak of the weakness of [Eure's] estate, his religion or [her godmother's] folly in making such a choice', and told her even less convincingly that the rumours of her imprudent chatter hadn't come from Mun but from someone else. Then he went on to plead with her to be careful: 'Good sister, take my counsel, be more careful of your words, and though you should think yourself a little slighted, yet, let me beg of you, take no notice of it. I know your aunt better than you do, and I am sure she intends well to you, if you do not lose her love by prating.'[29]

As that last remark suggests, there was an ulterior motive for Ralph's anxiety. Aunt Margaret was giving Peg an annual allowance of £20 and providing her with free board and lodging worth another £26 a year. Before she met Eure, she had promised that at some point in the future she would convert this into a lump sum, settling £900 on Peg outright. A family like the Verneys, plagued with money worries and facing the daunting prospect of finding dowries for six girls, could not afford to let such a generous gift slip away. And since Margaret's estate now passed to her husband, this meant that everybody – and especially Peg – had to be extremely tactful about the marriage, no matter what they privately thought about Eure.

As it turned out, Ralph needn't have worried. Eure was a decent man, and he had already insisted his wife should keep to her bargain and settle whatever she wished on Peg, which she did, in spite of being sorely provoked. In November 1639, three months after Ralph first censured his sister for gossiping about the Eures, the girl was at it again. This time she had been talking indiscreetly in front of the maids; whatever she said, her aunt was angry with her when she got to hear of it, as was Ralph, who told her to 'be more careful of your tongue hereafter. It is an unruly member, and I know you have made too much use of it, both against [Aunt Eure], and other of your friends.'[30]

Peg made light of the quarrel, telling Ralph it was all over now, and her aunt had forgiven her, 'which makes me wonder that so small a matter should come to your ear'.[31] But the following August she was responsible for yet another row in the Eure household, after talking to a gentlewoman servant rather too liberally, 'both of the unhappiness of your aunt's marriage, and her discontents and divers other things of that kind'. Once again Aunt Eure got to hear of Peg's carelessness; once again it was left to Ralph to remind his sister of how much she owed and depended upon her godmother. 'You are not only foolish, but ungrateful,' he told her. 'For you above all others (having received so many favours from that good aunt of yours) have most reason to conceal all things of that nature.'[32] He advised Peg to go and confess everything to her aunt straight away. If she had not said the things she was rumoured to have said, then all well and good. If she *had*, then 'I know nothing bad enough for you'. She maintained her innocence (didn't she always?), telling her sisters that she couldn't understand how 'these scurvy reports' could be attributed to her; and within a month or two, she and Aunt Eure were reconciled again.

It was not only family members who placed demands on Ralph's time. Friends and acquaintances would ask the well-connected Verneys to arrange marriages for their children, to negotiate property transfers, even to carry out simple errands. And if the friends were influential or close, or if his father expected it, Ralph would usually comply. It gave him an opportunity to practise the exercise of power, to place others in his debt, to enhance his reputation and – let's not be too cynical about seventeenth-century mores – to please his elders and himself.

A good example of this complicated mix of motives was provided by Eleanor Wortley. Eleanor was in her late forties; she had known the Verneys since the 1610s, when she came down from her family home in Yorkshire to marry Sir Henry Lee of Ditchley in Oxfordshire, a baronet and an old friend of Sir Edmund's. Lee died in 1631, and three years later she became a countess when she married Edward Radcliffe, 6th Earl of Sussex. Radcliffe, who was at least seventy-five, was the first of three elderly earls who would wed the widow (privately, the Verneys called her 'Old Men's Wife'). The couple leased Sir Francis Bacon's house at Gorhambury in Hertfordshire, a spectacular pile whose delicate walks and prospects, stately gallery and painted hall nevertheless failed to impress Eleanor, who dismissed Gorhambury as a dull place. Although they maintained a substantial household of their own, throughout her marriage to the Earl Eleanor turned her back on his own men of business and relied instead on Sir Edmund and Ralph to look after her affairs. Sir Henry Lee had left her a wealthy woman – she contributed a hefty £3000 jointure to her marriage with the Earl of Sussex. He had also left her with a son and a daughter, so there were trusts and property to be managed. Presumably 'my old lord', as she called her earl, was either not up to the task or not to be trusted to look after her personal interests and those of her Lee children.

Eleanor's ties with the Verneys were close, and they were ties based on real and reciprocal affection as well as mutual self-interest. Ralph was 'the best of men, so the best friend I have next your good father and mother', she wrote.[33] She was godmother to little Edmund, and 'my prayer for my sweet godson,' as she told Ralph, 'is that he may make as discreet and good a man as his father'.[34] Sir Edmund helped to draw up her will, and she consulted both men over prospective husbands for her daughter, Nan.

The Verneys also did their best to mediate between Eleanor and her own son, another Sir Henry Lee. Lee was eighteen when his mother remarried, and he resented the match and the loss to his estate of her £3000 jointure. Now twenty-three, with a young family of his own and a wife who heartily disliked her mother-in-law, he saw as little as possible of Eleanor. Like Sir Edmund, he went to join the King's army that gathered in the spring of 1639, but he made a point of not stopping at Gorhambury en route to York from his house in Chelsea. 'He promised to come this way as he went into the north, but he has failed me', Eleanor told Ralph miserably.[35]

The war proved fatal for Sir Henry Lee. Along with hundreds of other English soldiers he fell ill in camp that summer. The day after he returned home to Chelsea he came down with smallpox, and lay desperately sick for several weeks. But he rallied and his doctors were confident that he was going to pull through. Their confidence was misplaced, because on 23 July 1639 he died, leaving Eleanor distraught, not only at the loss of her dear boy but also at the fact that they would never have a chance to patch up their differences. 'They sent me word he was past all danger,' she wrote to Ralph from Gorhambury, 'and now they tell me he is dead.'[36]

Sir Edmund had gone back to the King in Berwick at this point, but Ralph went down to Chelsea on Eleanor's behalf to be present at the opening of Sir Henry's will, four days after the boy's death. It contained no words of consolation for the grieving mother. In fact it contained no words at all for Eleanor. Her daughter-in-law, Anne, was named as sole executrix; her grandchildren – two boys and a girl – were provided for; the Lee estates were placed in the hands of trustees during the eldest boy's minority. 'My Lady Sussex is not so much as named,' Ralph wrote to his father, 'which I am heartily sorry for, as I know it will trouble her extremely.'[37]

Eleanor coped with her grief by refurnishing Gorhambury, and in Covent Garden Ralph and Mary were bombarded with requests for help. Could Ralph find some suitable damask and send Eleanor some samples? Could he find her suitable satin that would do for the backs of her chairs, and also for curtains? 'When the chintz stuffs come in, if you see any pretty ones remember me I pray you for two or three pieces.'[38] (She uses the word 'chintz' here in its seventeenth-century sense of painted calicos imported from India.) Ralph was asked to find everything from carpets to wine glasses, to send them up to Gorhambury for her approval and to negotiate a good price: 'the carpet truly is a good one . . . if I can have that and the other for forty pound or a little more I would buy them'. And every now and then he was also required to negotiate returns, when goods proved not to be quite what she was looking for:

> The damask I have looked on and truly it is very good and well worth the money, but the colour I confess doth not please me for where I would employ it for is to make curtains for the room I intend my crimson figured satin for. And that is so pure a colour that it makes this damask look very dead and dull; therefore I beseech you, get the man to take it again.[39]

Ralph's precise, slightly fussy nature revelled in these errands for the Countess. When she sent him absurdly detailed directions for buying edging materials for a little bag she was making – silver lace about the width of threepenny ribbon with a few spangles, satin ribbon, ten yards of edging lace 'as slight as may be to edge the strings and but little silver in it' – he attended to the commission without batting an eyelid.[40] He bought her flower pots, pens and paper, a Venetian looking-glass and a new petticoat; and if he meticulously recorded his expenditure on her behalf and regularly presented her with the account, that was only what she expected.

In August 1639 Sir Edmund Verney asked Eleanor if she would consider sitting for a portrait. The timing – it was only four weeks since her son's death – suggests that he was trying to take her mind off her loss. Portraits were common currency among friends and relations: they conferred status not only on the sitter, but also on the owner, as Lord Howard of Bindon told the Earl of Salisbury, when he announced that he wished to hang a picture of the Earl 'in the gallery I lately made for the pictures of sundry of my honourable friends, whose presentation thereby to behold will greatly delight me to walk often in that place where I may see so comfortable a sight'.[41]

Sir Edmund had pulled off quite a coup: he had arranged for Eleanor to sit for Van Dyck, principal painter in ordinary to their majesties, and the greatest portraitist in England. A stream of aristocratic clients alighted at the Thames-side causeway which led to the urbane courtier-artist's 'shop of beauty' in Blackfriars – so many, in fact, that the studio was more like a production line than a romantic atelier.* Portraits were turned out by 'the glory of the world', as Herrick described him,† at a rate of just over one a week, with each sitter usually being allotted a series of

*Rare Artisan! whose pencil moves
Not our delights alone, but loves;
From thy shop of beauty we
Slaves return'd that entered free
(Edmund Waller, 'To Vandyck')

†On, as thou hast begun, brave youth, and get
The palm from Urbin, Titian, Tintoret,
Brugel and Coxu, and the works outdo
Of Holbein and that mighty Rubens too.
So draw and paint as none may do the like,
No, not the glory of the world, Vandyke.
(Robert Herrick, 'To His Nephew, to be Prosperous in his Art of Painting')

hour-long appointments at Blackfriars. At the first, Van Dyck discussed one or two ideas with his subject before putting him or her into the chosen pose; then he spent around fifteen minutes producing a drawing on a little piece of blue paper. After the sitting this drawing was scaled up on canvas by his assistants; the sitter's costume was also handed over to them so that they could begin painting it. The precise contribution – and even the identities – of Van Dyck's studio assistants was closely guarded, although the artist's customers were aware of their existence, sometimes complaining that a finished portrait owed rather too much to them, and too little to the artist himself.

Initially Eleanor was reluctant to sit for her picture, claiming modestly that she was no beauty and that the money would be wasted. (Van Dyck's rate was a reasonable £50–£60 for a full-length portrait, £30 for a half-length and £20 for head and shoulders.) Once persuaded, however, she proved an exacting client, issuing a string of requests to the artist via the hapless Ralph. It was decided that she should be shown wearing a sable over her dress, but she wanted Van Dyck to improve on the original: a clasp sent with diamonds would look very well. The gown she wore should be altered slightly, and if the end result was that she looked too rich and bejewelled, well, ''tis no great matter for another age to think me richer than I was'.[42]

But her main worry was that she was going to look too fat. She continually pleaded with Ralph for the artist 'to make my picture leaner' and for Ralph himself 'to make him trim it for my advantage'.[43] When it was delivered to Covent Garden in December, she was still fretting that she looked ugly. The picture was to be a present from Eleanor to Sir Edmund and Lady Margaret, but Ralph commissioned a copy (for £8) for Gorhambury. Eleanor begged him to 'see whether that man that copies out Van Dyck's could not mend the face'.[44]

Van Dyck was known for flattering his subjects. 'He took his time to draw a face when it had its best looks on,' said his near-contemporary Roger de Piles, diplomatically.[45] Sophia, the young Princess Palatine, was more forthright. Thinking that she knew her aunt, Henrietta Maria, from Van Dyck's pictures of her, she was astonished to find when they eventually met that the Queen was 'a little woman with long lean arms, crooked shoulders, and teeth protruding from her mouth like guns from a fort'.[46]

The artist clearly didn't flatter Eleanor enough. When her copy of the painting finally arrived at Gorhambury in April 1640, after a seemingly endless correspondence about the best way to transport it, she was horrified:

> Sweet Mr Verney . . . the picture is very ill favoured, makes me quite out of love with myself, the face is so big and so fat that it pleases me not at all. It looks like one of the winds puffing – but truly I think it is like the original. If ever I come to London before Sir Van Dyck go [he left England for his native Antwerp later that year], I will get him to mend my picture, for though I be ill favoured I think that makes worse than I am.[47]

The Van Dyck is now lost; it left Claydon when the Verney collection was broken up in the eighteenth century. However there is a picture hanging at Burghley House, near Stamford, which is almost certainly the copy which Ralph sent to Gorhambury in the spring of 1640. It shows an amiable, matronly woman in early middle age, draped in a sable stole and wearing an elaborate blue gown. Bodice and sleeves are spangled with huge pearls; there are pearls in her hair, and her jewellery consists of a pair of pearl earrings and a pearl necklace. She has a round face, with dark, slightly protuberant eyes and just a hint of a double chin; not quite 'like one of the winds puffing', but not conventionally beautiful, either. The sitter is undeniably attractive, though – and enigmatic in a way which is uncharacteristic of Van Dyck's other portraits of court beauties. *They* look proud, or beguiling, or serene, or sexually aware; Eleanor seems both extremely intelligent (as indeed she was) and also a little startled that the spectator should take the trouble to study her. The artist has managed to convey the fact that she is much more complicated than she appears at first glance. As she stares out so knowingly, so self-deprecatingly, there is just the hint of a smile on her lips, the barest suggestion that if she does not quite match up to our ideas of feminine beauty, the fault lies with us rather than her.

The picture undercuts her protestations and her modesty and her vanity, her laments that her face is 'so big and so fat' and her pleas that the artist should 'make my picture leaner'. It presents us with a woman who, while she is happy to exploit her sexuality, understands more about the world than we do, and excuses less.

While Van Dyck was busy trimming Eleanor's figure he undertook another Verney commission. The head of the clan also sat for his portrait. In contrast to the saga of Eleanor's picture, we don't know anything about the circumstances of its production, or even the precise date. However, we do know the three-quarter-length portrait of Sir Edmund was executed in the autumn of 1639 or early in 1640 and, since he cuts a decidedly martial figure, there can be little doubt that the immediate spur was the knight-marshal's desire to commemorate his exploits in the recent Scottish campaign.

He wears full plate armour and holds a baton nonchalantly in his right hand, while his left rests lightly on a helmet by his side – not the legendary pistol-proof pot, but a real helm, the light gleaming on the blue-black steel of its raised visor.

Sir Edmund's hair is still surprisingly auburn for a man of nearly fifty; perhaps he asked the artist to lose any traces of grey. It falls down in a mass of curls, and frames a face which, like Van Dyck's paintings of Charles I, manages to combine patrician hauteur with sadness. Rather than celebrating Sir Edmund's military prowess, it proclaims his determination to perform his public duty, no matter what his private thoughts might be.

In the background, storm clouds roll across the sky.

7

Fortune's Wheel is Ever Turning

*E*ngland was not used to war. The chaotic, faintly ridiculous border campaign against the Scots was enough to demonstrate that fact to even the most patriotic old soldier. But the nation's lack of military prowess was not a recent thing: back in the 1620s the great and the good had grumbled that 'this kingdom has been too long in peace . . . [and] the knowledge of war and almost the thought of war is extinguished'.[1] There was no standing army. Military traditions were weak. At the infrequent musters, local worthies bought their way out of the draft while convicts and vagrants were pressed into service. The county militias, 'scarce called forth to exercise either posture or motion once in four or five years', were ill equipped and ill trained; 'stout once a month they march, a blustering band,/And ever, but in times of need, at hand'.[2]

Nevertheless, for adventurous younger sons in search of glory and booty, war was not so very far away. Since the Defenestration of Prague in 1618, when Bohemian nobles threw two representatives of the Holy Roman Empire out of a window in Hradčany Castle and sparked off one of the most vicious conflicts the

Western world had ever seen, the Thirty Years War had offered plenty of opportunities to those who yearned for a soldier's life. What began as a Protestant rising against the Catholic Hapsburgs grew until it encompassed not only issues of religious freedom, but a bewildering melange of independence movements, territorial struggles and battles for economic supremacy which drew in most of Europe, from Scandinavia to the Balkans.

England's direct involvement was marginal. Frederick V, the Elector Palatine and the man to whom the Bohemians initially appealed as a champion of Protestantism in Europe, was roundly defeated by the armies of the Holy Roman Empire and Maximilian I of Bavaria's Catholic League at the Battle of the White Mountain near Prague in November 1620; and although Frederick's wife Elizabeth was the daughter of James I, the King was reluctant to come to the aid of his son-in-law, preferring to cast himself in the safer role of neutral mediator. When Charles I succeeded to the throne in 1625, he made some half-hearted and on the whole rather unhappy attempts to provide aid to those fighting against the imperial forces. Charles's uncle, Christian IV of Denmark, pitched in on the Protestant side in 1625, and the English agreed to subsidise the Danish intervention to the tune of 300,000 florins per month.

Smarting from his attempt to woo the Spanish Infanta in 1623, Charles also authorised a disastrous expedition against Philip IV of Spain. Led by Sir Edward Cecil, the force consisted mainly of pressed men, poorly equipped and poorly drilled. When they landed at Cadiz their first prize was a warehouse full of wine, which they promptly drank. 'In my life I never saw such beastliness,' wrote one of Cecil's colonels; 'they knew not what they did or said, so that all the chiefs were in hazard to have their throats cut.'[3] When they recovered and decided to retreat to their ships, the force came under heavy fire from the Spanish, causing those who still had muskets to panic and start firing in all directions as they scrambled into the boats. Cecil recalled ruefully that 'they proved rather a danger to us than a strength, killing more of our own men than they did of the enemy'.[4]

A second foray into Europe, this time an attempt by the Duke of Buckingham with an army of 8000 men to relieve French Protestants at La Rochelle, came to a similarly unsuccessful conclusion; and peace treaties with France in 1629 and Spain in 1630 effectively put an end to official English participation in the Thirty Years War.

But that didn't prevent enterprising outsiders from getting involved in the conflict. When Gustavus Adolphus of Sweden, the Protestant 'Lion of the North', was campaigning against the Empire in Germany in 1632, he commanded a colossal army of about 108,000 men. Of these, only 13,000 were Swedes and Finns; the rest were mercenaries, attracted from all over Europe by the prospect of fighting for Protestantism and against popery, by the rich pickings to be found among the corpses and burned-out homes of a brutalised civilian population – or by both. 'They fought only for spoil, rapine, and destruction,' Lord Brooke recalled in 1643: 'Merely money it was, and hope of gain.'[5] Between ten and fifteen thousand English volunteers fought in the Thirty Years War, mostly on the Protestant side; as many Irish enlisted in the predominantly Catholic armies of France, Spain and Austria; and it has been estimated that 25,000 Scotsmen fought abroad, around 10 per cent of the adult male population.[6]

Some confounded Brooke's low opinion of them: the Scotsman Robert Monro, for example, who commanded a regiment of Scottish mercenaries, had a well-developed notion of honour and religious principle. He believed it better 'to live honourably abroad, and with credit, than to encroach (as many do) on their friends at home'; and he fought first for Christian IV, and then for Gustavus Adolphus, simply because he was an ardent Presbyterian and believed that God was clearly on the Protestant side and against 'Catholic Potentates' and their idolatrous ways.[7]

A long way below Monro's moral high ground we can set Sydenham Poyntz, another veteran of the wars. Poyntz was an English Presbyterian who converted to Catholicism but still served as a mercenary with Protestant forces in Saxony; then, after being captured by the Catholic League, he happily changed sides and enlisted with the Spanish Imperial Army, where he rose to the rank of major general. Whatever his personal convictions, Poyntz was primarily motivated by the need for money, which he duly sent back to his wife in England, 'who it seems spent at home what I got abroad'.[8]

Henry and Mun Verney both served in the Thirty Years War, and both stood somewhere between the high-mindedness of

Monro and the easy pragmatism of Poyntz. The Verney family's fierce anti–Catholicism meant that service with the imperial army and its allies was unthinkable; both young men were with English companies who were helping the Dutch in their struggle for independence from Spain. But Mun's declaration when he arrived in the Low Countries in 1639 says it all: '[I have] vowed to myself never to return unless I get a fortune.'[9]

Neither Henry nor Mun dwelled in their letters home on the horrors they must have seen during their service. Nor would we expect them to, perhaps. But it is important to bear in mind what lurked behind their apparent nonchalance, their cheerful stories of horse races and wagers. The Thirty Years War was terrible. The brutality was unprecedented. Stories flew around of babies burned, of pregnant women disembowelled, of nuns raped and priests castrated. Even allowing for the hyperbole and the less fastidious times, it is clear that the atrocities perpetrated on unarmed civilians were shocking, with entire communities being killed in cold blood. 'I could never had believed a land could have been so despoiled had I not seen it with my own eyes,' wrote one traveller.[10] Magdeburg in central Germany, which was captured by the armies of the Catholic League in 1631, was entirely destroyed, and 24,000 men, women and children, or around 85 per cent of the population, were killed. A desire on the part of the Protestant armies to avenge the atrocities committed in Magdeburg led to an escalation of barbarity throughout the 1630s. Towns were taken and retaken again and again, as the hordes of mercenaries and freebooters surged out each spring in search of plunder. Commanders exacted 'contributions' from the citizenry, and took hostages to ensure that those contributions were paid; ordinary soldiers took whatever they could find, secure in the knowledge that they could kill and steal with impunity. And the winners were usually the merchants and tradesmen in neighbouring towns, who bought the soldiers' loot at knockdown prices. The Burgomaster of Magdeburg lamented that 'the most magnificent garments, hangings, silk stuffs, gold and silver lace, linen of all sorts, and other household goods' were peddled throughout the surrounding countryside after the sack of the city, and bought from desperate soldiers for a tenth of their real value.[11]

The sheer size of opposing armies, and the fact that they

remained in the field for years at a time, meant that they could only be supplied by stripping occupied territories. In Gustavus Adolphus's famous dictum, war sustains war: an army must be constantly on the move in order to supply itself. Once this lesson had sunk in, it led to scorched-earth policies on the part of retreating forces, adding to the miseries of local populations.

The worst of the fighting took place in Germany, where year after year opposing armies swept down on defenceless communities between the big set-piece battles. But the Low Countries saw their fair share of violence and by 1640 Henry and Mun had both joined an elite force of Englishmen who were familiar – far too familiar – with war. As storm clouds began to gather in the British Isles that spring and summer, this band of brothers smelled blood and began to drift home, a body of veterans waiting in the wings, battle-hardened and with first-hand experience of killing.*

Mun Verney spent the winter of 1639–40 in Utrecht and The Hague, angling for preferment and not getting it. In September he had joined a regiment of foot led by Colonel Sir Thomas Culpepper, and his desire for a commission was sharpened by the fact that his younger brother Henry, who was still with the garrison at Breda, had just achieved the rank of lieutenant.

The word 'achieved' needs some qualification here. Advancement may have required good leadership, sound judgement, coolness under fire and all those other qualities which made a good officer; but a man also needed money to buy the commission – Sir Edmund paid for Henry's lieutenancy – and the right friends, both in the regiment and at home. In the spring of 1642, for instance, when Henry was in The Hague with Henrietta Maria, who had come over to exchange crown jewels for arms in the

---

* The impact of the Thirty Years War on the English Civil War can be judged by the fact that all but four of the field army commanders, Royalist and Parliamentarian, had previous battle experience in Europe. Two of the exceptions were the King and Oliver Cromwell. (For the record, the others were the courtier Viscount Mandeville, a friend of the King who succeeded his father as Earl of Manchester in 1642; and the romantic but rather unsoldierly William Cavendish, Earl of Newcastle.)

run-up to the English Civil War, he attributed his failure to make captain to his family's politics. The opinion of the court, he told Ralph, 'is that my father and you are all for the Parliament and not for the King, which here I find they take not kindly'.[12]

Mun was keen to match his brother's progress, and as he settled into his winter quarters in Utrecht in 1639 it seemed as if he'd fallen on his feet. Colonel Culpepper was full of promises, talking warmly of his obligations to Sir Edmund for past favours received, and hinting that it would only be a matter of time – and perhaps a little money – before Mun got a company of his own.

It turned out that money was crucial in all of Culpepper's dealings. By the end of 1639 Mun was complaining that the man would do anything to line his own purse; he would forfeit his honour 'ten times in an hour to gain but sixpence'.[13] When a lieutenant in his company was cashiered, the boy pleaded with Ralph to persuade their father to stump up the £100 needed to secure him the post. But nothing came of it, and Mun grew more and more disillusioned with his commanding officer's venal behaviour. He urged his father to adopt a carrot-and-stick approach, citing the case of a fellow-officer whose influential father had given Colonel Culpepper a fright by letting him know he would be repaid in kind for his treatment of the man's son, whatever that treatment was. But the root of the problem was, that no matter what the colonel might say, he couldn't be trusted. 'I vow to God I cannot credit his fairest and greatest protestations,' Mun wrote, 'for I am sure his great god, Gold Almighty, is able to make him deceive the best friend he hath in the world.'[14]

Mun was a charismatic young man. He was idealistic, considerate, brave and decent – more like his father than any of the other brothers. Ralph, although only twenty-six, was already rather querulous, self-important, burdened with an impending sense of responsibility. Tom, the resentful second son, who saw himself as condemned to penury by an accident of birth, had no redeeming features: he was a thief, a cheat and a liar. Henry was indolent and hedonistic, a pleasure-seeker who would use his considerable charm – not *ruthlessly*, exactly, but instinctively and without qualm – to ensure that he got what he wanted. But Mun embodied the best qualities of the other three: he had Ralph's sense of right and wrong, Tom's wild daring, Henry's devil-may-care attitude to life.

And he brought to those qualities something of his own – an endearing openness in his dealings with others which was not all that common in seventeenth-century society, and an optimistic pragmatism which never descended into moral compromise. 'Fortune's wheel is ever turning' he once told Ralph, without the slightest bitterness; 'now it favours one and anon another'.[15]

By the spring of 1640 he decided Fortune's wheel wasn't turning his way. A winter with Culpepper's regiment had shown him that even if he did manage to obtain a lieutenant's commission – and the prospect was looking remote – he wouldn't be able to maintain it without being dishonest. Corruption was rife, and officers around him routinely supplemented their income by keeping false musters – that is, by drawing pay for deserters and dead men. No captain would have him in his troop unless he was prepared to commit such economies of truth.

Moreover, there was talk of something big happening back home. Over the winter rumours reached the camp at Utrecht that Anglo-Scottish relations were deteriorating again. Both sides were mobilising their forces. Charles I was openly trying to recruit Spanish and Irish troops; and, most astonishingly of all, he was so intent on financing another campaign against the Scots that he was actually prepared to summon Parliament, for the first time since 1629.

All of these rumours were true. Charles had always seen the Pacification of Berwick in June 1639 as a device to buy time, so that when, and not if, he resumed his campaign against the rebellious Covenanters his army would be better prepared and better equipped. He dismissed the leaders he blamed for his failure in the first Scotch War – Arundel and Holland – and began to listen more closely to the counsels of less moderate advisers, including the unpopular Archbishop William Laud and Thomas Wentworth, Lord Deputy of Ireland, whom Charles created 1st Earl of Strafford in January 1640. Strafford and Laud were united in their detestation of Puritanism, and Strafford was sure that the only way to subdue the recalcitrant Scots was by force. Under his guidance, the King began to raise a new army of ten foot regiments and six of horse, 13,000 men in all. He reasoned that when hostilities broke out again, the Scots would attack Edinburgh Castle before moving down to the border, so he ordered that the garrison there should be reinforced with English soldiers, who were smuggled in dressed as sailors, while powder and arms arrived in innocuous barrels of beer. (The citizens of Edinburgh weren't fooled: they refused to provide the Castle with supplies, and made the Englishmen's lives so miserable whenever they ventured out from behind the walls that half the garrison deserted.) Strafford and the King also ordered a general mobilisation, this time pressing men into service rather than relying on patriotism and the goodwill of local militias. Steps were taken to prepare a force of Irish troops for a seaborne invasion of Scotland, and the King entered into negotiations with Spain for the loan of several thousand battle-hardened Spanish mercenaries. Those negotiations came to nothing; nor did the plans to involve the Irish. But they showed that, while in 1639 he had hoped to frighten the Scots into submission with a display of shock and awe, he intended now to crush them.

The preparations for war depended on an adequate supply of money; and the obvious way to get that was to summon parliament and to bully it into voting subsidies. Writs went out in December, and on 13 April 1640 the two Houses met. Both Sir Edmund, who had sat in the last parliament, and Ralph, who had not, took their seats to hear the King and the Lord Keeper, Sir John Finch, argue that Scotland represented a threat to the kingdom which must be met by military force. And military force cost money – around £720,000 to be exact. The Commons were unconvinced; the mere fact that preparations were already in hand for raising an army made them uneasy, and a number of MPs were privately convinced that the King 'and his more confidential ministers' had secret intentions above and beyond the subjugation of the Covenanters: 'the chief one is to keep within bounds, by fear of these forces, the Parliament which they have decided to open.'[16] With admirable courage, MPs refused to pass the proposed fiscal measures until they had had a full and frank discussion of the King's behaviour during the years of personal rule.

Charles responded by dissolving what became known as the Short Parliament three weeks after it first met, and Strafford set about raising funds for the war among City merchants. 'Go on with a vigorous war, as you first designed, loose and absolved from all rules of government,'[17] he urged in the course of an emergency meeting of the King's advisers which was convened on the very afternoon that Parliament was dissolved.

War was in the air again. Bulstrode Whitelocke, a Buckinghamshire neighbour of the Verneys, noted in his diary that he 'as others did, furnished himself with a barrel of gunpowder, and bullets and twenty carbines, with swords and necessary provisions, and hung them up in his hall'.[18] Mun's despised colonel, Sir Thomas Culpepper, came back to England in March, joining a number of mercenary commanders who were gathering in London to prepare for the coming campaign. Mun himself lingered on in the Low Countries for another seven or eight weeks, before giving up all hope of preferment in continental Europe and returning to the Verneys' Covent Garden house. Once there, he kicked his heels while he waited to join his company. 'Here is no news but that divers officers have orders to march with their companies towards the north with all convenient expedition,' he told Ralph. 'I am not (as I yet understand) of that number, and that doth not a little grieve me, for by this means I shall be kept at rack and manger when others are high fed.'[19]

Mun was finally ordered to the border in July, but he soon found that the English army of 1640 was very different from the bands of 1639. The enlisted men under his command were more politicised, less deferential. They were fiercely anti-Catholic, mistrustful of their officers and deeply unhappy at the thought that they were being pressed into service against a Protestant nation and in support of what they called the 'episcopapacy'. On the march north Mun, whose Verney upbringing was more Protestant than most, found it politic to attend church with his men three times a day, simply to allay their suspicions that he might harbour Catholic sympathies. When he nodded off in church one day he woke to find them pointing at him and complaining loudly: 'had it been a minute longer, truly I do think I had been pulled by the nose'.[20] And that same day a fellow-officer had been dragged to the altar by his own men and forced to take the sacrament with them, simply to prove that he was no Catholic.

Mun got off lightly. All through the summer of 1640, as troops mobilised and moved north, there were violent incidents among a pressed and resentful soldiery who saw the world in simple Catholic-versus-Protestant-black-and-white. Altar rails, a potent symbol of exclusion, were ripped out of churches along the road and burned. Altars themselves were dragged down into naves to serve as communion tables rather than popish emblems; any window or carving which even hinted at idolatry – statues of Christ, decorated fonts, 'the picture of the Holy Ghost and a cross'[21] – was vandalised. As one soldier on the march north expressed it, if the King was fighting papists he and his men would fight on his side; but 'if the Scots fought against the papists, they would fight on the Scots' side'.[22]

Mun might make a joke of it, but officers in the King's army were hard put to keep their troops under control. In Faringdon, Berkshire, just a couple of weeks before he set out with his men, some Dorset soldiers on their way to the north had fallen out with their lieutenant, William Mohun, whom they suspected of being a Catholic. Matters came to an ugly conclusion after he slashed at an insubordinate drummer with his sword; he was chased into the street, 'where the soldiers beat him lamentably with their cudgels'. They dragged him through the town by his hair and threw him into a ditch. Remarkably, he survived this maltreatment and crawled to a nearby house for help; he was taken in, but when his men found out that they hadn't killed him, a mob of them burst into the house and cornered him. He tried desperately to fend them off with a knife, but they smashed his brains out on the spot and put his corpse in the local pillory. The men rampaged through Faringdon for two days and then scattered into the surrounding countryside – as did their frightened officers.

Mohun's murder sent shock waves through the military hierarchy. But although three soldiers were apprehended, and ten others named as participants in the murder in a royal proclamation, the troubles in the ranks continued. In July, when Mun was complaining to Ralph that he was having 'infinite trouble' with his men, 600 troops mutinied in Daventry, 'some alleging they would not fight against the Gospel, and others that they were to be shipped and commanded by Papists'.[23] Around the same time 160 Devon soldiers in Colonel Culpepper's regiment who were quartered at Wellington in Somerset became suspicious of their lieutenant, Compton Evers. Evers was reluctant to attend church services with them: deducing that the man must be a Catholic, they entered his lodgings, 'dragging him by the arms and legs down the stairs' and beat and stabbed him to death in the street. Then they robbed his corpse.

The civil authorities tended to be rather slow to respond to these outrages, which is quite understandable when one considers that they were faced with large groups of armed and violent men. (Devon was rather more efficient than some: when the 160 members of Evers' company deserted and drifted back to their homes, 140 of them were rounded up and thrown in gaol to await trial.) But if local magistrates could do little to quell mutinous behaviour, military commanders were more robust. The Dorset company to which the killers of William Mohun belonged finally arrived at the King's camp at Selby in Yorkshire at the beginning of August, still arguing with their surviving officers. Sir Jacob Astley, the King's Sergeant-Major-General, singled out one of the troublemakers: 'we arquebused him in the sight of the rest, some 340, whereupon they were all quiet'.[24]

Mun and his fractious force arrived at Newcastle upon Tyne in August, as both sides massed their armies and waited. This time he was the only member of the Verney family to go to the Scotch Wars. Sir Edmund's sciatica was troubling him so much that he had to go to Bath to take the waters again. Ralph kept him company; Henry was still with the garrison at Breda and Tom was in Barbados. Sir Edmund was due to travel up to join the King at the royal camp in York early in September, but it isn't clear if he actually made the journey.

If he did, he was too late for the war. Nor was he the only one: the Lord General of the King's forces in the north, the Earl of Northumberland, was too sick to command his troops; and the Earl of Strafford, who might have taken his place, was confined to his bed with an attack of gout. On 20 August a Scottish army led by Alexander Leslie launched a pre-emptive strike. Instead of laying siege to Edinburgh Castle or assaulting the garrison at Berwick-on-Tweed, the Scots crossed the border at Coldstream, sixteen miles south-west of Berwick, and pressed straight on towards Newcastle upon Tyne, sixty miles away. This was masterly: if Leslie managed to take Newcastle the English forces at Berwick would be cut off, and the Scots would command not only a major base for English military operations, but a vital seaport which supplied London with most of its coal.

On 27 August 12,000 Scots arrived at a ford at the village of Newburn on the north bank of the Tyne, just outside Newcastle. An English force of about 4500 men was waiting for them behind hastily prepared earthworks, and the next morning both Scottish and English cavalry watered their horses in the river within plain sight of each other, but without incident. That afternoon, however, a Scottish officer with 'a black feather in his hat' emerged from one of the thatched houses on the north bank and led his horse to water. While he waited, he stared straight across at the English trenches, whereupon an English soldier shot him and he fell off his horse.

That was the signal for the Battle of Newburn to start. Scottish and English musketeers began firing at each other; the Scottish cannon broke down the crude earthworks, and, as English infantrymen panicked and ran, cavalry poured across the river and through the breach. A group of Royalist cavalry officers mounted an heroic countercharge in an effort to prevent the Scots from establishing themselves on the south bank; Lord Henry Wilmot, a veteran of the Siege of Breda, dashed straight into the enemy and began laying about him, in spite of taking a pistol shot in the face.* Unfortunately for the English cause, his men didn't follow him. They retreated, riding right over their own fleeing infantry in the narrow country lanes and leaving 10,000 Scots to surge across the Tyne.

All things considered, there were relatively few fatalities – perhaps a couple of hundred on each side – but the English commander, Viscount Conway, decided his only course was to withdraw to Durham, and eventually to rendezvous with the rest of the King's forces at York. This would, of course, leave Newcastle undefended. 'For the love of Christ,' Strafford advised him, 'think not so early of quitting the town, burning the suburbs, or sinking of ships.'[25] Unfortunately he neither burned the suburbs nor sank the ships; but he did quit the town at five the next morning. Leslie's men marched into Newcastle. To all intents and purposes, the Second Bishops' War was over.

---

* Wilmot survived; he was taken prisoner by the Scots and returned later in the year. In 1644 he married the widow of Sir Harry Lee, Lady Sussex's estranged son. Stuart England was a small world.

The retreat from Newcastle was a chaotic affair, with men leaving behind supplies, munitions, even their clothes and personal possessions. Mun, who complained bitterly about the poor conduct of the war – 'we had neither cannon nor ammunition by us, but went on like sheep to the slaughter'[26] – lost everything he had in the world, except for a buff coat, a shirt, a cap and a few other odds and ends of clothing 'which were all of the very worst I had'.[27] He spent the next couple of months praying with a rather endearing candour for the resumption of hostilities. 'It hath undone me if war break off,' he told Ralph. 'Wish us better success and anything but peace.'[28]

He was destined to be disappointed. Dunbarton Castle at the mouth of the Clyde fell to the Covenanters the day they took Newcastle; Edinburgh Castle followed suit a few weeks later. Leslie's army continued to march south as Conway retreated before it. A proclamation commanded the trained bands south of the Trent to be 'in readiness with horse and arms, to serve His Majesty for defence of the kingdom'.[29] The Scots occupied Durham on 4 September. At this point they offered a cease-fire and Charles accepted, convening a Great Council of English nobles in York on 24 September. When it was rumoured that the Scots demanded a levy of £40,000 Mun's hopes were briefly raised – 'we have a company of noble lords that vow to pay them in leaden coin'[30] – but the Council had no stomach for war, and on 21 October the King submitted to the Scottish terms for an armistice, including daily payments of £850 to maintain Leslie's army until a final settlement was reached in London. Only Parliament could provide that kind of money, and Charles summoned the two Houses to meet at the beginning of November.

Sir Edmund was returned to Parliament for Chipping Wycombe, Ralph for Aylesbury. They were in familiar company. Sir Alexander Denton, Lady Margaret Verney's brother, sat for the town of Buckingham; John Hampden, Sir Alexander's brother-in-law, sat for the county. The MP for Banbury was a Verney cousin – Nat Fiennes, the Puritan son of the Puritan Lord Saye and Sele who had refused to fight for the King in 1639 if it meant invading Scotland. Sir Peter Temple of Stowe, who sat for Buckingham alongside Sir Alexander Denton, was a cousin – Margaret's mother,

Lady Susan Denton, was a Temple of Stowe. Frank Drake, who was married to Margaret's niece – the wedding had taken place at Claydon – sat for Amersham in Buckinghamshire; so did his elder brother, William.* Sir Roger Burgoyne, one of Ralph's closest friends, was a Member for neighbouring Bedfordshire.

And so the list goes on. Ralph had ties of blood or business with upwards of twenty of his fellow MPs; and considering he was so young, and that there were only 493 MPs in total, that's quite an impressive tally.† Moreover, most of them shared his anxieties about the road down which the King and his advisers were taking the country. Buckinghamshire was well known for its opposition to royal policies. Hampden was its most distinguished dissident (as well as one of its wealthiest), having been gaoled back in 1626 for his refusal to pay forced loans imposed by the King without the consent of Parliament. He had led the resistance to the imposition of ship money in 1637, arguing that, like forced loans, it violated ancient rights and liberties; and his influence is one reason why Buckinghamshire gentry were notorious for their reluctance to pay the tax. Sir Peter Temple had been placed under house arrest at one stage for his refusal to pay; Sir Alexander Denton, who was sheriff in 1637–8, was severely criticised by Crown agents for refusing to collect the levy. The Drakes were known dissidents and ardent Puritans, as were the Fienneses.

---

* To be accurate, Frank Drake didn't enter the House of Commons until May 1641, when he replaced William Cheyney, who had died the previous month.

† There are two caveats to be made here. One is that the political world of the 1640s was a small one, and the game of Six Degrees of Separation should be played with caution; it has been calculated, for example, that John Hampden had upwards of eighty relatives sitting in the Long Parliament, and probably many more, since Brunton and Pennington, who reached this figure in their *Members of the Long Parliament* (1954), gave up when they found that Hampden was also related to King Charles. Nevertheless, the basic point – that Ralph Verney had plenty of friends and relations in Parliament – deserves to be made.

The second caveat relates to the number of MPs in the Commons. There were indeed 493 Members when the writs went out in the autumn of 1640; but within a few months Parliament decided to restore seven boroughs to representation, and since each of these boroughs could return two Members each, the total number of MPs thus rose to 507.

Like Ralph, most of these MPs were fervent Protestants, uneasy at the direction in which the Church of England was moving, and equally uneasy with the King's arbitrary rule over the past decade. One or two were ambivalent, caught between personal conviction and loyalty to the Crown. They tended to be men with strong connections at court, like Sir Edmund; men who disapproved of Charles's policies but found it impossible to disapprove of the King himself. Of the fifteen MPs which Buckinghamshire returned to Parliament, no fewer than thirteen were at odds with royal policy; although when the battle lines were eventually drawn in 1642, several would choose to follow their king rather than their conscience.

On Tuesday 3 November, along with the rest of the 'Kings who sit at Westminster', as Mun called them,[31] Sir Edmund and Ralph took their seats in the Commons, duly swearing that Charles I was 'the only supreme governor of this realm' and that they would be 'true and faithful to the king and his heirs . . . and not to know or hear of any ill or damage intended him without defending him therefrom'.[32] That morning, instead of taking the customary processional route on horseback from the Palace of Whitehall into Westminster, the King elected to arrive relatively unobtrusively at Parliament stairs in the royal barge, where he was met by the Lords and conducted with great solemnity through Westminster Hall and into Westminster Abbey to hear a sermon from the staunchly loyal Bishop of Bristol, Robert Skinner. Archbishop Laud himself wrote a prayer for the occasion, asking God to 'give the King a heart of judgement, to do all that for his people which becomes a good, a gracious, a just, a pious, and a prudent king. And give the Parliament a heart of duty to do all that towards the King, which becomes an obedient, a religious, a moderate, a free, and a wise people.'[33]

Then, before the Lords and 'such Members of the House of Commons as pleased', Charles outlined his reasons for summoning what was to be his last parliament. He wanted the means to drive the 'rebels' back to Scotland. Once that was achieved, he would turn his attention towards redressing his people's 'just' grievances – although it was open to debate exactly how 'just' he considered the complaints about the conduct of the war, about the imposition of ship money, about his disregard for Parliament and his lukewarm support for Protestantism.

With the benefit of hindsight, the Earl of Clarendon later recalled that the day 'had a sad and melancholic aspect . . . which presaged some unusual and unnatural events'. More credibly, he also remembered that there was 'a marvellous elated countenance in most of the Members of Parliament' that week; they were eager for radical change, so that 'the warmest and boldest counsels and overtures would find a much better reception than those of a more temperate allay'.[34]

Ralph, whose three-week stint as an MP during the Short Parliament had given him a taste for affairs of state, was enthusiastic in his attendance in the House. He was temperamentally a conservative in politics, but his anti-Catholicism inevitably placed him in the Puritan camp. Radicals like John Pym, the MP for Tavistock, seemed to him to be speaking plain sense when they put the blame for the nation's troubles on Catholics, who sought to alter its religion; on corrupt elements in the Anglican clergy, who found 'a better doctrine in papists to serve their turns better than that of our church'; and on those who thought only of their own advantages, and would 'let in popery [and] Turkism too'.[35]

Ralph and Mary were now living for most of the time in Covent Garden with Sir Edmund and Lady Margaret, leaving William Roades to manage the Claydon estates. On 'gunpowder day', 5 November 1640, two days after the opening of Parliament and on the thirty-fifth anniversary of the Gunpowder Plot, Mary gave birth to another son, whom she and Ralph decided to name John.

Mary was twenty-four and this was her sixth full-term pregnancy in the past eight years. Her friends were all hugely relieved at the safe outcome. Back in August Lady Vere Gawdy, an old friend of the family, had written to lament that 'I must be absent from you when you lie down, but my prayers shall wait on you for a happy delivery'; and two days before the birth Eleanor told Ralph that 'the good news of your wife's safe delivery I long very much to hear'.[36] Maternal deaths among the gentry, while nowhere near as common as stillbirths or infant deaths, were a dreadful fact of life: 'rising of the lights' – postpartum pulmonary embolus – and the more generic 'death in childbed' accounted between them for one death in thirty-eight during the middle years of the seventeenth century. Stillbirths, miscarriages and infant deaths, which had already cost Mary three of her children, accounted for more than one in six.* Sister Susan Verney was to die in childbirth; and in the 1660s, when Betty Verney was married and pregnant, she asked her brother's daily prayers for her life as 'I grow extremely big, and am nearer my time', confessing that she was 'very fearful I shall die of this child.'[37] In the event she survived; the baby didn't.

John Verney did, and Jack, as the family called him, was soon packed off to Claydon with his nurse. He became his aunts' favourite plaything, while his father and grandfather played politics at Westminster.

Tom, meanwhile, had got himself into trouble again. In fact he was in gaol again. For debt, again.

The charitable interpretation of what happened to Tom in the winter of 1640–41 is that established Barbadians like James Futter took advantage of his lack of experience and talked him into buying poor land and unnecessary provisions. This was the line tactfully taken by Richard Gregorie, an agent who was representing Sir Edmund's interests in Barbados by the autumn of 1640. According to Gregorie, Tom was an innocent abroad: 'at his first coming hither, for want of good advice and knowledge of the place he run (as many others have and daily do) into many unadvised bargains for plantations, stock of hogs, turkeys . . .'.[38] In an attempt to placate as many of his creditors as possible, the young man sold up most of his land and with the little money he had left he bought a passage home in December 1640. Sadly, the unplaced creditors got to hear of his imminent departure; his chest and fresh provisions had actually been placed aboard a vessel bound for England when word got out and a group of planters to whom he owed money and cotton petitioned for his arrest. He was physically prevented from boarding the ship and

---

* Although these figures give us an insight into the perils of pregnancy in the mid-seventeenth century, both should be handled with care. They are drawn from John Graunt's pioneering demographic study, *Natural and Political Observations . . . upon the Bills of Mortality* (1662). But one must bear in mind a) that the Bills only relate to London and its suburbs; and b) that postmortem diagnosis was still in a raw state. Other itemised causes of death, for example, include fright, grief and 'itch'.

escorted to see the governor, Major Hunks, who threw him in prison in Jamestown until the matter was cleared up. The clearing up was done by Gregorie, by now the only man on the island that Tom could turn to for help. He agreed to pay off the boy's debts, charging them directly to Sir Edmund's own account.

Tom eventually arrived back in England in 1641, unrepentant, aggrieved that his creditors should treat him so badly and still cherishing dreams of reaping a fortune from his tattered and much reduced plantation. He persuaded his father to pay for his return to Barbados – Sir Edmund seems to have been quite keen to keep as much distance as possible between his errant son and himself – and while he was waiting for provisions and a suitable passage he turned his attention to recruiting a new workforce for his new start on the island.

There were professional agents who specialised in this kind of thing, as a writer on the colony of Virginia noted in 1649: 'The usual way of getting servants hath been by a sort of men nick-named *Spirits*, who take up all the idle, lazy, simple people they can entice.'[39] (John Sadler of Bucklersbury, who advised Tom's mother back in 1634 when she was kitting out Tom for his Virginia expedition, was just such an agent, telling Lady Verney then that he could have forty servants ready at a day's notice.) But Tom preferred to conduct negotiations himself, thereby avoiding a broker's fees. By the time he set sail again for the Caribbean in January 1642, he had on board with him a size-able party of local men, indentured agricultural workers whom he had recruited from the estates around Claydon.

He sold them the moment he reached Barbados.

Tom later tried to excuse his extraordinary behaviour to his father by saying he had fallen sick 'with an extreme burning fever' during the voyage, and that when he arrived in Barbados he was so weak that two of his men had to carry him ashore. While he was still recovering, six of them also came down with an ague and, fearing that he wasn't able to look after them prop-erly, he sold them all on to a broker, along with the goods he had brought over with him, 'in a lump'.[40]

The men didn't take kindly to this. Even according to Tom, who presumably played down their anger in his letter to his father, they 'bestowed many a wholesome curse upon me'. One tried to stab him. But there was worse to come: his assailant was one of three brothers who had signed indentures with Tom; a fourth had stayed behind in England, where he was in the Pye family household at Bradenham, about twenty-five miles south of Middle Claydon. Now Tom warned his father to steer well clear of Bradenham for a while, because the man had 'told me before my departure that in case he heard I sold [his brothers] that he would be the death of some of my generation at home, in case I came not myself'.[41]

In the same breath Tom asked Sir Edmund to procure another hundred men 'with the great help of Bridewell and prisons': there were good profits to be made in the trade.

No doubt it was a desire to avoid unpleasantness, coupled with an equal desire not to spoil a business opportunity, which led Tom to keep quiet about his servants. He certainly did his best to prevent word of their fate getting back to Buckinghamshire. If any of their friends or relations came to Claydon asking for news of the men, Will Roades was told to answer as succinctly as possible, and to give out that they had been temporarily assigned to another plantation while Tom journeyed back to England with cargoes of cotton and tobacco. If it came to it, Tom commanded poor Roades to lie. 'If [their friends] should tell you that I have put them off to other people, tell them it is not so, and endeavour to the utmost of your power to persuade them to the contrary.'[42]

As an afterthought, Tom told Roades to ignore the demands for money being made by the local brewer who had supplied his Barbados expedition with ale. 'Let him not be paid till my coming down,' he said airily, 'and then [his bill] shall be paid with use, but not in money but in very good blows.'[43] Creditors always brought out the worst in Tom.

8

This World is Full of Changes

The House of Commons sat in the thirteenth-century St Stephen's Chapel in the Palace of Westminster, given to them as their permanent chamber by Henry VIII in 1548 after the college of chaplains founded by Edward III to serve the chapel had been dissolved. Actually, the word 'sat' is somewhat misleading. St Stephen's was small – only 60 by 30 feet – and there was only room in its modified choir stalls for 250 or so MPs. Others might stand in the lobby or near the bar, but only the Speaker, William Lenthall, his clerk and the 'clerk's man' were guaranteed seats. Members were expected to leave space on the benches near the Speaker's chair for their more important colleagues, and woe betide those who didn't. One MP was censured for misconduct after placing himself near the Speaker's chair 'where none but privy councillors and men of distinction are wont to sit, to the great scandal of the house'. According to Ralph, he aggravated the offence by shouting 'Baw!' in the Speaker's ear when he disagreed with a point, 'to the great terror and affrightment of the Speaker, and of the Members of the House of Commons, and contrary to his duty and the trust reposed in him by his country'.[1]

With the exception of privy counsellors, men of distinction and the occasional boor, everyone had to find a place where he could. So it was perhaps just as well that absenteeism was astonishingly high. The Commons kept no records of daily attendance, but it seems to have averaged around 150, rising to about 350 for key votes. Those conscientious Members who turned up at 8 a.m., when the House opened for business, frequently had to hang around for an hour or more until the quorum of forty was reached. There were various reasons for the low attendance. Some MPs were old and infirm, or reluctant to go to the expense of keeping a household in London. Some were still in the north, serving with the King; others simply adopted the time-honoured practice of making themselves scarce whenever there was a vote which might entail their commitment to one political line or another.

The two Verneys were quite conscientious by the standards of the time. Sir Edmund was an old hand, having served in four parliaments since his return from Spain in 1624. Ralph was fresher, more enthusiastic and more ardent in his opposition to the arbitrary nature of the years of personal rule. Although neither was among those who moved motions or gave speeches, father and son both did their bit in the Commons over the winter and spring of 1640–41. Sir Edmund's name crops up among those investigating the jurisdiction of the courts of Canterbury and York, or on a committee looking into a bill 'for the Abolishing of Superstition and Idolatry, and for the better Advancing of the true Worship and Service of God'.[2] Ralph was involved in the committees considering bills to abolish trial by battle, to outlaw usury, to consider 'the Complaints of the Inland Posts, Foreign Couriers, Carriers, and Foot Posts . . . [and] the Rates and Prices for Carrying of Packets and Letters'.[3] When Sir Alexander Denton brought in a bill allowing him to break an entail and sell off some property in Oxfordshire 'for payment of his debts, and preferment of his younger children', Sir Edmund and Ralph were both involved in ensuring its safe passage through the House.[4]

Sir Edmund's commitments at court – and his divided loyalties – mean that he drifts in and out of the sketchy parliamentary records of the time. Ralph, on the other hand, *created* some of those sketchy records. The first weeks of parliament were taken up, as they usually were, with the hearing of petitions and counterpetitions in an attempt to make sense of election results which were sometimes confusing and often downright fraudulent. On a single day – 9 November 1640 – no fewer than a dozen MPs owned up to having been elected to two seats at the same time, and were accordingly asked by the House to choose between them. In a number of other cases, separate returns named different individuals as having been elected to the same seat, and enquiries had to be made to determine who had really been elected.

Ralph took a particular interest in the deliberations over one of the Buckinghamshire constituencies, Great Marlow. In the October election one return had named two Royalists, John Borlase and his stepfather, Gabriel Hipplesley, as Great Marlow's MPs, while another named Borlase and a well-known local Parliamentarian, Peregrine Hoby. A fourth candidate was the lawyer Bulstrode Whitelocke, who had an estate at Fawley, five miles west of Great Marlow. However, no one had thought to tell Whitelocke that his name had been put forward, and the first he heard about it was when 'a plain country fellow in mean habit' turned up at his chambers in the Inner Temple and informed him that he had received more votes than Borlase, but that the sheriff had nevertheless returned the latter.[5] The upshot was that Parliament declared the election void; and in a by-election held at the end of November, Borlase and Hipplesley were defeated and Hoby and Whitelocke were returned.

The matter didn't end there. Borlase complained to the House that he should have had Hoby's seat, and a committee was convened on 1 December 1640 to investigate. It was at this point that Ralph, who had been following the case with interest, found it so intriguing that he started to take notes of the proceedings, either for his own benefit or to make sure that when he told the story to his friends and relatives he would be able to remember all the details. As the affair dragged on into January, he carefully wrote down the opposing arguments. Borlase claimed that just before the by-election Hoby had been chosen sheriff for Berkshire, an annual office which apparently debarred him from standing.[6] He also alleged that Hoby's agents 'unduly procured voices by inviting to alehouses, &c'; and that they had one of the bailiffs arrested in front of the electors, so that 'divers were deterred by this means from giving voices for Borlase'.[7] According to Ralph's account of the proceedings, Hoby did not appear in a particularly good light. He admitted to being sheriff, claiming that Borlase had had him appointed without his knowledge to get him out of the race, and arguing that in any case there were precedents for sheriffs sitting as MPs. Neither argument cut much ice with the committee. Ralph also heard several witnesses come forward to confirm that one bailiff had indeed been effectively kidnapped on Hoby's orders, and that Hoby had punched another in the face and accused him of procuring votes against him.

Borlase *v.* Hoby dragged on into January 1641, in spite of the fact that John Borlase had managed to obtain a seat in Dorset at the beginning of the month.* Whitelocke's seat was confirmed, and Hoby was also eventually allowed to take his seat, but not until the end of his term of office as sheriff. But the case had given Ralph a taste for recording proceedings in the Commons: so when, one afternoon in February, a committee sat in the Exchequer Chamber at Westminster to discuss irregularities in the government of the Church of England, he was there, meticulously reporting the arguments for and against bishops, the references to biblical and historical precedent, the idea of divine right and the role of presbyters. As the committee's deliberations continued over the next two weeks, so did Ralph's terse, laconic notes. The following three entries are typical:

Presbyters are equal with bishops, i Thes. v. 12. Heb. xiii. 17. i Pet. v. 1. 2. 3. i Tim. [v.] 17. i Tim. iv. 14. Presbyters and bishops are all one.[†]

---

* He was chosen for Corfe Castle on 2 January 1641 after the sitting MP, Charles I's unpopular Secretary of State, Francis Windebank, fled to France rather than face charges relating to his 'many transactions on the behalf of the papists' (Clarendon, *The history of the rebellion and civil wars in England begun in the year 1641*, I, 235). Corfe Castle was controlled by Lord Chief Justice Bankes, who was Borlase's father-in-law.

† 15 February 1641 – John Bruce (ed.), *Notes of Proceedings in the Long Parliament*, Camden Society (1845), 9. The curious might like the full texts mentioned by

Dr Burges says, many things now claimed by bishops were no part of jurisdiction in primitive times, as admission to pastoral cures, which was not done by the bishops alone, but by the bishops and clergy.[8]

Bishops confirm little children, and old people, which they ought not to do.[9]

Over the next seventeen months, Ralph filled sixty-eight sheets of foolscap paper with his tight, neat handwriting. Many of the sheets were folded, so that they would sit on his knee in St Stephen's or fit easily into a pocket. Most of the writing was done in pencil. Only three sheets were in ink, and they all recorded proceedings of committees which usually met in less frenetic surroundings – the Star Chamber, the Court of Wards, the Exchequer Chamber – or even entirely outside the Palace of Westminster, in the Inns of Court or in the City. Some of the notes break off abruptly; others show signs that Ralph was nudged in the middle of a sentence and his pencil pushed across the page. It is fair to assume that he was writing down events as they happened, rather than piecing them together afterwards.

Ralph was not the only man in the Commons to take notes of its proceedings. At least five other MPs kept private journals for the early years of the Long Parliament, as did the Clerk Assistant, John Rushworth. But it was quite brave of Ralph: MPs

---

Sir Ralph. In the King James version, they are: 'And we beseech you, brethren, to know them which labour among you, and are over you in the Lord, and admonish you' (1 Thessalonians, 5: 12); 'Obey them that have the rule over you, and submit yourselves: for they watch for your souls, as they that must give account, that they may do it with joy, and not with grief: for that is unprofitable for you' (Hebrews, 13: 17); 'The elders which are among you I exhort, who am also an elder, and a witness of the sufferings of Christ, and also a partaker of the glory that shall be revealed: Feed the flock of God which is among you, taking the oversight thereof, not by constraint, but willingly; not for filthy lucre, but of a ready mind; Neither as being lords over God's heritage, but being examples to the flock' (1 Peter, 5: 1–3); 'Let the elders that rule well be counted worthy of double honour, especially they who labour in the word and doctrine' (1 Timothy, 5: 17); 'Neglect not the gift that is in thee, which was given thee by prophecy, with the laying on of the hands of the presbytery' (1 Timothy, 4: 14).

did not take kindly to having their deliberations documented. The official Commons journal, which was kept by Rushworth and the Clerk, Henry Elsynge, was limited to the recording of divisions, petitions, readings of bills, reports of committees and the membership of those committees, resolutions, orders and the like; debates, speeches made by Members and the proceedings of committees were carefully excluded. In other words, while obviously requiring its decisions to be recorded, the Commons most definitely did not want any publicity for the route which it took to reach those decisions.

Right at the beginning of the parliament, John Rushworth was ordered to take no notes without its command, except for orders and reports. When he was suspected (quite rightly) of continuing to put rather too much detail into those notes, a committee was appointed to examine them each Saturday. And throughout the period when Ralph was surreptitiously taking his notes, the House had bursts of anxiety about information being leaked to outsiders. Several times in March 1642, for example, Members complained that printed versions of their proceedings were circulating around London without their permission, and there were more calls for all note-taking to be prohibited. The lawyer Sir Simonds D'Ewes opposed the idea: 'Unless men's tongues may be restrained from relating as well as their pens from taking notes,' he said, 'I am sure this inhibition will be to little purpose.'[10] As one of the most dedicated note-takers in the Commons, he proved his own point by meticulously recording in his private journal this speech and those of several others, and continuing with his note-taking undeterred.

Ralph was less sanguine, it seems; on Friday 26 February 1642, a couple of weeks before the issue was raised in the House, he began to experiment with a cipher. It was a simple nonsequential substitution code, using numbers instead of letters: a = 14, b = 6, c = 10, and so on, with two blank numbers bringing the total up to 28. (A cipher which used only numbers between 1 and 26 would have been a bit of a giveaway.) His first entry showed that taking down coded notes from dictation was no easy task, but he managed to get the gist. A resolution that the college of Capuchin friars established by Henrietta Maria at Somerset

House should be suppressed came out as 'the cadhuchins houti [i.e., house] to be dissolued'. Even so, he only managed to stick it out for two days. Halfway through the session on Monday 28 February, during a heated debate on the King's refusal to cede control of the militia, he gave up, turned his paper over and reverted to his original unencoded English.*

Margaret Verney died at Covent Garden on 5 April 1641, with Sir Edmund and Ralph at her bedside. 'Good Puss' had been in indifferent health for some months, but she was only forty-six, and she left a young family, most of whom were still far from making their way in the world. Of the four boys and six girls, only Ralph – now Sir Ralph, in fact, having been knighted a few weeks earlier – was married; Elizabeth, her youngest child, was just seven years old.

Sir Edmund delegated the funeral arrangements to Sir Ralph. So did Lady Margaret, who in her will charged her son, rather than her husband or her Denton brothers, with making bequests and supervising the arrangements for her burial. She seems to have kept little amounts of money stashed all over the place – £1 15s. in an old glove, £1 11s. 4d. in a white dish, £4 9s. 6d.

---

* Although John Bruce published Sir Ralph's ciphered notes in 1845 'in the hope that the ingenuity of some reader may discover their meaning', no one has ever produced a deciphered version, as far as I know. So this may be a first: 'the cadhuchins houti to be dissolued. no extracts of letters to be aloued in this house. the prince is noh cometo greenhich three lette. three greate ships staiedinfrance gersea a letter from lord s albones. the kings answert th ourpetition about the militia. if aking offer to kil himselfe wee must noronly aduise but wrest the weapon from. a similitud of a de pilat. consciences corrupted.' With the exception of the last two sentences, which I haven't been able to identify, everything refers to discussions in the Commons on Saturday 26 and Monday 28 February 1642. For example, there was a rumour that the Prince of Wales had been moved to Greenwich in preparation for his departure to France; a letter from the Earl of St Albans about the state of things in Ireland was read to the House on the Saturday; and the reference to a king offering to kill himself relates to a speech on Monday in which an MP identified only as 'Sir W.' argued that control of the militia must be taken from King Charles, giving as an example 'if the king should be desperate and would lay violent hands on himself' (Willson H. Coates, Anne Steele Young and Vernon F. Snow (eds), *Private Journals 3 January to 5 March 1642* (1982) 482).

'in the black and white pocket'.[11] But most of her valuables were stored in 'my red box'. They included another £144 13s. 5d., and two miniatures, one of Sir Edmund and another of Prince Henry. Sir Ralph was to keep the picture of his father, and give to him the one of Prince Henry.

Margaret's bequests were straightforward. Sir Edmund was to have £100 'to buy what he pleases to keep for me'; and Sir Ralph's eldest boy was given another £100, which Sir Ralph should invest for him until his wedding and then spend on some good plate for his household. She showed a special interest in her grandson, still only five years old: he was also to have one of her diamond rings and some good holland sheets 'which were never yet washed'; and although she left a gilt tankard and a case of silver-handled knives to her husband, Sir Ralph was to ask that Sir Edmund leave them to the little boy. Sir Ralph and Mary's daughter Peg was given four 'very fine smocks' and a holland sheet. (The will was made in May 1639, before Jack's birth, and it hadn't been amended since, so no mention was made of the latest grandchild.) The household linen that belonged to Margaret should go to Sir Ralph and little Edmund instead of being sold – rather an odd bequest this, since one assumes it was still needed for the households at Claydon and Covent Garden – with only the coarsest stuff left to Sir Ralph's sisters. Mary was left six new smocks, some diamonds and a sable muff.

The rest of the legacies were conventional enough and as poignant as all such summaries of a person's life: there were small sums for the poor, for the household servants – 'if cook is with me give her some £3 and some of my worser gowns' – and for the Claydon rector; mourning rings for the family; little legacies for Henry and Mun.

There was something for everyone – everyone except Tom, that is. He never forgot it, and continued to demand the legacy that Sir Ralph had 'cheated' him out of for years afterwards, even when Sir Ralph told him straight that their mother had cut him out of her will because she was so angry at his appalling behaviour. This, Tom told his sister-in-law Mary with that nasty self-righteous piety which always rose to the surface when things weren't going his own way, 'was a most unchristianlike saying, for how could she make a happy end and bear malice to her death? . . . you and your husband would rather have the world question the salvation of our mother's soul than to pay me that small legacy she left me'.[12]

Margaret was anxious about how she would be remembered. She didn't care about monuments and memorials, asking only to be buried at Claydon church next to where Sir Edmund proposed to lie. But she did ask Sir Ralph to burn all her papers, and not to leave the task to anyone else. (She excepted her 'medicinal and cookery books' and a few other notes.) And she left detailed instructions about the preparation of her corpse, presumably because she felt so self-conscious about her scars:

> Let no stranger wind me, nor do not let me be stripped, but put a clean smock over me . . . and let my face be hid and do you stay in the room and see me wound and laid in the first coffin, which must be wood if I do not die of any infectious disease, else I am so far from desiring it that I forbid you to come near me.[13]

Sir Ralph and Mary also had the task of writing round to family and friends to let them know of Margaret's death. The immediate circle – or rather circles – around Claydon, Hillesden and Covent Garden were first on the list. Eleanor Sussex heard the news within days, for example, and immediately wrote back to commiserate with Sir Ralph over the lost of his mother and her dear friend: 'this world is full of changes. God fit us for his pleasure.'[14] The seventeenth century's ability to cope with loss is thrown into sharp relief in a second letter she wrote to Sir Ralph just two weeks later, in which she implied that the time for grieving was already past – 'I should not say anything to renew your sorrow' – and told him in passing how glad she was that 'you have Parliament business to take you off your sad thoughts'.[15]

The way in which Sir Ralph informed others of Margaret's death seems equally strange to modern sensibilities. He didn't get round to telling Mun, who was still with the army at York, for several months – and then he left the task to Mary, who had fallen sick along with young Edmund soon after her mother-in-law's death. Mun wrote a tender and sensitive letter back. ''Tis most true the loss of our mother was infinite but I'll not torture you by expressing it more largely', he told Mary. 'I have that great affection to you and yours that though you and my nephew are well recovered, yet I cannot but be much troubled that you have been sick; I pray God continue you in your health and give you all other happiness that this world can afford.'[16]

Even more bizarre than his offhand approach to telling his brother about their mother's death was the way in which Sir Ralph looked for the right words with which to break the sad news to an Irish friend of the family, the Countess of Barrymore. He found those words not in his own heart, but in a letter which James Dillon had sent to him mourning the death of Lady Sara Digby, daughter of the Earl of Cork, eight years earlier.

'My Lady Digby's dead', Dillon had written. 'My Lady Digby's dead; whom neither the tears of her father, nor the sighs of her husband, nor the prayers of the poor, nor the moans of her friends nor (in a word) the petitions and desires of all that ever knew or heard of her could withhold from the jaws of death. By death she is gone into an endless life. But I will now withdraw myself from these thoughts, and compose myself the best I can.'[17] Now Sir Ralph took out Dillon's letter and carefully copied the relevant sentiments. 'My dear mother is dead,' he wrote to Lady Barrymore, 'whom neither the sighs of her husband, nor the groans of her children nor the desires and petitions of all that knew her, could withhold from the jaws of death. By death she is gone to an endless life. But now I will withdraw myself from these sad thoughts . . .' Then, either because he felt uneasy at parroting ready-made emotions or because he thought he could improve on Dillon's prose, he reworked the letter. The groans, the sighs, the jaws of death remained, but now it read, 'You have lost a faithful servant and I a dear and careful mother. No sighs, no groans, no prayers could withhold her from the jaws of death. By death she is gone to an endless life. But now I will withdraw myself from these sad thoughts . . .'[18]

The Earl of Strafford went to a more public and more violent death five weeks after Lady Margaret. Sir Ralph was present throughout his trial for high treason and the subsequent debates in the Commons, frantically scribbling down his terse pencil notes on the proceedings, breaking off only to bury his mother at Claydon before rushing back to the House. He watched in Westminster Hall as Strafford flatly denied one charge after another, or argued a point of law or precedent, or broke down in the middle of his closing speech as he spoke of his children and his dead wife. 'Passion made him break off' was Sir Ralph's only comment.[19] He carefully noted down the names of the fifty-nine Members who voted against the Bill of Attainder which condemned Strafford to death, and raged along with the rest of the Commons at the news of a plot by junior army officers to free Strafford and mobilise Irish forces to come to the defence of the Anglican Church. He was among the first MPs to make the Protestation which was a result of the Army Plot, a loyalty oath in which he and most of the rest of the House vowed to maintain and defend the Protestant religion, the King and the power and privileges of Parliament.

Interestingly, Sir Ralph carefully wrote down the lengthy preamble to this Protestation, which lamented 'that the designs of the priests and Jesuits and other adherents to the see of Rome have of late been more boldly and frequently put in practice than formerly, to the undermining and danger of the ruin of the true reformed protestant religion in his majesty's dominions'.[20] Sir Edmund Verney was in the House and made the Protestation on the same day as his son, Monday 3 May 1641. Charles I was pressured into signing Strafford's Bill of Attainder on Sunday 9 May, and his chief councillor's execution took place on Tower Hill at noon three days later. Strafford died bravely, remarking on the scaffold that 'the omen was bad for the intended reformation of the state, [when] it commenced with the shedding of innocent blood'.[21] There is nothing to show whether or not Sir Ralph was among the thousands of spectators. Perhaps he was, because he missed that morning's session of Parliament; but he was back in the House by two o'clock to hear a debate on a bill to abolish the episcopacy.

There was more innocent blood to be shed that year, much more. On 23 October 1641, Sir Phelim O'Neill issued a proclamation at Dungannon, Co. Tyrone, on behalf of Irish Catholics. He declared that the English Parliament had usurped the royal prerogative and, intent on extinguishing Catholicism throughout the kingdom, was threatening 'to send over the Scottish army with the sword and bible against us'. O'Neill and his followers had therefore 'taken arms and possessed ourselves of the best and strongest forts in the Kingdom, to enable us to serve his Majesty, and preserve us from the tyrannous resolution of our enemies'.[22] He was overly optimistic – the plans for a general rising in Ireland had been discovered the previous day, and an attempt to take the crucial strategic garrison at Dublin Castle had already ended in disaster. But it was too late now for second thoughts. In Ulster, the insurgents quickly took Dungannon, Newry and Charlemont and, unable to dislodge Scottish garrisons in the main Ulster seaports, moved south to lay siege to the port of Drogheda in Co. Louth, a few days' march north of Dublin.

The rebels believed their actions would lead to a popular rising of native Catholics; so did Protestant English settlers, and as news spread a stream of frightened colonists began to pour into the relative safety of Dublin, where the Earl of Ormond was co-ordinating efforts to suppress the rebellion. Within weeks, other garrison towns across Ireland were opening their gates to refugees from the country.

To describe the factional politics of the 1641 Irish rising as labyrinthine is woefully inadequate. In one corner there were O'Neill and the Old Irish, Catholic nobles whose clans had seen their power gradually eroded by successive waves of English and Scottish colonists. In another were the Old English who had come over to Ireland with the expeditionary forces of Henry II and King John in the twelfth and thirteenth centuries and later, establishing themselves as major landowners. Many were also Catholics, the English Reformation having passed them by; but some, like the Earl of Ormond's ancestors, had found it expedient for the sake of their careers in public office to convert to Protestantism.

A third force were the New English, Protestants who had seen rich pickings in post-Reformation Ireland, and who positioned themselves to possess 'those places of honour, profit, and trust, whereof neither the Ancient Irish, nor the Old English, because they were Catholics, were capable'.[23] Then there were the Scottish Planters, hard-line Protestants who settled Ulster in the early seventeenth century, dispossessing the native Irish – and some of the Old English – in the process.

Throw into the pot a king, Charles I, who was torn between the need to suppress an unlawful rebellion and the prospect of raising a Catholic army in Ireland to quell his insolent subjects across the Irish Sea; an English Parliament desperate to prevent him doing exactly that; zealous Covenanters in Scotland who felt the same and who were, in addition, eager to protect the interests of their Planter brethren in Ulster; and a native Catholic aristocracy who had seen how the Covenanters had just fought off Charles I's attempts to interfere with their religious freedom and were prepared to follow their example. This was Irish *realpolitik* in 1641.

Quite apart from their different political perspectives, the Verneys' implacable hostility towards Catholicism meant that they were necessarily opposed to the rising: as far as Sir Ralph was concerned, it was 'utterly impossible to infuse any humanity into those pagan Irish'.[24] But the rebellion also had a personal impact. Aside from James Dillon, with whom Sir Ralph had all but lost contact over the past couple of years (and who was scarcely likely to renew their friendship at the moment, since the Parliament to which his old friend belonged had just condemned his father-in-law, the Earl of Strafford, to death), the Verneys had friends and family among the Protestant New English in Ireland. Sir Edmund's half-sister, Alice Turville, lived in Co. Cork with her husband, Sir John Leeke. One of their daughters, Anne, was married to Nat Hobart, the young London lawyer and family friend whose involvement in Sir Edmund's business ventures in the mid-1630s had nearly ruined him; another daughter, Dorothy, had been raised in the Verney household, and was currently a gentlewoman-in-waiting with Sir Edward and Lady Sydenham, Sir Edmund's next-door neighbours in Covent Garden.

Sir John Leeke's land was part of Castlelyons, an estate about twenty miles north-east of Cork city; and, as it happened, the Verneys were also on friendly terms with his landlord, the Earl of Barrymore, and more particularly with his wife. Lord Barrymore had been raised by the 1st Earl of Cork, who married him to his eldest daughter, Alice; Lady Barrymore visited England regularly throughout the 1630s in the company of her husband or her father; and while she was there she invariably spent time with Sir Edmund and Sir Ralph, taking the waters at Bath with them and socialising with them in London. Sir Edmund had a high opinion of her – he thought her 'very discreet and of great understanding'[25] – and she seems to have returned the compliment, habitually addressing him as 'Noble Governor' and asking his advice on a variety of matters. In 1639 Sir Edmund was instrumental in finding her a new gentlewoman – Magdalen Faulkner, a poor Denton cousin; and around the same time she asked him to send over a tutor for her little son, a 'monsieur, one that might teach him to write and a good garb . . . I like [your father] so well for a governor for myself', she told Sir Ralph, 'that I humbly desire he may choose one for my mad boy'.[26]

Almost as soon as the rising in Ireland started, stories began to circulate of the most appalling atrocities perpetrated by the native Catholics on Protestant landowners like the Leekes and the Barrymores. Pamphlets described in horrid detail how women were raped; how babies were pitchforked by drunken mobs, or ripped from their mothers' wombs and thrown into rivers and bogs; how men were hacked to death and their bodies fed to pigs. Pamphlets were sent from Dublin to England, with titles like *More News from Ireland of the Bloody Practices and Proceedings of the Papists of that Kingdom*, and woodcuts which with a ghoulish relish depicted priests murdering children. In Co. Antrim, rebels were said to have admitted to murdering nearly a thousand people in a single morning; in Armagh, a woman was forced to hang her own husband, while a young man was quartered alive and the quarters thrown in his father's face.

There was truth buried deep in this mythology of hate; it is generally accepted today that around 5000 Protestants lost their lives during the first months of the rising. Elements among the rebels were horrifically vicious, and their commanders found it impossible to control them, even when they wanted to – and there were plenty of times when they didn't, since they realised that terror was one of their most potent weapons. But the important thing was that Protestants all over the British Isles were ready and willing to believe the tales of rape and disembowelling. The English and Scottish already regarded the Irish peasantry as little more than violent, superstitious savages, a depressingly familiar attitude which, by dehumanising a native population, allowed the colonists to treat them as less than human. Now those prejudices seemed to be confirmed. As Sir Ralph told Lady Barrymore, 'those barbarous rebels . . . delight in cruelty, and take pleasure in insolency, above and beyond the worst of infidels'.[27]

In Cork, as elsewhere, aristocratic Protestant womenfolk began to leave not just the countryside, but the country itself. Sir John Leeke informed Sir Edmund that Murrough O'Brien, Earl of Inchquin – a local military commander whose ferocity against the rebels was about to earn him the title of 'Murrough of the Burnings' – was sending his wife and children to safety in England.* Other neighbours did the same.

The powerful Jephsons of Mallow Castle sent their women over to London. So did Sir William St Leger, the Lord President of Munster, who was soon to die of grief at the rising; and Viscount Kinalmeaky, second son of the Earl of Cork. Sir John reported that 'the virtuous Lady Kinalmeaky . . . can give our miseries to the life' when she saw the Verneys.[28] By the beginning of 1642, he reckoned that 'there are not any women of quality but are come for England'.[29] Those who didn't settle in London made their temporary homes in the West Country: a number of Sir John's friends had taken houses at Taunton and Minehead.

The Barrymores had just finished remodelling and fortifying their mansion at Castlelyons, with financial help from the Earl of Cork; for the time being, Lady Barrymore decided to remain there, prompting an anxious Sir Ralph to urge her to change her mind: 'Your stay there at this time, I confess, afflicts me extremely,' he wrote. 'Be pleased to come over and make us happy here.'[30] Sir John, who lived in the Lodge at Castlelyons, was reluctant to leave, but as the rebels began to establish a pattern of raids on Protestant estates as well as all-out attacks on garrison towns his

---

* During a pitched battle at Liscarroll in the summer of 1642, Inchquin's cousin, who was fighting alongside the rebels, came face to face with the Earl and had the better of him. But just as he was about to administer the *coup de grâce*, he remembered a promise made to his mother that he wouldn't shed his family's blood. This moment's hesitation was enough for the Earl, who had no such qualms and shot his cousin in the head.

wife insisted they take refuge in the walled port of Youghal, which was being defended by the Earl of Cork. 'My wife is in that extremity of fears (as cause she hath, poor soul),' he told Sir Edmund, 'that I must not delay longer.'[31]

In the meantime, the English began to organise a resistance which was as savage as the rebellion itself. Around 5000 Irish Catholics lost their lives in the counter insurgency measures. In Dublin, the Earl of Ormond was instructed to 'wound, kill, slay and destroy, by all the ways and means he may, all the said rebels, their adherents and relievers; and burn, spoil, waste, consume, destroy and demolish, all the places, towns and houses, where the said rebels are, or have been relieved and harboured; and all the hay and corn there'.[32] The Earl of Cork's clan took charge of defence in east Cork: the Earl himself was an old man of seventy-five, and 'full of distractions, not like the man he was' according to Sir John.[33] But his older sons, Lord Dungarvan, Lord Kinalmeaky and the twenty-year-old Baron Broghill, took up the fight with gusto. So too did Lord Barrymore, whose ties with the Earl of Cork made him a senior commander; he took the field with a troop of sixty dragoons and seventy lancers, joining up with forces led by St Leger and Dungarvan. Even the elderly Sir John Leeke begged Sir Edmund to use his influence to obtain him a commission at Youghal, although he seems to have been singularly ill prepared for battle, since he also asked his friend to send over a case of pistols and a sword with a guarded hilt, since he had neither.

These forces were soon matching the brutality of the Catholic rebels. Early in 1642 a group of Barrymore's supporters surrendered to a rebel force led by the Condons of Ballymacpatrick. Although they had been promised quarter, they were all killed, except for a single man who was left for dead. When the story got out, Barrymore vowed vengeance on the Condons. That March he took Curbeigh Castle, a Condon stronghold, and then moved on with Dungarvan to Ballymacpatrick, where his forces killed between 150 and 300 men, women and children. Fifty Condon survivors were dragged off to Castlelyons, where – according to a Catholic propaganda pamphlet – their hair and beards were set alight before they were hanged in the stables there, so that their relatives could not identify their bodies. 'My

Lord Barrymore . . . hath most bravely and loyally behaved himself,' Sir John told Sir Edmund, 'to the great terror of his countrymen.'[34]

This kind of tit-for-tat terror benefited neither side. The insurgents made a number of important gains, taking Clonmel, 'the key of Munster', and Dungarvan town and castle, Kilkenny, then Wexford and Waterford, from the last two of which Irish privateers mounted raids on English shipping. But they were unable to score any decisive military victories over the Protestant New English; nor were Ormond and his commanders able to suppress the rebels. What they needed to tip the balance in their favour was reinforcements, as Sir John was constantly pointing out to Sir Ralph and Sir Edmund. 'Oh! we sigh and grieve for the English forces,' he wrote in January 1642. 'We believe they will come, but the kingdom will be so near losing, or at least destroying, that the regaining will cost more blood and charge than the first conquest did or all the war in Queen Elizabeth's time.'[35]

The reason why reinforcements were slow in coming was that King and Parliament could not stop quarrelling for long enough to agree a coordinated strategy for dealing with the rebellion. News of it had reached the Commons on 30 October 1641, and MPs immediately appointed a committee to consider 'the raising and sending of men and ammunition from hence into Ireland'.[36] But the rising fuelled suspicions of a more widespread Catholic plot masterminded by Henrietta Maria, if not by the King. Nor did it help that five days later Phelim O'Neill produced a warrant, purportedly signed by Charles I himself, which gave royal approval for the Irish Catholics' actions. (He later admitted it was a forgery.) Certain that the rising was part of a wider Catholic conspiracy to take control of the three kingdoms, and thus suspicious that the King was grooming an army in Ireland for service against Parliament, John Pym and other leaders of the anti-Royalist faction in the Commons pressed for Charles's role as commander-in-chief of the army to be delegated.

They also presented up a long and impressive catalogue of grievances which had accumulated since the King came to the throne back in 1625. The Grand Remonstrance was grand indeed, amounting to 204 separate clauses and a total of 10,435 words: it steered Charles step by relentless step through his errors of judgement, his attacks on Parliament and liberty, his conduct of the wars with Scotland, his habit of surrounding himself with those 'whose proceedings evidently appear to be mainly for the advantage and increase of Popery'.[37] Pym in particular saw the events of the past sixteen years as part of a vast Catholic conspiracy. Through the tireless efforts of priests, Jesuits and other malignants, 'the violent distraction and interruption of this Parliament, the insurrection of the Papists in your kingdom of Ireland, and bloody massacre of your people, have been not only endeavoured and attempted, but in a great measure compassed and effected'.[38]

Sir Ralph had not spent much time in the Commons since the summer; or if he had, he had not heard anything worth recording. There is a gap in his parliamentary notes from 12 August 1641 until the following 17 November, only partly explained by the fact that the House was in recess from 9 September to 20 October. But at noon on Monday 22 November, when the Commons began their debate about the Remonstrance, he was on his bench and writing. He watched as Pym argued that 'the honour of the King lies in the safety of the people'.[39] He heard the radical Denzil Holles declare that 'if kings are misled by their counsellors, we may, we must tell him of it';[40] and diligently noted down John Hampden's more Delphic statement that 'when the woman shall be clothed with the sun, the moon shall be under her feet'.[41] (Hampden was talking about the need to reform the Church, and was in fact referring to Revelation 12: 1 – 'And there appeared a great wonder in heaven; a woman clothed with the sun, and the moon under her feet, and upon her head a crown of twelve stars'.) By midnight, when the House finally divided, he had stopped recording the arguments. Those against the Remonstrance, 148 of them, stayed in their seats; those in favour left St Stephen's Chapel and the 'Tellers for the Yea' counted 159. We don't know how, or even if, Sir Ralph voted.

But we can hazard a good guess. As the tensions between King and Commons came to a head, Sir Ralph found himself unequivocally on the side of Parliament and Protestantism. His father tried to straddle the divide, but he found it more and more difficult to reconcile his Puritan views with his position at court. Charles I had been in Scotland since August, either pleading with the Scots to stay out of English affairs or, as the opposition

believed, trying to win military support from the Scots if it came
to a fight with the Commons. Sir Edmund was with him for
much, if not all, of the time, in which case he may also have
been in the royal retinue when Charles rode into London two
days after the Commons voted for the Remonstrance. The City,
seeing his return as an indication that the Irish rising was about
to be quashed, gave him a rapturous reception – 'methinks the
king should love his people of England best, for sure their bounty
and obedience is most to him', Eleanor Sussex told Sir Ralph[42] –
but Charles, always adept at misinterpreting popular opinion,
decided this was an endorsement of his policies as a whole. He
refused to appear in the House of Lords, saying he had a cold,
and went off to Hampton Court, studiously ignoring the Grand
Remonstrance.

From that safe distance he ordered the removal of the guard
from around the Houses of Parliament, which the Commons
thought was a prelude to an armed assault on St Stephen's Chapel.
Then he reinstated it, which the Commons also thought was a
prelude to an armed assault on St Stephen's Chapel. Just before
Christmas he dismissed the Lieutenant of the Tower, Sir William
Balfour, and replaced him with an unsavoury character named
Thomas Lunsford – and again, the Commons braced itself for an
attack. There were anti-Catholic demonstrations in and around
Westminster Abbey, where the Dean, John Williams, was personally involved in repelling a group of apprentices intent on tearing
down the high altar; and there was a near-riot in Westminster Hall
on 27 December, when a crowd which had arrived to petition
the Lords was attacked by Lunsford and his soldiers and responded
by throwing bricks and tiles at them. The following day Charles
told the Lord Mayor, Sir Richard Gurney, to be ready to use the
trained bands to clear the streets 'with bullets or otherwise'.[43]

'I cannot say we have had a merry Christmas,' wrote one MP,
Sir Henry Slingsby; 'but the maddest one that ever I saw.'[44] The
madness worsened with the New Year. On Monday 3 January
the King decided to take the offensive, and sent a message to
Parliament demanding the surrender of five of the most articu-
late and vociferous of his opponents in the Commons – Pym,
Hampden, Denzil Holles, Sir Arthur Hazelrigg and William
Strode – and the leader of the Puritan faction in the Lords,

Viscount Mandeville,* on charges of high treason. The Lords refused, and appointed a committee to consider whether the charge against Mandeville was legal. The Commons, who had had advance warning of the charges when the rooms of Pym and Holles were sealed up by men acting under the King's warrant, reacted vigorously. They also answered that they would consider his message, but pointed out that 'being there was no charge delivered in against those five gentlemen, they have not delivered them'.[45] A conference was held with the Lords, the upshot of which was that a sergeant-at-arms was sent to arrest those responsible for the seals, and to break them open. Sir Ralph, who was as indignant as anyone that MPs should be treated in such a cavalier fashion, recorded that the Commons invited the Lords 'to join with us, because they had protested with us to defend the privileges of Parliament'.[46]

The next morning the Commons heard of a plan to take the five MPs by force, and when the House reconvened after dinner Pym and the others were ordered to leave, 'to avoid all tumult'.[47] Shortly afterwards the King appeared at the door of the chamber.

Sir Ralph was there, and his description of what happened next is a world away from his usual terse style. MPs immediately saw that Charles was not alone: he had brought his nephew the Elector Palatine, the Earl of Roxburgh and around a hundred armed men, 'desperate soldiers, captains, and commanders, of papists, ill-affected persons, being men of no rank or quality, divers of them being traitors in France, Frenchmen fled hither, panders and rogues', according to the outraged MP for Bridport, Roger Hill.[48] Hill's conviction, that this band had come 'to fall upon the House of Commons and to cut all their throats', was shared by many of his colleagues. And although Charles commanded his men to stay outside in Westminster Hall, the doors between the chamber and the hall were deliberately kept open, so that they could be seen plainly by Members, as could their swords and their charged pistols. The Earl of Roxburgh made sure of this by

---

* The correct title of Edward Montagu, son of the 1st Earl of Manchester, was Lord Kimbolton, since he had been created Baron Montagu of Kimbolton in 1626; but he was generally known by his courtesy title of Viscount Mandeville.

standing just inside the chamber door and nonchalantly 'leaning upon it', in Sir Ralph's words.[49]

Charles removed his hat and walked up to the Speaker's chair, where he stood looking around at the frightened assembly. 'And, after he had looked a great while, he told us, he would not break our privileges, but treason had no privilege; he came for those five gentlemen, for he expected obedience yesterday, and not an answer.'[50] Then he called the Five Members by name. When there was no reply, he turned to Speaker Lenthall and asked where they were.

William Lenthall was (inevitably) related to the Verneys. His brother was married to Sir Ralph's mother's first cousin, Bridget Temple. A successful lawyer, he was also a weak and notoriously venal man, not at all the stuff that heroes are made of. But in that single moment he gained for himself a place of honour in the history of Parliament. Kneeling down before the King, Lenthall begged to be excused from answering, saying he was a servant of the House, and had neither eyes nor tongue to see or say anything unless commanded by the House.

> Then the King told him, he thought his own eyes were as good as his, and then said, his birds were flown, but he did expect the house should send them to him, and if they did not he would seek them himself, for their treason was foul, and such an one as they would all thank him to discover.[51]

The King then assured the House, not altogether convincingly, that the fugitives would have a fair trial; and with that he walked out, 'putting off his hat until he came to the door'.[52]

Charles I's ill-judged attempt to arrest the Five Members caused chaos. The Commons adjourned, congratulating themselves on avoiding a bloodbath, and the next day they decided that, since Westminster was no longer safe, they would reconvene in the City, where popular anger at the King's recent moves might provide them with a degree of security. When Eleanor Sussex heard the news in Gorhambury, she expressed real fear of the violence that loomed. A staunch Puritan, she was scared that the Catholic uprising in Ireland would be duplicated in England, as Pym had foretold: 'I hope we shall not be killed,' she told Sir

Ralph; 'yet I think you are in greater danger than we are in the country. I pray God bless you with safety.'[53]

On Friday 7 January Sir Ralph attended a parliamentary committee in the Grocers' Hall north of the Poultry in the heart of the City. The MPs present resolved that 'the coming of the soldiers, papists, and others, with his majesty to the House of Commons on Tuesday, to take away some Members of the House, and, if that had been denied or opposed, then to fall upon the House of Commons in an hostile manner, was a traitorous design against the King and Parliament'.[54] Armed citizens came on to the streets, ready to repel any attack on MPs by the King's men. Parliament took control of the trained bands, appointing Philip Skippon, a veteran of the Dutch Wars, as major general in charge; and hundreds of sailors flocked into the City to offer their services as armed guards when MPs returned to Westminster the following week.

Now it was the King's turn to beat a retreat. He left Whitehall for Hampton Court on Monday 10 January. On Tuesday the committee which had been sitting in the Grocers' Hall, along with the Five Members and Viscount Mandeville, returned to a heroes' reception in the Palace of Westminster, accompanied by a fleet of boats bristling with weapons and several companies of the trained bands, who formed a guard around Parliament. 'I pray God direct all your hearts to do for the best for the good of us all,' Eleanor wrote to Sir Ralph. 'If we now be overcome we are undone for ever.'[55]

It was in the shadow of these events that Parliament had to grapple with the problem of the Irish rising. England needed to go to the aid of beleaguered Protestants, but even the most fervent Puritan conspiracy theorists jibbed at the notion of diverting money, men and munitions when it was looking increasingly likely that all three would be needed at home before the year was out. The solution finally adopted was to pay for a Scottish army of 10,000 men, which deployed in Ulster that summer, recapturing Newry, Dundalk and Dungannon from the rebels and reinforcing Planter enclaves. The English expeditionary force to Munster for which Sir John Leeke prayed so fervently didn't materialise. Instead, English regiments were sent over to Dublin and Munster in a piecemeal fashion, as reinforcements for the troops led by the Earl of Ormond and Murrough of the Burnings.

Mun, who had been kicking his heels with his sisters at Claydon ever since the failure of Charles's second campaign against the Scots, was one of the first to go. By the second week in December 1641 he had got himself a captaincy and set off for west Chester where his regiment was mustering, leaving behind in Buckinghamshire a lock of his hair as a keepsake. 'It shows so like a legacy that it has put a sadness into me,' thought Doll Leeke.[56]

An Irish crossing was an unpredictable business. Although the distance to Dublin from the Dee estuary outside Chester – 'Chester water', as it was known in the seventeenth century – was only about 150 miles, the voyage took four or five days, and more if the winds were against you. James Dillon nearly died during one of his journeys between England and Ireland: after waiting two or three days at Chester for a favourable wind, he boarded a vessel only for a sudden storm to break while he was still in harbour. 'The winds blew beyond measure high, and the rain fell down so violently and so fast as one might have thought the floodgates of Heaven had been set wide open.'[57] The passengers put ashore again, which was just as well since the ship foundered shortly afterwards – 'she had her bottom strucken out and was unseamed'.[58]

Mun's problems were more frustrating than Dillon's, if less dramatic. The wind was against the expedition, and he was left at Chester to kick his heels and listen to terrifying tales of atrocity. 'What a bloody age this is!' exclaimed the pamphleteers; and Mun agreed. 'Never was more barbarousness practised amongst the Heathen than they use now amongst men of very good quality,' he reported to Sir Ralph.[59] The latest story to outrage English Protestants concerned Sir Patrick Dunson, whose house in Armagh was broken into by insurgents at the end of November. According to a newsletter which was currently circulating in England, the rebels killed his servants and children and raped his wife in front of him. He laughed in their faces, apparently – rather a strange reaction, all things considered – whereupon

they did run upon him, and bound him with rolls of match fast to a board, so fast, that his eyes bursted out of his head, then did they cut off his ears, then his nose, then seared off both his cheeks; after that they cut off his arms, after that his legs, and yet (a wonderful thing to hear) was not this good knight dead, although he were in body so inhumanly mangled. Will, eye and vital spirits remain; then did they cut out his tongue, and afterward to put him out of his pain, they ran a red hot iron into his bowels, and so he died.[60]

Fuelled by such stories, Mun was eager to get to Ireland. He had to wait a whole month for favourable weather, while his colonel prodded him to use his influence with Sir Ralph to persuade Parliament to approve payment of the army's arrears. 'I believe it is a business you care not to meddle with,' Mun told his brother, 'and for my own part I will not at all press you to it.'[61]

In the New Year he finally arrived in Dublin, where the recently appointed governor of the city, Sir Charles Coote, was engaged in a series of counterattacks on insurgent positions in the surrounding countryside. Mun was immediately involved in one of these raids, as part of a force of 2000 footsoldiers and 200 cavalry which set out from Dublin on the night of 9 January 1642 to attack a rebel stronghold at Swords, a small town eight miles to the north. The party arrived at six the next morning, overran the Irish fortifications – 'more like a garden ditch than a trench,' said Mun dismissively[62] – and plundered the town, before setting it alight. There were only a handful of English casualties, and he reckoned the rebels lost 100 men, with the remainder, around 900, running away. Another contemporary put the death toll at Swords much higher, saying that 'our new English soldiers spared neither man, woman, or child therein, they got good store of good booty'.[63]

Mun's introduction to the pattern of slaughter was typical of the campaign. The rebels were poorly equipped and ill-disciplined, and they rarely came off best in the kind of formalised battle which the English forces offered them. Mun thought they were cowardly. 'Ireland is full of castles,' he told Sir Ralph, 'and truly strong ones, and thither the rebels fly, not daring to give us a meeting.'[64] He wasn't the last English soldier in Ireland to underestimate the potency of his enemy's hit-and-run guerrilla campaign.

In Dublin, Sir Charles Coote's tactics during the early months of 1642 consisted mainly of relieving beleaguered outlying garrisons and trying to eliminate insurgent strongholds within the Pale, and Mun was more than once involved in close-quarters combat against the rebels. In March, his men took part in an assault on the castle of Carrickmines to the south of Dublin. His own account of the attack was brief and matter-of-fact: 'We the last Monday stormed the castle of Carrigmaine and took it in, where the common soldier (though the service were most desperate) expressed as much courage and resolution as could be expected from brave commanders.'[65] Others on both sides were less reticent about what actually happened. Sir Simon Harcourt, a veteran of the Dutch and Scotch wars, took a small force to attack the castle, but found it better defended than he had thought, and sent back to Dublin for reinforcements. While he was waiting for them to arrive, the rebels taunted his men: at one point 'a brave daring fellow upon a white horse came out of the castle, and rode quite through our men, and then discharged his pistol in despite of all our men'.[66]

Harcourt, who was one of the most senior figures in the English army (he had actually come to Ireland with a commission to take over the governorship of Dublin, but Coote refused to give way to him), was shot in the left shoulder by a rebel sniper, and died the next day. In the meantime, the reinforcements arrived and broke down the castle gate, swarming into the courtyard and smashing open the main door. They killed every man, woman and child they found there, apart from a single Welsh maidservant. Her brother happened to be serving in Harcourt's regiment and he was one of the first through the door. One of the English officers tried to save a seven-year-old boy by hiding him in his cloak, but the child was killed in his arms. About 260 Irish died altogether, and the castle was then blown up.

None of this raised any comment from Mun, who was grown accustomed to such horrors. Two months later, after he lost twenty men during an assault on a castle near Trim, he and his troops put eighty rebels to the sword, blithely mentioning the action in passing in one of his letters home, and noting – as something exceptional – that 'like valiant knights errant, [we] gave quarter and liberty to all the women'.[67]

He was much more exercised about Parliament's refusal to stump up officers' arrears of pay. The reluctance he felt about lobbying Sir Ralph had vanished within weeks of his arrival in Ireland. Now every letter he wrote to his brother was filled with complaints: 'I pray let us know when you intend to send us money, or whether ye intend to send any . . . I admire how you think we live . . . Our soldiers have lived upon nothing this month but salt beef and herrings, which is so unusual to our men that came last out of England, that of our 2,500 men, I believe we have 500 sick; then judge what will be the event if money come not speedily.'[68]

Sir Ralph, who was perfectly capable of using his parliamentary influence for his family's benefit when it suited him, was able to be of some help; at the beginning of July Captain Edmund Verney was one of those named in a list of officers to whom the Commons decided to pay arrears after the Scottish campaign. Henry, who was still in the Low Countries, also benefited from Sir Ralph's intervention that summer. At the end of May Parliament ordered that 'Sir Ralph Verney shall have Mr. Speaker's warrant to transport one horse into Holland'.[69]

9

I Do Not Like the Quarrel

'*I* am much troubled to see things go as they do,' Aunt Eure wrote in August 1642. 'It will bring us all to ruin; neither papist, nor puritan, aye nor protestant but will be the losers by it.'[1]

The fear of war in England had been growing among the Verney clan, as it had throughout the country, since the King's attempt to arrest the Five Members at the beginning of the year. No one wanted it; no one seemed able to stop it. Up in Yorkshire, where she and her children were living with the Royalist Eure family, Margaret imagined the beat of distant drums whenever a door creaked, and wished with all her heart for the arrival of a Parliamentary delegation 'with the olive branch in its mouth, it would refresh and glad all our hearts here in the north'.[2] Eleanor Sussex, an ardent supporter of Parliament and Protestantism, told Sir Ralph on 29 January 1642, 'I pray God there may be agreement betwixt the King and his people'.[3]

Two days later, Sir John Hotham, at the head of one of the Yorkshire trained bands, occupied Hull for Parliament and took possession of its arsenal, the most substantial store of munitions in the north of England. Charles had removed his court from London to the more hospitable surroundings of York, and he arrived with a troop of cavalry at the gates of Hull in April. Hotham wouldn't let him in.

Over the spring and early summer both sides tried with less and less subtlety to rally support and arms for their causes. In a prolonged exercise in brinkmanship, both were coming to believe that armed force – or, at least, the realistic threat of armed force – was the only way to resolve the standoff. The Militia Ordinance, which effectively transferred control of the armed forces from the King to Parliament, was passed by Lords and Commons in March 1642, after Parliament decided the royal assent was no longer required for legislation. Not to be outdone, three months later Charles I resurrected the Commissions of Array, an obsolete device whereby the King could nominate gentry in every county and empower them to raise troops for his service. This was effectively a call to arms, and a thinly disguised declaration of war. There was an unedifying scramble to hide valuables, so as to avoid embarrassment if one side or another asked for donations to the war effort. 'I have put up my plate, and say it is sold,' confessed Eleanor Sussex.[4]

Confused and intimidated by commands to attend both royal and parliamentary musters, some men made themselves scarce and hoped the war would go away. There were brawls as one side or the other attempted to take control of a militia or commandeer the contents of a town magazine. At the end of June a group of Royalists met with heated opposition in Leicester when they tried to muster the trained bands; the only thing which stopped them from opening fire on local leaders was the weather, in the shape of a sudden downpour which extinguished the slow matches of the musketeers. (The Royalist Henry Hastings then held his pistol to the head of a Parliamentarian captain and pulled the trigger, but the gun was also too wet to fire.) A few weeks later, street fighting in Manchester between rival groups led to the death of a linen weaver named Richard Perceval, traditionally said to be the first casualty of the English Civil War.

On 1 August there was a bloodier skirmish at Shepton Mallet in Somerset, when twenty-seven men died. And a week later, a troop of Royalist cavalry led by a Captain John Smith rode into a Northamptonshire village at dawn looking for weapons, only to come face to face with a crowd of hostile locals. They asked a man whom he was for, and when he answered 'For the King and Parliament' they shot him dead. His friend protested, and he was slashed and shot. In the fire fight that followed, three or four more villagers were killed. 'It is strange to note how we have insensible slid into the beginnings of a civil war,' Bulstrode Whitelocke told his wife. 'From paper combats, by declarations, remonstrances, protestations, votes, messages, answers and replies, we are now come to the question of raising forces.'[5]

From February to the end of July 1642 Sir Edmund spent most of his time in London, where he was trying to arrange a marriage for his daughter Cary. Although she was only fifteen, with three older sisters still unwed, in the autumn of 1641 Cary had been suggested as a possible bride for Thomas Gardiner, a young captain of horse from Cuddesdon in Oxfordshire. His father, also Thomas, was a prominent pro-Royalist lawyer and the Recorder of London, 'a man of gravity and quickness that had somewhat of authority and gracefulness in person and presence' according to Clarendon.[6] Sir Thomas had been Charles I's first choice as Speaker of the House of Commons in the current parliament, but much to the King's chagrin (and his own) all of the four City of London seats had gone to opposition candidates, leaving him out of the Commons. Cary liked Captain Gardiner well enough; and the widowed and worried Sir Edmund wasn't about to pass up the chance to hand on the expense of providing for one of his six daughters. But the situation was complicated in the spring when Sir Thomas Gardiner was impeached for his part in opposing parliamentary control over the trained bands and asserting that citizens would be legally bound to support the King if he called on them, among other things. Sir Ralph, who was in the House when the charges were read, duly noted them down: the Recorder 'endeavoured to hinder the calling this Parliament, and now to destroy it . . . he pressed payment of ship money, and being told it was against the law, he said, "We shall find a law for it ere long" . . . He said, every man was bound by his allegiance to serve the King, and no charter could excuse them.'[7]

Marriage negotiations were already at an advanced stage – Eleanor Sussex declared rather disingenuously she was sure Sir Edmund would have called a halt to the match if they hadn't been – and the wedding went ahead. By the end of July, Cary was with her husband's family at Cuddesdon, and happily settling into the Gardiner clan. Thomas's grandmother was now 'my grandmother', his sisters were 'my sisters', while 'Sir Thomas and my lady bid me very welcome to Cuddesdon and said they wished it might be my own'.[8] Captain Gardiner was their eldest son, so the expectation – and the reason behind the cordial reception – was that one day it would be. Cary's task now was to produce an heir.

The couple didn't have much time together. 'I am neither Puritan nor Roundhead,' Gardiner told Mary Verney soon after the marriage; and within weeks of Cary's arrival at Cuddesdon her husband had left her to join the King's army at York.[9] 'He is 200 miles distance from me,' she wrote desolately to Sir Ralph. 'Think what a trouble it is to me which has so good a husband.'[10]

Although neither side had actually declared war, people were preparing in earnest. Sir Edmund continued to sit in Parliament as though nothing had happened, not as a particularly active MP, but as one who was playing his usual minor role in the workings of Parliament. He sat on the occasional committee, took messages from the Commons to the Lords, brought back their Lordships' replies. In June he formed part of a parliamentary delegation sent to wait on the French ambassador.

All the while he was preparing for the coming conflict. From Covent Garden he sent to Claydon for Will Roades to get his horses ready, and to send him arms and armour. Sir Ralph, who also remained in the London house – and was rather more active in parliamentary affairs – also wrote, asking Roades for pistols: 'my father tells me there is a pair that have white stocks, and part of the locks are blue, and they are very light'. He wanted them brought to London, together with bullet moulds 'and other implements belonging to them'.[11]

Soldiers were on the move everywhere. Cary, who was quick to imbibe the views of her Royalist in-laws at Cuddesdon, was outraged at the behaviour of Parliamentarian troops passing through Oxford, who were rumoured to have pillaged most of the colleges, 'and say when they have done they will see what pillage the country has'.[12] Cuddesdon was only five miles from Oxford, and, considering Sir Thomas Gardiner's reputation, Cary was understandably frightened for the future of her husband's family estates – and, indeed, for her own future.* At Claydon, Sir Edmund ordered Roades to arm himself, and to have carbines, bullets and powder at the ready: 'for I fear a time may come when rogues may look for booty in such houses'.[13] The steward was also to get in any rents and other moneys that were owing. Sir Ralph seconded this, telling Roades to prepare for trouble, to keep doors closed during the day and to have two men on watch in the village at night. These precautions would do 'until the times grow fuller of danger'.[14]

'Until', not 'unless'. By the beginning of August Sir Ralph was in no doubt that war was coming. Nor was Sir Edmund. 'We shall certainly have a great war,' he told Roades.[15]

And in the middle of all this misery there was a greater misery. When King Charles commanded those loyal to him to travel north, Sir Edmund Verney went north. He didn't approve of Charles's behaviour towards Parliament; he had a pathological hatred of Catholicism and believed that Charles had betrayed the Protestant cause in Ireland, but whatever his private feelings, his sense of honour would not allow him to disobey his king. As he told Edward Hyde at the end of August 1642,

> I do not like the quarrel, and do heartily wish that the King would yield and consent to what they desire; so that my conscience is only concerned in honour and gratitude to follow my master. I have eaten his bread and served him near thirty years, and will not do so base a thing as to forsake him; and choose rather to lose my life (which I am sure I shall do) to preserve and defend those things which are against my conscience to preserve and defend.[16]

Most of the family agreed with him. If they differed at all, it was only that *they* had not the slightest doubts about the righteousness of the King's cause. But there was one exception. Sir Ralph, the precious heir, the favourite child – Sir Ralph was for Parliament.

---

* Colonel Arthur Goodwin, whose men were causing Cary so much anxiety, did once confess that 'we are all the most abominable plunderers; I am ashamed to look an honest man in the face' (quoted in Charles Carlton, *Going to the Wars: The Experience of the British Civil Wars, 1638–1651*, 1992, 268).

'Old' Sir Edmund Verney of Pendley.

Long thought to be the only surviving
portrait of the Barbary Coast buccaneer
Sir Francis Verney, this is more likely
to date from the 1620s, and to show
his half-brother Sir Edmund.

The north front of
Claydon House as it was
in the seventeenth century.

Van Dyck's portrait of Sir Edmund Verney, knight-marshal of the King's household and, for the last two months of his life, standard-bearer to Charles I.

Margaret Denton of Hillesden, wife of Sir Edmund Verney. Lady Margaret was sensitive about exposing her scarred left arm, which makes this portrayal of her particularly intriguing.

Barbados, 'the best and healthfullest in all the western isles',
according to Tom Verney, who went there to seek his fortune in 1639.

A defendant kneels at the bar of the Commons. Only 60 feet by 30 feet, St Stephen's Chapel
could be rather crowded on those occasions when all 493 MPs decided to put in an appearance.

The Battle of Edgehill, 23 October 1642. This is a slightly fanciful depiction by the Flemish engraver Michael van der Gucht, who wasn't born at the time.

Sir Edmund Verney's ring, containing a miniature of Charles I.

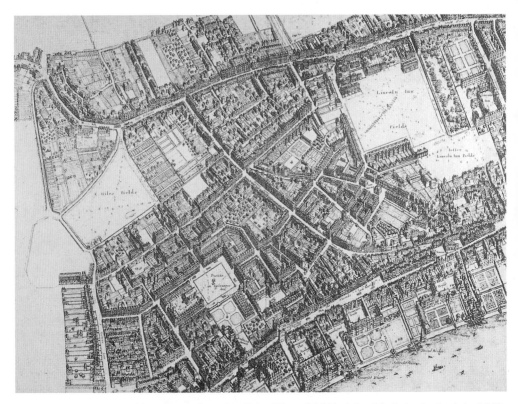

The western suburbs of London before the Great Fire of 1666. After his father's death in 1642, Sir Ralph Verney gave up the family's Covent Garden house and took a more economical establishment in Lincoln's Inn Fields.

The Siege of Drogheda, September 1642. More than 3,000 soldiers and civilians were killed when Cromwell's soldiers stormed the town. Mun Verney was one of the casualties.

His reasons were clear enough, and in other circumstances Sir Edmund would have applauded them. He wanted peace, he said, and he wanted 'our liberties'. Without peace there could be no hope of enjoying those liberties; but until the King confirmed the liberties, Sir Ralph couldn't bring himself to hope for peace. 'Both these together may make us all happy, but one without the other I must confess can never satisfy me.'[17] So when Sir Edmund went to join the King's army in Yorkshire, Sir Ralph stayed behind, grappling with his own moral qualms and fending off the anger of the entire family.

Things grew much worse after Monday 22 August 1642, the day on which King Charles declared war. Accompanied by a group of nobles, including his knight-marshal, the King rode into Nottingham Castle that evening and watched as a huge royal banner, 'much of the fashion of the City streamers used at the Lord Mayor's show', was unfurled from the highest tower of the castle. As the bright red pennant fluttered in the wind, bearing the royal arms with a hand pointing to the crown and the motto 'Give unto Caesar his due', a herald-at-arms read a proclamation setting out the King's reasons for raising the standard, namely 'to suppress the pretended rebellion of the Earl of Essex in raising forces against him, to which he required the aid and assistance of all his loving subjects'.[18] (Essex had been appointed Captain General of the Parliamentary forces the previous month.) And Charles I conferred on Sir Edmund Verney the title of Standard Bearer. The King was not particularly responsive to the feelings of his courtiers – otherwise one would say that this was an astute political manoeuvre, intended to confirm a waverer's loyalty. But unwittingly or not, he achieved exactly that result. The honour conferred on Sir Edmund may not have dispelled his doubts about the righteousness of the King's cause, but it strengthened his determination to remain loyal.

The standard-raising ceremony wasn't a wild success. The King insisted on making last-minute changes to the proclamation, and with all the crossings-out and amendments the herald couldn't read it properly. Then there was the unpalatable fact that while the assembled crowds dutifully threw their hats in the air and shouted 'God save the King!', they showed a marked reluctance to step forward and volunteer for military service. That night the standard blew down.

A couple of days later the drums and trumpets sounded again as the ritual was repeated, this time on a hill just outside the castle walls. When the herald announced the appointment of a standard-bearer, Sir Edmund stepped forward and declared to the crowd 'that they that would wrest that standard from his hand, must first wrest his soul from his body'.[19] At the same moment, 120 miles away in London, his eldest son stood up in St Stephen's Chapel and swore in a loud voice that he supported the Earl of Essex as Captain General of the Parliamentary army, and that he would maintain and assist him with his life and his estate.

The declaration of war sharpened the divisions within the Verney clan. They weren't the only family to be separated by ideology and loyalty, of course: 'parents and children, brothers, kindred, aye and dear friends have the seed of difference and division abundantly sowed in them.'[20] But the Royalist majority was relentless in the way it piled the pressure on Sir Ralph – and on his wife Mary, who admitted she 'never had more cause to be sad than now'.[21] At the beginning of September she received a vicious letter, ostensibly from Cary Gardiner at Cuddesdon. Not in her hand and probably written by one of the Gardiner in-laws, it called Sir Ralph a traitor for supporting Parliament, and went on to suggest that since he couldn't possibly believe in the justness of his cause, he must be hedging his bets: 'indeed, the world now accounts it policy for the father to be on one side and the son on th'other'.[22] As soon as she received the letter Mary sat down and wrote straight back, defending Sir Ralph's integrity and telling her sister-in-law she did not believe her to have written such a letter. 'If I knew whose it was I would tell you what I think of it.'[23]

But now Mary's Covent Garden neighbour Anne Sydenham, who was with the King's army in the Midlands, wrote a more subtle appeal for Sir Ralph's conversion. Anne and her husband Sir Edward, who had just taken Doll Leeke into their household, were good friends to all the Verneys, and Anne was particularly close to Mary, who confided that Sir Ralph was having problems reconciling his conscience and the duty he owed his family. After assuring Mary that she had no doubts about Sir Ralph's sincerity in siding with Parliament, Lady Anne went on to ask if he really understood the situation adequately:

Truly, my heart, it staggers me that he should not see clearly all their ways, being it is so apparent, for how 'tis for the liberty of the subject to take all from them which are not of their mind, and to pull down their houses, and imprison them, and leave them to the mercy of the unruly multitude – I cannot find that this is the liberty of the subject. Nor do I find that it is in God's law to take arms against their lawful king to depose him.[24]

Then, in a seemingly innocuous aside which contrived to remind Mary of the danger in which her husband's side had placed her father-in-law, while at the same time consigning Sir Ralph to eternal damnation, she sweetly said, 'My dear, if any of my friends fall in this quarrel I trust their souls will be happy, for sure 'tis lawful to fight for one's lawful king.'[25]

Doll Leeke joined in the campaign to convert Sir Ralph, with a plaintive directness which is more appealing than Lady Sydenham's elegant barbs. Referring to the King's recruiting drive, she told Mary that 'I for my part wish for no more men but your husband, and I do so heartily desire him that I dream of nothing else. I am confident that he will come. I pray tell him so . . .'[26] In her reply (which doesn't survive) Mary seems to have talked about how unhappy she was at the prospect of a war in which she would be the loser whichever side won. Doll's response was honest, but not comforting: she said that if the King was victorious, Sir Edmund would surely protect Sir Ralph; and if Parliament won, there would be no need for Mary to worry about her father-in-law, because he 'will hardly come off with his life'.[27]

Throughout their marriage Mary was always fiercely protective of her husband, and we don't know to what extent she kept these exchanges from him. But it didn't really matter: he was in any case thoroughly miserable by now, and increasingly isolated. Cary's husband, Thomas Gardiner, was a captain in the King's service. Aunt Margaret's papist husband, William Eure, was about to re-enter the army after Charles I, who needed all the friends he could get, discarded a parliamentary ban on Catholics serving in the military. At Hillesden, Sir Ralph's uncle, Sir Alexander Denton, looked like coming out for the King. So did his son, Sir Ralph's cousin. Brother Henry was with Queen Henrietta Maria in The Hague; when she returned to England in February 1643 he would come with her, taking up a commission which Sir Edward Sydenham obtained for him as major of horse in the Royalist army. Tom joined up on the King's side towards the end of 1642, bombarding Sir Ralph with patronising and self-righteous letters. 'I did always maintain that true Protestant religion which my father bred and brought me up in; next the King's prerogative, then the liberty of the subject, and last of all the just privileges of Parliament.'[28] And could Sir Ralph lend him £10?

Mun – easy-going, cheery Mun – took the news of Sir Ralph's defection the hardest of all. His company was fighting beyond the Pale when the King raised his standard at Nottingham, and he didn't hear about Sir Ralph until he returned to Dublin in September. When he did, he sent a sharp rebuke:

> Brother, what I feared is proved too true, which is your being against the King. Give me leave to tell you in my opinion 'tis most unhandsomely done, and it grieves my heart to think that my father already and I, who so dearly love and esteem you, should be bound in conscience (because in duty to our King) to be your enemy. I hear 'tis a great grief to my father. I beseech you consider that majesty is sacred; God saith, 'Touch not mine anointed'. It troubled David that he cut but the lap of Saul's garment. I believe ye will all say ye intend not to hurt the King, but can any of ye warrant any one shot to say it shall not endanger his person? I am so much troubled to think of your being of the side you are that I can write no more, only I shall pray for peace with all my heart, but if God grant not that, yet that He will be pleased to turn your heart that you may so express your duty to your King that my father may still have cause to rejoice in you.[29]

Sir Ralph was so upset and guilt-ridden that he refused to defend himself to Mun. He refused to explain himself; he refused to reply. He simply ignored the letter and cut his brother out of his life.

The deepest hurt was caused not by Mun's sermonising, but by Sir Ralph's rift with Sir Edmund. These two men, who loved each other so dearly, stopped speaking when, soon after the raising of the standard, Sir Edmund wrote and told Sir Ralph how unhappy he was about his son's choice of sides. The letter hasn't survived: Sir Ralph sent a copy to Eleanor Sussex at Gorhambury, who burned it as soon as she had read it and begged Sir Ralph 'not to write passionately to your father, but overcome him with kindness'.[30] Eleanor acted as a mother-confessor and intermediary. When Sir Edmund sent her a letter in the second week of September, she reported its contents to Sir Ralph gently, but honestly. 'His word was this of you,' she told Sir Ralph: '"Madam, he hath ever lain near my heart and truly he is there still."' However she didn't hide how angry and sad he was, and how troubled that Sir Ralph had declared for Parliament. '[He] said he had many afflictions upon him, and that you had used him unkindly.'[31]

Eleanor was full of good advice and calm common sense. Perhaps Sir Ralph's father was publicising his displeasure with his son to keep the King happy. Perhaps, considering the Royalist war effort was not going so well, his obvious melancholy was caused by other anxieties 'besides the difference betwixt you'. The important thing was not to worry too much, and to remember that if it pleased God to return Sir Edmund after the war was over, he and Sir Ralph would undoubtedly be reconciled in a moment. When the young man fretted that his so-called friends in the Royalist camp might encourage his father's antagonism for their own ends, she was full of sympathy: if Lady Sydenham, Doll Leeke and the others weren't doing all they could to heal the rift, 'they are the most vile unworthy people'.[32]

Along with the advice came the reassurance that Sir Ralph was doing the right thing. Although she certainly didn't look forward to war, Eleanor was never in any doubt as to which army had God on its side. Alone among Sir Ralph and Mary's close friends and family, she took their support for Parliament as a given, reminding Sir Ralph that no matter what Sir Edmund thought about his politics, as a good Protestant he had to respect his son for following his conscience. 'If you had failed in anything of duty or love to him it had been some just case of exception; but in going the way your conscience tells you to be right, I hope he hath more goodness and religion than to continue in displeasure with you for it.'[33]

★   ★   ★

The commencement of hostilities, when it finally happened, was more farce than ferocity. On 2 September 1642, 7000 Parliamentarian soldiers commanded by the Earl of Bedford briefly laid siege to Sherborne Castle in Dorset; but when the defenders fired at them, they ran away. Then the Parliamentarian colonel Sir William Waller mounted an assault on Southsea Castle near Portsmouth; the Royalist governor of the castle was so drunk that he had taken to his bed and when his men managed to wake him, he promptly decided to change sides. Later that week the King's nephew Prince Rupert, who had arrived from Europe in August with his brother Maurice and a group of English and Scottish veterans, sent word to the people of Leicester that he would sack their town unless they paid him £2000. Although this was standard behaviour for Thirty Years War mercenaries like Rupert, it didn't go down well with Leicester, whose citizens offered £500 and complained to King Charles.

The first real skirmish took place at Powick Bridge outside Worcester a fortnight later, when Prince Rupert and around a thousand cavalry confronted a similar number of Parliamentarian horse commanded by Colonel Nat Fiennes, the son of Lord Saye and Sele. Fiennes' men were trying to intercept a Royalist treasure convoy (consisting largely of silver plundered from Oxford colleges). They were too late – the convoy had already gone to join the King at Shrewsbury, leaving Rupert to defend its rear – and as Fiennes and his dragoons tried to cross the River Teme to enter Worcester from the south, Rupert's men charged them down, killing around 150 and putting the rest to flight before following the convoy north. The main Parliamentary force under the Earl of Essex occupied Worcester the next day. Although Powick Bridge was a minor action, it was significant for the way in which it boosted Royalist morale and established Rupert's reputation as a daring and impetuous cavalry commander.

Sir Edmund Verney was with the King throughout September and the first weeks of October, bearing a standard which was presumably rather more practical than the massive banner which had been raised at Nottingham. And he was with Charles's army when it left Shrewsbury on 12 October, heading for London and using the standard to attract recruits along the way.

A week later the Earl of Essex left Worcester in search of the King. The pursuit was cumbersome and slightly comical: the Earl of Clarendon later recalled that although both armies 'marched the same way, they gave not the least disquiet . . . to each other; and in truth, as it appeared afterwards, neither army knew where the other was'.[34] On Saturday 22 October the Royalists held a rendezvous and council of war at Edgecote, a Northamptonshire hamlet about seven miles north of Banbury (and still some seventy-five miles away from London). After deciding that a small force should try to take Banbury the next day while the King and the main body of the army rested, the council disbanded and everyone marched off to their quarters for the night. The King stayed at Sir William Chauncey's house in Edgecote, and Sir Edmund, who was serving with the King's Life Guards, lodged nearby. The Lord General, the Earl of Lindsey, put up a couple of miles away at a place called Culworth. Prince Rupert, General of the Horse, decided to lodge in the village of Wormleighton, five miles to the north.

Rupert arrived in Wormleighton that evening and rode straight into a party of Parliamentarian quartermasters who had been sent by the Earl of Essex to find billets for his own troops. The Prince's cavalry quickly took them all prisoner, and he sent a patrol to reconnoitre the surrounding area. That patrol came back to report that the Parliamentarian army was camped at Kineton, seven miles west, and at midnight he sent word to Charles I that the enemy were heading for Banbury. His advice was to move south to intercept them at a little ridge known locally as the Edgehill. At four on Sunday morning Charles replied to his nephew: 'I have given order as you have desired; so I doubt not but all the foot and cannon will be at Edgehill betimes this morning.'[35]

In fact it wasn't until two o'clock on Sunday afternoon – 'as fair a day as that season of the year could yield, the sun clear, no wind or cloud appearing'[36] – that the two forces finally faced each other across a tract of open countryside between Kineton and Edgehill. They were pretty evenly matched, with around 13,500 men each. Charles I held the higher ground on the ridge – an advantage which was all but cancelled out when his commanders spent the morning bickering over precedence and tactics. The mounted Life Guards, who were supposed to act as a reserve, took umbrage after someone called them 'the Troop of Show', and they insisted on taking up a position in Rupert's front line, leaving the King and the senior officers, including Sir Edmund Verney and the royal standard, protected only by a small body of foot guards and an escort of fifty Gentleman-Pensioners. Then Charles overruled the Earl of Lindsey's preference for a simple battle formation derived from the Dutch, and opted instead for one favoured by Prince Rupert and known as 'the Swedish Brigade' – whereupon his Lord General resigned on the spot and stormed off to stand with his own regiment of foot, which 'he desir'd might be placed opposite to that of the Earl of Essex, hoping thereby that he might engage him personally'.[37]

Realising that Essex had no intention of trying to storm the ridge, Charles moved his army down towards the Parliamentarian forces, drawing his five infantry brigades up in the centre of the field, with Prince Rupert in charge of 1700 cavalry on the right wing, and Lord Henry Wilmot on the left with just over 1000. By this time the King's army was only about 800 yards away from their enemy. Sir Edmund, who had breakfasted with the King at Edgecote that morning, carried the standard high as Charles, wearing a black velvet cloak over his armour, rode up and down the ranks encouraging his men: 'Your King bids you be courageous, and Heaven make you victorious.'[38] Unlike his King, Sir Edmund had decided that he was not going to wear any protective armour in battle, or even a heavy buff coat. We'll never know why.

Across the fields, the sight and sound of the Royalists cheering their King led Essex to give the order to open fire with his artillery, and for up to an hour both sides bombarded each other's lines, to little effect. Then, over on the Royalists' right wing, a solitary Parliamentarian horseman emerged through the pall of smoke which enveloped the battlefield and galloped right up to Prince Rupert, tearing off his orange scarf and announcing that his commander, Sir Faithfull Fortescue, intended to defect to the Royalists with his entire troop.

Fortescue – faithful by name but not by nature – duly brought his men over to the King's side. They discharged their pistols into the ground as they did so; and at this Rupert told his men to advance. He had given orders that they should keep ranks 'with sword in hand, to receive the enemy's shot, without firing either carbine or pistol, till we broke in amongst the enemy, and then to make use of our firearms as need should require'; and his men observed those orders to the letter.[39] They moved at a trot, a canter; and then, after the Parliamentarian cavalry facing them lost their nerve and discharged their carbines while they were still out of range, they broke into a gallop, drove straight through Essex's left wing – and kept going. Members of Fortescue's troop who hadn't been quick enough to remove their orange colours were cut down by their new allies along with the rest. The Royalists' second line, commanded by Sir John Byron, decided there was nothing more to be done except follow on behind; they 'could not be contained by their commanders, but with spurs and loose reins followed the chase'.[40] That chase continued into Kineton village, where Rupert's men got down to the serious business of looting Essex's baggage train.

Rupert's charge was mirrored on the left wing, more or less, by Lord Wilmot's horse. They too broke through the enemy lines; they too rode on to loot Kineton. In the centre, 10,500 Royalist pikemen and musketeers infantry advanced on the remaining Parliamentarian foot brigades, about 6400 strong. Both sides were at push of pike, the bristling hedgehogs of men shoving and jabbing at each other while their musketeers fired almost point-blank into the enemy's ranks.

The battle seemed to be going the King's way, although Essex's infantry were less easy to break than his cavalry. 'The foot of both sides stood their ground with great courage,' wrote Clarendon; '. . . and the execution was great on both sides.'[41] But Essex had kept back a reserve force of cavalry, which was led by Sir William Balfour; and seeing that Rupert and Wilmot were no longer in the field, Balfour launched a devastating charge at the Royalists' left flank, breaking through and pressing on towards the King's position and the main Royalist battery. Charles, who had been watching the battle from a piece of rising ground, marched down to urge his men on, 'thereby to prevent their entire defeat', having first ordered that the thirteen-year-old Prince Charles and his ten-year-old brother James should be taken further

off out of danger.* One of the King's footmen was shot in the
face by his side. In the thick of the fighting the Earl of Lindsey,
who at one point had been within pistol shot of the Earl of
Essex – 'which was the thing he most desired in the world',
according to Clarendon[42] – went down, his leg smashed by a
musket ball. Although his son, Lord Willoughby of Eresby, stood
astride his wounded father brandishing a pike in a desperate
attempt to keep the enemy back, both men were eventually taken.
Lindsey blamed his own inexperienced soldiers for his capture,
declaring that he would never take the field with boys again.
Nor would he – he died of his wound the next day.

In the aftermath of Balfour's charge Sir Edmund Verney became
involved in some vicious hand-to-hand fighting with Parliamentarian
soldiers from Sir William Constable's regiment of foot. Constable's
blue-coats were pouring up the hill through the gap made by
Balfour's cavalry, making straight for the Royalist cannon – and the
King's standard. Sir Edmund held his ground as, surrounded by
screaming men and powder smoke, his personal servant was killed
at his side by one of the blue-coats. He killed the man with his
own hands, and, still without armour or buff coat, managed to
account for at least one more of the enemy, wielding the standard
as a pike and breaking off its point in the man's body.

Then he went down.

The mythologising which enveloped Sir Edmund's death over
the following months makes it hard to piece together exactly
what happened next. His body was never found; according to an
old Verney legend, the soldiers were unable to prise the standard
from his cold, dead hand, so they duly hacked off the hand and
carried it away with them. (It seems to have been returned to
Claydon, however, since the ring given to Sir Edmund by Charles
I, containing the King's miniature, is still at the house.) His ghost,

---

* Charles told the Duke of Richmond to accompany the boys, but the Duke refused
to walk away from the fight. Then he commanded the Earl of Dorset to take them,
only for the Earl to swear 'that he would not be thought a coward for the sake of
any King's son in Christendom'. In the end the King gave 'an absolute command'
to Sir William Howard, the commander of his personal guard (J.S. Clarke, ed.,
The life of James II, collected out of memoirs writ of his own hand (1816), I, 15).

which within weeks was seen wandering the battlefield, also walked in the woods at Claydon – and occasionally in the house itself – searching for the lost hand. By the eighteenth century the story was that he had stormed right into the middle of the enemy's ranks, waving the standard high and urging the dispirited Royalists to follow him. Surrounded, he was offered his life on condition that he gave up the banner royal. This he could not do, he said. 'His life was his own, but the standard was his and their sovereign's, and he would not deliver it while he lived.'[43] He then single-handedly killed sixteen of his attackers with his sword before they brought him down.

The truth is probably more prosaic, but moving nonetheless. From all we know of Sir Edmund's personal courage and sense of honour, there can be no doubt that he fought hard to keep the standard: 'nor will I think you could wish me to leave anything undone when it falls to my turn to be in action', as he had told Sir Ralph when he went north for the First Bishops' War. But instead of charging down the hill brandishing the banner royal, and then selling his life dear for sixteen of the enemy, he was almost certainly shot by Arthur Young, an ensign in Constable's regiment, during the fighting around the Royalist battery. Young took up the standard – with or without Sir Edmund's hand attached – and carried it back to his own lines, where it was presented to the Earl of Essex and handed over to his secretary, Robert Chambers, for safekeeping.

It didn't remain with the Parliamentarians for long: a Royalist captain, John Smith, rode in among them disguised with an orange scarf and said it was 'unfit that a penman should have the honour to carry the standard'.[44] Thinking he must be one of Essex's officers, the secretary gave it up, and Smith carried it straight back to the King, who knighted him on top of Edgehill the next morning.*

When Sir Edmund fell, the battle was drawing to a close.

---

* Truth is the first casualty of war. This account of Smith's exploits is based on the memoirs of Edmund Ludlow, an officer in Essex's Life Guards. Royalist narratives describe how Smith charged in among the enemy with his rapier drawn, crying 'Traitor, deliver the Standard!' and tell how he stabbed Chambers, ran a cuirassier through and then rode off again, bearing his trophy.

Rupert's cavalry returned to the battlefield, and their arrival checked the Parliamentarian advance. By now it was getting dark, and both sides retired from the field. The next day Essex went back to Warwick, and Charles continued south to Banbury, and then to Oxford. Casualties on both sides amounted to about 1500 dead, with perhaps a similar number badly hurt.

Essex and the King both claimed victory. The first details Londoners heard of the outcome of the battle came from three officers from Essex's brigade, who arrived in the capital the next day, Monday, talking of great losses on Parliament's side and claiming that 'there were not four men or their companies escaped with life besides themselves'.[45] Eleanor Sussex wrote to Sir Ralph from her house in Chelsea, letting him know about the rumours. 'We heard yesterday there was great news come to the parliament, I fear no good; that the armies were met,' she said. 'The lord be merciful.'[46] It soon emerged that the three men weren't well placed to give an accurate account of the fight, since they ran from the field at the first shot and kept on running until they reached London. But more reliable news was coming in. On Tuesday 25 October, a rider from the Earl of Essex arrived at Westminster, having covered the eighty miles from the Parliamentarian camp at Warwick in just over a day. (The Commons voted him a reward of £20.) The man reported the death in battle of the King's knight-marshal; Sir Ralph, sick with fear, sent three messengers off to both armies to try and find out if the story was true.

Eleanor was distraught. 'The most heavy news of your worthy good father's death is come to me, for which I have the saddest heart and deepest wounded soul that ever creature had; he being I confess to you the greatest comfort of my life. I pray God fit me for another, for I am sure I shall never had more joy in this . . . I am in so miserable a condition that I cannot express my thoughts. My eyes are so full that I cannot say no more.'[47] Her main thought was that she wanted to be with Sir Ralph, even though the etiquette of mourning dictated that social visits were inappropriate. She begged to be allowed to see Sir Ralph before she left for Gorhambury the following week, 'for you are all the joy I have left me now'.[48]

Sir Ralph, who had avoided telling Eleanor about his father

until he knew the worst, wrote a misery-filled little note back to her. There was still no absolute certainty of Sir Edmund's death, he wrote, but he held out no hope for his father's survival; he would know more when his servants returned from the battle-field at the weekend. And he was eager to be with Eleanor, so long as there was no one else present. Now there were none of the eloquent and self-consciously literary phrases he had used when his mother died. 'I will not add to your grief by relating my own deplorable condition, neither can my pen express the miseries I am in,' he told the Countess. 'God's will be done, and give me patience to support me in this extremity.'[49]

Sir Ralph wrote this to Eleanor on Thursday 27 October. That morning the Commons received an official narrative of the Battle of Edgehill, sent by Sir William Balfour and five other senior officers in Essex's army. (It was compiled close by the battlefield; the Lord General himself had already gone back to Warwick, and was apparently too busy regrouping his army to write.) Although they claimed 'a blessed victory . . . upon the army of the cava-liers', the officers' account was quite even-handed, praising some soldiers on both sides for their gallantry, while noting that others – again on both sides – 'deserve to be hanged, for deserting and betraying, as much as lay in them, their party'. We don't know if Sir Ralph was in the House to hear the report read out, or how his fellow MPs reacted when they were told that 'Sir Edmund Verney who carried the King's Standard was slain by a gentleman of the Lord General's Troop of Horse, who did much other good service that day.'[50]

That same Thursday Sir Edward Sydenham wrote to tell Sir Ralph about his father's death. He explained that the last any of the King's side had heard of Sir Edmund was actually during the battle, when he was seen fighting at push of pike and using the banner royal as a weapon. It was only the following day, when the King sent a herald into Essex's camp, that the news came back he had been killed. 'For all our great victory,' Sydenham said, 'I have had the greatest loss by the death of your noble father that ever any friend did.'[51]

Sir Ralph was left to struggle with the reality of his father's death, the aching knowledge that Sir Edmund had been estranged from him during the last months of his life, and the terrible truth that the cause Sir Ralph had embraced with such high principle had killed the man he loved best in the world.

There was more pain to come. One of the servants he despatched to the Midlands came back on Sunday night, a week after the battle, with news from the Earl of Essex's army. There was no possibility of finding his father's body. The servant had asked twenty or more Parliamentarian nobles who had known his father personally, including the Lord General himself; no one had seen or heard of the corpse. Then the servant went round the entire district, going from church to church and questioning clergymen in the hope that one of them might remember burying such an illustrious man of quality. None did. Large numbers of the fallen were stripped, robbed and buried in the fields where they lay; and many of those who were given a Christian burial in one of the local churchyards had nothing to identify them. 'I am in every way unhappy,' Sir Ralph confided to Eleanor.[52] 'God's will must be done in all things,' she replied, wishing Sir Edmund might have had a decent burial at Claydon, but comforting Sir Ralph with the thought that his father was beyond caring about such things. 'I hope he is blessed and happy.'[53]

Part 2
Ralph and Mary

10

A Strange Cruelty

On the last Sunday night of 1643 an unhappy little family group stood shivering on the ice-cold quay at Rotterdam, still reeling from their hellish voyage. They had left England two days earlier, and endured rolling waves and a twelve-hour storm in the North Sea before finally arriving in the calmer waters of the Maas. Now, wrapped in furs against the bitter December winds and surrounded by piles of parcels and trunks, they waited in the dark while an agent arranged accommodation for them. Their papers said they were Mr Ralph Smith and his wife, accompanied by their two small children and two servants. Their friends and relatives knew they were the Verneys in exile. Their hearts told them they were strangers and afraid.

Things had gone from bad to worse for Sir Ralph in the fourteen months since Sir Edmund's death at Edgehill. When he took stock of his financial situation at the end of 1642, he discovered his father had left him in serious trouble. In spite of the drastic steps Sir Edmund had taken to rescue the family fortunes – mortgaging Claydon to Francis Drake and borrowing £1000 from

Aunt Isham, selling estate rental to Sir Ralph for £4000 and consolidating his sporadic marshal's income into regular payments from the alnage – he had still been borrowing heavily to stay afloat, and his legacy to Sir Ralph was a raft of debt amounting to close on £9000. Half of the estate income which now belonged to the new head of the family went straight into servicing this debt; and in addition, Sir Ralph had to find money to pay the annuities which Sir Edmund had so thoughtfully left in his will. Thomas had £40 a year, payable quarterly; Henry had £30 a year. Mun and the girls were bequeathed a one-off present of only £5 each, but Sir Edmund had been at pains to point out that this was because they were 'otherwise provided for', presumably by the terms of their mother's will. There were other legacies: £5 a year to be paid to a cousin, son of his uncle Urian; £15 a year to servants; presents of £20 for Doll Leeke, £40 for Sir Ralph's wife Mary, and £20 to Claydon's poor. Sir Ralph was sole executor.*

The situation was bad, but it was retrievable, given some careful long-term management. And Sir Ralph excelled at careful management. He sat down and drew up a schedule of debts – including the Claydon mortgage, which alone cost £500 a year – and he methodically devised strategies for paying them off. Various outlying parcels of land were earmarked for sale. He gave up Covent Garden for an equally fashionable but, one assumes, more economical address in Lincoln's Inn Fields – 'a pretty fine house' only just finished, which stood 'in the middle of the row where the Spanish Ambassador lies'.[1] If he economised for the next six years or so, he and Mary would still have nearly £1000 a year to live on, and this would double when the debts were paid off.

If only there hadn't been a war on. The economic effects of the Civil War were disastrous, especially in hotly contested battlegrounds like north Buckinghamshire. Both sides imposed swingeing taxes on landed families and their tenants, and both did their level best to collect them. Caught in the middle, some of Sir Ralph's tenants adopted the simple expedient of paying up and deducting the money from their rents. Many were, in any

---

* Henry Verney may also have received something from his mother's estate, since his annuity was actually £40 a year.

case, less able to pay those rents. Their crops were destroyed in the fighting; their cattle were stolen; their barns and hayricks were burned. Soldiers were billeted on them with little warning, and they often had to wait years for payment. All over the country landlords were forced to abate the rents due to them by one-third or more; at Claydon, rents dropped to 50 per cent of pre-war levels. To make matters worse, taxation was based on pre-war valuations. In a thirty-month period between October 1643 and March 1646 Parliament raised twenty-four tax levies on Claydon. Sir Ralph, or rather his bailiff, Will Roades, had to find £834, which swallowed up around half of the income from rents.

As a result, Sir Ralph wasn't able to keep up payments to his creditors. Some were initially sympathetic: Aunt Isham, for instance, acknowledged that Sir Ralph would never be able to pay at the normal rate of 8 per cent, and comforted him with the thought that 'it would be a sin in one to receive it, though you should freely offer it'[2] – but their goodwill wore off as they became anxious about the long-term prospects for repayment. The arrears of interest were added to the principal, and Sir Ralph's debts escalated alarmingly. He began to have problems not only in servicing these debts, but even in finding the money for various family annuities. And although by the end of 1643 Susan, Pen and Peg were all in their twenties, the rock-steady £400-a-year charge on the alnage by which Sir Edmund had provided for his daughters simply ceased in the confusion of war.

In the summer of 1643 Scottish Covenanters, worried that an unholy alliance of Ulster Catholics and pro-Royalist Scots in England was about to launch an invasion of Scotland, suggested to the English Parliament they should collaborate in the face of a common enemy. John Pym and the other leaders in the Commons were quick to see the advantages of bringing the armed might of Scotland into the war against the King, and a pact was negotiated with Edinburgh whereby in return for military aid the English Parliament agreed to implement Presbyterianism at home and to help enforce it in Ireland.

Sir Ralph, while still clinging to the political rightness of the Parliamentary cause, was one of those whose Puritanism could countenance bishops, so long as they behaved themselves. He belonged to what was described later that year as 'the moderate zealous Protestants, lovers (though desirous of some amendment) of the Common Prayer Book'.[3] He stopped attending the Commons that summer, while negotiations with the Scots were still in progress over a Covenant for England. The last reference to his presence at Westminster was in June when, ironically enough, he had taken another covenant, engaging with the rest of the House to support the forces raised in support of Parliament. When the final form of the Covenant was fixed, he wrote to inform the Commons that he was resolved 'for a while to retire to some such place, where I may have leisure enough to inform my judgment in high things wherein I am yet doubting'.[4]

Sir Ralph wasn't the only MP to have misgivings about the Scottish alliance and the religious concessions which Pym was prepared to make in order to secure Scottish military intervention. The Solemn League and Covenant was a high-risk strategy for Pym: it alienated the political moderates in the Commons who still hoped for some kind of reconciliation with the King, and it upset the religious moderates like Sir Ralph for whom an exclusively Presbyterian system smacked of fanaticism. (As one exasperated Scot said, 'A presbytery to these people is conceived to be a strange monster.'[5]) The choice pushed some MPs to leave for the King's court at Oxford; Sir Ralph's uncle, Sir Alexander Denton of Hillesden, seems to have gone over to the King's side around now. Others declared they just could not support the abolition of the episcopacy, and asked the House for official leave of absence so that they could take their scruples abroad with them. Army officers refused the Covenant, and were cashiered by their high-minded leaders.

The Royalists, busy forging their own alliance with Irish Catholics, were outraged at the attack on episcopacy. But faced with the prospect of a 20,000-strong Scottish army poised to cross the border and take arms against them, they would be outraged, wouldn't they? The tone of their indignation can be gauged from the opening arguments of an anonymous pamphleteer who railed against 'the impiety and unlawfulness of the new Covenant with the Scots', describing its instigators as 'the contrivers and prosecutors of that monstrous rebellion, which

hath been the deformed and unnatural issue that the hellish copu-
lation of Satan, with this wicked and adulterous generation . . .
hath brought forth'.[6]

Sir Ralph's anxieties over the Covenant were helped along by
the relentless criticism of his relations. Doll Leeke, who was still
with the Sydenhams, wrote a long and painfully frank letter in
August, telling him exactly what she thought of his behaviour,
again. 'I cannot choose but let you know my opinion of your
condition, which I think is so ill that it were want of friendship
in me to conceal it'.[7] Sir Ralph's heart must have sunk when he
read those opening lines. Doll berated him for taking the oath
supporting Parliament's army, predicted that his friends in the
Commons were bound to leave him in the lurch sooner rather
than later, and reminded him that his actions were causing suffering
to his wife and children and brothers and sisters. 'Whatsoever
your conscience has been heretofore, I now believe you see your
error, for it is impossible that you can still continue in so much
blindness'. His only hope was to come over to the King, bringing
plenty of men with him; rumours that he was poised to do so
were already circulating at Oxford. And when he came, as he
surely would, he must be prepared for a less than enthusiastic
welcome, because everyone in the Royalist camp hated him for
what had happened to his father. 'From their love to him proceeds
their hate to you, because you have continued with those that
killed him; this is the speech of many and I confess goes something near me to hear it.'[8]

She ended by urging that if Sir Ralph couldn't bring himself
to change sides, he should at least leave London and the Commons.

What she didn't know was that his thoughts were already
turning in that direction. He no longer attended at Westminster,
but when his absence led to rumours that he had gone over to
the King, he was quick to contradict them. 'Perhaps this my
absence may give occasion to some jealous spirits to suggest (as
formerly they have done) that I am gone to Oxford,' he told his
fellow-MP Sir Robert Reynolds; 'I confess I care not what such
men say, a little time will sufficiently discover those malicious
untruths and shame their authors.'[9]

On Monday 25 September 1643 over a hundred MPs trooped
into St Margaret's Westminster to subscribe to the Solemn League

and Covenant for the Three Kingdoms. All day, in an atmosphere of evangelical fervour, they listened to clergy from both sides of the border leading them in prayer and exhorting them to ever-greater acts of piety. One of the Scots gave 'a thing between a speech and a preach'[10] from his pew, finishing with a particularly dramatic image: 'Were that Covenant now painted upon the wall within the Pope's Palace, it would doubtless put him into Balshazar's quaking condition.'[11] Then the Independent minister Philip Nye climbed into the pulpit and read the Covenant aloud, swearing to preserve the reformed religion in Scotland, to reform religion in England and Ireland, to hunt out malignants and incendiaries and to pursue 'the extirpation of Popery, prelacy (that is, Church government by Archbishops, Bishops, their Chancellors and Commissaries, Deans, Deans and Chapters, Archdeacons, and all other ecclesiastical officers depending on that hierarchy), superstition, heresy, schisms, profaneness, and what-soever shall be found to be contrary to sound doctrine and the power of godliness.'[12] Like the congregation at a revivalist meeting, MPs raised their hands to heaven in unison to signify their assent – a procedure which Royalist critics found particularly uncouth and strange – and then filed into the chancel to set their names on a parchment roll 'with the Covenant entered upon it'.[13]

Over the coming weeks and months, those MPs who hadn't been present at St Margaret's, and who had not deserted to the King at Oxford, were asked, then urged, and finally ordered to take the Covenant. Those whose opposition to the King was primarily ideological, and who might be lukewarm Anglicans rather than zealous Puritans, found themselves in an awkward situation: they knew well enough that the price of Scottish military aid was the complete dismantling of the Church of England. But one by one they came in. Sir Roger Burgoyne signed, so did Sir Peter Temple, and Sir Ralph's cousin Francis Drake. The peers who remained in the House of Lords consented to sign, after a show of reluctance in the middle of October. Determined opponents in the Commons, including two of Sir Ralph's distant kinsmen, Sir Philip Parker and James Fiennes, waged a prolonged rearguard action in Parliament well into the New Year. They informed the Commons 'that some scruples stuck with them insomuch, that, as yet, they cannot take this Covenant'.[14] They went into the country to think things over; they were repeatedly ordered to take the Covenant; they were suspended from the House and threatened with expulsion; and eventually, in February 1644, Parker gave in, held up his hands to heaven and signed his name on the roll of parchment. There is no record in the *Journal of the House of Commons* of James Fiennes ever signing up, although it is fairly safe to assume he did since he remained an active MP.

Sir Ralph did not sign.

This was a brave decision. As brother Henry put it, Sir Ralph's friends did their best to be charitable and impute his actions to scruples of conscience; 'or else, believe it, by the carriage of your business they would account you mad'.[15] (He was more direct with Mun, saying simply that their brother was 'a goose'.) By flouting the orders of Parliament, Sir Ralph risked the sequestration of his estate – that is, the confiscation of the income from his property. The County Committee responsible for local sequestrations might leave a little for the maintenance of his dependants, but they would take all the rest. Worse than this, his refusal to take the Covenant meant he was highly likely to lose his seat in Parliament. A sitting MP could not be imprisoned for debt; but if he lost his parliamentary privilege, there was nothing to keep his clamouring creditors away from his door. By not putting his name to that parchment roll, Sir Ralph risked his good reputation, his family's future, everything he owned.

There are different kinds of heroism. Sir Edmund Verney was the hero of cavalier romance, careless of his personal safety, putting his honour before his life. His eldest son wasn't that kind of man. Fretful and querulous, uncomfortable in the hunting field and frightened at the thought of a battlefield, Sir Ralph always felt keenly just how different he was from his father and his three soldier-brothers. But his stand over the Solemn League and Covenant was breathtaking. It earned him a place in history.

It was typical of the man that in the very moment he threw everything away for a principle, he did it with care and method. He went to stay at Gorhambury with the newly-widowed Eleanor Sussex, whose elderly Earl had finally given up the ghost that July, and he began to prepare for exile. He had deeds drawn up to put his Buckinghamshire estates into the hands of trustees. The trusts, which covered two two-year periods until 1647, were

set up to pay creditors and family annuities, but they also transferred effective ownership of the income from Verney lands, so
that if the sequestrators did come knocking at Claydon, William
Roades would be able to show that the estate income no longer
belonged to Sir Ralph and was thus out of their reach.

Sir Ralph had decided to take his family to Rouen, and Roades
was charged with despatching bundle after bundle of goods from
Claydon up to the house at Lincoln's Inn Fields, from where
they were sent on to France via Amsterdam and Rotterdam.
Finally in November, everything was ready, and Sir Ralph and
Mary took Edmund and Peg over to the east coast, using a safe
conduct obtained from Parliament which required all concerned
'to permit and suffer Mr Ralph Smith and his wife and his man
and maid to pass . . . so they carry nothing of danger'.[16] Their
youngest boy, Jack, was only three years old, and they decided to
leave him behind at Claydon in the care of the housekeeper,
Frances Alcock, and the family nurse, Nan Fudd. Sir Ralph wrote
gloomily to Eleanor Sussex, 'I am now hasting to the ship, which
perhaps may be my grave.'[17]

He needn't have hurried. The family was stuck in Essex for
nearly a month while they waited for fair winds for France.
Several times they boarded a vessel, only for the winter gales to
force them back to shore. 'By which time,' Sir Ralph told Eleanor,
'I spent all my little stock of patience, and then seeing no hopes
of better weather, a ship or two being ready for Holland, I resolved
to come hither.'[18] Which was how they ended up on the quay
at Rotterdam in the last days of the year 1643.

The war coloured everything. In February 1643 Mun had been
hurt in a battle at Rathconnell, Co. Westmeath, when a bullet
hit him in the neck; fortunately it bounced off the collar of his
doublet, and left him with no more than a bad bruise.* His master
the Earl of Ormond negotiated a cease-fire with the Irish rebels

---

* 'At this fight at Roconnell, is to be observed the great hand of God, as this,
the bullet of the enemy hit many of our men, but dropped down without doing
any hurt at all' ('Journal of William Tucker, while in Ireland as Agent for English
Adventurers for Irish lands', in John T. Gilbert (ed.), *History of the Irish Confederation
and the War in Ireland, 1641–1643* (1882), II, 195).

in September, driven by the King's need to bring troops home for his own use; and that autumn Mun duly came back to England to fight for the Royalist cause. 'Though I come with as mortal a dislike to those you wish too well to, as any man that shall come over,' he told Sir Ralph, 'yet I pray be assured that I have as much affection towards you as any friend you have.'[19]

Henry had also joined the Royalist army, having tried and failed to get a place with the King's court at Oxford. But according to the Parliamentarian propagandists, at least, his career in the military was not going well. He had a very public quarrel in an inn with his major; and when the landlord – a friend of the major's – remonstrated with him, Henry apparently shot the man dead. Realising too late that this was a mistake, he deserted and gave himself up to the enemy, spending the autumn of 1643 as a prisoner at Portsmouth while Sir Ralph tried to have him released. He was eventually ransomed for £60, and enlisted once again in the King's army – with a different major, presumably.

Tom's military career was as eventful as his brothers'. Within weeks of joining the Royalist army he was captured at Chichester and ended up in the Fleet prison, from where he wrote furious letters to Sir Ralph demanding money: Lady Sussex wasn't alone when she said, 'I wish he were in the forefront of the next skirmish.'[20] Sir Ralph offered to buy Tom's freedom on condition that he took ship for Barbados again; but Tom refused to go, objecting that he would simply be exchanging one prison for another. He found another solution, in the shape of a wife. When Lady Sussex heard of the match, she leapt to the conclusion that Joyce Verney must be a poor woman of low birth on the principle that this was the only kind of bride Tom would attract.

She missed the point. He needed to get out of gaol, and he couldn't accomplish that with a wife who was either mean or poor. He used Joyce's dowry to buy his freedom, then deserted her and, according to one contemporary news-sheet, 'left his father-in-law in the lurch for him'.[21] When Joyce wrote to Sir Ralph for help, her new brother-in-law was not sympathetic, replying only she should have asked his advice *before* she married Tom; if she had, the match might have been avoided.

It was hard to say in 1643 exactly who was winning the war. Across the country, the fight was exploding into a thousand local feuds and score settlings — vicious little hedge fights and house burnings and lynchings. As far as the broader picture was concerned, the King probably had the best of it, securing half of England and almost the whole of Wales, although in the only big set-piece battle of the year, the Earl of Essex had managed to stall the Royalist advance on London at Newbury. The Parliamentarian cause suffered two important losses. John Hampden died in June 1643, six days after being shot in the shoulder during an action against Prince Rupert's men near Oxford, 'a most infinite loss', Lady Sussex wrote, 'being so religious and very wise a man'.[22] And John Pym, who was already sick with bowel cancer while he was supervising negotiations with the Scots over the Solemn League and Covenant, died on 8 December, six weeks before a Scottish army commanded by the Earl of Leven crossed the Tweed to come to the aid of Parliament.

With the King's headquarters at Oxford, and major Parliamentary garrisons at Aylesbury and Newport Pagnell, the north-west corner of Buckinghamshire which included Claydon and Hillesden was subject to constant raids and 'tax-gathering' expeditions from both sides. Then in January 1644, Hillesden was occupied by Parliamentarian troops. Lady Susan Denton was recently dead. Her son, Sir Alexander Denton, was away fighting for the King. But two of his sisters, Aunt Isham and Susan Denton, were living there, along with his younger children and the Verney girls. The Parliamentarian commander, a half-English, half-Scottish captain named Jeconiah Abercrombie, established himself in the house and issued a series of belligerent proclamations demanding that the locals bring in £40, and threatening that, if they didn't, 'I will come to fetch it, and will not leave you a cock to crow among you.'[23]

A couple of weeks later Abercrombie's men moved out; and soon afterwards Hillesden was occupied by Royalist troops. They were led by Colonel William Smith, a Buckinghamshire lawyer and MP who had taken the Covenant and then deserted the Parliamentarian cause for Oxford and the King. He set about fortifying the house and the little fifteenth-century church of All Saints which stood next door, pressing into service hundreds of men from the surrounding villages and hamlets. His plan was to create a huge system of earthworks, turning Hillesden into a virtually impregnable advance post from which Royalist forces based in Oxford could launch raids into Parliamentarian territory.

While the fortifications were under way, Colonel Smith and his men rustled cattle and stole money and goods from the surrounding farms to provision the garrison. His major, a bad-tempered character named Avignon, had his own troop of French and Walloon horse cavalry and an exaggerated sense of his own importance: he demanded that he and his troopers should have the biggest share of the loot, and imprisoned any soldier who disagreed with him. This caused a mutiny among the men at Hillesden, and Avignon was forced to backtrack rather hastily. In the meantime, an angry farmer – a tenant of Sir Alexander's relations the Hampdens – arrived on the doorstep to complain about the disappearance of his stock. He was told it would cost him a fine of £80 to get them back. So he went over to the Parliamentarian garrison at Aylesbury and demanded double that figure as compensation.

This stirred the garrison into action. At nine o'clock on the morning of Wednesday 28 February, the day of Buckingham Fair, a force of about 300 Roundhead dragoons rode up to Hillesden, hoping to take Smith's men by surprise and storm the house. Although the fortifications were nowhere near complete, the Royalists mounted a robust defence and, after exchanging a few shots and firing a barn and two cottages, the dragoons went back to Aylesbury.

But the episode brought Hillesden to the notice of Sir Samuel Luke, the governor of the garrison at Newport Pagnell, and he decided to organise a more serious assault on the house. Hearing that something was in the air, Sir Alexander Denton arrived home on Sunday 3 March, intending to evacuate his family and the Verney girls.

He was too late. The next morning he woke up to find the house surrounded by the enemy. One group of Roundheads had come over from Newport Pagnell with Luke; they had been joined by another contingent from Buckingham, led by Oliver Cromwell. Colonel Cromwell's force had camped at Claydon the previous night, before moving down to rendezvous with Luke's men and encircle Hillesden at dawn.

Although the house belonged to Sir Alexander, Colonel Smith was the garrison commander. He had at his disposal 263 men, including Avignon's Walloons and Tom Verney, who had come over from Claydon to see his sisters and been inadvertently caught up in the action, and five small artillery pieces, which he placed in the church. There was also a rather dangerous sounding cannon which his men had put together themselves – its barrel was a piece of elm bound with iron.

Smith didn't have much hope of holding out against Cromwell's force, and he knew it. His fortifications still weren't finished – the trenches were only knee-deep in places – and the perimeter was just too extensive for him to defend. While the women and children waited in one of the inner rooms and his troops manned their posts at the windows and on the earthworks, he sent out a messenger to treat with Luke and Cromwell. The man came back with the news that unconditional surrender was the only offer the enemy would accept. Smith refused, and the shooting started. It didn't last for long. The Parliamentarians stormed the trenches and pushed Smith's soldiers back towards All Saints'. Within minutes, the little medieval church had been overrun by Cromwell's troops, and Smith surrendered on promise of quarter. Cromwell and Luke ordered a thorough search of the house. The soldiers found money hidden behind some wainscoting in one of the rooms, and more up in the roof space under the leads. Shortly afterwards news reached them that a Royalist relief force was on its way from Oxford, so they set fire to the house and barns and beat a strategic retreat back to their bases at Newport Pagnell and Buckingham.

Sir Alexander and Colonel Smith were well-known figures on the Royalist side and, as MPs who had signed the Covenant and then gone over to the King at quite a late stage, they were both regarded with particular contempt by the Parliamentarians. It was only six weeks since Sir Alexander had been 'discharged and disabled for sitting, or being any longer [a Member] of this House, during this Parliament, for deserting the service of the House, and being in the King's Quarters, and adhering to that Party'.* As a result the taking of Hillesden was widely reported in the newsletters of the

---

* *Journal of the House of Commons* 3, 22 January 1644. Smith had been disabled six days earlier 'for deserting the Service of the Parliament, and going to Oxford, and continuing there in the Enemies Quarters' (*Journal of the House of Commons* 3, 16 January 1644).

day. The *Scotish Dove* said that Cromwell stormed the house, and offered quarter to those inside; the offer was accepted, but two of his men were killed as they moved in after the surrender, so he gave permission 'to put them to the sword that were refractory'. More than eighty French and Walloons in the garrison were killed.[24] *Mercurius Civicus* repeated the story about the French and Walloons, saying they 'peremptorily refused quarter' but claiming that only thirty were killed. *Mercurius Civicus* also noted with some disappointment that 'our forces gave quarter' to Denton and Smith '(though undeserving), leaving them to a judicial trial for their perjury and fallaciousness'.[25] *The Weekly Account* got the wrong house, claiming that the two men had been captured during an assault on Sir Cope Doyley's Greenlands, which lay fifty miles south.[26]

The Royalist *Mercurius Aulicus* offered a more colourful account of the assault and its aftermath. Sixty of the King's men were put to the sword in cold blood, apparently, including an eighty-two-year-old kitchen servant who flew into a rage at the disrespect shown to Sir Alexander Denton and attacked one of the soldiers with a cleaver. The surviving men, including Sir Alexander, William Smith and Tom Verney, were stripped and herded into the church of the Nativity at Padbury, a couple of miles closer to Buckingham. From there they were forced to watch as soldiers set fire to the house, its farms and hayricks. The women of the household, who included Aunt Isham, her sister Susan Denton and the Verney girls, were 'stripped almost naked, their attire pulled from their heads, necks, shoulders, to the very gloves, their heads beaten and cut with muskets, themselves dragged about the house, and then made to march up to the knees in dirt, the soldiers reviling them as they went along, called them "Bloody ammunition whores"', before they were put in a cart and sent off to Claydon.[27]

According to *Mercurius Aulicus* Aunt Isham, who was left in charge of the Verney girls and Sir Alexander's young children, petitioned the local garrison commander to at least leave her some milch cows and any part of the house still standing so that the children could have some kind of food and lodging: but the answer came back that 'surely the woman was asleep when she writ it, or else how could she dream of any mercy from them?'.[28]

Judging from the reports of those who were actually *at* Hillesden during the siege, *Mercurius Aulicus* was offering its readers a tabloid version of the truth. Twenty-one-year-old Pen Verney, who was certainly no friend to Parliament, was quite clear that 'we were not shamefully used in any way by the soldiers';[29] and Sir Alexander, while he thought that 'my children and nieces [were] not fairly used', nevertheless added, 'yet no immodest action'.[30] He reckoned that no more than nineteen men had been killed on both sides, which doesn't tally with any of the other contemporary accounts of the action – or indeed with Sir Samuel Luke's official report, which was sent up to Parliament and read on Tuesday 5 March, the day of the burning. Luke wrote that forty Royalists 'at least' were killed. But one thing Sir Alexander Denton was certain of – he was ruined. The house was destroyed, along with the stables, barns, farm buildings and surrounding cottages. The cattle were driven away, his money was gone, the wine was taken from his cellar. Even the park pales 'be every one up and burned or else carried away, and the Denton children like to beg'. He estimated he had lost £16,000. 'My comfort is I know myself not guilty of any fault.'[31] Small comfort.

One cannot help wondering about the realities of the assault on Hillesden. Not about the fighting – which was surely as chaotic and panicked as close-quarter combat always was, and always will be – but about what came afterwards. All the public accounts agree that Cromwell's men put to death some of the garrison after they had surrendered, but none of the women mention the fact in their letters. Did the soldiers wait until they had been led away over the fields to Claydon before they started cutting throats or hanging trussed prisoners from trees? Did the Verney girls hear the crying and shouting in the distance as their carts bounced along the lanes, and either not understand what it meant, or simply put it away from them?

If the women felt any distaste for the brutalities of war, two at least managed to put it aside. Susan Denton, Sir Alexander's forty-something spinster sister, had attracted the attention of Jeconiah Abercrombie when the Parliamentarians first occupied Hillesden in February. The fact that his army had just ruined her family, burned her home, imprisoned her brother and laid waste to his estates did not deter either of them: they were married that summer. 'Few of her friends like it,' said Aunt Isham shortly before the wedding. 'But if she hath not him she will never have any, it is gone so far.'[32]

Sir Alexander's eighteen-year-old daughter Margaret also found romance in the ruins of Hillesden. William Smith and Sir Alexander were brought down to London and called before the bar of the Commons twelve days after being taken by Cromwell's troops. Denton was committed to the Tower, Smith to the much less salubrious Poultry Compter, where the Speaker ordered that he be 'kept safe within his chamber and the gates of the prison, and no man suffered to speak with him, but in the presence of his keeper'.[33] Nevertheless, he managed to carry on a courtship of sorts with Margaret Denton, and the couple were married that July. 'You may think it a bold venture,' Aunt Isham informed Sir Ralph, 'but if these times hold, I think there will be no men left for women.'[34] Smith escaped from gaol in September, but he was quickly recaptured and sent to the Tower. His bid for freedom earned him a charge of high treason and his bride, her cousin Susan Verney and their aunt Isham an eight-day spell in prison. 'It was thought that I had a hand in helping of my new cousin out of prison,' said an indignant Susan Verney, 'but indeed I had not!'[35]

In February 1645 the Commons agreed that Colonel Smith should be exchanged for Sir Robert Meredith, a privy counsellor who had been committed to Dublin Castle for trying to persuade soldiers in Ireland to join the King's enemies. Smith survived the war, was made a baronet by Charles II and lived for another fifty years.

Others weren't so lucky. Jeconiah Abercrombie was killed by a raiding party outside Boarstall; he was buried at Hillesden, leaving his widow with a baby boy, his namesake. Sir Alexander Denton died of a fever on New Year's Day 1645, while still a prisoner of war in the Tower. His eldest son John had been killed the previous August, when a field gun exploded as he led an assault on Parliamentarian forces at Abingdon. 'Never did I hear of a more braver piece of service done [than his behaviour in battle],' said Aunt Isham; 'and if his life had been spared, the whole town had been his own.'[36]

Colonel William Eure, the Catholic who had caused the Verneys and the Dentons so much anguish when he married Sir Edmund's sister-in-law, was killed at Marston Moor in the summer of 1644.

'The gallantest man that ever I knew in my life,' said his widow,[37] who was left with two little girls, Margaret and Mary; a third, Lucia, had died in February 1643. The colonel was buried in York Minster on 7 July, and even the unforgiving Doll Leeke mourned his loss, although she couldn't resist a sideswipe – 'he had but one fault,' she said to Sir Ralph. 'I wish he had not infected his wife [with his Catholicism].'[38]

Cary's husband, Captain Gardiner, was shot dead in a skirmish outside Oxford in July 1645, leaving his widow disconsolate and pregnant; her brother-in-law, Henry Gardiner, was killed a few weeks later. With her husband gone, Cary's relations with her parents-in-law deteriorated rapidly. They made a string of excuses to avoid paying over her widow's jointure; and when she lost her only trump card by giving birth to a girl rather than a Gardiner heir – 'to all our griefs,' said Henry Verney[39] – they threw mother and baby out and packed them off to Claydon without a penny. She was eighteen.

All that Sir Ralph and Mary could do was watch from a distance as their old world was turned upside down. Letters from home announced each blow as it fell: friends and cousins were killed; sisters turned out of their homes or thrown into prison. At one point Claydon itself was threatened by bands of marauding troopers. Prince Maurice's men intimidated Verney tenants into paying their rents directly to them. The Royalist governor of Boarstall impounded timber, animals and carts from Claydon, and when Will Roades went to ask for them back, he was told that 'if they had my master they would slaughter him, for he was worse than those slain beasts, for he helped to slay his own father'.[40] Sir Roger Burgoyne reported a rumour that one side or the other intended to burn down Claydon: 'I hope God in his mercy will take that man [that intends it] out of the world before he be guilty of so devilish a sin.'[41]

It wasn't so long ago that the quarrel between Charles and Parliament was mere politics, less important than Sir Edmund's latest bout of sciatica. Now Sir Ralph and Mary were marooned in an alien land. Everything that defined who they were – their relationships, their status, their wealth, their home – was disintegrating, and they powerless to stop it.

The 'Smiths' had stayed in Rotterdam for a couple of weeks, recovering from their stormy North Sea crossing. It was a relaxed, cosmopolitan city, so relaxed, in fact, that English visitors were often scandalised by the way in which every sect, from Arminians to Anabaptists, could worship freely. Its main claim to fame among travellers was as the birthplace of Erasmus, 'the man that made the rough and untrodden ways smooth and passable', in Aubrey's gentle phrase.[42] His bronze statue by Hendrik de Keyser gazed benevolently down on the traders and merchants who thronged the busy market square. But Sir Ralph had little time for sight-seeing: most of his efforts were focused on ensuring that the family's possessions – twenty-six parcels of 'wearing apparel, linen, pictures, and other household stuff'[43] – arrived safely at Rouen without being rifled by customs officers.

An arduous 227 miles south-west of Rotterdam, the Verneys' new home was a thriving city with a population of around 60,000, which made the ancient capital of Normandy twice the size of Bristol or Norwich, England's second cities. Most travellers commented with rather grudging approval on Rouen's commerce – 'a town of great trade, being full of shops from one end to the other', according to one commentator[44] – but apart from the late-fifteenth-century Palais de Justice, no one had much praise for anything else. 'The houses without juttings or overlets, four storeys high, and in the front not very beautiful,' said Peter Heylyn in 1656.[45] 'Neither so handsome nor so pleasant a place as Caen' was the verdict of another visitor;[46] 'they have not built a fine Exchange,' commented a third.[47] Most robust of all was the cheerfully splenetic John Clenche, who said that as a result of the 'crowd of sluttish people, ill situation, and narrow streets', Rouen was 'most abominably filthy'.[48] Clenche was the epitome of the Ugly Englishman abroad: he also maintained that Rouen's 'best church was built by the English; and their best monastery is now of English women'.*

* *A Tour in France and Italy, made by an Englishman, 1675* (1676), 2. Clenche's chau-vinism extended to Paris, which he described as being not half as big as London (it was bigger), and filled with theatres that were 'much worse than ours'. French wines had no flavour, and were 'most of them tart and crabbed'; French men were 'withered', and French women 'thick lipped [and] flat-nosed'; even French horses were 'so strangely put together, that scarce any of them can either trot or gallop' (7, 22, 21).

Sir Ralph's decision to settle his family in Rouen was dictated partly by its proximity to England and partly by the presence of a Protestant community which equalled the Roman Catholic one in size. But the family couldn't settle. Peg fell sick with smallpox; Mun was shaken with a high fever and vomiting. Sir Ralph, confused and isolated, began to suffer from bouts of depression which would dog him for the rest of his life. 'The doubts and fears I have for my little family, together with the miseries of my native country, have made me so conversant with afflictions, that this world is grown tedious and life itself a burden to me,' he wrote to Doll Leeke.[49] He couldn't see any happiness or any prospect of it, he told Anne Hobart. 'Perhaps my being so seasoned with afflictions like the man whose continual looking through a green glass made all things seem green to him, so my perpetual troubles make all things appear sad and black to me.'[50] It was left to Mary to hold the family together.

Parliament seemed ever more enthusiastic about the Solemn League and Covenant. A roll call of 228 MPs who had signed up was published a few weeks after Sir Ralph and Mary arrived in Rouen, and stragglers continued to add their names to the roll throughout the summer. A flood of pamphlets appeared to counter Royalist charges of impiety and treason, employing those rather splendid rhetorical flourishes which characterised the writing of both sides during the war:

> However some men, hoodwinked and blinded by the artifices of those Jesuitical engineers, who have long conspired to sacrifice our religion to the idolatry of Rome, our laws, liberties and persons to arbitrary slavery, and our estates to their insatiable avarice, may possibly be deterred and amused with high threats and declarations, flying up and down on the wings of the royal name and countenance (now captivated and prostituted to serve all their lusts) to proclaim all rebels and traitors who take this Covenant; yet let no faithful English heart be afraid to join with our brethren of all the three kingdoms in this solemn league, as sometimes the men of Israel (although under another King) did with the men of Judah . . .[51]

Parliament ordered that the College of Physicians should tender the Covenant to all 'physicians, practitioners in physick, and apothecaries';[52] then to all barber-surgeons. Judges could not sit, lawyers could not appear before them, without having sworn the Covenant; ministers could not be ordained unless they produced testimonials showing they had taken it; vessels could not sail until the captain 'and all other officers and passengers in the said ship, do take the National Covenant before they be embarqued'.[53] Prisoners of war had to take the Covenant before ransoms or exchanges took place. A parliamentary committee was appointed 'to take into consideration the tendering of the National League and Covenant to English subjects, resident in foreign parts'.[54] Even King Charles himself wasn't exempt. When the Commons discussed proposals for peace in the summer of 1644, they made sure to include in the peace plan their wish that 'his Majesty . . . may be pleased to swear and sign the late solemn League and Covenant'.[55]

With all this zeal and fervour in the prisons and law courts and harbours, it goes without saying that dissidents were no longer tolerated in the House of Commons itself. In August 1644 it was reckoned that every Member who was ever likely to sign the Covenant had signed it, and the Commons declared that 'this House would not suffer any Member to sit in the House, till they took the National Covenant; and that justice may be done upon such as shall refuse to take it'.[56] And yet somehow Sir Ralph still managed to avoid expulsion, sequestration – even the mildest public censure.

He came close, however. The Buckinghamshire Committee was convinced he was a Royalist – and one can't really blame them, considering the political leanings of all the other Verneys. Representatives from the committee turned up at Claydon in the summer threatening sequestration, and the threat was only lifted because Will Roades was able to show the trust deeds as evidence that the estate legally belonged to others (actually Francis Drake, Sir Alexander Denton's brother John and Richard Winwood, a Buckinghamshire neighbour who was active in the cause of Parliament).

Sir Ralph's friends were exasperated. 'None will be in so sad

a condition as those that stand neuters,' said his brother Henry.[57]
Sir Thomas Parker, who was distantly related through the Temples
and the Fiennes, wrote to explain at length that neutrality was
no longer an option. Of course there were arguments on both
sides, he said; but Sir Ralph couldn't agree with both, and
whichever had most weight with him, no matter how slight the
imbalance, had the first claim on his loyalties. He owed it to God
to act in accordance with his conscience; but doing nothing was
not an action.

Sir Ralph replied with a rueful gentleness. He explained that
one of his main complaints about the Covenant was the way in
which it was forced on MPs with such severity, and cited Sir
Thomas Parker's kinsman, Sir Philip Parker, as a case in point.
(Sir Philip was one of those dissident MPs who had been bullied
into taking the Covenant after holding out against it for months.)
Ever since leaving England, he said, he had struggled to come
to terms with the commitment he was being asked to make; and
he was all too well aware of the risk he was running in refusing
it. But it always came back to the same thing: 'Rather than make
a solemn vow and covenant wherein I am not satisfied, I must
choose to suffer.'[58]

And suffer he did. In the summer of 1645, after a visit to Paris,
Sir Ralph moved his family to Blois in the Loire valley. They
had barely settled in when the news came through from Sir
Roger Burgoyne that Parliament had finally taken official notice
of Sir Ralph's absence. 'My friend is voted out.'[59]

The crunch had come on Monday 22 September, when a question was raised about parliamentary representation for Aylesbury.
Of the two MPs for the borough, Sir John Packington had gone
over to the King years ago; he was disabled from sitting back in
August 1642, two days before the King raised his standard at
Nottingham. Sir Ralph hadn't been fulfilling his parliamentary
duties for at least two years, and although Sir Roger had strenu-
ously defended him from accusations of having been seen in the
King's quarters, his absence alone was enough to convince the
House that it was time to elect two new Members for the borough.
The question was put 'whether Sir Ralph Verney shall be disabled
to sit as a Member of this House, during this Parliament'; it was

carried, and writs were issued for new elections.*

Sir Ralph was distraught at what he called 'one of the greatest and most inexpressible afflictions that ever yet befell me . . . God in mercy give me patience and forgive those that did it, without affording me the favour, nay I might say the justice, of a summons.'[60] Considering his friends both in and out of Parliament had been urging him for the past eighteen months to return home in order to save his seat, this was a little hard for them to swallow. But in any case, it was all too late now. He was described as a delinquent on the front page of *A Perfect Diurnall.*† He had lost his parliamentary privilege. If he went back to England and sought to argue his case, he risked being thrown into prison for debt. He couldn't sell off any land to satisfy his creditors, because of the threat of sequestration. He might settle with the sequestrators by paying a fine of at least two years' value 'according to the true value of his estate, before these troubles began'.[61] But a prerequisite for composition was the taking of the Covenant, and that meant his exile would all have been for nothing. He couldn't do it, even though 'this single thought must needs be heightened to a crime worthy of a total ruin'.[62] So he stayed in Blois with Mary, Mun and Peg, and contemplated the wreck of his life.

There were worse places to be than Blois, although John Clenche didn't think so. 'Has nothing good in it but its situation' was his only comment on the town.[63] Less jaundiced English eyes found Blois a charming place, with courteous, well-spoken

---

* *Journal of the House of Commons* 4, 22 September 1645. Symon Mayne and Thomas Scott, the men who replaced Sir Ralph and Sir John Packington in the Commons, were both hard-liners who were active on the parliamentary committee for Buckinghamshire. In 1649 both would put their signatures to Charles I's death warrant; and at the Restoration both were accordingly condemned to death as regicides. Mayne died in the Tower before sentence could be carried out; Scott went to the gallows bravely, his last words being that his was 'a cause not to be repented of'.

† 22–29 September 1645, 1: 'The House this day received the report concerning Sir Ralph Varney his delinquency; and the question being put; a vote passed for disabling him ever [to] sit in this present Parliament as a Member thereof.'

inhabitants. There was a stately public promenade, a handsome stone bridge across the Loire, good air and rich pastures – and, of course, the magnificent chateau built for François I in the 1510s and recently extended by François Mansart. There was a decent Protestant congregation and a moderate and educated minister, Paul Testard, who was prepared to take in pupils. Testard took on the education of Mun and Peg, closely supervised by Mary's gentlewoman-in-waiting, Luce Sheppard, and assisted by Claude Mauger, a young Protestant convert living in Blois who would later achieve fame as the best-selling author of a French–English dictionary and *Mr Mauger's French Grammar,* which went through twenty editions by the end of the century. Mauger turned out to be something of a mixed blessing: after he admitted taking in a Catholic lodger, Sir Ralph insisted that Mun should only be taught in the Verney home, to avoid contamination; but even this wasn't enough, and in the end he dismissed Mauger, calling him 'the greatest liar, notorious drunkard, and the nastiest sloven that ever was seen'.[64]

Mun's education focused on Latin; Peg's academic training is much less clear, but both children learned drawing, singing and music. 'Child, I have taken order with the guitar master to send me a fine guitar for you, when I send for it,' Sir Ralph told his son. 'But first I will see whether you deserve it or not; for if you have not studied it hard in my absence, a worse shall serve your turn and therefore I would not buy one here, till I have heard you sing, and play.'[65] Mum and Peg also had dancing lessons, until Sir Ralph decided he couldn't afford them: 'They have no use for it but for fashion and carriage.'[66]

In spite of such small economies, the Verneys lived well in France. In the summer of 1646 Sir Ralph and Mary took a tour down the Loire to Nantes, and then on to La Rochelle ('very ordinary, not having one good church', says Clenche) and Bordeaux, famous in the seventeenth century as one of the prime cities and fairest ports in all France ('one good street with two or three good houses in it', says Clenche; 'the rest of the town narrow and ill built').[67] Their friends in England, and the various English travellers who passed through Blois, kept them informed on the latest developments: Prince Rupert's surrender of Bristol in September 1645; the failure of the King's campaign and his surrender to the Scots at Southwell in Nottinghamshire the following May. Apart from the staunchly Royalist William Denton, Sir Ralph's contacts in England during his exile were, like him, firmly on the side of Parliament. Eleanor Sussex was not such a frequent correspondent as she had been in the past, perhaps because she was now moving in high political circles: in March 1646, six months after Sir Ralph's expulsion from the Commons, she took as her third husband the fifty-eight-year-old Earl of Warwick, *de facto* commander of the navy. Sir Roger Burgoyne, who regularly helped to organise the transfer of funds from London to Blois and did his level best to prevent Sir Ralph's sequestration, continued to sit as MP for Bedfordshire until he was secluded in a purge of moderates at the end of 1648. He kept Sir Ralph up to date with the latest political gossip, showing a robust relish for cloak and dagger. His more sensitive snippets of information were sometimes written in invisible ink; and his letters, which were still being addressed to 'Mr Ralph Smith' long after all of Sir Ralph's other correspondents had reverted to 'MonsieurVerney Chevalier Anglais', were often signed '9.14.3=9.16.10.4'. The signature translates as 'War Wick', which was Burgoyne's code name; and the cipher was the one Sir Ralph had toyed with when he was making his clandestine notes on Commons debates back in 1642. The Verneys still used it occasionally, but not as enthusiastically as Sir Roger, who switched without warning into cipher in the middle of otherwise normal letters in a disconcerting fashion. For example, in the course of one letter he suddenly said, 'Some imagine that 5.40.7.15−3.30.15.8.16.50.11.28.15.30= 6.8.30 = 40.27.40.14.4.15.30 =8.16.40.3=14.3.30.5.7.18.3.40=7.14.8.30.15.20.30.3.16.10.40.4= 11.15.28.40.15.3.14.20.40.20=I think you may believe this, although it be yet nothing but a premise.'* Indeed.

The irony was that, although Sir Ralph remained loyal to Parliament, it was his own side which was intent on ruining him. The long-suffering Will Roades was desperately trying to keep

---

* Sir Roger Burgoyne to Sir Ralph Verney, 3 January 1650; M636/10. The message reads 'the resigne [i.e. design − Burgoyne confused 'r' and 'd'] is make sir arthur haselrick generall'. The numbers 30, 40 and 50 are meaningless, and included just to throw code-breakers off the scent. Sir Arthur Hesilrige was commander of the Parliamentarian forces in the north-east; if Burgoyne meant that he was to replace Sir Thomas Fairfax as Lord General of the army, he was mistaken.

the estates at Claydon going, getting in what rents he could, paying taxes with whatever came to hand, fending off Sir Ralph's creditors and doing his best to placate Ralph's brothers and sisters. This last was a task in itself. All of the Verneys, even Henry, adopted a peremptory tone with the long-suffering steward: after one of Henry's demands for money was refused, he warned Roades that 'if you make me not satisfaction and post it in a way on sight of my letter, in a word you must not expect to have me for your friend'.[68]

Tom was much worse. After Roades offered him only half of his £10 quarteredge, the £40 annual allowance which was supposed to be paid to him at three-monthly intervals, he told the steward to 'wipe your arse with it', and threatened to turn up at Roades' door with a troop of soldiers. At other times he asked Roades for a loan of 50s., promising to repay him when his father-in-law stumped up his wife's outstanding dowry; he berated him for paying some of his quarteredge to 'my unfortunate wife' without permission; he ordered him to make over the annuity to a third party who had advanced Tom money to escape gaol and flee the country; and he begged the steward for money for food when he was once more in gaol: What I shall eat this day, being Monday, or how to live all the week till I can hear from you, God perish me, if I know as yet.'[69]

All this while, Roades was trying to hold Claydon together. At one stage he was selling wood from the estate to pay taxes, telling Sir Ralph that 'if I let it [i.e., the tax] run in arrears they will sell the wood themselves'.[70] The threat of sequestration was still hanging over Sir Ralph's entire estate, although the deeds of trust continued to stave it off, and he resorted to various ruses to keep the County Committee at bay. Over the winter of 1645–6, for example, Francis Drake was encouraged to secure his mortgage by taking possession of parts of Claydon.

But the deeds would reach the end of their life in 1647. And there were already signs that the radicals on the County Committee – men who mistrusted landed gentry like Sir Ralph and who were convinced that a man with so many Royalist connections could hardly be a friend to Parliament – were not prepared to wait that long. On 10 September 1646 lands which Sir Ralph owned at Brill, on the border with Oxfordshire, were sequestrated. A month later the committee ordered Will Roades to appear before them, bringing rents, leases and rent rolls for Claydon.

Friends were doing all they could to help, but it wasn't enough. Sir Ralph's situation demanded a personal appearance before the committee. Yet the moment he set foot in England he risked arrest and imprisonment, and he couldn't bear the thought.

There was another option. Sir Roger Burgoyne suggested that Mary could plead his cause: she was well able to 'use the juice of an onion sometimes to soften hard hearts'.[71] Sir Ralph was uncomfortable with this, but the idea received support from Uncle Doctor. After King Charles's surrender and the fall of Oxford, William Denton had succumbed to *realpolitik*. He had resolved to apologise publicly for 'attending the King . . . and adhering to the forces raised against Parliament', to pay a fine of £55 and to take the Covenant.[72] Now he urged Sir Ralph to send Mary back to England:

> I am clear of the opinion the best course you can take is to send over Mischief [their pet name for Mary] with all the speed you can, and to place yourself at Dieppe, or Calais, or some other maritime town where you may receive an account, and return answers with speed concerning your own business. Not to touch upon [the] inconveniences of your coming, women were never so useful as now . . . Instruct your wife, and leave her to act it with committees; their sex entitles them to many privileges . . .[73]

In November 1646 Sir Ralph took his wife and Luce Sheppard down to Rouen, where they waited to join a party heading for Dieppe. Their other maid, Bess, was left behind with the children in Blois. When they arrived in Dieppe, the weather was stormy in the Channel, and the strong winds meant further delays. Always a worrier, Sir Ralph fretted when he heard that only six weeks earlier forty-two ships had been cast away on the English coast during a bad storm. He entrusted Mary to a couple of English merchants, and gave her detailed instructions about who she must see in London, when she must write to him, the particular code words she must use in case her letters were opened –

'Clayford' for Claydon, 'Will Johnson' for Will Roades, 'Old Men's Wife' for Eleanor, Countess of Warwick, and so on.

On Friday 13 November he wrote to his brother Henry to say that they were still waiting for a ship, but Henry should let the rest of the family know – 'Mischief is coming'.[74]

11

Mischief

*M*ary was the perfect wife to Sir Ralph. She was bright while he was lugubrious; warm when he was cold; relentlessly cheerful when he teetered, as he often did, on the edge of depression. She was fiercely loyal, putting his own interests before her own, before those of their friends and relations, before even their children. Slightly built and enormously good-looking (Sir Ralph was neither) she preserved, in her portraits at least, a knowing, rather humorous expression, looking more intelligent than her husband – and often acting it.

But much as we might like Mary to be a pioneering seventeenth-century feminist, empowered by the vicissitudes of war, she was no such thing. She was empowered by circumstances, certainly; her role as petitioner and potential saviour of the Verney fortunes enabled her to use her judgement in a male forum, giving her a degree of responsibility which was usually reserved for the male head of the family. But we need to remember that she neither regarded herself as Sir Ralph's equal nor was regarded as such by others. She did as she was told and she deferred to his judgement. Nothing made her more angry than to hear him criticised; nothing pleased her as much as his approbation.

She wasn't the first wife to represent her husband before the feared Committee for Compounding, which sat in the spectacular setting of Nicholas Stone's Goldsmiths' Hall in Foster Lane. London at the end of 1646 was packed with Royalists and papists come to make their peace with Parliament and compound for their delinquency. And since many of them were as circumspect as Sir Ralph about actually stepping into the lion's den, a surprisingly large number sent their wives to plead their case. 'Women become pleaders, attorneys, petitioners and the like,' said Margaret Cavendish, Duchess of Newcastle, 'running about with their several causes, complaining of their several grievances, exclaiming against their several enemies.'[1] She took a rather jaundiced view of women's role as petitioners – 'our sex doth nothing but jostle for the preeminence of words' – but that was perhaps because when she appeared at Goldsmiths' Hall to plead for something from the sequestered estates of her exiled Royalist husband, she was too frightened to open her mouth and failed miserably. Writing after the Restoration, the scholar and teacher Bathsua Makin was more sanguine about the part which women played in the 1640s. 'When their husbands were serving their King and country,' she said, they 'defended their houses, and did all things, as soldiers, with prudence and valour, like men. They appeared before Committees, and pleaded their own causes with good success.'[2]

'Like men.' But they weren't men, and they were operating in a man's world. Let's not ignore the tremendous courage it took for a woman like Mary Verney to leave her husband and children, to cross the Channel and set up home by herself in London, to begin a remorseless round of doorstepping and lobbying of peers and MPs.

Mary landed on the Sussex coast at Rye towards the end of November 1646 and, after catching her breath for a couple of days at the home of the Cockrams, merchants she knew from Rouen, she and Luce Sheppard went on to London, arriving at their lodgings on 26 November. She was feeling poorly – 'neither the air nor the diet agrees with me'[3] – but she put on a brave face and said all the right things to the stream of visitors who arrived to pay their respects over the next couple of weeks. Lady Leeke came, and Aunt Eure (who was now Aunt Sherard, having found a Protestant captain, Philip Sherard, to replace her Catholic colonel); so did Frank Drake, timorous and anxious about the Claydon mortgage, and the faithful Sir Roger Burgoyne. Dr Denton turned up; and Henry, looking for money; and a rather harassed Will Roades, pursued by creditors. 'I have told him whosoever suffers, you must be supplied,' Mary reassured Sir Ralph.[4]

There had been some big changes in the Verney family's domestic circumstances over the past seven months. Mary's sister-in-law Peg was married at the beginning of May to Thomas Elmes, a prosperous gentleman from Warmington in Northamptonshire, who was knighted the same year. Peg had money of her own – the £1000 which Aunt Eure had settled on her, despite her runaway tongue – but Sir Ralph had put the money out at interest to provide an income for her until she married, and in the straitened times it was proving difficult to recall it. Elmes was willing to take Peg on the understanding that the money would sooner or later be forthcoming, and to offer her 'five hundred a year good security jointure', although he demanded £100 cash up front.[5] Henry helped to broker the marriage. He was quick to tell his older brother that 'I will not say I brought the young man to her, but I may boldly say had it not been for me and my credit she will acknowledge it had never been done.'[6] He meant credit in the literal sense, too: he borrowed the money in the expectation that Sir Ralph would reimburse him. The newly-weds settled down in Covent Garden.

Peg was twenty-two and, like her sisters, she was keen to leave the stifling environment of Claydon and become mistress of her own household. In the circumstances, her choice of husband was limited; and the fact that Sir Ralph, who as head of the family was supposed to be arbiter and chief negotiator, was in exile made her prospects even more problematic. But she chose a wrong 'un. Within weeks of her wedding she was struggling to cope with Elmes's jealous temper, and his violence grew worse with every passing month.

On 5 August 1646, almost three months to the day after Peg's marriage, her eldest sister Susan followed her to the altar. The groom, Richard Alport, was widowed, childless and kind but poor – so poor, in fact, that the couple started their married life in the Fleet, where Alport was imprisoned for debt. This time Henry did not approve; but that was perhaps because brother Tom had introduced them. The Verneys' kinsman Sir John Leeke, on the other hand, endorsed the match. Susan, who had been lodging with the Leekes in London for some time, was reckoned to be plain, and Sir John told Sir Ralph straight out that she 'was not a wife for many men, though it hath pleased God to infuse a great affection into the man from the desire to match into your family'.[7] Susan was happy enough at the prospect of marriage to Alport, but her financial situation was much more complicated than Peg's. She had a notional £1000 as a dowry from Sir Edmund's investment in the alnage; but Sir Ralph had borrowed against it, and he couldn't pay it back. She also owed the Leekes for her board and lodging; since leaving Ireland they had fallen on hard times themselves, and the £32 she owed them would make a big difference to their circumstances.

Sir Ralph did not behave generously to Susan. He kept Alport strictly to the latter's offer of a £200-a-year jointure, while haggling down the amount he had to pay towards his sister's marriage portion from £1000 to a mere £400. Alport had to consult his creditors at each stage of the negotiations, and letters often took an age to pass between England and France, so the whole affair dragged on for nearly two years. Sir John Leeke did his best to break the impasse, but it was the couple themselves who expedited matters. In July 1646 Sir Ralph admitted to Sir Roger Burgoyne that 'she had best marry him and that quickly too'; at the same time he told Sir John Leeke that 'if she have him not she is a lost creature'.[8] She may not have been pregnant (she miscarried the following summer) but Sir Ralph clearly had reason to believe that she and Alport had grown tired of waiting and embarked on a sexual relationship. They married at the beginning of August; Sir John Leeke gave the bride away. 'I was never so happy since my father died as I am now,' said Susan.[9]

There was a third Verney wedding in 1646. Around the beginning of November, only a few weeks before Mary arrived in England, Penelope Verney married a cousin on her mother's side,

John Denton of Fawler in Oxfordshire.* He was an eager suitor – so eager that he proposed without consulting his parents, and offered to take Pen without a portion, and with only a slight increase to the £40-a-year allowance which Sir Ralph was already paying her. Henry, who once again was acting as chief negotiator, apologised to Sir Ralph for going ahead with the marriage contract without obtaining his approval, but he needn't have worried. Sir Ralph was delighted. So was Pen, although not for the most romantic of reasons. According to Henry, 'she was sensible her portion lay in a desperate condition, besides, she grew in years and was not to all men's liking; these reasons made her so ready to yield'.[10] The groom came with a reputation as a drunk, but in the circumstances everyone, even the bride, was happy to believe that he had his drinking under control.

A wife beater, a gaoled debtor and a drunkard: the weddings of Peg, Sue and Pen are stark examples of how damaging Sir Ralph's moral stand was proving for the rest of the family. His exile meant he couldn't play a full role in finding suitable partners for his sisters; his parlous financial condition meant he had less to offer a prospective groom. Not to put too fine a point on it, he was grateful to anyone who would consent to take the girls off his hands. Perhaps the saddest thing about all of this is that they were, too.

Within days of arriving in London Mary was invited to Susan Alport's house for 'a very great dinner'.[11] But she did no other socialising, apart from receiving visitors. She didn't even go to Claydon to find Jack, the little son she had left behind when she fled to France three years earlier. Her whole energy was focused on discovering exactly what must be done to lift the sequestration and establishing or re-establishing contact with anyone who might prove useful. Through Aunt Sherard's influence she was introduced to Henry Pelham, an influential MP and lawyer who sat with her in his Gray's Inn chambers and gave the encouraging

* Not to be confused with John Denton their lawyer uncle, brother of Uncle Doctor and the late Sir Alexander; nor, of course, with Sir Alexander's dead son, yet another John Denton. John was a common name, and there were a lot of Dentons.

opinion that Sir Ralph was not liable for sequestration, since the only thing against him was his absence, rather than any active service in the King's cause. An hour-long interview with Old Men's Wife was less successful: although Mary dropped some very heavy hints about the role that powerful friends could have in bringing Sir Ralph's affairs to a happy end, Eleanor 'did not offer to engage herself for her husband nor any other courtesy'.[12]

With help from William Denton, Mary found out that she needed a certificate of sequestration from the Buckinghamshire Committee; and then she would have to petition Parliament. She was keen to avoid having her case heard before the Committee for Compounding. Never mind Sir Ralph's qualms about having to take the Covenant if he compounded; Mary was worried that the fine would be more than they could possibly afford. Everyone was talking about the 4th Earl of Dorset, who had just been told to pay a colossal £4360, and had responded by offering the Committee his whole estate for £6000 if they would also take on his debts.

Although she had only been in England for two or three weeks, the whole business was already starting to wear Mary down. She told Sir Ralph how disappointing it was to find that erstwhile friends now seemed reluctant to help: 'there is nothing of friendship left, but all the falseness that can be imagined . . . The greatest friendship one can expect from most here is not to be one's enemy.'[13] Like Sir Ralph, she put her faith in the kinship networks which had been so important before the war, not realising the extent to which ideology had taken over from the old alliances – or the suspicion with which her husband was regarded by his ex-comrades in the Commons.

Then there was the expense. Mary's London lodgings cost 12s. a week, and an extra shilling for Luce Sheppard's upstairs chamber. On top of this, Mary had to pay for fires, candles, laundry and all of their food. She found the cost of hiring coaches terribly dear, but town was so busy that it was impossible to get about on foot. A coach, or at least a sedan chair, was essential, and within days of her arrival in London she had spent so much that she had to borrow £50. Henry arranged the loan – and promptly took £20 of it towards the £100 he had borrowed for Peg's marriage to Sir Thomas Elmes.

Sir Ralph didn't help matters. Stuck in Blois and entirely dependent on Mary and Uncle Doctor for information about his case, all he could do was urge his wife to do more, to move faster, to spend less. 'I am sorry you did not put off Sue's invitation,' he told her; 'for feasting agrees not with your condition [i.e., her financial condition], not being able to return the like. Avoid it hereafter, and make some better use of your friends' love.'[14] She shouldn't have borrowed any money, he said. She should make as few visits as possible (how she was supposed to lobby the great and the good without visiting them, he didn't explain); and she must refrain from travelling by coach. 'One loseth time, and the other spends money.'[15]

As it happened, his worries about Mary wasting her time socialising and squandering her money on coaches were academic. Just before Christmas (which, incidentally, was cancelled that year as an 'ancient but superstitious custom') she fell ill with a fever which confined her to her bed for several weeks and left her weak and depressed.*

The weather was damp and rainy, without any of the bright, sharp frosts which went some way to clearing London's polluted air. 'I am so extremely oppressed with melancholic that I am almost ready to burst,' she wrote to her husband.[16] Just as she started to mend, Luce went down with the same fever, leaving Mary facing the prospect of being attended by a stranger for several weeks, something she hated. Then she found out she was expecting a baby.

It was her seventh pregnancy in fifteen years of marriage, so it wasn't exactly a novel experience. But it couldn't have happened at a worse moment. The business of lifting the sequestration looked likely to drag on for months, and it seemed quite possible that she would still be in England – and Sir Ralph in France – when her time came. 'The very thought . . . goes to the very soul

---

* MPs and peers made a point of sitting on Christmas Day, but few followed their example. An exasperated *Perfect Diurnall* pointed out there was no evidence at all for Christ's birth taking place on 25 December: 'What pity is it this nation should be so wedded to custom, and so hardly persuaded as well in this as other things to leave to the traditions (to say no worse) of their predecessors' (21–28 December 1647).

of me,' she wrote when she broke the news to him, 'for to be so long from thee and to lie in without thee, is a greater affliction than I fear I shall be able to bear.'[17]

Sir Ralph tried to reassure her, urging her to pray for strength and a happy outcome to the pregnancy, to trust in God's mercy and to submit herself to His will; he promised to do the same. If that makes him sound cold and unloving, nothing could be further from the truth. For all his querulousness, his stiff pomposity and his fretful, humourless manner with outsiders, Sir Ralph's relationship with Mary was tender, affectionate and still passionate, and he missed her desperately. She was 'my dear bud' in his frequent letters to her, as he was her 'dear heart' and her 'dear rogue'. Conscious that he sometimes nagged her to bring the business of the sequestration to a speedy conclusion, he would apologise: 'You must not think that I reprove you with any neglect in that point. But rather that I, groaning under the burden of thy absence, cannot but vent it on all occasions. Enough of this. My dear, adieu. Thine for ever.'[18]

When the pregnancy became common knowledge, their friends were mildly amused. Sir Roger Burgoyne told Sir Ralph, 'I can be no means excuse you for giving her such a farewell which I believe will stick to her this half year before she can be rid of it; nevertheless I shall pray for a blessing upon the fruit of your joint endeavours.'[19] The couple themselves exchanged tender ideas for naming the child. Mary decided that if it was a girl, Sir Ralph could give it any name he liked; but if it was a boy, she would have it called after him. He responded by saying that if it was a girl, Mary would be a good name; if a boy, then Richard. But not Ralph. And certainly not Tom.

The couple's letters are full of small domestic detail and painful sweet sentiment. Sir Ralph holds 'a huge, huge, huge feast which cost me very near three pistoles' for the Protestant minister and his family, the doctor and his family, and assorted others. (Domestic economies don't extend to Blois, obviously.) Their ten-year-old son Edmund announces that Mary must love England better than France, otherwise she wouldn't stay away so long. Eight-year-old Peg is driving Sir Ralph to distraction because she won't hold her head up straight. Mary must write to both, he says, and tell them to be good and stick to their studies – 'then make large promises what you will bring them out of England . . .'.[20]

For her part, Mary talks of maternity clothes and good midwives and christenings. She is scandalised at the grip Presbyterianism holds over the Church of England: there are no godmothers or godfathers any more; the liturgy is read 'in such a tone that most people do nothing but laugh at it'; and anyone who wants to receive communion is interrogated as to the details of their personal life by the Church elders, who ask such questions she would blush to describe them.[21]

The brothers and sisters irritate and amaze her. Peg, Susan and Pen, the newly-weds, are shockingly indiscreet. Tom's wife Joyce is worse: she storms right into the Fleet prison one day to demand money which Richard Alport owes her husband. She says she'll cut his heart out if he doesn't pay her, and swears she'll kick Susan. This provokes Alport to say something insulting about Tom, which Joyce promptly reports back, and Tom challenges his brother-in-law to a duel. Disaster is avoided by Uncle Doctor, who stumps up the debt since Susan can't and her husband won't.

The two younger girls, Mall and Betty, are eager to leave the rural delights of Claydon for London. Mary calls them both 'clowns'; she thinks their want of a proper disciplined upbringing is going to get in the way of their finding a husband. Eighteen-year-old Mall is clever, but 'as wild as a buck', according to Mary.[22] She is passed from Claydon to Peg to Cary and back to Peg again. 'Much the plainest of them all and about the height of Pen but reasonable straight,' is Mary's verdict.[23] When she informs Sir Ralph that there may be a suitor on the horizon, he presses his wife to do all she can to get Mall married off: 'she is like to stick long, unless you make that match with you know who'.[24] Mary should explain to 'you know who' that, while Mall might not be handsome, she has wit and she will make a good housewife.

Unfortunately 'you know who', a Mr Brown, was not convinced, and the match fell through. When Mall insisted on staying in London rather than Buckinghamshire, Sir Ralph blustered that 'while she is at my allowance, I expect [to] be made acquainted with all such motions'.[25] However, Mary pointed out that if he made Mall's life difficult she might decide to come and live in Blois, a prospect which made Sir Ralph considerably less

reluctant to have her visit with her sisters in London. She went
to stay with Susan Alport during the latter's confinement in the
summer of 1647 – and then left again rather quickly after Susan
accused her of making a pass at her husband Richard.

Mary grew to like Mall best of all the sisters. She admitted to
Sir Ralph that the girl was plain, but she had a good, easy-going
nature and was always willing to do anything for anybody – as
Richard Alport found out. Betty, the youngest sister, was equally
willing, but lacked Mall's redeeming features. Barely fourteen
when Mary came back to England, she had led an unusually
unsupervised life at Claydon, where she could sometimes be
found sitting on the lap of one of her uncle John Denton's
servants. Mary disliked her, calling her 'a pestilent wench', 'much
the worst natured and wilfullest of them all' and 'of a cross proud
lazy disposition'.[26] The girl demanded expensive clothes, expected
to be treated like an adult and threw extravagant tantrums when
she was crossed – familiar enough behaviour to anyone who has
a passing acquaintance with twenty-first-century adolescents.

Betty contrived to exasperate the entire family, and she was
passed from sister to sister, never staying with any of them for
long. 'Nobody that knows her is willing to take her,' said Mary.[27]
Peg Elmes wrote a very hurt letter to Mary in September 1647.
Betty had suddenly decided she was bored with her company
and left. 'She was so violent to be gone as that she resolved to
go home a-foot rather than to stay here.'[28] In the end, Uncle
Doctor found a private school in London which would take her
for £25 a year and, even though she threatened to kill herself if
she was sent there, that is where she was sent.

Mary refused to play the go-between in the incessant squabbling between the brothers and sisters; nor did she take much
notice of their clamouring for money, although her patience was
tried to the limit. The girls complained because Nan Fudd, Jack's
nursemaid at Claydon, refused to act as maid to them. Will Roades
had fallen out with the Middle Claydon rector, John Aris, after
Aris accused him of mismanaging his master's estates and slan-
dering him. Sir Ralph urged Mary to mediate between them –
all she said was, 'I cannot endure to interest myself in quarrels.'[29]
But quarrels interested themselves in Mary. Tom, having presented
her with his portrait as a gift in the hope that he might be able

to extract some money out of her, flew into a rage when she refused to advance him £5, and wrote an extraordinarily pompous letter in which he accused her of never having liked him. 'But since you have spewed up your inveterate malice against me, let me say with the proverb, "Devil, do thy worst".'[30] Uncle Doctor thought this was hilarious, and took to calling Mary 'Devil-do-thy-worst'. Mary returned Tom's portrait and forwarded his letter to Sir Ralph.

Henry also fell out with her. In March 1647, after several months of paying Mary compliments and running errands for her, he lost his temper over some money matters and made the mistake of criticising Sir Ralph. 'Believe me,' she told Sir Ralph, 'there is nothing puts me in so great choler as to hear thee taxed, that I know art so good and just to all.'[31] She was a formidable enemy, pressing her husband not to give Henry anything. She had the measure of Henry, too, telling Sir Ralph that the only thing he cared about was his own welfare and describing his kindness to her as being 'but from the teeth outward'.[32]

This constant pestering wore Sir Ralph down. He and Mary were both convinced, quite rightly, that as long as he owned Claydon, family and creditors simply would not believe there was no money. On at least one occasion Mary was embarrassed by having to explain to an irate creditor that 'we had fed by the plate and stuff that we had sold . . . and that considering what fortune I brought I was reduced to a very low condition.'[33] And another time Sir Ralph lost his patience and suggested that if the brothers and sisters would take on his debts and make sure he and Mary and the children were properly provided for, they could have Claydon – house, woods and all the rest of the land he inherited from their father. He wasn't serious, but he *was* exasperated.

Mary was impatient of anything and anyone that got in the way of her prosecuting 'the great business', as she called her quest to save Sir Ralph's estate. Advised by Uncle Doctor and Aunt Sherard, she initially tried to have the Buckinghamshire Committee lift the order of sequestration. This was a long shot – the local committee had no power to remove sequestration, and she was resigned to the likelihood that they would refer her back to the Committee of Lords and Commons for

Sequestrations in London, having stated the reason why Sir Ralph was being penalised. Even this was unduly optimistic: she hadn't reckoned on the County Committee's hostility towards her husband, nor on its determination to follow due bureaucratic procedure. She needed a certificate of sequestration, and they couldn't produce one without an order from London. This was procured by the end of February – 'those villains in the country might have given a certificate if they had pleased, without putting me to all this trouble,' grumbled Mary[34] – and Sir Ralph's case was set to be heard by the Committee of Lords and Commons on Friday 16 April 1647. Unfortunately, in the interval between obtaining the certificate from Aylesbury and petitioning the Committee of Lords and Commons, Parliament passed an order declaring that the committee could not hear cases 'that concern such persons as have been Members of this House in this Parliament'.[35] Mary and her friends either didn't know about this, or chose to ignore it and hope that Sir Ralph's case might be heard anyway. Either way, they were frustrated on the day.

Now Mary was faced with the task of petitioning the House of Commons itself to pass an order referring the matter back to the Committee of Lords and Commons. Influencing an entire chamber was a more difficult task than trying to persuade a dozen or so committee members; but it was nothing compared to the problem of actually getting the petition heard by Parliament in the first place.

No one in the family had any doubt that personal influence was the route to take. In Blois, Sir Ralph wrote letter after letter to Parliament men he knew, asking them to intercede for him. 'Absence is the only crime that can be justly laid unto my charge,' he told Sir Gilbert Gerard MP, an ex-Sheriff of Buckinghamshire and a very distant connection via the Hampdens:

Were you but well informed of the true grounds and reasons of it (and how much I have already suffered for it) I assure myself you would afford me your best assistance and advice to put a period to my future troubles . . . If you please to appear my friend and speak favourably in my cause, and not suffer base accusations to pass for proofs against me at the day of hearing, I am most confident your good example will draw others to be of your opinion.[36]

Sir Ralph also provided Mary with a list of names which made the most of old family connections and paid no heed to shifting political groupings. Old Men's Wife and her new husband were at the top of the list. Sir Ralph reckoned they could bring with them the Earl of Warwick's predecessor as Lord Admiral, the Earl of Northumberland; the Earl of Manchester, who had married first Warwick's daughter, and then his niece; Lord North, 'and perhaps more too'. In France the Verneys had struck up an acquaintance with the Earl of Devonshire, a lukewarm Royalist who had fled to Rouen in 1644; Sir Ralph thought he and his formidable mother, Christian Bruce, might persuade the Earls of Salisbury and Pembroke to his cause. Eleanor Warwick might be able to influence Lord Wharton because she was friends with his mother; Sir John Trevor, MP for Grampound in Cornwall, was connected to the Dentons through his marriage to a Hampden; Sir Roger Burgoyne and his father were related to John Browne, MP for Dorset. Mary must go to Lord Saye and Sele on her own account, pleading family ties with his wife, a Temple; 'and show your pedigree'.[37]

As she lobbied and visited and urged her friends to show 'courtesy' to her husband in his plight, Mary encountered two problems. The first was her ignorance of groupings within Parliament and the complex politics of early 1647. After a series of military defeats King Charles had surrendered, not to Parliament but to the Scots, who kept him prisoner for nine months before handing him over to Parliament in return for £200,000, part-payment of their financial claims against the English. He was currently under house arrest at Holdenby House in Northamptonshire. In the meantime the victors were trying to reach some kind of settlement amongst themselves, with Presbyterians demanding a strict orthodoxy and Independents in an uneasy alliance with army radicals to resist non-toleration. Ideological divisions were becoming much more important than distant family ties.

The second problem was that Eleanor Warwick – the linchpin in Sir Ralph's plan – was not the political force she had been when he and Mary left England. The Earl of Warwick was

considerably less biddable than the poor old Earl of Sussex, and
Mary found that Old Men's Wife now had 'very little power,
for she lives in the house like a stranger, and doth not meddle
with anything, only she gives two parts of three of her estate
for her diet. Her new husband hath not made her a penny jointure; neither did he ever give her anything but one ring of
diamonds.'[38] No wonder she was reluctant to commit her
husband's influence to Mary's cause when they talked in
December; she couldn't.

Mary visited Eleanor again in March 1647, the first time they
had met since her illness at Christmas. The Earl of Warwick turned
up with his brother, the Earl of Holland, who came straight over
to Mary and told her that 'all the service that lay in his power
he would be ready to do us'. Warwick sat like a clown and said
nothing.[*] When Sir Ralph heard, he was really disappointed,
ranting against 'that vinegar-faced fellow'. He told Mary he hoped
'we shall have no occasion to use him, and I should account it
a particular blessing to dispatch my business well, without being
beholden to him, or any such unworthy and ill-natured creatures'.[39] Given such intemperate language, it is little wonder that
he commanded his wife to burn all his letters as soon as she had
replied to them.

Mary gave birth to a boy on 3 June 1647. William Denton
attended her, and Mun and Eleanor were godparents when he
was christened two weeks later. The delay is a little odd: she had
promised Sir Ralph that a parson would be ready in the house
to christen the child the moment it was born; and it was so sickly
that everyone thought it would die, which was of course another
reason for moving quickly. She also disregarded Sir Ralph's wishes
on another matter, insisting on naming the boy after him. 'I will
not now dispute with you about his name,' he wrote to her, 'but
assure yourself you shall hear of it at large hereafter.'[40]

Against expectation, baby Ralph rallied, restored 'from death

[*]Mary Verney to Sir Ralph Verney, 11 March 1647; M636/8. Holland was one
of the leaders of the moderate party. He switched sides several times during the
1640s, and was eventually executed in 1649 after raising a regiment for the King
on the outbreak of the second Civil War. His enthusiasm for Sir Ralph's cause
may have been related to his own distaste for the radical party in Parliament.

to life beyond all people's imagination'.[41] The wet nurse Mary had hired was a local Buckinghamshire woman and was fretting to go home, so she decided at three weeks old that he was well enough to travel down to Claydon. She was not: she was suffering from sweats and pounding headaches, and Dr Denton refused to allow her to leave her lodgings.

So at the end of June, Mall Verney took the child and his wet nurse by coach to St Albans, where they were met by Will Roades and the nurse's husband with horses. (Mary didn't think the expense of coach hire for the entire journey was justified.) From there, the little convoy made its way forty miles to Claydon, stopping off at Tring overnight. It consisted of Will, with Mall riding pillion behind him; the nurse's husband on his own 'very easy-going horse', with the baby tied to him with a garter; a footman going beside them; and the wet nurse, riding one of the Claydon horses.[42]

Mary followed a month later. She had been keen to stay in London and push ahead with her suit, but the political situation was more confused than ever. The day after her son was born, troops arrived at Holdenby House and removed the King, to forestall a projected countercoup by the Presbyterians in the Commons and their Scottish allies. Mary's friends were leaving the capital; there was talk of war breaking out again, and as she told Sir Ralph, 'everybody adviseth to see how the army and Parliament agree' before she made another attempt to have her petition heard.[43]

Claydon was not a happy place. Will Roades and Mr Aris were still not speaking, although the rector's wife was only too keen to speak to the poor bailiff, yelling at him in an unseemly manner in front of Mary. The house furnishings were in a dreadful state, with feather mattresses gnawed by rats, fire irons and kitchen spits so eaten with rust that they were beyond repair, linen worn out and the dining room chairs in rags. Part of the problem was depredations caused by soldiers who had been billeted in the house, but one can't help wondering exactly what the Verneys' housekeeper, Frances Alcock, had been thinking of to allow the house to fall into such a state. Perhaps she was thinking of love: a few weeks after Mary arrived at Claydon Mrs Alcock married a local cowherd, although she stayed on as housekeeper because Sir Ralph thought it would not be fitting for Mall and Betty to board at her husband's house, 'for he is but an ordinary grazier and a mean condition man'.[44]

Mary's reunion with her son Jack was a muted affair. They had been apart for nearly four years, and during that time the boy had been cared for by Mrs Alcock, his nurse Nan Fudd, and whichever of his aunts happened to be at Claydon. His mother was a stranger to him, as he was to her. But perhaps because of his easy-going upbringing, he adapted well enough to her, following her round like a puppy from the moment she arrived. For her part, she was pleased enough with his cheery attitude – 'though 'tis my own I must needs say he is an extreme witty child'[45] – but considerably less pleased with his general development. His learning had been neglected, he had a speech impediment and his legs were crooked, which she put down to the fact that his carers let him eat anything he liked. Some parental supervision was called for, and she told Sir Ralph that the boy would be better off with them in France.

The baby, who in line with contemporary practice was fostered out with the wet nurse until he was weaned, fell sick soon after she arrived at Claydon, but once again he picked up. 'Poor child,' Mary said, 'I pray God bless him and make him a happy man, for he hath had but a troublesome beginning.'[46] She changed to another wet nurse and, after carrying out an inventory of the goods at Claydon and going through the accounts with Roades, she left the two boys, spent a few weeks with Aunt Sherard in Leicestershire, and then went back to London and the great business. Every Thursday she wrote home to Blois, telling Sir Ralph how things were going, whom she had seen, what the latest gossip was about their friends or the political situation. He wrote just as regularly, his letters a mixture of affection, obsessive anxiety and petulance. 'Had I but one letter to write a week, I would not miss answering the least particular,' he told her after she hadn't responded to one of his many queries about the estate. 'If you cannot answer it presently you commonly forget it, and the reason is, because you will not take a note of remembrance.'[47]

Sir Ralph had reason to be peevish. So far, the deeds of trust he had arranged back in 1643 had stalled the effects of the sequestration process by stating that interest on the family debts had first call on estate income. But the second and last deed was due to expire on the last day of November 1647. If that happened with the sequestration still not lifted, the rents which fell due in March 1648 would be confiscated by the County Committee. Apart from a small sum set aside for Sir Ralph's dependants, the money would be lost.

He was so desperate to avoid this that with six weeks to go to the end of November he told Mary she would have to forge a third deed. And that was what she did. She sent for the originals and used them to make a copy ostensibly dated 1 December 1643 and running for twelve months from 1 December 1647. She forged Sir Ralph's signature and chose as 'witnesses' people who had known him in 1643, but who were now either dead or safely out of the country. Sir Ralph told her she could discuss what she was doing with Uncle Doctor, 'but with no other creature whatsoever'.[48] No wonder. Forgery had been a capital crime since 1634, and she could have hanged if the ruse was discovered.

While Sir Ralph sniped at Mary for not answering his letters properly, she also complained. Towards the end of October 1647 she took him to task because for weeks now the regular letters from Blois hadn't mentioned a word about Edmund and Peg. Why was that? Were they well?

They were not well. They were sick with dysentery, and Sir Ralph didn't want to distress her. Edmund recovered, but Peg didn't. Right at the end, this eight-year-old child lay on her bed and told her maid that she could have her clothes after her death. Then she asked her father and brother to pray for her soul, and died.

If Sir Ralph hadn't dared to tell Mary when her children were ill, his nerve failed him completely when it came to telling her that Peg was dead. He didn't have the courage; he didn't have the words. So he asked William Denton to break the news: 'Oh Dr., Dr., my poor Peg is happy but I am your most afflicted and unfortunate servant. Tell me how and when this shall be made known to her mother.'[49] Uncle Doctor went straight round to Mary's lodgings when he received Sir Ralph's letter; but on the way he met his own wife Kate, who had just had word from Claydon of another tragedy.

Without any warning, baby Ralph had gone into convulsions

and died. Kate had just this minute told Mary, and when Denton walked into her chamber he found her lying on the bed crying. In an unbearably poignant gesture, she turned to him and confessed through her tears that she was worried about Edmund and Peg; it was a month or more since her husband had mentioned them in his letters. 'I thought it better to make but one business of both,' Denton told Sir Ralph; 'and so I let her know how happy her girl was.'[50]

She fell apart. For two days she lay in her bed and raved. She didn't know her friends, she was desperate to go home to Sir Ralph, she cried that this double blow was too much for her to bear. Then on the third day she got up, paced her chamber and turned her thoughts back towards accomplishing her mission. Miserable as she was, desperate though she was to be with Sir Ralph in Blois, she convinced herself that she couldn't go home until that happened. She must put her faith in God:

> For He gave [my children] to me and He took them from me, and I hope and I trust He will in His good time deliver me out of all my troubles and give my mind some quiet and bring me to thee; for until I am with thee I cannot take any content in any thing in this world. For the truth is, I would not to gain the greatest riches in this world be so long again from thee as I have already been. But as soon as I am able to go abroad I will follow thy business night and day.[51]

Sir Ralph was not so resilient. For a year he had kicked his heels in France while his wife and friends worked to extricate him from a muddle of his own making. He was impatient and frustrated at Mary's lack of progress, anxious about the outcome, miserable about their long separation and – crucially for someone to whom method and order were an essential part of life – he was not in control of events. The deaths of Peg and the baby son he had never seen pushed him over the edge, and he despaired of ever having his affairs sorted out. 'Court hopes undid my father,' he told Mary, 'and Country hopes (for so I may call these that we now gape after) are like to undo me.'[52] If she wasn't going to succeed in her mission, she must tell him and have done – he couldn't bear the waiting any longer. At the same time he hatched a wild scheme to leave Edmund in Blois, change his name and go travelling alone in Italy and the Levant. 'I doubt not but my good God both can and will bring me to his heavenly rest,' he told Denton, 'whether I die in the midst of Rome or in the deserts of the heathens.'[53] And it would be best for all concerned if he did die: then at least Mary and the two boys could enjoy his estate, since the widows and orphans of delinquents were rarely pursued by the Committee for Sequestration.

A few weeks after confiding his plans to Uncle Doctor he wrote and told Mary. And Mary was furious. For several days, and several sleepless nights, she thought about the best way to respond to her husband's announcement that he was going away. Then she sat down and wrote a long, angry and passionate letter. How could he have so little respect for her feelings, after everything they had been through? Where was the sense in having their little family divided 'in four separate places'. Was he trying to break her heart? 'I confess I did believe thou haddest had other thoughts of me than to think I could brook such a proposition. No, my heart, you must not whilst I live have any such design without your resolve to take me along with you, and then live in what part of the world you most fancy . . . I am not able to say one word more but that at this time there is not a sadder creature in the world than thy own dear M.'[54]

Mary's rebuke seemed to work, in that Sir Ralph gave up his dreams of escape and oblivion. But another calming influence was the knowledge that the great business was on the move again. In November Mischief and Uncle Doctor came to the conclusion that the only way to make any progress in the Commons was by bribery. Initially Mary was reluctant to go down that route, not because she had scruples, but because she didn't have money. She had been selling off bits and pieces to raise cash all year: her watch, 'one of the finest in London', went for £26, for example – not bad, since 'it would not go at all'.[55] But her living expenses were a constant worry. She had already left one set of lodgings because the woman insisted on letting the entire house as a single entity, and it cost her too much; she now had two rooms with a Mrs Brooks, two doors above the Golden Fleece tavern in Charles Street, which cost 14s. a week. Then there were unavoidable obligations. She owed Uncle Doctor for looking after her when she had her baby. A sum of £20 seemed reasonable to her, but Sir Ralph insisted on £30; and even then he told her to make it clear this was just an interim payment until times improved. If the Doctor absolutely refused to accept the money, Mary was to buy him a present of 'six trencher plates and a pair of little candlesticks', and to be sure to give something to Mrs Denton and their daughter.[56]

So a bribe of £40 or £50, which was the going rate, represented a considerable outlay. 'Where we shall get the money I vow I know not,' she told Sir Ralph.[57] Dr Denton wasn't going to let a little thing like that stand in his way. He reckoned that if he offered £50 to his cousin, who was sister-in-law to Speaker Lenthall, the petition might be heard. A week later he'd managed to get the price down to £40, and word came back that Friday 17 December was the day appointed.

It was touch and go. According to Denton, who was hovering around in Westminster Hall, the Commons had so much pressing business to attend to that Friday that no one thought the Verney petition stood the remotest chance of being heard. Among other things John Ashe, the chair of the Committee of Goldsmiths' Hall, was bringing in a long report on fines and compositions of nearly twenty delinquents; each case had to be heard and the committee's recommendations approved. As Ashe passed through Westminster Hall on his way to St Stephen's Chapel, Denton and Francis Drake, who had agreed to move the petition, collared him and asked him to sit quiet while Drake moved it. He refused, but when they explained how little parliamentary time it would take he agreed to move it himself, which he did, slipping it into the middle of his report. With 'some but not much regret', according to Denton,[58] the Commons agreed that 'the whole business touching the sequestration of the estate of Sir Ralph Verney, be referred to the examination and consideration of the Committee of Lords and Commons for Sequestrations: to examine, hear, and determine the same, according to the Ordinances of Parliament in that behalf'.[59]

Mary found £40 and paid it out that day. 'You may imagine for what,' she told Sir Ralph, 'and truly I was never better contented to pay any money in my life than I was to pay that.'[60] Everyone was confident the sequestration would be lifted, but Mary was determined to cultivate friends on the committee. The case was due to be heard on Christmas Eve, but she and Denton managed to have it deferred for a couple of weeks because the Earl of Warwick and several others had gone into the country and weren't due back until the beginning of January. 'Though it be a clear case, yet it is policy to have most Lords there,' said Denton.[61]

Mary entertained MPs to dinner and haunted Eleanor Warwick's house nearly every day for a week in the lead-up to the hearing. At long last, on Wednesday 5 January 1648, more than fourteen months after Mary left Sir Ralph at Dieppe, the case was heard. It was not quite as open and shut as she had anticipated – the committee argued fiercely over the rights and wrongs of Sir Ralph's actions for three hours – but in the end the vote went Sir Ralph's way, by a majority of 'eleven to three or four'.[62] The sequestration was lifted.

Mary went straight round to Eleanor Warwick's house that night to thank her and her husband. Family and connections had made a difference after all; so had her own determination. The next morning she wrote to tell Sir Ralph the good news, as did Denton and Sir Roger Burgoyne, who urged him 'to add life to your intentions and let them turn to resolutions of casting once more an eye upon your unhappy country'.[63] That was a little premature: Sir Ralph couldn't come home until he had made arrangements with his creditors, but at least he could begin the process. Denton made sure that certificates were immediately presented to the County Committees of Buckinghamshire, Oxfordshire and Berkshire, compelling them to accept that the sequestration was no longer in force and that Sir Ralph's estates in those counties were free of restriction.

Then, on Sir Ralph's behalf, he set about renegotiating the debts and selling off parcels of land. Creditors were given two choices: they could either accept land at pre-war values (much greater than they were now) in which case they would be given land to the full value of the principal plus all the accrued interest; or they could have cash, in which case Sir Ralph would only pay the principal and half the interest. Almost everybody opted for cash.

It was a long process, and Denton worked hard to rescue Sir Ralph's fortunes for another four years. In the meantime, though,

Mischief prepared to go home. She settled accounts in London during January and February, shopped for clothes and presents for Sir Ralph and Edmund and their friends in Blois, and made arrangements for Jack to be brought down to her. She asked Will Roades to find her a 'handsome mastiff dog . . . it must be a very large and quiet dog', to take back to France,[64] and packed up her trunks and bundles and boxes.

Sir Ralph fussed and worried and looked forward to their reunion, but he was still emotionally fragile, and every now and then his grief over Peg burst through. 'I loved her at least equal too (if not above) any child I had, and truly she deserved it, for there was never a better, nor more patient babby born,' he wrote. 'Till now I never knew what a grief it was to part with a child.'[65] Mary suggested he send bracelets of Peg's hair to all six of his sisters.

He came down to Dieppe to meet her at the end of March 1648, but she fell sick in London with 'a miserable fit of the stone' and had to postpone her journey for some days.[66] In the second week of April she finally embarked at Rye, with Jack, Luce, Will Roades (who had been ordered to bring the estate accounts to France so that his master could go through them with him) and, presumably, the large mastiff.

On Monday the 10th, Mary was reunited with Sir Ralph. They had been apart for more than sixteen months. She sent word that he was to look in the great trunk in her closet at Blois for her black silk gown, and to be sure to bring it with him when he came to meet her.

12

Oh My My Dear Dear

*I*n August 1649 the Royalist news-sheet *Mercurius Elencticus* carried a front-page story about the exploits of an enemy of the crown called 'Varney'.[1] The author told how Varney had recently broken into his own brother's study and robbed him before fleeing to France, where he stole a horse and was forced to take refuge in a monastery. He pretended to the monks that he was a 'zealous Catholic', and this, coupled with the fact that he was known to be the son 'to so honourable a gentleman, as Sir Edmund Varney', ensured him a warm welcome. He repaid this hospitality by stealing 'sundry rich vestments, pictures, and other things consecrated to a holy use, and of great value, wherewith he fled to Calais, and there sacrilegiously sold them'. With the money he went to Holland, where he joined up with the Royalists in exile – and informed on them to the 'rebels' in Westminster. Found out and forced to run for his life, he came back to England and his masters in Parliament, 'where ever since he hath lived under their protection and pay, to betray men'.

This was not the first time Tom Verney had appeared in the pages of *Mercurius Elencticus* (for, of course, it was he). Three weeks earlier the newsletter had named him as the most dangerous of a group of paid informers who were making a trade out of betraying Royalists to Parliament. In spite of being the son of the King's standard-bearer, he had 'strangely degenerated from the true worth of his father, as having betrayed many gallant gentlemen of the King's party'. His aim in all this treachery, according to *Mercurius Elencticus*, was 'to get his brother's estate, it being at the devotion of the rebels, because of his loyalty to his sovereign'.[2]

The cavalier news-sheet was often cavalier with its facts. It confused Mun and Sir Ralph, for example, announcing that Tom's elder brother was currently 'an eminent commander' with the Marquis of Ormond in Ireland. So in other circumstances one might be inclined to be wary of such a lurid attack on a man's reputation.

But Tom was capable of anything. Over the previous couple of years he had deserted his pregnant wife Joyce, forged Will Roades' name on a bond and sold the furniture out of Sir Ralph's London house. As his lack of reputation made it harder for him to secure credit, so he moved further and further into the twilight world of Stuart criminality. 'His ways and courses have not only made him as a stranger to his own family, but almost to all gentlemen,' an exasperated Mun informed Sir Ralph in August 1647.[3] And he did indeed go to France in the spring of 1648, around the same time that Mary returned to Blois. This was partly to get away from his 'most turbulent and ill-disposed wife', as he described her,[4] but chiefly to escape the law, after he was found out forging some deeds. His companion was his brother-in-law, Sir Thomas Elmes, who was also keen to escape England and his own marriage to Peg, which was in difficulties after less than two years. According to Susan, 'poor Peg has married a very humoursome cross boy as ever I saw in my life, and she is very much altered for the worse since she was married; I do not much blame her for being so altered, because sometimes he makes her cry night and day.'[5] Elmes's bad temper turned to violence, and he took to hitting Peg. She stood up to him – when William Denton tried to step in and mediate, even he was shocked at the language which passed between them – but according to Henry, who also tried to make peace between the couple, Elmes behaved erratically, 'by fits very bad and devilish jealous, now and then for an hour strangely fond'.[6] Henry found that speaking 'big words' kept him quiet for a while; but Henry couldn't always be on hand in the Elmes's Covent Garden household.

Elmes walked out on Pen in 1648, and Tom, ever quick to spot an opportunity, persuaded him to pay for the pair of them to travel in France. Whether or not the story of the monastery had any truth in it, Tom certainly did get into serious trouble in France. He ran up more debts, signed Elmes's name to a bill of exchange and ran back to England to avoid prosecution. By the time *Mercurius Elencticus* put his name on its front page, he had turned *agent provocateur*, writing to the Leveller John Lilburne, who was imprisoned in the Tower, with an offer of 3000 or 4000 men and a suggestion that Lilburne might like to provide Tom with a list of his supporters in Buckinghamshire. Lilburne actually met with Tom, but stories about his lack of scruples were common knowledge around London and, when the Leveller repeated them to his face, 'the gentleman (with the impudentest and undaunted countenance that I have seen) denied all'.[7]

In November 1649 Tom was on the run again, leaving the country as fast as he could and making hurried arrangements for Will Roades to pay his £10 quarteredge, which seems to have been all he had to live on. 'You are very sensible of my deep engagements; and how narrowly I was looked after,' he told Will. 'It was high time for me to take my journey.'[8] Six months later he was back in England and in the fourteenth-century Gatehouse prison at Westminster, whence he had been sent by Thomas Elmes. By now he was a master of the begging letter, which he elevated to an art form – a perfect blend of misery and righteous indignation, blame and contrition:

> I take God to witness [he told Roades] I have lived upon bread and beer and nothing else for Thursday, Friday and Saturday last, and a Sunday all day nothing, till night, then a man out of charity gave me . . . meat. Had I money to remove myself to a better prison, I did not much care; but the cursed damned lawyers will not look up and trust for a week's space. Neither will any of my unkind kindred lend me sixpence; I have solicited them over and over, and all to no effect.[9]

Could Roades lend him five pounds? And quickly?

That autumn Tom turned Parliamentary informer. When the estate of the staunchly Royalist Duke of Hamilton came before the Committee for Compounding, Tom gave evidence that in 1643 the Duke had come to Oxford of his own accord to present the King with propositions from the Scottish government. Unfortunately for him, someone took exception to Tom's testimony and pointed out that Hamilton's creditors, who were eager to get their hands on his estate, had given Tom a new suit and £50 to give his evidence.

Tom's brother Mun was in Ireland when *Mercurius Elencticus* published its story in August 1649. He was now Colonel Sir Edmund Verney, having been knighted by the King in 1643 and promoted from major the following year. Still resolved that 'my sword must be my best livelihood',[10] he saw action during the war at Chester, where he was lieutenant governor, and when the King was defeated he followed his master, the Marquis of Ormond, into exile in France. 'You are the loadstone that may draw me all over the world,' he told Ormond, 'and I am in pain until I am with you.'[11]

Mun went with Ormond when the Marquis returned to Ireland in September 1648 to try to form a coalition with Irish Catholics. Although Charles I was executed in January 1649 – 'we are now in the maddest world that ever we mortals saw,' said Uncle Doctor[12] – Ormond continued to rally troops to the Stuart cause, and his forces had some success, particularly in Leinster, where they captured Drogheda and Trim and gradually closed in on the remaining Parliamentarian garrison at Dublin, which was held by Cromwell's 'noble friend and companion in labours'[13] Michael Jones, with a force of some 8000 men. By the end of July 1649 the Royalist army – including Mun, who was now a lieutenant colonel in Ormond's regiment of foot – was camped at Rathmines, a couple of miles to the south of the city, and having a relaxed time of it. Ormond was not a great disciplinarian: he was said to keep 'a great inn of play, drinking, and pleasure, [rather] than a well-ordered camp of soldiers'.[14] A degree of urgency was given to their siege by the news that Cromwell was poised to set sail from England with a large relieving force. If Ormond's troops didn't capture Dublin before he arrived, they certainly wouldn't take it afterwards.

Soon after nightfall on 1 August a party of 1500 Royalists led by Ormond's second-in-command, Patrick Purcell, set out from Rathmines to seize the strategically important Baggotsrath Castle, which commanded the meadows below Dublin. It was only a mile away, but Purcell got lost in the dark and didn't arrive at his objective until the next morning. Ormond, who had been up all night writing despatches, rode over at eight o'clock to find that the castle was still unfortified, with no trenches dug or earthworks thrown up. There seemed to be quite a lot of activity taking place among the Parliamentarians across the meadows, too. Nevertheless, he trotted back to Rathmines and went to bed.

At ten that morning he was woken by gunfire. Jones had launched a counterattack with more than 5000 men, overrunning Baggotsrath and pushing straight on to Rathmines. Troops were running everywhere – chiefly away from the fighting, and up into the Wicklow Hills 'where some of them were bred, and whither they knew the way but too well'.[15] Ormond's cavalry commander, Sir William Vaughan, tried to organise a defence of the camp, but was killed. Jones claimed to have taken more than 2500 prisoners and slain 4000 Royalists. Within days, the news reached England that Mun was one of the dead.

Uncle Doctor wrote to Sir Ralph and Mary in France. Mun's regiment of foot and Vaughan's regiment of horse were at the forefront of the action, he said. Mun's men 'were killed all on a heap, not one of them as I can hear but fought it out to the last even against horse and foot'. Mun died with them and was buried alongside Vaughan. The word was, the death of such a valiant soldier grieved even his enemies. 'Jones himself when he saw him struck his hands on his breast, and said he had rather have had him alive than all the prisoners he had.'[16]

None of this was true. Dr Denton, whose relish for gossip led him on more than one occasion to serve up rumour as fact, had got it quite wrong. Sir Ralph's brother was alive and unharmed. When Jones and his soldiers descended on Rathmines like the wolf on the fold, Mun was several miles away on the north bank of the Liffey, and he made his escape up the coast to Drogheda, thirty miles away, taking 400 infantrymen with him. They joined the Royalist garrison there, and waited for Cromwell.

Cromwell landed at Dublin on 15 August, after a crossing which made him 'as sea-sick as ever I saw any man in my life', according to the Puritan minister Hugh Peter.[17] One of his first acts was to issue a declaration against drunkenness and profanity. Further reinforcements arrived a week later, and on 31 August he mustered a force of 9000 men, eight regiments of foot and six of horse, in the fields to the north of Dublin, and marched north, arriving before the gates of Drogheda on 3 September.

While the Parliamentarians waited for their heavy guns to catch up with them, Mun and his comrades organised the occasional raid. 'Our men are all in heart and courage, having still had good success in our salleys,' he wrote in a despatch to Ormond, who was camped twenty-five miles away at Trim, Co. Meath. He was calm and unruffled, describing how he held daily staff meetings with his 'most intimate comrades', Colonels Warren and Wall, both of whom commanded regiments of foot. 'I have not in my life known more diligence and circumspection than in these two gentlemen, to discuss how best to conduct the defence,' he told Ormond. '. . . We do little fear what the enemy can do forcibly against us.' But there were hints of disquiet. Although Mun and the other senior officers claimed to be confident about their ability to repel Cromwell's force, he told Ormond that the biggest talking point among the rest of the garrison was how they were going to be relieved, and ended his despatch by urging that Ormond's forces should advance towards Slane, ten miles to the west, thus drawing off Cromwell's men. 'Certainly they could much less maintain their siege.'[18]

By the next day, a Monday, Cromwell's heavy guns were in place just across the valley overlooking the south-eastern corner of the town. He called on Drogheda to surrender, warning the garrison and the townsfolk that 'if this be refused you will have no cause to blame me'.[19] The garrison commander – and Mun's immediate superior in the town – was Sir Arthur Aston, a Catholic and a professional soldier who was both high-handed and peculiarly accident-prone. As Governor of Reading in 1643 he had been rendered speechless when a roof tile hit him on the head;

he had his horse shot under him at the Battle of Newbury, was stabbed in the side during an Oxford street brawl and lost a leg to gangrene after he fell off his horse trying to impress some women with his equine skills in 1644.

But whatever else Aston was, he was no coward; and although the native Irish in the garrison were deserting in droves and ammunition was running short, his response to Cromwell's ultimatum was to boast that anyone who could take Drogheda could capture hell itself.[20]

Later that day hell came to Drogheda, as Cromwell's artillery bombardment began. The town straddled the River Boyne, and the Parliamentarians concentrated on taking the south bank, hoping that they would be able to secure the drawbridge which linked it to the north. It was a formidable task. The town walls were 20 feet high and defended by twenty-nine guard towers, and Aston had created a complex system of earthworks and trenches within them. But Cromwell had heavy siege guns, the like of which had never been seen before in Ireland; and by the following afternoon those guns had breached the south-eastern defences.

Mun's role in the fighting isn't mentioned in any of the contemporary accounts. All we hear is that he 'behaved himself with the greatest gallantry that could be'.[21] It seems likely that he and his men were among the troops who waited in the smoke and rubble for the inevitable assault. It came at five o'clock. Three regiments of Parliamentarians swept across the valley, only to be forced back by the entrenched Royalists. Their commander, James Castle, was shot in the head by a Royalist musketeer. After the attackers were repulsed again, Cromwell himself led his reserves into the breach, and this time they broke through. Mun lost both of his friends: William Wall was killed trying to hold the line; Colonel Warren had his legs blown off by a cannon ball.

At this point, Sir Arthur Aston should have pulled his survivors back to the north bank of the Boyne and raised the drawbridge. This would at least have bought the defenders a little more time, and prevented Cromwell's troops from sweeping through the entire town. But he didn't. He chose to make a last stand at a palisaded fort called the Mill Mount, which stood only 200 yards from the breached wall. Cromwell described what happened next:

The enemy retreated, divers of them, into the Millmount: a place very strong and of difficult access, being exceedingly high, having a good graft and strongly palisaded. The Governor, Sir Arthur Aston, and divers considerable officers being there, our men getting up to them were ordered by me to put them all to the sword. And indeed being in the heat of the action, I forbade them to spare any that were in arms in the town, and, I think that night they put to the sword about two thou-sand men.[22]

It was a bloody massacre. Roundhead officers who offered quarter to any defenders had their orders countermanded by Cromwell himself, who was determined to make an example of Drogheda. Aston was killed, and his killers fought among themselves over his artificial leg, which was said to be made of gold. Many of the Royalists who did try to make it back across the drawbridge were overtaken by Parliamentarians and cut down. About a hundred barricaded themselves into the tower of St Peter's church in the heart of the main town. After a failed attempt to blow it up with powder, John Hewson, who commanded one of Cromwell's five regiments of foot, told his men to pile all the seats in the church directly under the tower and set them alight. The fugitives were burned alive, 'and so at once men and bells and roof came all down together, the most hideous sight and terrible cry that ever he was a witness of at once'.[23]

There was little organised resistance, and certainly none to match the terrifying brutality of Cromwell's battle-hardened professionals. Pockets of fighters were ruthlessly hunted out by soldiers using children as shields. At least two groups of Royalists barricaded themselves into towers on the town walls, and one continued to shoot at the soldiers in the street below, hitting several. When they surrendered, their officers were all 'knocked on the head' in Cromwell's words; every tenth enlisted man was killed; and the rest were shipped off to Barbados. Royalists in the second tower, which was probably part of the fortified West Gate, were all spared because they hadn't given fire; they were also destined for Barbados.

Thomas Wood told his brother, the antiquary Anthony Wood,

how he had found a group of women hiding in the vaults under one of the town's churches:

> One of these, a most handsome virgin and arrayed in costly and gorgeous apparel, kneeled down to Tho. Wood with tears and prayers to save her life: and being strucken with a profound pity, took her under his arm, went with her out of the church, with intentions to put her over the works and to let her shift for herself; but then a soldier perceiving his intentions, he ran his sword up her belly or fundament. Whereupon Mr Wood seeing her gasping, took away her money, jewels &c, and flung her down over the works.[*]

By the next day, when the carnage was over, Colonel Hewson reckoned that more than 3000 bodies lay in the streets; Cromwell said there were 1000 dead in and around St Peter's church alone, all 'put to the sword fleeing thither for safety'.[24]

Mun wasn't one of the casualties. Unlike Wall, Warren and Aston, he got through the fighting unhurt and somehow managed to escape the bloodletting which followed, although he didn't escape the town. Within days, Ormond was informed that although Cromwell had ordered no quarter given, a number of Royalists were saved by their enemies, and that his lieutenant colonel was one of them. Perhaps Mun belonged to the group from the West Gate which was spared by Cromwell. Perhaps he was just lucky.

His luck was about to run out. Three days after Mun surrendered, he was walking in the streets of Drogheda with Cromwell and some others, when a Parliamentarian officer who had a passing acquaintance with him called him aside for a private word. Mun went over to talk to him, and without warning the man stabbed him. He died where he fell.

Cromwell remained in the town for the rest of the week, issuing dire threats to the Royalist garrisons at Dundalk and Trim before heading back to Dublin on the Saturday. The threats

---

[*] Andrew Clark (ed.), *The Life and Times of Anthony à Wood*, (1961), 62. Although Thomas Wood was in Cromwell's army during the Siege of Drogheda, he had also fought on the Royalist side, serving as a trooper during the English Civil War with Captain Thomas Gardiner, Cary Gardiner's husband.

worked. With the dreadful example of Drogheda before them, both garrisons fled, which was exactly the purpose of his behaviour after the siege. 'The enemy was filled . . . with much terror. And truly I believe this bitterness will save much effusion of blood, through the grace of God.'[25]

The only known portrait of Mun Verney was painted by Justus van Egmont in Paris in 1648, when he was about thirty-one. It shows a weedy, unprepossessing young man with a weak chin and a receding hairline. He doesn't look like a hero. In fact the only martial thing about him is the armour he wears. How unfair that is. Mun was his father's son – physically brave, determined to do right, excited by the prospect of danger. But he had something else which one wouldn't expect to find in a professional soldier: a generosity of spirit, a kindness and an openness which none of the other Verneys possessed. Even today his killing still seems pointless and spiteful, his death a peculiar loss.

The news of Cromwell's victory spread quickly across Europe, and his own account of the action in a letter to Speaker Lenthall was published by order of Parliament on 2 October 1649, along with a 'list of the officers and soldiers slain at the storming of Drogheda'. Mun's name came second on the list, below that of Sir Arthur Aston. His friends Wall and Warren were there; and right at the bottom were 'two thousand five hundred foot soldiers, besides staff officers, chyrurgeons, &c and many inhabitants'[26] But in Blois Sir Ralph and Mary didn't hear anything definite for months. They had either read or been told about Cromwell's letter, and the fact that it mentioned survivors being shipped to the West Indies 'makes me more confident of dear Mun's being alive', Sir Ralph told a friend at the end of October.[27] A day or two later he confessed that he was still 'between hope and fear concerning dear dear Mun'.[28]

At the end of November his worst fears were confirmed when a letter arrived from James Buck, an impoverished member of the exiled Marchioness of Ormond's household at Caen, relating the circumstances of Mun's death at Drogheda. The letter was kindly enough, and Buck promised vengeance against the killer; but, ironically, his chief purpose in writing was to tap Sir Ralph for the sum of five pistoles and eight livres (about £4 10s.) which he claimed Mun had owed him. Even in death,

Sir Ralph's siblings continued to clamour for money. He didn't pay up.

Dearly as he loved his brother, Sir Ralph had more pressing worries. His 'dear bud', his Mischief, was sick. Mary had been taken ill not long after returning from England, losing her sight temporarily and suffering what Sir Ralph described as 'a kind of apoplexy or lethargy'.[*] She recovered, but she remained rather frail, and her French doctor, a kinsman of the Protestant minister in Blois, recommended bleeding her. William Denton, who was following her progress closely from England, advised that if she must be bled, 'let it be under her parlous [in the old sense of 'mischievous'] tongue'.[29] In the summer of 1649 Sir Ralph took her to the hot springs of Bourbonne-les-Bains in the Haute-Marne; from there they went to Paris, where they received frantic letters from Blois warning them that Jack was sick with a high fever. But Dr Testard bled him and the fever broke, so they stayed on in Paris while Mary shopped for the kind of luxury goods which were only available there – trimmed gloves, a fan, an enamelled box. Sir Ralph kept up a running joke with English friends about her dominant role in their relationship: 'she wears the breeches and will do what she list,' he said.[30]

But the joke hid his worry. She was still sick, and he toyed with the idea of taking her south for the winter. That didn't work out – he wanted to go down to Montpellier on the Mediterranean coast, a town famous with the English for its mild climate and its Protestantism, its physic schools and its 130 apothecaries' shops ('the streets insufferably narrow,' said John Clenche[31]), but there was an outbreak of smallpox there, and in the end the couple decided to go straight home to their children in Blois.

In the meantime, the bad news kept flooding in. First there was Uncle Doctor's announcement that Mun had been killed at Rathmines; then the stories about the taking of Drogheda. Sister Pen wrote to ask for the pair of holland sheets 'that was given to me by my mother': her father-in-law had just died intestate,

[*] *Memoirs of the Verney Family* (1907) I, 447. The phrase recalls Falstaff's remarks in *2 Henry IV*, I, 2: 'This apoplexy is, as I take it, a kind of lethargy, an't please your lordship; a kind of sleeping in the blood, a whoreson tingling.'

so that everything in the house went to her mother-in-law, including the linen.[32] Word came from Rotterdam that Tom had been there, and had managed to borrow £63 from an English merchant, Mr Boulds, by using Sir Ralph's name. 'He told him that he had bills coming from England but he is since run away from here.'[33] Could Sir Ralph honour the debt? Sister Susan, who hadn't been in touch with Sir Ralph for months, wrote him a long and graphic account of her recent pregnancy:

> Ten weeks since I was brought to bed; my child was dead born, it was a boy. I had a very sad and weak time of it, for ever since before I was churched I have been under the surgeon's hands with my breast[s]. Both of them did break, I had five holes in one, and one great one in the other. I have endured much pain and misery with them, for a long time not able to turn me in my bed, nor put my hands to my head. I thank God I am now able to put on a wide waistcoat but all this while I have sat up in a cloak. I am now able to go up and down my house, but not out of doors . . .[34]

Rather too much information there, one feels. And all the while, Mary's health was failing. She was tired all the time now, and suffering from debilitating bouts of diarrhoea; her fingers felt dead and her nails were blue. Dr Testard suggested she might have scurvy, and by November an anxious Sir Ralph was writing to England to ask William Denton if Testard was right. Uncle Doctor didn't agree with the diagnosis, but he approved rather grudgingly of the treatment – a daily dose of horseradish and scurvy grass or spoonwort 'should be very good for her whether she have the scorbic [scurvy] or not'.[35] Denton argued that the blue nails and numbness were caused by obstructions which prevented her natural heat from reaching her extremities. He prescribed plenty of exercise and recommended that she take up tennis.

Tennis wasn't going to help. By Christmas Mary had developed a dreadful and persistent cough, and Dr Denton mentioned consumption, a word which the seventeenth-century applied not only to tuberculosis, but to any wasting disease. She may have had some form of cancer, but the way in which her illness presented itself was more consistent with mitral stenosis, a narrowing or obstruction of the opening of the mitral valve which separates the upper and lower chambers on the left side of the heart. Usually brought on by rheumatic fever, it is something of a rarity in the developed world these days. Symptoms include the peripheral cyanosis which led Testard to think of scurvy, general lethargy, transient ischemic attacks (which may have caused Mary's temporary blindness), coughs and other respiratory problems. Its effects can be exacerbated by pregnancy; as it progresses, the patient becomes increasingly at risk from atrial fibrillation, embolism and congestive heart failure. Surgical intervention – the only treatment – was not even dreamed of in seventeenth-century England: in 1649 it was only twenty-one years since William Harvey published *De Motu Cordis*, and many medical men were still sceptical about his theories on the motion of the heart and the circulation of the blood.

Friends in England and France were constantly asking after Mary. Lady Mary Herbert, one of the Royalists in exile who hovered around the court of Henrietta Maria in Paris, wrote with the good news that she had managed to sell some hangings for Sir Ralph, and said she would be 'extreme glad' to hear of his wife's good health.[36] She was to be disappointed: Mary was too ill even to attend church, and Sir Ralph organised communion and a sermon for her at their lodgings 'after the honest old way at home'.[37]

Denton sent out a parcel of books, which showed a distinctly catholic (as distinct from Catholic) taste in politics and theology. There was *A Manual of Private Devotions* and *A Manual of Directions for the Sick*, both by the great anti-Calvinist Bishop of Winchester, Lancelot Andrewes; *Of the Laws of Ecclesiastical Polity* by Richard Hooker, seen at the time as a hero of moderate Protestantism; *A History of Independency* by the West Country pamphleteer Clement Walker, who argued against the radicals in Parliament and for a settlement with the King. There were also more subversive works, such as *The Jugglers Discovered*, the Leveller John Lilburne's attack on 'the turncoat, Machiavell practices and underhand dealings of Lieutenant-General Cromwell and his son-in-law Commissary General Ireton, and the rest of their Hocus Pocus faction'.[38] *Eikonoclastes*, John Milton's justification of the King's execution, was on Sir Ralph's reading list (he already had English and French

editions of *Eikon Basilike*, the book which purported to be Charles
I's spiritual autobiography). Then there was William Prynne's
Historical Collection of the Ancient Parliaments of England and several
books by the Somerset divine William Sclater, whose *Papisto-
Mastix, or Deborah's Prayer Against God's Enemies*, was particularly
recommended by Uncle Doctor. 'One of the best books I ever
read,' he told Sir Ralph; 'short and strangely convincing.'[39] He
urged Mary to leave off her romances and apply herself to the
reading of it, a long sermon on the miraculous way in which
the nation was delivered from Guy Fawkes and the Gunpowder
Plot of 1605. If it had succeeded, said Sclater, 'we might have
been plundered in gross superstition and idolatry; have been
worshipping of images, cringing to crosses, adoring of crucifixes,
blathering to a saint, rumbling of our beads, wandering in some
pilgrimage; all overrun with the rank weeds of well-worship,
angering our God of jealousy, and irritating the just wrath of
Heaven; or else all dragg'd unto racks, or stakes, or dungeons, to
fire, and faggot, or other exquisite tortures; the proper badges of
that Romish Antichrist, that man of sin.'[40]

Mary was better off sticking to her romances. But the list is
interesting, if earnest, and entirely consistent with Sir Ralph and
Mary's inclinations: thoughtful, serious, rabidly anti-Catholic and
moderately Protestant.

In January Mary rallied a little. Dr Testard prescribed a diet of
asses' milk, an idea which worried Uncle Doctor. He advocated
bleeding her first, either under her tongue again or by making
an incision in her jugular. (The mind boggles.) If she wouldn't
consent, then she should at least have leeches applied to her
throat. And the asses must be fed with turnip tops from the
Verneys' own garden in Blois.

Denton was no country quack. He had been court physician
to Charles I from 1636 until the mid-1640s; and he was one of
the most respected doctors of his day. Both he and Dr Testard,
of whom much less is known, were only following established
medical practice: 'Asses milk is universally preferred for the treatment of consumptives because of its cleansing qualities,' wrote
Gideon Harvey in *Morbus Anglicus: or, The Anatomy of Consumptions*
(1666). 'And to render it the more effectual, it's advisable to seed
the ass with restringent and detergent herbs, as yarrow, plantain,

vine leaves, knotgrass, bramble-bush leaves, &c.'* And according
to his own lights, Denton was providing sensible advice: although
asses' milk had powerful detergent properties, it was not nour-
ishing – hence the turnip tops.

The past is a foreign country; they do things differently there.
That goes way beyond the practice of medicine. In March 1650,
when Mary's brief remission was over and she was resuming her
downhill road, Sir Ralph asked Uncle Doctor to help him find
another English maid to help in the household. Denton's reply
still has the power to shock:

> Because you writ me that you were in love with dirty sluts, I
> took great care to fit you with a Joan that may be as good as
> my lady in the dark, and I hope I have fitted you a penny-
> worth. I will whilst she stays take her into my house and
> observe what I can, but Luce [Sheppard] is very confident she
> will match your cock, and she should know . . .[41]

Denton always did have a gift for the inappropriate remark, and
throughout their long friendship he delighted in getting a rise
out of Sir Ralph. And even Mary laughed at times about her
husband's liking for pretty maids. But that was a tender teasing
between lovers. This is much more difficult. There is not a shred
of doubt that Uncle Doctor cared deeply about Mary Verney.
'Pardon my passion for her,' he once told Sir Ralph, 'for if she
be so worthy of your love, you cannot blame me if I think her
so of mine.'[42] Nor is there any doubt at all that Sir Ralph was
desperately in love with his wife. So perhaps this is just a terribly
misjudged, laddish joke.

Except it doesn't feel like a joke – or at least, if it does, it feels
like a shared joke between two men who really see nothing
wrong with the idea of fucking a servant girl while your wife
lies dying in the next room. I wish I'd never seen that letter.

The asses' milk and leeches did Mary no good. After the short

---

* Pp. 235–6. Harvey went on to say that '*Platerus* records several cured by Womans
milk suck'd warm out of the Breast; and among the rest there was one, that throve
so well with his Wives milk, that he purposely got her with child again to prevent
his want of milk for the future.' Mary's regimen was not so bad, perhaps.

remission her condition began to deteriorate again, and by April this bright, energetic young woman, just thirty-four years old, was wasting away to nothing. Too weak even to lift a pen, she suffered from recurring bouts of fever, and had a terrible cough which nothing could alleviate. Her mouth was so sore that all she could take was milk and jellies; and the diarrhoea was back (which is hardly surprising, considering her diet). Sir Ralph was frantic. Just how frantic can be judged by the fact that at the beginning of May 1650 he wrote for help to John Cosin, Protestant chaplain at Henrietta Maria's court and well known as a Laudian whose views were dangerously close to popery. Although he was committed to the Anglican Church, Cosin's brand of Anglicanism was anathema to Sir Ralph: as vice-chancellor of Cambridge before the war, he had introduced ritualism and vigorously criticised Puritans as 'locusts ascending out of the bottomless pit, the very form of the beast, hellhounds'.[43] Now Sir Ralph sat in his study at Blois, listening to Mary coughing her life away, and wrote a heart-rending letter to the author of the notorious Laudian *A Collection of Private Devotions* (condemned by Prynne as *Cosin's cousining Devotions*), a man whom the Commons had described as 'author and abettor of Popish and Arminian innovations'.[44] He told Cosin that he was sending a little box containing forty livres (about £3), and begged for his prayers that 'God in his own good time will be graciously pleased to restore [Mary] to her health and strength again'.[45]

The seemingly interminable sadness of terminal illness played itself out. Nancy Denton, Uncle Doctor's young daughter, wrote a chirpy little note to Mary, saying how sorry she was to hear of her illness, 'but that now you are in a very good way for your recovery'.[46] Lady Mary Herbert sent a recipe for chocolate, still a rarity in western Europe and hailed as a universal panacea which among other things cured consumption and the 'cough of the lungs'.[47] Initially sceptical, Sir Ralph decided that Mary should try it, and began to fret over the right dose, the best time of day to take it, the length of time to wait after one meal and before the next. Mary liked to drink chocolate at four in the afternoon. Was this all right, as long as she fasted for two or three hours afterwards?

Uncle Doctor told Sir Ralph what in his heart he already

knew. Mary could drink chocolate whenever she liked; it wouldn't make any difference. 'I much doubt she hath not no long time here. We [doctors] are miserable comforters, but it is fit you should both know the worst.'[48]

There it was, out in the open. Mischief was going to die. Denton had been privately convinced of it for some time now, but he had hoped she might live through the summer. Now he doubted it, and when he heard that she had been fitting, he was sure. So he did something which in an age more intimate with mortality seemed less peculiar than it does in ours. He wrote her a long and uplifting letter, exhorting her to prepare herself for the inevitable, to give herself willingly to God. 'Corn cannot live except it be buried in the earth . . . death and sickness are but the fire through which we must pass . . . to the city of the living God, the heavenly Jerusalem and to an innumerable company of angels.'[49] He left it to Sir Ralph to decide whether or not Mary should read these words of hope, but in the event there was no decision to be made.

At three in the morning of Friday 10 May, Mary died. 'With what a religious and cheerful joy and courage this now happy and most glorious saint left this unhappy and most wicked world,' Sir Ralph told his uncle later, when he was able to think clearly.[50] In the immediate aftermath of Mary's death he was less fluent: all he could scrawl was 'Oh my my dear dear'.[51]

When Dr Cosin heard of Sir Ralph's bereavement, he sent him a copy of his *A Collection of Private Devotions*, which has an entire chapter on 'prayers at the point of death':

> Go to thy rest, O my soul, for the Lord hath upholden thee. From death to life; from sorrow to joy; from a vale of misery, to a paradise of mercy.[52]

While Mary's soul set out on its long journey, her body stayed at home, and for a disturbingly long time. Sir Ralph had her embalmed, and locked the corpse in a room by itself while he made arrangements to have it transported back to Claydon for burial. Mary remained in that room for nearly six months before being shipped over and interred in the family vault on 20 November 1650. Sir Ralph, who still went in fear of being gaoled by his creditors, stayed in France, although he was determined to be buried with her, so that they could go hand in hand to heaven together. He understood that at the Resurrection husbands and wives would no longer be considered as married, but he still hoped 'that we who ever from our very childhoods lived in so much peace, and Christian concord here on earth, shall also in our elder years for the full completing of our joys, at least be known to one another in heaven'.[53]

There were unpleasant legal complications over the death. France subscribed to *droit d'aubaine*, whereby the King had a right to all the personal property of a deceased alien; and under French law a wife was entitled to one half of a couple's estate. An unnamed court favourite – referred to by Sir Ralph only as 'this cunning catchpole'[54] – had begged the grant of the *droit d'aubaine* in Mary's case, sending Sir Ralph into a panic. He sold off as many of his goods as he reasonably could and distributed the rest among friends for safekeeping, while he tried (successfully, as it turned out) to have a stop put on the grant.

Mary's death devastated Sir Ralph: 'This, oh this, far exceeds all my other misfortunes, and hath put me upon so many several resolutions that now I know not what to resolve upon.'[55] Those misfortunes would have destroyed a stronger man. Over the past ten years he had lost both of his grandmothers, his mother, his father, his daughter, a son he never even saw, his 'best beloved brother',[56] his home, his fortune, his reputation. His wife had kept him going through all of this. She 'was not only willing to suffer for and with me here, but by her most exemplary goodness and patience both helped and taught me to support my otherwise almost insupportable burden'.[57] Now she was gone, and he didn't know where to turn. In an attempt to understand why God had punished him so ruthlessly and completely, he sat down and wrote out a list of all his past faults and transgressions, from a church window he had broken as a boy, to a brewer's bill for 40s. which he hadn't paid. He sent this review of his life off to Dr Denton with a request 'to tell me plainly wherein you have observed me to be faulty, and especially whether any man hath or is like to suffer unjustly either by or for me'.[58]

Denton responded with just the right combination of levity and straight talking which made him such a good friend to Sir

Ralph. He told his nephew that the catalogue of sin was nothing in comparison with his own faults – 'Oh, that my soul were guilty of no higher!'[59] – but he nevertheless took the opportunity to point out one of Sir Ralph's most irritating character flaws, his ability to take offence at the most trivial thing and then to hold a grudge for far too long. Then he suggested Sir Ralph could make amends by being reconciled to four people he was currently not speaking to: Parson Aris, Aunt Isham, Nat Fiennes and his brother Henry. Sir Ralph had no problems with the first three, but he jibbed at making friends with Henry, who had fallen out with him over money. He announced that he forgave his brother for the things Harry had said and done to hurt him, but he spent considerably longer in enumerating those things than in proclaiming his forgiveness. Harry's 'tongue and pen, not only on a sudden, but also after long deliberation, hath been no less bitter than unjust against me (though I am bound to forgive him as I thank God I do), yet . . . I am no more obliged to continue an old, or enter into a new strict league and friendship with him than to trust a man that by all the ways and means he can hath endeavoured to deprive me of my life or (which is far more precious) my good name.'[60] No matter what he might say in his grief, forgiving family slights was a step too far.

Sir Ralph's thoughts turned back to the scheme he had hatched when Peg died. He decided that he would travel in Italy, perhaps even to North Africa. Family memories of Uncle Francis and his dramatic flight still had a powerful effect on his imagination, as his friends were only too well aware. 'You are now going to see the Pope,' wrote Sir Roger Burgoyne; 'I am confident that the next will be the Turk.'[61]

13

Giro d'Italia

The *giro d'Italia* was an exciting prospect. To an earnest English Protestant like Sir Ralph, it was also a little frightening. 'Here he shall find virtue and vice, love and hatred, atheism and religion in their extremes,' warned James Howell.[1] On the one hand there was the thought of visiting a country which was reckoned to have civilised the whole world – not once, but twice. 'If the ancient Italians had their rare architects, statuaries, painters,' said Richard Lassels in his *Voyage of Italy*, 'the modern Italians have their Brunelleschi, Palladio, Fontana, and Cronaco in architecture; their Bandinelli, Donatello, Olivieri, and Bernini in sculpture; their Raphael, Michelangelo, Titian and Sarto in painting.'* The intellectual twin peaks of Imperial Rome

---

* Richard Lassels, *The Voyage of Italy* (1670) I, 8. Most of the names on Lassels' list are still familiar. Simone del Pollaiuolo Cronaca (1457–1508) was a Florentine; his masterpiece is generally reckoned to be S. Francesco al Monte. The Mannerist sculptor Baccio Bandinelli (c. 1493–1560) was routinely mentioned in the same breath as Cellini and Michelangelo by seventeenth-century commentators. Pier Paolo Olivieri (1551–99) is best known today for his colossal statue of Pope Gregory XIII in S. Maria in Aracoeli, Rome.

and the Renaissance were a powerful draw, especially to a university-bred gentleman like Sir Ralph whose education had consisted entirely of studying the classics and commentaries on the classics. Italy had come to take second place to France as arbiter of polite culture over the past couple of decades, but as far as architecture and the arts were concerned it was still pre-eminent. Its gardens were legendary, its palaces and churches so stunningly beautiful that, as an ambassador from the Low Countries once told the Duke of Florence, they 'deserved to be seen never but on holy-days';[2] its sculptures so lifelike that they confounded the senses. John Raymond, who made the *giro d'Italia* in 1646–7, illustrated the astonishing power of Italian statues with the story of the female allegories of Youth and Old Age which decorated a tomb in St Peter's; Youth was so beautiful that one day a praying Spaniard could stand it no longer and, getting up from his beads, he dashed over 'to expiate his sense on that Niobe-like lady'. As a result, a veil of black marble now preserved Youth's modesty; Old Age remained naked, as a deterrent to anyone else contemplating inappropriate acts of auto-eroticism.[3]

Against all this culture the tourist had to balance the potential danger of travel. The traditional route over the Alps through either the 6893-foot Mont Cenis pass or the 6590-foot Simplon was terrifying enough – 'most hideous mountains, covered with snow, on all sides precipices, monstrous rocks, passages over narrow bridges, cataracts of water . . . [a] strange and unusual landskip'.[4] Not to mention the marauding bandits and gangs of ex-soldiers hardened by the Thirty Years War. Then there were the Italians themselves, jealous, suspicious, ready to slip a phial of poison into your wine or a stiletto into your heart at the least imagined slight. And the moral pitfalls: it was well known that Italy's dissolute ways were able to deprave the best natures, to turn a saint into a devil. Florence was notorious for its Machiavellian approach to politics; Naples for its 30,000 registered prostitutes; Venice for its debauchery and its homosexual culture. And as a result, there were plenty of Englishmen who travelled to Italy for the express purpose of falling into one or other of these pits.

Rome was a more serious matter. For most of the early seventeenth century the Papal States in general were officially off-limits to the English; those who did dare to venture into the heart of

Catholic darkness were advised not to speak their own language in public, not to set foot in churches while there was a service in progress, not to linger for more than a few days, not to tell the truth if they were questioned about their religion. In a rich and varied life, the traveller George Sandys rode into Cairo on camelback, fought hand to hand with Powhatan Indians in the forests of Virginia and battled with Arab bandits in the deserts of Palestine. But he didn't dare stay in Rome for more than four days, for fear of being corrupted. William Lithgow, the traveller who buried Sir Ralph's uncle Francis at Messina, faced up to shipwreck on Chios and attacks by Algerian slavers; but he hid for three days in a Roman attic in case he encountered the Inquisition. In England people still talked about John Mole, tutor to the young Lord Ros, who was imprisoned by the Inquisition in 1608 and left to languish in a Roman gaol until his death thirty years later.

Relations with Rome were less strained by the time that Sir Ralph set out for Italy in 1651, not least because of the influence of Charles I's widowed queen, the Catholic Henrietta Maria. Protestants were entertained at the English College on the Via Monserrato, and those who did fall foul of the Inquisition often found that their interrogators adopted a surprisingly relaxed approach. "'*Siete Catholico?*' Are you a Catholic?' the Inquisitor asked one English traveller, 'without adding *Romano*, to my much content and safety, whether on purpose or unwittingly he did it I cannot say. But I could honestly and with truth say I was a Catholic, as I did, but not a Roman Catholic.'[5] Nevertheless, Sir Ralph was anxious enough about religious persecution to write to John Kirton, a doctor friend he had known in Paris who was now living in Florence, to ask if it was as dangerous as he'd heard to bring an English Bible and a couple of books of devotions into Italy. The best advice he could get in Blois was that he should wait until he arrived and then have them sent over to some English gentleman who had just left the country, so that if the parcels were opened by searchers, 'neither he that sent them, nor he that they are addressed unto, is within their reach'.[6]

Sir Ralph being Sir Ralph, his preparations for the adventure were painstaking and protracted. To begin with, there were decisions to make about the household in Blois. He had no intention of taking his boys with him. Jack, whose tenth birthday was on 5 November 1650, was much too little; and although Mun was four years older, Sir Ralph reckoned the boy was 'too young to profit by his travel, and his body too thin to endure it'.[7] He also had two other children to look out for: Luce Sheppard had gone back to England before Mary's death, and now she returned to Blois with Mary and Margaret, Aunt Sherard's little girls by William Eure. (There should have been a third girl: Uncle Doctor's daughter Nancy Denton was supposed to be travelling with them, but she fell sick in England at the last moment and had to be left behind.) Aunt Sherard was busy producing sons for her new husband, and she decided it might be better if her Eure daughters spent some time away from their home at Misterton in Leicestershire. She was also keen to have Mary Eure touched for the King's Evil, and the nearest available crowned and anointed King was Louis XIV. Last but not least, she saw a stay in France as an educational opportunity for both girls, as she told Sir Ralph:

> I shall desire your care of them that they may be taught what is fit for them as the reading of the French tongue and to sing and to dance and to write and to play of the guitar . . . I have kept a strict hand over them, so I desire as Lucy [Sheppard] may, and not to leave them at any time alone with any of their masters that teacheth them their exercises, for too much familiarity will give them too great a boldness.[8]

Luce and the girls stayed in and around Paris for several months, hoping for a glimpse of the King, before moving on to Blois when their money ran low in the late summer of 1650. Sir Ralph was still trying to arrange for the removal to Claydon of his wife's corpse, still trying to clear debts which, in spite of William Denton's success in negotiating deals with the major creditors, amounted to between £4000 and £4500. He thought once again of selling up and turning his back on England for ever, but the depressed state of the land market deterred him.

Things were slowly improving, however. Rents began to rise again at home, and with the upturn in the economic situation creditors were not so desperate for their money. (And after August 1651, when Parliament passed an act limiting the maximum rate of interest to 6 per cent, lenders who still had money out at the old rate of 8 per cent had a positive incentive *not* to demand repayment of their loans.) Early in 1651 Sir Ralph found lodgings for Luce and the Eure girls with a Madame Juselier; Jack went to Madame Testard, widow of the Protestant minister, on the understanding that Luce would keep an eye on his studies. Sir Ralph eventually decided that Mun should travel with him after all, in spite of his youth and his frailty. But he wanted adult company. 'If I could possibly meet with some good friend, whose design (like mine) were to seek his fortune in a foreign land, it might be a comfort and advantage to us both,' he told Dr Denton. 'But considering how unfortunate I have lately been, in the loss of my most dear, most incomparable companion, how can I think to meet with any man so miserable as myself?'[9]

With such a cheerful outlook it was perhaps just as well that in Italy 'he is accounted little less than a fool who is not melancholy once a day'.[10] In fact there were plenty of English exiles in search of travelling companions who passed through Blois over the winter of 1650–51. Some were young men trailing around France with their tutors in tow, such as Charles Needham, teenage son of the 2nd Viscount Kilmorey, 'my very good acquaintance and a fine youth', according to Sir Ralph.[11] Others were committed Royalists, like Sir Philip Monckton, who had barely escaped England with his life after being captured during the second Civil War; the Earl of Downe, another active Royalist, who had left England after selling off his estate to pay his composition fines; and Sir Henry Newton, who had fought alongside Sir Ralph's father at Edgehill. Newton was a particularly engaging character: he had just hunted down the kidnapper of his cousin Jane Puckering, who took her to Flanders and attempted to force her into marriage. In the process he fought a duel with the Royalist agent Joseph Bampfield, who had asked Sir Henry's sister-in-law to marry him in spite of already having a wife.*

---

* Newton eventually inherited Jane Puckering's fortune. It was somewhat depleted, having been sequestrated in 1646 on the novel grounds that, although her father died in 1637, he would obviously have been a Royalist if he had lived to see the war.

Newton, who stayed with Sir Ralph in the autumn of 1650, talked fondly of playing chess and drinking while he talked divinity and mathematics with 'the noble squires of the strong fireside fromage table'.[12] Those noble squires included a Monsieur Du Val, a cultured but rather mysterious figure who travelled regularly between France and England, and was said to have a wife in each country; and two English exiles who became Sir Ralph's travelling companions during the *giro d'Italia*. One was Thomas Cordell, an impecunious tutor who made a living of sorts from teaching the sons of Royalist exiles and had taken a notion to Luce Sheppard.

The other, William Gee of Bishop Burton in Yorkshire, fulfilled Sir Ralph's requirements for a man 'so miserable as myself'. It isn't known what brought Gee to Blois, but he was also newly widowed; his teenage wife, Rachel, had died in March 1650, two months before Mary, which gave them a common interest in grief. He had just commissioned a sculptor named William Wright to carve her monument for the church at Bishop Burton, the Gees' family seat. It is still there, a powerful and rather disturbing piece of work – she gazes blankly out from her shroud, while a small child kneels beside her. Her grandmother was a Temple of Stowe, which made Gee a relation – a distant relation, to be sure, but a relation all the same. These things mattered to Sir Ralph.*

Sir Ralph, Mun and William Gee set off on their Grand Tour in March 1651. Cordell was acting as bear leader to a group of three young men and had to stay behind, but there was a chance that he and his charges might meet up with the group later on in Italy. They travelled south to Bordeaux, Toulouse and Carcassonne, and for a while they thought about crossing the Pyrenees into northern Spain; but stories of plague and famine deterred them, and they went instead to Montpellier, where they

---

* Some family relationships were more welcome than others. Tom's formidable wife Joyce was rumoured to be either dead or separated from her husband and living in Italy. Sir Ralph was anxious in case it was the latter, writing to England to find out exactly where she might be, 'for I neither desire to visit her nor to be visited by her' (*Memoirs of the Verney Family* I, 546). Whatever her fate, she disappeared from the Verneys' lives around this time, never to be seen again. At one point Tom mentioned having a wife in Malaga, but it is not clear whether he was referring to Joyce.

arrived in May. Then, having looped around the southern edge of the Massif Central they came to Lyons in mid-July and settled there for the summer.

Lyons was a pleasant place, famous for its *hôtel de ville*, which was reckoned to rival Jacob van Campen's masterly new Town Hall in Amsterdam, and for the great clock in the church of St John, which had a cock that crowed and brass angels that appeared when it struck the hour. ('Ridiculous,' said John Clenche.[13]) Sir Ralph had arranged to have his letters forwarded here, along with an awesome array of clothing – almost all of it marked with an 'R.V.', an 'E.V.' or just a plain 'V' in black silk, blue silk or white thread, as if he and his boy were off to boarding school. There were six lace nightcaps, two plain nightcaps, three pairs of cambrick boothose, two lined holland waistcoats and two dimity waist-coats, and a rather fetching set of taffeta nightgowns, nightcaps and velvet slippers, all in black; also a black leather needle case with a gold needle, pins, blue thread, shirt buttons and tape.

Everyone urged Sir Ralph to travel light. Dr Kirton wrote to say, 'Bring no sheets and as little luggage as you can, that's my advice';[14] and an anonymous friend who provided him with hand-written instructions for travel in Italy pointed out that the carriage charges for one's 'valeze' were five sols per pound, and that was just from Paris to Lyons. 'The less you carry the better, for the smallest things will weigh heavy at that rate before you get to Italy.'[15] Among other things, Luce Sheppard packed thirty peaked nightcaps, six serge and six calico under caps, black taffeta garters, two gold toothpicks and combs and powder for his day- and night-periwigs. Perhaps this was what travelling light meant to the seventeenth-century gentleman.

Along with the nightcaps and toothpicks, Sir Ralph arranged for the latest copies of a weekly English newsletter, *A Perfect Diurnall*, to be sent to him at Lyons. They contained the odd news item of personal interest: he must have felt a twinge to read that Parliament had resolved 'that the Court of the Knight Marshal held in Southwark (commonly called the Marshal's Court) be from and after the first of August next, absolutely dissolved and taken away'.[16] And perhaps there was a surge of moral outrage when he saw that Jane Puckering, whose abduction and forced marriage Sir Henry had set out to avenge, was back safe in England

and had appeared in court at Maidstone, where she gave evidence of how her kidnappers held her up in Greenwich Park with pistols and swords, and 'set her upon the pommel of the saddle on horse-back before one of their company, who galloped away with her to Joseph Welch', who threatened to kill her 'if she yielded not to his desire to marry him'. Welch was not in court.[17]

Otherwise, the news consisted of an unrelenting catalogue of war and disaster. Earthquakes had swallowed up Santiago in Peru and completely destroyed Manila in the Philippines. A French army 10,000 strong was massing on the border with Flanders. Henry Ireton, who had been in charge of the Parliamentarian army in Ireland since Cromwell's recall to England the previous year, had crossed the Shannon and was laying waste to Connaught. There was an insurrection in South Wales at the end of June, when Royalist insurgents in Cardiganshire heard a rumour that Charles Stuart had an army within forty miles of them, and that the entire nation was about to rise up in support. The rebellion was swiftly put down by local Parliamentarian cavalry, but in other areas known to be sympathetic to 'Generalissimo Charles Stuart', as the *Diurnall* contemptuously called him, troops of horse were moving into posi-tion to prevent any further shows of defiance.

And it was the movements of the Generalissimo that provided the *Diurnall*'s big story. In one of the more complicated twists in an already complicated story, on 1 January 1651 the young Prince Charles was crowned King of Scotland, the nation which had sold his father to the English for £200,000 less than three years earlier. Now '*their* king' (the *Diurnall*'s other favourite term for Charles) was massing an army near Stirling, while Cromwell moved his forces between Stirling and his own base at Linlithgow, hoping to provoke the Royalists into a fight. Charles and his generals refused to rise to the bait, and in August the *Diurnall*'s jibes gave way to an anxious call to action when it emerged that the Royalist army had outmanoeuvred Cromwell and crossed into England: 'Let us not now be guilty of losing all our travails, labours, blood and other expenses, through unbelief, or supine negligence . . . Our desire is, that all honest, true and well affected hearts in all places apply themselves armed to their faithful officers, and wait orders.'[18]

Another war in England was an appalling prospect, and Charles Stuart's defeat by Cromwell at the Battle of Worcester on 3

September came as a relief, not only to Parliament but to the majority of the population. Sir Roger Burgoyne wrote and told Sir Ralph about the great victory a week later, adding that 'the King of Scots escaped very narrowly but we expect every day to hear of his being taken'.[19] He was unduly optimistic. Even as he wrote Charles was on the road to Bristol disguised as a manservant; he sailed for France and safety a month later.

Of more pressing concern to Sir Ralph than the King of Scots' military ambitions was the situation on the Franco-Italian border. For almost twenty years hostilities between Savoy and Piedmont had meant that the Mont Cenis crossing was out of bounds to all but the bravest travellers. Things were quieter now – or at least that was what Sir Ralph had thought – but in June the Duke of Savoy's troops invaded Asti in the north of Piedmont, 'and do already begin to enter their enemies' country with strong parties'.[20] The Governor of Milan mobilised his forces and prepared to take the field against the Savoyards, and Sir Ralph and his party waited in Lyons to see what would happen.

The established practice among travellers was to avoid the war zone by going down to Marseilles and sailing to Genoa, making the *giro d'Italia* and returning over the Simplon Pass to Geneva. This was the route which the anonymous writer of Sir Ralph's directions for travel advised him to follow. He should take a boat from Lyons down the Rhône to Avignon, then travel overland to Marseilles, where the English Consul, Daniel Codgell, would help to arrange a passage along the coast to Cannes or Nice. He should stock up there with food and wine, because it would be cheaper than in the other coastal towns along the route, and then negotiate passage to Genoa (where the best inn was run by an Englishman named Zacchary) and Leghorn.

Sir Ralph decided against this, perhaps because of his friend's warnings against the avarice of the sailors who plied the coastal waters, 'those troops of boatmen who raise a tempest in the house, and shipwreck their consciences and your purses, before they set out'. It was necessary to set a guard on provisions in case the 'irrational sea-calves' helped themselves to them; one mustn't let them hoist sail, because they charged extra to row; 'and let them not launch too far into the sea, for fear of pirates'.[21]

The path over the Alps was hardly less hazardous, but that's what the travellers decided to take. They left Lyons at the end of September 1651, reached Geneva by 14 October and crossed the Simplon four or five days later.

It is hard to appreciate the essential strangeness of the alpine landscape to a Buckinghamshire gentleman. There was nothing to be seen but snow, 'which hath laid there beyond the memory of man, and as some say ever since the Flood'. [22] They hired a guide – everyone did – and there were poles set up to mark the path, but even so their horses sometimes sank up to their shoulders and lost their footing, so that everyone fell sooner or later. The steepest part of the mountainside was too much for the horses, and eventually the riders had to dismount and crawl up foot by foot.

It was a dangerous route – as another traveller said twenty years later, 'a man need but stumble once for all his lifetime'[23] – but the group managed to negotiate the pass and avoid the precipices. On the Italian side the trail descended gradually through pine forests, meadows and hamlets until eventually they reached more congenial terrain. Another five days' ride brought them to Milan which, 'for the mighty circuit of her walls, the great number of churches, is before any other city in Italy said to be the Great'.[24] Dr Kirton advised Sir Ralph that Turin was pretty safe, even though a Spanish army was camped there and preparing to defend itself against the French; but he warned that the roads around Alessandria, halfway between Milan and Leghorn, were full of danger. It was best to move in convoy with other travellers. The tourists reached Leghorn at the end of October 1651, and then rode down the coast to Pisa, where they met up with Cordell and his three young gentlemen, who decided to leave their own party and join up with the Verneys and William Gee in Florence. Sir Ralph was pleased with the arrangement, Mun less so, since his father agreed with Cordell that the boy should bring him his Latin translations every morning for marking.

There was only one place to stay in Florence if you were an Englishman in the 1650s – Signora Anna's house, close by Brunelleschi's Santa Spirito on the south bank of the Arno. Anna, who only took in English travellers, was a Florentine institution: Dr Kirton recommended Sir Ralph to go straight to the lodgings of 'Signora Anna Inglese' when he arrived in the city; the author of Sir Ralph's 'Directions for travel' agreed, saying that she 'entertains her countrymen like princes, both for chamber and diet'.[25] The tourists stayed for a month.

'Fail not to see the Duke of Florence's garden of simples,' said the author of the 'Directions','and his gallery of rarities of all sorts.'[26] The Uffizi's galleries contained wonders even then: the Emperor of China's robe, Hannibal's helmet and Charlemagne's sword; Christ's Passion done in amber and a nail half turned to gold by alchemy; a curious chastity belt and a magnet so powerful it could suspend eighty pounds of iron. Then there was Michelangelo's *David*, which stood at the entrance to the Palazzo Vecchio, and its companion, Bandinelli's *Hercules*. (Opinion was divided over which was the better sculpture.) Amannati's huge and not altogether successful Neptune Fountain, an allegorical tribute to Duke Cosimo, was another favourite sight, as of course was the Duomo, 'which I conceive either for the exquisiteness of the work, or worth of so vast a bulk of red, black and white marble, to be the fairest cathedral without, that ever man laid eyes on'; and the Medici Chapel at San Lorenzo, 'which is so glorious, that whosoever enters, will even imagine himself in some place above terrestrial'.[27]

These words were written by John Raymond in 1648. Sadly, we don't know what Sir Ralph or Mun thought. Neither felt the need to describe their experience of Florence – or of any of the other cities they visited in Italy, come to that. Judging from the surviving correspondence, Sir Ralph was more anxious about the whereabouts of various items he had bought in Leghorn – a Turkish razor, a pound of good tobacco, some Turkish coffee. He was also eager to know exactly what he was supposed to *do* with the coffee, which was making its first appearance in western Europe. 'Send me the receipt of it, and a little of the seed that I may see it, and how long the drink will keep after 'tis made, and how long the seed will last good,' he asked a Leghorn merchant.[28] The answer came back promptly, along with a sample of ground coffee and a few roasted beans in a paper twist:

Now if the seed will serve your turn, that is also to be had; which being heated over the fire or in a frying pan until they are brown as some few you will see in the paper, then they must be beaten to powder . . . To make the drink, take a pint of water and boil it a little; then put in two spoonfuls of the powder letting it boil by a soft fire for half hour and it is made. The seed will keep a good while and not perish.[29]

Sir Ralph also asked the merchant for olives and jars of olive oil, some of which he sent as a present to Uncle Doctor in London.

Shortly before Christmas 1651 Sir Ralph, Mun, Gee, Cordell and Cordell's three gentlemen moved on to Rome. By now they were following the established conventions of the mid-seventeenth-century *giro d'Italia*, which dictated that English travellers overwintered in the Holy City, making a foray south to see the natural wonders of Naples – 'a noble, rich kingdom, but a bad people'[30] – but concentrating on Rome itself. 'He that would see Rome may do it in a fortnight, walking about from morning to evening; he that would make it his study to understand it, can hardly perfect it in less than a year.'[31]

Sir Ralph and Mun spent Christmas there watching the ceremonies and celebrations, the midnight masses and Nativity puppet shows, 'the multitude of scenes and pageantry'.[32] On Christmas Day, Pope Innocent X sang mass, guns were fired from the battlements of Castel Sant' Angelo and Christ's crib was exposed in the ancient basilica of Santa Maria Maggiore.

As soon as the holidays were over, the Verneys carried on down to Naples. It was six or seven days' ride away, and the route was reckoned to be the most dangerous passage in all Italy on account of the *banditti* who preyed on the unwary; but they travelled without incident and arrived safe in the first week of January 1652.

Naples was as far south as most foreigners went. The mountains and the isolated agricultural communities of Calabria held no charms for urbane seventeenth-century tourists, and the Verneys were no exceptions. They were content to admire the region's natural wonders from a distance – the islands of Capri and Ischia, which could be seen across the bay, and the 'burning mountain' of Vesuvius, about seven miles to the east. A favourite destination between the city of Naples and Vesuvius was Virgil's tomb, a curious cave said to have been burned out of the hillside by the intensity of the poet's gaze. The city itself was noted for its curious houses, which had flat roofs which could be walked on; for the fragment of an ancient Roman temple at the Theatins' church; and for the number and opulence of its churches generally. The Gothic cathedral was admittedly rather ancient, 'and therefore out of the mode a little: yet it hath a modern chapel which is very beautiful'.[33] The beauty stemmed largely from frescoes by Domenichino, less than twenty years old, but the chapel's fame came from the fact that it housed the tomb of the fourth-century bishop and martyr Januarius and was the scene of a remarkable and oft-repeated miracle. At regular intervals throughout the year a glass phial supposed to contain the saint's congealed blood miraculously turned to liquid, sometimes even bubbling and frothing. In 1670 Richard Lassels (a Catholic) reported that a French nobleman was converted from Calvinism to Catholicism on the spot by the sight of this wonder. Sir Ralph was not.[*]

Father and son were back in Rome by 22 January, and in Rome they remained with Gee and Cordell until after Easter. The *giro d'Italia* determined that tourists spent Holy Week in the Holy City, before travelling to Venice for the celebration of the Feast of the Ascension. There is a comic irony in the way that the itinerary of earnest Protestants like Sir Ralph was wholly dictated by a desire to see the pageantry with which the Catholic Church celebrated Christianity's major festivals. Less amusing (and a little more complicated) is the mixture of appalled fascination and contempt which those ceremonies provoked in Protestant hearts. John Evelyn's characterisation of Holy Week in Rome as 'busy devotion, great silence, and unimaginable superstition' was typical.[34]

The usual course for an extended stay in Rome was to negotiate with a reputable *pensione* for board and lodging; the going rate was anywhere between 10 and 20 crowns a month. Sir Ralph, Mun and their cousin Gee took rooms in one house, Cordell and his three gentlemen in another, but they were so close to each other 'that we are seldom asunder', as Sir Ralph told his friend in Blois, Monsieur Du Val.[35] That wasn't necessarily such a good thing: Gee and Cordell fell out over something, and although they were back on speaking terms quite soon, yet 'they read no more mathematical lectures together'.[36]

Once settled in, the next step was to hire a guide from the army of 'Sights-men' who made a living showing tourists around

---

[*]The miracle of St Januarius and his liquefying blood still takes place in the cathedral at Naples today.

the city's monuments: legendary antiquities like the 'stupendous fabric' of the Colosseum, and the Pantheon, 'the admiration of the whole world';[37] modern marvels such as the Palazzo Barberini, the work of Maderno, Borromini and Bernini; and St Peter's, consecrated only twenty-six years earlier and still waiting to reach perfection with the completion of Bernini's great piazza. In the Vatican library, visitors were shown letters from Henry VIII to Anne Boleyn, 'beginning commonly with "My Darling", or a lascivious expression';[38] and in the Sistine Chapel they marvelled at Michelangelo's *Last Judgement,* 'of a vast design and miraculous fancy'.* At churches across the city they shook their heads incredulously at the stone on which Abraham sacrificed Isaac, St Thomas's doubting finger and some of the thirty pieces of silver given to Judas. But they still went to see them.

Quite a lot of Sir Ralph's time seems to have been taken up in running errands for friends and keeping track of his financial affairs in England and Jack's educational progress in Blois. He went to great lengths in both Rome and Naples trying to track down the works of the botanist, chemist and physician Pietro Castelli, which William Denton had asked him to look out for. Uncle Doctor's efforts to retrieve Sir Ralph's fortunes were paying off by now, and, although his debts still amounted to around £7000, the estate could just about handle a figure like that, which meant the way was open for him to return to England. The news of Jack's education was less optimistic; his schoolmaster gave up teaching, leaving Luce Sheppard to find another master for him, and Luce was uneasy about Madame Testard's ideas of child-rearing. A letter to her would 'stir up her care of Mr. John. Not that I find she is careless of him, indeed; but Sir, you know how the French govern their own children as concerning giving them raw fruit [a diet frowned upon by the English] and hearing him practise his guitar and wearing of gloves.'[39] Around the same time Jack began to write to his father making all sorts of promises to reform, to study harder, to keep better company.

Easter Day in 1652 fell on the last day of March. On Good Friday relics of the Passion, including St Veronica's handkerchief – which

---

* William Bray (ed.), *The Diary of John Evelyn* (1907), 18 January 1645. Evelyn mentioned in passing that 'the roof also is full of rare work'.

retained the image of Christ – the lance used to pierce Christ's side at Calvary and a piece of the True Cross, were exposed at St Peter's; and that night there was a procession of flagellants, who paused every three or four steps to beat themselves with knotted whipcord, 'whilst some of the religious orders and fraternities sung in a dismal tone, the lights and crosses going before, making altogether a horrible and indeed heathenish pomp'.[40] On Easter Day itself there were artillery salutes from Castel Sant' Angelo, and virtually the entire city gathered in front of St Peter's, where the Pope celebrated mass and more relics were uncovered.

A few days later Sir Ralph and Mun set out for Venice, leaving William Gee and Thomas Cordell behind in Rome. It was a long journey – well over 300 miles – and the pair stopped off for several days at Bologna, arriving in Venice in time to explore a little and settle themselves in for the great Marriage to the Sea which took place (as it still does today) every year on the Feast of the Ascension. It was a remarkable spectacle. At eight in the morning the Senate processed in their scarlet robes to the Doge's Palace, where they met the Doge, Francesco Molino, and conducted him down to the shore and into a slave galley, which rowed him and his senators out into the lagoon. A fleet of gondolas and other small craft flocked around them, 'richly covered overhead with sumptuous canopies of silks and rich stuffs, and rowed by watermen in rich liveries, as well as the trumpeters. Thus foreign ambassadors, diverse noblemen of the country, and strangers of condition wait upon the Doge's galley all the way long, both coming and going.'[41] When he arrived at the appointed place, Molino threw a ring into the sea without any further ceremony, saying only in Latin, 'We espouse thee, o sea, in testimony of our perpetual dominion over thee'. And with that, he returned to mass and a great feast at the palace.

The ceremony was only the starting point: for the next ten days the whole of Venice celebrated carnival. Foreign and domestic merchants gathered in their droves; gallants strutted and preened; noblewomen struggled to keep their balance on their alarming high-heeled pattens, sometimes as high as a man's leg, as they showed off their jewels and their curious hairstyles. Everyone who visited Venice commented on the outré appearance of these 'walking May Poles'.[42] Evelyn, who was in the city at Ascensiontide 1645, was particularly intrigued:

> The truth is, their garb is very odd . . . They wear very long crisped hair, of several streaks and colours, which they make so by a wash, dishevelling it on the brims of a broad hat that has no head, but a hole to put out their heads by . . . their sleeves are made exceeding wide, under which their shift sleeves as wide, and commonly tucked up to the shoulder, showing their naked arms, through false sleeves of tiffany, girt with a bracelet or two, with knots of points richly tagged about their shoulders and other places of their body, which they usually cover with a kind of yellow veil of lawn very transparent.[43]

The sight of these Venetian noblewomen tottering around on their *choppines* under the steadying influence of flanking maidservants led one wit to describe them as *mezzo carne, mezzo legno* – half flesh, half wood.

Sir Ralph was ready to leave Venice when the great Ascensiontide fair was over. He bought a few souvenirs, including the famous Venice treacle, a concoction of upwards of seventy ingredients, including pickled snakes and opium, which was renowned throughout Europe as a cure for 'stone, dropsy, coughs, phtisick, spitting of blood, swooning, leprosy, gout, madness from the bite of a mad dog, all poisons, plague, cholic, plague of the guts, many diseases peculiar to women, and a hundred more'.[44] He packed off a few leaden pots of this nostrum to Aunt Isham, who wasn't quite sure what to do with it, but thanked him politely.

At the end of May father and son took one of the eastern passes over the Alps, reaching the Protestant stronghold of Basle by 8 June, from where they went on to Amsterdam and then to Flanders.

What did they get out of their *giro d'Italia*? Mun was rather too young to make much of the experience. It isn't surprising that his upbringing in France had a much greater impact: as an adult in Buckinghamshire he used French whenever he wrote to his father, for example. But Italy also confirmed Sir Ralph's own predilection for France. He neither spoke nor wrote a single word of Italian the whole time he was in the country, and his verdict on the tour was that 'though Italy is more pleasant to be seen than France, yet (to say truth) France is much better to dwell in, than Italy'.[45]

But along with the olives and the tobacco, the Venice treacle and the Turkish coffee beans, Sir Ralph acquired something more intriguing – designs for a family monument which he intended should stand in the chancel of Middle Claydon church.

In the aftermath of Mary's death, his immediate and perfectly natural plan had been to put up a grandiose monument to her memory. Even before she was buried, he wrote from Blois urging the long-suffering Dr Denton to make a tour of the most fashionable tombs in London and report back on what was suitable; at that stage, however, he was undecided between a single statue 'of her alone whose memory is so precious to me' and a more complicated monument which would also commemorate his mother, his father, his dead children and, when the time came, himself and his two boys.[46] Denton was unenthusiastic, partly because he had enough to do in keeping up a busy medical practice and negotiating Sir Ralph's debts without running around procuring designs from tomb-makers; and partly because he didn't think the erection of an ostentatious and expensive memorial gave the right messages to creditors. He sent a sketch plan of the chancel out to Blois and advised Sir Ralph to be content with something less ambitious, like the simple pedimented wall plaque which marked the passing of Uncle Doctor's grandfather in Hillesden church.

In other circumstances Sir Ralph might have listened; but it just so happened that Cousin Gee was on hand in Blois, full of enthusiasm for the shrouded figure of his own late wife which William Wright had just produced. Mary must have one just like it, and done by 'Mr Wright of Charing Cross' if possible.[47]

A tomb like Rachel Gee's tomb, in which a life-size effigy lay full length on a raised stone table, would cost around £80, including transporting it and setting it up in the church. Something similar 'but perhaps not so well cut' might be had for £50. But there was a problem: it would take up rather a lot of space, and the Claydon chancel was only 14 feet wide by 12 feet deep. Sir Ralph was keen on the idea of Mary being portrayed in her winding sheet, and another option he considered was to have her standing upright on a flaming urn, rather like Nicholas Stone's famous monument to John Donne in St Paul's Cathedral. She could be placed, with her hands raised to heaven, in one of a pair of arches on one side of the communion table, and he could fill the other arch when his time came. This way, there would be room for a second memorial to Sir Edmund and Lady Mary on the opposite wall.

Denton was told to go and have a look at 'Dr. Donne's and the other tombs at Paul's or Westminster or elsewhere',[48] and then to open negotiations with Wright or other suitable masons. He must show them the layout of the chancel, get them to produce and cost designs; and he was not to forget to mention that Sir Ralph intended to commission a monument to his parents at a later date.

This was all a bit much, even for the good-hearted Uncle Doctor, and as far as we can tell he simply ignored Sir Ralph's demands. Luckily for them both, Sir Ralph's French friend Monsieur Du Val moved to England in the summer of 1651, and he happened to take lodgings in the Drury Lane home of the mason-sculptor Thomas Burman. Burman may not have fitted Sir Ralph's description of him as one of the best stone-cutters in London, but he had a reputation for good work and reliability; and like many statuaries in the puritanical climate of Commonwealth England, he was not exactly overburdened with projects, which suggested he would be cheap (as did the fact that his wife was reduced to taking in lodgers). It made sense to everybody – particularly William Denton – that Du Val take over Sir Ralph's project and that Burman be commissioned to produce designs.

Those designs reached Sir Ralph in February 1652, while he was in Rome. He didn't like them, so he turned to an Italian artist to come up with something better. Tantalisingly, we don't know the man's name: all we have is Sir Ralph's statement to Denton, whom he was continuing to pester with requests for information about sources of stone, that 'the man that should draw the design of the tomb as I directed is so employed by the Pope's officers about shows for Easter that I cannot get it done yet; but I am promised it in [a] few days'.* By this stage Sir Ralph had

---

* 1 March 1652; (M636/11). Sir Ralph wanted his uncle to find out about the quality of stone coming out of Sir Thomas Coghill's quarries at Bletchingdon in Oxfordshire. Seventeen years later Coghill's daughter Faith became the first wife of Christopher Wren.

resolved on having two monuments – one for his wife and himself, the other for his mother and father – made at the same time, reasoning sensibly that since they were to face each other across the chancel, both the materials and the design should match.

A week after Easter 1652 he sent sketches to Denton, asking him to check them and then to pass them on to Du Val and Burman, who after having his own designs rejected was to be asked to execute those of the anonymous Italian. Burman accepted but did nothing about the job over the summer of 1652, pleading other commitments. Denton lost his temper and said he wasn't going to have anything more to do with the plan – 'the business of the tomb is Paul's work, which I cannot attend to'[49] – and Du Val was left to negotiate with his dilatory landlord and to keep Sir Ralph informed about progress.

The Frenchman was bombarded with questions, which he duly passed on to Burman. What was the difference in price between black, white and coloured marble? (White cost 16s. a foot, black and coloured only 10s.) What were the relative merits of marble and alabaster? (Alabaster was cheaper at 7s. a foot, and a life-size figure would cost only a quarter of its equivalent in marble.) What was dearest, black marble or basalt, and 'which of them is hardest to work, will last longest, and hold its polishing best?'[50] (There wasn't much to choose between them.) While he waited, Sir Ralph changed his mind yet again about the design, opting now for a big single monument, 11 feet wide and 18 feet high with life-size alabaster figures or busts of his parents and his wife, the whole crowned with the Verney arms 'with mantle, helmet and crest carved, painted and gilt'.[51] Since neither the Italian draft designs nor Burman's own have survived, it isn't clear to what extent the London carver was adapting the scheme Sir Ralph had acquired in Rome.

What *is* clear is that by October 1652 Burman had finally come up with a price for the job – £200, including packing up the thing in chests and transporting it 'either by water or land to the appointed place'.[52] That was too much for Sir Ralph: he asked Du Val to persuade Burman to reconsider, but in December the man was still refusing to compromise.

Sir Ralph decided it was time to come home. He had been away for nine years now. Denton's herculean efforts on his behalf meant he was no longer in danger of being thrown into the Fleet prison by his creditors, while national politics had settled down somewhat after Generalissimo Stuart's rout at Worcester the previous year. He was unhappy with the way Will Roades was managing the Buckinghamshire estates, the more so since reports were reaching him that Roades was drinking heavily and failing to keep him informed about events at home. There was already some tension between landlord and bailiff, because Roades had flatly refused to come to France to discuss the estate accounts shortly before Sir Ralph left for Italy, and Sir Ralph had reacted by stripping him of quite a lot of his powers and setting Frank Drake, John Denton and William Denton to make regular inspections of his accounts.

The feud with the rector had also plumbed new and vitriolic depths. In 1651 the Reverend Aris published one of his sermons, which he called *The Reconciler*. There wasn't much reconciliation evident in the four-page open letter appended to the sermon, though. Addressed to 'Mr Ro:' and entitled 'A Charm for Slanderous Tongues', the letter accused Roades of being a lying, sneaking coward, among other things.[53]

Sir Ralph's presence at Claydon would calm things down and help to bring his erring steward to heel, but the main reason for his decision to return was the need to revise his will, drawn up before he and Mary left the country back in 1643. The *giro d'Italia* hadn't cured him of his melancholy: he was thirty-nine on 9 November 1652, and he had fallen seriously ill with a fever in Antwerp that autumn. Death might strike at any moment.

There were arrangements to make. Sir Ralph didn't think it was a good idea for Jack and Mun to be educated together. 'Besides the snarling and disagreement I have oft observed between brothers that are so kept in couples,' he said, 'their age and humours are so different, that I know they will do much better asunder.'[54] So Jack was removed from Madame Testard's care and packed off to a grammar school at Barnes in Surrey, run by a Royalist cleric named James Fleetwood who had served at Edgehill. Mun stayed in the Low Countries: Sir Ralph found him a tutor in the shape of Dr Robert Creighton, a humourless Laudian-in-exile who had been chaplain to Charles I at Oxford.

'In all my life I was never thus alone,' he told Uncle Doctor; 'for when my dear wife went over, I had two children and a family [i.e. household] which is now reduced to a little (very little) footboy. I need not tell you how sad this makes me.'[55] But he wasn't alone for long. In January 1653 he travelled over to England from Brussels in company with Cousin Gee, who had joined him there, and the wife, son and daughter of another relation he had met in Brussels, Robert Spencer. (Gee married the daughter two months later.)

Like Mary before him, Sir Ralph decided to spend some time in London before heading for Claydon, and William Denton found him lodgings near Covent Garden, two furnished first-floor rooms and a study for 15s. a week. Friends and relations queued up to pay their respects: Roger Burgoyne rather sweetly said that the sight of his dearest friend 'will make my old legs to caper, and with excess of joy';[56] Pen and Peg rushed to tell their brother all about their financial difficulties. Henry sent his apologies: he was in the retinue of the 2nd Earl of Peterborough, Henry Mordaunt, and the Earl was in the country visiting friends, 'so that until that be over, he will not dismiss me on no pretence whatsoever, though I pleaded with him on this occasion modestly for my liberty'.[57] Tom was also pleading for his liberty, although to a different authority – he was in gaol again.

Rejected by her Gardiner in-laws, with a seven-year-old daughter and still only twenty-six, sister Cary had married again. John Stewkeley was a good-hearted widower with four teenage children of his own and a rather lovely country estate, Preshaw, a few miles south-east of Winchester. When Sir Ralph returned to England she already had one child by Stewkeley, a son named for his father, and she followed this with six more. The marriage was a long and happy one, although Cary refused to part with either her Gardiner surname or her status as the widow of a knight. For the rest of her life she remained 'Aunt Gardiner' to the Verney family and 'Lady Gardiner' to the rest of the world.

Sister Susan wasn't as lucky as Cary. After two stillbirths, Susan Alport had a difficult third pregnancy. She gave birth on 1 February 1651, crying 'Now I thank God I am delivered' and calling her husband to kiss her. The child lived for an hour; Susan drifted in and out of consciousness for three hours, and then died at midnight. 'I am yet a willing prisoner to my grief in my disconsolate and now altogether comfortless chamber,' wrote her husband. It didn't remain altogether comfortless for long, however: five months later the now twice-widowed Alport married one of William Denton's stepdaughters, leading Sir Ralph to express the wish that the girl would live long enough 'that she may prevent the trouble of his fourth wooing'.[58]

Sir Ralph stayed in London for several months. One of the first things he did after he had settled in was to fire Thomas Burman and hand over the long awaited Verney monument to the master-mason who had taught Burman his craft. Edward Marshall, whose yard was in Fetter Lane, was an altogether more significant sculptor than Burman. He was a past Master of the Mason's Company, with a dozen first-class funerary monuments to his credit. It may not be a coincidence that one of the best, an alabaster wall monument in which Marshall shows the subject, Henry Curwen, standing upright in his shroud and flanked by cherubs, is in the church of St Mary's, Amersham, where Frank Drake's family was also buried.

Just as important as Marshall's artistic credentials was the fact that he was both businesslike and cheap. He agreed to execute the tomb, including alabaster figures of Sir Ralph's parents, his wife and himself, for £130, 'the carriage of the work by land and water to be done at the charge of Sir Ralph Verney . . . and also the brick, lime, sand and scaffolding to finish the work in the country'.[59] And he promised to have the entire monument set up in the chancel at Claydon by 21 October 1653.

Edward Marshall's work still dominates the interior of Claydon church. Hardly anything is left to show from the drafts Sir Ralph obtained in Rome, and nothing at all of the idea for macabre shrouded corpses that were so fashionable in the mid-seventeenth century. Instead, Marshall produced an understated and very English display of portrait busts in niches of black marble beneath a broken pediment – Sir Edmund and Lady Margaret on the top shelf, Sir Ralph and Mary below them. They flank a drapery with an inscription proclaiming that the edifice is 'sacred to the memory of Sir Edmund Verney who was Knight Marshal 18 years and Standard Bearer to Charles the first in that memorable battle of Edge Hill where he was slain on the 23rd of October 1642, being then in the two and fiftieth year of his age'. The same inscription honours Lady Margaret, 'by whom he had six sons and six daughters', while a black marble panel below it talks of Mary, 'wife of Sir Ralph Verney (eldest son of the said Sir Edmund and Lady Margaret) by whom she had three sons and three daughters whereof only Edmund and John are living'. The panel commemorates her burial at Claydon on 19 November 1650, and announces that this is also where her husband 'intends to be buried'.

What are we to make of Sir Ralph's act of filial and conjugal piety? Because the intended memorial to Mary has turned into something quite different – a proud advertisement of his father's royal connections and glorious death in the King's cause. The tremendous grief Sir Ralph felt initially at his wife's death has passed, and she is no longer the sole focus of his devotion. It is shared with his parents – and, because he is memorialised and yet still living, it is an illustration of his own self-pity. Guilt must have played a part, too, and the memory of his strained relationship with his father in the months leading up to Edgehill; so must the absence of Sir Edmund, the fact that his body was never recovered. The monument can be seen as a poignant attempt to fulfil in stone the wish Sir Edmund expressed in his last will and testament, that his body should be 'interred in the chancel of the parish church of Middle Claydon'.[60] But it also suggests that, in commemorating the Standard Bearer, Sir Ralph's allegiances were shifting away from the Parliament which had almost destroyed him and towards, not the Royalist cause exactly, but towards family. He had put principle before blood, and it had brought him nothing but misery. Now it was time to show the world that blood mattered.

Part 3
Mun and Jack

14

None but Princes

W hen he first arrived in England, Sir Ralph's intention was to set up home in London, keeping a
cook, a maid to wash his linen and clean the house,
a coachman, a footman and a page. As a widower whose sons
were both living away from home, he had no use for a country
seat. Mrs Alcock and her ordinary grazier of a husband could
continue to run the house at Claydon, while Roades managed
the estate. Their master would spend no more than three or
four months in the country each year.

But within weeks of his return Sir Ralph discarded the idea.
No matter how he tried to fight it, Claydon had a powerful hold
over his imagination. It represented stability and shelter after so
many years of trouble:

The purling springs, groves, birds, and well-weav'd bowers,
With fields enamelled with flowers,
Present their shapes; while fantasy discloses
Millions of lilies mix'd with roses . . .

Thus let thy rural sanctuary be
Elizium . . .[1]

There were also sound practical reasons for spending more
time on the estate, the chief one being that he was now so
unhappy with Will Roades's performance as steward that he felt
it necessary to become a full-time landlord. So instead of setting
up an expensive permanent establishment in London, he decided
to take lodgings as and when he needed them. There were plenty
of offers: for example, Uncle Doctor's son-in-law William Gape
obligingly said that Sir Ralph was always welcome to stay with
him and his wife in Covent Garden. They only had the one bed,
but it didn't matter as long as Gape slept in the middle.

As part of his preparations for his return to Buckinghamshire,
Sir Ralph bombarded the hapless Will Roades with queries. How
much linen was there in the house? How many of the beds had
curtains? Was there any cutlery left, any kitchen equipment? 'I
presume there are dishes, pie-plates, candlesticks, basins, wooden
trenchers, beer and wine glasses, great and small candles.'[2] No
servant was to be allowed to smoke – 'it only stinks up my
house' – and no workmen were to disturb his peace. 'Repair the
chicken house next the slaughter house quickly as you and I
agreed, that I may not be troubled.' Roades was to put all the
locks and the glass in the windows in order. He should 'glaze
the parlour and my study by it, the dining room and best chamber.
Tell me if the water pipes are in order, and let the cistern be
clenged . . . Make [my tenants] welcome, and being they have
nothing but bread, cheese and drink, it must be good and in
plenty too, or else they may justly blame both you and me.'[3]

Sir Ralph had an ulterior motive for keeping the Claydon
tenants happy. He had decided to complete the enclosure of open
fields and commons around Claydon, a process begun by Sir
Edmund Verney back in the 1620s. Forty-two of the fifty-three
farms on the estate were less than 50 acres, and more than half
of those were less than 20 acres. Such small units weren't amenable
to modern agricultural practices – indeed, as Roades was
constantly pointing out to Sir Ralph, some of them were hardly
viable – and that meant low rents or, in the worst cases, bank-
rupt tenants and no rents at all. Almost as soon as he returned

to England Sir Ralph began to seek his tenants' agreement to enclose the commons and renegotiate their leases, often entertaining them lavishly as he did so. He then put up fences, dug ditches and set hedges to establish larger pastures; and rents went up accordingly. It has been estimated[4] that enclosure may have cost Sir Ralph around £600, but that it raised his estate income by some £300 a year – quite a return on his investment.

He and Roades managed to retain the goodwill of the majority of tenants, although a few left to seek their fortunes in London, and there were one or two rumblings of discontent at the changes. In April 1656, for instance, cottagers who were unhappy that Sir Ralph had given them a new cow-close some distance from the village in exchange for the commons where they had been used to pasturing their cattle, threatened to drive the animals across the enclosed fields to reach it, since that was the most direct route. Roades, who for all his real and imagined faults was always sensitive to the importance of keeping the community happy, suggested Sir Ralph might provide a close nearer to the village.

Predictably, it was Parson Aris who caused most trouble over the business. Sir Ralph had rather sneakily waited until the parson was away from home before he allowed Roades to open negotiations with his tenants. At the same time he met with Aris in London and persuaded him to sign a forty-year lease on his glebe and tithes in exchange for £80 a year, without mentioning his plans for enclosing the estate. Aris was furious when he realised that Sir Ralph and Roades had got the better of him, and demanded an extra 20 per cent. After more than a year of wrangling, Mrs Aris went behind her husband's back and suggested that Sir Ralph bring in as independent mediator Edward Butterfield, the rector of the nearby village of Preston Bissett. 'But Mr Aris not knowing anything of this, you must carry it so,' he informed the rector at the beginning of October 1654, 'as if you came only to visit him.'[5]

Butterfield was a decent man, and although he reckoned the business of mediation to be a thankless office which was likely to lose him friends on both sides, within weeks of his first visit to Aris's parsonage he had persuaded both parties to agree to a settlement. On 3 November 1654 Aris agreed to accept £91 a year for the contested lease.

The parson continued to fight with Roades – and with Sir

Ralph, too. He complained when cattle ate his beans, blaming the steward for not putting up fences even though he had been told to do so. Sir Ralph was stung into writing a searing letter to Roades: 'I cannot yet foresee how you can possibly excuse it . . . and I shall be no less sorry than ashamed to have the world see my commands so slighted by my own servant.'[6] Then Aris complained that pigs belonging to Roades's brother, who was one of Sir Ralph's tenants, had eaten his corn. When he set his dog on the pigs, the man threatened to shoot the dog, and hinted that he would quite like to shoot the parson as well.

Death would finally bring an end to the quarrelling. An influenza epidemic in the summer of 1657 carried off both Aris and Roades. Sir Ralph replaced the latter with a local farmer, Hugh Holmes, who was reckoned to be diligent and careful, and whose wife was a servant at Claydon House. He acted as the Claydon steward for the next ten years. Reverend Aris's place was taken by Edward Butterfield, the clergyman who had helped over the enclosure of the parish glebe. Poor Butterfield needed all his mediation skills even before he moved in, since Aris's widow refused to leave the parsonage and took to her bed: in the end, the only way he could gain possession was by marrying her. He remained rector of Middle Claydon until his death in 1679, when he was succeeded by his son William. A grandson had the living after him, and the three generations of Butterfields presided over the parish for an unbroken 102 years.

As well as completing the enclosure of the Claydon estates, Sir Ralph threw himself with enthusiasm into the remodelling of Claydon House. His old home, largely the product of the Giffards' Tudor tenancy with various haphazard extensions, looked hopelessly tired and old-fashioned in comparison with the hôtels and chateaux of Mansart and Lemercier, the palazzi of Carlo Maderna and Borromini. It needed a lift of some sort.

This was Sir Ralph's first opportunity to really take possession of his inheritance. The fourteen months between his father's death at Edgehill and his family's departure for France at the end of 1643 were a miserable, frightening time for him and Mary; then, he had needed all his wits simply to keep one step ahead of the cruel game being played out around him. Now he could take stock and set about putting his own mark on Claydon. He built six new almshouses next door to the church, brought in a piped water supply and contracted with a brickmaker for some half a million bricks. Then he sent to Rouen for the second edition of Pierre Le Muet's *Manière de bien bastir pour toutes sortes de personnes* of 1647. Le Muet's Paris mansions, including the Hôtel d'Avaux in the rue de Temple (1644) and the Hôtel Comans d'Astry on the quai de Béthune (1647) would have been known to Sir Ralph; the *Manière de bien bastir*, which had first appeared in 1623, was a popular collection of designs for houses large and small, from a three-storey town house on a plot 12 feet by 21½ feet to a mansion with flanking pavilions. It also contained practical advice on the placing of 'doors, windows, chimneys, beds, stairs, and other conveniences; with their just measures for the best advantage both of commodiousness, health, strength, and ornament'.[7]

The 1650s are traditionally supposed to have been lean years for English architecture. Royalists were in no position to build, so the story goes; they were all in exile or in debt or in both. Parliamentarians and Puritans were much too serious minded to fritter away huge sums on something as worldly as a country seat. The politically uncommitted were still reeling with shock at the violence of the 1640s and anxious about what the future held for them: architecture was hardly a priority.

In reality, the situation was rather more complicated. The victors naturally built to consolidate their position and to celebrate their victory. Cromwell's attorney-general, Edmund Prideaux, extensively and expensively remodelled the medieval Forde Abbey in Dorset in the decade before his death in 1659, for instance. The regicide and President of the High Court, John Lisle, rebuilt his wife's country seat at Moyles Court in Hampshire around the same period. John Thurloe, secretary to the Council of State and head of intelligence from 1652 to 1658, commissioned the London surveyor Peter Mills to design Wisbech Castle in Cambridgeshire, which was a perfect example of the mannered classicism which flowered during the middle years of the seventeenth century. Mills' Thorpe Hall in Huntingdonshire, built for Cromwell's Chief Justice, Oliver St John, was another.

The vanquished had different motives for their architectural adventures. Some built as a gesture of defiance. In 1653 Sir Robert Shirley, lamenting that 'all things sacred were throughout the nation either demolished or profaned', put up a new church at Staunton Harold in Leicestershire, declaring in an inscription over the entrance that he had 'done the best things in the worst times and hoped them in the most calamitous'. (They were destined to grow more calamitous yet: Shirley died in the Tower in November 1656.) Other Royalists had to repair the damage brought about by war: Sir Ralph's cousin Mun Denton, the eldest surviving son of Sir Alexander Denton, married an heiress and poured his wife's money into rebuilding Hillesden after the siege and fire of 1644. And others still built because there wasn't much else for them to do. So Sir Justinian Isham, a kinsman of the Verneys whose family's allegiance to the King during the wars excluded him from politics in the Commonwealth, retired to his country seat, the Elizabethan Lamport Hall in Northamptonshire: between 1654 and 1657 John Webb created a beautifully restrained new set of rooms at Lamport where Isham could entertain friends like Sir Ralph. In the south of Buckinghamshire the Royalist poet Edmund Waller celebrated his own return from French exile in 1652 with a change of heart (his 'Panegyrick to my Lord Protector' praises his kinsman Cromwell as a new Augustus) and a change of architecture. Hall Barn, Beaconsfield, which he put up on his family's estate in the early 1650s, is a wonderful Dutch-inspired dolls' house of a building, square and high with dormer windows in a hipped roof and crowned by a cupola.

We don't know as much as we'd like about Sir Ralph's remodelled Claydon House, which was completely swept away by his great-grandson in the eighteenth century. It is clear that the bulk of the work was carried out between 1654 and 1656, and it certainly involved taking down some of the older parts, building new chimneys and inserting dormers. The undated pencil drawings of Claydon mentioned in Chapter 1 might relate to the remodelling, but they equally well may refer to one of Sir Edmund's attempts to renovate the house. They certainly show a sixteenth-century building which has been given a not altogether successful facelift at some point in the seventeenth century. The centre of the entrance façade is set back between two wings, with a flight of steps leading up to a central doorway and balustraded openings above it on the first and second storeys. On the ground floor of the wings the windows are paired and linked by a common sill, but the separateness of the two windows in the pair is emphasised by each one having a prominent keystone above it. On the first and second floors a wide broken pediment spans the pair, but the span is so wide that the device looks clumsy and amateurish. The south front, which looked towards the churchyard, has a couple of French-looking bull's-eye windows; the west front shows an idea for a colonnade with three semi-circular openings and niches. The whole thing seems too piecemeal, too half-hearted for what we know of Sir Ralph's tastes in the 1650s. Compared to Webb's elegant addition to Lamport or even Peter Mills' rather heavy treatment of Thorpe Hall, it is so crude that one hopes the drawings do depict Claydon before rather than after his remodelling.

Sir Ralph had an abiding passion for the gardens at Claydon, mindful perhaps of Bacon's famous pronouncement that gardening is 'the greatest refreshment to the spirits of man, without which buildings and palaces are but gross handiworks'.[8] Even before he arrived at Claydon his instructions to Roades included the order to plant plenty of 'ordinary useful herbs'; and 'if there is no borage nor burnet, plant or set it quickly'.[*] The park and orchard were planted up with cherry, fir, walnut, alder, yew and ash. His friends on the Continent were asked to help him stock the estate: William Gee offered to get hold of lime trees in Flanders, and William Wakefield, a merchant he knew from his time in France, said he could send over 800 white poplars. Luce Sheppard, who was still in Blois, was asked to buy grape and melon seeds, different varieties of lettuce and cabbage, and Spanish cardoon ('the best and fairest comes from Tours').[9] A friend sent sweet briers and fig sets in exchange for some young walnut trees, chestnut and almond; Sir Ralph planted mulberry trees and asparagus plants, roses, blue and white violets, sweet marjoram and lemon thyme, and set up new stone seats from which he could look out on his handiwork.

There was considerable interest in horticulture and husbandry during the 1650s, and a steady stream of manuals was issued and

[*]May 1653; M636/12. As its name suggests, the young leaves of the salad burnet, *Poterium sanguisorba*, were used in salads. Burnet was also grown for its medicinal properties: it 'openeth the stoppings of the liver, causeth urine, and helpeth the jaundice, and with white wine and honey it unbindeth stitches of the ribs and teats' (William Langham, *The Garden of Health*, 2nd edn, 1633, 110). Borage was thought to be an antidote for melancholy, among other things.

reissued to cater for the demand. Two Elizabethan works, Leonard Mascall's *Countryman's New Art of Planting and Graffing* [i.e. grafting] and Thomas Hill's *Gardener's Labyrinth*, were republished in 1651. Editions of the *English Improver Improved, or, the Survey of Husbandry Surveyed* appeared in 1649 (twice), 1652 and 1653. Its author, a Parliamentarian captain named Walter Blith, dedicated the work to Cromwell, promised to make the poor rich and the rich richer, and placed the blame for the degenerate state of English husbandry on 'the reign of many abominable lusts, as sloth and idleness, with their daughters, drunkenness, gaming, licentious liberty'.[10] Sir Hugh Plat's Jacobean classic, *Floraes Paradise Beautified*, was reissued in 1652 as *The Garden of Eden, or, An Accurate Description of all Flowers and Fruits now Growing in England*, and went through at least four more editions before the Restoration.

As with the remodelling of his family home, Sir Ralph's decision to reconstruct the gardens around it stemmed from a desire to make Claydon his own. And a knowledge of gardening was part of a gentleman's cultural apparatus: the new editor of Plat's *Garden of Eden* explicitly stated in his preface that his readers 'may not only advance their knowledge and observation when they walk into a garden, but discourse more skilfully of any flower, plant, or fruit than the gardener himself'.[11] There was also the reassuring fact that good husbandry could, as Walter Blith had pointed out, make the poor rich and the rich richer. But it isn't too far-fetched to think that, in creating his orchards and flower gardens, his groves and avenues, Sir Ralph found a way to assert control over a world which had destroyed his family and ruined his life. In taming nature, he was making sense of a world turned upside down. There was comfort in that.*

★   ★   ★

* Marvell expresses the same sentiment in his poem to Lord Fairfax, 'Upon Appleton House':

> 'Tis not, what once it was, the *World*;
> But a rude heap together hurl'd;
> All negligently overthrown,
> Gulfes, Deserts, Precipices, Stone.
> Your lesser World contains the same.
> But in more decent Order tame . . .
> (Canto xcvi)

The political situation in England was still fraught with danger. In May 1654 the government uncovered a plot to assassinate Cromwell as he travelled in his coach from Whitehall to Hampton Court and the ringleaders were arrested and executed. In January 1655 the Lord Protector dissolved the parliament he had called five months before, when its Members proposed to reduce the army. He was convinced that a strong military presence was still needed.

And so it was. At the beginning of March 1655 strange rumours of Royalist risings began to circulate. There were reports that the King of Scotland was at Hull; that his brother, James, Duke of York, had landed at Bristol. The stories were dismissed as the work of 'malignant spirits who use all their art and industry to hinder the peace of the nation'.[12] But a week later those stories were borne out as Royalist insurgents all over the country attempted to provoke a popular rising.

The rising ended in farce. Cavaliers gathered at Marston Moor in Yorkshire on the night of Thursday 8 March 1655, but they went home again when they saw that, instead of the 4000 comrades they had been told to expect, fewer than a hundred men had turned out to march on York. (Someone had got the date wrong.) The same thing happened in Nottinghamshire, and at Morpeth in the north-east. Royalists intending to storm Shrewsbury were rounded up and imprisoned the day before they could assemble; others who were supposed to take Chester Castle decided against the idea at the last minute. Only in Wiltshire did 200 rebels actually go through with the planned rising, and even then they left it until the following Monday to march on Salisbury, where they took the sheriff hostage and declared for Charles II before running for Royalist strongholds in Cornwall. By this time Parliament was prepared for them, and they only got as far as the little town of South Molton in Devon before they were overpowered by a troop of soldiers from Exeter in some vicious house-to-house fighting.

The March rising had never posed a serious threat to the Protectorate; most of the rebels were rounded up over the next couple of months and either executed or transported to the West Indies. But the government was rattled; and Cromwell, who had until now pursued a policy of 'healing and settling' towards malignants – the seventeenth-century equivalent of Truth and

Reconciliation – cracked down hard. Royalist sympathisers in the City of London and Westminster were ordered to leave in case plotters against the Commonwealth 'make use of such dangerous and discontented persons'.[13] All over the country anyone of quality who might conceivably support the Stuart cause came under suspicion, and William Denton wrote to warn Sir Ralph that the Verney name alone might be enough to put him in danger.

He was right. On 13 June 1655 a troop of soldiers turned up at Claydon. They arrested Sir Ralph and confiscated all the pistols and swords in the house. The soldiers treated him with courtesy, but there was no charge and no explanation. He was taken first to Northampton and then down to London, where he found he was part of a general round-up of potentially dissident nobles and gentry. Some were imprisoned in the Gatehouse at Westminster, others at Lambeth Palace; Sir Ralph went to St James's Palace, where he was put in a chamber over by the Tennis Court and guarded day and night – 'which is usual to none but Princes', he told Vere Gawdy with pride.[14]

Friends did their best to comfort him, although their best was not really all that good. The ever-optimistic Doll Leeke wrote that 'my despairing nature is apt to fear the worst';[15] Will Roades urged him to have faith in Jesus Christ, and reminded him that 'afflictions while we live in this vale of misery must continually be looked for, but if you suffer afflictions here for righteousness' sake, happy are you in your sufferings'.[16] Aunt Isham announced she was confident Sir Ralph was innocent of being involved with the insurgents, although she hardly gave him a glowing testimonial: 'you are too discreet as to have had a hand in the last rising'.[17] Tom wrote an entirely insincere letter saying that 'perhaps you may imagine I rejoice at your misfortune, and at your restraint. In truth I do not.'[18] And Roger Burgoyne tried to make a joke of the whole matter. 'I pray you know,' he wrote tongue in cheek, 'that I will have nothing to do with any prisoner of that nature [i.e., a rebel], till he hath cleared himself before my Lord; therefore as you would avoid my censure, acquit yourself like an honest man.'[19]

Sir Ralph wasn't good at seeing the funny side of things, even at the best of times. A few weeks before his arrest he had fallen out with Cary Gardiner and her husband when his attempts to retrieve Pen's chaotic financial affairs kept him from standing godfather to their daughter, and John Stewkeley teased that he was too busy running after widows to be with them. On that occasion he retreated headlong into pomposity – 'I thought it utterly impossible my kindness, charity and honour should all be called in question' – but the Stewkeleys knew him too well to do anything other than shrug off the rebuke.[20] Now he chose to take Sir Roger Burgoyne's jokey remark at face value, and fired off an angry response which brought the two men closer to a quarrel than they had ever been. Within days both had realised their mistake and apologised, Burgoyne for being such an 'unworthy clown', Sir Ralph for taking offence so easily. 'Either you or I or both of us are grown notable drunkards,' he said, 'and know not what we write.'[21]

The weeks dragged by, with no indication that Sir Ralph was going to be charged, or brought to trial, or even questioned about his loyalty to the Protectorate. He was treated quite well. At the end of August, for example, he complained that there was no room at St James's for his servant Robert Kibble and that the man had to go off to lodgings near Charing Cross each night; the authorities granted him permission to move into his widowed Aunt Abercrombie's house, which was within the jurisdiction of the garrison.

As time went on other suspects were released, some with much stronger links to the insurgency than Sir Ralph. Sir Frederick Cornwallis, who had been with Charles II in exile, was allowed home; so was Sir Ralph's rabidly Royalist kinsman Sir Justinian Isham. Sir Ralph was careful to maintain some distance between himself and the other internees: when Doll asked the newly liberated Cornwallis for news of her cousin he could give her none, because, he said, Sir Ralph took his meals alone and refused to mix with the other prisoners. At the same time he had powerful friends in the government camp. Nathaniel Fiennes was a member of the council of state, and around the time of Sir Ralph's arrest was made one of the keepers of the great seal; and although Eleanor Warwick's husband didn't wield the same influence as he had when Mary was lobbying the couple back in 1648, he was still close to Cromwell. Thomas Hammond, a prominent figure in Parliamentarian circles who was married to a Temple, wrote to the authorities about 'a cousin of my wife's, Sir Ralph Verney', saying he was sure that Sir Ralph's arrest was a mistake and that he was certainly no delinquent. 'He was sitting in the Parliament house when his father was killed at Edgehill, and sent in voluntarily two horses into the Parliament's army.'[22]

But someone somewhere in government was convinced of Sir Ralph's Royalist sympathies, and the only way he could secure his release was by agreeing to be bound over. He refused to countenance the idea; he had, after all, done nothing wrong.

The whole affair threatened to turn into a repeat of the business about the Covenant. By the autumn, however, he began to waver as he realised he was the only prisoner at St James's Palace who still stood out against the bond. All the others had either signed or indicated their willingness to sign. So on Thursday 4 October, 113 days after his arrest, he gave in and agreed to be bound over for a year in the sum of £2000. He was released the next day.

Everyone congratulated him on his liberation. Vere Gawdy comforted him with the thought that 'there is a sovereignty in honour which no usurpation can depose; you are safe in that'.[23] Aunt Sherard sent him a present of a mare, because 'you should be well mounted to bring you through the deep ways'.[24]

Those ways were set to grow deeper. The Protectorate's response to the March risings extended beyond the internment of suspected malignants. All news-sheets were suppressed except for *Mercurius Politicus* and the *Weekly Intelligencer*, both of which were consistently pro-government; the authorities clamped down on hunting and racing, pursuits which were thought to offer disaffected Royalists perfect cover for clandestine plotting. And the country was divided into twelve districts, each governed by a major-general who was answerable only to the Lord Protector, and who was charged with raising a local militia and with suppressing unlawful assemblies and disarming malignants. These measures were to be paid for by a 10 per cent tax on Royalists – the people who had made them necessary in the first place.

Even though the war had been over for years, there was still a lot of bitterness, still a hard line between victors and vanquished. Despite the Protectorate's efforts to bring about reconciliation, most Royalists steadfastly refused to put the past behind them. 'There is nothing they have more industriously laboured in than

this,' wrote an exasperated Cromwell: 'to keep themselves separated and distinguish'd from the well-affected of this nation; to
which end they have kept their conversation apart as if they
would avoid the very beginning of union; have bred and educated
their children by the sequestred and ejected clergy, and very much
confined their marriages and alliances within their own party, as
if they meant to entail their quarrel and prevent the means to
reconcile posterity.'[25] He had a point: when Sir Ralph dared to
suggest to Sir Justinian Isham that a Puritan physician might make
a good husband for one of his daughters, the Ishams reacted with
horror. In these degenerate times, they said, it was vital to make
a stand against the 'sea of democracy'; and that meant keeping
their family 'pure and untainted from that mongrel breed, which
would feign mix with them.'[26]

Sir Ralph managed to stay on good terms with both the 'sea
of democracy' – as represented by Eleanor Warwick, Roger
Burgoyne and Francis Drake, the Fiennes and the Temples – and
malignants like Isham, brother Henry and sister Cary, the entire
Denton clan, and the various exiles he knew from his time in
France. But in spite of this delicate balancing act, his reputation
as a disaffected Royalist continued.

The County Commissioners responsible for levying the decimation tax had a simple way of deciding who was and who was
not a malignant. If a man had had his estate sequestrated by
Parliament, it followed that he was a Royalist and thus liable for
the tax. Sir Ralph's sequestration had been lifted by the Committee
of Lords and Commons in January 1647, and the Buckinghamshire
Committee had been formally notified of the decision four
months later. But the fact that it had been imposed at all was
enough for the Commissioners, and he was duly summoned to
appear before them at Aylesbury in the spring of 1656, and to
bring a valuation of his estate.

Sir Ralph applied for a certificate from the old Sequestration
Committee stating that he had never been sequestrated, and peti-
tioned Cromwell directly to have his name removed from the
list of Buckinghamshire gentry who were to be taxed. But
Cromwell only referred the matter back to the Commission at
Aylesbury. Sir Ralph was ordered to appear before the
Commissioners and to bring with him 'particulars of my estate

real and personal'.[27] He prepared for the worst, laying off the
men who were working on the house and gardens at Claydon,
telling Mun – who was still on the Continent – to 'contract your
expenses into a narrower compass',[28] and making out a valuation
of the Middle Claydon estate which, at just over £722, was
conservative, to say the least.

The Commission was chaired not by the major-general for
the region, Charles Fleetwood (who was busy with affairs of
state), but by his deputy for Buckinghamshire, a cousin named
George Fleetwood. Everyone did their best to be fair, but the
Commission had its terms of reference and its members were
determined to stick fast to them. Sir Ralph's opening gambit was
to walk in and demand an adjournment on the grounds that his
original sequestration was a mistake. The Commissioners asked
him to leave the chamber while they discussed the idea; but when
he was called back in, he was told there was nothing they could
do. 'They had only authority to charge all that were sequestered,
not to acquit them; they were not judges whether I was justly
sequestered or not.'[29] So could they please see the valuation?

His next ploy was to argue that Cromwell was considering his
case; they should at least suspend their decision until they had
heard what the Protector had to say. Again they asked him to
leave them to their deliberations. Again they called him in and
said it was not in their power to wait. They did agree not to
insist on immediate payment of the tax, giving him until their
next meeting in three weeks' time. If in the meantime he could
have the charge lifted, 'they would be well pleased'. Sir Ralph
wasn't happy with this – it was much harder to have the tax
taken off once judgement had been given – but he was also
anxious for his reputation. 'Twas not the money I stood upon,'
he reported to William Denton later, 'but the mark of delinquency.' The Commissioners also consented not to put down his
name as a malignant in the official record. They instructed the
clerk 'only to take short notes of all that concerned me, but not
to enter it in any book, till my Lord Protector's pleasure were
known upon my petition.'[30]

A second petition went to Cromwell, this time supported by
seven of the Commissioners, who certified that his original sequestration had been lifted by Parliament. But it did no good. The

petition was referred back to Aylesbury, just as the first; and after another hearing on 3 July, the decision to levy a charge on Sir Ralph was confirmed. To add insult to injury, he was barred from entering London for the next six months, along with all the other dangerous and disaffected Royalists.

The major-generals soon overreached themselves. On Christmas Day 1656, John Desborough, major-general of the West Country and brother-in-law to Cromwell, brought in a bill 'for continuance of a tax upon some people, for the maintenance of the militia'.* His intention was to turn the decimation tax into a permanent levy on Royalists – 'Let us lay the saddle upon the right horse,' he told his fellow MPs[31] – and he purposely avoided the word 'decimation', so that the 10 per cent rate could be raised as necessary. This was too much for the moderates, who argued against the unfairness of a tax which punished the well-behaved majority of cavaliers for the actions of the few, and pointed to the illegality of a levy that rode roughshod over the 1652 Act of Oblivion, which had promised a pardon to peaceable Royalists for any actions committed prior to the Battle of Worcester. At the end of January 1657 Desborough's bill was defeated by 124 votes to 88. The major-generals were relieved of their roles as regional governors soon afterwards and Cromwell, under growing pressure to assume the crown, abandoned the experiment of military rule.

This was small comfort to Sir Ralph. It took a strong man to hold fast to a cause which, having first killed his father and then sent him into exile, now falsely imprisoned him and demanded that he pay for the privilege of being disgraced. But although he railed against the incompetence of a system which could get things so wrong so consistently, he *still* didn't give up his commitment to Parliamentary rule. He refused to turn out in support of Monck, when the general marched past Claydon in February 1660 on his way to break down the gates of London and declare for a free Parliament. When his entire family, brothers and sisters, cousins, aunts and uncles, were cheering Charles II's return, he

---

* *The Diary of Thomas Burton*, I (1828), 230. William Denton reckoned that Desborough had deliberately chosen 25 December to introduce the bill because, although Christmas was banned, the less earnest MPs had gone home to celebrate, leaving only hard-liners in the Commons.

couldn't bring himself to celebrate the restoration of a regime which it had cost him so much to oppose – although he did accept a baronetcy from the King in March 1661, after reminding him of his father's heroic death at Edgehill and his own harsh treatment at the hands of the Commonwealth. (Everyone was a trimmer that year.)

Writing soon after the Restoration to one of his Protestant friends in Blois, he hoped for peace 'under our good and gracious King, whose virtues are more honour to him than his crowns, and whose zeal and constancy in religion are like to make him the head and protector of all the reformed churches in Europe'.[32] That was a forlorn hope; Charles II was no Prince Henry. But it does offer the clue to Sir Ralph's reluctance to give up on Parliament throughout the 1650s, no matter how it served him – his continuing conviction that whatever served the interests of Protestantism was best for him and best for his country.

Stuck in the Low Countries, Mun Verney deeply resented the fact that his father had taken Jack back to England at the beginning of 1653 and left him behind. He didn't get on well with his tutor Robert Creighton, an intellectual Scot whose rigid approach to life and learning made Sir Ralph seem positively carefree by comparison. And no sooner had his father gone than the teenager experienced that rigidity in an all too literal sense, when Dean Creighton decided with Sir Ralph's blessing that it was time to correct the boy's slouching posture. Mun was taken to see Skatt, a Utrecht doctor with an international reputation, according to Creighton: 'Young people have been brought to him from further than the utmost parts of Shetland or the Orcades, even from Swedeland, Denmark [and] Holstein.'[33] Dr Skatt diagnosed a curvature of the spine. He fitted Mun with a tight iron harness which encased his torso front and back, and told him he must wear it day and night. It was lined with leather and went over a linen undershirt, which helped a little to prevent chafing; but still during Mun's weekly sessions with the doctor, when Skatt removed the harness so that he could change the stinking shirt, the boy could see that his skin was rubbed raw and bleeding.

After six months of torture Mun was 'of his crookedness almost wholly restored';[34] but he was ordered to continue with the harness for another nine months at least. Over the hot summer of 1653 Skatt allowed his patient to spend two or three days out of the thing, a concession which Creighton thought quite unnecessary: the corset was really very light, he said, 'and I think might well be borne at all times, and were far better borne, than left off at any time till the cure be finished'.[35] Easy for him to say.

Creighton was a hard master with high standards and a low opinion of his student. Even the pathologically earnest Sir Ralph was driven to ask him to ensure Mun got out a little more and had an opportunity to refine his social skills in polite company. It was necessary for a boy of his age and his class to study men as well as books, 'or else his learning may make him rather ridiculous, than esteemed', he reminded the Dean; 'a mere scholar is but a woeful creature'.[36]

Mun was capable of being a woeful creature without going to the trouble of scholarship. Each morning Creighton rose at six, called him at seven and returned at eight to find him sound asleep, 'and seldom can I get him up before nine'. He was so used to being instructed that at sixteen he was incapable of private study, and would do nothing unless Creighton was actually in the room with him. Instead, the boy lolled around until noon, 'his breast unbuttoned, his breeches unclasped, his stockings untied about his heels'. In winter he hovered over the fire; in summer he sat 'in a chair so ill-favouredly that you would take him for a scullion'.[37]

He was civil enough, and reasonably well behaved. He didn't keep bad company, he didn't swear or smoke or drink. If he went in search of whores every now and then, that was to be expected. Sir Ralph's only comment to Creighton on the subject was that the boy shouldn't consort with 'women of evil fame' too frequently, in case he caught something. But besides his laziness, he seemed – to the Dean's unrelenting eye, at least – to be lamentably backward in his learning. In response to Sir Ralph's worries that the seeds of a conversion to Rome might have been sown in the boy's mind during his time in Blois, Creighton answered that Mun must surely be a true Protestant, since he certainly understood nothing of any other religion. 'It is to me admirable,' went on the Dean, '[that] those that in your house of Blois perverted him should so ill ground him.'[38] Sir Ralph in his turn was just as hard on the boy. When, after two years' tuition at Utrecht,

Mun moved to The Hague and told his father that letters should
be directed 'For Mr Edmund Verney at Mr Bates in the sign of
the Samson in die Pots in den Hagh', Sir Ralph tore into him:

> You should have said 'At Mr Bates his House or Shop or
> Lodging', or some such like place, or 'tis not good English.
> Secondly 'In the sign of the Samson' is nonsense; it shoud have
> been 'At the sign'. Your very French phrase might teach you
> to write better sense, and English too, but that you are so care-
> less that you mind nothing. 'Tis no less a wonder than a trouble
> to me to see that at near nineteen years of age (though no
> care, nor cost hath been wanting for your breeding) you are
> not yet able to write a superscription of a letter. For shame,
> be not still thus childish.[39]

This wasn't altogether fair. Mun was no genius, but he could
read and speak Latin and he had some Greek. The *giro d'Italia* had
given him a working knowledge of Italian; he was learning Flemish
and he was fluent in French. Under Creighton's supervision, he
read Sallust and Livy, and probably Caesar and Quintilian as well.
And while owning a book is not the same as reading it, the fact
that he had works by Seneca, Virgil, Lucian and Justin implies a
degree of willing – as does the fact that he also owned Sir Richard
Hutton's *Young Clerk's Guide* (1649), a popular collection of
templates 'for all sorts of indentures, letters of attorney, releases,
conditions, &c, very useful and necessary for all, but chiefly for
those that intend to follow the attorney's practice'.[40] Perhaps the
rocky state of Sir Ralph's affairs in the 1640s had prompted him
to ensure that Mun had a working knowledge of the law.

It wasn't really a lack of academic progress that bothered Sir
Ralph; it was his son's attitude. Mun was being trained for a
purpose; how he presented himself to the world, how he coped
with responsibility, were of supreme importance for the family
fortunes, since the future of the Verneys rested with him. An inept
or irresponsible heir was the next worst thing to no heir at all.
He would find it hard to attract the heiress which was every
father's object of desire for his eldest son; he might squander his
inheritance, or neglect the management of his estate.

So Sir Ralph was constantly urging Mun not only to study

but to acquire polite and gentlemanly virtues; otherwise he might as well come home and mind the sheep. Even if he did buckle down to his studies, and still 'prove a lazy sloven, or a wilful clown', Sir Ralph commented, 'all his other good qualities will but make his follies more observed and laughed at'.[41]

It was to no avail. When Mun finally came home to Claydon in May 1655, eleven and a half years after he left England, he was still a wilful clown, still a lazy sloven. Worse, he managed to combine these qualities with an airy arrogance and an over esti-mate of his own worth which was bound to set him on a colli-sion course with Sir Ralph. 'Hitherto my father hath not given me any education whereby I might be rendered accomplished in body and mind,' he told a friend, with a frightening contempt for the truth:

Nay further, though I am naturally inclined to be that which the Italians call *un Virtuoso*, he never did so much as coun-tenance me therein, but hath continually opposed me. Considering these premises aforesaid my industry will labour under a great difficulty of acquiring a title above an honest elder brother, which nowadays is accounted but little above a silly fellow, yet I think myself capable of deserving much better . . .[42]

We can smile at the familiar world-weariness of adolescence. We might find it less amusing if the future of our family depended on a wilful clown like Mun.

15

Mend Me or End Me

It was different for Jack Verney, who as a thirteen-year-old was described by an aunt as 'the sobrest youth that ever I did see'.[1] Jack was first reserve; he had fewer responsibilities than Mun, and if he also had fewer prospects at least he had more freedom to choose how he spent his life. The biggest choice he had to make was what career to follow: the days had long passed when younger sons could expect to be provided for, and if he needed a reminder of *that* he had only to look at the struggles of his two impecunious uncles, the one an inveterate sponger, the other a whining thief. As he wrote *pace* Uncle Tom many years later, ''Tis often the fate of gentlemen's younger children to be a clog to their families.'[2]

Jack was determined not to follow in their footsteps and be a clog. At James Fleetwood's school in Barn Elmes he showed an aptitude for arithmetic, but Fleetwood was barred from teaching as a delinquent in 1655 and Sir Ralph moved Jack to a school in Kensington. Its proprietor, Samuel Turberville, was less sanguine about Jack's academic progress than James Fleetwood had been, announcing that the boy was poor at writing and grammar, and 'an indifferent Latin author'; but in contrast to Dr Creighton's experiences with his brother, he was 'very laborious and industrious to redeem the time that is past and irrecoverable, and very observant of my advice'.[3]

Jack enjoyed Kensington. Instead of sleeping in a dormitory with seventeen boys as he had at Barn Elmes, he shared a chamber with one other pupil. He could ride over to Windsor, and there were regular visits to Dr Denton and Mun. The aunts and great-aunts doted on him: he was tall and good-looking, and he dressed well. Pen thought he was 'so fair that if he were in woman's apparel he must look lovely in it'.[4] London excited him, in contrast to Claydon, a 'grievous dull and sad, lamentable mournful place'.[5] But he was impatient, and he knew his own mind. 'One must have some living nowadays,' he told his father; and when Sir Ralph tried to push him towards the law he argued that he would rather be apprenticed to a tradesman. 'I do verily think that I am a great deal fitter to be [in] some trade than to be a lawyer.'[6]

The middle years of the seventeenth century saw some heated arguments over the plight of younger sons of the gentry like Jack. In 1628 James Earle's *Micro-cosmographie* offered the kind of vignette which Uncle Tom would have relished. After making the reference to Jacob and Esau which seems to have suggested itself to almost every writer on the subject, Earle declared that the typical younger brother had his father to thank for his troubles: 'he tasks him to be a gentleman, and leaves him nothing to maintain it.'[7] All he had to live on is an annuity; if it stretched to it, he might go to university and then into the Church. 'Others take a more crooked path . . . the King's highway, where at length their vizzard is pluck'd off, and they strike fair for Tyburn.'[8] Soldiering in the Low Countries was another course; at least as a poor gentleman of a company, 'rags and lice are no scandal'. But the younger brother's best bet – really the only chance to improve his fortunes – was to find himself a rich widow.

Gentry attitudes towards primogeniture were hardening during the first half of the century, to the extent that many educated people believed a father was legally obliged to leave the bulk of his estate to his eldest son. Younger brothers who were unwilling to buckle down and find a career for themselves – like Henry and Tom – and unable to entice a rich widow – again, like Henry and Tom – were left to rail against the accident of birth which had left one sibling with so much and the rest with so little. The younger brother was a symbol of discontent and envy, or of injustice and inequality, depending on one's point of view. Levelling radicals in the Commonwealth used the term 'elder brothers' as shorthand for landlords and enclosers who had 'by the murdering and cheating law of the sword, stolen the land from younger brothers, who have by the law of Creation, a standing portion in the land, as well and equal with others'.[9] The anonymous author of *The Representative of Divers Well-Affected Persons in and about the City of London* (1649) included among his proposals for reform one which would set aside two-thirds of a man's estate for his eldest son, and divide the rest between his remaining children. In 1655 another pamphleteer, 'Champianus Northtonus', argued for a more 'harmonical division and proportion' of a father's fortune, and then went so far as to suggest that younger brothers should emigrate en masse and set up a colony of their own, with its own government, its own decrees and constitution.*

That same year, the case of Freeman Sondes made the conflict between elder and younger brothers a talking point all over the country. On 7 August, Freeman, who was eighteen or nineteen at the time, crept into his elder brother's chamber and, motivated by a fit of jealousy, killed him with a cleaver; he then went to his father, confessed what he had done and tried to kill himself. Sir George Sondes stopped him but the boy was taken to Maidstone assize and arraigned; he pleaded guilty and was hanged on 21 August.

The Sondes affair provoked a flurry of pamphlets about a father's duty towards his children. Some of the comment was so grotesquely unfair to Sir George that he felt moved to defend himself in print, and his *Plain Narrative to the World, of all Passages upon the Death of his Two Sons* (1655) not only offers a dignified glimpse into his

---

* 'Champianus Northtonus', *The Younger Brother's Advocate: or a Line or Two for Younger Brothers* (1655), 16. Anyone who thinks that the idea of a colony of younger brothers sounds fanciful should know that Thomas Hughes, author of *Tom Brown's Schooldays*, actually set one up in Tennessee in 1879. It failed – apparently because the colonists preferred to spend their time playing tennis and putting on amateur dramatics instead of working on the farm.

broken heart, but also demonstrates some of the dilemmas which faced gentry with more than one son. 'I am sure no man ever endeavoured or laboured more to persuade a son to take to something, than I did [Freeman],' he wrote. 'I was earnest with him to study the law, or to be a merchant, or any thing, so he would be something.'[10] He inherited nearly £4000-worth of debts from his own father, and was left to provide for a younger brother, six half-brothers and a half-sister. He paid off the debt and managed to find annuities of £100 for his brother, who was a law student, and his eldest half-brother, whom he sent travelling. The second he sent to Leiden to study medicine; the third went to the Low Countries with money to buy a commission; the fourth and fifth were apprenticed to merchants, and the sixth to a woollen draper in Paul's Churchyard. The sister had £40 a year.

Sondes' account of his treatment of his siblings provided a pretty accurate survey of the career opportunities available to Jack Verney as a younger son – only the Church of England is missing. And unwittingly or not, Sondes placed those opportunities in an order of precedence which fellow-gentry like Sir Ralph would have recognised, with the law and leisure at the top, following by physic, soldiering, and finally Jack's chosen path, commerce.

The seventeenth century couldn't quite make up its mind about trade. Some commentators argued that being a merchant and a gentleman was a contradiction in terms, and that 'the first mistake belonging to business is the going into it'; others grudgingly accepted that it was a necessary evil for younger sons, but that even so 'being made an apprentice according to our custom is a blot at least in every man's scutcheon'.[11] Others embraced the world of business with pride: the antiquary Gervase Holles, for example, declared that 'I shall ever esteem it more honour to be descended from a merchant than from any other civil profession whatsoever.'[12]

Something of this range of responses can be found in the Verneys' circle. Mun, who was growing to be quite a snob, disapproved of his brother's ambitions. On the other hand, Dentons and Temples had gone into trade; and Sir Ralph, although he was uneasy at the prospect of having a merchant for a son, reassured himself with the thought that such a move involved no loss of status. 'If this were not so,' he reasoned, 'the nobility, as well as the gentry, would not make their younger sons apprentices, as diverse lords have done.'[13] In this he was echoing Dudley North's remarks that, while the military, the law and physic were suitable professions for the sons of gentlemen, 'neither is merchandise to be condemned, whereunto in foreign lands persons of the most honourable condition do apply themselves'.[14]

Jack had something more glamorous in mind than being apprenticed to a woollen draper in Paul's Churchyard. He wanted to travel to far-flung lands with one of the big monopolies: the Russia Company; the Eastland Company, which traded with the Baltic; the East India Company; the Levant Company. But which one?

Sir Ralph did nothing about Jack's ambition for three or four years, leaving the boy to improve his Latin and his grammar in Kensington under Samuel Turberville's guidance. Perhaps he hoped his son might discover a liking for the law after all; but if he did, he was disappointed. 'I am afraid that you are a little displeased with your worm for desiring to be an apprentice,' Jack told him in May 1659.[15] The following month he agreed to send Jack, now eighteen, to a school which specialised in commerce and accounting.

He consulted his merchant acquaintance William Wakefield about the right apprenticeship for his son. Wakefield took the request very seriously, visiting Jack at his school and examining him in his arithmetic and accounting. He came away impressed with the teenager's abilities, but he didn't have anything particularly encouraging to say about his career prospects. England had been at war with Spain for four years, so the lucrative Spanish markets were effectively closed to English merchants; and the Baltic trade, in which Wakefield himself had been raised, was not going well. Barbados, the Caribbean and New England offered high returns, but with such high attendant risks that 'I should never advise any friend of mine to breed up his son to it'.[16] (Nor would Sir Ralph, when he remembered Sir Edmund's unhappy experience with Tom and Barbados.) The West Indies, the East Indies and the Levant also bred high failure rates: not one man in three managed to thrive, and those merchants who did could command as much as £500 for an apprenticeship.

Wakefield confessed he didn't know what to suggest. Sir Ralph's request for advice was 'of more hazard and difficulty than ever anything you put me upon before'. But he was clear about one thing – speed was of the essence, since already some reputable merchants would think that Jack was too old to start an apprenticeship. 'It [is] high time, if you intend your son for a merchant, speedily to look out for a place for him.'[17]

Sir Ralph took the hint. Sir Roger Burgoyne put him in touch with his brother-in-law Alderman William Love, a Levant Company merchant who traded through Aleppo in Syria; and although Love wouldn't take Jack, he suggested the boy might do well with another Levant Company trader, Gabriel Roberts, who had premises on Threadneedle Street in the City. Gabriel asked £400 for the seven-year apprenticeship, which was a little on the steep side. He stipulated a two-week probationary period and agreed to release Jack immediately if Mun died. Sir Ralph had to provide Jack's next suit of clothes and sign a £1000 bond as security against theft. Sir Ralph agreed to his terms, the indenture was sealed on the last day of December 1659, and Jack became a merchant's apprentice.

The origins of the Levant Company dated back to 1581, when Elizabeth I granted a monopoly on trade with the Ottoman Empire to a small group of merchants looking for new markets, after being forced out of Italy by Spanish hostility and high tariffs at Venice, and out of the Barbary Coast by civil wars in Morocco. The Company prospered; by the 1630s it was accepted as 'the most flourishing and most beneficial Company to the Commonwealth of any in England of all other whatsoever'.* It exported goods to the value of £250,000 every year; and in the lead-up to the Civil War the cargo of just two of the Company's outward-bound vessels was valued at £200,000. The bulk of these exports were in English broadcloth, with nearly 30,000 pieces going out yearly, around half to the main factory at Constantinople and half to Smyrna and Aleppo, where the cloth was sold on and taken by caravan to the markets of Persia. Less important stations were maintained on the islands of Cyprus in the Mediterranean, Zante and Cephalonia in the Ionian Sea, and at Patras on the Greek mainland.

---

* Lewis Roberts, *The Marchants Mapp of Commerce* (1638), 80. Roberts is echoing contemporary opinion, although since he was a leading light in the Levant Company (see below), he was hardly an impartial witness.

The glamour and prestige of exotic alien cultures beyond the boundaries of Christianity, the enjoyable frisson at the idea of trading with the Turk and the prospect of high returns for a relatively small outlay meant the Levant was the company of choice for the sons of the gentry. Vere Gawdy's son was apprenticed to the Turkey merchant Thomas Barnardiston (who was charging around £300 in the 1650s) around the same time as Jack was apprenticed to Gabriel Roberts; Lord North had bound his son Dudley to another, Thomas Davis, in May 1658, at a cost of £350 without sureties.

Sir Ralph may have had to pay more, but he had the better bargain. Jack's master was well connected. His brother William was out in Aleppo, trading both on his own account and in partnership with Gabriel; two of the Roberts sisters were married to Levant merchants; and until his death in 1641 their father, Lewis, had been one of the Company's most influential members, and a well-known economic theorist. Lewis Roberts' *The Marchants Mapp of Commerce* was the standard handbook for merchants who needed information on weights and measures, rates of exchange and local commodities everywhere from Amsterdam to Zanzibar; and *The Treasure of Traffic, or, A Discourse of Foreign Trade*, which was published the year he died, 1641, made a convincing argument for recognition of the contribution commerce made to the wealth of the nation, and of the navigators and merchants who risked their lives in trade:

> And if true nobility should have taken its foundation, (as the judicious and learned have observed heretofore) from the courage of men, and from their valour, there is no vocation, wherein there is so many useful and principal parts of a man required, as in these two, for they are not only to adventure and hazard their own persons, but also their estates, goods, and whatever they have, amongst men of all nations, and customs, laws, and religions, wheresoever they are inhabited.[18]

It wasn't only Gabriel's reputation and connections which made him a good choice for Jack. Apprentices were often treated worse than servants: they were made to serve at table and to do the most menial tasks, such as keeping the garden tidy and emptying the slops. If they disobeyed their master or his wife, or even the maid, they were beaten, and the court records of the seventeenth century are full of tales of abuse and humiliation: an apprentice whose hip was broken with a boat hook; another who was beaten so severely that he couldn't stand upright, and was still spitting blood two weeks later; another who was beaten, salted and then forced to stand naked by a fire; a girl apprentice who was stripped, hung up by her thumbs and whipped twenty-one times.[19]

Jack's experience with Gabriel Roberts was not at all like that, partly, to be sure, because of the boy's gentry background, but also because Roberts was a decent, humane master who took his responsibilities seriously. He taught Jack to keep accounts, and allowed him to eat with the family. And the boy loved his work. He loved the writing of bonds and bills, the stripping and weighing of the great parcels of silk which came back from Aleppo in return for the bales of cloth that went out there. 'I assure you,' he told his father, 'that I never delighted in any play when I was at school as I do in this trade.'[20] Above all, he looked forward to travelling out to the Levant. Roberts initially intended to send him to Smyrna, which by now was handling the lion's share of the Ottoman trade, but by the autumn of 1661 he had settled on Aleppo where, as William Love reported to Sir Ralph, 'he hopes your son will be a noun substantive'.[21]

Jack's brother had a destiny which was at once less exotic and more pressing than becoming a noun substantive in the souks of Aleppo. Mun had to make haste to rescue the Verney fortunes by marrying an heiress, and to secure them for the future by fathering a son.

Although there was as yet no bride on the horizon, family, friends and servants were already looking forward to the wedding within weeks of Mun's return to England in 1655. Aunt Sherard told Sir Ralph she hoped the boy would find a good wife with 'a portion answerable to your desires'. Even Will Roades said he was praying that God would bless the next master of Claydon 'with a Rebecca in nature if not in name'.[22]

The problem for Sir Ralph was that he didn't think his son was much of a catch. He told anyone who would listen that Mun was clumsy and clownish, 'not at all nice either in point of beauty or of breeding';* and he warned Lady Warwick, when she mooted the idea of a match with her young granddaughter, that the boy was 'no courtier, nor no complimental man'.[23] For his own part Mun took little interest in the courtship rituals being rehearsed around him, preferring to spend his time and his father's money whoring in the taverns and brothels around Newgate.

Perhaps that was because within the immediate family circle models of conjugal bliss were rather hard to find. Sir Ralph remained locked into his widower's grief; every year he set aside the anniversary of his wife's death as a day of meditation and prayer, routinely complaining that he could no longer hope for any happiness in this world and shying away from the idea of marrying again, in spite of being urged to do so by all and sundry. Uncle Tom's wife was dead or deserted; Uncle Henry showed not the slightest wish to give up his amiable, aimless bachelor existence.

Of Mun's five surviving aunts, Betty was still single. Just three years older than her nephew, she continued to irritate her siblings, with the exception of Cary Gardiner, who had a soft spot for her. 'Truly, sister,' an exasperated Sir Ralph told Cary after she had tried to excuse Betty's sulks and tantrums for the umpteenth time, 'if you yourself were of such a humour, that you should sit wishing for death and sigh and sob and pout yourself into a sickness, could you then with any confidence expect a more than common consideration? . . . I must confess your proportion of good nature doth very far exceed my own.'[24]

Cary was the only married aunt with anything like a happy relationship. Pen's drunken and impoverished husband John Denton was routinely violent towards her – 'it is not long since that upon a slight occasion, he did kick me about the house' – although she was capable of giving as good as she got.[25] At one point, after a big family get-together at Claydon, there was an embarrassing scene in the middle of Aylesbury as the couple tried to board the coach back to London. It was raining hard and Denton pushed his wife out of the way in his haste to secure an inside seat; she punched him in the face, and he was left to ride behind the carriage, soaked to the skin and nursing a black eye which made him the laughing stock of his friends.

---

* 'Nice' here means particular, fastidious.

Peg's marriage was worse. She and Sir Thomas Elmes had achieved a reconciliation of sorts after he left her and went to France with Tom in 1648. But it didn't last: they agreed to separate in 1657 and Peg went to live with Cary and her husband at Preshaw, leaving Sir Ralph to spend the next decade trying either to reconcile them or to persuade Elmes to give his estranged wife enough to live on with honour.

A marriage which failed so publicly was quite a scandal. But it was Mall Verney, easygoing, wild-as-a-buck Mall, who really set tongues wagging. By 1654 she was twenty-six years old, still single in spite of attempts to find her a husband, and living with just a maid in lodgings in London on the £10 quarterly allowance which Sir Ralph paid her. She was just as eager to please as she had been as a teenager, when sister Susan had thrown her out of her house for flirting with her own husband, and she had attracted a string of men friends who were keen to spend time with her, but markedly less keen to declare themselves as suitors. They included a Colonel McShane; Charles Goode, a friend and patient of William Denton's, who lived in a country house down at Maldon in Surrey; and a young Welshman named Robert (known otherwise as Robin) Lloyd, who worked with his brother Francis in the Covent Garden shop of Denton's son-in-law, the apothecary William Gape. Gape not only supplied Sir Ralph and his family with pills and powders, he also doled out the quarteredge on his behalf to Tom and Mall; and he usually employed Robin Lloyd for the task.

In August 1654 Mall began to complain of feeling ill with colic or the dropsy. She took a massive dose of 'physic', but this only made her worse. By the end of the month it was obvious that her belly was swollen. Uncle Doctor watched her closely, and the more he watched the more convinced he became that she was pregnant and that the medicine she took had been an attempt to bring on an abortion. All his cynicism and urbanity vanished in an instant as he struggled between horror and compassion. 'I am at my wits end to know what to do or say,' he confessed to Sir Ralph, who was at home in Buckinghamshire. Mall faced 'shame, imprisonment, beggary (not having wherewithal to buy rags to wrap a child in), alienation from all her friends . . . and I want foremost to express the ugliness of it towards God and man.'[26]

If a woman in seventeenth-century England chose to conceal a pregnancy, it was harder than one might think to discover it. Gowns were loose-fitting; expectant mothers put on less weight than they do today; and the normal test in close-knit country communi-ties – a straightforward demand by female neighbours to examine the suspect's breasts – was hardly appropriate in Mall's case. She was a Verney, not a maidservant or some farm worker's daughter.

No one dared to confront the girl – fornication was not a charge to be levelled lightly – but everyone was desperate to know if Denton's fears were justified, who the father was and whether or not Mall was secretly married. Henry was sure that the responsibility for his sister's ruin lay with McShane, Goode or Robin Lloyd; Uncle Doctor thought it might be Lloyd or the colonel, 'or both, but I most suspect the first'.[27] When Cary Gardiner heard the news from Sir Ralph, she prayed McShane was the culprit; he came from a respectable family and they might avoid scandal by pretending they were already husband and wife. Otherwise, perhaps Charles Goode could be persuaded. But if Lloyd was the father, said Cary, 'I wish her banished rather than marry him.'[28] Whatever happened, her sister must stay in London, where at least she might remain relatively anonymous. If she sought refuge at Claydon – or worse still, in Cary's house at Preshaw in Hampshire – her dreadful secret would be all over the country within days.

After weeks of family conferences, William Gape was finally delegated to raise the subject with Mall, who came straight out and confirmed Dr Denton's worst suspicions. She *was* pregnant, she said, and she wasn't married. It turned out that the father was Robin Lloyd, but whether she also admitted as much to Gape at this stage isn't clear. It wasn't mentioned as fact within the family until after she had the child. One can't help remembering with unease that midwives routinely interrogated unmarried women in labour about the identity of the father. Mall put herself in the hands of a local brothelkeeper who was of course well used to dealing with unwanted pregnancies; the woman would farm out the baby when it was born, but Mall would need money to pay her for her help, to employ a nurse, to buy things for the baby and to settle her debts at her lodgings.

She was in a desperate position. Technically, she and Lloyd had committed a criminal offence: under a 1650 Act 'for suppressing the detestable sins of incest, adultery and fornication', they could both be committed to gaol for three months and bound over to keep the peace for a year. That was unlikely, but money was a more pressing problem. Winter was coming on – it was now early October – and she was near her time. Denton believed she had only a couple of weeks to go, in fact, and that 'she will be brought a bed in the street, or as openly' unless something was done.[29] At his suggestion, Gape advised her to throw herself on Sir Ralph's mercy. If she agreed to be discreet about the birth, to find a more respectable carer and to go to Ireland or Barbados as soon as the baby was born, her brother might just be persuaded to stump up the money she needed.

So she wrote to Sir Ralph, taking care not to spell out the details in case her letter fell into the wrong hands:

> Brother, I have an earnest request to you concerning my own condition. For my recovery, here is a one that will undertake to cure me and in a short time for a matter of twenty pound, and they desire but half beforehand and the rest when I am well. I should not beg of you to do so much for me, but that I have been assured by so many that have been cured by the same party. I sent my uncle [Dr Denton] word of it by Mr Gape to see how he doth approve of it, and I do not find that he doth dislike it, so I ventured to beg this favour of you. Truly brother, if you please but to disburse so much for me I shall ever acknowledge myself obliged to you; and if [it] please God to send me recovered, I will go to any place that you shall desire me; or do anything that you think fitting for me. I will refuse no offer of yours. Any other kingdom I will travel to if you do approve of it.[30]

Guided by Dr Denton, who reckoned the girl would agree to go 'Tom o'Bedlam's journey, twenty leagues beyond the wide world's end', if she were only given the money she needed, Sir Ralph agreed.[31] He waited more than a week to tell her so, and even then he was so angry he didn't trust himself to write directly to his sister, dealing instead through Gape. But Mall didn't care what he thought, so long as she had the financial support she asked for. She immediately wrote back to him saying she would do whatever he bid her: she placed herself completely at his disposal. And if she was scared of what lay ahead for her, she refused to let her fear overwhelm her. 'I have a heart that will go through a great deal of pain,' she told her brother. 'I am in hope that I may over-come it all – it will either mend me or end me.'[32]

Mall moved into more discreet lodgings where she could be cared for by a midwife when her time came; Robin Lloyd left Gape's shop, either voluntarily or otherwise; and his brother Frank Lloyd agreed that he and his wife would take on the child, so long as Robin made some provision for expenses. People were gossiping, not least because Mall had, in Gape's elegant phrase, 'so publicly showed her great belly'; but that couldn't be helped.[33] Memories were short and with luck the whole affair would be forgotten once she was packed off to Ireland or the Americas. ('The Bermudas is much better than Ireland,' said Uncle Doctor.)[34] She gave birth to a healthy boy around the beginning of November 1654.

So far, so good. But once her immediate problem was solved, Mall began to have second thoughts about leaving her old love for the New World, and decided it was time to renegotiate terms. The opening shot was fired in January, after Sir Ralph showed reluctance to allow her to take her maid with her when she went abroad. Cary Gardiner received a letter which purportedly came from the maid to her mother, suggesting that if she left her mistress's service she might come down to look for a position in Hampshire. Cary recognised Mall's handwriting, which was not sinister in itself since an illiterate maid might well have relied on her mistress to write her letters for her. But what really star-tled Cary was the thought that although the girl could easily get another position in London, she was intending to settle near her own seat at Preshaw. 'If she come into these parts she will discover all passages,' Cary told Sir Ralph. 'I would not have her come down by no means.'[35]

Of all the Verney clan, Cary was the one who was most shocked at Mall's pregnancy, the one who was determined that the scandal shouldn't be spread abroad. 'Pray God it may ever be concealed,' she said.[36] The letter was an unwelcome reminder that, although Mall was dependent on her family's goodwill, she was quite capable of manipulating them to her advantage.

The agreement was that she should stay in her lodgings until the end of February 1655, with Sir Ralph authorising William

Gape to pay her 10s. a week and 14s. a month for a nurse. Once the baby was handed over to Frank Lloyd she was to leave London for a destination of Sir Ralph's choosing, with or without her maid. She gave up the child readily enough, but she couldn't bear to live without Robin. February passed, then March, as she pleaded with Gape for more time and more money. She claimed to have found herself a place in service where she could easily meet up with her lover and plan their wedding, telling Gape she was looking for a promise from Sir Ralph 'to continue her annuity unto her, and then to her R'.[37]

She didn't know her brother very well. His immediate reaction to being crossed like this was to refuse to have anything more to do with her. Gape was instructed to give her no more money; the other sisters were forbidden to help her (not that they were in much of a position to do so – Pen Denton, whose husband was currently languishing in Oxford gaol, reckoned that 'no creature that begs from door to door can live in a meaner condition than I do').[38] From now on, she was Robin Lloyd's responsibility. Let him look after her.

Except that he didn't. Perhaps the couple quarrelled, or perhaps Lloyd just didn't have any money. But less than three weeks after Sir Ralph stopped Mall's weekly allowance she heard that her brother was in town and staying with the Leekes in Russell Street, just round the corner from Gape's Covent Garden shop. She didn't quite have the courage to confront him, but she did leave him a pitiful letter, pleading for him to reconsider. She understood why he jibbed at the idea of supporting two people, she said; but now there was just the one (it isn't clear if she was referring here to the loss of her baby or the loss of her lover). And yet still he would give her nothing. 'Brother, as I have deserved hard usage so I have received; for I have endured more hardship than I am able to express with my pen. Now my earnest request to you is that you will please to let me know whether you will allow me a livelihood or no; if you do not I must starve, neither shall I have a place to lie in.'[39] She described herself as a castaway from the family, treated more harshly than others who were just as unworthy but who ate at Sir Ralph's table every day. She promised to leave town if only he would give her the money to do so; she begged him for help. 'Brother, you had dealt more charitably with me to a' laid the extremity of the law against me at the first than to a' relieved me for the present and to suffer me to starve now.'[40]

Sir Ralph held out for another month or two, and like the ruined maid in a broadside ballad Mall threatened to haunt him, to waylay him in the street, to come up to Claydon and perish at his door. 'I am confident that your dogs eat that as I would be glad of, if I had it.'[41] He finally agreed to resume her quarteredge around the middle of July 1655, but on strict terms.* A proportion of the money would be held back to pay off her creditors, and, unless she was absolutely desperate, Gape was not to advance her money against the next quarter – if she was allowed to keep drawing against future allowances, he asked the apothecary, then 'how doth she suffer for her impudence?'[42]

There is a handwritten certificate among the Verney papers which states baldly that on 2 November 1655 Mr Robert Lloyd and Mrs Mary Verney were joined in matrimony in the parish church of Paddington by Anthony Dodd, minister. Dodd had a reputation for conducting irregular marriages, several of which were declared void in 1655 and 1656: that may or may not be significant. It didn't stop Mall's begging letters. Two weeks later she wrote to Sir Ralph for money for clothes, a plea she repeated the following March. 'If you do not please to help me I am confident I must go naked,' she declared.[43] She – or rather Gape – had paid off most of her debts by now, but Sir Ralph didn't soften, so she asked Tom, of all people, to intercede for her. It did no good: although Tom assured his brother that Mall and her husband were all set to leave London for the house of a doctor of divinity a hundred miles away, Sir Ralph delegated his servant Robin Kibble to respond concerning the 'unfortunate party [who] hath so often deceived and abused him already, that he can neither credit her words nor intentions; but he will speak with Mr Gape about her and therefore he desires you would not trouble yourself hereafter to write to him concerning her, or her affairs.'[44]

The begging letters continued. In September 1656 Mall wrote

*It was at this time that Tom finally heard about his sister's misfortune and threatened, in that pompous way he had, to lie in wait for Lloyd and vindicate Mall's honour. Perhaps the prospect of another scandal was too much for Sir Ralph.

to say the rent was due, and she hadn't got it, so yet again she must 'both starve and die in the streets'.[45] For the first time she signed her letter 'Mary Lloyd', a fact which made Sir Ralph shudder. Six months later she told him she was pregnant again, and eager to travel into her husband's country of Wales, where all things were cheaper. As usual, she wanted money – an advance against her next quarteredge, and a commitment from Sir Ralph that he would continue to pay the allowance to any friend in London she might nominate, so that she could borrow against it. This was too much:

> I shall not grant her request [he told Gape], nor shall any importunity draw me to it, and so tell her. For if I once promise it, if he whom she calls her husband either pawn or sell it, I may be compelled to make it good, upon my promise. Therefore bid her think of no such thing, for I shall never make such a promise.
>
> But if she do go this journey (which I do not believe she intends) you may tell her I have entreated you to pay her according to my former order, and till I recall that order, whether she go, or stay, upon her acquittance, you will pay it accordingly. You know this is not the first time she hath pretended a resolution to go out of town, and I believe she intends this no more, than she did others formerly.[46]

Hard words; and on the last count, at least, he was proved wrong. After another request for money to cover their travelling expenses, on 3 April 1657 Mall and 'he whom she calls her husband' finally decamped for Wales and passed out of Sir Ralph's life. He continued to pay Mall's quarteredge until her death in 1684, but brother and sister never met again.

16

Perfect Empress of My Heart

*F*or Sir Ralph, Mall's fall from grace was only one scene in a bigger melodrama. While she was refusing to leave her Robin and simultaneously threatening to turn up at Claydon unless she received some money, her brother was under arrest on suspicion of treason; while she was enlisting Tom's help to beg new clothes, and promising for the umpteenth time that she and her husband were preparing to leave London, Sir Ralph was trying to prepare for his appeal against decimation.

There were other woes. Tom himself was cooking up get-rich-quick schemes, which always seemed to require an advance on his own quarteredge. In May 1655 he announced that his dead father-in-law had entered into a bond with him for £600; if Sir Ralph could just provide him with the funds to pursue the case in the courts, he was sure of a successful outcome. Then he became involved in a plan to sink a mine in the north of England; if only his brother would invest in 'my mineral discoveries', the venture was bound to make them both rich.[1]

But Sir Ralph's most pressing problem wasn't Mall, or Tom,

or even a hostile government. It was Mun. The boy showed no interest in finding a bride; worse, he showed a persistent lack of respect for his father. When Sir Ralph was called to his decimation hearing the month after Mun arrived back in England, for example, one of the charges he had to answer was that he had sent money to the Royalist court in exile, and that he had purposely kept Mun in Holland to act as his agent in the matter. Instead of rushing to give evidence in his father's defence, as he was asked to do, Mun said he was very sorry but he wouldn't be able to attend the hearing because he had met up with some gentlemen who had invited him over to Norfolk for a while.

Sir Ralph was understandably hurt, and ordered Mun to attend him in London at once. The boy didn't turn up, and there followed a farcical series of exchanges in which Mun became more and more mysterious, offering to meet with his father on neutral ground without servants present, but refusing point blank to obey him. This infuriated Sir Ralph. After Mun's go-between failed to arrange a venue for this proposed secret meeting, with only days to go before the decimation hearing, he wrote thus:

> Well Mun, if it be your absolute resolution, after the receipt hereof to persist in your own wilful ways, and contrary to my command, conceal yourself still from me, I shall quickly cast you off, and though now my life and quite probably my fortune lie at stake, I shall rather choose to hazard both, than seek to you to preserve either, for the advantage of such a son as shall thus highly, wilfully, and unhandsomely, provoke his father.[2]

The pair made up again a few weeks later, after Sir Ralph's decimation had been lifted, but they continued to bicker on and off until December, when a huge quarrel threatened to wreck their relationship for good.

The indirect cause was Uncle Henry, who tried to broker a marriage between Mun and the daughter of Lady Longueville. The Longuevilles, who lived at Wolverton in the north of Buckinghamshire, offered a portion of £4000, and in return Lady Longueville stipulated that she expected Sir Ralph to provide the young couple with an allowance of at least £600 a year. This

was too much: he was prepared to offer no more than a tenth
of the dowry – £400 – which the Longuevilles, and several of
his own cousins, thought to be too mean. He stood firm: 'By
reason of my father's debts, I am necessitated either to expect
more money with my son, or allow him less maintenance.'[3] Lady
Longueville refused to come up with a better offer, and negotiations ground to a halt in the middle of December 1656, with
Sir Ralph commenting rather uneasily that the Longuevilles were
letting it be known all over Warwickshire, Northamptonshire and
Leicestershire that he was treating his son badly.

Mun agreed with them. He was living in lodgings in London
and existing on handouts from his father, since Sir Ralph refused
to give him an allowance until he either married or came of age.
There were no signs of the former happening, and he had another
year to wait for the latter; yet, as William Denton informed Sir
Ralph, 'L'argent he wants, and l'argent he must have.'[4] Uncle
Doctor, who always did his best to moderate Sir Ralph's hard
line towards the rest of his family, advised him to make proper
financial arrangements for the boy straightaway.

Mun didn't exactly go out of his way to reassure his father
that he was mature enough to deserve a regular allowance. He
was still being secretive, and he sometimes disappeared for long
spells without offering a word of explanation. Then there was a
mysterious woman who kept turning up at Denton's house
demanding to see the boy. She wouldn't say who she was or how
she knew him, only that she was come about the £10 he owed
her from his time in Holland. In December 1656 she stopped
calling, leading the doctor to speculate that Mun had paid her
off – perhaps this was why he was in need of cash?

Whatever the reason, Mun's pleas for 'l'argent' grew more insis-
tent. Denton urged Sir Ralph to be reasonable. 'If an allowance
would not be a means to lead him to a way of living little pleasing
to you, I should please him in it.'[5] With scant regard for the truth,
he even claimed that Mun was living a wonderfully orderly and
well-regulated life in London, spending his days at home in his
lodgings and his evenings with the Dentons. But Sir Ralph
remained adamant, once more blaming the dreadful state of affairs
in which Mun's grandfather had left the family, as he usually did
when he suspected he was being mean.

That excuse led the boy to suggest some of the money being laid out on the remodelling of Claydon would be put to better use in his purse – a jibe which really hurt Sir Ralph:

> As for my buildings, I see I have already lost one great part of the contentment I took in them, which was, that you should find that what money I did expend, was laid out for your advantage, and to make the house more handsome and convenient for you and yours. But since I see you are not sensible of that benefit . . . I shall not debar myself of any expense that I think moderate to supply any extravagancies that you either have or shall commit.[6]

Familiar conflicts between parsimonious fathers and rebellious teenage sons were being played out all over the country, even back in the seventeenth century. But there was no doubt that, buffeted by Mun's resentment, Sir Ralph's righteous indignation and the inability of either to understand the other's point of view, the relationship between the two men was in serious difficulties.

It received another blow a few days after this exchange, which took place at the beginning of December. Mun had given out that he wouldn't be able to join the family over Christmas because he was going off on another of his mysterious journeys out of London. But shortly before Christmas, someone – it isn't clear who – informed Sir Ralph that the boy was still in town, and living in a tavern near the Old Bailey as 'Theodore Berry' (the name of his lute master in Utrecht).

This fuelled Sir Ralph's resolve to keep his son on a tight financial rein. But there was worse. Mun was in hiding because he was ill with gonorrhoea. In the weeks leading up to Christmas he had contracted a sore throat, a high fever and a blinding headache, and one of his testicles swelled until it was bigger than his fist. Reluctant to consult Uncle Doctor, he chose instead to go to a surgeon (surgeons were in any case more experienced than physicians in treating venereal disease), and the man prescribed a course of treatment which was nastier than the original complaint. Mercury was the standard treatment for syphilis, and since seventeenth-century medicine assumed that gonorrhoea and syphilis were different types of the same disease, it was common to prescribe it for the less serious ailment as well. So Mun was bled and purged and poulticed, and then told to take an apothecary's shopful of mercury-based pills, potions and enemas.

By Christmas Eve he was really frightened for his life, and in so much pain that he thought he would lose his mind. As he lay in his lodgings, sweating and puking and applying mercury poultices to the affected parts, a letter arrived from his irate father announcing that since 'Theodore Berry' couldn't be trusted, Mr Berry had no chance of receiving any kind of allowance from him.

Christmas Day was Mun's twentieth birthday. Filled with rage and self-pity, he crawled out of bed that morning and vented his spleen in a letter which, as Sir Ralph said, later, 'had better been unwrit'.[7] He told his father everything – not even sparing the details of his swollen testicle – and likened himself to Job for the pains and torments which afflicted him. Unfortunately, whereas Job came to 'abhor myself, and repent in dust and ashes', Mun seemed to think it would be more appropriate for Sir Ralph, rather than himself, to engage in self-loathing and repentance. After admitting that 'women are the original cause of my suffering', he laid the blame for everything at his father's door. If Sir Ralph had provided him with money of his own, he would have been cured long ago. He could only conclude either that his father's judgement was at fault, in which case 'I pray to God to guide you so well in future that you do not fail in other things'; or that he had deliberately set out to ruin his son and heir. If this were true, then 'I will have to take good care of myself and seek to look after myself the best I can'.[8]

The letter went to Claydon, but Sir Ralph was spending Christmas and Twelfth Night with Aunt Sherard and her husband at Whissendine in Rutland, so Mun's febrile rant didn't reach him for several weeks. When it did, he was livid with rage. He translated part of the letter (which was in French, as were most of Mun's letters to his father) and sent it to Denton for comment and advice.

In the meantime Mun wrote again, making things even worse. He was feeling much better, he said, and he really would like an allowance. He would also like Sir Ralph to pay his surgeon's fees. In spite of his father's silence, he was sure he must have received the Christmas Day letter – 'otherwise I would rewrite it for you word for word'.[9]

If this was his idea of making peace, it was not a success. Sir Ralph's reaction was to behave exactly as he had when Mall fell from grace: he simply refused to answer his son's letters or to send him any money. This time, however, his anger was mixed with real pain. 'For his dear mother's sake I would gladly love him,' he confided to William Denton, 'but he will not let me.'[10] He urged his uncle not to lend any money to 'Mr Berry', as he called the boy with heavy sarcasm, swearing that if he did he needn't look to Sir Ralph for repayment. Then he sat down to compose a retort which would achieve just the right blend of paternal disappointment and paternal wrath. Draft after draft was peppered with words and phrases like 'sorrow', 'the horror of your crime', 'your dear mother'. The final version was sent care of his uncle, with a note asking him to read it and, if he approved, to send it on. In its entirely it read as follows: 'When I see a submission and sorrow more suitable to your crime, I thank God I can forgive it, though you have most highly and strangely provoked your father, R.V.'[11] That was all.

Denton refused to pass on the note. The patient mediator had already been to see Mun several times since Christmas. He had told him what a fool he was, how he needed to mend his ways before his sexual activities ruined his life, how deeply he had hurt his father. And he told him to apologise, which the boy did, albeit rather half-heartedly. He wrote that he was sorry if he had done anything to cause his father displeasure, and if Sir Ralph would reassure him that he wasn't angry, 'you will make my heart leap for joy'.[12]

This missed the point rather. But Denton urged Sir Ralph to swallow his pride and accept the apology:

Suppose you should stand upon a submission more suitable to his crime, and he should not answer your expectation, I will not ask you what *can* you do to him (for I know you may do what you will) but what *will* you do to him? You cannot but suffer with him. Even your making of it public will be a torment to you, and to take notice of it, and not go through stitch with it, it will be an allay to your sovereignty. Go, kiss and be friends.[13]

Denton's counsel prevailed. Sir Ralph couldn't quite bring himself
to kiss and be friends with his son, but he realised the sense of
what his uncle was saying, and he duly sent Mun a polite enquiry
about his new harness, recently fitted by Skatt, and an equally
polite request to supervise the despatch of some trees from London
to Claydon. He closed with the clearest sign of all that their
differences were behind them: 'Shortly there shall be some money
sent to the Dr. for you, from your loving father R.V.'[14]

Marriage would solve all Mun's problems at a stroke. Sir Ralph
would have to give him an allowance, and he could legitimately
maintain a household in London, free from his father's prying
eyes. Denton reminded him of this during their talks, and dragged
him off to meet Sir William and Lady Luckyn and their daughter
Elizabeth, 'a pure virgin eighteen years old, tall, slender, straight,
handsome, with as much sweetness in her aspect as I know not
more anywhere'.[15] The Luckyns were Essex gentry with money
to spare – Sir William was prepared to give a portion of between
£5000 and £10,000 if he could be convinced that the Claydon
estates were worthy of it and that his daughter and son-in-law
would have a respectable amount to live on during Sir Ralph's
lifetime.

Denton was smitten by both the girl and the fortune, and hasty
steps were taken to turn Mun from a clown to a gentleman. He
had dancing lessons, violin and lute lessons. Sir Ralph urged him
to keep his Skatt harness out of sight when visiting the Luckyns,
in case it prejudiced the matter. Denton and Lady Anne Hobart
both despaired of his appearance, and begged Sir Ralph to buy
him some decent clothes: 'Truly I am ashamed to see how he
goes, not at all like your son,' complained Lady Hobart, 'for he
has nothing new like any other young man, neither hat nor
clothes, nor linen . . . I dare say your man wears better.'[16] Sir
Ralph wasn't persuaded; he was inclined to wait until Easter,
when the new fashions came in, he said. Lady Luckyn sent her
sister round to the Dentons' house to have another good look
at Mun and to make a few preliminary enquiries about Sir Ralph's
estates and the likely size of any settlement, and a second meeting
between the two youngsters was set up for Easter Monday in
the Temple Gardens. Uncle Doctor spent Easter Day ensuring

Mun would be properly dressed and coaching him in what to say and how to say it.

Mun remained completely uninvolved in all of this, content to leave the entire matter in the hands of his great-uncle and his father. Sir Ralph was impressed at the metamorphosis from rebel to obedient son (which was Mun's intention) and promised to come up to town the moment his presence was required at the negotiating table. 'Since you leave the matter of treaty so wholly unto me, I shall not only the more cheerfully appear in it, but the more willingly comply in any thing that's reasonably desired.'[17] The reality was that Mun didn't have strong feelings either way about the marriage. He couldn't say he liked Elizabeth; neither could he say he disliked her. If the wedding went ahead, that was all to the good – so long as he got his settlement – but if it didn't, it wouldn't break his heart.

That was just as well. With his lack of enthusiasm, his crooked figure and his clownish manners, Mun was hardly a figure of romance, and when the Luckyns began to hear stories about Mall and – worse – about Uncle Tom, they started to have second thoughts about marrying into the Verney family. After the Easter meeting in the Temple Gardens the couple don't seem to have seen each other, and by the summer the match-making circus had moved on once again.

The target this time was Alianora Tryon, the adolescent grand-daughter of Eleanor Warwick. Eleanor's star was currently in the ascendant: her husband had spent years in the political wilderness after Parliament abolished the office of Lord High Admiral back in 1649, but he was now closer to Cromwell than ever before. At the latter's second investiture as Lord Protector at Westminster Hall in June 1657, it was Warwick who acted as sword-bearer, and Warwick who helped to invest the Protector in his robe of purple velvet, lined with ermine. The following November, Warwick's grandson and heir married Cromwell's youngest daughter, Frances.

Eleanor's family tree had grown progressively more compli-cated over the course of her three marriages, and Alianora belonged to a flock of grandchildren and step-grandchildren she had acquired along the way. The child's mother was Eleanor's daughter by her first husband, Sir Henry Lee of Ditchley Park in

Oxfordshire; her father was stepson to Eleanor's brother, Sir Edward Wortley, which meant that Eleanor was the child's great-aunt as well as being her grandmother. Wortley promised to contribute a sum of £500 plus £100 a year for five years to Alianora's portion – not much beside the £5–10,000 which Sir William Luckyn had been prepared to give with his daughter, or Lady Longueville's £4000. But that was a negotiating position. More money could be brought to the table in the right circumstances.

This time Sir Ralph led the hunt. At the end of July he heard that Alianora was staying in Warwickshire, and took Mun for a viewing. They missed her by a few days; she had gone to Ditchley to spend the rest of the summer with her cousin, Sir Harry Lee, and his mother Ann, who was now married to the exiled Royalist Henry Wilmot, Earl of Rochester. Undaunted, father and son regrouped at Claydon and then travelled up to Ditchley for a meeting which, according to Sir Ralph, was a tremendous success. Mun was so enamoured of Alianora, he told Eleanor Warwick after they returned home, that they had extended their stay by several days. In fact if the boy had had his way, they would be there still: 'he is so much taken with Mrs Tryon that if you please to suffer him to be her servant, he will ever acknowledge your favour'.[18]

Eleanor was pleased. She liked the idea of a union between her family and Sir Ralph's, and she wrote to Alianora to tell her so. The Countess of Rochester thought that Mun was an excellent young man, remarking with approval that 'he carried himself with that prudence and discretion all the while of his being at Ditchley both to his mistress and everybody else, that he must in justice gain both my high esteem and all that do belong to me'.[19] And Alianora herself wrote a little note to Mun, thanking him for his kind words to her.

Mun was not so keen. Taking the advice of his friend Thomas Hyde, who counselled that he should 'let her estate be settled by agreement before you make love',[20] he avoided further visits to Ditchley that summer and left his father to make excuses for him. Sir Ralph was at pains to explain to John Cary, the chief negotiator on Alianora's side, that it was only because so many relations had descended on Claydon on purpose to see Mun that the boy hadn't been over to visit her; he hoped his absence wouldn't be misinterpreted. Autumn came and went, with proposals and counterproposals passing backwards and forwards between Sir Ralph and John Cary, and every now and then a member of the clan putting forward the name of another girl recently come on the market. But at the end of November, just when everything was on the verge of being settled, Mun abruptly declared that he didn't want to marry Alianora after all.

He had fallen in love.

The object of Mun's desire was Aunt Sherard's teenage daughter, Mary Eure. They had first met when she came to study in Blois with her sister Margaret, and they renewed their acquaintance over the summer of 1657. In November, Aunt Sherard sent both girls to stay with the Dentons in Covent Garden, in the hope that 'Pussy's Mad Eure', as Peg referred to herself, might find a husband. She was the more beautiful of the two, but she had already driven several eligible suitors (and her mother) to distraction through saying 'she will and then she will not', and by laying down strict conditions for courtship. She announced that she was only interested in a man with a good estate; a man who had no father or mother living, so that she wouldn't have to contend with in-laws; and a man who had fought on her dead father's side during the war. But while men queued up to woo her, Mun fell head over heels for her quiet, prim sister. 'I find him much more taken with her,' Sir Ralph told Aunt Sherard, 'than ever I thought he could have been with any woman.'[21]

Sir Ralph and Uncle Doctor were both delighted at the prospect, and Alianora Tryon was unceremoniously dumped. Aunt Sherard was not so keen, but rather than upset Sir Ralph with a frank assessment of his son's charms, she argued that the young people were too closely related (they were second cousins) and that in any case she had 'no mind to part with her daughter as long as she lived'.[22] She blamed Sir Ralph for the whole muddle, hinted that he had been scheming for this ever since she consigned her daughters to his care in Blois, and came rushing up to London to take both girls back to Whissendine.

Mun persevered. Declaring his love for Mary to anyone who would listen, and describing her admiringly as a 'solid, judicious wench'[23] (one hopes he did a little better than that to her face) he asked the rector of Claydon to act as go-between and to assure Aunt Sherard that her objections to second cousins marrying were groundless. The Reverend Edward Butterfield, who was new, eager to please and about to wed himself (having just decided that the only way to get his hands on his rectory was to marry his predecessor's widow, Mrs Aris), set off to ride the seventy miles from Claydon to Whissendine on 15 March 1658.* He took with him a love letter from Mun telling Mary that 'every joint in your body, and every perfection of your soul, are inventoried in my heart'; and a financial offer from Sir Ralph.[24] Neither did much good. Mary thought the rector was a joke, and laughed at him; her mother conceded Butterfield's point about the moral probity of a marriage between second cousins, only to shift her ground and claim that a French doctor had told Mary sex would be fatal to her.

Mun didn't take the news well. He blamed the poor rector for having 'an extraordinary sneaking countenance and way with him',[25] and suggested (to Dr Denton, at least) that if Mary *were* to have sex with him, it would do her the world of good. No prizes for sensitivity there, then.

He didn't give up. Begging Aunt Sherard to pardon him for being so forward – 'your daughter [is] the first and only love my youth ever had or shall have'[26] – he bombarded Mary with appeals to reconsider, appeals which were given the requisite eloquence by his lawyer friend Thomas Hyde, who wrote them for him to copy out. She was 'perfect empress of my heart';[27] he was her slave, her captive. By resolving to lead a single life she was going against God and against nature, and in any case it would be bad for her health, and his own. A denial from her was like a dagger in his heart.

> My dearest mistress,
> Startle not, I beseech you, at the title; for it is yours and none but yours, and my pen may be pardoned for writing what is

---

* In 1658 Sir Ralph pulled down the old parsonage, which stood next door to Claydon House, and replaced it with a new one about a quarter of a mile away. No doubt his intentions were good, but the fact that he also managed to put some distance between himself and Butterfield's formidable new wife was an added bonus.

so deeply engraven in my heart. Cast, I beseech you, an eye of pity upon your slave, whom your perfections have made the most miserable creature in the world. Your virtues have such absolute dominion over my soul that it can think of nothing but Mrs Mary Eure. I think that I am writing this at Claydon, but I can scarce believe it, for there is more of me at Whissendine than in Buckinghamshire: and you will be persuaded it is so, when I assure you that as often I make any addresses to my God, my saint, even your sweet self interposes between my maker and me.[28]

After weeks of this, Mary finally spelled out what everyone else had suspected for some time. If she married anyone, it wouldn't be her cousin, and 'if he write or speak a thousand times it will not prevail with me at all'.[29] Still Mun kept up the assault. She stopped accepting his letters, so he sent them hidden in notes from her uncle, Dr Denton. She begged Sir Ralph to make him see sense, but nothing Sir Ralph did or said could shake the boy from the conviction that if only Mary would agree to see him in person, he could win her over. She flatly refused to allow him up to Whissendine, writing that this might give him some small encouragement, 'which I am resolved shall never be given you',[30] so he plotted to ambush her in the street and literally throw himself at her feet when she and her mother came to London. His nerve failed at the last minute.

This one-sided love affair carried on for years. When Oliver Cromwell died in September 1658, Mun was pleading with his Uncle Henry to put in a good word for him with Mary. When Cromwell's son and successor as Lord Protector was preparing to open Parliament in January 1659, Mun was sending his manservant to Whissendine with yet another request for a meeting with Mary. Richard Cromwell was ousted, the major-generals came and went, Charles II returned in triumph to take the throne; and Mun pined for love. In August 1660, two years and nine months after he first decided that Mary Eure was his one true love, Mun was still asking Hyde to help him out, by composing one last appeal.

Sir Ralph was in an awkward position. He liked the girl, he wanted the match and he was quite pleased (not to say surprised) at his son's ability to play the devoted lover. But the fact remained that Mun needed to marry and father an heir; moping around and mumbling about how he was slave to the perfect empress of his heart wasn't helping matters along. He fired a warning shot in the summer of 1658, by which time it was probably dawning on him that Mary Eure was a lost cause: he hinted that if Mun didn't get a move on, perhaps *he* might remarry. This would mean a widow's jointure for his new wife, whoever she might be, and – if she bore him children – provision for a second family. All of this would have to come out of the estate. Mun knew this would be a financial disaster; but what could he do?

What he could do was remember his duty and forget Mary Eure. There were various desultory attempts to find him a more willing bride. Lady Mary Springett, who was married to the Quaker Sir Isaac Penington, had a daughter who was available; so did Mrs Utbut, a wealthy City widow. There were other widows without daughters; and Uncle Henry, when he could tear himself away from his primary occupations – horseracing and trying to obtain a place at court – swore he would 'make it my study night and day in my little progress to find out a lady suitable to thy liking and merit'.[31]

On 10 August 1661, Sir Ralph's neighbour, William Abell, died. The wealthy son of a well-connected London vintner,* Abell was High Sheriff of the county and lord of the manor of East Claydon, a village about a mile from Middle Claydon. He dropped dead unexpectedly while attending Buckingham assizes, leaving behind a widow, an estate worth about £800 a year, and a twenty-year-old daughter named Mary.

Edward Butterfield rode straight over to East Claydon to offer Mrs Abell his condolences. She was upset and there were relatives everywhere so that it was hard to have a moment alone with her; but as he was leaving, Butterfield hinted gently that

* William Abell senior had powerful friends. When he was arrested for debt in 1651 (he had borrowed £3600 for the use of the Vintners' Company and not paid it back), he was immediately released into the custody of his two sons, leading to questions in Parliament about 'the inconveniences and scandals arising by granting of such undue liberty' (*Journal of the House of Commons* 7, 19 January 1653).

perhaps Mun Verney might have a role to play in her step-daughter's future. He went back to give the same hint the next day, and the next. By 15 August – only five days after William Abell's untimely death – Mrs Abell had agreed to broach the subject with Mary, and the rector was confident that 'if there be a liking between the young folk, it may be a match'.[32]

And there *was* a liking between the young folk. Mary Abell was unaccountably smitten with crookbacked, clownish Mun; he was equally smitten with her fortune. He was urged on by his father, for whom this really was a marriage made in heaven – an unencumbered young heiress with an estate which bordered on his own and which, at current rates of interest, was equivalent to a dowry of £16,000. So Mun put thoughts of the one Mary behind him and did his best to woo the other, much to the relief of Aunt Sherard, who was quick to wish him well in his new endeavours. 'I hope there will be no stop of it,' she said.[33]

The financial side of the negotiations went less smoothly than Sir Ralph would have liked. The Verneys managed to see off Mary's uncle Richard Abell, first establishing that his brother had broken entails which would have entitled him to all or part of the estate; and then, when he suggested the girl might come and live with him, vigorously supporting her decision to remain at East Claydon with her mother. He went home empty-handed. But there were more formidable adversaries to deal with, in the shape of another uncle, George Gale, a proctor in the Doctors' Commons;* and Mrs Abell's uncle Sir Robert Wiseman, advocate-general and author of *The Law of Laws, or, The Excellency of the Civil Law above All Other Humane Laws* (1656). They were both good men, genuinely anxious to protect the interests of a widow and an orphan, and they weren't about to let Mary agree to anything which might damage those interests.

Wiseman's task was to make sure that Mrs Abell received a reasonable jointure from her husband's estate, while Sir Ralph and Mun tried to keep it as low as possible. Gale was the chief negotiator. He had no objections to 'the great business', as he

* The Doctors' Commons, more properly the College of Advocates and Doctors of Law, was beside St Paul's Cathedral; it housed the ecclesiastical and Admiralty courts and was a focus for civil law.

called it, reassuring Mary that 'I very well approve of your choice, for I conceive him to be a deserving gent and that he will be a suitable match for you.'[34]

Mun kept a foot in both camps. It was to his advantage for Sir Ralph to make the largest possible settlement on the couple when they married, and he egged Mary on to push Gale into taking a hard line with his father, dictating her letters to him and even instructing Gale directly. At the same time he tried to manoeuvre Mary into agreeing a marriage settlement which favoured the Verneys until, when Gale pointed out rather testily to her that one draft drawn up by Sir Ralph's advisers contained nothing at all to her advantage, she told Mun that he had to stop issuing orders to her lawyers.

The negotiations went on for nearly a year. Mary was in love: she wore Mun's ring in public, and his picture; she blushed when she heard his name. On Valentine's Day she was reluctant to play the old game of drawing one's future husband in case the name on the rolled-up piece of paper wasn't his. (It was.) According to Butterfield, who was a regular visitor at East Claydon, she 'both speaks of him with much pleasingness, and seems to delight to hear of him'.[35] In return, Mun said the right things, and wrote the right letters to 'my most passionately beloved Mistress'.[36]

But his heart wasn't really in it. He said he would visit Mary, and then he didn't. He promised to take her and her stepmother to London, and then he didn't. By the summer of 1662, just as the dealing between Gale and Sir Ralph was reaching a critical stage, there were whispers around Claydon that there was not going to be a marriage after all, that Mun had changed his mind. Butterfield was first irritated and then really angry with both the father, whom he blamed for dragging his feet over the settlement, and the son. 'Why will you destroy your family,' he raged at Sir Ralph, 'and render all the cost and pains you have been at in beautifying Claydon fruitless?' As for Mun, he had 'gained the affection of an honest gentlewoman, whom if you should wrong by an inconsiderate breach, you will never be able to answer it while you breathe; and look to it, never any prosper that are guilty of treachery of that kind'.[37]

Either Butterfield's words pricked the Verneys' consciences or – more likely – Sir Ralph and Mun decided that Uncle Gale's

terms were not going to improve. A fortnight later, on Tuesday
1 July 1662, Edmund Verney and Mary Abell were married at
Westminster Abbey, beneath the spectacular vaulting of Henry
VII's Chapel. Saints and angels looked down in benediction from
the walls as they knelt, surrounded by the tombs of kings and
queens, to be reminded that it was a husband's duty to give
'honour unto the wife as unto the weaker vessel', while brides
must 'submit yourselves unto your own husbands as unto the
Lord: for the husband is the wife's head, even as Christ is the
head of the Church'.

They signed their marriage settlement the same day. Sir Ralph
gave the couple an estate at Middle Claydon worth £600 a year –
exactly the sum which Lady Longueville had demanded and Sir
Ralph had refused six years earlier. But then Mary Abell's fortune
was worth four times what Lady Longueville had offered by way
of a dowry.

Mun and Mary also had the use of her East Claydon estate
and, once they had come to terms with Mary's stepmother (who
was still living there), they could move into the Abell house. The
settlement only provided Mary with a widow's jointure of £350
a year in the event of Mun's predeceasing her – which was rather
miserly considering what she had brought to the marriage – but,
crucially, Uncle Gale successfully insisted that the Abell estates at
East Claydon were to return to Mary if the couple had no children, and that she could then dispose of them as she wished.

Jack Verney turned twenty-one in November 1661, and his departure for the Levant was fixed for the following spring. On
Christmas Day Sir Ralph sat down with a list which Gabriel
Roberts had supplied of the items 'to be bought for Jack when
he goes to Aleppo'.[38] He would need a cloth suit for the winter,
when temperatures dropped to the low forties Fahrenheit, and a
black silk suit for the summer; six pairs of shoes, of which four
were to be of white Spanish leather; silk stockings, woollen stockings and linen stockings (nineteen pairs in all); twelve pairs of
socks, two white doublets and twelve pairs of white gloves; an
assortment of handkerchiefs, hats and caps; and a sea chest to
hold them all.

Over the next few months this list grew. Jack wanted to take his viol, a good supply of strong waters, and some Claydon cheeses, 'which I hope to carry to Aleppo, they being there in great esteem'.[39] He needed sheets and pillowcases, a hammock for the voyage, three padlocks for the sea chest, a leather hat box. Sir Ralph bought him some reading matter: a Bible, of course, along with Thomas Gery's *Holy Meditations upon God* and a copy of Lancelot Andrewes' *A Manual of Private Devotions*, which Uncle Doctor had sent out to him in France thirteen years earlier when Mary was dying. Sir Ralph also included Jeremy Taylor's *The Rule and Exercises of Holy Living*, 'in which are described the means and instruments of obtaining every virtue, and the remedies against every vice, and considerations serving to the resisting all temptations'.[40]

It was bound together with Bishop Taylor's *Holy Dying*, a spiritual self-help manual for those who found themselves facing imminent death. Jack might never come home – that was an open secret. That winter Sir Ralph had the boy's likeness painted by Gilbert Soest. At least he would have something to remember him by.*

Jack's thoughts were turning to more venal matters. Mun's courtship had made him think hard about his own future and his brother urged him to find out their father's intentions towards him before he left England. So in January, having waited until Sir Ralph had left London for the country, he wrote him a letter. Slipped in neatly between the latest news from town (he had just bought two hats, two combs and a pair of silk stockings) and the latest news from Leghorn (Algerian pirates had taken two merchantmen and killed the captain and six crew of a third), was a diffident query:

> Accidentally discoursing with a friend of mine, who is not unknown in those things we discoursed of; at last our discourse fell upon my (intended) estate by which means some words

---

* In January 1662 Jack sat at least twice for Soest, whose studio was off Cursitor Street at the end of Chancery Lane. Sir Ralph doesn't seem to have been happy with the result: in March, Jack told him he had been back to Soest 'to sit for the mending of my picture but he saith he can mend it without my sitting and that it is altogether needless' (26 March 1662; M636/18).

passed which causes me to desire of you to know about (I say about) what estate you intend me at first and last.[41]

In a postscript he confessed that the 'friend' was Mun.

Jack was rather frightened of his father, with good reason: Sir Ralph could be a hard and unforgiving parent, and he was at his worst when his authority over the family was questioned. Jack had his reply a few days later:

> As to what you desire about knowing what estate I intend you at first and last, I confess you may well think I cannot but wonder at your simple curiosity. I do not understand what you mean by 'first', for now you are going to a place where I presume your gains will not only keep you, if you behave yourself well, but I hope you may lay up money too; or else the great charge I was at when I bound you (and since too) was but ill bestowed.[42]

Sir Ralph assumed that simply by carrying out Gabriel Roberts' commissions in the Levant, Jack would earn enough to set up in business without the need for more capital. That was wishful thinking, although it was a mistake made by many fathers of would-be merchants. But it wasn't the thought that Jack wanted even more money that made him angry. It was the boy's impertinence:

> You must know children do not use to catechize their fathers what estate they intend to leave them; nor indeed can I tell you, if I would; for 'tis like to be more or less as you carry yourself towards me, and towards your master. If you are dutiful to me, and by your civility, care, and industry promote your master's good, and your own too, I shall do my utmost for you, and think it all too little for you. But if you keep lewd company, and by drinking, gaming, or your own idleness, lose your reputation, be confident you will thereby also lose my affection, and your portion too.[43]

Jack received the rebuke with equanimity. He realised he had crossed a boundary he should not have crossed; in his next letter to his father he kept to safer territory – specifically, the arrangements for sending two cases of vines and a parcel of melon seeds to Claydon. As far as we know, he never broached the subject of his inheritance again.

On 26 March 1662 Jack heard that the *Dover Merchant*, on which he was to take passage for Aleppo, was due to set sail from Gravesend in two weeks' time. The King had given permission for the Royal Navy to escort a convoy of merchantmen through the Channel, and the *Dover Merchant*'s captain planned to rendezvous off Deal with a vessel bound for Smyrna and 'all other ships that can be ready then to set sail'.[44] There was a delay of a couple of weeks, but by the end of the month Jack had sent his belongings aboard ship at Gravesend and said his goodbyes to Sir Ralph and Mun. 'Yesterday I returned from Gravesend, where I parted with my poore brother, who is gone for Aleppo,' Mun told Mary Abell.[45] Not quite gone: Jack then rode post the sixty miles down through Sittingbourne, Canterbury (where 'I went to the cathedral and there heard service said and sung by the choristers') to Deal.[46]

The convoy had gone on by the time he arrived; but fortunately the *Dover Merchant* and two other vessels weren't ready to leave. Hindered by contrary winds, they were still waiting to enter Deal harbour and take on their passengers. At three o'clock on the afternoon of 4 May the three ships came into the Downs, and the next morning Jack set sail for the Levant. At the last minute Mun sent him a note: 'I should rejoice very much to hear you were arrived at your journey's end, because I should hope in God to see your sooner return . . . the love of Heaven be with you and bless you, my dear brother.'[47]

17

All the Physic in the World

*M*un and his bride spent their honeymoon in London, lodging at the Golden Spread Eagle in Fleet Street. Although Mary was taken ill within days of the wedding, she quickly recovered, and over the last two weeks of July 1662 they paid the expected courtesy visits to most of the Verney relations, and to rather fewer of Mary's kinsfolk. And they generally enjoyed each other's company, while Mun muttered good-naturedly to his father about all the expense involved in taking his new wife to the playhouse or buying new clothes for her, maintaining her maids and dishing out money for coach hire. At the end of the month they went back to Buckinghamshire and settled for the time being at Claydon, while Mun began to negotiate with Mrs Abell over taking possession of the White House in neighbouring East Claydon, where the young couple intended to set up home.

The first months of marriage were a trying time for Mary, as they were for most brides of her age and class. She was separated from friends and family; learning to meet the physical and emotional demands of a sexually experienced partner; and, to top it all, she was little more than a guest in an established and unfamiliar household. If there was no possessive mother-in-law to disapprove of her, there was an army of aunts and female cousins who owed their allegiance – and their financial well-being – to Sir Ralph for the moment, and to his heir Mun in the future. They watched for the first slip, the first sign of disloyalty, the first real or imagined slight.

The situation wasn't unusual, and a more confident character could have turned it to her advantage, just as Mun's mother had done thirty years earlier. Like that other Mary, the girl might have revelled in her new status as saviour of the family fortunes and mother-to-be to the next generation of Verneys. She might have gone out of her way to obtain her father-in-law's affections, while contriving to remind the female dependants that when he died she would be in a powerful position which could work both to their advantage and to their detriment.

But Mary Abell didn't possess the strength and resilience of her dead mother-in-law, and that soon became embarrassingly obvious. There was a massive gathering of the Verney clan at Claydon in September 1662 to welcome the bride into the family. Sir Nathaniel and Lady Hobart came up from London along with Lady Hobart's unmarried sister, Doll Leeke; Sir Roger Burgoyne rode over from Warwickshire, bringing his brother with him; Aunt Isham was there, and two of Mun's five surviving Verney aunts, Cary Gardiner and Peg Elmes. Mall Lloyd rarely left Wales, and in any case she wasn't welcome at Sir Ralph's house; and no one thought to invite Betty or Pen Denton. Pen wrote to say she was coming anyway, and when Sir Ralph replied that there simply wasn't room, she confessed that her real reason for wanting to be at Claydon just then had nothing to do with the party: her drunken husband had tried to stab her, and when she and her maid locked themselves into their chamber, he yelled 'that he should never be at rest till he had washed his hands in my blood'.[1]

As the family and friends ate pickled sturgeon and oysters, drank the claret and canary that Sir Ralph offered them and picnicked on eggs, bacon and beer in the woods, they couldn't help noticing that the task of being the new Mistress Verney was proving rather too much for Mary Abell. Before their arrival she had been taken ill for the second time in two months – no doubt the usual knowing looks were exchanged within the family – and she was shy about joining in the fun. Initially this seemed appropriate behaviour in a young bride. But her modesty grew until she was really quite odd – withdrawn and moody one day, and gripped with fits of hysterical laughter the next. Mun grew anxious for his wife's sanity. His father, who hated anything to disturb his carefully regulated life, was frankly appalled: this wasn't at all what he had imagined when he and Butterfield bullied Mun into a match with their pretty and eligible neighbour.

Everyone else pretended not to notice, and when the party broke up after more than a week Mary's behaviour returned to normal. And if the clan was surprised at her odd ways, they soon found something else to gossip about. Mun's marriage had had a dramatic effect on poor Betty, who by now was a twenty-nine-year-old spinster, still vaguely neurotic and still eager to be the centre of attention. In October she declared that she was dying. She also told anyone who would listen that she had been shamefully neglected by her family, 'cast off, and forsaken, and left to herself, no continuance showed her, nor care taken of her'.[2] Hardened to her behaviour, Sir Ralph and his siblings didn't pay much attention to this, but at the end of the month rumours reached Mun that she was determined to throw herself away on Charles Adams, an impoverished clergyman five years her junior, for whom she had fallen when she saw him preaching in her local church.

Mun told his father and his father did nothing, a course of action he had cause to regret a couple of weeks later, when it emerged that Betty was married. She wrote Sir Ralph a contrite letter offering to go down on her knees and beg his forgiveness for marrying without permission from the head of the family; but she still confidently expected that he would find a lucrative living for Adams, and while the clan offered their condolences to Sir Ralph for Betty's folly in marrying beneath her, they muttered behind his back that he only had himself to blame.

The fuss caused by Betty's clandestine marriage took some of the pressure off Mary. Her melancholy lifted, and when Nathaniel and Anne Hobart invited Sir Ralph to take lodgings in their Chancery Lane house for the winter, Mun decided that he and Mary would also move in with the Hobarts for a few months.

The capital held more charms than provincial life in Buckinghamshire, and the two Hobart girls, Frances (known as Frank) and Nancy, would be company for Mary.

In the spring of 1663, while the three Verneys were still lodging at Chancery Lane, Mary's hysteria returned. She acted in an aggressive and challenging manner towards everyone in the house, and by the third week in March her shouting and laughing fits were so bad that a distressed Sir Ralph fled to Claydon, leaving Mun and the Hobart women to deal with the problem. His sister Peg Elmes was cross with him for running away – 'you may not frighten me with your sad looks', she told him – and the Hobarts begged him to come back.[3] But it was no good. He sent his best wishes for Mary's recovery, and some puddings for her breakfast. But as far as he was concerned, it was out of sight, out of mind. And vice versa.

It was not clear what provoked Mary's outbursts, but her husband was almost certainly at the heart of it. His unenthusiastic courtship had made her wonder about his feelings even before the marriage, and now she was convinced that he was seeing other women behind her back. 'Zelotipia [a morbid jealousy] is got into her pericranium,' Uncle Doctor informed Sir Ralph in a characteristically elegant turn of phrase. But he followed it with a much starker warning: 'I do not know what will get it out.'[4] The irony is that she was probably right. Throughout their married life Mun was routinely and conventionally unfaithful to his wife. But that was beside the point: if she couldn't cope with his philandering, the fault was hers for failing to understand the rules of the game. Lord Halifax put the matter in a nutshell in his *Advice to a Daughter*:

> Next to the danger of committing the fault [of adultery] yourself, the greatest is that of seeing it in your husband. Do not seem to look or hear that way: If he is a man of sense, he will reclaim himself; the folly of it, is of itself sufficient to cure him. If he is not so, he will be provoked, but not reformed.[5]

The proper reaction to a husband's infidelity was a dignified silence, which would 'naturally make him more yielding in other things: and whether it be to cover or redeem his offence, you may have the good effect of it whilst it lasteth'.[6] This was more than just a piece of male wish-fulfilment (although it certainly was that); it was a clear statement of how the majority of men *and* women in Mary's social milieu expected a wronged wife to behave. When the minister in Westminster Abbey had asked Mun if he would, 'forsaking all other, keep thee only unto her', the groom, along with the rest of society, was quite clear that this was not to be taken literally. The bride's mistake was to think that it was.

After a brief respite at the end of March, Mary followed a spiral down into madness, pursued by demons. On Friday 3 April 1663, Anne Hobart wrote to Sir Ralph to say that 'my cousin Verney is fallen into her laughing fit again and I fear it is worse much than the last year'.[7] The previous Sunday she had been a little withdrawn, but she was more cheerful during the week and declared to Doll Leeke that she would always be so from now on. Then the hysteria came back with a vengeance. Unsure of how to proceed, Uncle Doctor, who was treating her, called in a distinguished colleague, the Padua-trained physician and Fellow of the Royal Society George Ent. But Mary showed no respect to Ent, nor to Denton, nor to any of the men in the Hobart household. She 'laughs more than before, speaks more boldly, descants upon bystanders . . . and few escape her'.[8] Even if she were cured, Denton believed that there would always be a worry that her illness would return. On Thursday 9 April Mun wrote to his father and said what no one else had dared to say: his wife was mad.

Uncle Doctor purged Mary and then bled her under her tongue. Unsurprisingly, she was reluctant to submit to further treatment, but he insisted. Anne Hobart and Doll Leeke wrote regularly to Sir Ralph, keeping him up to date with his daughter-in-law's progress, or lack of it. Mun was angry and confused. Doll was sure that if only Mary realised what was wrong with her she could begin to make some progress; and Sir Ralph tended to agree with her. From the safety of Claydon he urged his son to persuade Mary to pull herself together: 'I doubt all the physic in the world will not cure her, unless she strive against her melancholy, and in a good measure prove her own doctor.'[9]

Attitudes towards mental illness and its treatment in Restoration England still tended to revolve around the theory of humoralism first formalised by the ancient Greeks. This maintained that flowing through every human being were four vital fluids, or humours, each with its own characteristics. There was blood, 'a hot, sweet, temperate, red humour',[10] which was produced in the liver from the most temperate constituents of digested food, or chyle; and phlegm, which was cold and moist, and made – also in the liver – from the colder part of the chyle. Yellow bile, or choler, was hot, dry and bitter, and gathered in the gall bladder. Lastly there was black bile, or melancholy: this was 'cold and dry, thick, black, and sour, begotten of the more feculent part of nourishment, and purged from the spleen'.[11] Any sickness was the result of an imbalance between these humours. So an overproduction of blood, which was hot and moist, resulted in a fever, and this fever could be alleviated by bleeding the patient until a healthy balance was restored.

By the Restoration more advanced medical men had begun to question the truth of humoral pathology, helped along by William Harvey's account of the circulation of the blood (published in 1628 as *Exercitatio Anatomica de Motu Cordis et Sanguinis*), and some pioneering canine splenectomies carried out in London and Oxford during the 1650s. (If a creature could live without a spleen, and hence without any means of producing black bile, where did *that* leave the idea of a balance between the four humours?) Doctors also started to be critical of other established tenets of psychiatry. Anxiety, feelings of suffocation, choking sensations and other symptoms of hysteria had long been thought to be caused by the uterus moving up through a woman's body until, in extreme cases, it blocked her throat. (The complaint was thought to be exclusively female; its male counterpart was hypochondriasis.) The Oxford physician Thomas Willis was sceptical: 'the body of the womb is of so small bulk, in virgins, and widdows, and is so strictly tyed by the neighbouring parts round about, that it cannot of itself be moved, or ascend from its place, nor could its motion be felt, if there were any . . .'.*

---

* Thomas Willis, *An Essay of the Pathology of the Brain and Nervous Stock* (1681), 77. William Harvey's own ideas about how to treat female hysteria were depressingly conventional. He blamed 'over-abstinence from sexual intercourse', and ordered the parents of one young patient to 'take her home, and provide her a husband' (Robert Boyle, *Some Considerations touching the Usefulnesse of Experimental Naturall Philosophy* (1663), part 2, 73).

But Willis, who placed the pathology of hysteria firmly in 'the brain and nervous stock',[12] and was thus one of the first to propose a connection between mental illness and nerves, was far ahead of his time, and uterine displacement as a cause of hysteria in women was still being taught in the late nineteenth century. An age which still believed in magic and astrology was slow to discard the conventional orthodoxies;* and most Restoration physicians continued to divide madness into two categories: mania, which was traditionally the result of too much choler; and melancholy, which, as its name suggests, was the result of too much black bile. Even those who were coming to regard the humoral pathology with suspicion still found themselves unable to dispense with its legacy which taught that, just like any other ailment, mental illness was essentially a *physical* condition. Changes in diet, bleeding and the application of purges and emetics were the standard responses – 'let vomitives lead the van,' pronounced Sir Theodore Turquet de Mayerne, royal physician to Charles I, in a letter of advice to a hypochondriacal patient[13] – and every doctor had his own particular recipes, from pimpernel juice taken through the nostrils to suppositories of Castilian soap. The following cure for depression, from Robert Burton's *The Anatomy of Melancholy*, hints at magic in its insistence on using a virgin ram:

> Take a ram's head that never meddled with an ewe, cut off at a blow, and the horns only taken away, boil it well, skin and wool together; after it is well sod, take out the brains, and put these spices to it, cinnamon, ginger, nutmeg, mace, cloves, *ana ℥ss* mingle the powder of these spices with it,

---

* Take the astrologer Nicholas Culpeper's diagnosis of the causes of madness: 'I. If the Sun be author of the distemper, as he may be if he be Lord of the house ascendent, sixth or twelfth houses, the distemper comes through pride, ambition, vain-glory. 2. If it be Jupiter, it comes through religion, some idle priest hath scar'd the poor creature out of his wits. 3. If it be Venus, love, luxurious expense, or something else of like nature is the cause. 4. If Mercury be the afflicting planet, the sick is pestered with a parcel of strange imaginations, and as many vain fears attend him; great vexation or study, or both is the cause' (*Culpeper's astrologicall judgment of diseases*, 1655, 107–8).

and heat them in a chafing-dish of coals together, stirring them well.[14]

The sufferer should eat the result with bread for fourteen days, taking no wine.

A harsh regime of discipline was a common response to madness, an attempt to impose behavioural norms on those whose most obvious symptom was a refusal to abide by them. Treatments ranged from sedation and stern words to more violent attempts at a cure. One such was a development of the medieval practice of ducking witches. The hapless victims were stripped naked and their hands bound behind their back; a rope fastened to a pulley was tied to their feet, and they were blindfolded and placed on a bench, with their back towards a big tub of water. The rope was then yanked hard and without warning so that they toppled backwards into the tub, where they were left dangling with their head and shoulders submerged. Even the most enthusiastic advocates of this particular form of shock therapy admitted that it was a good idea to clear things with the local magistrate beforehand, 'since some through fear, or because they are not strong enough to stand out this method, may miscarry and die'.*

Fortunately for the mentally ill there was occasionally a dose of common sense to accompany the spiced brains and supposi-tories. The nonconformist minister Timothy Rogers, who himself had a history of breakdowns and depression, urged people to treat melancholics with pity and compassion, and not to dismiss their complaints as nothing but imagination and fancy. 'It is a real disease, a real misery that they are tormented with: and if it be fancy, yet a diseased fancy is as great a disease as any other; it fills them with anguish and tribulation.'[15] Thomas Sydenham, the Parliamentarian cavalry officer who became one of the most

---

* Franciscus Mercurius van Helmont in *The Spirit of Diseases* (1692), describing a method of treatment pioneered by his father Joannes Baptista van Helmont. Even more startling than the therapy was the means used to revive the half-drowned patient – 'the thrusting of a knife-sheath that had the point cut off, into their fundament, and some blowing through the same, till the water gushed out of the mouth' (*The Spirit of Diseases*, 43).

famous of all seventeenth-century physicians, once 'cured' an aristocratic patient whose melancholy failed to respond to any of the more conventional treatments by ordering him to consult a Dr Robinson in Inverness. There was no Dr Robinson, and when the irate patient returned to London after a round trip of nearly 1150 miles and demanded to know how Sydenham dare abuse his confidence by sending him on a fool's errand, the doctor pointed out that the nobleman's eagerness to see Dr Robinson had preoccupied him as he rode north, and his rage to get his hands on Sydenham had similarly occupied him during his ride south, with the net result that he had completely forgotten his depression. And Robert Burton himself, whose *Anatomy of Melancholy* – that wonderful and weird compendium of aphorisms and anecdotes – was so popular that it went through five editions between its first publication in 1621 and his death eighteen years later, gave some admirably sensible advice to the melancholic along with his suspect recipes: 'Be not solitary, be not idle.'[16]

Mary seemed to have made a full recovery from her first bout of melancholy by the summer of 1663, but there were still problems which couldn't just be put down to a normal period of readjustment following the wedding. Even for a young bride she was unusually hesitant when it came to social matters. It was Mun, for example, who wrote her letters to relatives; she duly copied them out and signed them as if they came from her. But in spite of her delicate state, everybody endorsed Edward Butterfield's hopes, couched in what to modern ears seems a rather direct manner, when he told Mun that 'I should be glad to hear that Mrs Verney is ill of a great belly'.[17]

At the end of September the couple accompanied Sir Ralph and Aunt Peg Elmes on a trip to see their old friend Vere Gawdy at Crosshall, forty miles north-east of Claydon on the border of Bedfordshire and Cambridgeshire. Sir Ralph, Peg and Mary were back at Claydon by the first week of October, but Mun went up to Ely to see Uncle Doctor, who was staying there. His purpose was to invite Denton down to Claydon for a while, but he also confided that Mary was still suffering from attacks of jealousy. Denton counselled, quite naturally, that she really needed to keep them under control, although he was surprisingly cheery about the matter: barely a week after hoping that 'she hath left Mrs Zelotipia behind'[18] when she left Crosshall for Claydon, he was joking to Sir Ralph that he was going to tell Mary that the real reason for her husband's trip to Ely was 'to meet one of his pretty doxies there by agreement'.[19] He had no doubt she would believe him, either.

The family received two pieces of bad news that autumn, although both were clouds with silver linings. At the beginning of November Pen Denton's husband John dropped dead. He was not missed, and it was all Sir Ralph could do to stop himself from speaking ill of the dead. He advised his sister to do the same, 'for though you have been unhappy in him, yet he was a gentleman and your husband, and 'twill be your honour to conceal his faults'.[20] John Denton's faults were of a kind which were hard enough to conceal – witness his fist fight with Pen in the middle of Aylesbury marketplace – and even the solemn and punctilious Sir Ralph couldn't resist calling his death a deliverance.

The second crisis also involved a deliverance of sorts. For the past couple of years Tom Verney had been eking out a miserable existence in London, still supported by the £40-a-year allowance which Sir Ralph paid him quarterly in accordance with their father's will, and begging and borrowing whatever he could from whoever was soft enough to believe his tales of woe. He was single again, Joyce apparently having died in Spain in the 1650s (although some of the Verneys had their doubts about this). And as always, he was refusing to take responsibility for his reduced circumstances, whining instead that he was unlucky in his birth, unlucky in his education, unlucky in his travels. He also took to passing the time in his appropriately named lodgings, the Holy Lamb in Fleet Yard, by studying his Bible, which in his grubby hands became not a force for moral or spiritual renewal but just another instrument for extracting money from his hapless relations. For example, he quoted to Sir Ralph Christ's words at the Last Supper – 'A new commandment I give unto you, That ye love one another; as I have loved you, that ye also love one another' – and then asked his brother what better way there was to express one's love for each other than by acts of charity? He used the first general epistle of John to support another plea to Sir Ralph for money: 'Whoso hath this world's good, and seeth his brother have need, and shutteth up his bowels of compassion from him, how dwelleth the love of God in him?' Best of all was his reinterpretation of Genesis, as he followed up a request to Sir Ralph for money to buy new clothes with the assertion that God 'promised Abraham to grant him his suit for the righteous' sake'.[21]

Sir Ralph was exasperated, but he paid Tom a small weekly allowance and occasionally guaranteed his credit so that his brother could borrow against the next £10 instalment of his annuity. Towards the end of 1661 Tom had looked in vain for a way out of his troubles by obtaining the command of a ship named the *Bonaventure*, which was bound for Jamaica in the New Year. This came to nothing, but in April 1662 he hatched a plan which seemed an answer to Sir Ralph's prayers: he announced that he intended to take ship for Jamaica with the 'Earl of Windsor' (actually Thomas Windsor, Baron Windsor, who had just been appointed governor of the colony). He threw out the crumb of hope that he would almost certainly die during the voyage, so he wouldn't need much. Just £40 for goods and clothes, to be precise; plus £3 6s. 6d. to pay for his passage; plus £10 in ready money for when he arrived in Jamaica; plus another £3 for extraordinary provisions on the voyage. He wanted food for his soul and his mind: Jeremy Taylor's *Holy Living* and *Holy Dying*, bound together in one volume;* a recent book of prayers and devotions entitled *Of the Daily Practice of Piety*; and George Sandys' *Travailes, containing a history of the originall and present state of the Turkish Empire*. And he wanted food for his body: a 20lb earthenware pot of butter, four 12lb cheeses, three Westphalia hams; a sealed jar of oil; a bushel of meal in a padlocked cask, to prevent pilfering during the voyage; and 20lb of beef suet.

Sir Ralph was torn between a longing to see the back of his brother and the conviction, born out of bitter experience, that there must be a catch. He told Tom frankly that he didn't believe he would go to the Indies – this was simply another ruse to extract money from him. Tom countered by saying Sir Ralph

---

* Sir Ralph received this list just as he was putting together Jack's provisions for the voyage to Aleppo. Tom's reference to Bishop Taylor's *Holy Living* and *Holy Dying* is probably what gave Sir Ralph the idea to place a copy in his son's luggage.

could arrange to have everything delivered directly to the master of his ship. It was still too much of a risk for Sir Ralph, although he agreed to stand guarantor for the money and, if Tom never come back, to pay it out to his creditors at the end of a fixed term. But only if Tom didn't ask him for any more. If he did, the whole agreement was null and void.

Tom jumped at this. His idea was that Sir Ralph would guarantee to pay the money he borrowed (from a man named Madgwick) at the end of six months, and that he would reimburse him if and when he returned from Jamaica, having made his fortune. There was some urgency in the matter: although it was less than two weeks since he had first mooted the idea to Sir Ralph, Lord Windsor's fleet was already gathered in the Downs, and likely to sail within days.

Then, just as everything seemed to be settled, Tom made a stupid mistake. Again and again Sir Ralph voiced his worry that his brother didn't really intend to leave the country, and that he was going to put the money to entirely different uses. Finally Tom lost his temper and *demanded* that Sir Ralph supply his needs. To Sir Ralph, the difference between a request and a demand was the difference between yes and no, and he immediately took offence. On 23 April 1662 Tom rushed round to his London lodging in Covent Garden and managed to repair some of the damage, but Sir Ralph felt he needed a reminder of who held the upper hand in this relationship: he would now wait a year, rather than six months, before paying the debts incurred in preparing for the voyage. Tom agreed – what choice did he have? – but he suggested that neither of them should actually mention this change of plan to Madgwick. When he was safe on board ship in the Downs, he would write a begging letter to Sir Ralph; this would immediately invalidate the agreement between Sir Ralph and Madgwick, and if the latter wanted to see his money again he would be forced to agree to any 'new' terms Sir Ralph cared to impose.

It is not altogether clear what happened next, but it seems that Sir Ralph refused to have any part in this nasty little piece of dishonesty, Madgwick pulled out and the Windsor's fleet sailed for Jamaica without Tom. Within seventy-two hours he had bounced back with a new plan: although he was now forty-six, he was going to resurrect his military career by joining the King's Life Guards. He would obtain a buff coat, sword and belt from a local pawn shop, but again looked to Sir Ralph for help with the rest of his equipment – a horse, a saddle and bridle, a case of pistols and a carbine. There was just one thing he had to check before he entered the King's service – whether or not it was true that Life Guards enjoyed immunity from arrest.

They didn't, and so Tom remained at the Holy Lamb in Fleet Yard, bombarding Sir Ralph with begging letters, self-pity and threats of suicide all through the summer of 1662. Most of his efforts were focused on his continuing need to get himself a new suit. Not surprisingly given his record, he found it hard to obtain credit, but by the beginning of June he had managed to acquire 12 yards of material, which he was paying for at 3s. a week – money which should have gone to pay his rent, as he freely and somewhat wistfully acknowledged to his older brother. Sir Ralph's tailor made the suit up for him – at Sir Ralph's expense – and even Mun was approached for 20s. for 'a border' to finish it off.

That autumn Tom's preoccupation with his appearance was explained. He had found another wife. The unlucky bride was Elizabeth Kendall, the eldest daughter of an established Derbyshire family who had lived at their seat, Smisby Manor, for centuries. Two Kendalls had fallen at the Battle of Bosworth in 1485, fighting for Richard III; another, Elizabeth's grandfather, is still commemorated, along with his wife and sixteen children, by a fine monument in Smisby church. According to Dr Denton, who bumped into the newly-weds at the playhouse early in December 1662, Elizabeth brought between £400 and £500 to the match, with £50 a year and the expectation of more in due course. Tom himself put her portion at £1200.

Although the marriage was common knowledge among the Verneys and their friends, Tom said nothing at all to them about it. Indeed, he went to some lengths to conceal it from them all. It wasn't until three months later, in February 1663, that he finally wrote to Sir Ralph to inform him of his change in circumstances. Why Elizabeth's family had allowed her to marry such an impoverished charlatan now became obvious – he had lied through his teeth about his financial status. 'I would not have my wife to be sensible of my wants,' he told Sir Ralph with his usual disarming candour, 'because I have hitherto possessed her with the contrary.'[22] Unfortunately for Tom (and, ultimately, for Elizabeth too), the wedding had done little to alleviate those wants. In fact it rather looks as though the Kendalls managed to beat Tom at his own game. Most of Elizabeth's £1200 portion was tied up in different ventures, and her husband was left to unravel them all as best he could. This proved to be a hugely complicated task, so that quite early on he was forced to admit that 'I fear some part if it will never be paid'.[23]

Just over £550 had been put out to a City merchant named George Abney, and secured against property which Abney owned in Leicestershire. Tom moved to foreclose; Abney responded by threatening to take out an injunction preventing him from proceeding in common law; and Tom, who didn't have the means to pay counsel, was stuck.

Then there was a question of the mineral rights to some waste-land in Cardiganshire; and Tom dashed off to South Wales to obtain a lease to the land and claim his wife's inheritance, talking excit-edly of lead mines and potash works. Shortly before he left London he sold his annuity in order to raise cash, confident that at last his ship was about to come in. The purchaser was Dr John Colladon, one of the Queen's physicians and a man who was not averse to speculation. (In September 1663, for example, Pepys recorded in his diary that Colladon had entered into a partnership with Elizabeth Pepys' father over a patent 'to prevent and cure the smoking of chimneys'.[24]) According to Tom, the deal was that Colladon would pay him £120 and the annuity would change hands only when the Welsh lease was secure. But as with all of Tom's financial affairs, the truth was much more complicated, and much harder to untangle. It later transpired that Colladon had agreed to pay £200, not £120; and that he had already given Tom £20. There was also a ques-tion of another £300, the cash element of Tom's Kendall dowry, which he put up as a bond against corroboration of his title to the annuity. The pair lodged their contract with a lawyer named Gamlin, and Tom went off in search of his fortune.

Things didn't go well and by the spring of 1663 he was writing a begging letter to William Denton. 'I have made it my whole business to get this lease, which I have accomplished,' he claimed;

'but to deal truly with you (knowing you are a person endued with very much reason) I want three pounds towards the fetching of it.'[25] He was being economical with the truth – the lease steadfastly refused to materialise, and in the meantime Dr Colladon persuaded the attorney to release the annuity contract to his care, and took it round to show to Sir Ralph, threatening to sue him if he continued to pay the quarteredge to his brother.

Sir Ralph quickly told his man of business to stop Tom's next payment, and Tom flew into a panic. He consulted a lawyer in Gray's Inn and, when the lawyer told him to forget about it, he fired off an anguished letter to Sir Ralph. 'I perceive you have an intention to stop that small pittance my father left me,' he wrote, 'under a pretence of my passing it away to Dr Colladon.' That was just not fair, he said: the mere fact that Tom had sold his birthright to another man was no reason for Sir Ralph to stop paying it to him:

> My counsel's opinion was that the attorney played the knave in parting with the writings contrary to the trust that was reposed in him, and would not suffer the doctor to commence a suit against you, or me; but rather would advise him to arrest me, thinking thereby to gain my consent for his parting with the writings, then afterwards he may happily prefer a bill in chancery against you to see what you will answer to it. But my counsel sayeth, that you may (if you please) give him such a choking answer that he will have very small encouragement to meddle with you any further, because (if I sell over and over again) you are tied to pay it to none but to me.[26]

It was not clear to Sir Ralph exactly why Colladon and his lawyer might have Tom arrested, but Tom nevertheless went into hiding, begging Sir Ralph in the meantime not only to pay him half a year's annuity which was due to him, but also to advance another year's worth. Otherwise he was going to have to kill himself again, 'for I am now so over loaden with grief and groan under the heavy burthen of it, that I fear, I shall hazard the making my self away, if you should not answer my expectation. Pardon me (I beseech you) for this my last expression, being it proceeds from a most sad and dejected heart.'[27]

This was written on 8 October 1663, more than two months after Tom received notice of Sir Ralph's decision to withhold his quarteredge. His exasperated brother refused the advance point blank, and Tom grew desperate. He gave up hope of holding the moral high ground and confessed that he intended to run for Ireland, taking ship at Minehead as soon as ever he could. He begged his brother just to pay his lodging bill 'and to lend me twenty pounds to carry me for Ireland, not upon the account of my annuity, but as a real debt and I shall own that for a very great favour'. And if Sir Ralph could manage a little more for warm clothing, he would be eternally grateful. 'My clothing is very thin . . . the ways are very bad, and the weather wet.'[28] At the same time he touched both his nephew Mun and his brother Henry for £2 each.

Four days later Tom confessed to Sir Ralph the real reason for his sudden desire to leave the country. It had nothing to do with Colladon. Some months earlier the London friend with whom he had lodged the £300 of Kendall dowry had, 'like a traitorous Judas', let it be known about town that he was holding Tom's money, and a horde of creditors descended like locusts. The first Tom knew of it, a court order had been obtained and his precious £300 was gone.

Worse was to follow. Determined to revenge himself on the 'Judas', Tom and an associate lured his erstwhile friend to an out-of-the-way place, where they 'gave him a knave's mark for this his villainous deed'.[29] The place evidently wasn't out of the way enough, because a hue and cry was immediately raised and Tom had to run for his life while his partner in crime held off their pursuers. With that sense of puzzled indignation which characterised so many of Tom's dealings with his fellows, he told his brother that the pair were forced to fly their victim 'to prevent his malice'[30] — as though having been beaten up, the man really had no right to complain of the fact.

So it wasn't John Colladon and his attorney from whom Tom was running. It was the Lord Chief Justice, who had issued a warrant for his arrest. The reason he intended to sail from Minehead rather than the more convenient port of Bristol was that he was known in Bristol: he was frightened he might be recognised and hauled back to London. (And here again he was being economical with the truth, as we shall see.) He pleaded for money, while at the same time forbidding Sir Ralph to pay a single penny of his annuity to Dr Colladon while he was away, and threw himself on his brother's mercy: 'If you please to pity me so far as to take this into your consideration, I shall own my safe deliverance (under God) from you.'[31]

Sir Ralph came up with the cash. He immediately advanced Tom £10 against his quarteredge. And once he had it, the fugitive from justice disappeared.

In November 1663 Sir Ralph once again migrated to Chancery Lane for the winter, and once again Mun asked Lady Hobart if he and his wife could lodge with them, too. If she was agreeable, they would arrive at the beginning of December and stay until the New Year; and they would bring an extra maid, Bess King, who would look after the couple's chamber, keep their clothes clean and provide some extra help for Mary, who by now was several months pregnant. Butterfield's wish for a 'great belly' had been answered, and relations were congratulating Mun, Mary and Sir Ralph, and sending 'hearty wishes of a fruitful issue, for your mutual comforts'.[32]

Undeterred by the dramas of the previous spring, Lady Anne welcomed Mun, Mary and Bess King (in spite of the fact that on a previous visit to Chancery Lane Bess had scared her own maids out of their wits with her wild ghost stories). This was partly due to the Hobarts' desire to honour Sir Ralph as head of the Verney clan by doing a favour to his son and heir, in a culture where favours were currency. It was also down to Lady Anne's good housekeeping: the Chancery Lane house was too big for the Hobarts' needs, the rent was high at £55 p.a. and the Verneys came as paying guests. But Anne was genuinely fond of the family, and excited at the prospect of another visit from them. She had their chambers cleaned and decorated, instructed her maid to lie in the beds to air them, and checked the rates at various local stables. Her recommendation was for one in Magpie Yard, just off the south side of Fleet Street: terms were reasonable, and the staff were honest and civil enough for no less a legal luminary than Judge Edward Atkyns, one of the three Barons of the Exchequer, to have kept his coach with them for the past fourteen years.

Certain furnishings had to come from Claydon. There was no spare quilt for Sir Ralph's bed, and Lady Anne asked if it wasn't too much trouble to send up some curtains and a valance for Mun and Mary. The couple were to have quite extensive lodgings: the great chamber was turned into their bedroom, and they had 'the low room' as a parlour where they could entertain, 'for we did want that very much last year'.[33] Mary's maids, Bess and Jane, were to have their lodgings in the closet where their mistress's trunks were kept.

Perhaps Anne's decision to provide Mun and Mary with their own apartment was motivated by a reluctance to spend too much time in their company after their last visit. Perhaps she just felt they needed privacy – in November or early December Mary lost her baby, and, while miscarriages were treated with stoicism in Restoration England, this one heightened everyone's awareness of her delicate emotional state.

The couple arrived in London at the end of 1663 and settled into their lodgings. There are hints here and there that they weren't entirely happy: a couple of days after Christmas, for example, Reverend Butterfield was urging Mun that 'if you can but find true content in one another, things will go much the better with you'.[34] But there were no untoward incidents to mar the New Year, and when Sir Ralph went home towards the end of January, leaving his son and daughter-in-law with the Hobarts, there was no suggestion that he was running from Mary's odd behaviour.

Soon after he left, however, the girl developed a bad cough. Within a day or two it was obvious that she had measles, and a particularly violent case at that. She had diarrhoea, respiratory problems and a dangerously high fever, so that she hardly slept at all for five nights, and had to be forcibly prevented from getting out of bed and wandering off in her delirium. Mrs Abell was informed and asked to pray for her stepdaughter; Uncle Gale came regularly to see how she was; and Dr Denton was called in, along with the court physician George Bate.

Lady Hobart was convinced Mary was going to die. So was the girl's distraught husband, who spent his days praying for her safe deliverance and his nights keeping watch over her on a pallet in their bedchamber. Sir Ralph pressed him to have a care for his own health. 'Go walk in the garden, as often as possibly you can,' he urged his son. 'For I do not like you should be always in the chamber: for though you have had the measles, and I do not fear your having them again, yet it may be hurtful to you other ways.'[35]

By the second week in February 1664, Mary had recovered from the more distressing physical complications, but her fragile mental health was not so easily mended. At the height of her illness, when she was scared that she was going to die, she begged Mun to forgive her for being so difficult, and made all sorts of promises to turn over a new leaf if she was spared. As the news of her condition and her reaction to it spread, friends and relations responded in different ways. Doll Leeke, whose fondness for Mun and eagerness to please Sir Ralph made her less than sympathetic to Mary, was horribly indifferent to the girl's suffering. As far as she was concerned, it was a blessing in disguise:

I hear she is very sensible of the ill opinion she has had of her husband. I pray she may live to deserve the kindness he has ever paid her. I am sure he will be willing to remit all that is past and if she lay her humour aside, she has so many good things in her, it will be a great contentment to him, and satisfaction and pleasure to all that love him . . .[36]

Parson Butterfield was also pleased, but for a different reason. He was impressed with how upset Mun had been when he thought he would lose his wife, and he reckoned that this trial would help to shore up the couple's crumbling relationship. Moreover, Mun's display of emotion might finally cure the girl's fits of jealousy, by demonstrating to her just how deeply he cared.

Doll was firmly of the opinion that Mary bore sole responsibility for the problems of the past eighteen months – and that if the fault lay with her, so did the solution. 'As she gets strength,' Doll wrote to Sir Ralph, 'I hope that melancholy opinion will wear off, for if she has cured herself of her jealousy all things else I am confident will be easy to her'.[37] Be grateful to your husband for marrying you, in other words, and turn a blind eye to his infidelities. Thank God your life has been spared, and learn the rules of the game.

Tragically Mary was incapable of abiding by those rules. She loved her husband, and she wanted him to love her, forsaking all others. 'Those which are jealous,' said Robert Burton, 'if they be not otherwise relieved, proceed from suspicion to hatred, from hatred to frenzy, madness, injury, murder and despair.'[38] Mary stayed with the Hobarts to convalesce into the spring, and Mun stayed with her until the end of March. But as her physical health improved, her mental health deteriorated. While Mrs Abell, who seems to have been blissfully ignorant of her stepdaughter's psychological state, was blithely congratulating her on getting over the measles and urging that a cheerful heart and a good opinion of herself were all that she needed to make her happy, Mary was losing her mind and her friends in dramatic fashion.

To begin with, the hysterical fits of the previous year returned. They became so bad that by 20 March 1664 Mun, who had been such a devoted husband while his wife had an identifiably physical condition, lost patience with her. He followed his father back to Claydon and simply left her behind to the care of the anxious and nonplussed Hobarts. To begin with, Lady Anne was relieved at his going: she thought his presence was only making things worse for his wife, particularly since he was getting so angry with her. But with his departure Mary's behaviour, which had been challenging enough when she was depressed, became even harder to cope with. She took to yelling at Lady Anne and her daughters; she hated them all, she wished she had never come to London, she wished she had never left her stepmother's side. On 27 March, a Sunday, Lady Anne wrote to Sir Ralph in some distress:

> As the weather is windy and stormy abroad we have had our share with my cousin within. She has been very ill humoured and by fits, I may tell you, mad. She has cried and screamed and singed and railed on us and poor doctor too. Now Bate is all in all with her; she says she thinks in her heart he is not yet corrupted. But there is [no one] but her maid Jane but longs for her death. She does say such things as flesh and blood never heard.[39]

Mary, who had cried for days when Mun returned to Buckinghamshire, now announced that she was going to write and demand that he let her go home to her stepmother. She was going to give him a piece of her mind, she told Lady Hobart, who was naturally upset at her violent tempers and the way in which she ranted at her and her daughters, but rather more worried by the girl's withdrawal from normal social discourse and her growing obsession with her maid Jane. There was no one else she could depend on but Jane; if she had her fortune at her disposal now, she would give it to Jane; only two people in the world loved her, Mrs Abell and Jane. Lady Hobart recounted to Sir Ralph in shocked tones that Jane was more than all the world to Mary: 'she now lies with her', she said.[40]

At the beginning of April, Anne sent a confidential letter to Sir Ralph. Mary and Jane had just gone wandering off to Lincoln's Inn Chapel without bothering to wash or to dress properly, 'so dirty 'tis a shame to see them'.[41] Soon after they got back to Chancery Lane Dr Denton arrived and gave Mary a good telling-off for going out in public in such a state. She reacted by dismissing him and demanding to see Dr Colladon, a move which was rather ironic, considering that Colladon was currently pursuing her uncle-by-marriage through the courts and threatening to take her father-in-law to the Chancery court over the disputed annuity. Or perhaps it was her way of getting back at her in-laws?* Jane was now the only person she could bear to have by her. She fed the servant girl with her own hands, and drank to her, and slept in the same bed with her. 'So much dearness I never saw,' wrote Lady Hobart.[42] Bess King, on the other hand, was subjected to violent attacks. Mary bit her and tore at her hair if the maid tried to restrain her in any way.

Neither Mun nor Sir Ralph showed any sign of coming up to London, and, lumbered with a seriously disturbed young girl, the Hobarts were beginning to worry about what people would think. The Abells were well connected, and those connections were circling: Sir Robert Wiseman, that uncle of Mrs Abell's who also happened to be a distinguished civil lawyer, came round to see how Mary was faring and how the Hobarts were treating

---

*Anne Hobart actually writes of 'docker coryden'; but given that medical circles in Restoration London were extremely small, it seems safe to assume she's referring to John Colladon.

her. Lady Anne was appalled to hear her cousin announce that everyone was trying to poison her; and when Wiseman sent his man round a few days later to check on her state, Mary flew into a frenzy, insulting Lady Anne and her daughters and hinting darkly that she might have recovered with better care, but that the Hobarts had their own reasons for keeping her where she was. There was no way she could thrive at Chancery Lane, she told Wiseman's servant. She wished she had never seen any of the Hobart women's faces.

On 4 April Mary got hold of a knife and threatened to rip open her own belly with it; Anne Hobart begged Mun to come back from Claydon, and ordered that his wife should never be left unattended. The next day, Tuesday, was Mary's twenty-third birthday and Dr Denton, who hadn't taken his dismissal too seriously, decided that she should have a party. He was, as he put it, 'cocksure she puts on and assumes much, very much, of these vastly extravagant humours',[43] and reckoned that if she would only cheer up, all would be well. When she gravely told him that she was going to die very soon, he gave her a pound in gold and said she must give him £40 in return if she survived forty weeks. Now he and his family turned up at the Hobarts' house for supper to celebrate Mary's birthday and drink her health. According to Peg Elmes, who joined the party, it was a rather strained affair – 'I wish I had cause to say we did it with joy'[44] – but Mary did consent to come down from her room for half an hour, and she behaved herself quite well in front of her guests.

The next night she was worse than ever. Dr Bate, who came to attend her, said he wasn't going to come at night any more; she beat her precious Jane out of bed and out of her chamber, and raved and screamed. In the morning she attacked Lady Anne, who hid all the knives and scissors in the house for fear of what she would do with them. Dr Denton, although he still suspected her of being wilful and taking out her frustration at Mun's absence on the Hobarts, began to take a more pessimistic view of things. Only half-joking, he talked of her being not mad, but diabolically possessed, and stated quite categorically that, while Mun must come back to Chancery Lane, it wasn't safe for him to sleep with his wife. He voiced this opinion in a letter to Sir Ralph, but had the opportunity to repeat it to Mary herself on the

Thursday after her birthday, when he arrived at the Hobarts' to find that she had dressed herself and was halfway down the stairs, determined to go to church. (It was Holy Week.) He lost his temper and ordered Bess to take her back to her room by force; there he told her in plain terms that she was mad, 'and was now to be used as those in Bedlam, and that her maids should be put away and strangers put to her to master her, and that I would not venture her husband to sleep between a pair of sheets with her'.[45] The girl went quiet, convincing Denton that 'rough means will prevail best and most with her'.[46]

Mun arrived on Good Friday, but the reunion was not a success. His wife told him she was pleased to see him, because she was going to die soon. Then she tried to throw herself out of a window and, when she was prevented, she picked up a pin and made to swallow it, saying that she had to go to hell. Mun was horrified at the way she had deteriorated in the three weeks since he had seen her last. He begged his father to come up to town – something which Sir Ralph quietly but firmly refused to do – and sent for Mrs Abell and Uncle Gale. Mary just gave up. She decided that she was bewitched, and accused Lady Hobart of putting the evil eye on her. She was also desperately upset because Mun would not lie with her. But she stopped the raving and laughing and screaming which had been so distressing (and which, truth to tell, were the main reasons why the fastidious Sir Ralph was still so reluctant to visit the Chancery Lane house), and simply lay alone in her room, the window of which was now securely boarded over. She wouldn't eat; she wouldn't drink; she wouldn't take any medication at all. She just lay quietly in the darkness and moaned to herself, while every day she grew thinner and weaker. 'Her thigh is no bigger than Bess's arm and as limp as can be,' wrote Lady Anne on 13 April. 'At this rate she cannot last.'[47]

One of the most telling indications of the seriousness of Mary's state is the fact that everybody around her thought she was insane, and said so. That was not a claim which anyone made lightly in the seventeenth century, and particularly not anyone in the Verneys' position. It is worth recalling just how serious the situation was. Mun was the heir, and an important reason for pushing him into marriage with Mary, apart from her fortune, was the need for him to produce an heir of his own to secure the succession. Now he was saddled with a mad wife. There was, of course, no possibility of a divorce. If the couple did manage to procreate, their offspring would in all probability be tainted with their mother's madness. It was in the blood. (This was why Dr Denton and the Hobarts prevented Mun from sleeping with his wife – they feared for his safety, but they were also convinced that there could be no hope for a child conceived in such circumstances.)

Mary's madness meant that the future of the Verney family looked precarious indeed. In an attempt to secure the Abell estates, Sir Ralph and Mun pushed her into changing the original marriage settlement. This had stipulated that if there were no children East Claydon would be hers to dispose of; now their lawyers added a codicil agreeing that whoever survived the marriage would have the right to dispose of the estate as they wished.

But the line still had to be secured. Doll Leeke – loyal, tactless, terrible Doll – expressed what everyone else was thinking but dare not say, when she wrote to Sir Ralph in the middle of May to commiserate. 'Nothing but death can free her from that disease,' she said, 'which will be a blessing to her, and to us all.'[48]

18

She Doth Not Rave

*M*un's most urgent problem was to decide what exactly he should *do* with his wife. He was anxious about the cost of Mary's care: 'She has two nurses who watch over her day and night,' he wrote: 'all this costs me a lot of money, but even if it ruins me there is no cure.'[1] The Hobarts wanted her out of the house, and on behalf of the Abells, Sir Robert Wiseman was also pressing for her to be removed. It is unlikely that he gave much credence to her stories of poisoning and bewitching, but the fact that she was becoming more distressed with every week she spent at Chancery Lane was enough to convince him she would be better off elsewhere. However, it was out of the question for her to go back to her mother; neither he nor Gale would allow it, and for his part he wouldn't have her to stay with him for a hundred pounds. (After she attacked Lady Anne on one occasion, Mary sent for Sir Robert's man and begged him to take her away with him. He brushed her off by saying there was no room for her at Wiseman's house.)

Dr Denton also thought she should leave Chancery Lane, but he advised against taking her back to Buckinghamshire, more on

Sir Ralph's account than anyone else's. 'You must never think of her living at Claydon,' he told Sir Ralph, 'for I know you cannot endure to think that she should come to any mischief in your house, and you can never be sure she will not mischief herself or somebody else.'[2] At one point he suggested that Mun should leave her with an allowance and go off travelling abroad, and he was adamant that, while there may be no need for a complete parting of the ways, husband and wife certainly should not live under the same roof. 'It will puzzle all the wits [of] you and all the friends you have to know what to do with her,' he wrote.[3]

Where could she go? The options were limited. Confinement for madness was a last resort in seventeenth-century England. The state didn't get involved in the business at all, except when a lunatic's family specifically petitioned the Lord Chancellor on the grounds that the sufferer was incompetent to manage his or her affairs. Even when that happened, in the words of the eighteenth-century jurist Sir William Blackstone:

> The lord chancellor, to whom by special authority from the king, the custody of idiots and lunatics is intrusted, upon peti-
> tion or information, grants a commission . . . to enquire into the party's state of mind; and if he be found *non compos*, he usually commits the care of his person, with a suitable allowance for his maintenance, to some friend, who is then called his committee.[4]

The crown held no views on the incarceration of lunatics. The process Blackstone is describing is all about the administration of an estate, and there was no need to petition for a writ *de Lunatico Inquirendo* in Mary's case, since Mun already had her fortune in his hands. Families looked after their own, and when they were unable to do this without help, their local communities did their best to support them. The village fool who prowled around a parish by night or fell prey to shrieking fits and delu-sions was carefully managed by his or her peers, only chained as a last resort, and released at the least sign of lucidity. The parish paid for their food and welfare; the parish made sure their dependants were looked after.

Medical care was less common, and there was little or no

distinction drawn between mental disability and mental illness: if there was observable dysfunction, and it impaired an individual to such an extent that they could not look after themselves, then it was the community's job to look after them. If it didn't, then leave well alone.

The nation's only public madhouse was the vast and decaying Bethlehem Hospital off Bishopsgate, in the north-east corner of the City of London – the 'Bedlam' which Denton had thrown in Mary's face when he tried to scare her into behaving herself.* Founded in the thirteenth century, the Priory of St Mary Bethlehem soon acquired a reputation for taking in distracted patients, and when it was closed down during the Dissolution, the Mayor and Corporation of London bought the site from Henry VIII and re-established it as a hospital which specialised in caring for the insane. But although Bedlam was big, it only held fifty inmates, and it was not a suitable place for young heiresses. It catered mainly for paupers, who were kept for a year and then discharged. Scant attention was paid to therapeutics, as James Carkesse, a patient in Bedlam under Dr Thomas Allen, described in 1679: 'I'll tell you his way of proceeding,/All you, that here shall enter;/Purges, vomits and bleeding,/Are his method of cure at a venture.' Carkesse also recorded the routine violence used to subdue inmates in Bedlam: 'I ordered his keeper, at large,/On occasion to ply him with blows,/That what jugular did not discharge,/The mad blood might come out at his nose . . .'[5]

Such treatment was unthinkable for Mary, not only because of its cruelty, but also because of its public nature; the fact that patients were chained and on view to anyone who cared to wander into the hospital was enough to rule it out. The relations of even the most disturbed patient would jib at putting them on display if they had the means to avoid it, like the madman described in the 1640s as being 'so distracted, that at last it was held fit to have him away to Bedlam; yet for some credit sake, his friends so prevailed, that he was not put into the common condition of

* If the idea that there was only a single institution to take the insane of an entire nation seems surprising, we should remember that there were only two endowed medical hospitals in England – St Bartholomew's and St Thomas's, both in London.

the madmen there, but was kept private in the house of one that endeavours the cure of such persons.'[6]

The only reasons for imprisoning a lunatic were that they were a danger to themselves or to others, or that they were unable to look after themselves. Mary's behaviour since the end of March had shown that she fitted the bill on both counts, and a private house where she was under constant supervision seemed the obvious choice for her until she recovered her senses. But the situation called for extremely delicate handling. Both Mun and his father were keenly aware of how it would look if, having so recently got their hands on the Abell estates, they seemed to be imprisoning their young benefactress in a madhouse. ''Tis best to let her own friends dispose her,' Sir Ralph told his son, 'for that will give more satisfaction to all that side.'[7] Uncle Gale was due in London on Tuesday 19 April 1664 (although in the event he was delayed by more than a week), and Mrs Abell arrived the following day, to be met by Mun with his coach half a mile out of town and taken straight to see her stepdaughter. Sir Ralph himself was still reluctant to leave Claydon; in spite of his son's increasingly desperate pleas for him to come to Chancery Lane, if only to provide advice and moral support, he kept putting off his journey:

> I find you wish me at London [he wrote to Mun], and were it in the least kind advantageous to you or your wife to have me there, I would come away at a minute's warning. But since I can do neither of you two any good, perhaps I may stay here a few days longer, in hopes to hear some better tidings of her. For the truth is, it afflicts me so much here, that I [am] not very desirous to come nearer, for though she speaks sensibly, and that you think she doth not rave, yet I hear she often makes a very noise so that she is heard by the neighbours, and that must needs increase the grief of any man that hears it.[8]

In the end, it took reproachful words from Peg Elmes and some stern ones from William Denton to shame Sir Ralph into doing his paternal duty. Uncle Doctor was particularly firm: everyone was at a great loss to understand his absence, and his son was 'strangely concerned for want of you'.[9] Sir Ralph reluctantly returned to Chancery Lane at the beginning of May.

By this stage Denton had cut off all of Mary's hair. The girl was taking a little milk and trying to eat something, and was quiet from her screaming, according to Lady Hobart, 'but still speaks the bitterest things as ever was heard'.[10] Mun was still paying for the two nurses and struggling to decide between different regimes of care and the competing claims of doctors, kin and private madhouses. Sir Robert Wiseman advocated a house in Aldersgate Street run by a man named Lentall, but Mun was unhappy with the fact that Lentall took in several patients at a time and the general public were in and out of the place, heightening the risk that tongues would wag. Then a maid employed by a Mrs Beckerstaff came round to Chancery Lane. The maid had previously worked for Mrs Abell and had got to hear of Mary's illness; she had told her mistress, and her mistress had sent her straight round to the Hobarts to recommend that Mun see a woman named Clerk. Apparently the Beckerstaffs' teenage daughter had been in much the same state as Mary until four years ago, when she was treated by Mrs Clerk, responding so positively that 'she hasn't had any strange moods at all since the coronation'.[11]

Mrs Clerk was sent for, and confirmed Mrs Beckerstaff's account. She said she was prepared to take on Mary's care, that she would have her well again in two months, and that the charge would be £20, payable only when she was cured. The doctors were sceptical, and advised against it; Mary was a person of quality, and she deserved more than a local wise woman with her mysterious recipes. Mun was tempted, but he didn't dare do anything without the approval of his in-laws, and neither Uncle Gale nor his father had turned up yet. When he broached the idea in a letter to Sir Ralph, the latter was unenthusiastic. He admitted that women like Mrs Clerk had good success, and frequently cured those who had been failed by conventional medicine; but 'unless her own friends desire and advise it, 'twill not be fit for you to put her to her to be cured, for if any ill accident should follow, all the world would blame you for it.'[12]

We know surprisingly little about seventeenth-century madhouses. Some were run by physicians. In 1674, for example, Dr James Newton was advertising his house 'on Clarken-well Green' as a therapeutic haven for the distracted and the melancholy. But

many madhouses boasted of the fact that they were *not* run by
medical professionals. In a cynical culture where self-interest was
king, it was considered inappropriate for those who stood to benefit
from a patient's protracted stay to be in charge of their treatment.
(Dr Newton felt obliged to point out that he laboured to cure
both rich and poor 'rather than keep either in my house for advantage'.[13]) So the day-to-day care of the insane was often left to
women like Mrs Clerk, or clergy, or ordinary families.

The autobiography of Exeter clergyman George Trosse offers
an insight into what might be in store for Mary. In 1656, when
he was twenty-five years old, Trosse was plagued by a voice saying
'Yet more humble, yet more humble'. He took this to be God
and, convinced he was such a grievous sinner that God wanted
to destroy him, he went to great lengths to shut the voice out,
tying his door 'with a particular sort of a knot' and keeping his
eyes and mouth tightly closed for days on end. He lay on his
bed listening to different voices – 'fairies, who, I thought, were
in the wall, and there conversed and were merry together'. Trosse's
friends heard of a person in Glastonbury who was experienced
in dealing with cases like his; they sent word to him and he
agreed to treat Trosse if they could get him to his house. So they
did, by putting him up on a horse behind a 'very stout strong
man' and binding them together; and, after an appalling fifty-
mile journey in the course of which Trosse became convinced
he was being taken into Hell, he arrived at the Glastonbury
madhouse. The chief feature of his therapy seems to have involved
keeping him in a room for several weeks with his hands and legs
manacled, until 'at length, through the goodness of God, and by
His blessing upon physick, a low diet, and hard keeping, I began
to be somewhat quiet and composed in my spirits; to be orderly
and civil in my carriage and converse, and gradually to regain
the use of my reason'.[14] Thus cured of his psychosis, he went
home to Exeter, with no more outward show of his ordeal than
the scars left by his prolonged chafing against his leg irons.

Mun's favoured option was something along these lines, as long
as his wife's rank and dignity were respected. 'I will never consent
to putting her in a public place or a place free to take any other
person into safe hands while she is within,' he said. 'But if I take
a private dwelling and abide by exactly what the doctors order,

Mary Blacknall, wife of Sir Ralph Verney.

Ralph and Mary's daughter Margaret, who died of dysentery in Blois while her mother was away in England trying to rescue the family's finances.

Cary, the fourth of Sir Ralph Verney's six sisters.

'Uncle Doctor' – William Denton.

Sir Roger Burgoyne, one of Sir Ralph's dearest friends and a fellow MP in the early years of the Long Parliament.

Anne Hobart, one of the Verneys' Irish cousins. Sir Ralph and his family lodged at her Chancery Lane house in the 1660s.

Mun Verney (1636–88), a complicated mixture of lecherous clown, tender father and loving husband.

Jack Verney. Sir Ralph arranged for Soest to paint this portrait of his son in 1662, a few months before the boy left for the Levant.

Aleppo in Syria, Jack's home for twelve years. 'Arrogant, it laughs in the face of Time...'

The old Royal Exchange, where Jack learned his trade as apprentice to the Levant Company merchant Gabriel Roberts.

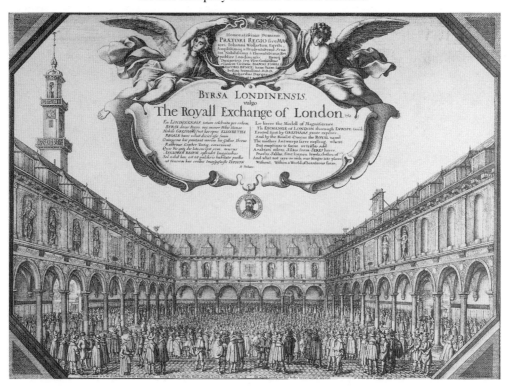

Jack the prosperous London businessman.

Elizabeth Palmer, 1st wife of Jack Verney and the love of his life. 'No man breathing can have more love for you than myself.'

Mary Lawley, 2nd wife of Jack Verney. The black page is probably Peregrine Tyam, whom Jack acquired through his connections in the Royal African Company in 1689, when the boy was six years old. (*Right*) Elizabeth Baker, 3rd wife of Jack Verney.

Sir Ralph Verney by Sir Peter Lely.

Most Deare Father.

According to your Commands
I doe heare send you this same, which is for
noe other reason whatsoever then to exresse, or rather to
fulfill my duty, w.ch is to ritte in too returnes oweee
and soe I doe and will doe accordingly, hoping by fulfilling
all my dutyes, I shall now and heareafter obtaine your
blessing, and that will bee a very greate comfort
and satiffaction unto

Honoured ffather

London
July y.e 20.th
1659

Your most Humble
and most obedient
Sonne

John Verney

Filial piety: a letter from eighteen-year-old Jack Verney to his father, Sir Ralph, 20 July 1659.

The Verney monument in the Church of All Saints, Middle Claydon.

I think that is much better.'[15] The trouble was that the doctors couldn't agree, although that's not so surprising, considering how many of them were involved in the case. There was William Denton and George Ent and George Bate; also a Dr Nurse or Norris; and Dr Colladon, although after a single house call his services were dispensed with, and he went back to the business of suing Sir Ralph. Wiseman and Gale seem to have thought that even this cabal of physicians was not good enough. They pressed Mun to engage the services of Sir Francis Prujean, a past president of the College of Physicians who lived by the Old Bailey, and whose reputation as a doctor was riding very high indeed at the moment, because the previous autumn his special cordial had cured Catherine of Braganza of typhus.

The women on the Verney side were not convinced of Prujean's worth. Lady Anne favoured the Clerk woman, while forthright Doll Leeke said that 'in my opinion they take a very ill way with her to send her to Dr Prujean's. I never heard of any he cured.'[16] Sir Ralph advised Mun to do whatever his in-laws suggested: 'If her friends desire Dr Prujean's advice, you must needs have it.'[17]

In the middle of all this confusion, with doctors and madhouse-keepers competing for business, relations trying to keep up appearances, Mary moaning to herself in her boarded-up chamber and Mun desperate to know what to do for the best, Tom Verney's wife, Elizabeth, turned up at the Hobarts' house.

She had a baby with her.

When Tom fled the Chief Justice's warrant in the autumn of 1663, he made no reference to his wife of twelve months, and he certainly didn't mention any child. Little wonder. He had abandoned Elizabeth in Bristol when she was pregnant with their baby; this was the real reason why he was anxious to keep away from the place. Moreover, he had left her with no money and no means of support, having borrowed as much as he could from her friends and family and taken all of her portion that his creditors hadn't got their hands on. Left without so much as sixpence, Elizabeth had begged a relation of hers, Sir Verney Noel of Kirby Mallory Hall in Leicestershire, to advance her £50 which he had promised to leave her in his will. Thirty pounds of this went on her lying-in at Bristol; another ten she had to repay to a kinsman 'that trusted us'. And now the remaining £10 was spent. Her father was in no position to help her, she said – he was in fact going to sell up the family home of Smisby Manor the following year – and only Sir Ralph's influence could prevail on Tom. Her friends had promised to find him honest employment if he would consent to come back to her and their baby. 'I hear he is not so far off as he pretends,' she told Sir Ralph. 'If you would please to encourage him to come to me and give us some little assistance, [that] will be as great a piece of charity as you can perform.'[18]

Rumours of this unhappy development were circulating in London by April 1664, when Harry Verney warned Uncle Doctor that Elizabeth was intending either to leave the child for the parish to care for in Bristol, or to present it to Sir Ralph and tell *him* to look after it. She didn't quite do that – or, if she did, Sir Ralph handed the baby back to her – but she did turn up on the Hobarts' doorstep and her friends petitioned him to pay a good part of Tom's annuity directly to her for the upkeep of their child.

Elizabeth made much the same suggestion. She asked that she should have £20 a year – half of the annuity – to pay for the child's upbringing in Bristol, so that she wouldn't have to rely on parish relief. After all, as Sir Ralph told her errant husband, she had been 'so much injured and abused by you already, and . . . you have gotten her portion, and so made her utterly unable either to help the child or feed herself, she having nothing now left but what her own friends in charity bestow upon her.'[19] As if this weren't bad enough, Dr Colladon was pressing Sir Ralph to pay over the annuity which he had bought from Tom – the same annuity to which Elizabeth was laying claim. His lawyers were threatening to bring a suit against Sir Ralph unless he immediately received satisfaction over his claims on the estate.

This was too much. Twice in the past – once when he lost his little daughter and baby son, and again when his Mary died – he had come very close to walking away from his responsibilities. The impulse to give up brokering and managing and mediating between squabbling members of the family was always close to the surface in him, and during the early part of May he began to think about leaving Claydon – leaving Mun and his mad wife, leaving Elizabeth and her starving child, leaving Dr Colladon and his lawsuits, and escaping to the Continent.

Vere Gawdy and Doll Leeke heard the news from their servants, after one of Sir Ralph's men brought some dogs up to Crosshall and mentioned in passing that his master was thinking of moving to France for a time. Doll was distraught and, assuming that it was the prospect of being saddled with Mary for the foreseeable future which was driving Sir Ralph to despair, reassured him that so long as Mun made sure she was well looked after, she didn't need to feature at Claydon. Lady Gawdy was much more severe. 'If you forsake your own country and should go beyond [the] sea,' she told Sir Ralph, 'you would be very unjust to your son, yourself and to all that have the honour to be related to you.'[20] He should seek consolation in his faith and remember that he wasn't the first person to have a son marry into madness. He had done his best for Mary. 'Do not destroy yourself by discontent.'[21] Doll wrote again, comforting him with the thought that Mary was probably going to die.

It worked. Sir Ralph pulled himself together, thanked Vere Gawdy for her sound advice, and fired off a stern letter to Tom, who was skulking near Kinsale in Co. Cork. He was so angry that he refused to have any direct communication with him now; instead he wrote down exactly what he wanted said, word for word, and gave it to his secretary, Henry Fowkes, to copy out as if it came from him. Through the agency of Fowkes, Sir Ralph pointed out that he had been 'very lately pressed again and again in a more than ordinary manner by your wife herself'; and that Colladon was threatening to sue. Tom needed to come up with a response to these conflicting and mutually exclusive claims, so that his elder brother 'may rest quiet from these importunities'.[22]

Fowkes's letter crossed the Irish Sea just as one from Tom was on its way to Sir Ralph. It followed the usual pattern of indignant self-justification and bare-faced begging. 'Sir, is my conceal-ment occasioned by or for reason of any treason, murder, or felony committed against his majesty, or any of his liege people? You cannot but judge me innocent therein.'[23] (He had obviously forgotten that he had confessed to assaulting his Judas of a friend the previous autumn.) If he had fled the country to escape his debtors, he wasn't the first or the last to do so. Sir Ralph was to give no credit to any scandalous reports that may come to his notice, but to pass them on to Tom, who would happily risk prison to return 'to purge and acquit myself'. Then came the punch line. Could he have an advance on his quarteredge? There was no mention of Elizabeth or the child.

The child, abandoned by its father, forgotten so completely by posterity that it has neither name nor gender, ceased to be a problem. It died in the spring of 1664, soon after it was introduced to its Uncle Ralph. 'I hear it hath pleased God to take away the child,' Sir Ralph told Tom, 'so that I shall say no more of it.'[24] But he did say that Elizabeth still wanted money – now just £14 or £15 to defray the expenses she had laid out for the baby in Bristol.

Tom's reaction was chilling, even by his low standards. The only way he could be compelled to assign any part of his annuity to Elizabeth, he said, was for her to pursue a long and expensive suit in chancery. She was of course in no position to do that, and even if she were, she would have to serve him with a subpoena. 'But I am not easily to be found out, and death may take away the one as it hath done the other before I make a return homewards.'[25] Fowkes was never to mention his wife to him again.

With that, Elizabeth disappeared from sight, rather as Tom's first wife Joyce had done fifteen years earlier. She did pop up again every now and then, looking for financial redress: more than forty years later, when Sir Ralph and Tom were both dead, she was still begging the Verneys for help.

The business with Dr Colladon dragged on for months. Sir Ralph continued to pay Tom his quarteredge (which was never quite enough) and sought legal advice, which was to repay the doctor the £20 he had given to Tom in the first place, and to hope that he would settle at that and reassign the disputed annuity back to Tom. Colladon was very, very angry by now, but he realised the wisdom of cutting his losses and agreed to the deal, which was signed and sealed over the summer of 1665. Tom, who was sent the release document in Ireland with orders from Sir Ralph to sign it without delay, expressed the sincere hope that Colladon might die of the plague. He also agreed to the settlement (as well he might), although he threatened to kill the doctor if he ever managed to get back to England, explaining that 'the unworthiness of this rascal deserves a stab, for it is pity the earth should bear such a villain'. He returned the release straight to

Sir Ralph with his signature and a postscript of unforgivable banality: 'When cloudy storms are gone and past/Then crumbs of comfort come at last.'[26]

The cloudy storms which had threatened Mary's life had also begun to recede. By the beginning of May 1664 Mun had yielded to the wishes of her kinsfolk (and the advice of his father) and brought in the famous Dr Prujean. 'This skilful and learned doctor', as John Evelyn called him, was well known in court circles, and for more than his medical successes. He was a noted virtuoso with a considerable art collection (including a Carracci *Magdalen*), and his own laboratory and workshop. He was also an accomplished musician: Evelyn, who visited him in 1661 in the course of a day hunting out curiosities, was particularly impressed when the doctor played to him on a stringed instrument 'by none known in England' called a polythore.[27]

When Mun went to Prujean for advice about Mary the doctor was in his sixties and just married to a wealthy widow. His approach to psychiatric care differed little from that of Denton, Ent and the rest: he prescribed powders to sedate Mary, and purges, emetics and enemas to restore her to health. He advised against consigning her to a private madhouse, perhaps because she was much calmer than she had been at the height of her illness in April; instead, a woman was hired to provide round-the-clock care at the Hobarts' house. And, if anything, his attitude towards Mary was harsher than Dr Denton's had been. Indeed, he was so severe with her that even Doll Leeke, who was still loudly praying for the girl's swift death, was moved to beg Sir Ralph to 'let not that doctor use her any more so roughly'.[28]

As far as Mun was concerned, Prujean's strict regimen was a necessary evil. For most of the spring he had been content to leave Lady Hobart and her daughters to make decisions on Mary's day-to-day care. Now he settled into Chancery Lane – and into the role of devoted husband – and concerned himself with every aspect of her care. He even wrote personally to Prujean when Mary had not moved her bowels for four or five days – 'my wife hath not gone to the stool since Sunday by her own confession, but I believe not since Saturday'[29] – asking if he should order from the apothecary another of the enemas which the doctor had prescribed during an earlier bout of constipation.

By the end of May, Mary had begun to recover her wits; whether it was because of, or in spite of, Prujean's combination of enemas and what we would call tough love is hard to say. She was still fragile; and, as her condition improved, Mun's patience deteriorated, so that the Hobart girls, Frank and Nancy, took him to task for snapping at Mary whenever she showed the slightest sign of her old behaviour. 'You will quickly lose the great reputation you have gotten of being a good husband,' Frank Hobart told him, 'which will be a great dishonour to you and I hope you will be more noble than to trample upon what is in your power.'[30] Mun's short temper was understandable: he wouldn't be the first or the last spouse to channel their relief at their partner's recovery from illness into frustration that it wasn't happening more quickly. And his irritability can't have been helped by the fact that everyone was still insisting the couple abstain from sex, something his friends found hilarious. When Frederick Turville, a distant cousin and one of his wilder drinking companions, wrote from Dublin to ask Mun to deliver a letter to a red-haired mistress in Charing Cross, he gleefully seized the opportunity to remind the young husband about his forced abstinence: 'I would venture to trust you with more younger flesh, but I remember you are a prohibited person at home, and therefore you are more dangerous abroad.'[31] This doesn't necessarily mean that Mun was finding sexual release outside the conjugal bed that summer; but it doesn't mean he wasn't, either.

By August 1664 Mary was well enough to leave the Hobarts' house. It was nine months since she had first arrived there. Having at long last concluded the negotiations over Mrs Abell's departure from the White House in East Claydon (she agreed to £30 a year and kept the silver plate, but left behind all the books), Mun and his wife finally settled into their marital home. It was more than two years since they were married – two desperately miserable years in which Mary had suffered melancholy, miscarriage, measles and madness. Now she was back at the White House, where she had lived for most of her life, and everyone hoped the familiar surroundings would complete her return to normality. Sir Ralph, who had gone down to Hampshire to stay with sister Cary at Preshaw for a few weeks, was keen to know from Mun how she was coping:

> I very much desire to hear how your wife is now, and whether she begins to mind her household business, and ordering her family [i.e., the servants]. In earnest you must persuade her to it by all the ways you can, and commend her doing of it at all times. And though she do not do it well, yet you must commend her for it, and keep her to it still; for as her condition is, I had rather she should do it, though she do it ill, than anybody else, though they do it well. Believe me, though you lose by her doing of it, yet you will gain ten times as much by it another way, for if she would be brought to employ her mind about it, I am confident it would do her more good than all her physic. Therefore I pray put her to it, and let her govern the whole family, and let her give order for everything in it, and not trust to others to do of it, but do it herself.[32]

He went on to urge that Mary should have her own household account book. Mun could reckon the accounts once a week – every Friday night was best – while Mary could do them as often as she liked. The important thing was that she kept busy. 'For if anything under heaven do her good, 'tis employment, a full and constant employment.'[33] That would be much more effective than all the physic she was taking.

And she was taking a lot of physic – so much that her bouts of self-imposed isolation, when the effects of her purges and emetics prevented her from socialising, were becoming the talk of the county. But it was only natural: she and Mun were both hypersensitive to the least sign that her illness was returning. After she drank too much wine one afternoon, for instance, he was convinced not that she had a hangover, but that that she was 'disturbed', and he didn't relax until the next morning when she took one of her powders and returned to normal. Gradually, however, she left off the medication. The female attendant who had been looking after her was dismissed at the end of September, by which time Mun could tell her Uncle Gale that Mary was 'in very good health every way, and hath already quite left off taking physic'.[34]

Sir Ralph continued to worry over his daughter-in-law. Echoing

Burton's 'Be not solitary, be not idle', he was very keen that she should not only be kept busy with the house, but must also have female company about her. Mun went along with this, but without too much success. The rector's wife, Mrs Butterfield, came to stay at East Claydon for a couple of months, but left before Christmas. Luce Sheppard was invited to move in for a while, but she couldn't come until the New Year, and then she could only stay until February. The Wisemans recommended a Mrs Felton, who seemed ideal – until she found out the nature of Mary's indisposition and demanded a new chambermaid to help her and an increase in her agreed salary from £10 a year to £12.

In the meantime, and in spite of the occasional lapse, Mary was steadily evolving into a conventional Restoration housewife. That autumn she threw herself into refitting the house at East Claydon, and wrote entirely conventional letters to Aunt Elmes, who had agreed to shop for her in London. She decided to work some new bed hangings in dimity and green crewel; she ordered new furniture for the drawing room and new hangings for her closet. Mun was proud – not to say relieved – when she managed to behave herself in company without saying anything odd or outrageous. He made sure to tell everyone what a good housekeeper she had become, and his relief was shared by the entire Verney clan: 'I hear she looks to her house well and grows a pretty housewife and delights in it,' Lady Hobart told him approvingly.[35]

The really big test came with the couple's first Christmas in the White House. They decided (or rather Mun decided) to make an impact on the neighbourhood by entertaining on a lavish scale. Sir Ralph was spending the holiday period in London with the Hobarts as usual, so his French cook, Michel Durand, was sent over to East Claydon. Mun brewed strong ale, purchased a quantity of cheap claret for the tenants' dinners (there were three – one for East Claydon, one for Middle Claydon and one for the couple's poorer neighbours), and 'bought more fruit and spice than half the porters in London can weigh out in a day'.[36] After a slight relapse in the middle of December – 'I pray humour her all you can till this public time is over', an anxious Sir Ralph told his son[37] – Mary behaved herself perfectly, and the only casualty was Mun's purse.

Her rehabilitation was all but completed in the summer of

1666, when she fell pregnant. A son and heir, Ralph, was born the following February. Then came Edmund in 1668; and Mary, born in 1675. Their mother would always be fragile, and she suffered from bouts of depression for the rest of her life. But she managed a life of sorts.

So what does one make of Mary Verney's madness? Diagnosing her is quite a task, in spite of the wealth of surviving material. For one thing, the realm of discourse appropriate to a twenty-first-century discussion of mental illness did not exist in Restoration England; and the vocabulary of madness used by Mun and his father, by a distraught Lady Hobart or a coolly detached medical professional like William Denton, is alien and imprecise. Most importantly, we never hear Mary's own voice. Our understanding of what *she* thinks about her husband, about her attempts at self-harm, about the precious Jane or the wicked Lady Anne, is always mediated, always interpreted by others.

The most benign interpretation of her behaviour – and also the most banal – is the one favoured by Dr Denton. A young heiress who is besotted with her new husband finds that he doesn't return her feelings. Placed in an unfamiliar milieu, left for long periods with strangers, she doesn't receive the attention she thinks is due to her; and her frustration manifests itself in increasingly challenging behaviours. She broods on her husband's absences and the reasons for them. She is moody and sullen. She has 'laughing fits'; she is abusive to her elders, she won't do as she is told and, as those around her grow more concerned and more exasperated with her, the sequence of disappointment, anger and drama repeats itself, gathering momentum as it goes. Exhausted, she finally calms down and, once she is returned to her old home and to a degree of intimacy with her husband, she stops sulking and gets down to the business of being a good wife.

If she were a character in a novel, then we could – and pro-bably would – take this idea several steps further and see Mary as a case study in female disempowerment: a rebel against the sexual conventions of her age, determined to seek some kind of equality in marriage and, when she couldn't find it, withdrawing deep inside herself. According to this interpretation, the male-dominated society against which she fights wreaks a terrible revenge. Denton, Prujean and the other doctors pathologise what is no more than socially undesirable conduct: as a result she is stigmatised and degendered by having her head shaved, denied sexual fulfilment within marriage while her husband is free to find it elsewhere, sodomised with enemas and bullied into conforming until, after months of intolerable pressure, she emerges as a good housewife who can keep her household accounts and keep up appearances in county society. The feminist mutineer becomes the Restoration equivalent of a Stepford wife who wants nothing more than to have babies and to discuss dimity with her elderly female in-laws.

But we can't reinvent Mary Verney as an anachronistic feminist heroine, no matter how persuasive the idea might be. She was not a character in a novel. She was a real person, she was scared and confused – and she was almost certainly mad.

There are a number of pointers to the fact that Mary's actions went beyond a form of social discourse which merely flouted convention. For one thing, there is the way in which those around her describe her behaviour as madness. During her first serious episode in the spring of 1663, Mun says that she has 'relapsed into her madness'; while she was in the throes of the second, Lady Hobart described her as being 'by fits I may tell you mad' and later as 'stark mad'; Denton said she was 'insane' and told her to her face 'in plain terms that she was mad, and was now to be used as those in Bedlam'.[38] In seventeenth-century England these words were not euphemisms for 'difficult', or 'rebellious'. Madness was a frightening thing. A terrible thing.

Another indicator of the seriousness of Mary's condition is the fact that she is described as lacking insight into what was happening to her, one of the criteria for diagnosing mental illnesses like schizophrenia today. 'I fear she is not to be alleved,' said Doll Leeke; 'she does not apprehend her conditions, which is her great misfortune.'[39] Her doctors were also puzzled, which suggests something out of the ordinary. What did Denton mean exactly when he characterised her behaviour as 'diabolical'? And, in the end, we have the evidence of that behaviour itself: the zelotipia and the self-harm, the eating disorder, the screaming and laughing fits. Lady Hobart is a witch who has put the evil eye upon her; she and the medical profession are conspiring to kill her. There is the hint – just a hint – from Anne Hobart that Mary looked to her maid Jane for some kind of social and sexual comfort when her husband denied it to her, such an obvious and deliberate transgression of the cultural code on the part of a twenty-three-year-old from her particular social background in the middle of the seventeenth century that it suggests an abnormal psychopathology rather than an unconventional woman throwing over the traces.

In the parlance of twenty-first-century psychology, Mary may have been suffering from a paranoid personality disorder, a schizoaffective disorder or a mood disorder with psychotic features. She may even have been schizophrenic: delusions, disorganised speech, grossly disorganised behaviour and social dysfunction are all diagnostic criteria which point to a schizophrenic episode. But in the end, we have to guess. And in the end, we mustn't let the problems of clinical diagnosis obscure the awful reality of what happened to Mary, the fear and confusion and misery. Nor should we underestimate the impact of her illness, which spread until it enveloped Mun and Sir Ralph, Anne and Nat Hobart and their daughters, Mrs Abell and Sir Robert Wiseman and Uncle Gale and Uncle Denton, Doll Leeke and Peg Elmes. Their reactions were very different: some wanted her cured, others wanted her chained or removed from their sight – or dead. The entire clan was profoundly affected by this poor little rich girl who lost her heart and then lost her mind.

19

The Levant Trader

*I*skenderun is a thriving commercial port on the Turkish coast, about 150 miles north-east of Cyprus. With its own oil refinery and steel plant, it is not exactly a prepossessing spot, and in the twenty-first century it is easy to forget that it has a distinguished history dating back to 333 BC, when it was founded by Alexander the Great after his victory over the Persian king Darius III on the nearby plain of Issus.

Iskenderun's significance for this story is that in the 1660s it was the seaport for Aleppo, which lies about 100 miles inland; and so it was here at that Jack Verney finally disembarked on 25 July 1662, eighty-one days after he set sail from England in the *Dover Merchant*.

The 5000-mile voyage was an awfully big adventure for a twenty-one-year-old. Soon after leaving the Downs in May, the *Dover Merchant* passed the Earl of Sandwich's fleet escorting Catherine of Braganza to England for her marriage to Charles II and a lifetime of disappointment and humiliation.* Although the wedding wouldn't take place for another two weeks, Jack already called her his Queen.

A few days later the little convoy encountered a naval squadron bound for home with a report of the situation in Tangier, which had recently been acquired from Portugal as part of Catherine's marriage settlement, a move that was being hailed as a great step forward in securing the Strait of Gibraltar against the depredations of Barbary pirates. A Moorish force under the rebel leader 'Abd Allāh al-Ghailān was presently intent on occupying Tangier, and the passengers and crew of the *Dover Merchant* can't have been too thrilled to hear that the Moors had just slaughtered 220 Englishmen in sight of the harbour.

The convoy crossed the Bay of Biscay and negotiated the Strait of Gibraltar without incident and without meeting any of the corsairs and renegades who plied their violent trade, just as great-uncle Francis had done fifty years before. As a precaution against marauders, the ships hugged the southern coasts of Spain and France, perhaps calling at Marseilles. By mid-June the *Dover Merchant* had put in at Leghorn on the coast of Tuscany, where Jack and his fellow-passengers were able to break their journey for three weeks. Declared a free port by the Medici in 1593, Leghorn (Livorno) was a hub for trade in the Mediterranean, and its harbour was a regular destination for ships from the Barbary coast, Venice and the Levant. At any one time four million crowns' worth of English goods could be found lying on its quays, and both English and Dutch merchants regarded it as having overtaken Venice as the major trading port in the region. This was partly because it was much more accessible than Venice – with a good wind a ship could reach Leghorn from England in twenty-four days, while it took three times as long to navigate round the heel of Italy and up the full length of the pirate-infested Adriatic Sea – but mainly because duties and transport costs were up to five times higher in Venice. By the 1660s it was the norm for the Levant Company's general ships en route for Aleppo to

---

* Looking back on her marriage twenty-five years later, Catherine wrote that 'there were then reasons for my coming to this kingdom, solely for the advantage of Portugal, and for this cause and for the interests of our house I was sacrificed' (*DNB*).

call in at Leghorn to take on fresh water and provisions, and perhaps to engage in some unofficial trading.

Jack took advantage of the break to indulge in a little tourism. Leghorn was famous for its great arcaded piazza, said to be the inspiration for Inigo Jones's Covent Garden (Jones was here in about 1600). It was invariably filled with slaves and slave-traders, 'Turks, Moors and other nations . . . some buying, others selling, others drinking, others playing, some working others sleeping, fighting, singing, weeping, all nearly naked, and miserably chained'.[1] Drunks could gamble their liberty on a throw of the dice: if they won, they walked away with a few crowns; if they lost, they were chained and led away to the waiting galleys, 'from whence they seldom returned'.[2]

Jack didn't linger. Pisa was only sixteen miles north, and within a day or two he headed off to visit the city, 'as much worth seeing as any in Italy' according to John Evelyn.[3] Pisa was celebrated for the baptistery of San Giovanni and its beautiful cupola, which had such astonishing acoustics 'that the voice uttered under it seems to break out of a cloud';[4] it was famous for the Ducal Palace, the Exchange, the cathedral of San Stephano. But then, as now, the city's greatest attraction was the cathedral's twelfth-century campanile, 'the falling tower which travellers boast of (and not undeservedly) as one of the most marvellous things they see in the voyage of Italy'.[5] The tower was already leaning at a five-degree angle. 'How it is supported from falling,' wrote Evelyn after a visit in 1644, 'I think would puzzle a good geometrician.'[6]

By chance, Jack had arrived in Tuscany in time for the Festival of St John the Baptist in Florence, and after a short stay in Pisa he travelled sixty miles east 'to see those sights which are at St John's tide'.[7] The patron saint of Florence's feast day on 24 June was famous for the spectacular procession from the Piazza della Signoria to the Piazza San Giovanni, ending up before the great doors of the Baptistery. The centrepiece of the procession was the Cart of St John, a 30-foot-high structure filled with niches containing children and crowned with a pauper draped in skins, who was paid a few lire to impersonate the saint. 'St John' perched precariously atop the moving tower while he ate, drank and rained coins and sweet-meats down on the enthusiastic crowd. There were fireworks, brawls, and usually a minor riot: a good time was had by all.

Jack spent nine days in Florence altogether, returning to Leghorn on 30 June. He immediately wrote a brief note home, mentioning his trip without going into details, merely confessing that it had left him 'somewhat tired'.[8] The *Dover Merchant* set sail again a few days later, travelling down the western coast of Italy and through the Strait of Messina. It touched at Cyprus and reached Iskenderun on 25 July 1662.

Scanderoon, as the English called Iskenderun, was essentially a storage and distribution point for Aleppo, which lay three days' journey inland. Goods bound for the trading centre were unloaded here, checked and placed in warehouses before being taken on the final leg of their journey by camel or mule. In the 1660s the town boasted English, French and Venetian factories, a run-down mosque beside the sea and a Greek orthodox church presided over by an old priest, who eked out a living by teaching local children to read and write and showing his church to the rare visitor. The churchyard contained an ominously large number of English graves.

Scanderoon was notorious as one of the most unwholesome places in the eastern Mediterranean, a morass of bogs, fogs and frogs. 'One of the worst airs in the world' was how one merchant described it to a young apprentice bound for the Levant, urging him to leave the city the moment he disembarked. 'An hour's sleep either by day or night is almost certain death to a stranger.'[9] Fevers and heavy drinking kept the death-rate high among the 'Franks', as the Turks called all European merchants without discrimination. In 1658 the Levant Company, which had kept an agent or factor-marine here since the 1590s, cheerily ordered the current factor-marine to take on an assistant 'for mortality's sake';[10] new arrivals noticed that the European factors in Scanderoon had yellow complexions, livid eyes and distended bellies; and any ship's captain who was forced by circumstances to spend a summer in the port might reckon to lose a third of his crew to sickness.

The town was set in a marshy plain and surrounded by high hills which kept the sun out until nine or ten in the morning. When it did appear the temperature rose rapidly, staying in the humid eighties all summer. By day, the air was heavy with the stench of decomposing frogs, huge things that came into the town in a fruitless search for water when their bogs dried up, crying like ducks and then expiring. At night, packs of howling jackals roamed the streets. There were lions and wild boar in the hills, and porcupines, which always fascinated new European arrivals, who responded to them as they usually did to rare and curious creatures – by eating them. A 'very savoury meat' when roasted was the verdict of one seventeenth-century traveller.[11]

The arrival of the Company's general ships was a major event. It usually only happened once a year, and everything depended on it. General ships – and *only* general ships – brought out the bales of dyed West Country cloth which were sent by Company members in London to their factors in Aleppo; anyone wishing to send goods to the Levant by any other means had to pay the Company a prohibitive 20 per cent surcharge. Seventeenth-century economic theorists argued strongly against the export of bullion or ready money, so merchants also shipped out the 'money goods' such as indigo, pepper, cochineal, sugar and tin, which could be sold in Aleppo to buy goods for the European market: Persian silks, mohair from Turkey, and grogram (a coarse silk and mohair mix). These in turn were sent home in the general ship.

The moment a vessel like the *Dover Merchant* hove into view, the Company's factor-marine sent the eagerly awaited news of its safe arrival to factors in Aleppo. The usual method was by homing pigeon, a practice which never failed to amaze newcomers from Europe. Thomas Dallam, who was in the Levant in 1599, described how it worked:

> As we were sitting in our merchant's house talking, and pigeons were a-feeding in the house before us, there came a white cote pigeon flying in, and light on the ground amongst his fellows, the which, when one of the merchants saw, he said: 'Welcome, Honest Tom', and, taking him up, there was tied with a thread under his wing, a letter, the bigness of a twelve pence, and it was dated but four hours before.[12]

The bales of cloth took a great deal longer than four hours to travel from Scanderoon to Aleppo. The road was difficult and infested with bandits, who were only too aware that there were easy pickings to be had when Company ships came into port. A few years after Jack's arrival a factor wrote home to tell his principal about 'the Arabs in great numbers grievously infesting these parts . . . our last caravan was robbed by them in sight of Aleppo, but being mostly gross [i.e. common] goods they left them basely mangled and abused and scattered for some miles; the finest with all the camels they carried away'.[13] For security, camel trains or mule trains had to be mustered, guides and mounted guards had to be hired, weapons and munitions gathered and distributed – every man in the caravan was armed, and there might be 600 or more carriers and perhaps fifty armed guards to accompany them. A factor could wait for months, even years, before the circumstances were right to chance the journey.[*]

New apprentices were usually moved inland much more quickly. Within twenty-four hours of landing on Turkish soil Jack was in a party of horsemen heading towards Bylen, a little village six miles to the south-east of Scanderoon. He spent the night of 26 July in 'this strange built town', as one of his contemporaries described it, 'standing upon cliffs of rocks, [with] one house as it were on the top of another, for six or seven houses high'.[14] Before sunrise the next morning they were on their way again, over little bridges with toll houses 'where you must call and drink a dish of coffee, and give them half a dollar at least';[15] across plains where buffalo grazed alongside vast flocks of brilliant-white pelicans, and through dusty villages where women with painted bellies and pierced nostrils came out to stare at the bizarre sight of Franks passing by. They slept the next night in tents and were up around two in the morning, picking their way along rocky tracks and over steep mountain passes. At last their path took them over the brow of a high hill; and there, spread out below them to the east and gleaming white in the sun, were the towers and gardens of Aleppo. It was to be Jack's home for the next eleven years.

★   ★   ★

[*] 'You little think what trouble we have in procuring camels to bring up the goods,' wrote one eighteenth-century factor. 'I some time have had cloth at Scandaroon 8 or 10 months after its arrival and was almost 2 years in getting up 600 slabs of lead' (anon. to Messrs. Teasdaile & Townson, 25 September 1755; in Ambrose, 'English Traders at Aleppo (1658–1756)', *Economic History Review* 3, 2 (October 1931), 252). Factors also delayed the movement of goods quite deliberately to manipulate the Aleppo markets, which tended to go down whenever a general ship came in.

The city looked beautiful in the distance. It was built on a group of low hillocks, so that it seemed to undulate across the plain, like the river – little more than a stream, really – which ran past it and provided its inhabitants with fresh water. A high wall, three or four miles round and pierced by seven gates, defined the perimeter; and within there were brilliant white houses of stone, all with flat roofs, interspersed with cupolas and a profusion of tall, slender minarets – more than anyone could count – from which the muezzins chanted the azan to call the faithful to prayer five times each day. There were cypress trees everywhere, and inviting gardens and orchards, 'wherein grow all manner of garden-stuff, apples, pears, plums, apricots, peaches, cherries, figs, pista-chios, and other things'.[16]

Towering over the city on a steep-sided 150-foot-high mound of its own was the citadel, one of the most ancient and magnif-icent fortresses in the Levant. Hittites raised a temple there a thousand years before Christ; Abraham was said to have milked his goats there; poets celebrated the fort as

> A citadel whose base was embraced by the Pleiades
> while its peaks surpassed the orbit of Gemini;
> Its watchtower would be counted among the celestial
> bodies were it only to move in their courses;
> Arrogant, it laughs in the face of Time . . .[17]

Rebuilt by al-Zahir Ghazi, son of Saladin, around the beginning of the thirteenth century, its sloping walls formed a vast moated ellipse, 450 by 325 metres at its base tapering to 285 by 160 metres at the top. The ramparts were faced with polished limestone and behind them lay al-Zahir Ghazi's palace and two mosques.

When Jack and his companions passed through the city gates, closer inspection showed that Aleppo wasn't quite so impressive. The walls were in poor repair and broken down in places. So were many of the houses, and so was the citadel. Swallowed up by the Ottoman Empire during the short but aggressively expan-sionist reign of Sultan Selim I (1512–20), when Egypt, Palestine, Mecca and Medina also came under Turkish control, Aleppo's dilapidated state was usually attributed by expatriate Franks to inherent Turkish idleness – 'only the English keep their houses in good repair', wrote one prim (English) visitor in the 1670s[18] – although the fact that the region was prone to earthquakes can't have helped. The Aleppo which Jack Verney came to know so well was wiped out in 1822, when an earthquake demolished two-thirds of the buildings and killed 20,000 inhabitants.

Entrance to the citadel and to the many mosques was forbidden to all Franks, but there were still plenty of impressive and intact pieces of architecture to see. The souk was a complicated maze of narrow cobbled streets, its main thoroughfare closed and roofed with a series of stone arches, with shops on each side and gates at either end: it was full of hustling, bustling traders all day, closing down around nine each night. Then there were the private mansions of the Turkish governing class – each one a palace fit for a king, according to European merchants – and the houses of the Jewish and Armenian middlemen who acted as go-betweens for the Franks and the Turks, taking a brokerage of 1 per cent on the goods they handled. (Turks hardly ever dealt directly with Europeans.) An English naval chaplain, Henry Teonge, described the interior of a house in the Jewish quarter which he saw in May 1676:

> a spacious room, in the midst of which was a large fountain, with four cocks flinging up water and falling into the fountain; which was a square about eight yards in compass. And each end of the room was also a four-square; and ascended three or four steps, the square being spread over with rich carpets, and velvet and plush long cushions, richly embroidered with gold, lay close on to another round about the carpets.[19]

Finally, there were the khans – combined warehouses, stables, trading areas and living areas. In plan, a typical khan was rather like an English college, with everything arranged around a central gated quadrangle. The warehousing and stabling was usually on the ground floor behind a colonnade, with the residential quarters on the floor above and set back behind a covered gallery. The English factory (using the word as Jack and his contemporaries did, to mean an establishment for traders carrying on business in a foreign country) had several khans: the most important was the Khan al-Jumruk, which stood behind massive oak doors just off the Souk al-Attarin and about halfway between the Citadel and Bab Antakya, the great western gate out of the city.

The Levant Company had maintained a presence in Aleppo since the sixteenth century, and its agents had settled in the Khan al-Jumruk back in the 1580s. There were at least fourteen English merchants living there ten years later, and by 1638 Lewis Roberts, the father of Jack's master Gabriel Roberts, reckoned that Aleppo had grown to be 'the most famous city in all the grand signior's dominions, for the wonderful confluence of merchants of all nations and countries, that come hither to traffic'.[20] Besides the native cottons and grograms which were traded there, silks came in from Persia, gems from India and spices from Arabia. Annual caravans arrived from Basra and Mecca and even from the Indies, although with the rise of the East India Company the importance of Aleppo as a conduit from India was declining and, in a remarkably slick piece of market management, the Levant Company was now buying Indian silks and calicos in London and exporting them to Persia via Aleppo. 'This town,' wrote Lewis Roberts, 'is found to be the great magazine of all Persia, India and Arabia commodities; the merchants whereof come hither in great troops and caravans, with their camels laden with the rich wares of those several countries, and make their returns in the commodities of Europe.'[21]

When Jack arrived there were around fifty English factors in the city. They shared Khan al-Jumruk with agents from France and the Netherlands; the Venetians lived next door. The Levant Company's consul in Aleppo, a wealthy merchant named Benjamin Lannoy, had his lodgings in the khan. Robert Frampton, later to become the Bishop of Gloucester, had been the Company chaplain in the city since 1655, although, because the Turks wouldn't allow any new Christian churches to be built outside Constantinople or Smyrna, his chapel was a makeshift affair, just a room set aside in the consul's lodgings.

Jack's first reaction to being thrown into such an exotic and alien culture was to fret. His living expenses were much greater than he had hoped, and he didn't know where he was going to find more money, unless his father might invest in some cloth and send it over for him to sell. His hair fell out in tufts, and he wrote anxiously home for a periwig to cover his head: '[I] must go in the Turkish mode before it comes.'[22] (The Turks customarily shaved their heads.) He didn't have any riding harness: could Mun send him out a saddle, stirrups, a little bit and some reins? He broke the bridge of his precious viol and tried to glue it back together, not very successfully. Not that it mattered – there was nowhere in Aleppo to buy new strings. He hadn't managed to find the melon seeds which his father had asked him to send to Claydon. *And* he had written home three times, from Leghorn, from Scanderoon and from Aleppo, without having a single letter from anyone in England.

The boy was homesick. Who could blame him? He was among strangers, in a strange land and a strange culture. Franks were encouraged to keep themselves to themselves in Aleppo, and for their own safety there was effectively a dusk to dawn curfew; so the khan was his entire world. He was a long, long way from home, and communications with his family were wildly hit and miss, dependent as letters were on passing travellers and home-bound merchants. His request to his father for a periwig was sent on 22 October 1662, and didn't arrive in London until just over four months later. A letter he wrote to Mun from Leghorn didn't arrive at all.

Responding to the letters which did find their way to Buckinghamshire, Mun did his best to reassure his brother, and in the midst of all his worries about Mary he carried out his errands with great care. 'I have sent you all you desired and more,' he wrote to Jack in May 1663:[23] he despatched a crimson velvet saddle with a cover for it, stirrups, horse cloths, pads, snaffles, a bit and bridle and two sets of reins. He also sent out five replacement bridges for Jack's viol and two boxes of assorted strings. Jack asked him to take the money for all these things out of a debt which Lady Hobart owed him, and which he expected her to discharge direct to Mun. In a sardonic postscript to his letter, Mun said that 'My Lady Hobart hath paid me nothing and I believe never will.'[24]

Kind as he was, Mun couldn't resist playing the worldly-wise older brother, and along with the harness and the strings he sent a little homily:

I think that I have forgot nothing which might conduce to your recreation in the things which you writ for, and pray

God I may not repent it for I should be very sorry that any thing should draw you from endeavouring to thrive in your calling, which although it be not such as I did wish you, yet since it was your choice, swerve not therefrom, but withal remember you are a gentleman, and show yourself upon all occasions to be a man of worth and courage, otherwise I shall never own you, for I hate a poltroon, you know. Dearest brother, I cannot discourse often with you, therefore I take upon me to advise you a little with my pen, to labour hard towards the improvement of your talents, and to fly idleness and debauchery and never be so foolish as to be persuaded to any evil or unbefitting thing whatsoever, and if I hear that you do behave yourself like a man of discretion and honour I will justify your actions and assist with my sword and fortune in any ground of the earth against any men breathing.[25]

'I hate a poltroon, you know.' Mun excelled at this kind of pomposity. And he couldn't resist ramming home his point a few weeks later, when he wrote again promising that he would venture some capital in Jack's business – something he never did – and announcing that he intended to encourage Jack in his work, 'especially if I find that you carry yourself handsomely and labour diligently and worthily, hating all vice, and searching after virtue'.[26] And by way of reward for all this good advice to attend to his labours and not be distracted by fripperies, would Jack be good enough to send him a Turkish scimitar or battle-axe or a set of Persian bow and arrows?

The young Levant trader reacted with asperity. 'I humbly thank you for your advice and kind expressions,' he told Mun. '[They] cannot at present be answered in any other terms but by copying of them out again in my own name.'[27] But he was more anxious about looking the part of a factor. During the early seventeenth century, Franks wore Turkish costume – it was cooler and it helped them to merge into the landscape and avoid hostile encounters with the locals. However, by the time Jack arrived in Aleppo, some factors were wearing a hybrid of Turkish dress with European hat and wig; while others, and particularly the English, had become doggedly Frankish in their dress, no matter how inappropriate that might be.

Judging from Jack's correspondence, the absence of the right clothes worried him rather more than his brother's good opinion of him. In the summer of 1663, just a year after he arrived, he wrote home to say that he no longer needed the periwig he had asked for – he'd managed to find one in Aleppo – but he did want a proper beaver hat with a broad brim and not too high a crown; everyone was wearing beaver hats, but at £7 each they cost twice the price they could be had for in England. He asked for a knee-length black silk suit with open sleeves; a close-fitting grey cloth coat also 'long to reach to the knees'; a cloth suit – 'any colour but black' and no ribbons; high stockings which should be either red or the same colour as the cloth suit; a red waistcoat; a pair of chamois drawers; and some winter shoes with heels no more than two fingers higher than the soles.[28]

Jack was also eager to have the right gloves sent over from England, and one pair at least was for the sake of his health rather than his vanity. He needed heavy gauntlets for riding, and soft suede for every day; but he was most anxious to have a pair of white knitted gloves to protect his hands during the sultry summer nights, when along with his fellows he slept out on the flat roof of his khan and was plagued by sandflies. Their bite was the cause of one of Aleppo's most notorious gifts to the Franks: cutaneous leishmaniasis. Variously known as 'Aleppo Button' and 'Aleppo Boil', this was (and still is) a nasty infection which first showed itself as a raised, red area of skin, growing in size until it developed into an ulcer that could remain for up to two years before it finally healed.

In spite of – or perhaps because of – his homesickness and his eagerness to fit in with the other factors, Jack settled down quite quickly to his work. The usual arrangement was for the Company to license a three-year apprentice like Jack to operate as a factor on his own account, provided his master gave his blessing. Gabriel Roberts' plan was for Jack to work alongside John Sheppard, an associate and one of the most powerful grandees in Aleppo. Sheppard was in partnership with Gabriel's brother William, and also worked as a factor for a string of influential principals back in England.

Jack's duties as a factor were largely dependent on the arrival of goods in Aleppo. The general ships which the Levant Company hired usually arrived in June or July, but not every merchant consigned cloth to every general ship and there might be a period of several years when Gabriel Roberts sent nothing. When the pigeons came into the Company khan in Aleppo with the news that the bales had arrived, it was Jack's job to travel down to Scanderoon to check them for sea damage, arrange for their transport to Aleppo and harangue the factor-marine into ensuring they were kept dry and secure in the meantime. Gabriel would supply an invoice along with the bales to show how much the cloth had cost him, thus giving Jack an idea of the kind of price he should be looking to get in Aleppo. (A frequent complaint among factors was that greedy principals sometimes sent falsely inflated invoices, forcing them to sell at a higher rate than the market warranted.)

Whether or not he managed to get a good price depended on a whole range of variables. Matching the colours of the cloths to the demands and fashions of the Levant market was crucial: red was always popular, because it was used in making caps and breeches, and the general rule was the brighter the colours, the better. One Aleppo factor in 1658 advised his principal to buy white Worcester cloth and dye it for the Levant into different greens, bright violets and rich burgundies. Quality was just as important: '[Be] very careful they be well and even dyed, free from all spots.'[29]

Jack's master also had to pay attention to packaging, and one of Jack's jobs was to keep Roberts informed as to what was saleable at any one time. The bales were wrapped in wax cloth or brown paper and covered at either end with canvas or calico to protect them from water damage during the long voyage; but a brightly coloured outer wrapper of silk or buckram made them more attractive to the brokers and shopkeepers in the Aleppo souks. Factors urged their principals to package their cheaper cloths in tillets of silk or yellow buckram to entice buyers, and even the more expensive bales could benefit from similar treatment. 'The want of silk tillets for your fine cloth hath been a very great hindrance to its sale,' one of Jack's fellow-dealers told his principal in London. 'Although it betters not the cloth yet it pleases customers, especially seeing the generality are so imbaled [which] makes some that are ignorant put the less esteem on the cloth being in plain tillets.'[30]

Sales were also affected by supply and demand. When the Company ships came into Scanderoon in the summer, the price of English cloth in Aleppo went down. The astute factor would hold on to his principal's stock for as long as possible, waiting for prices to rise and hoping to goodness that a French or Dutch vessel didn't arrive before a deal had been struck. There was an element of brinkmanship; good intelligence was vital and the market was extremely sensitive. If a member of the English factory (or any other factory, come to that) lost his nerve and unloaded a substantial amount of cloth at a knock-down price, the effects were felt by everyone:

> Trading continues here very dead, as you may imagine, one of this factory having sold to Jacob shopkeeper in the bazaar . . . 170½ cloths at 1¼ lion dollars and very good cloth giving two years time, and not to begin payment till one year be expired . . . This bargain makes people of the country give out that the general ships will arrive in two months; it is much to the prejudice and disesteem of our cloth, being distributed to most shopkeepers and cap makers in town.[31]

(The Dutch lion dollar, which was replacing the Spanish dollar as the standard money of account in the Levant while Jack was there, was a silver coin of fluctuating value. English merchants usually reckoned it as four English shillings.)

Besides shifting Gabriel Roberts' brightly coloured bales of cloth, Jack also had to buy silks and grograms for his master to sell on the London markets. When the enormous caravans from Gilan and Basra, sometimes as many as 3000 camels long, emerged from the desert and set up camp at the city gates, Jack and his fellows were already in the souks, bargaining with the Greeks, Jews and Armenians who occupied the commercial twilight zone between Moslem and Christian, Ottoman and Frank. In an ideal world Jack would be able to sell his master's cloths for cash, and offer that cash for the Persian silks that would end up as suits for London merchants and stockings for their wives and their whores.

But Aleppo was not an ideal world and, in the words of one historian of the Levant Company, good business 'did not mean selling at a high price, but selling to someone who could pay'.[32]

Straightforward cash deals were rare; it was more common for Frank factors to barter their cloth for silk, adding a little ready money as a sweetener. In spite of fears that brokers would default, factors sometimes had to give credit – a practice which was condemned by principals back home and also by the Company's governing body, which periodically prohibited factors from 'trusting' and ordered them to take oaths signifying their agreement to abstain from the practice. The smart factor found ways of getting round this oath. Some simply ignored it; others hit on a system of taking cash for cloth and then immediately 'lending' it back to the broker for a fixed term.

Jack was good at his job. With his black silk suit and red waistcoat, his broad-brimmed beaver-skin hat pulled down over long, curling locks which had grown back thicker than ever (leading him to discard the periwig) he soon became a fixture in the English factory. Gabriel Roberts was pleased with him, and the Company chaplain, who was briefly back in England in 1666–7, had nothing but good to say about the boy when he bumped into Sir Ralph in Chancery Lane.

But although Jack worked hard and did well for Gabriel Roberts, he didn't prosper. A factor could charge around 2 per cent on transactions, and with other commissions and storage charges he might be able to bring this up to 6 or 8 per cent. The received wisdom in commercial circles was that in this way a young factor could live entirely off his master's business. With hard work, sound business sense and a little luck, he could amass enough capital within a few years to begin trading on his own account, so that by the time his seven-year apprenticeship was over he would be able to set up as a merchant.

In practice, you needed some start-up capital of your own, and Jack's father hadn't given him any. That was bad enough, but, to make matters worse, just about the only member of the English factory at Aleppo who didn't think much of Jack was his associate John Sheppard, who from the outset felt threatened by the younger man. Gabriel Roberts' intention was that at the end of Jack's apprenticeship Sheppard should take him into full partnership, with the two factors splitting the proceeds of all their business fifty-fifty, a common precaution among merchants, designed to minimise the complications which could arise if a factor died. However, Gabriel traded in association with his brother William Roberts, who had spent time in the Levant, where he had become firm friends with Sheppard. William returned to London around the time that Jack arrived in Aleppo (it's quite possible that Jack was meant to replace him there); and when he heard that Gabriel was planning to divide trade equally between Jack and Sheppard, the two brothers had a huge quarrel. William refused to countenance the idea that Sheppard should give away half his commission, and reported to his comrade in Aleppo that 'my denial caused betwixt us a great difference and after that a great strangeness, in so much that had not private friends interceded, I had parted and left his house'.[33]

The brothers were soon reconciled, agreeing that for the time being any business they sent to Aleppo *together* would be consigned jointly to Jack and John Sheppard, even though, as William admitted, this would do little more than cover Jack's expenses and living costs. Sheppard didn't need to worry: besides the Roberts brothers, he also acted for a string of wealthy merchants in England, most notably Sir Thomas Bludworth, 'the great trader of them all,' said Jack. '[He] sends generally above twice as much as any of the rest.'[34] Bludworth, who was a Lord Mayor of London, an MP and a Master of the Vintners' Company, was reckoned to have a personal fortune of £3000 a year. (He eventually sent his eldest son out to Aleppo as a factor: the boy burst a blood vessel and died in 1679.)

Jack didn't have Sheppard's contacts, either in the City or in the Levant, and Sheppard wasn't about to share them voluntarily. Worse, William Roberts conspired with his friend behind Gabriel's back to keep the commission from the brothers' joint ventures out of Jack's pocket, so that he was forced to survive solely on the commission he got from goods sent out by Gabriel Roberts alone.

It was an anxious time. Jack's dreams of making his fortune in the Levant, proving himself to his father and returning to England a rich man were not turning out as he'd hoped. On the second anniversary of his arrival in Aleppo he confided in Sir Ralph that 'I hope on the arrival of our next general ship, which may be about five months hence, to hear that this business of partnership is effected and writings drawn up accordingly, which would be very joyful news.'[35]

The joyful news was not forthcoming, although back in England Sir Ralph was doing his best to help. As Jack was writing to him, he was arranging for £200 to be invested in cloth which Gabriel Roberts would send out to Aleppo on the next ship. (He would also send out ventures worth £122 11s. 6d. in 1666 and £200 in 1667.) He settled some land on Jack in December 1664, and consulted with various City friends 'who understand the way of merchants much better then myself, for I must confess I know it not'.[36] They advised him to speak directly to Gabriel Roberts about the partnership, which Sir Ralph duly did: and Gabriel, who had Jack's interests at heart throughout the boy's apprenticeship, was shocked. 'He spake very well, and handsomely of you,' Sir Ralph told his son, 'and seems to be much troubled that you have not been so fairly dealt withal as he expected. And since 'tis so, he assures me he will do his utmost for your advantage. And I am confident this ill usage will make him the more studious, and careful to promote all that may tend to your profit.'[37] Sir Ralph particularly asked Jack to obtain a list of the principals who sent out goods to Sheppard – 'we know not who they are that consign their goods to him'.[38] The implication was that, once he and Gabriel Roberts had this information, they could start to bring pressure to bear on them.

Things hadn't improved by the summer of 1667, more than six months after Jack's apprenticeship had ended. 'My dependency [is] now only to one man (my master), who if God should take from this world I must return home, for a farthing more I should not get in this country,' he told his father.[39] Sheppard had offered a third of the factor's business, but Gabriel Roberts turned him down, insisting that Jack should have a half-share. William Roberts promised to consign his goods to both factors, but this was just a ploy to keep Gabriel happy.

Jack was desperate. He would accept 40 per cent of the business if it was offered, he said. He asked his father to suggest that Mun might invest £1000 in him; but, knowing Mun's precarious financial position rather better than Jack did, Sir Ralph didn't even mention the idea to him. Then Jack hinted that William Roberts was taking a cut from Sheppard's commission. That was a highly unethical practice, even in those less regulated times, and he was careful to say that *others* were spreading the rumour – 'really I believe not, but do rather impute it to pride and a stubborn will of ruling'.[40] He also floated the idea with his father that perhaps a 'gift' of fifty pieces of gold would help William Roberts to be a little more accommodating.

In March 1668, Gabriel Roberts at last came to an understanding with his brother and John Sheppard over Jack's future. They agreed that Sheppard would take Jack into partnership, not on equal commission, but with a four-sevenths/three-sevenths split in the older man's favour. On 28 July 1668, exactly six years after he arrived in the Levant, Jack received the liberty of the Levant Company to trade on his own account in Aleppo.

Mun's anxiety that his brother should not deviate from the straight and narrow – something which he himself did rather often – was a common theme running through books of advice to young apprentices abroad and the history of Franks in the Levant. Seventeenth-century merchant's handbooks contained plenty of guidance for young men enjoying their first taste of independence in foreign lands. 'What winneth a man by whoredom?' asked one: 'Even but a momentary pleasure; a present sorrow to his mind; a perpetual sickness to his body; and eternal damnation (without hearty repentance and amendment) to his soul.' Drinkers fared no better. The mouth of a youngster who abused alcohol would 'receive twice so much bitterness as it had before delight' – a rather neat description of a hangover – and the drinker 'shall become corrupt as the toad, and shall return to vomit with the dog'.[41]

Seventeenth-century observers differed on whether the celibate collegiate setting of the khan inspired sobriety or high living – and, indeed, on just how celibate it was. Henry Maundrell, who was in Aleppo in the 1690s, painted quite a rosy picture of everyday life among the English factors. 'Our way of life resembles, in some measure, the academical,' he wrote. 'We live in separate squares, shut up every night after the manner of colleges. We begin the day . . . with prayers; and have our set times for business, meals, and recreations . . . we want not divertisements; and these all innocent and manly. In short, 'tis my real opinion, that there is not a society out of England, that for all good and desirable qualities, may be compar'd to this.'[42] But Maundrell was the Company chaplain, and the young men of the factory may not have been entirely open with their resident clergyman. A contrasting view was offered by the Levantine adventurer Laurent d'Arvieux, who remarked on the lavish hospitality offered by rich merchants, and particularly the English. 'One can add nothing to the magnificence of the feast, nor to the quantity of wine drunk. They smash and break everything to do honour to those to whom they drink, and the debauch is sometimes carried so far that finding nothing more to break they light a great fire and fling on it hats, wigs, coats, even shirts, after which these gentlemen are forced to remain in bed until other garments have been made for them.'[43] In 1687 the factor Nathaniel Harley remarked rather wistfully that Aleppo wasn't what it used to be, 'all sorts of vice being now as much discouraged as formerly promoted, and seems every day to be more and more disliked'.[44]

Any kind of social contact between Frank and Turk was actively discouraged by the authorities. One visitor to Aleppo in the 1670s counted only three prostitutes in the city, much to his surprise. There was some intermarriage between European factors and women in the Greek and Armenian communities, but not much;* and to engage in a sexual relationship with a Moslem woman was in theory punishable by death, although in practice the sentence was usually commuted to a hefty fine. This did not stop Franks from speculating freely about the sexual predilections of the Ottomans, who were reputed to be 'generally addicted, besides all their sensual and incestuous lusts, unto sodomy, which they account as a dainty to digest all their other libidinous pleasures'.[45] Nor did it stop the factors from lusting after Moslem women, whose unavailability only made them more desirable. Jean

---

* The case of Sam Pentlow, a merchant in the English factory at Smyrna, shows why. 'Sorry Sam' died in 1679, having married a Greek woman and settled down in a villa of his own outside town. When his English executors tried to ship his estate, his widow and his children back to England, they were arrested, threatened with torture and heavily fined for helping the sultan's subjects to leave the Empire without official permission.

Dumont, whose *A New Voyage to the Levant* first appeared in English in 1696, got really quite excited as he described the antics of local belly dancers who 'wriggle their backs, roll their eyes, seem to swoon away, and put their bodies into a thousand obscene postures, which the most shameless strumpets in Europe would hardly be persuaded to imitate'.[46] As a corrective to this we have the more prosaic and probably more accurate views of Lady Mary Wortley Montagu, who in 1717 commented on how male accounts of the Levant invariably 'give you an account of the women, which 'tis certain they never saw, and [talk] very wisely of the genius of the men, into whose company they are never admitted, and very often describe mosques, which they dare not peep into'.[47]

The *otherness* of the Levant is something which was constantly being impressed on Jack and the other members of the English factory. The consul, Benjamin Lannoy, employed a footman who walked before him when he went to visit the Kadi or the Pasha, carrying a silver-tipped staff, a common enough ritual in diplomatic circles. But whenever he ventured out into the streets, he was escorted by two janissaries, members of the elite military corps which constituted the standing army of the Ottoman Empire. Their protection was required because the more devout Moslems had a distressing habit of shoving Franks, hurling abuse without warning and spitting on them as they passed by. Nor was it only the consul who needed an armed escort: few merchants were brave enough to wander round the city unless they were accompanied by at least one janissary.

The clash of cultures was a perennial source of conflict and misunderstanding, and neither side made much effort to empathise with the other. The Turks tended to regard all Franks with contempt: under Islamic law, the world was divided into those who lived in Islamic states and were governed by Islam, the *dàr ül-islàm*, and those who did not. Non-Moslems entering Moslem territory had few rights: they could be killed or enslaved, and only if they accepted the authority of Islam – and paid a poll tax – would they be given protected status. Merchants from the Levant Company and its European rivals were reluctant to go this far, and since the fourteenth century, when Venetian merchants first negotiated privileges in the region, European countries had developed a system of 'capitulations' in the Ottoman Empire, whereby certain foreign nationals were granted exemptions from certain elements of Islamic law. England's capitulation dated back to the 1580s, although it had been renewed and its terms revised several times since.

Frankish merchants were regarded by the Ottomans as a necessary and lucrative evil. The district where they lived was called the pig quarter, and throughout the Levant they were habitually referred to as swine. During a heated exchange with the French ambassador at Constantinople in 1666, the Grand Vizier, Fazyl Ahmed Pasha, suddenly burst out, 'Do not I know you, that you are a giaour, that you are a hog, a dog, a turd eater?'[48]

The Franks were equally contemptuous of the Turks, whom Jack referred to in his letters home simply as 'heathens'. Few factors bothered to learn either Arabic or Ottoman Turkish, the mixture of Arabic, Persian and Turkish in which the Ottoman Empire conducted its official business. The vast majority of Europeans held that their hosts were 'avaricious and covetous of money above all the nations of the world', in the words of one seventeenth-century traveller, who went on: 'They never observe their promises, unless it be with advantage, and are naturally prone to deceive strangers; changing their conditional bargains, as time giveth occasion to their liking.'[49] When not sodomising their servants, the Turks were generally believed to sit around on their sofas all day smoking tobacco and sipping coffee, 'so that their whole life is a continual revolution of eating, drinking, and sleeping, intermixt with some dull recreations'.[50]

Not surprisingly, the picture Jack painted for his father of his own leisure activities in the Levant showed him to be pure as the driven snow. In March 1663, eight months after he arrived in Aleppo, he took advantage of a quiet period to set out with twenty other English factors for the Holy Land. The group travelled overland to Scanderoon, by ship down the coast to Jaffa and then overland again to Jerusalem, where the established procedure for Franks was to halt at Bethlehem Gate, send in a messenger to the Ottoman governor asking for permission to enter and then, after dismounting and giving up their arms, to head for the Franciscan friary which offered bed and board to European pilgrims. There were established sights, including the Church of the Sepulchre (which was guarded by janissaries and cost four-teen dollars a head for admission); Jeremiah's cave and the sepul-chres of the Kings; and, outside the city walls, Mary Magdalene's house, Lazarus's tomb and 'the mountainous desert into which our Blessed Saviour was led by the Spirit, to be tempted by the Devil'.[51] There was also a time-honoured tradition of having one's arm tattooed with a Jerusalem cross: history doesn't record whether Jack opted for this, although he did make sure to obtain a certifi-cate signed by a Father Bernard, proving that he had made the trip. Visitors could tour sacred biblical sites like the pasture where the shepherds were said to be watching their flocks when the Angel of the Lord brought good tidings of great joy; Gethsemane and Potter's Field; and the Chapel of the Ascension on Mount Olivet, then in use as a mosque. 'There are many other holy places about Jerusalem which the Turks pretend to have a vener-ation for, equally with the Christians,' wrote one cynical seven-teenth-century pilgrim: 'and under that pretence they take them into their own hands. But whether they do this out of real devo-tion, or for lucre's sake, and to the end that they may exact money from the Christians for admission into them, I will not deter-mine.'[52]

Jack's pilgrimage, a round trip of some 800 miles, took about two months, and by May 1663 he was back in Aleppo and reas-suring a rather querulous Sir Ralph that 'my recreation in this country shall never be immoderate nor at unseasonable times'.[53] During the rest of his stay in the Levant his travels were usually connected with business. In 1670, for example, he spent a month in Cyprus, a major cotton exporter and a permanent outstation of the Company since the 1630s. But when business was quiet, he also took the time to explore the country around Aleppo. Several times a week during the summer, the English factory rode en masse into the Plat Valley, four miles out of town, where they picnicked and hunted gazelle and hare, partridge, woodcock and snipe. The hunt was well organised, with a master, two assis-tants and a pack of dogs – native greyhounds, because imported English dogs couldn't cope with the heat. There was also a jokey sub-Masonic fraternity, variously called the Knights of the Malhue or the Knights of the Valley of Salt, into which new members were inducted by the consul with much sword-waving and bad poetry.* Other pastimes in the khan and in the country included music making, bowls and – improbable though it seems – cricket.

Jack was eager to please his family. He found the melon seeds his father wanted, and sent off bags of them, along with pistachios, for the garden at Claydon. He did his best to meet Mun's demands for Levantine artefacts, of which the most notable – apart from the bow and arrows and the Persian scimitar – was a silk suit complete with turban. (The thought of the portly Buckinghamshire squire parading around the White House at East Claydon in Turkish costume is only slightly less incongruous than that of his brother hitting a six across the plains of Antioch.) In return, there were polite, newsy letters from Aunt Peg or Aunt Cary. Mun rarely confided in him or told him anything of home. 'My wife presents her service to you, and [thanks you] for your consideration,' he wrote in August 1664, after Jack had enquired about his brother's bride. 'She hath miscarried and hath since laboured under divers diseases these three quarters of a year so that I have no child as yet, but she begins now to recover apace, and I hope in God that she will bring me many boys and girls.'[54] He didn't mention Mary's madness.

Of the three Verney men, Sir Ralph and Mun had always been close to each other, with Jack trying for the approval of both. Ever since being left behind, first at Claydon as a three-year-old when the rest of the family went to France, then again when his father and brother went to Italy, he had remained on the margin; and now his long voluntary exile only widened the gap between him and the others.

---

* The following example is more than enough:

> Now hear what you're obliged to do,
> You noble Knights of the Malhue,
> Or as some others please to call't,
> Brave Knights of the Valley of Salt.
> First you must love and help each other,
> With the affection of a brother.
> Anger or wrath must not appear
> To have a motion in your sphere . . .
> (Henry Teonge, *The Diary of Henry Teonge . . . Royal Oak* (1927), 154)

Sir Ralph was consistently hard on him. He berated Jack for not writing more often, an accusation which hurt the young man deeply so that he begged to get back into his father's good graces, 'the beloved son of a most loving father'.[55] The whole twelve years he was out in the Levant he kept looking for reassuring signs of his father's love, to the extent that after one long-distance spat he asked outright that Sir Ralph should continue his 'fatherly affection' in spite of the fact that his long absence from home might 'cause love to faint and turn into remembrance'.[56] Sir Ralph's affection for his son often showed itself as disapproval: even in 1673, when Jack was a successful factor with nearly eleven years' experience in Aleppo behind him, he was still criticising his son for ignoring his business and wasting his time in idle pleasures. Again, Jack was hurt, and showed it: 'Were there any pleasures in this country, I had leisure enough to enjoy it for of eleven years I have been in exile, full seven of them have not brought me in employment enough to reap my expense in meat, drink and clothing, and for the pleasures I can't think of any . . .'[57] All he ever did was to ride out into the countryside at dusk twice a week, and even this wasn't much fun since the entire factory rode huddled together for protection against brigands.

A great deal of Sir Ralph's criticism was a mask for his anxiety about a son who was far from home and out of reach; when-ever he was worried, he tended to get petulant and grumpy. The unreliability of communications between Aleppo and England meant that for long periods neither father nor son received any word of the other. On two occasions, Jack heard nothing from home for more than two years. The first, when plague was raging in England, made him frantic with worry: 'As I am unfortunate not to have received any letters from you which might assure me of your health and wellbeing in the late dreadful mortality, so I imagine myself fortunate that I have not received any advice from any other friends to the contrary,' he wrote to his father in May 1666; 'though this lack is but a small comfort to what the former would be . . .'[58] Sir Ralph, who would sometimes send two copies of a letter to Jack by different routes in the hope that at least one might reach Aleppo, was just as anxious in his own way when plague swept through the Levant in the summer of 1669. Tens of thousands died, trading was suspended and most of the Franks fled up into the Bylen Mountains, two days away from Aleppo, leaving only a skeleton staff behind in their khans.

Jack was one of the unlucky ones left behind: he had been sick for three months with malaria the previous year, and now he came down with plague and was ill for nearly a month before pulling through. Others were not so lucky: the disease spread into the surrounding villages and towns, and by the time it had run its course in the September of 1669, twelve of the English factors had died.

Once he had recovered, Jack wrote to reassure his father, from whom he had not had a word for over a year. The young Levant trader added a poignant little postscript which speaks volumes for the isolation and misery which the distance from home still provoked in him: 'My respects to those of my relations that have not forgotten me.'[59]

20

Natural Bias

enry Verney's career, if it can be called such, epit-
omises the plight of the gentry-born younger son
of the generation before Jack. Less principled than
Sir Ralph, more principled than Tom, he was charming, amiable
and basically honest. But he had the tastes and appetites of a
gentleman, an income which wasn't sufficient to support them
and a disinclination to earn his own living. That was not a happy
combination.

Henry had come out of the army back in 1644, having finally
decided that the soldier's life was not for him, and he spent the
next few years drifting from one Verney household to another,
doing small favours, acting as business agent, carrying out commissions in return for his diet and a little something extra. He went
first to Aunt Ursula, the widow of the piratical Francis; but an
unpleasant misunderstanding over £20 (which Sir Ralph finally
reimbursed her) led him to move to Misterton and the hospitality of Aunt Eure. Rural Leicestershire proved too quiet for
him, and he soon went to London, where he looked after Sir
Ralph's interests for a short time.

In spite of some heavy hints, Henry's exiled brother was not prepared to subsidise his lifestyle in the capital, and he reluctantly returned to Aunt Eure and Misterton. But his dealings on Sir Ralph's behalf bore fruit the following year, 1645, when he obtained possession of a lodge in the park at Oatlands in Surrey.* This probably came through the good offices of cousin Frank Drake, with whom he had been negotiating about the mortgage on Claydon. He suggested to Sir Ralph that sisters Pen and Mall should come to live with him at the old Tudor palace, so that they might learn a little breeding. Pen went, but Mall didn't fancy it, because the lodge stood all alone and, reported Henry, it 'was in my absence melancholy'.[1]

Oatlands was dismantled and disemparked in the early 1650s, a victim of the 1649 Act for the Sale of the King's Lands. Long before he could be evicted from his lodge, however, Henry went home to Claydon, where he kept an eye on the estate and sent regular news reports to Sir Ralph in Blois. He took the lead in arranging marriages for his sisters, advanced money to them when the need arose, and indulged enthusiastically in the family pastime of bullying Will Roades. 'You have more disobliged me in failing of your promise of giving to my sister Denton than I can express,' he told the long-suffering steward on one occasion.[2]

Henry's help always came at a price. Family was important to him, but his chief loyalty was to himself. When Sir Ralph gave him their dead father's clothes and told him to share them equally with brother Mun, for instance, 'he was very partial in his dividing', keeping the best for himself.[3] 'I find he is all for his own ends' was how Mary Verney expressed it to her husband in one of her letters home to Blois; and again, 'He cannot mind any business long but where himself is concerned.'[4] Henry went to great lengths to keep in Sir Ralph's favour, telling tales on his brothers and sisters if it served his own interest, taking the credit for every successful manoeuvre in the battle to keep Claydon from the full consequences of sequestration, talking himself up as Sir Ralph's only true friend in England – and living like a gentleman on Sir Ralph's money while he did so. 'Truly he is at a most mighty height both in his diet and attendance and all things else,' Mary

* Sir Ralph and Mary's secret name for Henry was 'Lodge'.

reported to her husband. 'I believe he fouls more linen in one week than you do in three.'[5]

Mary didn't like Henry very much (but, with the exception of Mall, she didn't like any of Sir Ralph's brothers and sisters very much). And she didn't exactly hide her feelings from her husband. 'As for Harry, I have a worse opinion of him than I have room in this paper to express,' she wrote at one stage.[6] He was always after money, and he seemed to think he knew what was best for Sir Ralph's fortune, and also that he had a right to part of it. That presumption irritated Mary and enraged Sir Ralph, causing a major rift in 1647, when Henry was tactless enough to complain that it wasn't fair for the eldest son to get everything.

From this point on Henry's role as his brother's agent and adviser declined, with Sir Ralph turning to his uncle William Denton to mind his business affairs in his absence. Henry continued to live at Claydon into the early 1650s (when he couldn't find entertainment anywhere else), but it was years before Sir Ralph forgave him for daring to question his role as head of the family.

That didn't make Henry a bad man. It was the doctor who provided the fairest account of his character. 'I think he is put to his shifts to live, which makes him do more unhandsome things than otherwise he would do,' he told Sir Ralph, 'and his choler transport[s] him many times beyond the natural bias of his heart.'[7]

An advantageous marriage was the obvious solution for a personable gentleman in his position, but either because he was unlucky in love or because he didn't find the idea of married life congenial, this just didn't happen. In 1648 there was some gossip in the Verney clan about his having found a bride; but whoever she was, she was dismissed as unsatisfactory and nothing came of it. Then, in 1649, he was seen about town with a widow, and once again the clan held its collective breath – especially when she began to show a suspiciously big belly. Henry said nothing about his intentions. The London rumour-mongers, on the other hand, said plenty, most of which revolved around their conviction that the widow's own son-in-law was more likely to be the father of any new babe. Pregnant or not, the widow also disappeared abruptly from Henry's life.

His real love was hunting and racing, as it had been ever since he was old enough to ride. In the summer of 1655 he was out after deer near Stowe in company with his kinsman Sir Richard Temple and two of Temple's friends – Oliver Cromwell's son Richard, and his son-in-law John Claypole. (Unreconstructed Royalist though Henry was, the hunt transcended political differences.) Henry's favourite hunting dog, Hector, was nearly killed in a struggle with a buck, and conducted himself so bravely that Claypole 'would not be denied the dog to breed on, so much against my will, I was forced to present him'.[8] A couple of years later, when a position in the Protector's household fell vacant, Henry automatically turned to Richard Cromwell and John Claypole for help. He failed, but only because Cromwell had decided not to fill the place after all. The cultivation of important men was another means of getting on in the world.

Horseracing offered the same opportunities to mix in exalted circles, while the heavy betting that accompanied it helped him to eke out his £40-a-year annuity. But the 1650s were lean years. In 1654, and again in 1655 and 1658, the Protectorate ordained that because 'the restless and implacable enemies of this Commonwealth' were inclined to take advantage of the 'concourse of people at horse races and other such-like meetings, that they may the better carry on their pernicious ends to involve these nations in new troubles', horse races were prohibited.[9] Gaming was not exactly encouraged, either. It was denounced from the pulpit as a crime against society, 'a strong knot of wickedness, a conspiring of vices, a consort of disorders, a bold and scandalous profession of mischief';[10] and a statute of 1657 outlawed all forms of betting and fined gamblers double the value of their winnings, with half the fine going to the Protectorate and the other to the loser. 'If proclamations march forth thus thick, and all sports put down, and the gentry not permitted to meet,' complained Henry, 'I am sure my fortune will be to break.'[11]

With the return of the King in 1660 Henry remembered his Royalist past and tried, like so many others, for some kind of preferment. For a short while it looked as if he might go back into the army and command a regiment at Windsor, where the Earl of Peterborough's son had just been made governor in return for his loyalty to the crown. When he heard he would have to settle for less than a colonel's commission he dropped the idea, to Sir Ralph's disgust. 'These punctilios are not to be stood upon by younger brothers,' he said, 'especially at this time when so very many persons of worth and honour do rather choose to take what they can get, than be left out of all employment.'[12]

Luckily for Henry, the Restoration restored more than a monarchy. Racing was resumed in the two kingdoms in 1661 – Haddington, just outside Edinburgh, was quickest off the mark, holding its first post-Commonwealth race on 29 May 1660, the day that Charles II entered London – and by 1662 Henry was riding regularly at meets all over the south and east of England. His companion on some of these outings was the influential Charles Stuart, 3rd Duke of Richmond, whose father, Lord d'Aubigny, had died with Sir Edmund Verney at the Battle of Edgehill. Together they were at Newmarket at Christmas 1662, riding the six-mile course together.

After John Denton died unlamented by the Verneys in 1663, Henry moved in with the widowed Pen, who had always been his favourite sister, just as he was her favourite brother. The family referred to her as 'Harry's Dame', and decades later she was proud to say that 'from my childhood I have loved my brother Harry Verney'.[13] Living at her expense in her Covent Garden house, he was able to dedicate a lot of time and money to the welfare of his horses, although since they were kept at Claydon at Sir Ralph's expense, it was usually his elder brother's time and money. He sent Sir Ralph a constant stream of instructions about 'the only horses I have to trust to for Newmarket . . . Good brother be careful of them.' They must be blooded three or four times a year. The grey's feet are tender, and he can't be left to the local blacksmith. None of the horses should be tethered or left out in the heat of the summer sun: 'Tis the night's dew, scope, fresh water and liberty that must cure them.'[14]

If Henry was content to train his horses from a distance, at least he raced them himself. Racing in Restoration England was not the preserve of professional jockeys.* Grooms sometimes rode

* The *OED*'s first instance of 'jockey' in the modern sense of the word dates from 1670, although before the Civil Wars the word was being used to describe someone who manages or has to do with horses.

for their masters, but it was more common for gentry, nobility and even royalty to saddle up. In March 1663, for example, Henry's friend the Duke of Richmond won £100 at Newmarket in a race against the Earl of Suffolk, in spite of having fallen badly earlier in the day. Thirteen years later, also at Newmarket, Charles II won the Town Plate (which he had himself instituted in 1665), after riding in three heats and a course, or final. Racing really *was* the sport of kings in those days.

Most races pitted just two riders against each other over a marked-out course of four, five or six miles. It was usually only the bigger, more organised events which involved three or four heats and a course. The heats were qualifying events – no horse which had not won a heat could take part in the final course – but the same horses rode in all of the heats, with only a half-hour break in between. Manuals of the day were full of the most meticulous preparations for race day. Riders were advised to break a raw egg into their horse's mouth, to soak his snaffle in sweet wine and to 'provoke him by all means imaginable, to empty before he runs'. They were told to wash his tongue and nostrils with vinegar, even to urinate in his mouth. 'And as you are about to lead him out, put an half pint of Muscadine [muscat wine] in a horn, and give it him.'[15] To take the taste away, presumably.

Prizes were modest – a silver flagon worth £15, spoons valued at £20, a piece of plate worth £40. The wagers, however, were anything but modest. On one day, Henry saw 'three good matches' at Newmarket, in which a Mr Elliott won £400 and Lord Sherard nearly £300. 'My Lord Lovelace lost £600 of his horse.'[16] That wager alone was roughly equal to a London maidservant's wages for 200 years, gone in a single day.

In spite of his addiction to the sporting life, Henry was never robust. He fell sick at the end of March 1662, so sick that he was unable to drag himself along to the Duke of Richmond's wedding at Whitehall, even though he was the only gentleman to have the honour of being invited. One didn't lightly snub a duke, and he managed to attend Richmond at dinner that day – only to leave the table in rather a hurry. He tried again that evening, when he sat down to supper with his patron and sipped a mess of broth. He was still poorly several days later, but the prospect of a day's racing at Roehampton stirred him rather more than Richmond's wedding: as Pen said to Sir Ralph, whenever Henry 'does hear of a race that is to be run, that will carry him the world over'.[17]

He was ill again in the summer of 1671, with a creeping sickness that caused pain in his stomach and back. He was spitting blood and complaining of a prolapsed anus 'which troubles me much and occasions my great weakness'.[18] Pen said he had the glanders, but it was no joking matter. Dr Denton had left town, so she brought in the internationally famous Oxford physician Thomas Willis, who had recently been persuaded by the Archbishop of Canterbury to set up practice in St Martin's Lane. Willis prescribed regular doses of 'the waters' and purged Henry, but he was past help. On 22 August, 'knowing the uncertainty of this mortal life', he made his will. Four days later he slipped into unconsciousness, and William Denton, now returned to town, reckoned he had no more than forty-eight hours left to him. He was exactly right: on the afternoon of Monday 28 August Henry died, leaving Denton to hope 'we may be all fitted for dissolution'.[19] He was fifty-three years old.

Henry left his favourite sister a healthy fortune of more than 700 guineas. She buried him in Claydon church and commissioned a monument from the prominent Holborn mason William Stanton, the bill for which she tried to pass on to Sir Ralph. The rest of the family were mildly shocked, especially since Henry hadn't so much as mentioned him in his will. As Lady Anne Hobart put it, 'your brother is dead and not left you a pair of gloves but they say you must bury him at your charge'.[20] Sir Ralph was sanguine. He gave Pen permission to bury their brother in the family vault, stipulating only that the coffin must be leaded; but he refused point blank to pay for the monument. He also begged to be excused from coming down to London to accompany the coffin back to Claydon. His man was sick, and he was none too well himself. 'I am sure that (considering my present condition) all reasonable persons will excuse me.'[21]

The Verneys were sorry for Henry's passing, but they weren't brokenhearted. Mun announced the news to Jack in Aleppo simply by saying that 'my Uncle Henry Verney and my father's cook . . . are both lately dead'.[22] Pen was the only one who really missed him. She told Sir Ralph she wanted to be buried next to Henry in the vault at Claydon; and when her wish was granted twenty-four years later, she still had by her a picture of their father with Henry's likeness painted on the reverse, and a little silver spoon marked with the letters H. V.

One day in 1657, Dr Denton and his wife Kate were travelling home when their coach was pulled over and they were robbed. Neither of them was hurt, and the family treated it as a huge joke. The aunts teased Pen Denton with the theory that her favourite brother was one of the highwaymen, a slur which made her leap to his defence, but which rather pleased Henry himself.

Robbery wasn't always so funny. In June 1652 John Evelyn was riding back from Tunbridge Wells to London when two men armed with long staves leaped out at him from behind a hedge, dragged him into the woods and stole his money, his rings and his boots. They left him bound hand and foot, tormented with flies, ants, and the sun; and it was several hours before he managed to untie himself and go for help. He was lucky. John Talbot, an Essex curate walking through the Inns of Court one evening in 1669, was chased into a garden by a group of men (and a woman, Sarah Swift, who yelled 'Kill the dog'). They knocked him down and 'laying him on the ground, clapping some of their hands to his mouth, others kneeling on his breast whilst one of them took him by the throat and with his own knife that they had taken out of his pocket' cut his throat and stripped him of his money, his rings and his clothes.[23] When everyone − even a curate − carried a knife, if only to cut up his or her food, the slightest brawl was life-threatening, and deadly violence was commonplace. Cary Gardiner's stepson William Stewkeley was forced to go into hiding in France after he was involved in a fight in which a man was fatally injured, while a friend of her stepdaughter, Ursula, a young man named Charles Turnor, narrowly escaped hanging for murder. (The fact that his father was an eminent judge may have had something to do with it.) Aunt Sherard's son-in-law Thomas Danby was killed in a tavern brawl in London; so was one of the Temple boys.

Historical homicide rates are notoriously unreliable, but recent estimates suggest that in Restoration England they stood at around six per 100,000 of the population − more than four times the rate in the United Kingdom in the first years of the twenty-first century, and about 10 per cent higher than current rates in the United States.

Attitudes to crime were subtly different. A county family with a strong puritanical streak, the Verneys were what the Victorians would call 'respectable'. But Susan's husband Richard Alport was in gaol for debt when they married. Tom was in and out of gaol, also chiefly for debt, although he periodically crossed the line from civil offence into outright criminality. And, according to Mun at least, one of the Temples of Stowe, to whom the Verneys were related through their Denton kin, was tried for having fourteen wives at once, and only narrowly escaped hanging.

At least two of the Verney cousins were real criminals. One was Mun's friend Frederick Turville or Turberville, a distant relation (Sir Ralph's Verney grandmother had been married to a Turville before she met his grandfather). In the 1650s Fred stayed with both Sir Ralph and with Nat Hobart, and although Sir Ralph never saw any evidence of vice or crime, the man was reputed even then to be an unsavoury character. In 1660 he was up for trial on an unspecified charge, which he obviously managed to escape, since four years later he was in Dublin, with a red-headed mistress in Charing Cross.

Then in the summer of 1666, Fred was convicted of burglary and other capital crimes at Hertford Assizes. Sir Ralph had a soft spot for him, but he was estranged from his own family and the Turvilles wouldn't intervene to help him, much to the disgust of the Hobart daughters, whose grandmother was a Turville. Frances Hobart in particular railed against 'those barbarous uncles that did make it appear by their jingling proceedings that they designed his death all along, which I believe will light heavy upon them'.[24] One of the barbarous uncles did go to him and urge him to confess his crimes, but he refused, saying 'he had lived ill but he would not die like a knave nor ruin a family'. According to Frank, his own sister refused to beg for his life: 'she said let him be hanged'.

And so he was. The heartless sister wouldn't even visit him in Hertford gaol. His only friends at the last were a priest who heard his confession (he died a Catholic, which might explain his family's rejection of him) and a mysterious woman, perhaps the red-headed Charing Cross mistress he mentioned to Mun in 1664. 'That woman that was continually with him till his death did bury him in the church yard,' Frank Hobart told Sir Ralph afterwards. 'I know not what she is, but never any woman had a greater kindness for any man than she, and has spent all she has, and sold all to her skin for him.'[25]

Apart from the fact that he was convicted of burglary (and that the victim and his servants declared it was their wish that he should die), we don't know too much about Fred Turville's criminal career. But there was another robber in the family, Dick Hals, who took a more colourful journey to the gallows and about whose exploits we know a great deal.

Dick was the son of an Irish naval captain, William Hals, who had property in Barbados, and the nephew of the sisters Anne Hobart and Doll Leeke. After his father's death and his mother's remarriage he was brought up in England by Doll, and in 1655 he 'put on his gown' and became a law student.[26]

Dick was eighteen. Sir Ralph, who had a low opinion of him, was sure he wouldn't last the course at the law – and he was right. Within a few months the boy had spent his year's allowance of £20 and given up his studies. That was sad, but not exactly unheard-of, and his aunt marshalled the family's connections and set about finding him a job as a lawyer's clerk. Soon after that, he went back to his mother in Ireland, and apart from the odd vague reference in Doll's letters to him being in one spot of trouble or another, the next we hear of him is after the Restoration, when he was going by the name of Captain Granger and languishing in Newgate Prison. He begged Mun Verney to come and visit him, and although he didn't specify the nature of the charges against him, they were obviously serious: a £100 reward had led to his being betrayed 'by a treacherous friend', and he was facing the gallows. 'But till I see you, I shall be silent,' he told Mun mysteriously.[27]

The Dutch War which broke out in 1665 may have saved Dick's life. By the summer of 1666 he was out of Newgate and in the navy, serving aboard the *Revenge*. He saw action in the Four Days' Fight off the North Foreland that June. But he hoped for a promotion that didn't materialise, and he hadn't the money to bribe the clerks at the Navy Office. Before the year was out he was in trouble again, and Lady Hobart was asking Sir Ralph to 'let me have one of your whitest wigs and you shall have a new one for it. It is to help away a friend. You shall know all hereafter.'[28]

From this picaresque point on, Dick's life descended into a succession of scenes from *The Beggar's Opera*. On the run after a series of highway robberies, he escaped arrest by leaping from a second-storey window, leaving his clothes behind him. Then he married 'a sailor's wife at Wapping'.[29] One assumes he meant a sailor's widow, but who knows?

February 1671 found him in Exeter gaol. He had been bound over on a minor charge, and the authorities didn't know he was wanted elsewhere; but he hadn't any money, and so he had to wait until they found out, or until his friends in London could be persuaded to put up his bail. To Sir Ralph he announced he had written to 'your brave son for a winding sheet, that in it I may with my body wind in the eternal remembrance of his abounding spirit'.[30] And to Mun himself he lamented that the 'over-ruling hand of fate nicked me in the bud, when I least thought of harm, and in a place where I never did any'.[31]

He managed, somehow, to escape justice again. Then at four o'clock one morning in April 1672, bailiffs burst into his London lodgings and dragged him off to Newgate, having first 'robbed me of every pennysworth of my ill-gotten goods', he noted indignantly.[32] He was kept in a cell without pen and paper, a fire, or even a candle to see by, and then brought before Judge William Morton, whose name was a byword for the harsh treatment of highwaymen. Unfortunately for Dick, it was also the name he had recently adopted as his alias. No doubt it seemed quite funny at the time, but Morton didn't see the joke. He was condemned to hang, along with three other members of his gang.

The judicial system in Restoration England was infinitely flexible, and being convicted and sentenced for a capital crime was not at all the same thing as being hanged for it.* The Recorder

---

* A study of capital crimes in East Sussex, for example, shows that only 30 per cent of cases in which the accused either confessed or was convicted ended in execution (Cynthia B. Herrup, 'Law and Morality in Seventeenth-Century England', *Past and Present* 106, February 1985, 106, fn. 9). Herrup suggests the execution rate varied between 20 and 40 per cent.

of London made recommendations to the Crown regarding mitigations and reprieves for those condemned to death, so Dick's Aunt Hobart bribed the Recorder's clerk (who was also his nephew) to intercede on his behalf and 'make the Recorder my friend'.[33] At least, she *said* she would give him a bribe, and Dick was told that his name would appear on a general pardon. But the 'gratuity' did not materialise, the irate clerk swore he would stir up his uncle and within a couple of weeks Dick was crossed off the list of reprieved felons.

It isn't clear what happened next. While he awaited his fate Dick talked of facing further indictments, of making a daring escape ('but this place is made past all hope'[34]), of pleading to be transported to Virginia, of being sent to the galleys of Tangiers. His amazing luck held, though. His old captain from the *Revenge* heard about his plight and, with another Dutch war in progress, secured his release from Newgate on the understanding that he would 'engage for my future deportment (which is much) and carry me with him to sea'.[35]

Once free, Dick changed his mind about going to sea, resolving instead to fight with the French in the Low Countries. Then he changed his mind about that, too, and went back to his old ways – a route which led him inexorably to gaol. This time it was Chelmsford, where he was told that the only way to save his life was to turn king's evidence. So he did. He informed on his accomplices, he informed on his acquaintances, he informed on 'all persons I did or do know that use the pad'.[36]

This was a far cry from the romantic highwayman whose daring exploits had fascinated the family. For a time it seemed as if Dick's copious confessions might not be enough to save him, and he watched terrified as the Chelmsford hangman began to make preparations for his execution. He whined that 'all the miseries which attend humanity have fallen on my head . . . Could they not as well have pressed me or hanged in my state of innocency, I mean, while I was a pure thief, without blot or blemish, as to make me stink in the nostrils of my old associates?'[37] But yet again, his friends managed to secure his release at the last minute; and yet again he was arrested within a matter of months, as those old associates vowed to kill him for betraying them.

That was in 1675. The pattern of crime, arrest, intervention and release continued unchanged for the next ten years, except for one rather unlikely interlude in the late 1670s when Dick found a job as a court bailiff. 'He is very honest, and I hope will keep so,' wrote the ever-optimistic Aunt Hobart. 'He is to oversee all the baileys, for they have cheated highly. He receives all the money of the court . . .'[38] History doesn't record what he did with that money, but he had gone back to his old ways by the early 1680s. His wife gave up on him, and in 1683 he talked wildly of taking service with the Hapsburgs against the Ottoman army laying siege to Vienna. 'All that troubles me is my little boy, but God is able to provide for him. I would if I could.'[39]

In 1685 Dick was living in Stepney, and it was there that his luck finally ran out. That spring he and three or four others broke into the home of Alexander and Elizabeth Handerson, assaulted them and stole three gold rings and a silver cup. Dick was caught, along with another known thief, Peter Roach, and the pair were indicted on charges of felony and robbery and sent to Newgate to await trial.*

The first Sir Ralph heard of this was two days before the Old Bailey sessions began, when a letter arrived from Newgate: 'I have no great news,' Dick told him with a show of nonchalance, 'but only that I think to die next week.'[40] He and Roach appeared in the Justice Hall on 29 April before Sir Thomas Jenner, the Recorder, and the Lord Mayor, Sir James Smith. There was strong evidence brought against them, and the jury didn't hesitate to find them guilty 'of felony and robbery both'. (Seventeenth-century juries didn't have much of an opportunity to hesitate – trials lasted around half an hour each, and it was common for between fifteen and twenty to be heard in a single day.) At the end of the three-day session, they were brought forward along with another thirty-nine men and eight women, to hear their sentences pronounced: fourteen were to be transported; eight were 'burnt in the hand';† four went to the pillory; and the

---

* Roach was also convicted of attacking and robbing a man on the road to Bow 'with some others'. Dick Hals wasn't named in this indictment.

† In other words, they escaped punishment by claiming benefit of clergy. Successful claimants were branded on their thumbs to ensure that the benefit wasn't claimed more than once.

remaining twenty-three, including Dick and his accomplice, were condemned to hang. A week later Jack Verney, by now back in England and living in London, was watching as the cart carrying his cousin and the other condemned prisoners wended its way through the narrow streets from Newgate to Tyburn.

There was no scaffold at Tyburn in those days, just a gibbet. Dick was given the chance to stand in the cart and make a last speech to the crowd (there is no record of what he said); then he was blindfolded, the noose was placed round his neck and the cart was pulled away. 'I wish I could have saved him,' said Mun. 'I pray God rest his soul in heaven.'[41]

One of the intriguing features of Dick Hals's career – apart from the evidence it provides of the haphazard way in which the judicial system operated – is the reactions of Sir Ralph, Mun and the rest of the clan to his crimes. We can understand that his aunts Doll Leeke and Anne Hobart were determined to see the good side of their wild young nephew; it's more surprising to find that the others neither condemned him for his crimes nor excluded him from their social circle. No one raised an eyebrow when Dick wrote to congratulate Mun and Mary Verney on the birth of their first child: 'God make him a better man than his father; that's blessing enough.'[42] Lady Vere Gawdy, who knew all about his chequered past from Doll Leeke, was perfectly happy to have him to stay with her at Crosshall when he came out of Newgate in 1672 with a commuted death sentence. He appeared at family weddings. Even the ultra-respectable Sir Ralph was only mildly surprised when Anne Hobart arrived at Claydon for a visit, bringing with her her daughter, her grandson, her two maids – and her highwayman nephew. In fact there was a greater sense of disgrace and dismay among the Verneys when Aunt Margaret Pulteney married a Roman Catholic than there was when Cousin Dick was sentenced to hang for highway robbery.

The thief as romantic hero, while not yet risen to the heights he would achieve in the eighteenth century, was already a stock figure in popular culture. There was a general consensus that the threat posed by robbers and highwaymen was on the increase. Observers lamented the fact that the roads were infested with them, and it seemed that every day brought news of another

outrage perpetuated against innocent travellers. And the experience of crime and its consequences wasn't confined to the
victims and their families. The mass executions of malefactors
which took place at Tyburn eight or nine times a year were
public rituals, watched by hundreds, even thousands, of spectators. In July 1669 the cart carrying one group of prisoners from
Newgate to the gallows couldn't reach its destination for the
press of people, and the condemned men and women had to
complete their last journey on foot. And violence sometimes
spilled over into the streets. In November 1677, for instance,
there was a gun battle in the Strand after a gang of highwaymen
was recognised while they were drinking in a tavern. One fired
off his pistol at the constables who tried to arrest him, and
received a ball in his shoulder from 'a resolute Gentleman of the
Guard'.[43] Such behaviour was outrageous; and polite society
agreed (in theory at least) that criminals like these deserved
nothing but the noose:

> The miserable fate which they suffer'd was but their deserved
> due, since all the Royal Indulgence which some of 'em have
> receiv'd, was only an inlet to the perpetrating more and greater
> villainies, even to a defiance of justice drawing her sword;
> wherefore as their unparalleled insolence insulted over the laws
> of God and Man, by taking an unaccountable pride and ambi-
> tion in breaking both, we ought not to be sorry at the hangman's
> meritorious act of sending such case-harden'd villains out of
> the land of the living.[44]

But there was still a true-life crime kind of fascination with the
lurid details of wrongdoing. It provided reassurance for those
who remained within the law, defining social boundaries by
demonstrating who was outside them. There was also a sneaking
admiration for the wrongdoer, an acknowledgement that transgression has a glamour all its own. Tracts purporting to record
the dreadful exploits of 'gentlemen of the pad' deliberately
mythologised their subjects by weaving episodes from popular
literature into their tales (Boccaccio's *Decameron* was a particular
favourite). And life mirrored art: at the beginning of the seventeenth century the last speech of a condemned highwayman on

the gallows was full of remorse and penitence; by the end of the century he was expected to show insouciance at the prospect of being 'turned off' into eternity. The celebrated highwayman Claude Duval stood on the gallows at Tyburn in 1670 and thanked the women of England for their attempts to intercede with the authorities:

> How mightily and how generously have you rewarded my little services? Shall I ever forget that universal consternation amongst you when I was taken, your frequent, your charge-able visits to me at Newgate, your shrieks, your swoonings when I was condemned, your zealous intercession and impor-tunity for my pardon? You could not have erected fairer pillars of honour and respect to me, had I been a Hercules, and could have got fifty sons in a night.*

This was good, but it was pretty tame in comparison with the crowd-pleasing bravado of some Georgian highwaymen, like Dick Turpin, who had a joke with the hangman and then threw himself off the gallows; or Jeremiah Abershaw, who carried a flower in his mouth and made the hangman wait while he removed his boots. (When asked why, he replied that his mother had always said he would die with his boots on, and he was determined to prove her wrong.) But Claude Duval was an anti-hero, not a villain. Just as clerks and storekeepers would later read about the exploits of outlaws in the Wild West and fancy themselves as Jesse James or Billy the Kid, so spotty London apprentices and fat country squires fantasised about being Duval, while ladies and maidservants wandered what it might be like to be made love to by such a celebrated swordsman.

---

* [Walter Pope], *The Memoires of Monsieur Du Vall: containing the History of his Life and Death, Whereunto are Annexed His last Speech and Epitaph* (London, 1670), 14. Duval's epitaph begins,

> 'Here lies Du Vall: Reader, if Male thou art,
> Look to thy Purse; if Female, to thy Heart.
> Much havoc has he made of both: For all
> Men he made stand, and Women he made fall' (*ibid.*, 16).

Dick Hals was no Claude Duval, but there was still a vicarious thrill to be obtained by having a highwayman in the family. And there was a more serious side to the Verneys' acceptance of him. Dick consistently saw himself as a victim: his first stay in Newgate was the result of his being 'betrayed'; his last, he put down to 'the malice of [a] gaoler and [the] overheat of a Chief Justice'.[45] To a Puritan family like the Verneys, however, crime was a sin and Tyburn the last earthly stop on a path which began with a failure to control one's vices and ended in Hell. 'Of sloth comes pleasure, of pleasure comes riot, of riot comes whoring, of whoring comes spending, of spending comes want, of want comes theft, of theft comes hanging.'[46] The individual was answerable for the consequences of his or her own actions; but sin nevertheless required the possibility of forgiveness and redemption.

Dick's occasional attempts at reform were usually connected with religion. While he was in Chelmsford gaol the clergy made him resolve 'to hate for ever the company and name of a thief'.[47] He held on to his religious principles for a year or two, it seems: when he was at a particularly low ebb in 1676 and surrounded by the 'sin and vice' of London, he told Sir Ralph, 'I trust my newborn grace will defend me and itself from participating this sink of humours and disorders.'[48] The fact that Dick didn't consider himself beyond redemption softened the family's attitude towards him. He was weak rather than evil, a sinner who had lost his way rather than a brutal armed robber.

Another factor softened the family's response to their criminal cousin. Dick was *likeable*. He was friendly and pleasant to Mun, polite and respectful to Sir Ralph, witty, articulate, unfailingly grateful to anyone who bailed him out of gaol or sent him a few pounds for food and clothing. Social historians sometimes forget how important that is. One could forgive a man a lot, even armed robbery, if only he was an agreeable companion.

Mun Verney had always dreamed of cutting some figure in the world – of standing for Parliament, or taking up soldiering. He was made a commissioner for the Buckinghamshire militia in 1660, along with Eleanor Warwick's grandson, Sir Harry Lee, and her new husband, the erstwhile Parliamentarian 2nd Earl of Manchester, whom she had married after Warwick's death left her temporarily without an earl. (It was a characteristically astute move which kept her at the heart of national affairs after the Restoration: Manchester's lukewarm support for Cromwell readily translated into an enthusiastic welcome for Charles II, who made him Lord Chamberlain and showered him with honours.) In an excess of patriotic zeal brought on by the Dutch War of 1672, Mun even fantasised for a while about going to sea until his father told him not to be so stupid.

There was a strong element of playacting in Mun's dreaming. He dressed up in the Ottoman costume Jack had sent him from Aleppo and practised in the gardens at East Claydon with the 'Persian scimitar or battle axe or Persian bow and arrows',[49] a romantic renegado like his great-uncle Francis, but without the element of danger. When war threatened, he yearned to take up arms for the King, but showed more concern about having the right uniform than about the rightness of the cause:

> Though I carry a soldier's mind yet I hate any servile bade, neither do I understand the livery which [the King] makes his peculiar guards wear, to be the only pattern becoming all other soldiers to follow in their habits, for that's as everyone fancies, so that there is no necessity for the generality of martial men to fall into such extremes as to be in the King's Guards' peculiar livery, if they will wear a habit soldier-like . . .*

The role Mun adopted with the greatest gusto was that of the old-fashioned country squire. Like Sir Edward Hartfort in Shadwell's *Lancashire Witches* (1682), 'a worthy hospitable true English gentleman, of good understanding and honest principles',[50] Mun dispensed lavish hospitality to friends and neighbours and revelled in being both arbiter of justice within his community and a mainstay of traditional values. Like Hartfort,

---

* Mun Verney to Sir Ralph Verney, 16 July 1677; M636/30. The correct dress for a gentleman-soldier was a subject which exercised Sir Ralph as much as his son. He told Mun that a Suffolk baronet had been laughed out of Whitehall for wearing the livery of an officer in the Guards, and begged for a picture of his son 'in a buff coat, or in armour with all my heart, but not in a suit like the officers of the Guards' (16 July 1677; M636/30).

he thought 'twas never good days, but when great tables were kept in large halls; the buttery-hatch was always open . . . and a good smell of meat and March-beer, with dog's turds and mary-bones [marrow bones] as ornaments in the hall'.[51] Like Hartfort (and like his own father), Mun's life was grounded in a belief in 'our English religion, and our English principles',[52] and he loathed the French in general and Louis XIV in particular. He lamented that young men slavishly affected French manners and fashions, so that 'we Englishmen are justly styled apes of the French'.[53] (This from a man who habitually wrote French to his own father!) When a French man-of-war went down in the summer of 1679, he was sorry for the poor men who were lost, but still wished 'all this French King's ships at the bottom of the sea and lost for ever'.[54]

This bluff country squire, who hunted, drank and entertained with such enthusiasm, weighed over 280lb and couldn't put his boots on without help. He laughed at himself for being so fat, saying he needed a stronger horse than most men, and that he didn't dare to go out on foot in case he sank down into the Buckinghamshire clay. It is as if he *became* a stock character from literature, the kind of squire who fifty years later was satirised by Pope as a well-meaning oaf 'whose laughs are hearty, though his jests are coarse/And loves you best of all things – but his horse'; who a hundred years later appeared as the irascible Squire Western in Fielding's *Tom Jones*.*

In another respect Squire Verney remained frighteningly true to type. If he needed help to take off his boots, he certainly found it – in the stews of London, the farms and cottages of Buckinghamshire, East Claydon itself. He often went up to town, and when he did he usually left Mary and the rest of the family behind, refusing to tell them exactly where he was going or when he would be back. 'Neither will I be confined to time or place,' he announced airily, 'for that were to render myself, who am

---

* Pope's satire was rooted in reality. Witness Jack Verney's son-in-law Thomas Cave, who said he preferred hunting to matrimony and complained to Jack in 1704 about his wife's pregnancy: 'In the night the little brat kicks, my wife coughs . . . and I am put to it to quiet both . . . With other suffering comes the loss of many of my hounds by the murrain' (Thomas Cave to Jack Verney, 15 October 1704; M636/52).

master of a family, a prisoner to it.'[55] The reality was that he remained unremittingly unfaithful. One of his wife's favourite maids was the eighteen-year-old Jane Avery, who came from the nearby village of Quainton, once part of the Verney estates. She was also Mun's mistress. 'My faithful sweet Jinny,' as he called her, was eventually married off in 1678 to an Oxford painter, George Harris, perhaps after she became pregnant. When she died at the beginning of 1679, Mun was deeply upset, telling his father how grieved he was to hear of her death. And considering the high moral tone Sir Ralph usually adopted when faced with evidence of Mun's character flaws, his response to the news of Jinny Harris's death was surprisingly mild:

> I am very sorry for the death of [Jane], for I must needs confess she carried herself as well as I have known any one of her birth and breeding: and had she not been very good natured, she would have imposed much more upon you. But now you see neither youth nor health can secure as against the Jaws of Death; therefore let us all endeavour to amend our lives, and God grant this may be a warning to us, to forsake all our vices, and become new men, and then God will bless us here, and reward us with heaven hereafter.[56]

There's a hint of male camaraderie here; a suggestion lurking beneath the mixture of relief, regret and gentle reproof that Sir Ralph the ageing widower wasn't guiltless when it came to sexual conduct.

In the same breath as he mourned the passing of Jinny Harris, Mun complained to his father about another of Mary's maids. Betty Phelps was expecting his child, and he was desperate to get her out of the way: 'I wish she had a place and so were gone from me.'[57] Sir Ralph couldn't help – he pointed out that no gentlewoman would take the girl in her condition – and eventually Betty was packed off to London to lodge with her mother. She had a son, John, and Mun kept up the relationship. He was still seeing her five years later, when Sir Ralph received a rather nasty anonymous letter informing him of the fact:

> It is admired by many persons of quality in this town that you give the Esquire such allowances to keep a whore in town.

He hath been seen often to visit her and now 'tis understood to be his maid Miss Betty Phelps. She lodges near him. When he is dead his name will quickly rot, for he hath made it stink already. Many of your friends are troubled at it . . .[58]

Sir Ralph's reaction to this is unknown; but it was certainly common knowledge in the family that Mun had fathered a number of bastards; Betty's John was one of at least three who survived him.

Sleeping with your wife's maidservants was inconsiderate. It wasn't so unusual, though. One thinks, for example, of Samuel Pepys' affair with his wife's teenage maid, Deb Willet. But while we have Pepys' own vivid account of what happened when his wife found him with his hand up Deb's skirt – Elizabeth's tears, her threats to slit Deb's nose, the way she arrived at her husband's bedside in the middle of the night shaking with jealousy and brandishing a pair of red-hot tongs – we know nothing about how much Mary Verney knew or suspected about Mun's infidelities.

What we do know is that throughout the 1670s and 1680s Mary's behaviour was as erratic as it had been during the first years of her marriage. For long periods she functioned normally, although she was often listless and withdrawn, spending her days lying in bed and prowling the house at night, calling for her maids. Occasionally, though, she exploded into violence, swearing at her husband, kicking and punching him. She swallowed glass, she put her hands through the lattice windows in her chamber, she hid knives and scissors in her bed. On one visit to Middle Claydon she embarrassed the family by wandering out of the church in the middle of Reverend Butterfield's sermon, then drifting back in and walking round and round the font.

The family accepted that she was insane, and made the best of it. When she needed help, Mun hired gentlewomen-servants and nurses; and if he sometimes benefited from their ministrations as well, that isn't to say he didn't care about her. He was prepared to try anything that might cure her. At one point he even brought in a local wise woman, who produced the head of a hare and told him Mary should wear it bandaged to her forehead for three or four days and nights. The melancholy hare's brain would draw off the melancholy from hare-brained Mary, after which it must be 'put into the feathers of a pillow whereon the party grieved must lie as long as they live'.[59] And just to give a touch of respectability to a magical cure, the wise woman ordered that prayers should be said for Mary in church, on six consecutive Sundays.

Mun laughed at the idea. He still tried it, although he didn't care to have the banns of madness proclaimed in East Claydon, sending instead to 'some by-church remote from all her relations', and asking the congregation to pray for an unnamed 'person of condition who labours sorely under a melancholy distemper'.[60]

It would be easy to dismiss Mun as a lecherous buffoon slouching round East Claydon in his Turkish turban; a fat, dreaming clown who longed for romance and escape, and found it with wet nurses and whores. But the clown drank good French wines, read Dryden, studied international politics rather more assiduously than his pronouncements on the French might indicate. The lecherous buffoon was endlessly patient with his lunatic wife, and kind and considerate to less fortunate family members. In 1665, for instance, Doll Leeke fell sick with breast cancer, and Mun immediately invited her to stay with him and his wife at East Claydon. Always grateful for acts of kindness from her wealthier kin, and for the most part dependent on their generosity, she took him up on the offer and appointed herself Mary's companion. That winter her condition worsened and she moved in with her niece, Lady Smith, one of Anne Hobart's daughters. Mun rode over to the Smiths' house at Radcliffe again and again to see her until her death that February, which she bore with 'magnanimity and truly Christian patience'.[61]

He was also a very proper father to his three children, although his letters are an uncomfortable reminder that sooner or later we turn into our parents. His eldest boy, Ralph, once dared to suggest that he might have a say in his own future. Mun's response might have come straight from the pen of his own father. 'I will not be taught by my cradle how to breed it up; 'tis insolence and impudence in any child to presume so much.'[62]

He paid more attention to the formal schooling of his three children than his own father had. Both young Ralph and his brother Edmund – 'Munsey', as the family called him – were sent to school twelve miles away at Bicester in Oxfordshire. The fees were £16 a year. Neither boy was a particularly diligent scholar: Ralph kept asking to come home, and Munsey's behaviour was so bad that Mr Blackwell, the master of the school, wrote to East Claydon to complain that he was 'idly and evilly inclined'.[63] He was also prone to wander around at night when he was supposed to be in bed – and he defaced Blackwell's books.

Ralph, who was a delicate boy, was sent to Winchester College at the age of sixteen. He only lasted a few months: Mun wouldn't let him return after the summer holidays of 1682 because he heard that the headmaster had described him as a blockhead 'before a great deal of company at table openly at London'.[64] Munsey was entered at Trinity College, Oxford, in January 1685. His father was clear about his reasons for sending him to university: 'I hope in God you will take to some honourable profession of your own accord, if not I am resolved you shall be of a mean one, for of some profession, high or low, I will make you.'[65] Mun painstakingly made sure the boy's trunk was filled with new clothes, a new knife and fork and an awesome collection of fruit and sweet stuff – eighteen oranges, six lemons, 316 of brown sugar and one of white, a pound of brown sugar candy and 402 of white sugar candy, four nutmegs and 'one pound of picked raisins, good for a cough'.[66] After all this paternal kindness the young student wasn't quite quick enough in announcing his safe arrival in Oxford, and earned himself a sharp reprimand:

> Child, when I take any journey I always write unto my father by every opportunity a perfect diurnal of my voyage, and what else occurs worthy of remark. I writ to you a letter this day seven-night when I sent you your trunk and box but never had any answer nor account from you since. Which is such a piece of omission in you, to say no worse, that I believe neither Oxford nor Cambridge can parallel. For why I should be thus neglected by my son I cannot imagine. Indeed I look upon it as an ill omen, that you should commit such a gross solecism at your first entrance into the University against your loving father.[67]

Mun and Mary's youngest child was named for her mother, but she was known as Molly by the whole clan. She was sent to school in Chelsea in 1683, when she was eight years old. There is a sweet vignette in the Verney letters of her spending the day at Bartholomew Fair with her father, and then being taken round the tombs of Westminster Abbey (a favourite outing for tourists then, as now), before she was deposited at Mrs Priest's school at Great Chelsea. Based in Gorges House, a spacious and good-looking Jacobean mansion set in its own grounds next door to the Duke of Beaufort's house, this famous boarding school for young ladies was originally founded by a singer, James Hart, and the court violinist Jeffrey Bannister. In November 1680 the *London Gazette* announced that 'Josias Priest, Dancing Master, who kept a Boarding-School of Gentlewomen in Leicester-fields, is removed to the great School-House at Chelsea'. Priest kept on both Hart and Bannister, and his wife Frances was schoolmistress, although she was busy giving birth to so many children that the Priests' could have filled a schoolroom themselves. Between 1665 and 1693 she had nineteen of them – one of whom, two-year-old Susanna, fell into a tub of water and drowned in 1684. 'Such little children should never be left alone,' commented Sir Ralph when he heard.[68]

By the time Molly arrived at the school at the beginning of September 1683, Priest's contacts in the world of the arts meant that it had become one of the more fashionable educational establishments in the country, a lot more fashionable than Mr Blackwell's school in Bicester, anyway. Josias Priest had been a well-known figure on the Restoration stage. He appeared in Dryden's *Sir Martin Mar-All* in 1667, and was named as one of the choreographers of a spectacular musical adaptation of *Macbeth* in 1673; he was friends with the playwright Thomas D'Urfey and the composers John Blow and Henry Purcell. On 17 April 1684 his pupils put on the first public performance of the earliest surviving English opera, Blow's *Venus and Adonis*.* One of Priest's daughters played Adonis; Miss Baker, 'a Dutch young gentlewoman' acted Venus, and a Miss Helsham took the role of Cupid. Molly was probably in the chorus; her Uncle Jack came to see the performance, and paid threepence for a printed copy of the libretto. Five years later Priest and his pupils staged the first known performance of Purcell's *Dido and Aeneas*; D'Urfey wrote the

---

* It had been performed privately for the King the previous year.

epilogue, which was spoken by 'Lady Dorothy Burk', and, again, it is quite possible that Molly Verney took part.*

Music, singing and dancing played a large part in Molly's education. Priest's fees were reasonable − £5 for a year's board and schooling − but there were rather a lot of extras. A bill dated 20 January 1685 shows that, in addition to the fees, Mun was charged 5s. for 'music', and another five for 'singing', plus a shilling to Mr Hart. (This was still much cheaper than individual tuition: six years later, after Molly had left Priest's school, she took private dancing lessons from him at 30s. a month.) When the child also wanted to learn how to japan boxes − then particularly fashionable − her father was told it would cost an extra guinea for lessons and 40s. more for materials. He didn't demur at the cost: 'Though they come from Japan and from never so far, and look of an Indian hue and odour I admire all accomplishments that will render you considerable and lovely in the sight of God and man.'[69] And marriageable, he might have added.

* D'Urfey's 1691 comedy, *Love for Money: or the Boarding School*, is said to be based on Priest's establishment. The sub-plot involves two of the girls running off with their singing master and dancing master: the playwright indignantly denied rumours 'that I lived at a boarding school near London all last summer, and in return of their hospitable civility, write this play ungratefully to expose 'em' [Preface].

21

Good Husbandry

*I*n the autumn of 1673 Jack Verney decided it was time to return home. He was nearly thirty-three; he hadn't seen his family for eleven years; and making a living in the Levant was not getting any easier. His partner John Sheppard was now in business with Sir Thomas Bludworth's son as well as with Jack, and the suspicion was that Sheppard was concentrating his money and effort on his new venture at the expense of his trading with Jack. In any case, trade had been quite slow in the late 1660s and that meant London merchants, Gabriel Roberts included, were tempted to cover short-term losses by taking on more apprentices at £300–400 a time. Every summer now the Company's general ships disgorged a fresh batch of pasty-faced young factors at Scanderoon. If it was mannerly to mind these ambitious and enthusiastic youngsters until they found their feet, it was prudent to watch them carefully once they had.

All these things slowly convinced Jack that his future lay in England rather than Aleppo. He had managed to accumulate a tidy sum of money over the years – £6000 according to his own account, although Mun reckoned he was worth a great deal

more – and he was confident he could put this and his considerable knowledge of the Levant business to good use by going
into trade on his own account on the London markets.

There was no great hurry, though. He sailed from Scanderoon
around the end of 1673, and instead of making the entire voyage
in one of the Company's ships, he disembarked at Leghorn and
travelled overland along the coast, via Genoa, Toulon and
Marseilles, before heading north to Lyons. Wherever he went, he
carefully noted down the best places to stay – 'at Marseilles the
best inn is Monsieur Fagot's at the Blackamoor's Head (now
commonly called L'Hostel de Malta)' – and also those which
offered the best value. At Lyons, for example, he acknowledged
that the French Crown, where Germans usually stayed, was a
good inn; but the Three Kings was better value for money. 'Your
diet at the former is near a crown a day, but if you go to the
Three Kings agree with the landlady beforehand and 'twill not
cost you above 45 sols a day.'[1]

Jack also took time to do some sightseeing, embarking on a
French version of the Grand Tour he had missed out on twenty
years earlier, when his father took Mun to Italy and left him
behind at Blois. He visited the ancient crypt beneath the Provençal
church of St Maximin to see the bones of St Mary Magdalene,
and clambered up the 'vast and terrible rock' outside Sainte-Baume
to enter the cave where she was said to have spent the last thirty
years of her life: it was now a chapel, 'with some few rooms clacht
up against the face of a rock, like a bird cage upon the side of a
wall'.[2] In Marseilles he toured the new hôtel de ville and the
celebrated royal arsenal (although the main attraction for him was
'the pretty, clear-skinned airy women'[3]). At Lyons, he was introduced to the virtuoso Nicolas Grollier de Servière, whose closet
of rarities was famous all over Europe. Monsieur Servière, who
was nearly eighty when Jack met him, showed visitors round in
the wheelchair he had invented for himself – a considerable novelty
at the time – and delighted in explaining his mechanical and
mathematical curiosities. They included a perpetual motion
machine, an engine 'for casting bombs to a great certainty', clocks
and dials of all kinds, and a curious revolving reading wheel fitted
with shelves, on each of which lay an open book. One of the
most intriguing items in his collection was a little desk-top device

where, 'let any person touch a little ball that is put on a needle (men's passions and affections being writ on the brim of a round board), it immediately turns to that inclination whereto he is most subject'.[4] A trip to de Servière's estate was essential for visitors to Lyons; but in a flattering reciprocal gesture, the distinguished old virtuoso came several times to call on Jack at his lodgings in the town, eager to hear a young merchant's stories of life in the Ottoman Empire.

From Lyons, Jack travelled north to Moulins to visit the magnificent Montmorency tomb designed by François Anguier twenty-five years earlier; then on to Nevers – famous for the production of little glass figures of people and farm animals – and the galleries and gardens of François I's chateau at Fontainebleau, before settling for a while in Paris.

It was an exciting time to be in the French capital, with Louis XIV and Colbert intent on turning it into the cultural centre of Europe. Architecture, as François Blondel told the King, 'will fill your territories with so many magnificent buildings that the whole world will look on in wonder'.[5] And over the past decade or so the whole world had been given plenty of reasons to look on in wonder. François Mansart's domed Val-de-Grâce, one of the most breathtaking churches in the whole kingdom, was younger than Jack; Blondel's own triumphal Porte Saint-Denis, celebrating Louis XIV's victories over the Rhine and the Low Countries, was brand new. Claude Perrault's coolly classical east façade to the Louvre was just about complete; while fourteen miles to the south-west of the city, the Palace of Versailles was still a building site, and the Sun King was eight years off deciding to make it the seat of government.

Jack visited everything – Versailles and the Louvre, Val-de-Grâce and the Porte Saint-Denis. He climbed the steeple of Notre-Dame and looked out over the city; he rode in the Bois de Vincennes, and stood on the battlements of the old fortress of Vincennes where Henry V of England died in 1422. He walked in the Place Royale, ancestor of the piazza at Covent Garden, and gazed on the sick and dying who lay two in a bed in the wards of the great Hôpital de Paris, founded by Louis IX in the thirteenth century.

Jack had grown up in France. There had been a time when it was more familiar to him than his homeland. Even so, you can't help wondering how much of a shock this eager reacquaintance with European culture was to a man who hadn't been further west than Cyprus for the past twelve years. But his first sight of London, which he reached in the early summer of 1674, was more shocking still. Four years after he left England for the Levant – at two o'clock on the morning of Sunday 2 September 1666, to be precise – a fire broke out in a baker's shop in Pudding Lane, in the south-east corner of the City and a few hundred yards from the Tower of London. Fanned by gale-force winds and fuelled by the authorities' inability to organise themselves, the flames raged out of control for days, destroying more than 80 per cent of the capital. Virtually every one of the landmarks Jack had known as a young apprentice were lost: St Paul's Cathedral and the Guildhall; the Custom House by London Bridge, the Excise Office on Bartholomew Lane, the warehouses that lined the Thames; forty-four company halls, eighty-six churches and well over 13,000 houses. The Royal Exchange on Cornhill, where the entire merchant community gathered to do business and where Jack had first learned his trade, was completely destroyed.

His family and friends had got off quite lightly. Sir Ralph and Mun were both safe in Buckinghamshire when the fire broke out, and the house and premises of his master, Gabriel Roberts, stood just outside the fire zone. But Lady Hobart had nearly lost her mind as the flames crept closer and closer to her own Chancery Lane house: 'I am almost out of my wits,' she wrote to Sir Ralph. 'I fear I shall lose all I have and must run away . . . O pray for us!'[6] Cary Gardiner and her husband lost valuable investment property; so did the apothecary William Gape, and his father-in-law William Denton, whose wife Kate became so depressed at the loss of houses which had brought her an income of £86 a year that for a while Uncle Doctor was at his wits' end. 'She cries all day long,' he said. 'I shall take what care I can of her, but all in my power cannot make it good to her.'[7]

In the event, the Hobarts' house in Chancery Lane was saved; Kate Denton got over her loss; and by the time Jack arrived in London, a new city was emerging from the ashes of the old. A Custom House designed by Christopher Wren was finished in 1671, at a cost of more than £9000. The Guildhall was usable by then, in spite of the destruction of its massive oak roof, which had glowed for hours after the fire moved on 'as if it had been a palace of gold, or a great building of burnished brass'.[8] And merchants moved into a rebuilt Royal Exchange on 28 September 1669, with shopkeepers following two years later amid general celebrations for the restoration of the city's commercial heart:

> Our merchants which our shops do greatly store,
> From Asia, Africk, and the Indian Shore,
> With pearls and diamonds, and such other ware
> Which in our country are esteemed most rare;
> These do aver, and give it under-hand
> In all their travels, or by sea or land
> From east to west, from north to southern side
> There's not the like, in all the world so wide.[9]

The area around St Paul's was still being cleared; the foundation stone of Wren's magnificent new cathedral wouldn't be laid until the summer of 1675.* Around 3000 houses were either unbuilt or unoccupied. Others were restored and in use, their uniform façades of red brick a dramatic contrast to the jumble of timber-framing and jettied gables familiar to Jack before he left. Only a handful of the City's churches had been rebuilt, and most of those lacked their towers and steeples: the population worshipped in twenty-seven temporary wooden 'tabernacles', simple sheds equipped with communion table and pulpit and put up in church-yards next to the ruins. London was a strange and fragmented landscape.

But it was here, rather than Buckinghamshire, where Jack's future lay. When he first arrived in England he lodged with Gabriel Roberts, who was renting Carpenters' Hall (one of only seven of the Livery Companies' fifty-one halls to survive the fire). Although he soon moved a couple of hundred yards west to Bell Alley off Coleman Street, where he lodged with a wool merchant named William Fitzakerley, the Roberts family remained good friends to him. In November Gabriel's brother William, who had

---

*Foundation *stones*, to be precise. The first was laid by the master mason Thomas Strong, and the second by master carpenter John Longland. The date was 21 June 1675.

obviously put behind him his quarrel about Jack and John Sheppard, helped him to become a freeman of the Vintners' Company. Three weeks later, on 15 December 1674, he was made free of the Levant Company.

Gabriel and William Roberts were currently heavily involved in the Royal African Company, founded in 1672 to export metals, weapons and textiles to West Africa in exchange for slaves for the plantations in America and the West Indies. When Jack came back to England, both men were shareholders and members of the twenty-four-strong Court of Assistants, which met once or twice a week to conduct the Company's business. Gabriel Roberts went on to hold the African Company's two most senior posts, being elected Deputy Governor in 1676 and Sub-Governor in 1678. (The governorship automatically went to the King's brother, James, Duke of York.) Jack followed in the Roberts' footsteps, buying shares in the Company and, in 1679, being elected an Assistant. He was a conscientious attender, devoting every Tuesday and Thursday to business at 'the African House' in Leadenhall Street and often staying there from early in the morning until late at night. Attendance fees for Assistants were £30 a year.

The Royal African thrived. In the three years from the end of 1673 to the end of 1676 its exports were valued at more than £116,000, while its ships delivered 9043 slaves to Jamaica, Barbados and Nevis at an average price of nearly £19 a head. Its fortunes fell in the 1690s, but for those who were there at the beginning, dividends and rising stock prices gave an annual return of about 12 per cent. Jack invested heavily, and by 1679 he owned 700 shares in the Company. But just as important as profit was the way in which his connection enabled him to mix with London's most influential merchants. Fellow-Assistants included MPs for the City, past, present and future Lord Mayors, and an assortment of Directors and Deputy Governors of the East India Company and the Hudson's Bay Company. These men were the masters of Jack's mercantile universe. They ruled London, and financed the Crown.

Jack's trading activities were concentrated on the market he knew best – the Levant, which was picking up in the 1670s. The Levant Company's cloth exports, which had averaged 13,672 cloths a year during the period 1666–71, went up to 20,075 a year in 1672–7, an increase of almost 50 per cent. Jack sent out English broadcloths in return for silks, cottons, spices, even opium. ('Endeavour to learn to know drugs,' was the advice given by one Levant merchant to his apprentice: '. . . there is often a great deal of money got by them.'[10]) Four or five times a year he ventured goods on the long and dangerous journey through the Mediterranean in the Company's general ships to Constantinople, Smyrna and Aleppo. He hung around the Exchange and the new Custom House, gathering the latest intelligence. He visited different merchants of his acquaintance to discuss the market. He talked in coffee houses to ship's captains recently returned from the Levant. His world revolved around profit and loss. So did his relationships.

As a younger son with money of his own, Jack had much more freedom than Mun in choosing a wife. That's not to say he could manage without his father's blessing, and he told Sir Ralph straight out that he would never marry without it. His need for parental approval was as powerful now as it had been the day he left for Aleppo, and it says a lot about their relationship that, although Jack was thirty-three years old and a rising man of business, his father invariably addressed him in letters not as 'John' or 'Dear Jack', but simply as 'Child' – a form he still used twenty years later, when the 'child' was fifty-three with children of his own. In contrast, Sir Ralph always addressed Mun by name.

Jack began to look around for a wife within weeks of his return to England, reasoning that 'at a man's first coming from Turkey . . . estates are least known and rumours run high'.[11] By August 1674 he was in negotiations with a draper named Edwards, who lived in Basinghall Street with his nineteen-year-old daughter. She was no beauty, but she was 'a sober, discreet and godly young woman';[12] her widowed father had a fortune of between £10,000 and £15,000 and a specialised knowledge of the cloth trade which would, Jack thought, 'be of good advantage to me in his advice and skill when I buy that commodity'.[13]

Gabriel Roberts acted as intermediary. He arranged that he and Jack should 'accidentally' bump into Edwards and his daughter while all four were promenading in the fashionable Drapers Gardens, next door to Carpenters' Hall. Jack noticed that even though Edwards had promised that the girl should know nothing of Jack's interest, she wore a new gown for the occasion; but apart from that her dress was plain and unadorned, which he noted with approval: 'In Turkey we say, if you want a horse buy a lean one, and then you'll see what fatness (that creature's ornament) would have hid from you.'[14] He decided that while her looks were unlikely 'to prefer her to the title of a Duchess' – a reference to Charles II's mistress Louise de Keroualle, who had been created Duchess of Portsmouth twelve months earlier – Miss Edwards would do, so long as her father could come up with a big enough dowry.*

Hardly the language of love. Jack pursued his suit in a desultory fashion, going to visit Miss Edwards in Basinghall Street a couple of times over the next two weeks and bargaining hard with her father over the marriage settlement, while simultaneously scouting around for a better match. In the end Edwards' offer of £2000 now, an annuity of £100 after his death (he was over sixty) and another £100 on the birth of each child, was rejected. And so was the sober, discreet and godly Miss Edwards.

The episode convinced Jack that there was no rush to find a partner; no need to breed, as there had been for his brother. Many merchants delayed marriage until they were in their forties; some remained bachelors all their lives. For the time being, he could devote his energies to establishing himself in trade, enjoying himself as the mood took him with whores and servant maids.

For the next five years he did just that, taking a polite but detached interest whenever one of the aunts came up with a bride for him, fathering at least one bastard child, spending most of his time in building up his business. In the late summer of 1679, his father wrote from Buckinghamshire to tell him about fifteen-year-old Elizabeth Palmer, who was visiting relations in the neighbouring village of Steeple Claydon. She was an attractive girl – tall and straight with an oval face, full lips and an open, faintly amused look about her. She danced well; she played organ, guitar and harpsichord; and she had a well-connected father, another Ralph, who owned a house in Little Chelsea, and had property in Leicestershire and Hertfordshire and a respectable fortune.

---

* Years later Jack's verdict on the bride of an acquaintance was 'not a beauty but her portion is one thousand pounds' (7 July 1686, M636/41). At least he was consistent.

Elizabeth didn't have quite the same pedigree as the Verneys – one of Jack's aunts rather spitefully said that her mother had once been 'a pitiful chambermaid' to another of the aunts[15] – but she had at least one famous forebear, her great-uncle Baldwin Hamey, a distinguished and childless physician who had died in 1676 leaving her a portion which was rumoured to be in the region of £6000. (It was actually £1000.) Sir Ralph Verney urged her merits, saying she was 'handsome enough for a wife . . . [and] of a jolly good humour',[16] and Jack agreed to ride over to Little Chelsea one Sunday and sneak a look at her in church.

Little Chelsea in the 1670s was a small but well-to-do village straddling the parish boundary between Great Chelsea and Kensington. It was still surrounded by open fields and considered by those who lived in the more cosmopolitan western suburbs to be rather isolated. But there were some substantial houses, including Ralph Palmer's own eighteen-room mansion, which he had bought for £350 in 1671. The hamlet had no church of its own, and the family worshipped in St Luke's, Chelsea, where Palmer and his uncle Hamey were distinguished benefactors, and where Hamey's friend, the theologian and philologist Adam Littleton, was vicar.

Littleton's sermons, in which he railed against both popery and 'the foolish and outrageous zeal and odd practices of our fanatic brethren', were famous.[17] But Jack hadn't come to St Luke's to be lectured about the virtues of Anglicanism and the *via media*. He was there to judge for himself whether a match was worth pursuing.

And the moment he saw Elizabeth, this calculating, cynical middle-aged merchant fell head over heels in love. His aunts could snipe at the girl's background; her own relatives might shake their heads in disapproval at the twenty-five-year age gap. He didn't care. None of that mattered. Within weeks he had secured a formal introduction and opened negotiations with her father. He took Elizabeth to the theatre, and visited her at home, where he scratched a message in her window with his ring, 'I live and love EP'. He told her that 'no man breathing can have more love for you than myself'.[18] He begged a lock of her hair.

The only thing he didn't do was to allow his passion to blind him to the financial niceties of the marriage settlement. Ralph Palmer was a hard negotiator, but so was Jack. The bargaining took nearly eight months, with each side playing an increasingly

perilous game of brinkmanship. At one stage, Palmer barred Jack
from seeing Elizabeth, and he had to send Gabriel Roberts down
to Little Chelsea to mediate for him. At another, just when everything seemed settled and all the wedding clothes were bought,
Palmer surprised Jack with a demand for a £4000 bond as surety
for Elizabeth's jointure, half of which was to be payable even if
the marriage didn't take place. Without that bond, the whole
business was at an end, he said.

Jack held his nerve. He told Palmer he would have to talk to
the Verney family lawyers. If they consented to it, fine. If not, 'I
would never do it, let there be what end he pleased.'[19] The two
men had words, but in the end it was Palmer who backed down.

The final settlement was complicated and finely balanced. Jack
wanted a dowry of £4000; Palmer negotiated him down to
£3000. Land at Wasing in Berkshire which Jack's mother had left
him formed part of his contribution to the marriage; but if he
died without male heirs, it would revert to the Verneys. If Elizabeth
was widowed, she would receive £2000 from Jack's estate *and*
one-third of his business and personal wealth, in accordance with
the custom of London. If there were no sons, any daughters of
the marriage were offered a cash sum – £3000 if there was only
one, and £4000 split between them if there were more. But the
daughters could turn down the cash in favour of a third share
in their father's business wealth.

Throughout the lengthy negotiations, necessarily carried out
through agents and lawyers, Jack turned to his father for advice.
Sir Ralph helped when he could, but on matters of form he
referred him back to Gabriel Roberts – Sir Gabriel, as he now
was, having been knighted in January 1678. Jack should follow
Sir Gabriel's advice on how much to pay the lawyers, and whether
or not to abate the bill for engrossing which the lawyer's clerk
would put in, and what wedding presents to buy for his prospective parents-in-law. Sir Ralph was growing old and uncertain;
but he was also conscious that the cosmopolitan commercial
circles in which his son moved were not his own. They did things
differently there.

Jack confirmed that difference unwittingly in the weeks leading
up to his marriage. In the middle of April 1680 Sir Ralph wrote
to warn him that Lady Hobart and her daughter were upset

because Jack hadn't taken them down to Little Chelsea to meet the Palmers. 'Expect a storm about it, and appease it if you can,' he told his son, 'for 'tis not good to dispute with any lady, especially relations.'[20] Lady Hobart, now a widow, had moved with her two unmarried daughters from the Chancery Lane house she had shared with her husband Nat to a place 'next door to the black balcony in Holborn Row, in Lincoln's Inn Fields'.[21] And Sir Ralph had moved with her, in the sense that he still lodged with her whenever he came to London. He was anxious that she shouldn't be vexed.

It soon became clear that the trouble went deeper than a forgotten invitation. The Hobart women were angry because Jack hadn't confided in them about his courtship, and they were still angry when Jack went over to Holborn Row to make peace a couple of weeks later. Egged on by either Frank or Nan Hobart – Jack was careful not to say which daughter in his letters to his father, describing her only as 'a prouder implacable spirit, who hath so much breeding as to be civil, but not so much good nature as to be really kind and affectionate'[22] – Lady Anne told him off for not showing her more respect. Her sense of being slighted was exacerbated by the fact that while she had been kept in the dark about the match, William Denton's daughter Nancy knew all about it. She had been down to Little Chelsea a few days earlier to look over the bride-to-be, and was busy telling the rest of the clan what a nice girl Elizabeth was: 'I do verily believe she will make a very good wife and a very good daughter-in-law.'[23] She thus managed, deftly and charmingly, to advertise her intimacy with Jack and to infuriate older women like Lady Hobart who weren't party to the business.

The knives were out. Jack told his father that, although Nancy was impressed with what she saw, 'another person was pleased to tell me that Mrs E. P. had ferret eyes (which I think she hath not) and that her face was [so] full of pimples (to use her own expression) that there were a thousand in it'.[24] He was hurt and slightly bemused, having never, he said indignantly, seen more than three spots at a time on the face of his beloved.

Lady Hobart was still cross with Jack at the beginning of May, by which time Aunt Pen was complaining to Sir Ralph that the couple hadn't been to visit her yet. This was another mistake: Pen was now the wife of a wealthy Irish knight, Sir John Osborne, with an apartment in the Palace of Whitehall, a coach of her own and a place on the fringes of court society. These connections alone meant she should not be neglected.

Although it was fashionable to marry quietly, Jack did himself no favours by agreeing with Ralph Palmer that the wedding should be a very private affair. Wearing their old clothes and attended by only the bride's parents, her brother and her aunt, the couple were married in Henry VII's Chapel at Westminster Abbey on the morning of 27 May. The wedding was conducted by Dr Littleton, who, as well as being vicar of St Luke's, Chelsea, was also a prebend at the Abbey; and afterwards the party took off to the Rummer Tavern in the City, where they dined on chicken, goose, rabbit, fish, artichokes and a dish of peas, with strawberries and cherries to finish.

Within days, Jack had managed to upset yet another of the Verney matrons. After leaving the Rummer, he and Elizabeth killed time until all the Palmers' Little Chelsea neighbours were safe indoors for the night by calling in to see Aunt Gardiner, who was now living in London with her husband and children. They didn't say a word to her about their marriage, having decided to enjoy each other's company for a few days and then publicise the match when they appeared together at St Luke's, Chelsea, the following Sunday. That kind of modesty was perfectly acceptable, and when the news broke Aunt Gardiner and her daughters joined the swarm of Verney kin who drove over to Little Chelsea to pay their respects to the newly-weds. But Jack and Elizabeth were required to reciprocate these visits in strict order of precedence.

They didn't. One week after the wedding Aunt Gardiner called on Cousin Nancy and discovered her entertaining Jack and Elizabeth, even though they had not yet paid *her* a formal visit as a married couple. Her nephew's failure to observe the proprieties annoyed her; but just three days later Elizabeth was at Nancy's house again, left there while Jack did business in the City. News of this second slight made Aunt Gardiner crosser than ever, and threatened to cause a rift in the Verney clan. From Claydon, Sir Ralph remonstrated with his son and urged him to 'use all the art you can to make up this unhappy breach' with his aunt.[25] Jack should have left his bride with her rather than

Nancy, 'for both her relation and quality required you should go first to her'.[26]

For his part, Jack couldn't see what all the fuss was about. Nevertheless, rather than disobey his father, he agreed after some coaxing to take Elizabeth on a series of formal visits to Aunt Gardiner and other elderly relatives. None of them was at home, but that wasn't the point.

Jealousy played a big part in both these episodes. Nancy was married to George Nicholas, whose father had been Secretary of State to both Charles I and Charles II, and who had left him a quarter-share in the Surveyor-Generalship of Customs. The Nicholases and their three children lived in Covent Garden with Nancy's widowed father William Denton, now retired from medical practice and devoting his time to writing anti-Catholic tracts.[*] George's involvement with the Custom House made him useful to Jack, but it was Nancy who was Jack's real friend. A few months younger than him, she was funny, vivacious and hospitable. She was also a great favourite with Sir Ralph. He was her godfather (and godfather to her daughter). She called him 'Dear Parent', and styled herself in her letters 'your dutiful child and best girl'. In return, he sent her down compliments, avuncular advice and a regular supply of treats from Claydon: snipe, lark and so much venison – the ultimate mark of favour – that one of the Hobart women was led to remark rather bitchily that 'she eats it as others eat beef: three times a week, baked, boiled, roasted and potted'.[27]

The older women in the clan didn't like Nancy. (In another argument shortly after the wedding, Aunt Gardiner described her as a 'whore'.) They saw her as a competitor, a rival, a threat to their relationship with Jack and Sir Ralph; they were unhappy with the way she brushed aside their conventional notions of respect

---

[*] He was currently working on *Jus Caesaris et ecclesiae vere dictae or, A treatise wherein independency, presbytery, the power of kings, and of the church, or of the brethren in ecclesiastical concerns, government and discipline of the church: and wherein also the use of liturgies, tolleration, connivence, conventicles or private assemblies, excommunication, election of popes, bishops, priests what and whom are meant by the term church, 18 Matthew are discoursed : and how I Cor. 14. 32. generally misunderstand is rightly expounded : wherein also the popes power over princes, and the liberty of the press, are discoursed.* The title says it all, really.

and precedence and propriety. She seemed pushy and impolite. But Jack was just as impatient with the old ways as she was, and this impatience was at the heart of his skirmishes with Lady Hobart and Aunt Gardiner. Like Cousin Nancy, he was reluctant to conform to a set of social norms which were outmoded and cumbersome. The hard-headed Levant merchant simply didn't understand why he and his bride shouldn't spend their time with whomever they pleased, and the rows made him very sensitive about his wife's reception in the family. When Elizabeth went off without him to Buckinghamshire in September 1681 to visit with Dentons, Smiths and Temples, he wrote, not altogether joking, to say 'I hope you were made much of at Hillesden, Radcliffe and Stow, otherwise the ladies there lose their reputation with me.'²⁸ And years later he was still careful to inform his father whenever Elizabeth visited with Aunt Gardiner. The old kinship networks which were so vital to Jack's father's generation mattered less than commercial contacts and amusing friends; and if pressure from the aunts and Sir Ralph's displeasure forced him to pay lip service to those networks, that was all it was – lip service. Times were changing.

For the first year of their marriage Jack and Elizabeth lived with the Palmers. But Little Chelsea was five miles west of the City, and Jack soon grew tired of the cold and cumbersome commute, which involved him in a walk along muddy lanes into Great Chelsea and then a slow boat trip along the Thames. Once there, it was often easier to spend the night in town – not a particularly satisfactory situation for an enthusiastic new bridegroom – and by the autumn of 1680 he was looking to lease somewhere in the City where he and Elizabeth could set up their own home. He was prepared to lay out around £50 a year, but for that he also wanted warehouse space for his cloths and other goods.

There was no shortage of spare accommodation in London: the rebuilding programme which began after the Great Fire had been almost too successful, and several thousand properties were still unlet. Jack looked first at a new house in Basinghall Street, just behind the Guildhall and only a couple of streets away from Sir Gabriel Roberts' lodging at Carpenters' Hall. It was a typical town house, with a narrow street frontage and a ground floor consisting of business premises at the front and a parlour behind, a large dining chamber filling the first floor and two bedchambers on the second. The lease was £40 a year.

Sir Ralph recommended a similar house in the north-east corner of the City, which was available at £50 a year with gardens and coach-house. The problem was that although a home in the City was convenient for Jack's business – both of these houses were within easy walking distance of the Exchange and the Custom House, the Levant Company's premises at Ironmongers' Hall and the Royal African Company's meetings in Leadenhall Street – it would place the couple a long way from the cluster of Verney relations and connections in the western suburbs, and even further from the Palmers in Little Chelsea. And notwithstanding Jack's impatience with his aunts, proximity to kin was important. Sixteen-year-old Elizabeth was expecting their first child: she would naturally rely on the support network provided by her family, and the Verneys provided a support network of sorts for Jack himself. Sir Ralph and Mun both came up to town for weeks, even months, at a time, usually lodging at Lady Hobart's house in Holborn Row on the north side of Lincoln's Inn Fields (although Mun spent rather more time lodging with his mistress Betty Phelps). Uncle Doctor and George and Nancy Nicholas lived in Covent Garden; so did Jack's cousin Alexander Denton, the current squire of Hillesden, and his wife Hester, and another Buckinghamshire kinsman and neighbour, Sir Richard Temple of Stowe. Aunt Gardiner and the Stewkeleys were close by, Aunt Osborne a little further away in her lodgings at Whitehall, although she too had a house in Covent Garden.

Jack wanted to be close to his family, but not too close. He wanted to be in reach of the Palmers, but he had had enough of living with them. His solution was to lease a house halfway between the City and his 'Piazza' kin. In the spring of 1681 he and Elizabeth moved into a house 'at the first wooden balcony on the left hand near Holborn in Hatton Garden'.[29]

Like most of the housing schemes in the western suburbs, Hatton Garden was a fairly recent development. In 1576 Elizabeth I's Lord Chancellor, Sir Christopher Hatton, put up a mansion in the orchard of the Bishop of Ely's medieval palace (much to the irritation of the Bishop, whose successors were still trying to reclaim the property ninety years later). But the Hattons fell on hard times, and in 1659 Hatton House was dismantled, its bowling green and privy gardens were swept away and foundations were laid for speculative housing. Hatton Street, as it was then known (the neighbourhood was Hatton Garden), was initially laid out under the guidance of the surveyor Edward Woodroffe, who after the Great Fire would collaborate with Sir Christopher Wren on the rebuilding of St Paul's Cathedral and several of the City churches. Running north from Holborn to Hatton Wall, by 1664 it was already lined with more than fifty properties; when the development was completed thirty years later, there were 282 good-sized houses, along with another ninety more modest dwellings in the yards and courts behind them.

Jack and Elizabeth rented their new home, which stood at the south end of Hatton Street, from a lime dealer and property developer named Benjamin Cole, who was also building four more houses at the northern end. In what had become the normal pattern for the seventeenth century, the Hatton family offered sites to speculative developers like Cole, who usually took leases of forty-two years or fifty-one years and paid an annual ground rent based on the site's position and the amount of street frontage. The plots on Hatton Street itself went for 4s. a foot; those in the less prestigious cross-streets could be had for 3s. Most of the early lessees built houses at their own expense and then, like Cole, sublet. Rents could be more than £50 a year – Jack and Elizabeth paid £53 5s., later reduced to £45 – and that made Hatton Garden a good investment for developers. Since the standard width of the houses on Hatton Street was 22 feet, and a decent house could be built for around £500, a speculator could cover his costs and move into profit within eleven or twelve years. Quite a few of the 110 speculators who leased plots were directly involved in the building trades – bricklayers, carpenters, masons and the like – and no doubt their contacts helped them to keep costs down.

The neighbourhood was fairly well-to-do. It was popular with merchants, including Sir Arthur Ingram, a fellow-Assistant at the Royal African Company, and Sir Benjamin Bathurst, Governor of the East India Company and also an Assistant at the Royal African. At one time or another Jack and Elizabeth were neighbours with the Bishop of Norwich and the Countess of Drogheda; the anti-Catholic lawyer Sir George Treby, who had led the

Parliamentary Committee which investigated the Popish Plot; and Dr George Bate, the royal physician who had tried to treat Mary Abell during her first serious bouts of madness in the early 1660s. The neighbourhood also had its own eminent quack, George Jones, who sold his famous Friendly Pills every Monday, Tuesday and Wednesday out of his corner house 'three doors from the sign of the New Hole in the Wall, over against Baldwins Gardens, near the George'.*

The street even had its own notorious crime: one Sunday evening at the end of December 1678 twenty men burst into a gentleman's house and locked up his family at pistol-point before ransacking the place and stealing nearly 400oz of plate and between £15 and £20 in ready money. Five were subsequently arrested for the 'Great Robbery in Hatton-Garden', along with a woman who had tried to sell the plate to a broker; all six were convicted and hanged at Tyburn three weeks later.†

Mun, who took an older brother's delight in finding fault with everything Jack did, pronounced the house too small. Built of brick, like all the other Hatton Garden houses (this was one of the covenants which the Hatton estate placed on new building) it was three storeys high plus attics, with a wide oak staircase, casement windows, a carved wooden entrance-doorway and two rooms on each of the main floors. Jack's warehouse occupied one of the ground-floor rooms; the other was a wainscoted parlour.

---

* Jones claimed that his Friendly Pills 'are the true tincture of the sun, and have dominion from the same light; for as the sun at its appearance giveth nourishment to all creatures, so do my Friendly Pills give present relief, comfort and nourishment to all mankind. They cause all complexions to laugh or smile in the very time of taking them, especially sanguine. They work seven several ways in order; first, by sleep. Secondly, by little breathing-sweat. Thirdly, wind downwards. Fourthly, by stool. Fifthly, by urine. Sixthly, by cheering the spirits. Seventhly, by strengthening the whole body in the very time of taking' (*George Jones of London, student in the art of physick and chyrurgery for about thirty years*, 1675, 1).

† On the gallows one of the convicted men confessed that 'the first eminent sin which I can remember was the breach of the Sabbath. Then I proceeded to keep company, where I learned to curse and swear, and profane God's holy name; lying and adultery, drunkenness, and disobedience to my mother' (*The Behaviour, Confession and Execution of the Twelve Prisoners that Suffered on the 22 January 1678/9*, 1679, 5). Let that be a lesson to us all.

There was a dining room, a withdrawing room and the couple's bedchamber above. Then they had to fit in a nursery: their first child, named for its mother, was born in 1681. Three more babies were born in quick succession: Mary in 1682, Ralph in 1683 and Margaret in 1685. Room also had to be found for the servants: the Verneys' establishment included a footboy, a manservant, a nurse, a cook-maid and a liveried coachman. When Jack tentatively suggested to the cook-maid that she might sleep in a passageway between the two attic rooms, she refused to countenance the idea.

But if there wasn't much space, the rooms were well appointed. The drawing-room walls were hung with tapestries chosen by Sir Gabriel Roberts, and the hearth was set with fashionable Dutch tiles. The parlour had gilt-leather hangings. There were pictures by Sir Godfrey Kneller of Jack and Elizabeth, and Sir Ralph sent portraits of himself and his father Sir Edmund.

'London is a place that affords many fine things,' Sir Ralph warned his son; 'but they are not to be had without money.'[30] Jack was always careful with his money – Aleppo had taught him that – and there were times when even his thrift-conscious father despaired of him. 'You will never be the richer for this kind of good husbandry,' an exasperated Sir Ralph once told Jack after he travelled on horseback all the way from London to Wasing in Berkshire – some fifty-odd miles – because he refused to pay out twopence a day for a post chaise. 'I had rather paid double, nay treble that money, than not have had a chariot.'[31]

That's not to say Jack and Elizabeth lived like paupers. The couple kept their own coach, a particularly expensive status symbol in an urban setting where it was much easier to get around on foot, or by barge or sedan. When the farrier's charges, the coachman's wages and the livery were added together, the coach cost him £80 a year. Food, wine, beer and coal came to £3 a week, or £156 for the year. In 1683 Elizabeth's personal expenses were £55; Jack's were £45. A nurse cost £20, Elizabeth's lying-in when she was expecting their second child another £20, and clothes for the two children another £20. The rent was £53 5s. and the water company's charges £3 5s. Along with some other bits and pieces, household expenses added up to £480. That was a good bit less than the £800-plus laid out each year by another

London-based Levant trader, Dudley North, but it was still ten times the income of a family of the middling sort.

The couple enjoyed London life to the full, going to plays, entertaining and being entertained by Nancy and George Nicholas, the Palmers, the Piazza folk. They went to watch the King and his court at Whitehall, and attended civic ceremonies in the City. They visited fashionable watering places like Epsom and Bath, and wore fashionable clothes: a flowered muslin cravat and a black velvet coat for Jack, white gauze and black silk for Elizabeth. They promenaded with the ton along Tunbridge Wells's leafy Upper Walk, 'where pleasures of the town and country meet'.[32]

And they enjoyed each other with a passion. 'I long to see thee,' wrote Elizabeth, eighteen and pregnant with her third child, when Jack was away in Buckinghamshire; 'I would not live this life always without you for all the world.'[33] He returned her 'every-thing that the lovingest of husbands can express to the best of wives, and love to the little ones, not forgetting the kicker in the dark'.[34] She called him 'Dearest Joy', and when they were apart declared that 'all pleasure to me I find is nothing without you'.[35] He wrote to her as his 'Dear Heart' and 'Dearest Dear', told her how he could spend all day reading her letters, and longed to substitute the ten thousand kisses she sent him in one letter with half a dozen real ones: 'but for this vacancy we'll have the more when I return to you'.[36] Well off, attractive, socially confident and deeply in love, the couple had everything.

Except time. Elizabeth died suddenly on 20 May 1686, one week short of her sixth wedding anniversary. Jack was left to bury the twenty-one-year-old love of his life in the chancel at Claydon church, and to bring up their four children as best he could. The eldest was five, the youngest less than a year old.

'Our life is but a vapour,' says Jeremy Taylor in *The Rule and Exercises of Holy Dying*, one of the books which Jack took with him when he set out to the Levant. It is 'phantastical, or a mere appearance; and this but for a little while neither; the very dream, the phantasm disappears in a small time, like the shadow that departeth, or like a tale that is told, or as a dream when one waketh . . . Perfumes make our heads ache; roses prick our fingers.'[37]

22

Without Escutcheons

*O*n 22 May 1685, Sir Ralph Verney watched a new King address both Houses of Parliament. Seated on his throne in the Lords and 'adorn'd with the Royal Ornaments' James II, the first Roman Catholic monarch of England for sixty years, reassured his subjects that 'I fully declare my opinion concerning the principles of the Church of England, whose members have shewed themselves so eminently loyal in the worst of times, in defence of my father, and support of my brother, of blessed memory; that I will always take care to defend and support it.'[1] Then he asked them for money.

One might have thought Sir Ralph's experiences with the Long Parliament and the Solemn League and Covenant would put him off politics for life; and indeed, after a failed attempt to be elected to the Convention Parliament of April 1660, he had turned his back on the Commons for more than twenty years. He didn't like the expense of a contested election; he didn't like the corruption and bribery involved; and he didn't like losing.

He was returned as one of Buckingham's two Members in Charles II's eight-day Oxford Parliament of March 1681 (his neighbour, Sir Richard Temple of Stowe, was the other), although his decision to stand for the borough had more to do with keeping out an unsuitable rival candidate, the libertine and free-thinker Charles Blount. When Charles II died suddenly on 6 February 1685 and the new King, James II, summoned a new parliament for 'the settling of my revenue, and continuing it, during my life, as it was in the life-time of my brother',[2] Temple urged the seventy-two-year-old Sir Ralph to stand again for Buckingham.

Sir Ralph hesitated, weighing his anti-papist leanings and his strong sense of civic duty against his reluctance to do anything which caused him any inconvenience; and for a while it seemed as if inertia would win out. James's conversion to Catholicism had been public knowledge since 1676 (and it had almost certainly taken place some years before that); but in spite of the new King's religion Sir Ralph was prepared to give him the benefit of the doubt; he was not one of those who automatically opposed him on religious grounds.

In any case, he wasn't at all sure that he would be able to secure a majority this time round. In 1681 the mayor of Buckingham had been a friend of the Verneys, Nathaniel Kent; now it was a mercer named Hugh Ethersey, who was known to dislike Sir Ralph and his politics. Since the electorate of Buckingham comprised just the mayor and twelve aldermen, Ethersey's opinion mattered quite a lot. Moreover, the Verneys weren't popular in the town: some of the townspeople still harboured a grudge against Sir Ralph's father for lowering its status by having the assize moved to Wycombe half a century before, while Sir Ralph's own high-minded refusal to distribute money and ale at past elections had done nothing to endear him to traders or drinkers.

But while he hummed and ha'd, word reached Claydon that Sir Richard Temple had asked his godson, Alexander Denton of Hillesden, to stand in his place. Out of loyalty to his Verney kin Denton refused, but Temple's behaviour so incensed Sir Ralph that he decided he would stand after all. He also agreed to be a little more accommodating in his electioneering. He was, he said, 'content to entertain the mayor and aldermen before the elec-tion in a reasonable manner, to join Sir Richard [Temple] in giving £10 or £20 apiece to the poor, to pay all charges on the day and, after it, to treat the mayor and aldermen and their wives at a dinner'. But he was not prepared to treat the mob 'at all the alehouses in the parish and to make them drunk, perhaps a month beforehand, as is usual in too many places upon such occasions. I shall not join in that expense. I had rather sit still than gain a place in Parliament by so much debauchery.'*

The election was a fight between James II's court faction and the anti-Catholic, independently minded landed gentry who made up the majority of the country party – between Whigs and Tories, as the two factions were becoming known.† Sir Ralph was for the country, but in a moderate sort of way. Temple's position was less clear: he had switched sides several times since the Restoration, and in the late 1670s was clearly in sympathy with the court party – in fact in 1679 he had been publicly accused of being a Roman Catholic. The truth was, he was a trimmer. None of the Verneys trusted him, or even liked him very much; but he was kin, and he was a powerful figure in Buckinghamshire affairs.

He was also skilled in the murkier waters of seventeenth-century political campaigning. Before an election could take place, a writ had to be delivered to the sheriff or mayor ordering the election of knights, citizens and burgesses to represent county, city or borough in the coming parliament: no writ, no election. When writs were issued at the beginning of March for James II's new parliament, Temple and Mun Verney were in Uxbridge on their way home from London. Temple arranged for the Buckingham writ to be handed over to him, and popped it into his pocket – where it stayed until he judged the moment right

---

* *Memoirs of the Verney Family* (1907), II, 381. Sir Ralph had a serious political concern here, which had nothing to do with his puritanical principles and his parsimonious nature. To court the popular vote was to acknowledge its existence, and hence to legitimise its calls for a more democratic franchise of property owners in the borough. He was not prepared to do that.

† 'The latter party have been called by the former, whigs, fanaticks, covenanteers, bromigham protestants, &c.; and the former are called by the latter, tories, tantivies, Yorkists, high flown church men' (1681 – Narcissus Luttrell, *Brief Relation* (1857) I, 124).

for the election to proceed. It was another seventeen days before he finally handed the paper over to Mun, who passed it on to the mayor. The opposition was outraged. It had obviously slipped their memory that they had tried the same trick at the last election – except that *they* kept the writ for five weeks.

Sir Ralph and Temple were pitted against Viscount Latimer, the eldest son of the Earl of Danby, and Sir John Busby of Addington, sometime colonel of the Buckinghamshire militia and 'a most mighty Tory'.³ Busby was stopping off to entertain Mayor Ethersey every time he passed through Buckingham. Latimer offered £300 towards a new town hall (which is probably the origin of the story that Sir Ralph himself funded the building of the town hall around this time).* Latimer was also happy to pay for dinners for the aldermen, but he was reluctant to come down from London to campaign in person. That gave Sir Ralph an edge. He made the seven-mile journey in from Middle Claydon to show his face on market days, and did his best to be charming whenever he visited Mayor Ethersey or treated the aldermen and their wives to dinner.

The campaign was a family affair. Mun coordinated support for his father among the local gentry. Anyone riding through East Claydon on the road from Aylesbury to Buckingham – anyone who might be useful in the Verney interest, at least – was invited to stop and take a glass of sack. In London, Jack did his best to gather intelligence. At the beginning of April he reported to his father that, while he was with Cousin Nancy Nicholas in Covent Garden, she produced a handwritten newsletter from Buckingham and passed it over to him, having first rather ostentatiously torn off the signature and tossed it into the fire. Jack read that the author of the newsletter claimed that Sir Ralph and Latimer had six votes apiece – with one voice undecided.

The minute Nancy left the room, Jack dived into the fire and grabbed the crumpled signature, which had bounced off a lump of coal and landed on the hearth. It belonged to a man named William Baker, who was married to the mayor's daughter and thus well placed to know about aldermanic voting intentions.

---

* Buckingham Town Hall was rebuilt in the eighteenth century. It had been a pawn in the election game since at least 1661, when Sir Richard earned the nickname 'Timber Temple' for promising to provide wood for its rebuilding.

Temple's victory in the polls was never in doubt, but agents of Latimer and Busby were fighting Sir Ralph for the second seat, and they set about securing that deciding vote any way they could. One of the twelve aldermen, Henry Hayward, was the Verney's barber; he was generally reckoned to be in the Verney camp. So when he was abruptly arrested for debt and put in the Fleet prison, Mun suspected skulduggery. He paid the barber's debts and brought him back to Buckingham, to find he wasn't quite as grateful as everyone had hoped. He preferred, he said, to see exactly what was on offer before he committed himself to either side.

By the end of March Sir Ralph was fed up with the whole business. 'I have no desire to be a Parliament Man,' he confessed to Jack. 'I wish I had stuck to my first resolution of declining it.'[4] And again in the first week of April, 'I wish I had never been concerned in the business, for 'tis not only chargeable, and wonderful troublesome, [but it] forces me to omit those things that are necessary in respect of my health.'[5] A single vote could decide the matter; and as Mun told Jack, 'all means are used to lay my father aside if possible. But I hope we shall prevail.'[6]

The odds against a Verney victory lengthened a week later, when one of Sir Ralph's staunchest supporters among the twelve aldermen was threatened with imprisonment for defaming a public official. The trouble started in the George Inn at Buckingham, when Mayor Ethersey gave the aldermen the news that Lord Latimer would stump up for a new town hall – if they elected him. George Dancer, a tanner who was very definitely in the Verney interest, said he didn't hold with that kind of blatant bribery, and accused Ethersey of putting his desire for a new town hall before his loyalty to the Crown. There was a stand-up row between the two men, with Dancer calling Ethersey a 'shatterbrain' and a 'rascal', and the mayor swearing he would 'throw off his gown or rout him'.[7] What Ethersey did do was to walk out of the inn and denounce Dancer to the Lord Chief Justice's office. He also accused another of Sir Ralph's supporters, the former mayor Nathaniel Kent, of laughing at him behind his back and referring to him and one of his henchman as 'Alderman Ape and Alderman Scrape'.[8]

The mayor's civic dignity was obviously important to him. But there were more sinister political forces behind the denunciation.

By levelling a charge of public defamation against Dancer, Ethersey set in motion a legal leviathan which might culminate in Dancer losing office or worse; in the short term, it meant that the Lord Chief Justice's office would shortly send a tipstaff to Buckingham to arrest the tanner and take him up to London for questioning. As soon as that happened, Ethersey would hold the election. And Sir Ralph, deprived of that 'single voice' on which everything depended, would lose.

Jack was deputed to protest directly to the Lord Chief Justice about the plot, and at the same time to talk with the mayor's brother John, a London attorney, in the hope that he might bring the mayor round. John Ethersey owed Jack a favour – he had recently recommended him for a post with the Grocers' Company – but the interview did not go well. The lawyer was 'a rude, passionate fellow' who disliked Sir Ralph as much as his brother. He told Jack to his face that his father had 'never spent twenty shillings in Buckingham in twenty years', and that he had called the town of Buckingham 'a nest of bastards and beggars'.[9]

The Chief Justice was not likely to be sympathetic to Sir Ralph's cause, either. He was Judge Jeffreys, who within a matter of days would be raised to the peerage for his efforts in securing a majority in Parliament for the King's cause.* As far as Sir Ralph was concerned, Mayor Ethersey was already wholly governed by the Lord Chief Justice; but the hope was that by making the Dancer affair public before it went too far, they could shame Ethersey and his friends into giving up their plan to have their fellow-alderman arrested.

Jeffreys had an interest in Buckinghamshire, having recently built himself a country house at Temple Bulstrode, about forty miles south of Buckingham. For the moment, his attention was focused on the outcome of the contest for the county, where there were three candidates for the two seats: Viscount Brackley, a popular moderate with a father who was Lord-Lieutenant of Buckinghamshire; a young man from Newport Pagnell named Thomas Hackett; and Tom Wharton, a longtime thorn in the side of James II. Brackley's position meant he was almost bound to

---

* He was created Baron Jeffreys of Wem on 16 May 1685, and took his seat in the Lords when the new parliament opened three days later.

be returned, and the real contest was between the innocuous Hackett and Wharton, whom Jeffreys was determined to keep out of Parliament at all costs.

Tom Wharton was a colourful character. He was one of the party which tried throughout the early 1680s to have James excluded from the succession because of his Catholicism. His passion for horseracing matched Henry Verney's, and he was better at it: at St Germain-en-Laye in 1683 he beat a field consisting of some of the best in Europe, winning a prize of £850 and the admiration of Louis XIV, who sponsored and watched the race. His passion for debauchery matched Mun's, and he was rather better at that, too, although it had almost been his undoing in 1682, when he and his brother had got drunk and vandalised the parish church at Barrington in Gloucestershire. After cutting the bell ropes, breaking the font cover and ripping the church Bible, he had then 'pissed against a communion table [and] done his other occasions in the pulpit'.[10] A public confession and fifty guineas were enough to appease the Bishop of Gloucester, but Wharton's political opponents never let him forget the incident as long as he lived.

Such a reputation for dissolute behaviour was hardly likely to endear him to Sir Ralph as a suitable candidate for Parliament, but the old man was charitable. 'I am confident that he will serve the King and the country faithfully, though he is wild enough in drink and I am troubled at it,' he said when he heard Tom was standing. 'But who lives without great faults?'[11]

The explanation of Sir Ralph's uncharacteristically tolerant attitude was simple enough: Wharton's wife was the heiress Anne Lee, the great-granddaughter of his old friend Eleanor Manchester, *née* Warwick, *née* Sussex, *née* Lee, *née* Wortley. Sir Ralph was Anne's guardian, and he had personally arranged her marriage to Wharton. The couple had dined with him at Claydon. It turned out to be a deeply unhappy relationship, with Anne suffering periodically from seizures and Wharton flaunting his mistress in public, but kin mattered. Faults must be glossed over, friends must be supported, even if it roused the anger of powerful figures like Jeffreys.

Which it did. The county franchise was much harder to manage than the borough, since instead of a baker's dozen of aldermen there were several thousand freeholders to be persuaded, bought

off or intimidated. But the Lord Chief Justice did his best. He
began by telling Ethersey to postpone the Buckingham election,
so that if Thomas Hackett lost in the county he could be thrust
into the borough at the last minute. When the poll opened in
Aylesbury in the second week in April, the Lord Chief Justice
was there in person. As it became clear that too many of Wharton's
supporters had turned up to cast their votes for their man, he
decided to move the whole election to friendlier territory. Sir
Ralph arrived in the town to find he was too late to vote:

> Mr Wharton having many more voices than Mr Hackett, my
> Lord Chief Justice got the Sheriff to adjourn the poll to
> Newport [Pagnell] (which is 15 very long miles from hence)
> in the heart of Mr Hackett's friends, and 'tis thought it will
> be adjourned on Saturday morning from thence to Buckingham
> where Mr Hackett has a good many friends . . . Most are of
> opinion that this adjournment will lose my Lord Brackley 2
> or 300 voices, that cannot go so far. Therefore my Lord Brackley
> is against it, but my Lord Chief Justice like a torrent carries
> all before him. Some say that if Mr Hackett is worsted in these
> parts, then my Lord will get the Sheriffs to adjourn it to
> Beaconsfield, where my Lord Chief Justice has an interest,
> being not far from his house . . .[12]

Sir Ralph couldn't face the prospect of riding those '15 very long
miles' to Newport Pagnell, although plenty of Wharton's friends
did, only to find that the landlords and landladies of every inn
and lodging house in the town claimed they had no room and
barred their doors to them. Fortified by thoughts of Wharton's
deep purse – his marriage to Anne Lee had brought him £8000
in cash and an annual income of £2000 – they camped out that
night in the fields in their hundreds. By the end of the first day's
polling in Newport Pagnell it was obvious that, local or not,
Hackett didn't have a hope of winning; and on Friday 10 April
1685, Wharton and Lord Brackley were returned for the county.

   According to Sir Ralph, the Lord Chief Justice was furious at
the result and 'in his passion fell upon many of the gentry, but
most upon me, though I was not there'.[13] Jeffreys accused him
of being a trimmer and swore to warn Lord Keeper North of

his unreliability in politics. On the following Monday Tom Wharton won the £80 Plate at Brackley races.

There was a temporary halt to campaigning after the Newport Pagnell poll while everyone turned their attention to the coronation of James II at Westminster on St George's Day. 'Many comes from beyond [the] sea to see it, which you may guess the reason of,' muttered Aunt Gardiner darkly.[14] Her own house was full of friends and relatives who had come up to London for the occasion. Both of Mun's boys were staying with her, so that they could see the spectacle of James and Mary of Modena processing on a carpet of blue cloth from Westminster Hall to the Abbey, 'arrayed in their royal robes furred with ermines, the King with a velvet cap, and the Queen a rich circle of gold on her head; all the nobility in robes of crimson velvet with their caps and coronets in their hands, and the rest who formed the proceeding being richly habited'.[15] The day wasn't without its surprises: the crown slipped as it was placed on James's head; and then the King's Champion, Sir Charles Dymoke, rode into Westminster Hall to give the traditional challenge to anyone who disputed James's right to the throne, and threw down his gauntlet with such enthusiasm that he fell off his horse. (The shocked silence that followed was broken by a snort from the Queen, trying to stifle her laughter.) There were a few mutterings at the fact that communion was omitted from the coronation service, but there was no tumult, no capering Jesuits, no bolts of lightning, and at the end James and Mary returned to the Palace of Whitehall 'with all imaginable splendour and expressions of joy'.[16]

James had insisted on having the coronation before Parliament met, believing he was not really King until the Archbishop of Canterbury placed the crown on his head. Now that was done, and Parliament was summoned to meet on 19 May. In Buckingham, Sir Ralph and his supporters were still facing an election. They were confident of a majority, albeit a slender one. 'I believe I shall have seven votes,' Sir Ralph told Jack.[17] 'All imaginable endeavours have been used to get over any one of his seven voices,' said Mun. 'But they are as firm to us as rocks.'[18]

The big problem was that Jeffreys and Mayor Ethersey were still trying to turn out George Dancer and Nathaniel Kent. Jack did the rounds of lawyers, looking for an opinion on the legality of disenfranchising them at such a crucial juncture. Once they realised their advice would be used to thwart the will of such a powerful figure as Jeffreys, however, those lawyers didn't want to know. 'In vain I played with the gold in my fingers,' wrote Jack after an unsuccessful interview with the normally independently minded attorney Henry Pollexfen. 'Reason signifies nothing. He will have nothing to do with such matters.'[19]

Faced with the prospect of losing, Sir Ralph grew more and more grumpy. But in end it was the rather more independently minded aldermen of Buckingham who secured his election. Angry at central government's attempts to interfere in local affairs, they stood shoulder to shoulder and refused to accept the threatened expulsion of two of their colleagues. Sir John Busby, the 'most mighty Tory', didn't stand; nor did the luckless Thomas Hackett. Lord Latimer didn't turn up for the vote, which took place at the town hall on the morning of Friday 15 May, four days before the new parliament was due to meet for the first time. Sir Ralph distributed £25 worth of largesse on the day (and more than twice that in total), and it paid off. 'Sir R.T. and myself were elected at Buckingham without noise or trouble,' he informed Jack that night. The result was as close as could be: 'The whole twelve electors signed the book for Sir R.T. and seven signed for me, after which the mayor sent for us up into the town hall, and declared the election and sealed the indenture or return with the town seal.'[20] No doubt Ethersey did his best to look pleased. But it didn't matter. Sir Ralph rested over the weekend and then set off for London and Parliament. He asked Jack to go round to his landlady in Holborn Row as quickly as possible, 'and give her the key of my chamber, and desire her that her maids may lie in my bed to air it'.[21]

James II's parliament sat until the beginning of July, and then again for nine days that November. Sir Ralph attended regularly, and served on three parliamentary committees: one to discuss a bill for relief of poor prisoners; another which looked at an Act 'to disable minors to marry without the consent of their fathers or guardians';[22] and a third on a bill which sought to allow the parishioners of St Anne's, Soho, to raise funds for the completion of their new church. He set off for Westminster each day from his lodgings in the Holborn Row house (now occupied by a Captain Paulden and his wife Rebecca – Lady Hobart had died some years earlier); and unless the sky was clear and the air mild he made a point of travelling the two miles by coach, worrying meanwhile that the cobbled streets were shaking it to pieces.

While he spent his mornings in the Commons and his afternoons deliberating on clandestine marriage and church fundraising in the Speaker's Chamber, the awful and pointless drama of Monmouth's Rebellion was being played out: first at Lyme Regis, where the young Protestant Duke landed on 11 June 1685 and declared war against James, 'as a murderer, and an assassin of innocent men; a popish usurper of the Crown; a traitor to the nation, and tyrant over the people';[23] then in the ditches and fields of the Somerset Levels, where his ragtag army was routed by the King's forces at the beginning of July; and finally on Tower Hill, on the morning of Wednesday 15 July. The House had adjourned for the summer by then, and Sir Ralph had gone home to Claydon; but Mun, who was lodging in Lincoln's Inn Fields while Uncle Doctor treated him for gout, sent home an account of Monmouth's execution, which he had from one of Aunt Gardiner's former servants:

> On the scaffold there were four divines, the Bishops of Ely, Bath & Wells, Dr. Tenison and Dr. Hooper. [The Duke] said little but answers, and did sometimes turn from them when they asked him several questions, one after another [the divines were trying without success to persuade Monmouth he should go through his sins and repent of them one by one]; but he died very resolutely, neither with affectation nor dejectedness, but with a courageous moderation. The executioner [to whom the Duke had just presented six guineas to do his business well] had five blows at him; after the first he looked up, and after the third he put his legs across, and the hangman flung away his axe, but being chid took it again and gave him 'tother two strokes; and severed not his head from his body till he cut it off with his knife.[24]

Monmouth's rebellion wasn't popular. Bonfires were lit across the country to celebrate his defeat, and even Judge Jeffreys' 'bloody

assizes' that September, at which 200 of the rebels were executed
and another 2000 or so transported to the West Indies, did little
at the time to evoke public sympathy. Most people seem to have
rallied behind the Crown and supported the status quo.

The Verneys were no different. Their attitude towards James as
Duke of York and as King had swung back and forth, along with
the rest of England. In 1679, for example, Mun criticised the
Exclusion Bill, saying that no mortal had the right to disinherit
the God-appointed heir to the throne. The next minute he was
cheering James's departure for Brussels, telling Sir Ralph, who
had been feeling poorly but was now recovered, 'that your
distemper should leave you, and the Duke of York, England,
much about the same time, is a mercy, which makes me merrily
and trebly sing, Gaudiamus and Halleluia; and I pray that the one
be never suffered to trouble you more, nor the other this nation
again'.[25] By the end of the year, he was approving the fact that
'his Majesty hath determined the succession in the Duke of York,
with much reason in my thoughts'.[26] Now that James was on
the throne, the virulent anti-Catholicism which ran deep in Sir
Ralph, Mun and Jack was tempered with a strong desire for
stability and – in Sir Ralph's case, certainly – a conviction that
even a popish King was better than another civil war. And anyway,
to puritanically inclined gentry like Sir Ralph, the hard-working
and high-principled Dismal Jimmy offered a wholesome alter-
native to his brother's idleness and debauchery. Within days of
his accession, commentators noted with approval that 'the face
of the whole court was exceedingly changed to a more solemn
and moral behaviour; the new King affecting neither profaneness nor buffoonery'.[27] His insistence that the Church of England
was safe in his hands also helped Sir Ralph to look on the bright
side, and he doubtless agreed with the thoughts expressed by the
Earl of Peterborough in a letter to his old kinsman, Sir Justinian
Isham: 'Never king was proclaimed with more applause . . . I doubt
not but to see a happy reign.'[28]

The reign was anything but happy. From the outset James was
intent on placing Catholics on an equal footing with Anglicans;
and that set him on a collision course with the majority of his
subjects. Having established a solid majority in the Commons –
although not among Buckinghamshire MPs – he made sure he

could do without Parliament by persuading it to grant him revenues of £1.2 million a year for life. Then, after Monmouth had been crushed, he refused to accept that Catholic officers recruited to put down the rebellion were ineligible on account of their religion: 'having had the benefit of their services in such a time of need and danger, I will neither expose them to disgrace, nor myself to the want of them, if there should be another rebellion to make them necessary to me'.[29] When both Lords and Commons objected to this blatant flouting of the Test Acts, which excluded Protestant and papist nonconformists from all civil and military office, the King prorogued Parliament. Then he dissolved it. Determined to repeal the old penal laws and the Test Acts, he issued a Declaration of Indulgence suspending the penal laws, and tried to weed out dissent by purging corporations and commissions of the peace. He framed three questions for lord-lieutenants to put to their deputies and other office holders in the counties − justices of the peace, militia officers and the like. Would they, if elected to Parliament, vote for the repeal of the penal laws and the tests? Would they support candidates who were willing to do so? Would they support the Declaration of Indulgence by living friendly with those of all religious persuasions?

Most answered 'yes' to the last question, but 'no' to the first two, suggesting that they were happy to 'live friendly' with nonconformists, but rather less happy to see them wielding public office. Sir Ralph refused all three questions, and was removed from the county bench because of it. He didn't really mind. 'I shall have the less trouble,' he wrote. 'My years require a writ of ease, and I shall be very willing to sit still.'[30]

But as the King's efforts to bludgeon his subjects into submission grew ever more crude and high-handed, Sir Ralph watched and prayed. James ordered a second Declaration of Indulgence to be read from every pulpit in the country: Sir Ralph recorded with complacency that there were 'none about us that read it, but two very ordinary persons, having but poor livings'.[31] When the Archbishop of Canterbury and the Bishops of St Asaph, Ely, Chichester, Bath and Wells, Peterborough and Bristol published a petition urging James to withdraw the Declaration, and he imprisoned them on charges of seditious libel in the summer of

1688, Sir Ralph asked God 'to make them firm to do that which may most conduce to his glory and the good security of the Church of England'.[32] Bonfires were lit in Buckingham when they were acquitted.

Mun was in poor health all through the 1680s. Hard drinking and obesity were taking their toll, and he suffered badly from gout and an ulcerated leg, both of which inclined him to the occasional petulant outburst. Yet he was generally an indulgent father, more affectionate to his three children than Sir Ralph had been to him and Jack. His aspirations for them, however, were clear and conventional. Young Ralph's job was to prepare for the time when he inherited the Verney estates. As the younger son, Munsey had to make his own way, and he must go to university. Molly needed to learn the accomplishments which would attract a good husband. All three had their futures determined by birth and gender.

But those futures weren't in Mun's gift. In the autumn of 1685, Aunt Gardiner was asked to help find a wife for nineteen-year-old Ralph, who, like his father before him, was keen to marry and gain a degree of financial independence. Aunt Gardiner came up with a few suitable candidates – 'inclinable to be fat, sings prettily' was her verdict on one girl[33] – but nothing had been settled when, at the end of January 1686, the boy fell sick with a fever. The family were staying in Lincoln's Inn Fields and they naturally turned to Dr Denton, who brought in the royal apothecary James St Amand.* In spite of their best efforts Ralph grew worse, and the conviction grew on Mun, quite rightly as it turned out, that he was going to lose his son and heir. Early on the morning of 10 February he dashed off a frantic note to his mistress Betty Phelps: 'I am a man oppressed with sorrow, my son Ralph is a dying, I cannot come to you,' he wrote. 'But I love you.'[34] A few hours later the boy was dead.

Mun was too ill and too upset to attend the funeral. His brother Jack and their cousin, John Stewkeley, accompanied the coffin on its journey back to the family vault at Claydon, while Mun

---

* St Amand was apprenticed to William Gape in 1660; he took over Gape's Covent Garden business when his master retired.

turned for comfort to Betty. Her discreet note of condolence provoked an outburst of emotion. 'While you continue your sincere love, and constancy, and fidelity to me,' he told her the day after young Ralph's death, 'I will for ever love you really from the bottom of my heart.'[35] At the same time he ordered her a pair of mourning shoes, sent her food – a dozen rice puddings and a dozen black puddings – and gave her money for her rent. And because the Verneys were going into close mourning for Ralph, he asked that she do the same, along with 'my little son John his brother by you'.[36]

Mun's own health wasn't improving, either – his hands shook and the ulcer on his leg kept him bedridden for weeks at a time – and in the aftermath of Ralph's death he fretted over Munsey, who was still at Trinity. He forbade him to come up to London that May – the month Jack's wife Elizabeth died – because there were 'many scurvy fevers' about the town.[37] He forbade him to go swimming until the weather warmed up, 'for fear of catching harm'.[38] He forbade him to pat any dogs, in case they were rabid. He worried when he heard that the boy was 'grown very melancholy',[39] and whenever there were stories of sickness in Oxford. When word reached him in London that there was smallpox at Trinity, he immediately ordered Munsey to Claydon:

I would have you leave Oxford and go keep your grandfather company at Middle Claydon. As soon as I hear from you on this subject, I'll order horses to fetch you away. I would have you prefer your welfare and health before the honour of speaking in the Theatre, and so God bless you and be careful of yourself.[40]

The 'Theatre' he mentioned was Wren's Sheldonian. Munsey had been chosen to declaim verses during the Acts, 'one of the noblest and most honourable things a gentleman can do while he stays at the university', as he told his father.[41] But the thought of his son catching something obsessed Mun. When he heard that a troupe of actors were in Oxford, he sent Munsey more anxious advice:

I am unwilling that you should go to see them act, for fear on your coming out of the hot playhouse into the cold air, you should catch harm, for as I did once coming out of the Theatre at a public Act when it was very full and steaming hot, and walking abroad in the cold, and gave me such a cold that it had liked to a' cost me my life. Your best way in such a cold is to go home to your own chamber directly from the playhouse, and drink a glass of sack. Therefore be sure you send your servant at your hand for a bottle of the best canary and keep it in your chamber for that purpose. Be sure you drink no cooling tankard nor no cooling drinks whatsoever.[42]

Not smallpox, but the death on 10 July of John Fell, Bishop of Oxford and Dean of Christ Church, led to the cancellation of the Acts that summer, and Munsey never did get to speak his verses. In September, his tutor complained that he was missing lectures; and a couple of weeks later he came close to being sent down after staying out of college all night. Luckily for him, another smallpox scare sent all the students home, and by the time he returned his sins had been either forgiven or forgotten by the college authorities.

Mun was stern with him, but nothing like as stern as his own father would have been. He remained in a state of anxiety about Munsey's health and welfare, convinced that something dreadful was bound to carry him off. All his hopes now rested on him.

'How joyful I am that you are well,' he wrote to his son in May 1687. 'I need not tell you that I wish you a long continuance of health, when I do assure you that I reckon it my chiefest felicity in this world.'[43]

It was Tuesday 4 September 1688, and Sir Ralph Verney was fed up.

Everyone was sick, or worried, or both. Including him. He had just been forced to take an emetic for the sake of his health, and he had missed an important meeting with the manipulative Sir Richard Temple in Buckingham. His grandson Munsey was recovering too slowly in Oxford from a summer fever which had almost killed him. News had just reached England of a massive earthquake which had destroyed Smyrna: several Frank merchants had been killed, and in London Jack was bracing himself for the aftershock, which was bound to be felt on the Exchange. Jack was also fretting, along with everyone else, at the news from Holland, where the King's son-in-law, Prince William of Orange, was reported to be preparing an invasion force. Drums were being beaten around Wapping Dock to call sailors to service, and the authorities were commandeering small vessels on the Thames for use as fire ships if war broke out.

Tom was sending begging letters again – this time from South Wales, where he had settled on his return from Ireland. And sister Cary Gardiner was poor and depressed – so depressed that she had just announced her intention, at sixty-two, to emigrate to the West Indies.

The death of Cary's husband John Stewkeley four years earlier had left her short of money, a deficiency she tried to remedy by betting at cards. In order to finance her gambling she was always trying to borrow money from Sir Ralph, from friends and neighbours, from her own children – and she hated the advice that accompanied each loan. 'You are in no way qualified for a gamester, but lie at the mercy of all that play with you,' Sir Ralph had warned her. 'I must needs tell you with a brother's freedom, that you are now come to the brink of the precipice, and nothing can save you but a timely retreat.'[44] She ignored the warnings – 'what qualifications a gamester should have I am a stranger to, but what does become a gentlewoman as plays only for diversion I hope I know'[45] – and now her circumstances were so straitened that she was resolved to leave her debts behind her. In 1684 she had threatened to go and hide in a poor part of London; now she went a step further and announced that she was going into exile in the New World.

Sir Ralph would have none of this 'unusual and unheard of kind of retirement'. 'You shall become the public talk of the nation,' he scolded her, 'by leaving your children unprovided of any manner of settlement and absconding from them, as if you perfectly ran away.'[46] She must think no more about it.

Any hint of family scandal was particularly unwelcome just now, because the ton was already agog at the marital mishaps of Alexander Denton, Sir Ralph's godson and the current squire of Hillesden. For several years Alexander's wife Hester had been involved with a 'T.S.', who came from an otherwise respectable gentry family in Stepney. She had had at least one miscarriage

by him, having commanded her maids not to say a word about
her pregnancy to her husband; now she was heavily pregnant by
'T.S.' again and had deserted Alexander, taking money, jewels and
plate to the value of £500. The business reached the courts in a
very public fashion, with Hester petitioning James II's Commission
for Ecclesiastical Causes for maintenance, and Alexander not only
offering a vigorous defence against the action, but threatening to
have her prosecuted for theft. It was all very embarrassing.

But all these inconveniences, the ailments and anxieties and
family scandals, were about to be put into perspective in a terrible
fashion. Just after eight o'clock on the morning of Tuesday
4 September 1688, Mun's groom arrived over from East Claydon
to say his master wouldn't wake up. Could Sir Ralph come immediately?

When he arrived at the White House just before nine, Sir
Ralph found his fifty-one-year-old son and heir in a deep coma.
A local surgeon was sent for and Mun was bled, but the blood
was cold and watery. Empress of Hungary water, an early version
of eau-de-cologne, was applied; it had no effect. Nothing they
tried made any difference, and at ten o'clock Sir Ralph sent word
to Jack that his brother was dead. Jack was to procure the services of the London undertaker William Russell, well known for
his ability to preserve corpses; and he was to get him quickly,
because Mun's body 'will not keep'.[47]

Mun had always been complaining about his health. Although
he was relatively young, he had told Aunt Gardiner several times
that he thought he was near his end, and others in the clan were
concerned about him. His swollen leg kept him bedridden for
long periods, and his oldest son's death in 1686 had hit him very,
very hard. But Sir Ralph, who saw more of him than most, was
not prepared for this. He had been convinced his son's problem
was bladder stones, which were painful but rarely fatal. Only the
day before, Mun had been at the races on Quainton Meadows
with his daughter Molly and his cousin Cary Stewkeley, who was
helping to take care of his melancholy wife. They had had a great
time, and Mun had come home that evening and written a letter
to Jack, telling him all about how Alexander Denton's man had
won the silver plate; how a drunk fell off his horse; how a child
was run over and almost killed. He finished by promising 'I have

a story to tell in the next sheet that [will] fill it up, and so I shall conclude this who am your most loving brother.'[48] Now that story would never be told.

Sir Ralph had suspected for some time that Mun was living beyond his means, and the moment prayers were over he went into his son's study and began to work through his papers. The picture of Mun's finances that emerged over the next couple of hours was far worse than he had ever imagined. His son had owed money to everybody: £350 to William Denton and £700 to Denton's son-in-law George Nicholas; £200 to cousin Cary Stewkeley and £100 to Aunt Adams. He owed £160 to Sir Ralph's own steward, William Coleman, and a whopping £1170 to William Butterfield, who had succeeded his father Edward as parson of Middle Claydon in 1679. All in all, Mun had died with bonded debts of £4455, a sum that didn't include interest, servants' wages or outstanding tradesmen's bills. A sum that couldn't conceivably be paid.

Sir Ralph went home to Middle Claydon that night and, in a white-hot rage that overwhelmed his grief, he wrote another letter to Jack. His brother's funeral was going to be a private affair; it would take place at night 'without escutcheons, or inviting of neighbours to attend with their coaches, which is very troublesome and signifies nothing'. Sir Ralph had heard it was possible to hire a hearse and pall cheaply in Oxford, and that might be a good idea, but only at the right rate. He totted up the names of everyone in Mun's household on the back of a playing card: including Mary and the two surviving children, there were sixteen. 'And therefore it will be very chargeable to put them all into mourning.' He wasn't inclined to bother himself, arguing that it hadn't been the fashion for fathers to go into mourning for their children when he was living in France. But he asked Jack to ask around and find out if it was the custom. If it *was* expected of him, then could Jack establish how it could be done at the cheapest possible rate? He finished by providing the measurements for the coffin – 6 foot long by 15 inches deep by 25 inches wide at the elbow, which seems quite small for such a big man – and by urging that William Russell send down a coffin as quickly as possible. 'The body purges very much at all places.'[49]

There is nothing strange about a bereaved father escaping into the minutiae of mortality. And it was certainly true that if you weren't careful, death could turn into an expensive business. The hire of a black velvet pall alone might cost 20s. or more; gloves, hatbands and scarves had to be found for the mourners, and vast quantities of black cloth were needed to deck the walls and furniture. As Sir Ralph pointed out, if the neighbouring gentry were invited they would all have to be entertained: red or white wine mulled with sugar and cinnamon was usually dished out both before they left for the church and after they returned. Funeral escutcheons alone – paper to hang in the hall at East Claydon, and silk to drape over Mun's pall – could cost six or seven pounds. Then there were mourning rings. When John Evelyn's daughter Mary died of smallpox in 1685, he distributed sixty rings to her friends and relatives. Some were more expensive than others, but gold and black or white enamel would cost a pound or more for each ring.

But Sir Ralph's fretting over detail wasn't just an escape; it was a way of venting his rage. He was so angry with Mun: angry at him for dying and leaving the future of the Verneys in the hands of a teenage boy; angry at the miserable condition in which he had left his family. A few days later the seventy-five-year-old head of the family buried his son and heir privately, by torchlight. Mad, widowed Mary – whatever her wishes were for her husband's remains – didn't figure in the business at all. Three weeks after Mun's death, Sir Ralph had her officially declared lunatic, partly for her own protection, but also in an attempt to secure the Abell estates for the Verneys in the unlikely event that her two surviving children predeceased her. For the benefit of the Commission of Lunacy, Sir Ralph stated she had been insane for the past seventeen years. She continued much as she always had, wandering to church when the mood took her, lying alone in her damp, darkened bedchamber all day when it didn't.

Jack came down for his brother's nocturnal funeral, and a bewildered Munsey was summoned back from Oxford and informed that his legacy was debt. 'I am at present in such trouble by my being as it were a steward to my father's creditors,' he told his Uncle Jack.[50]

Unlike Sir Edmund, and Henry, Mun had no monument in Claydon church. There was nothing to commemorate his passing.

It was left to Aunt Gardiner to provide his obituary. Referring to Mun's womanising, she told Sir Ralph that 'you may comfort yourself that he had but one crime, which he did not believe to be great; so not a sin against conscience. And he had many virtues to palliate that; more than most men have.'[51]

That's not such a bad epitaph.

At the end of October, Munsey Verney watched anxiously as 500 Irish foot soldiers marched past the gates of East Claydon en route for London. A few days later Sir Ralph was woken at two in the morning by a messenger informing him that by that afternoon he must provide men and horses for the county's trained bands, which were mustering fifteen miles away at Stony Stratford. There had been a sense of menace in the air for weeks now. On the King's birthday, 14 October, the sun was eclipsed at its rising. The following Sunday public prayers were read in the churches against invasion by the Dutch, as food prices spiralled out of control. An angry mob stormed a newly built Catholic chapel in the City and rased it to the ground. On 3 November a massive Dutch fleet – the largest invasion force England had ever seen – sailed through the Strait of Dover. The crowds who gathered on the cliffs to watch its passing could just make out the words on William of Orange's banner as it rippled in the sea breeze: 'I will maintain the Protestant religion and the liberties of England.'

On 5 November, Jack Verney's forty-eighth birthday, the Prince of Orange landed with 13,000 men at Torbay in Devon and marched up to Exeter, where he waited. 'The Prince marches slow,' Cary Gardiner told Sir Ralph; 'his reasons is not known.'[52]

The Prince's reasons were actually pretty straightforward. He wanted his father-in-law to give up the throne without a fight. And James II, having marched as far as Salisbury Plain before realising friends, courtiers, officials and troops were all falling over themselves in their hurry to change sides, did just that. 'The papists in offices lay down their commissions and fly,' wrote John Evelyn in his diary. 'It looks like a revolution.'[53] James packed his wife and their six-month-old son off to France, and then fled himself, disguised in a black wig and an odd pair of boots. His boat ran aground at Faversham and was boarded by fishermen, who stole his valuables and his breeches before sending him back to London. He finally left the capital, never to return, on 18 December, just as William of Orange arrived. ''Tis said he wept as he left Whitehall,' wrote Jack; 'the P. of Orange is at St James'.'[54] Cary Gardiner reported that Sir Richard Temple, ever the trimmer, had gone over to the Prince after waiting to see which side offered the most advantage; 'but those as goes in now signifies little but are rather laughed at'.[55]

Sir Ralph and Sir Richard were both returned to the Convention Parliament of January 1689, which Prince William called to settle the issue of the Crown. There was a dispute about the validity of the Buckingham poll: the defeated candidates claimed that due notice of the time of the election hadn't been given, which led to a lengthy investigation by the Committee of Privileges.* The two men managed to hold their seats, although this turned out to be a mixed blessing for Sir Ralph. In a rerun of his disastrous stand against the Covenant forty-five years before, he decided he could not vote that James II 'having withdrawn himself out of this kingdom, has abdicated the government' and that the throne was thereby vacant.[56] It wasn't true. So he was

---

* The evidence to the committee offers an insight into the practice of elections in the 1680s. John Upston, the under bailiff, testified that Mayor Ethersey, having received the Prince's letter about nine or ten o'clock on Saturday 5 January, 'gave him order to go to the respective houses of the twelve capital burgesses, (by whom elections of Members for Parliament had always been made) on Sunday after evening prayer, to give them notice to meet him on Wednesday following, at 10 o'clock in the morning, at the Town Hall, to elect two burgesses for the Convention; and that they should also meet him the next morning, being Monday, in the Town Hall: which notice, on Sunday, after prayer, he accordingly gave; and spake with ten of the said burgesses themselves at their houses; and left the like notice at the other two burgesses' houses, viz. with the wife of Mr Henry Robinson; and the servant of Mr Mason. And that this had been the constant and usual way of giving notice for election to Parliaments in all his time; having been, ever since the restoration of King Charles the Second, under bailiff there. And being further asked, whether it was not the custom to leave notice in writing; he declared, that it was always left by word of mouth, with themselves, or some of their family; and not otherwise. And further said; that all the Thirteen did accordingly meet at the Hall on Monday morning; and also on Wednesday morning, when the Election was made. And that twelve of them gave their voices for Sir Rich. Temple and Sir Ralph Verney' (*Journal of the House of Commons* 10, 19 April 1689).

placed on a blacklist of unreliable subjects, a trivial thing in comparison to the consequences of his refusal to take the Covenant forty-five years earlier, but yet another example of his determination to put principle before political career.

When a new parliament was called the following year, Sir Ralph stood again for Buckingham. But in the middle of his campaign and just nine days before the poll he discovered that Sir Richard Temple, the great trimmer, had lost patience with his principles and lost confidence in his ability to win the election. As he had in 1685, Temple had gone behind his back and invited Alexander Denton to stand instead; and this time Denton accepted. That was a betrayal, and while Sir Ralph wasn't desperate to sit in Parliament again, he was hurt and angry that two neighbours and friends could jettison old ties of kinship and personal loyalty in such a cavalier fashion. Without their support he didn't stand much of a chance in the town, and after a difficult interview with Denton, who came to see him at Claydon the night before the poll and begged him to give up the fight, he agreed to withdraw. 'I had not enough voices to carry it,' he told Jack; 'and the bailiff was so much my cousin Denton's friend that I believe he would have returned him if he had had but two voices.'[57]

The Verneys were shocked, and they joined forces to reassure Sir Ralph. Cary Gardiner declared that Alexander Denton could no longer be regarded as 'a man of any principle of justice, honour, or goodness'. Her brother was 'too kind to him as has treated you unworthily,' she said. 'I know my own sentiments of him.'[58] Jack reckoned both Denton and Temple were beyond the pale: 'these are men that never consider past obligations.'[59] The words were meant to comfort, but the truth was that a new ruthlessness was the order of the day. Friendship came second to expediency in local and national politics. Times had moved on, and they had left Sir Ralph's generation behind.

A few weeks after the election, which Denton and Temple won, their opponents having withdrawn so that the three old friends could fight it out amongst themselves, an arbitrary fate gave the Verney fortunes another twist. After a miserable five years in which Sir Ralph had had to endure the death of his grandson and namesake, the death of his much-loved daughter-in-law

Elizabeth, the death and near-ruin of his eldest son – after all this, there was more. Cary Gardiner wrote from London that Munsey Verney was sick with smallpox. Four days later the boy was urged to make his will, which he did. The next day, 28 February 1690, he died, leaving Jack the heir to the Verney fortunes.

23

He Grows Weary

*O*n 10 July 1692, Jack Verney married for the second time, and once again his wedding took place in Henry VII's Chapel at Westminster Abbey. His bride was Mary Lawley, the statuesque thirty-one-year-old daughter of a Shropshire baronet. We don't know Mary's reasons for marrying, although being a thirty-one-year-old spinster probably ranked high on her list. Jack's motives were clear. He wanted a mother for his children, who were now seven, nine, ten and eleven. And the death of Munsey, while making him heir to the Verney estates, placed a certain amount of pressure on him to secure the line; another son would be a great comfort if anything should happen to his nine-year-old boy, Ralph.

Then there was the money. Jack was quite wealthy by now. He had diversified out of the Levant trade into land – his Wasing property alone brought in over £260 a year in rentals – and into finance and investments. It is hard to say exactly how much he was worth in the early 1690s, but it was enough for him to invest £500 in government funds in 1690, £900 in 1691–2 and another £500 in 1692–3; enough for him to put out £3450 on a mortgage in Oxfordshire and to lend £2350 to the Royal African Company. He was an astute observer of the markets, and marriage was another venture, another opportunity to make a profit. Now the heir to Sir Ralph's baronetcy, he was better placed to make a good bargain than he had been in 1680, when he was an up and coming City merchant; he could expect to attract a bride from a better family than the Palmers, as indeed he did.

The courtship was a protracted affair. Aunt Pen Osborne was a neighbour of the Lawleys, who had lodgings at the Palace of Whitehall next door to the Banqueting Hall. In the summer of 1691 she suggested that Mary might be worth a look, and as a first step Jack contrived an informal meeting with her father, Sir Francis Lawley, at the Rainbow on Fleet Street. Lawley was a shareholder in the coffee house, one of Jack's regular haunts; but when it came to it he found the setting too public and left without broaching the subject of marriage. Nothing much happened until that December, when he visited the Lawleys at home and was introduced to Mary, whom he found 'handsome enough'.[1] Again he said nothing of marriage, but Sir Ralph, Sir Francis Lawley and their lawyers met several times to discuss the business early in 1692, and Jack finally proposed in late February or early March.

Negotiations over the financial details carried on through the spring, and by the beginning of June the Verneys and the Lawleys reached an agreement. Mary's portion was to be £3000, the same as Elizabeth Palmer's had been; her jointure was £400 a year. The sticking point seems to have been security for the jointure and provision for any sons of the marriage. In the end the two sides agreed that Jack should add £6000 to his wife's portion, and that the entire sum should be invested in land within 100 miles of London, which would finance the jointure and provide estates for male heirs of the marriage.

This looks at first sight to be a victory for the Lawleys. (Sir Ralph certainly thought the £400 jointure was overgenerous.) But the acquisition of land was already one of Jack's objectives; in effect, he was given an extra £3000 to do something which he intended to do anyway. Mary's family had only a life interest in her portion; if she died childless they would lose the entire amount.

Which is exactly what happened. The marriage lasted only two years, during which time Mary gave birth to a son, John, who died in infancy. She was pregnant with their second child in the summer of 1694 when she succumbed to smallpox. Jack rather guiltily sent the Lawleys £100 to pay for mourning clothes, 'because they lose their daughter, and portion'.[2]

The couple's short-lived marriage was happy enough. Mary was popular with the clan, who endorsed Jack's opinion of his new wife as a clever and 'extraordinary sweet natured woman'.[3] The Palmers welcomed her as the stepmother of their four grandchildren, at the same time thanking Jack rather touchingly 'for your staying so long single'.[4] Aunt Osborne took the credit for bringing about the match, and reassured everyone that Mary would be kind to her stepchildren (always a sensitive issue in such situations). Nancy Nicholas told Sir Ralph that 'the more I see your daughter so much the more I like her'.[5] Jack marked the marriage by putting his servants into new liveries, refurbishing his coach, and altering his arms 'by putting her coat with mine'.[6] He also showered 'Mrs Lamb' (his pet name for her) with expensive gifts.* He gave her diamonds, characteristically remarking to his father that they were cheaper now than when he married his first wife; he gave her a breast jewel worth £100 and a silver dressing table set; and he gave her that quintessential fashion accessory, a black pageboy.

The child, who had arrived from Guinea in 1689 when he was about six, was probably acquired through Jack's connections in the Royal African Company. Christened Peregrine Tyam at All Saints, Middle Claydon (and buried there in 1707), he waited on Mary, ran errands for her and carried notes around town. Jack treated him quite severely, judging from the fact that when he brought messages round to Sir Ralph's lodgings and had to wait for an answer, Sir Ralph was always careful to write and tell his son he was responsible for the delay, and not to blame the boy. Perry hovers nervously behind Mary, wearing a jewelled slave collar, in a portrait which Jack commissioned to celebrate the marriage.

The couple lived in Hatton Street – Jack renewed the lease on his house in 1693 – and followed much the same kind of social life as Jack and Elizabeth had done. They saw a lot of Sir

---

*Mary's nickname had nothing to do with the nursery rhyme, which first surfaced in the nineteenth century.

Ralph, who dined with them regularly when he was in town. He still lodged on Holborn Row, paying a rent of £30 a year for the privilege; and he still locked his chamber and left the key at Hatton Street whenever he went back to Buckinghamshire. Although they only lived a ten-minute walk away from each other, father and son exchanged almost daily notes, sometimes full of gossip and news, sometimes no more than terse invitations given and accepted or refused. Two such notes from 5 October 1692, on a day when Sir Ralph was packing up to leave for Claydon, give an idea of their tone:

Sir

I send Perry to bring me word how you do; and to desire your company at dinner with me today. I return you many thanks for the pigeons you were pleased to send us yesterday.

Little news is stirring, only, two of the King's fireships and a merchant ship are lost by stormy weather off Dunkirk and all the men drowned. In the Downs a well boat is cast away but the men all saved except one, and in the Downs is also cast away a pinnace belong to the Chatham wherein were eleven men, who are all drowned.

Which is all from

Sir, your most obedient son

John Verney

Child

Pray thank my daughter kindly for her invitation but I cannot possibly dine with you today, but God willing will be with you in the afternoon. I am very sorry for our losses at sea. I have no news but that my cousin Ann Hobart is come to town, and I am in such a hurry in putting up my things that I can say no more.

Yours

RV*

---

* Jack Verney to Sir Ralph Verney and Sir Ralph Verney to Jack Verney, both 5 October 1692; M636/46. A well boat was a fishing boat provided with a well or tank for transporting live fish. Lady Anne Hobart was dead, so the Ann Hobart Sir Ralph mentions is presumably her daughter Nan.

The Verney correspondence from this period also contains a sweet little message from Jack's ten-year-old son Ralph, who has clearly been instructed to write his grandfather a thank-you letter:

Honered Granfather
This is to present my umble duty to
You and to give you many thinks for
Keeping of my lettel hors and for my
Cheeses and I am in hopes yt I shall heare
That you are well after your iurney
And pray present my umble cervis to all
My frinds and pray accept of thes few
Lines from your most o Bedient granson
To command
Ralph Verney*

For Sir Ralph the early 1690s were marred by the behaviour of another less dutiful grandchild. He had always had a soft spot for Mun's daughter Molly, and she worked that grandfatherly affection for all it was worth. The Verneys spent an inordinate amount of time discussing suitable clothes for her: when she was only four years old, her father had his servant looking for the right kind of collars for her and agonising over the choice of silk or worsted for her frocks. When she was fourteen Aunt Gardiner, who was looking after her, was pleading with Sir Ralph to pay for black leather gloves, a black crepe coat and some taffeta: 'which things if she could be without I would not write for them'.[7] When Munsey died Molly seized the opportunity to beg her grandfather for some decent mourning clothes and a tippet (which alone would cost five or six pounds). Sir Ralph agreed, giving her permission to buy the best she could. 'Child, you see how desirous I am to please you, and I doubt not but you will be as willing to please me.'[8]

---

* Jack's son Ralph Verney to Sir Ralph Verney, 13 June 1693; M636/46. I may have been unfair to Ralph junior by not modernising his spelling and punctuation, as I have with all the other Verney letters; but it seems even more inconsistent to correct 'lettel hors' but leave 'many thinks' and 'o Bedient' unaltered. Sorry, Ralph.

Unfortunately, he was wrong in that. Molly's grandfather acted *in loco parentis* for her. Her mother was in no state to make decisions about her future, and all her choices in life were subject to Sir Ralph's close scrutiny. Aunt Gardiner's daughter Cary Stewkeley, who had moved into East Claydon after Mun's death to care for Mary, warned him in 1692 that Molly was unlikely to marry purely for money, no matter how her grandfather chided her. For a time she was in love with the friend of a cleric who was courting her mother's maid, much to Sir Ralph's distress. To forestall an inappropriate marriage, he arranged a match for her with Robert Dormer, a lawyer whose father had estates at Quainton in Buckinghamshire; but she was unable to summon up much enthusiasm for Mr Dormer.

In the summer of 1693, everyone found out why. On 16 June she walked out of her Uncle Jack's house in Hatton Street, where she had been lodging, leaving a note behind her:

> I have been for some time married to Mr Kelyng, and upon his desires am now gone to live with him at his mother's (in Fisher Street in Red Lion Square). I hope you will excuse my not giving you notice of this before as well as my abrupt leaving of your house. I was in fear of putting you in a passion, the sight of which my temper cannot very well bear.[9]

There was nothing wildly unsuitable about Molly's new husband. John Kelyng came from a very well-known legal family: his grandfather, Sir John Kelyng, had until his death in 1671 been Lord Chief Justice of the King's Bench; his father, also now dead, was a King's Counsel and a sergeant-at-law. John's mother Philippa was the daughter of the Italian diplomat Alessandro Antelminelli, who had served as English representative of the Grand Duke of Tuscany for nearly forty years.

The problem was money. Sir Ralph had been quietly paying the interest on Mun's debts for years, but he was distinctly disinclined to pay off the debts themselves. They would have to wait for Molly to find a wealthy husband, and John Kelyng was not wealthy. There was also the matter of East Claydon's long-term future. The settlement worked out when Mun married Mary Abell in 1662 stipulated that the Abell estates should go to the couple's male heirs; failing that, to any daughters of the marriage. The deaths of young Ralph and Munsey had not only made Molly an heiress (and made her grandfather regard impoverished suitors with deep suspicion); it also raised the prospect of East Claydon being lost to the Verney family for ever unless Sir Ralph and Jack – who had an interest in the matter himself now – could work out something during negotiations over Molly's marriage.

The clandestine marriage put that out of the question, and Molly was quite right to be worried about how the family would take her news. They were all angry at first, but the eighteen-year-old was so contrite, and so obviously in love – Kelyng, she told her grandfather, was 'the only person in the world I thought capable of making me happy'[10] – that one by one they relented. Jack forgave her. Her mother, insofar as she understood what had happened, forgave her. Aunt Gardiner forgave her: she described her first encounter with the young couple, who called round to see her within days of moving in together, as 'the saddest meeting I ever had with her; [it] made my children stand like mutes being so full of grief'.[11] The old lady gave Kelyng a piece of her mind, and then settled down to the task of persuading her brother to accept the girl back into the family.

Because it was Sir Ralph, predictably, who was most intransigent when it came to forgiving Molly. 'Mall Kelyng's stolen wedding', as he called it, hurt him deeply.[12] She offered to go down on her knees in front of him and plead for his pardon, but he wasn't moved. She wrote him sad little letters: 'I cannot live in your displeasure and unless you design the breaking of my heart for an atonement, I beg of you, Sir, no longer to defer your blessing.'[13] Kelyng reassured Sir Ralph that he was no fortune-hunter. Aunt Gardiner said it might have been worse: the Earl of Suffolk's daughter had just married a manservant. Lady Gardiner also tried some blatant emotional blackmail. 'Dear brother,' she begged, 'harken to all of us as makes our request to you in your granddaughter's behalf.' Molly was terribly distressed, she warned him; her lunatic mother Mary was in no position to plead her cause. And 'should my niece fall into her mother's distemper, the malicious world would say you caused it. So, dear brother, let her have your pardon and blessing.'[14]

Sir Ralph wasn't to be won over so easily. He was the girl's guardian and, in truth, Molly had made a grave error in marrying without his consent. Commentators and conduct books were all clear on this. It was 'one of the highest injuries [daughters] can do their parents, who have such a native right in them, that 'tis no less an injustice than disobedience to dispose of themselves without them'.[15] Lord Halifax's advice was that the parents' right to choose their daughter's husband might not be fair, but it was the way of things; a woman had to make the best of it. The author of *The Ladies' Dictionary* went further, declaring that a match made without parental consent was 'the greatest piece of rebellion, as well as ingratitude'.[16]

Over and above the fact that Molly's 'stolen wedding' had thrown the future of the East Claydon estates into doubt, it was the challenge to his authority which really irked Sir Ralph. This always brought out the worst in him, and he never really forgave Molly. He eventually and grudgingly accepted the marriage, but made sure the girl only received an allowance, rather than coming into possession of the East Claydon estate.

She died, aged twenty-one, in February 1696, shortly after giving birth to a little girl. Sir Ralph was godfather, and for a while it seemed as though the babe would survive; but she followed her mother three months later. With these deaths, the Verney–Abell line came to an end, and in accordance with Mun's marriage settlement Sir Ralph and Jack handed over East Claydon (and custody of the lunatic Mary) to the Abells that summer. By now Mun's widow was barely in touch with reality. She was withdrawn and depressed, and when Cary Stewkeley broke the news of Molly's death, she 'said not a word, but her eyes filled with tears, and I think that she understood'.[17]

In the meantime the Verneys were having to contend with another defiant woman. Aunt Gardiner had a big family: there was Peg, her daughter by her first husband, Thomas Gardiner; five daughters and a son by her husband, John Stewkeley, and three stepdaughters and a stepson which he brought with him from his first marriage. At least two of the girls were married; another was betrothed to an Islington clerk, William Vickers. Peg, the oldest at fifty, was almost blind and lived with her mother. Cary Stewkeley had gone as nurse-companion to mad Mary at East Claydon. Penelope Stewkeley had been acting as a reluctant companion to her Whitehall godmother, Aunt Osborne. 'My lady only wants me to wash up her old crepe and suchlike work,' she complained.[18] Like Cary, Pen was being nudged inexorably into the role of poor relation, condemned to be little more than a servant, dependent for the rest of her life on the whims of others.

So it came as something of a shock to her family when at the beginning of August 1695 she suddenly announced that she had slept with William Vickers. Not once, not twice, but often. Very often.

It isn't clear what prompted Pen's admission. Perhaps the pair had been discovered, or perhaps she feared she was pregnant (she wasn't). Perhaps it was simply that she had fallen in love and wanted to marry her clerk. But Jack, Sir Ralph and Aunt Gardiner – not to mention Vickers' fiancée – were all outraged at her conduct, and deeply suspicious of the timing.

Because, as it happened, Pen's godmother had recently made her will. Aunt Osborne was a wealthy and important woman, and the will was very detailed: her corpse must be taken up to Claydon in a hearse drawn by six horses and followed by a coach with another six horses; a trust was to be set up to distribute money annually to six poor men of Buckingham, who in return must wear gowns of green cloth and silver badges with Sir Edmund Verney's arms on them. There were small personal bequests to most of the Verney clan as well as to Aunt Osborne's aristocratic friends in Whitehall – the Earl and Countess of Lindsey, the Countess of Plymouth, the Countess of Carnarvon. The Earl of Lindsey got 'my bed lined with lemon coloured sarsenet with the counterpane of lemon colour and four cushions, in case I die in his Lordship's chamber'.[19] Nancy Nicholas got the silver spoon marked with Henry Verney's initials. Peg Gardiner was left Henry's silver watch and the picture of him with Sir Edmund on the reverse (curious things to give a blind woman). Peg Adams, daughter of Lady Osborne's sister Betty, got ten lottery tickets. Four of the Gardiner girls were bequeathed 'all my little bracelets, jewels and rings to be equally divided between them'.[20] Pen Stewkeley got her aunt's clothes, a pair of silver candlesticks with snuffers – and 'all such money, plate and goods which shall remain undisposed of'.[21] In other words, Aunt Osborne left the bulk of her considerable estate to her niece and goddaughter.

Aunt Osborne was quite poorly in the summer of 1695 – she died on 20 August, a couple of weeks after Pen confessed to her affair – and there was no doubt in the minds of the Verneys that Vickers was after Pen's money. He was 'one of the worst of men,' said Jack.[22] Sir Ralph corrected him: Vickers was 'the very worst man in the world'. Nor was his niece allowed to hide behind the role of wronged maiden:

> I thought Pen had had more wit, and more honesty [he said]; more grace, and more modesty, than to be guilty of such crimes with him, whereby she hath utterly ruined herself, and (as much as in her lies) brought shame and infamy upon her sisters, and her whole family; so that she cannot expect any kindness or indeed to be willingly seen by any of her relations, or be owned by any of them.[23]

Aunt Gardiner went to Jack for help. Vickers was insisting on marriage, and threatening to bring Pen before an ecclesiastical court on a charge of fornication if he was thwarted. What was to be done?

Jack set out three options. Pen could stay put and refuse to marry, although an appearance before the spiritual court would involve a physical examination by midwives, and she was not prepared to countenance that. She could leave London, change her name and go into hiding. Or she could marry Vickers, having first secured her fortune in such a way that he couldn't get his hands on it.

Everyone talked as though Pen Stewkeley was the victim in all this. She had been stupid; she had been deceitful and wanton; and she had fallen into the clutches of a bad man. That may well have been how she portrayed herself to her mother, but it wasn't true. She knew exactly what she was doing, and she knew she wanted Vickers for a husband. The couple married that summer and, as far as we know, they lived happily ever after – or at least until 1719, when Vickers died. Although Jack took steps to ensure he couldn't squander Pen's inheritance, he didn't hold it against the Verneys. In fact he baptised Jack's grandson and granddaughters, and when Pen died in 1740 – still a widow – she made Jack's son her executor, left him William's portrait along with her own, and asked to be buried 'as near the body of my late dear husband as conveniently may be'.*

There was something both poignant and farcical about Aunt Osborne's end. As she lay on her deathbed at Whitehall in August 1695, she suddenly begged her friend the Countess of Lindsey to fetch her a Catholic priest. Nancy Nicholas heard about this at second-hand and immediately wrote to warn Sir Ralph to brace himself. Then, remarking that 'we cannot be too cautious where souls are concerned', she wrote to the Countess to assure her that no matter how it looked, Lady Osborne didn't really mean it. The appeal, she said, had been made 'in lightheartedness' – a weird choice of phrase, considering the woman was slipping in and out of consciousness and obviously dying. 'I beseech your ladyship not to gratify her in this request, not that I think her capable now to make any judgement of any religion, but Sir Ralph is of a great age, and I fear such a shock now might hasten his end.'[24] Clandestine marriages, fornicating nieces, dying sisters and dead grandchildren were upsetting, but they were part of the natural cycle of things. A Catholic convert in the family was altogether more serious. Pen Osborne went to heaven attended by her own Anglican vicar, the conservative William Lancaster. She died a Protestant, whether she liked it or not.

Seventeenth-century England was pretty clear about how its women should behave. Modesty, meekness, compassion, courtesy and piety were 'those general qualifications, which are at once the duty and the ornament of the female sex'.[25] Conduct manuals advised girls that 'obedience in young virgins is very comely'.[26] The paragon of female virtue is 'very discreet, wise, and prudent in her actions; not passionate, nor retentive of anger, never over merry, but modestly grave and composed . . . Her discourse . . . always pertinent and useful, not at all loquacious.'[27]

If the rich and varied relationships of the Verney women tell us anything, it is that the ideal of womanhood constructed by male writers was just that – an ideal, a wish, a hope. The Verney

---

* Prob/11/706. In his own will (Prob/11/433) Vickers left £5 each to two poor children of Westminster, William and Anne Robinson, and £200 to his wife's maid Elizabeth Harris. An uncharitable soul might wonder if marital fidelity was high on his list of virtues.

men are straightforward: Sir Edmund, his sons Sir Ralph and Tom and his grandsons Mun and Jack all made arranged marriages for money. Sometimes the marriages worked, sometimes they failed. Unhappy or not, the men were able to seek extramarital solace whenever they felt like it; and we know that some, if not all of them, did just that.

But what are we to make of the women? Because it wasn't just Molly, the heiress who eloped and married for love, who broke with convention; or Pen Stewkeley, the spinster who slept with and then married her sister's unsuitable boyfriend. There was Aunt Eure, the widow who scandalised the Verneys' entire social circle by marrying a Roman Catholic; Sir Ralph's sister Susan, who started her married life in the Fleet prison; Peg Elmes, who decided to separate from her violent husband, and Pen Denton, who according to the family broke her heart for joy when hers died. Mall became pregnant by a servant and eventually married him. Betty ran away with a poor clergyman. Even Cary, the ultra-genteel Cary, contrived to flout orthodoxy in her own small way by insisting on retaining her first husband's name when she married her second and remaining a Gardiner when she should have been a Stewkeley. It was only Sir Ralph's wife and his mother who didn't rebel. And they didn't need to: both women were in successful and intimate relationships with the head of the family – and both were in positions of power as a result of those relationships.

The social historian automatically looks for patterns and trends, and I suppose we can find them if we look hard enough. We could point to the absence of a dominant male figure in the lives of Sir Ralph's sisters when they were growing up. The same holds true for their niece Molly, whose adolescence was marred by the sudden deaths of her father and her two older brothers, not to mention her mother's insanity. We could speculate over the impact of the Civil War, of Sir Ralph's puritanical brand of Anglicanism, of the lax moral climate at the Restoration court. We could blame society.

The most delightful thing about all this is that the Verney women *did* confound expectations of polite female behaviour with such cheerful vigour. Driven variously by love, passion, courage, stubbornness and a fear of spinsterhood, they simply refused to do as they were told. They may not have been typical, but if Mall and Molly and Pen Stewkeley and the rest teach us nothing else, they demonstrate that no matter what commentators *said* about the submissive position of women in seventeenth-century England, the reality of individual experience was at once more complicated and more compelling.

Sir Ralph Verney had a long, bad death. By the time he reached his eightieth birthday in November 1693 his health was poor, and Jack fretted about his coughs and colds and aches and pains whenever the two men were apart for any length of time. Not trusting his father, Jack tended to look to the Claydon servants for reliable information on Sir Ralph's condition when he was in the country. 'I thank you kindly for the information you give me of my father's health,' he wrote to Sir Ralph's steward William Coleman. 'If he mends I shall hear it from himself but when he is bad he saith nothing.'[28]

Sir Ralph spent the Christmas of 1695 in London, and didn't return to Claydon until the following July. He was eighty-two, and not surprisingly he complained of various aches and pains. His face and hands were swollen and he felt terribly tired, so tired that he couldn't even be bothered to discuss estate business with Coleman. This was so uncharacteristic that the anxious steward contacted Jack. But Sir Ralph's son had made a point of keeping out of Claydon. He was always happy to carry out errands and commissions in London, effectively acting as Sir Ralph's agent there; but he rarely came up to Claydon more than once a year, and he hadn't visited his father in Buckinghamshire since Aunt Osborne's funeral the previous summer. In any case, there was a strong support network gathered round Sir Ralph. Peg Adams, his sister Betty's girl, had recently come to live with him, ostensibly to convalesce after a serious illness, but in reality because she was an impoverished spinster looking for a role and a home.* Cary Stewkeley was still looking after Mun's widow Mary over at East Claydon, and she was a regular visitor. Coleman lived in; and the half a dozen or so household servants were loyal and

---

* 'As for anybody falling in love with me,' she once told her uncle rather touchingly, 'I can't expect that, which have none of that which all the world values – I mean money' (Peg Adams to Sir Ralph Verney, 16 October 1693; M636/47).

capable. Jack was in the middle of negotiating for his third wife – Elizabeth Baker, the eighteen-year-old daughter of a merchant who lived next door in Hatton Garden. And he had a cold. So he told Coleman how sorry he was to hear of his father's condition, asked to be kept informed of any changes, and left it at that.

In August 1695 Sir Ralph seemed to be mending, and on Sunday 9 August Cary came to walk him over to morning service. The expedition ended in confusion and embarrassment: Sir Ralph had a sudden attack of diarrhoea in the middle of Parson Butterfield's sermon and had to run out of the church. He made his way home; then he was sick. He drank a little water and vomited again. By the time Cary found him he was so weak he had to be carried up to his chamber.

She stayed with him until about seven that evening. 'I think that he went to stool nine or ten times as I was there; and he told me that it was as thin as water, and that it ran down into his very shoes.'[29] He was racked with fits of vomiting and too weak to feed himself, and she thought him so poorly that she had better sit with him through the night. But Sir Ralph ordered her back to East Claydon, and when she returned the next morning he was a little better. The swelling in the old man's face and hands had gone down, his stomach had settled and he managed to take a little burnt claret 'with things done in it to stop a looseness'.[30] He was well enough to offer dinner to Alexander Denton when he called with his cousin and some friends, although he didn't go downstairs, entertaining them instead in his dressing chamber. It was thought prudent for his manservant Richard to sit up with him on Monday night, but the diarrhoea and sickness had eased by Tuesday. Cary decided nevertheless – and very much against Sir Ralph's wishes – to inform Jack about the latest events. 'I should not have forgiven myself if I had not let you know how ill your father was.'[31] And as soon as he received Cary's letter Jack dropped everything and rushed down to Claydon.

He brought his son with him, and stayed for three weeks. Everyone was determined to be cheerful and positive, as though saying how well Sir Ralph was would make him well. Only Jack was pessimistic. He told Nancy Nicholas that his father was dying, and gave a equally gloomy prognosis to Elizabeth Baker. Nevertheless, Sir Ralph rallied at the beginning of September and Jack went back to London, only to hear within days that the old man had had a serious relapse. The diarrhoea was back, and now it was coupled with a bad cough, and Sir Ralph was complaining about a pain in his side. Elizabeth Lillie, who had been the housekeeper at Claydon for years, wrote a distressed letter to Jack on 6 September:

> Ever since you left Claydon my master has grown weaker and weaker every day. His looseness still continues and his stomach quite fails him now and he doth not rise till after eight o'clock in the morning and lies much upon the bed all day. He is much weaker than when you were at Claydon and complains of a pain of his hip always when he coughs. Truly, Sir, my concern is very great for him to know what to get him to eat, for he will not now care to eat anything or drink. He grows weary of all that I can imagine to make for him.[32]

It is hard to know exactly what was killing Sir Ralph. Taken one at a time, his symptoms might suggest kidney or liver problems, heart failure, perhaps a stomach tumour or a prostate cancer with secondary bone cancer. Together they don't point to a single cause. It was as if his system was slowly shutting down. He was dying of old age.

Jack didn't go back to Claydon. Over the following weeks the tone of the letters he received from Mrs Lillie, from Peg Adams, from Cary, grew less panicky and more resigned. The picture they give of Sir Ralph's protracted end is frankly heart breaking. He lay in bed every day till late morning, when he was carried into his dressing room and cajoled into eating a few spoonfuls of broth. Then he was carried back to his chamber to lay down in his clothes all the afternoon, 'so while the maids make [his bed] he is undressing ready to go into it again'.[33] He couldn't even bring himself to get out of bed to say his prayers at night. He was fading away before them, 'a perfect skeleton, as Mr Hodges [his secretary] says, and complains mightily of his weakness that he can scarce sit up'.[34]

But he wouldn't die. Peg Adams wrote excitedly to Jack of every small victory, every slight sign of improvement. One day Sir Ralph manages half a porringer of broth; he has obviously begun to mend. Another day he eats two boiled eggs – a clear indication that his health is improving. 'He looks better and speaks better as we all thinks he has done a good while,' she said.[35] No one was convinced. Cary Stewkeley was more realistic. On Sunday 13 September she told Jack quite simply, 'I mayst tell you the thoughts of them that sees him, says that they wonder that he is alive. For my part, sometimes I think that he may live some time yet; and then soon after, I am of another mind.'[36]

Still Jack didn't come to see his father, either because he felt there was nothing he could do, or because he couldn't bear to see him in such a state. At least Sir Ralph wasn't asking for him. Quite the reverse – he gave instructions that Jack shouldn't know how ill he was, so Peg Adams had to send her bulletins in secret. On Sunday 20 September he dictated a letter to Charles Hodges, sending down a dozen empty bottles and asking his son to have six filled with good white wine and six with the best claret, 'for my own drinking'.[37] His only comment on the state of his health was to say he was getting weaker. In fact, some neighbours who called that day to pay their respects told Peg that from the look of him they couldn't see him lasting another three days.

Soon after they left that Sunday Sir Ralph complained of a fever, which grew worse over the next couple of days, until on Tuesday he was drifting in and out of consciousness. His cough was terrible, his speech was rambling and disconnected and it was no longer possible to get him to take any food at all. Cary Stewkeley arrived on Tuesday, bringing her nightclothes with her. Her uncle was not in any state to order her back to East Claydon now, and she sent word back that she was staying by him until the end. Even the determinedly optimistic Peg finally stopped pretending that there was going to be a happy ending. On Thursday 24 September she wrote a miserable letter to Jack: 'God knows, I believe it can't be many [hours] before the sad news of his departure will be sent, believing it not possible for him to continue till another post, nothing now passing down his throat. And in this sad condition which he lies in, I can't think it a kindness in his friends to desire his life.'[38]

Sir Ralph fell into a coma at two that afternoon. Parson Butterfield was called in, and the prayers for the dying were said at the old man's bedside. 'We humbly commend the soul of this thy servant, our dear brother, into thy hands, as into the hands of a faithful Creator, and most merciful Saviour; most humbly beseeching thee, that it may be precious in thy sight.' A few minutes before midnight, Sir Ralph died.

The next morning Peg wrote to let Jack know that at last his father had 'left this miserable world for endless joy and felicity'.[39] He sent round straight away to William Russell, the undertaker who had dealt with the aftermath of Mun's sudden death; and Russell despatched his son-in-law, a plumber and a cart which held a lead-lined coffin covered in black baize and a hamper with the materials needed to prepare the body.

The undertaker also offered to make all the arrangements for Sir Ralph's funeral, but before that could happen Jack had to decide exactly what form it was going to take. He gathered some relations round him at Hatton Garden – probably George and Nancy Nicholas – and opened the sealed will his father had made in February 1695. It was short and simple, with no surprises. He was asked to honour some small annuities to servants and a promised payment of £500 to Aunt Adams; but apart from these bequests, Sir Ralph had left him everything – all of his landed estates, all the household goods, all the pictures and plate and personal effects. He also left his son a title, since Jack inherited the baronetcy.

On the surface Sir Ralph's instructions for his funeral seemed equally straightforward. He wished to be buried in the Verney vault under the chancel of Middle Claydon church, 'as privately and with as little pomp as may be'.[40] But Jack was thrown into a quandary. He *had* planned to commemorate his father's passing by inviting forty or fifty of the neighbouring gentry to a big county funeral, but that hardly counted as burying him 'as privately and with as little pomp as may be'. If he invited some of the neighbours, he risked offending the others.

So he plumped for a private night-time burial, contriving to offend just about everybody. Mrs Lillie told him right out that the family's reputation in the county would suffer. Peg Adams pointed out that someone of Sir Ralph's standing needed gentlemen to carry him to his grave. Aunt Gardiner was fretful: she agreed her brother wouldn't want 'streamers and those kind of fineries',[41] but surely there was a happy medium between a furtive private burial and a grand theatrical production? Cary Stewkeley, now returned to East Claydon to nurse Mary, was caustic: 'Let me know when my dear uncle is buried,' she wrote, 'that I may steal out to wait on his body to the grave, since it is so private.'[42] But nothing anyone said made the slightest difference.

This wasn't a matter of Jack's notorious good husbandry: he was genuinely trying to carry out his father's wishes, although no doubt he was relieved to find that obligation and inclination came together so neatly. He decreed that the quasi-public areas of Claydon – the hall, screens passage and entrance porch – should be hung with black baize, 'likewise the Brick Parlour from top to bottom'[43] and the chancel and pulpit of All Saints, where the funeral was to take place. He provided mourning for the servants, and ordered escutcheons and a hatchment for 'over the great fore door'. He posted an announcement of his father's death in Buckingham. But he also told Coleman to keep quiet about the date of the funeral, which was to take place on 9 October – otherwise 'one friend will tell another and so all the town and country will know'.[44]

The ninth of October was a cold Friday, wet and windy. Jack had brought his four children down to Claydon the day before; it was the first time he set foot in the house as master. Aunt Gardiner was too frail to make the journey. She regretted it, but she was in any case convinced she would soon be reunited with 'the best of brothers . . . that I believe [to be] a blessed saint in heaven'.[45] She underestimated her powers of persistence; if the reunion ever did take place, it wasn't until 1704, when she was buried next to her husband in the Stewkeley vault at Bray in Berkshire. Aunt Adams, who doesn't seem to have been invited to the funeral, attended her own in 1721, after living a grumpy and impoverished widow for nearly forty years. Uncle Tom – 'my relation whom I never saw in my life,' said Jack, 'though he

hath had many a pound from me' — certainly wasn't invited.[46]
He lived on in an exile of sorts in Wales until 1707, still dreaming
dreams of riches, plotting vengeance on his creditors, begging for
an advance on his quarteredge.

But there were plenty of mourners to see Sir Ralph laid to
rest that night. Jack and his children were there. The service was
taken by William Butterfield, whose father had come to the
Middle Claydon parsonage nearly forty years before. Mrs Lillie
and William Coleman and Peg Adams were there. Cary Stewkeley
stole out from East Claydon, as she had promised: she wasn't
invited back to the house after the service, and caught a cold on
the way home from the wind and the rain beating in through
the window of her carriage. ('It was so dark we durst not put
up the glass.'[47]) The Middle Claydon villagers turned out in force
to show their respect to their landlord of more than fifty years.
And if they were also anxious to demonstrate their loyalty to his
successor, who was something of an unknown quantity, they
needn't have worried. Jack would be a decent enough landlord,
although his outlook remained that of a London merchant and
he would always be governed by profit rather than his father's
feudal sense of social responsibility. He paid off the family's debts,
married the girl next door (who complained constantly about
his meanness), sat twice in Parliament and in June 1703 was
created Baron Verney of Belturbet and Viscount Fermanagh, both
in the Irish peerage.

There were others watching Parson Butterfield as he recited
the Order for the Burial of the Dead in the flickering October
candlelight: Pen and Henry, Elizabeth Palmer and Mary Lawley;
Sir Ralph's mother Margaret, and his 'most dear, most incomparable companion' Mary, the love of his life. They are still there —
not only the Verneys whose bodies lie sealed in lead beneath the
chancel, but all of them. Sir Edmund Verney, tired of searching
disconsolately for his missing hand, and looking down indul-
gently from the monument his son erected as homage, penance,
memorial; the soldier son who was named for him and who died
so casually in the ruins of Drogheda; sisters Susan and Mary and
Peg, who made such disastrous marriages; even Sir Ralph's
outlawed Uncle Francis, whose remains still lie in the grounds
of a Sicilian hospital.

'We brought nothing into this world,' said Butterfield, as the congregation, seen and unseen, looked on. 'And it is certain we can carry nothing out.' The seventeenth-century Verneys left themselves behind.

We should be grateful.

Acknowledgements

Many people have helped me with the writing of this book. My special thanks are due to Sir Edmund Verney and the Claydon House Trust for their kindness in allowing me to quote so liberally from the Verney papers; and to the staff of the Manuscripts Room at the British Library, for their patience and good humour over many months.

On a personal note, I want to thank Dan Franklin of Jonathan Cape, and Jake Morrissey of Riverhead Books, for their encouragement and support; my agents Felicity Bryan and Irene Skolnick, who between them continue to enrich my life; Tricia Lankester, whose advice and enthusiasm for *The Verneys* have made all the difference; Catherine Henaghan, whose ability to provide instant translations of arcane French texts astounds me; Dr Bob Cramb and Dr Jo Cudmore, for sharing their medical knowledge; Kevin Simpson, who talked me through a seventeenth-century bout of madness; and Louise Silverton, who helped me to appreciate the perils of seventeenth-century childbirth.

First and last my thanks, as always, to Helen.

Source Notes

References to the Verney papers are to the sixty reels of micro-filmed letters held at the British Library and classified as M636/1–60. The spelling and punctuation of these and other primary sources have been modernised in the text.

Introduction

1   G. Lipscomb, *The History and Antiquities of the County of Buckingham* (1931–47), I, 183–4.
2   S. R. Gardiner, in Francis Parthenope Verney and Margaret M. Verney, *Memoirs of the Verney Family during the Seventeenth Century* (1904), I, xi.
3   John Bruce (ed.), *Notes of Proceedings in the Long Parliament . . . Taken in the House by Sir Ralph Verney, Knight* (hereafter *Notes of Proceedings in the Long Parliament*), Camden Society 31 (1845), xiii.
4   John Bruce (ed.), *Letters and Papers of the Verney Family*, vi–vii (hereafter *Verney Papers*).
5   Historical Manuscripts Commission, 7th Report (1879), xiv.

6   C. H. Firth,'Memoirs of the Verney Family during the Civil War', *English Historical Review* 8, 31 (July 1893), 579.

7   The two girls, who were born on a grand tour of Europe, were each named for their birthplace. Florence was born at Villa Columbaia, Florence; Parthenope was the Greek name for Naples. Presumably 'Naples Nightingale' was too much, even in 1819.

8   Mrs Cecil Woodham Smith, *Florence Nightingale* (1950); in E. D. Mackerness, 'Frances Parthenope, Lady Verney (1819–1890)', *Journal of Modern History* 30, 2 (June 1958), 131.

9   Tom Verney to Sir Edmund Verney, 4 June 1635; Mun Verney to Ralph Verney, 21 February 1635; Margaret Eure to Ralph Verney, 18 May 1639; Sir William Uvedale to Ann Temple, May 1635; all M636/3.

10   Howard Robinson, *Britain's Post Office* (1953), 25.

11   *Ibid.*, 38.

12   N. H., *The Ladies' Dictionary* (1694), 260.

13   Angel Day, *The English Secretary* (1599), 1.

Chapter 1

1   William Lithgow, *The Totall Discourse, of the Rare Adventures, and painefull Perigrinations of long nineteen Years Travayles* (1632), 397.

2   *Ibid.*, 398.

3   *Ibid.*

4   *Historical Manuscripts Commission Salisbury* 17 (1938), 115.

5   *Ibid.*

6   *Journal of the House of Commons* 1, 26 March 1606.

7   Sir George Carew to the Earl of Salisbury; *Memoirs* I, 48.

8   R. Cottington, *A True Historicall discourse of Muley Hamets rising to the three Kingdoms of Moruecos, Fes, and Sus* (1609), cap. xv [no pagination].

9   *Ibid.*,

10   *Historical Manuscripts Commission Downshire* 2 (1936), 160.

11   *Ibid.*, 186.

12   Philip Gosse, *The History of Piracy* (1968), 121.

13   Robert Adams to his father, Capt. Robert Adams, writing from Salé in Morocco, 4 November 1625; reprinted in Daniel

J.Vitkus (ed.), *Piracy, Slavery, and Redemption: Barbary Captive Narratives from Early Modern England* (2001), 349.

14 Edward Webbe, *The rare and most wonderfull things which Edw. Webbe an Englishman borne, hath seene and passed in his troublesome travailes* (1590), 18 [no pagination].

15 John Bruce (ed.), *Verney Papers* (1853), 100.

16 Lithgow, *Totall Discourse*, 358.

17 *Ibid.*, 397.

18 Bruce, *Verney Papers*, 102.

19 David Lloyd, *Memoires of the lives, actions, sufferings and deaths of those noble, reverend, and excellent personages, that suffered . . . for the Protestant religion* (1668), 352.

20 Arthur Wilson, *The history of Great Britain being the life and reign of King James the First* (1653), 52.

21 Sir Charles Cornwallis, *The Life and Death of our Late Most Incomparable and Heroique Prince, Henry Prince of Wales* (1641), 98.

22 Sir Francis Bacon, 'The Praise of Henry, Prince of Wales', in Joseph Devey (ed.), *The Moral and Historical Works of Lord Bacon* (1866), 494.

23 Roy Strong, *Henry Prince of Wales and England's Lost Renaissance* (1986), 76.

24 Bacon, 'The Praise of Henry, Prince of Wales', in Devey (ed.), *Moral and Historical Works*, 493.

25 Strong, *Henry Prince of Wales* (1986), 49.

26 *Historical Manuscripts Commission Portland* 9 (1923), 10.

27 *Calendar of State Papers, Venetian*, 1603–7, 514.

28 Michael Drayton, *Poly-Olbion* (1612), preface.

29 John Nichols, *The Progresses, Processions, and Magnificent Festivities of King James I* (1828), II, 490.

30 14 September 1611, S.P. Spain, 18/184.

31 Sir Francis Bacon, 'Of Nobility', *Essayes and Counsels, Civil and Moral* (1664), 71.

Chapter 2

1 *The Kings Maiesties Speach To the Lord and Commons* (1609), 7.

2 Norman E. McClure (ed.), *The Letters of John Chamberlain* (1939), II, 343.

3 C. P. Hill, *Who's Who in Stuart Britain* (1988), 17.

4   Sir Richard Graham to Sir Edmund Verney, June 1622; in John Bruce (ed.), *Verney Papers*, 106.

5   *Ibid.*

6   S. R. Gardiner, *History of England from the Accession of James I to the Outbreak of the Civil War, 1603–1624,* V (1908), 9.

7   Elisabeth Bourcier (ed.), *The Diary of Sir Simonds D'Ewes, 1622–1624* (1974), 102.

8   S. R. Gardiner, *Prince Charles and the Spanish Marriage: 1617–1623* (1869), II, 339.

9   William Wood, *Considerations upon the Treaty of Marriage between England and Spain* (1623), 3.

10 'Sir Richard Wynn's Account of the Journey of Prince Charles's Servants into Spain in the Year 1623', in Thomas Hearne, *Historia Vitae et Regni Richardi II* (1729), 300.

11 *Ibid.*, 301.

12 *Ibid.*, 303.

13 *Ibid.*, 303.

14 *Ibid.*, 304.

15 *Ibid.*, 305.

16 *Ibid.*, 322.

17 James Howell, *Instructions for Forreine Travell* (1642), 86.

18 Sir Ralph Winwood, *Memorials of Affairs of State in the Reigns of Queen Elizabeth and King James I* (1725), II, 74.

19 Sir Charles Petrie (ed.), *The Letters, Speeches and Proclamations of King Charles I* (1935), 10.

20 *Relacion de la Entrada que el Principe de Gales* (1623); in Henry Ettinghausen, *Prince Charles and the King of Spain's Sister: What the Papers Said* (1985), 7.

21 H. M. Colvin, *The History of the King's Works* (1982), IV, 248; quoting S.P. 14/144, no. 11.

22 'Sir Richard Wynn's Account . . .', 328.

23 *Ibid.*

24 *Ibid.*, 332.

25 Peter Verney, *The Standard Bearer: The Story of Sir Edmund Verney, Knight-Marshal to King Charles I* (1963), 61.

26 Charles and Buckingham to James I, 20 August 1623, in Petrie (ed.), *Letters, Speeches*, 28.

27 James Howell, *Epistolae Ho-Elianae* (1655), I, 134.

28 Christopher Hibbert, *Charles I* (1968), 82.

29 Anon., 'Hell in Epitome' (1718).

30 *Calendar of State Papers, Domestic Series* (hereafter CSPD) 1629–31, 281.

31 Samuel Sorbière, *A Voyage to England, Containing Many Things Relating to the State of Learning, Religion, and other Curiosities of that Kingdom* (1709), 16.

32 Count Lorenzo Magalotti, *Travels of Cosmo III, Grand Duke of Tuscany* (1821), 367.

33 Verney, *Standard Bearer*, 86.

34 Bruce, *Verney Papers*, 116.

35 Thomas Gataker, *A good wife Gods gift and, a wife indeed – two marriage sermons* (1623), 8.

36 Robert Wilkinson, *[The] merchant royall a sermon preached at WhiteHall before the Kings Maiestie, at the nuptialls of the right Honorable the Lord Hay, and his Ladie, vpon the twelfe day last, being Ianuar. 6. 1607* (1613).

Chapter 3

1 Orders in John Bruce (ed.), *Verney Papers*, 140–41.

2 *Ibid.*, 142.

3 Lady Margaret Verney to Mary Wiseman, June 1629; M636/2.

4 Mary Wiseman to Lady Margaret Verney, 20 June 1629; Mary Wiseman to Mary Verney (*née* Blacknall), June 1629; both M636/2.

5 John Crowther to Ralph Verney, 21 September 1631; M636/2.

6 J. H. Bettey (ed.), *Calendar of the Correspondence of the Smyth Family of Ashton Court, 1548–1642*, Bristol Record Society 35 (1982), 63.

7 John Crowther to Ralph Verney, 23 December 1631; M636/2.

8 Stephen Porter, 'University and Society', in Nicholas Tyacke (ed.), *The History of the University of Oxford*, IV: *Seventeenth-Century Oxford* (1997), 68–9.

9 Bodleian MS Ballard 49, f.172r; in Porter, 'University and Society', 68.

10 John Crowther to Ralph Verney, 6 November 1631; M636/2.

11 *Ibid.*

12 *Ibid.*, 18 December 1631 and 23 December 1631; both M636/2.

13 *Ibid.*, 18 December 1631; M636/2.

14 James Dillon to Ralph Verney, 12 June 1633; M636/2.

15 Ralph Verney to James Dillon, 22 February 1634; M636/2.

16 James Dillon to Ralph Verney, 19 March 1634; M636/2.

17 Ralph Verney to James Dillon, 1 April 1636; M636/3.

18 Sir Edmund Verney to Ralph Verney, 30 March 1636; M636/3.

19 *Ibid.*, 5 January 1635; M636/3.

20 *Ibid.*, 30 March 1636; M636/3.

21 *Ibid.*

22 John Smith, *The Generall Historie of Virginia, New England and the Summer Isles . . . from their first beginning An: 1584 to this present 1624* (1624), 29.

23 Alexander Brown, *The Genesis of the United States* (1897), I, 356.

24 William Crashaw, *A sermon preached in London before the right honorable the Lord Lawarre, Lord Gouernour and Captaine Generall of Virginea, and others of his Maiesties Counsell for that kingdome, and the rest of the aduenturers in that plantation* (1610) [no pagination].

25 John Sadler to Lady Margaret Verney, 30 July 1634; M636/2.

26 Susan M. Kingsbury (ed.), *The Records of the Virginia Company of London* (1906–35), III, 299.

27 John Sadler to Lady Margaret Verney, 30 July 1634; M636/2.

28 *Ibid.* There is still a Merchant's Hope church at Hopewell, Va., a relic of a plantation in Martin's Brandon parish which Barker bought in the 1630s.

29 Mary Verney to John Sadler, 1 August 1634; M636/2.

30 John Smith, *Advertisements for the unexperienced Planters of New-England* (1631), 28.

31 William Bradford, *History of Plymouth Plantation, 1620–1647* (1912), I, 149.

32 Smith, *Generall Historie of Virginia, New-England and the Summer Isles* (1624), 27.

33 *Ibid.*

34 *Ibid.*, 34

35 Lyon Gardiner Tyler (ed.), *Narratives of Early Virginia* (1907), 285.

36 Tom Verney to Ralph Verney, 13 June 1635; M636/3.

37 *Ibid.*, 24 August 1635; M636/3.

38   Tom Verney to Sir Edmund Verney, 11 October 1635; M636/3.
39   *Ibid.*, 22 October 1635; M636/3.
40   Tom Verney to Ralph Verney, April 1636; M636/3.
41   *Ibid.*, 15 July 1636; M636/3.
42   *Ibid.*, 4 August 1636; M636/3.
43   *Ibid.*, 8 April 1637; M636/3.
44   Tom Verney to Sir Edmund Verney, 12 February 1638; M636/3.
45   *Memoirs* I, 89.
46   Tom Verney to Ralph Verney, 22 July 1638; M636/3. 'Don' in this sense is an archaic word for a gift or donation.
47   *Ibid.*
48   *The office of Christian parents shewing how children are to be gouerned throughout all ages and times of their life* (1616), 231.
49   Edward Lawrence, *Parents' groans over their wicked children* (1681), 73.
50   *Memoirs* I, 91.
51   Lawrence, *Parents' groans*, 21.
52   Mun Verney to Ralph Verney, 25 August 1636; M636/3.
53   Henry Wilkinson to Ralph Verney, 26 December 1636; M636/3.
54   Sir Edmund Verney to Mun Verney, April 1637; M636/3.
55   John Crowther to Ralph Verney, 23 July 1637; M636/3.
56   Sir Edmund Verney to John Crowther, 18 July 1637; M636/3.
57   Mun Verney to Ralph Verney, 12 August 1637; M636/3.
58   Henry Verney to Ralph Verney, 19 April 1637; M636/3.
59   Mun Verney to Ralph Verney, 21 December 1638; M636/3.

Chapter 4

1   Ralph Verney to Nancy Denton, 27 July 1652; M636/11.
2   Ralph Verney to William Denton, 1652; M636/11.
3   *Ibid.*
4   1684 edn, prefatory 'Letter to her Husband'. There were eight editions of *The Mother's Legacy* in the seventeenth century alone.
5   Robert Burton, *The Anatomy of Melancholy*, (ed. Holbrook Jackson), New York Review Books (2001), part 3, 118.
6   Thomas Middleton, *A Trick to Catch the Old One* (1608), I, i.

7   Pen Verney to Ralph Verney, 3 June 1643; M636/5.

8   Mall Verney to Mary Verney, September 1647; M636/8.

9   Sir Edmund Verney to Lady Margaret Verney, 28 March 1637; M636/3.

10 Mun Verney to Ralph Verney, 15 December 1638; M636/3.

11 For instance, Sir Edmund Verney to Mary Verney, 20 August 1635; M636/3.

12 Sir Edmund Verney to Ralph Verney, 19 May 1638; M636/3.

13 *Ibid.*

14 Raymond A. Anselment, '"The Teares of Nature": Seventeenth-Century Parental Bereavement', *Modern Philology* 91 (August 1993), 33, fn 23.

15 Sir Edmund Verney to Ralph Verney, 19 May 1638; M636/3.

16 Mun Verney to Ralph Verney, 24 November 1638; M636/3.

17 Sir Edmund Verney to Ralph Verney, 13 March 1635; M636/2.

18 *Ibid.*, 4 August 1636; M636/3.

19 Anon., *A Narrative of the Draining of the Great Level of the Fens* (1660), [no pagination].

20 Sir John Leeke to Sir Edmund Verney, 4 February [1636]; M636/3.

21 Albert J. Loomie (ed.), *Ceremonies of Charles I: The Note Books of John Finet 1628–1641* (1987), 230.

22 Godfrey Davies, *The Early Stuarts, 1603–1660* (1952), 69.

23 Christopher Hibbert, *Charles I* (1968), 141.

24 William Laud, *Works*, eds J Bliss and W. Scott (1847–60), VI, 57.

25 Inigo Jones and William Davenant, *Britannia Triumphans* (1638), 20.

26 *Ibid.*, 1.

27 William Prynne, *Histrio-Matrix* (1633), 256.

28 *Ibid.*, 258.

29 Richard Mocket, *God and the King* (1616), 79.

30 *Ibid.*, 81–2.

Chapter 5

1   The Earl of Pembroke and Montgomery to Sir Edmund Verney, 7 February 1639; in John Bruce (ed.), *Verney Papers*, 205.

2 Bruce, *Verney Papers*, 198.

3 Lord Deincourt to Margaret Pulteney, 24 May 1638; M636/3.

4 Margaret Pulteney to Ralph Verney, 28 May 1638; M636/3.

5 Lady Susan Denton to Ralph Verney, 16 March 1639; M636/3.

6 Edward Hyde, Earl of Clarendon, *The History of the Rebellion and Civil Wars in England* (1888), I, 154.

7 *CSPD* 1640–41, 212.

8 Clarendon, *History of the Rebellion*, I, 161.

9 Mun Verney to Ralph Verney, 21 March 1639; M636/3.

10 Prob/11/190.

11 Sir Edmund Verney to Ralph Verney, 1 April 1639; M636/3.

12 John Rushworth, *Historical Collections . . . in Five Parliaments* (1721), II, 908.

13 Sir Edmund Verney to Ralph Verney, 4 April 1639, 1 April 1639; M636/3.

14 *Ibid.*, 4 April 1639; M636/3.

15 Ralph Verney to Sir Edmund Verney, 1 April 1639; M636/3.

16 Sir Edmund Verney to Mary Verney, 9 April 1639; M636/3.

17 Sir Edmund Verney to Ralph Verney, 28 April 1639; M636/3.

18 Margaret Pulteney [Eure] to Ralph Verney, 18 May 1639; M636/3.

19 Sir Edmund to Ralph Verney, Easter night, 14 April 1639; M636/3.

20 John Aston, 'Diary', in J. C. Hodgson (ed.), *Six North Country Diaries*, Surtees Society 118 (1910), 6.

21 Thomas Windebank to his father, Secretary Windebank, 19 April 1639; *CSPD* 1639, 58.

22 Arundel to Secretary Windebank, 20 April 1639; *CSPD* 1639, 65.

23 Sir Edmund Verney to Ralph Verney, 25 April 1639; M636/3.

24 4 Henry IV c.13, in Mark Charles Fissel, *The Bishops' War; Charles I's Campaigns Against Scotland, 1638–1640*, 21.

25 Sir Edmund Verney to Ralph Verney, 1 May 1639; M636/3.

26 *Ibid.*, M636/3.

27 *Ibid.*, 9 May 1639; M636/3.

28 *Ibid.*, 11 May 1639; M636/3.

29 John Aston, 'Diary', 8.

30 Ralph Verney to William Denton, 10 May 1639; M636/3.

31 Ralph Verney to Sir Edmund Verney, 10 May 1639; M636/3.

32 Sir Edmund Verney to Ralph Verney, received 18 May 1639; M636/3.

33 John Aston, 'Diary', 13.

34 Sir Edmund Verney to Ralph Verney, 22 May 1639; M636/3.

35 *Ibid.*

36 John Aston, 'Diary', 12.

37 *CSPD* 1639, 78–9.

38 *Ibid.*, 165.

39 Edward Norgate to Thomas Reade, 3 and 4 June 1639; *CSPD* 1639, 271.

40 Edward Norgate to Robert Reade, 5 June 1639; S. P. 16/423/29.

41 William Denton to Ralph Verney from Chillingham, 11 June 1639; M636/3.

42 Sir Edmund Verney to Ralph Verney, 4 June 1639; M636/3.

43 *CSPD* 1639, 272.

44 John Aston, 'Diary', 23.

45 Sir Edmund Verney to Ralph Verney, 4 June 1639; M636/3.

46 *Ibid.*, 5 June 1639; M636/3.

47 *Ibid.*, 9 June 1639; M636/3.

48 Sir John Borough to Secretary Windebank, 12 June 1639; *CSPD* 1639, 304.

49 Sir Edmund Verney to Ralph Verney, 11 June 1639; M636/3.

50 *Ibid.*, 15 June 1639; M636/3.

51 *Ibid.*

Chapter 6

1 Lady Susan Denton to Ralph Verney, 21 May 1639; M636/3.

2 *Ibid.*; M636/3.

3 Ralph Verney to Lady Susan Denton, 22 May 1639; M636/3.

4 Ralph Verney to Sir Edmund Verney, 18 June 1639; M636/3.

5 *Ibid.*; M636/3.

6 William Denton to Ralph Verney, 11 June 1639; M636/3.

7 *Ibid.*, 26 June 1639; M636/3.

8 Tom Verney to Sir Edmund Verney, 10 February 1639; M636/3.

9 *Ibid.*

10 *Ibid.*

11 *Ibid.*

12 *Ibid.*

13 *Ibid.*

14 *Ibid.*

15 *Ibid.*

16 *Ibid.*

17 *Ibid.*

18 James Futter to Sir Edmund Verney, enclosed with Tom Verney to Sir Edmund Verney, 20 May 1639; M636/3.

19 Tom Verney to Ralph Verney, 20 May 1639; M636/3.

20 Tom Verney to Sir Edmund Verney, 20 May 1639; M636/3.

21 Tom Verney to Lady Margaret Verney, 10 February 1639; M636/3.

22 Tom Verney to Sir Edmund Verney, 20 May 1639; M636/3.

23 Sir Edmund Verney to Tom Verney, July 1639; M636/3.

24 Mun Verney to Ralph Verney, 28 January 1640; M636/4.

25 John Bruce (ed.), *Verney Papers*, 262.

26 Lady Susan Denton to Ralph Verney, 29 October 1639; M636/4.

27 *Ibid.*, 26 April 1638; M636/3.

28 Mun Verney to Ralph Verney, 5 January 1639; M636/3.

29 Ralph Verney to Peg Verney, 16 August 1639; M636/3.

30 *Ibid.*, 4 December 1639; M636/4.

31 Peg Verney to Ralph Verney, 1 December 1639; M636/4.

32 Ralph Verney to Peg Verney, 3 August 1640; M636/4.

33 *Memoirs* I, 147.

34 Lady Sussex to Ralph Verney, January 1639; M636/3.

35 *Ibid.*, May 1639; M636/3.

36 *Ibid.*, 25 July 1639; M636/3.

37 Ralph Verney to Sir Edmund Verney, 27 July 1639; M636/3.

38 Lady Sussex to Ralph Verney, 12 November 1639; M636/4.

39 *Ibid.*, March 1640; M636/4.

40 *Memoirs* I, 154.

41 D. Piper, 'Some portraits by Marcus Gheeraerts and John de Critz reconsidered', *Proceedings of the Huguenot Society* 20, 2 (1960), 212.

42 Lady Sussex to Ralph Verney, 18 January 1640; M636/4.

43 *Ibid.*

44 *Ibid.*, 1 December 1639; M636/4.

45 Roger de Piles, *The Art of Painting and the Lives of the Painters* (1706), 306.

46 H. Forester (trans.), *Memoirs of Princess Sophia, Electress of Hanover* (1888), 13.

47 Lady Sussex to Ralph Verney, April 1640; M636/4.

Chapter 7

1 Sir Edward Cecil, in Charles Dalton, *The Life and Times of Sir Edward Cecil* (1885), II, 399.

2 William Barriffe, *Military Discipline: or, the yong artillery man* (1635), 2; John Dryden, *Cymon and Iphigenia.*

3 Sir William St Leger to the Duke of Buckingham in Dalton, *Life of Sir Edward Cecil*, II, 200.

4 Dalton, *Cecil*, II, 221.

5 Brooke, Robert Greville, Lord, *A worthy speech made by the Right Honourable the Lord Brooke, at the election of his captaines and commanders at Warwick Castle* (1643), 6.

6 These figures come from Charles Carlton, *Going to the Wars: The Experience of the British Civil Wars 1638–1651* (1992), 19, Much of what follows on British veterans in the Thirty Years War I owe to Carlton's excellent account.

7 Robert Monro, *Monro his expedition with the worthy Scots regiment . . .* (1637), 36, 75.

8 Richard Bonney, *The Thirty Years' War 1618–48* (2002), 68.

9 Mun Verney to Ralph Verney, 4 September 1639; M636/4.

10 Carlton, *Going to the Wars*, 18.

11 Bonney, *The Thirty Years' War*, 74.

12 *Memoirs* I, 116.

13 Mun Verney to Ralph Verney, 16 December 1639; M636/4.

14 *Ibid.*, 9 November 1639; M636/4.

15 Mun Verney to Ralph Verney, 9 April 1640; M636/4.

16 *Calendar of State Papers, Venetian, 1636–39*, 605.

17 PRO S.P. 16/452/31.

18 Ruth Spalding (ed.), *The Diary of Bulstrode Whitelocke 1605–1675*, Records of Social and Economic History, New Series XIII, British Academy (1990), 121. Whitelocke referred to himself in the third person throughout his diary.

19 Mun Verney to Ralph Verney, 21 May 1640; M636/4.

20 *Ibid.*, 31 July 1640; M636/4.

21 Mark Charles Fissel, *The Bishops' War: Charles I's Campaigns Against Scotland, 1638–40, 268.*

22 PRO S.P. 16/466/23.

23 *CSPD* 1640, 476.

24 Astley to Edward, Viscount Conway, 5 August 1640; *CSPD* 1640, 559.

25 Bodleian Library, Clarendon S.P. 19, 171v.

26 Mun Verney to Ralph Verney, 10 September 1640; M636/4.

27 *Ibid.*, 12 October 1640; M636/4.

28 *Ibid.*, 10 September 1640; M636/4.

29 James F. Larkin and Paul L. Hughes (eds), *Stuart Royal Proclamations* (1983), II, 732.

30 Mun Verney to Ralph Verney, 19 October 1640; M636/4.

31 *Ibid.*

32 The first phrase is from the Oath of Supremacy, required by the Act of Supremacy of 1559. The rest of the quotation comes from the Oath of Allegiance which MPs were also required to take under the terms of the Oath of Allegiance Act 1609.

33 3 November 1640, *CSPD* 1640–41, 242.

34 Edward Hyde, Earl of Clarendon, *The History of the Rebellion and Civil Wars in England* (1888), 239–40.

35 Speech by John Pym to the House of Commons, 7 November 1640; in Conrad Russell, *The Fall of the British Monarchies 1637–1642* (1991), 216–17.

36 Vere Gawdy to Mary Verney, 16 August 1640; Lady Sussex to Ralph Verney, 3 November 1640; both M636/4.

37 Betty Adams to Ralph Verney, 18 March 1664; M636/19.

38 Larry Gragg, 'A vagabond in paradise: Thomas Verney in Barbados', *History Today* 45 (August 1995), 44.

39 William Bullock, *Virginia impartially examined and left to publick view* (1649), 14.

40 Tom Verney to Sir Edmund Verney, 17 April 1642; M636/5.

41 *Ibid.*

42 Tom Verney to Will Roades, 21 May 1642; M636/5.

43 *Ibid.*

Chapter 8

1 John Bruce (ed.), *Notes of Proceedings in the Long Parliament*, Camden Society (1845), 156. The MP, who is referred to only as 'T.T.', was either Thomas Toll of King's Lynn, or Thomas Tomkins of Weobley in Herefordshire.

2 *Journal of the House of Commons* 2, 13 February 1641.

3 *Journal of the House of Commons* 2, 11 and 19 March, 10 February 1641.

4 *Journal of the House of Commons* 2, 2 June 1641.

5 Ruth Spalding (ed.), *The Diary of Bulstrode Whitelock 1605–1675* (1990), 122.

6 Although Hoby was well known in Great Marlow, his home was Bisham, just across the Buckinghamshire–Berkshire border.

7 Bruce, *Notes of Proceedings in the Long Parliament*, 3.

8 *Ibid.*, 10. Cornelius Burges was one of the ministers appointed by the Commons to preach to them. His writings included *The Fire of the Sanctuarie newly uncovered, or, a Compleat tract of zeale* (1625).

9 *Ibid.*, 12.

10 Vernon F. Snow and Anne Steele Young (eds), *The Private Journals of the Long Parliament: 7 March to 1 June 1642* (1987), 57.

11 Will of Lady Margaret Verney, 2 May 1639; *Memoirs* I, 224.

12 Tom Verney to Mary Verney, April 1648; M636/8.

13 *Memoirs* I, 227.

14 Lady Sussex to Sir Ralph Verney, 12 April 1641; M636/4.

15 *Ibid.*, 26 April 1641; M636/4.

16 Mun Verney to Mary Verney, 2 July 1641; M636/4.

17 James Dillon to Ralph Verney, 27 July 1633; M636/2.

18 Sir Ralph Verney to Lady Barrymore, 7 June 1641; M636/4.

19 Bruce, *Notes of Proceedings in the Long Parliament*, 43.

20 *Ibid.*, 70–71.

21 David Hume, The *History of England from the Invasion of Julius Caesar to the Revolution in 1688* (1778), V.

22 'Declaration of the objects of resistance of Sir Phelim O'Neill', in John D'Alton, *History of Drogheda* (1997), 222–3.

23 Richard Bellings, in John T. Gilbert (ed.), *History of the Irish Confederation and the War in Ireland, 1641–1643* (1882), I, 2.

24　Sir Ralph Verney to Lady Barrymore, 13 November 1641; M636/4.

25　*Memoirs* I, 124.

26　Lady Barrymore to Sir Ralph Verney, 18 February 1639; M636/3.

27　Sir Ralph Verney to Lady Barrymore, 13 November 1641; M636/4.

28　Sir John Leeke to Sir Edmund Verney, 10 January 1642; M636/4.

29　*Ibid.*

30　Sir Ralph Verney to Lady Barrymore, 13 November 1641; M636/4.

31　*Memoirs* I, 230.

32　Tom Reilly, *Cromwell: An Honourable Enemy* (1999), 20.

33　Sir John Leeke to Sir Edmund Verney, 10 January 1642; M636/4.

34　*Ibid.*, 4 March 1642; M636/4.

35　Sir John Leeke to Sir Edmund Verney, 10 January 1642; M636/4.

36　*Journal of the House of Commons* 2, 1 November 1641.

37　'The Petition of the House of Commons, which accompanied the Remonstrance of the state of the kingdom', S. R. Gardiner (ed.), *The Constitutional Documents of the Puritan Revolution 1625–1660* (1906), 202.

38　*Ibid.*

39　Bruce, *Notes of Proceedings in the Long Parliament*, 122.

40　*Ibid.*, 124.

41　*Ibid.*

42　Lady Sussex to Sir Ralph Verney, 29 November 1641; M636/4.

43　PRO S.P. 16/486/99; in Conrad Russell, *The Fall of the British Monarchies 1637–1642* (1991), 432.

44　Russell, *Fall of the British Monarchies*, 441.

45　Bruce, *Notes of Proceedings in the Long Parliament*, 137.

46　*Ibid.*, 138.

47　*Ibid.*

48　Willson H. Coates, Anne Steele Young and Vernon F. Snow (eds), *Private Journals of the Long Parliament, 3 January to 5 March 1642* (1997), 11–12.

49　Bruce, *Notes of Proceedings in the Long Parliament*, 139.

50   *Ibid.*

51   *Ibid.*

52   *Ibid.*

53   Lady Sussex to Sir Ralph Verney, 10 January 1642; M636/4.

54   Bruce, *Notes of Proceedings in the Long Parliament*, 140.

55   Lady Sussex to Sir Ralph Verney, 10 January 1642; M636/4.

56   *Memoirs* I, 278.

57   James Dillon to Sir Ralph Verney, 24 October 1631; M636/2.

58   *Ibid.*

59   Mun Verney to Sir Ralph Verney, 11 December 1641; M636/4.

60   Anon., *The Bloudy Persecution of the Protestants in Ireland, being The Contents of severall Letters brought by his Majesties Post from Ireland, November the 21, 1641* (1641), 12.

61   Mun Verney to Sir Ralph Verney, 18 December 1641; M636/4.

62   *Ibid.*, 4 March 1642; M636/4.

63   Henry Jones, *A Perfect Relation of the Beginning and Continuation of the Irish-Rebellion* (1641 [January 1642]), 8.

64   Mun Verney to Sir Ralph Verney, 4 March 1642; M636/4.

65   *Ibid.*, 29 March 1642; M636/4.

66   Anon., *The Last True News from Ireland . . . Wherein is declared many great overthrowes and defeates given to the rebels, likewise the manner how a great castle called Carricke Mayne (within 6 myles of Dublin) was taken by the English* (1642), 3.

67   Mun Verney to Sir Ralph Verney, 22 June 1642; M636/4.

68   *Ibid.*, 4 March 1641; M636/4.

69   *Journal of the House of Commons* 2, 24 May 1642.

Chapter 9

1   Margaret Eure to Sir Ralph Verney, 22 August 1642; M636/4.

2   *Ibid.*, 7 May 1642; M636/4.

3   Lady Sussex to Sir Ralph Verney, 29 January 1642; M636/4.

4   *Ibid.*, 19 June 1642; M636/4.

5   W.A. Day (ed.), *The Pythouse Papers: Correspondence Concerning the Civil War . . .* (1879), xvii.

6   Edward Hyde, Earl of Clarendon, *The History of the Rebellion and Civil Wars in England* (1888), I, 220.

7   John Bruce (ed.), *Notes of Proceedings of the Long Parliament*, 167–8.

8   Cary Gardiner to Sir Ralph Verney, 28 July 1642; M636/4.

9   Sir Thomas Gardiner to Mary Verney, 17 June 1642; M636/4.

10   Cary Gardiner to Sir Ralph Verney, 4 September 1642; M636/4.

11   Sir Ralph Verney to Will Roades, 9 June 1642; M636/4.

12   Cary Gardiner to Sir Ralph Verney, 28 July 1642; M636/4.

13   Sir Edmund Verney to Will Roades, 10 July 1642; M636/4.

14   Sir Ralph Verney to Will Roades, July 1642; M636/4.

15   Sir Edmund Verney to Will Roades, 2 August 1642; M636/4.

16   Edward Hyde, Earl of Clarendon, *The Life of Edward Earl of Clarendon . . . written by himself* (1857), I, 135.

17   *Memoirs* I, 254.

18   Anon., *A true and exact Relation of the Manner of his Majesties setting up his Standard at Nottingham, on Monday the 22. of Aug. 1642* (1642), 5.

19   David Lloyd, *Memoires of the lives, actions, sufferings and deaths of those noble, reverend, and excellent personages, that suffered . . . for the Protestant religion* (1668), 352.

20   Henry Oxinden of Deane, 27 January 1642; in Martyn Bennett, *The Civil Wars in Britain and Ireland 1638–1651* (1997), 113.

21   Captain Thomas Gardiner to Mary Verney, 5 September 1642; M636/4. Gardiner is quoting Mary's words back to her.

22   Anon. to Mary Verney, 5 September 1642; M636/4.

23   Mary Verney to Cary Gardiner, 23 September 1642; M636/4.

24   Anne Sydenham to Mary Verney, 2 September 1642; M636/4.

25   *Ibid.*

26   Doll Leeke to Mary Verney, 7 August 1642; M636/4.

27   *Ibid.*, 1 September 1642; M636/4.

28   Tom Verney to Sir Ralph Verney, 10 January 1643; M636/5.

29   Mun Verney to Sir Ralph Verney, 14 September 1642; M636/4.

30   Lady Sussex to Sir Ralph Verney, 9 September 1642; M636/4.

31   *Ibid.*

32   *Ibid.*, 18 September 1642; M636/4.

33   *Ibid.*

34   Clarendon, *History of the Rebellion*, II, 356.

35   Bartholomew Elliott G. Warburton, *Memoirs of Prince Rupert and the Cavaliers including their private correspondence* (1849), II, 12.

36 Clarendon, *History of the Rebellion*, II, 352n.

37 J. S. Clarke (ed.), *The life of James II, collected out of memoirs writ of his own hand* (1816), I, 10–11.

38 Peter Verney, *The Standard Bearer: The Story of Sir Edmund Verney, Knight-Marshal to King Charles I* (1963), 198.

39 Sir Richard Bulstrode, *Memoirs and Reflections* (1721). Bulstrode's account of the battle is reprinted in Peter Young, *Edgehill 1642* (1967), 266.

40 Clarendon, *History of the Rebellion*, II, 361.

41 *Ibid.*, 353n.

42 *Ibid.*

43 Lloyd, *Memoires*, 352.

44 C. H. Firth (ed.), *The Memoirs of Edmund Ludlow, Lieutenant-General of the Horse in the Army of the Commonwealth* (1894), I, 43.

45 *Speciall Passages*; in Peter Young, *Edgehill 1642*, 116.

46 Lady Sussex to Sir Ralph Verney, 25 October 1642; M636/4.

47 *Ibid.*, 27 October 1642; M636/4.

48 *Ibid.*

49 Sir Ralph Verney to Lady Sussex, 29 October 1642; M636/4.

50 Sir William Balfour *et al*, *An Exact and True Relation of the Dangerous and Bloudy Fight, Between His Majesties Armie, and the Parliaments Forces* . . . (1642), 3, 7, 5.

51 Sir Edward Sydenham to Sir Ralph Verney, 27 October 1642; M636/4.

52 Sir Ralph Verney to Lady Sussex, 31 October 1642; M636/4.

53 Lady Sussex to Sir Ralph Verney, 31 October 1642; M636/4.

Chapter 10

1 Lady Sussex to Sir Ralph Verney, 30 March 1643; *Memoirs* I, 293.

2 Elizabeth Isham to Sir Ralph Verney, 9 May 1643; M636/5.

3 Thomas Ogle, 24 November 1644; *Camden Miscellany* 8 (1883), 3.

4 Sir Ralph Verney to Sir Robert Reynolds, November 1643; M636/5.

5 Robert Baillie, *Letters and Journals* (1775), II, 117.

6 Anon., *A Brief Discourse, declaring the Impiety and Unlawfulness of the new Covenant with the Scots* (1643), 5–6.

7 Doll Leeke to Sir Ralph Verney, 10 August 1643; M636/5.

8 *Ibid.*

9 Sir Ralph Verney to Sir Robert Reynolds, November 1643; M636/5.

10 Sir Roger Burgoyne to Sir Ralph Verney, 25 September 1643; M636/5.

11 *A Perfect Diurnall*, 25 September to 2 October 1643, 2.

12 'The Solemn League and Covenant', in S. R. Gardiner (ed.), *The Constitutional Documents of the Puritan Revolution 1625–1660* (1906), 268–9.

13 *A Perfect Diurnall*, 25 September to 2 October 1643, 2.

14 *Journal of the House of Commons* 3, 2 November 1643.

15 *Memoirs* I, 330.

16 30 November 1643; M636/5. As a precautionary measure, Sir Ralph also obtained a pass from the Royalist side.

17 Sir Ralph Verney to Lady Sussex, November 1643; M636/5.

18 *Ibid.*, 21 December 1643 (31 December according to the Gregorian Calendar which was in force across Catholic Europe); M636/5.

19 Mun Verney to Sir Ralph Verney, 24 October 1643; M636/5.

20 Lady Sussex to Sir Ralph Verney, 30 January 1643; M636/5.

21 *Mercurius Veridicus*, 27 February to 5 March 1644, 6.

22 Lady Sussex to Sir Ralph Verney, 30 June 1643; M636/5.

23 *Mercurius Aulicus*, week ending 10 February 1643 [i.e., 1644], 3.

24 *The Scotish Dove, sent out and returning*, 1 March to 8 March 1644, 6.

25 *Mercurius Civicus*, 29 February to 7 March 1644, 2.

26 *The Weekly Account*, 29 February to 6 March, 1644, 6.

27 *Mercurius Aulicus*, 3 March to 9 March 1644, 4–5.

28 *Ibid.*, 6.

29 Pen Verney to Sir Ralph Verney; March 1644; M636/5.

30 Sir Alexander Denton to Sir Ralph Verney, 28 March 1644; M636/5.

31 Reverend Henry Roundell, 'Hillesden House in 1644; *Records of Buckinghamshire II* (1863), 97.

32 Elizabeth Isham to Sir Ralph Verney, 13 July 1644; M636/5.

33 *Journal of the House of Commons* 3, 16 March 1644.

34 Elizabeth Isham to Sir Ralph Verney, 15 August 1644; M636/6.

35 Susan Verney to Sir Ralph, 10 October 1644; M636/6.

36 Elizabeth Isham to Sir Ralph Verney, 15 August 1644; M636/6.

37 Margaret Eure to Sir Ralph Verney, 4 November 1644; M636/6.

38 Doll Leeke to Sir Ralph Verney, 25 August 1644; M636/6.

39 Henry Verney to Sir Ralph Verney, 5 October 1645; M636/6.

40 *Memoirs* II, 37.

41 *Memoirs* I, 322.

42 John Aubrey, *Aubrey's Brief Lives*, ed. Oliver Lawson Dick, Mandarin (1992), 103.

43 14 January 1644; M636/5.

44 Richard Ferrier 'The Journal of Major Richard Ferrier M.P., while travelling in France in the year 1687', *Camden Miscellany*, N. S. 53, IX (1895), 38.

45 Peter Heylyn, *A full relation of two journeys, the one into the main-land of France, the other into some of the adjacent ilands performed and digested into six books* (1656), 19–20.

46 Ferrier, 'The Journal of Major Richard Ferrier', 38.

47 Anon., *A New Journey to France* (1715), 118.

48 John Clenche, *A Tour in France and Italy, made by an Englishman, 1675* (1676), 2.

49 Sir Ralph Verney to Doll Leeke, March 1644; M636/5.

50 Sir Ralph Verney to Lady Anne Hobart, 7 March 1644; M636/5.

51 *An Ordinance of the Lords and Commons assembled in Parliament; with instructions for the taking of the League and Covenant . . .* (1644), 9–10. This exhortation was to be read in every church in the nation, along with the Covenant itself.

52 *Journal of the House of Commons* 3, 27 February 1644.

53 *Ibid.*, 16 October 1644.

54 *Ibid.*, 3, 4 March 1644.

55 *Ibid.*, 17 August 1644.

56 *Ibid.*, 10 August 1644.

57 *Memoirs* I, 326.

58 Sir Ralph Verney to Henry Parker, 6 December 1644; M636/6.

59 Sir Roger Burgoyne to Sir Ralph Verney, 24 September 1644; M636/6.

60 Sir Ralph Verney to Sir Roger Burgoyne, 20 October 1645; M636/6.

61 *Journal of the House of Commons* 4, 12 August 1645.

62 *Memoirs* 1, 329.

63 Clenche, *Tour in France and Italy*, 11.

64 Sir Ralph Verney to J. Coke, 30 June 1650; M636/10.

65 Sir Ralph Verney to Mun Verney, 5 July 1648; M636/9.

66 Sir Ralph Verney to Mary Verney, 7 March 1647; M636/8.

67 Clenche, *Tour in France and Italy*, 13, 14.

68 Henry Verney to Will Roades, 22 February 1647; M636/8.

69 Tom Verney to Will Roades, 29 April 1650; M636/10.

70 Will Roades to Sir Ralph Verney, February 1646; M636/7.

71 Sir Roger Burgoyne to Sir Ralph Verney, 15 January 1646; M636/7.

72 *Calendar of the Committee for Compounding*, 1576.

73 William Denton to Sir Ralph Verney, August 1646; M636/7.

74 Sir Ralph Verney to Henry Verney, 13 November 1646; M636/7.

Chapter 11

1 C. H. Firth (ed.), *The Life of William Cavendish . . . by Margaret, Duchess of Newcastle* (1890), 20.

2 Bathsua Makin, *An Essay to Revive the Antient Education of Gentlewomen* (1673), 25.

3 Mary Verney to Sir Ralph Verney, 3 December 1646; M636/7.

4 *Ibid.*

5 Henry Verney to Sir Ralph Verney, 13 April 1646; M636/7.

6 *Memoirs* I, 422.

7 Sir John Leeke to Sir Ralph Verney, 21 August 1645; M636/6.

8 Sir Ralph Verney to Sir Roger Burgoyne, 21 June 1646; Sir Ralph Verney to Sir John Leeke, 21 June 1646; both M636/7.

9 Susan Alport *née* Verney to Sir Ralph Verney, 20 August 1646; M636/7.

10 Henry Verney to Sir Ralph Verney, 1 October 1646; M636/7.

11 Mary Verney to Sir Ralph Verney, 3 December 1646; M636/7.

12 *Ibid.*, 10 December 1646; M636/7.

13   *Ibid.*

14   Sir Ralph Verney to Mary Verney, 29 December 1646; M636/7.

15   *Ibid.*

16   Mary Verney to Sir Ralph Verney, 7 January 1647; M636/8.

17   *Ibid.*, 21 January 1647; M636/8.

18   Sir Ralph Verney to Mary Verney, 21 February 1647; M636/8.

19   Sir Roger Burgoyne to Sir Ralph Verney, 11 February 1647; M636/8.

20   Sir Ralph Verney to Mary Verney, 10 March 1647; M636/8.

21   Mary Verney to Sir Ralph Verney, 11 March 1647; M636/8.

22   *Ibid.*, 25 March 1647; M636/8.

23   *Ibid.*, 4 March 1647; M636/8.

24   Sir Ralph Verney to Mary Verney, 28 February 1647; M636/8.

25   *Ibid.*, 24 March 1647; M636/8.

26   Mary Verney to Sir Ralph Verney, 15 April 1647 and 20 May 1647; both M636/8.

27   *Ibid.*, 20 May 1647; M636/8.

28   Peg Elmes to Mary Verney, 28 September 1647; M636/8.

29   Mary Verney to Sir Ralph Verney, 26 August 1647; M636/8.

30   Tom Verney to Mary Verney, 16 July 1647; M636/8.

31   Mary Verney to Sir Ralph Verney, 25 March 1644; M636/8.

32   *Ibid.*

33   *Ibid.*, 4 November 1647; M636/8.

34   *Ibid.*, 28 February 1647; M636/8.

35   *Journal of the House of Commons* 5, 23 March 1647.

36   Sir Ralph Verney to Sir Gilbert Gerard, 10 March/28 February 1647; M636/8.

37   Sir Ralph Verney to Mary Verney, 31 January 1647; M636/8.

38   Mary Verney to Sir Ralph Verney, 14 January 1647; M636/8.

39   *Memoirs* I, 354.

40   Sir Ralph Verney to Mary Verney, 27 June 1647; M636/8.

41   Mary Verney to Sir Ralph Verney, 1 July 1647; M636/8.

42   Mary Verney to Will Roades, 25 June 1647; M636/8.

43   Mary Verney to Sir Ralph Verney, 1 July 1647; M636/8.

44   *Memoirs* I, 378.

45   Mary Verney to Sir Ralph Verney, 7 September 1647; M636/8.

46   *Memoirs* I, 380.

47   Sir Ralph Verney to Mary Verney, October 1647; M636/8.

48 *Ibid.*, 17 October 1647; M636/8.

49 Sir Ralph Verney to William Denton, 3 October 1647; M636/8.

50 William Denton to Sir Ralph Verney, 28 October 1647; M636/8.

51 Mary Verney to Sir Ralph Verney, 4 November 1647; M636/8.

52 Sir Ralph Verney to Mary Verney, 8 December 1647; M636/8.

53 Sir Ralph Verney to William Denton, 27 October 1647; M636/8.

54 Mary Verney to Sir Ralph Verney, 16 December 1647; M636/8.

55 *Ibid.*, 18 March 1647; M636/8.

56 Sir Ralph Verney to Mary Verney, 10 October 1647; M636/8.

57 Mary Verney to Sir Ralph Verney, 11 November 1647; M636/8.

58 *Ibid.*, 20 December 1647; M636/8.

59 *Journal of the House of Commons* 5, 17 December 1647.

60 Mary Verney to Sir Ralph Verney, 20 December 1647; M636/8.

61 William Denton to Sir Ralph Verney, 23 December 1647; M636/8.

62 *Ibid.*, 6 January 1648; M636/8.

63 Sir Roger Burgoyne to Sir Ralph Verney, 6 January 1648; M636/8.

64 *Memoirs* I, 394.

65 Sir Ralph Verney to Mary Verney, 5 December 1647; M636/8.

66 *Memoirs* I, 396.

Chapter 12

1 *Mercurius Elencticus, Communicating the unparralell'd Proceedings of the Rebels at West-minster, and the Head quarters, discovering their Designes, reproving their Crimes, and advising the Kingdome,* 6–13 August 1649, 1–2.

2 *Ibid.*, 16–24 July 1649, 1–2.

3 *Memoirs* I, 405.

4 Tom Verney to Will Roades, 4 October 1646; M636/7.

5 Susan Verney to Sir Ralph Verney, 16 July 1646; M636/7.

6 *Memoirs* I, 423.

7   Lilburne's account of the affair appears in his *Preparative to a Hue and Cry After Sir Arthur Haslerig* (1649), 9–14.

8   Tom Verney to Will Roades, 24 October 1649; M636/10.

9   *Ibid.*, 29 April 1650; M636/10.

10 Mun Verney to Sir Ralph Verney, August 1647; M636/8.

11 *Memoirs* I, 400.

12 William Denton to Sir Ralph Verney, 21 February 1649; M636/9.

13 Wilbur Cortez Abbott (ed.), *The Writings and Speeches of Oliver Cromwell* (1988), II, 177.

14 *Aphorismicall Discovery*, II, 102; in Richard Bagwell, *Ireland Under the Stuarts* (1909), II, 186.

15 Bagwell, *Ireland Under the Stuarts*, II, 185.

16 William Denton to Sir Ralph Verney, 16 August 1649; M636/10.

17 Hugh Peter to John Bradshaw, 16 August 1649; *Essex Institute Historical Collections* 72 (1936), 327.

18 *Memoirs* I, 413–14.

19 Bagwell, *Ireland Under the Stuarts*, II, 193.

20 *DNB*. The remark is also attributed to Sir Phelim O'Neill, the Catholic rebel leader who unsuccessfully besieged Drogheda in 1641–2.

21 James Buck to Sir Ralph Verney, 18 November 1649; M636/10.

22 Oliver Cromwell to William Lenthall, 17 September 1649; Abbott, *Writings and Speeches*, II, 126.

23 Anon., *A Brief Relation of that Bloody Storm at Drogheda* (1649); in Tom Reilly, *Cromwell: An Honourable Enemy* (1999), 75.

24 Oliver Cromwell to William Lenthall, 17 September 1649; Abbott, *Writings and Speeches*, II, 128.

25 Oliver Cromwell to John Bradshaw, 16 September 1649; Abbott, *Writings and Speeches*, II, 124.

26 Anon., *Letters from Ireland, relating the several great successes it hath pleased God to give unto the Parliament's Forces there, in the Taking of Drogheda, Trym, Dundalk, Carlingford, and the Nury* (1649), 14.

27 Sir Ralph Verney to Sir Henry Puckering Newton 21 October 1649; M636/10.

28 Sir Ralph Verney to William Denton, 4 November 1649; M636/10.

29 William Denton to Sir Ralph Verney, 7 June 1649; M636/10.

30 Sir Ralph Verney to Margaret Sherard, August 1647; M636/8.

31 John Clenche, *A Tour in France and Italy, made by an Englishman, 1675* (1676), 16.

32 Pen Denton to Sir Ralph Verney, 16 December 1649; M636/10.

33 Edward Roscarrock to Sir Ralph Verney from Rotterdam, 22 December 1649; M636/10.

34 Susan Alport to Sir Ralph Verney, 11 August 1649; M636/10.

35 William Denton to Sir Ralph Verney, 15 November 1649; M636/10.

36 Lady Mary Herbert to Sir Ralph Verney, 24 November 1649; M636/10.

37 Sir Ralph Verney to Mr Hatcher, 13 December 1649; M636/10.

38 *The Jugglers Discovered, in Two Letters Writ by Lieut. Col. John Lilburne, prerogative prisoner in the Tower of London* (1647), 1.

39 William Denton to Sir Ralph Verney, 27 December 1649; M636/10.

40 William Sclater, *Papisto-Mastix or, Deborahs Prayer Against God's Enemies* (1642), 56–7.

41 William Denton to Sir Ralph Verney, 7 March 1650; M636/10.

42 *Ibid.*, 10 April 1648; M636/9.

43 BL Harley MS 7019, fol. 63r.

44 *DNB.*

45 Sir Ralph Verney to John Cosin, 25 April 1650; M636/10.

46 Nancy Denton to Mary Verney, 9 May 1650; M636/10.

47 Capt. James Wadsworth (trans.), *Chocolate: or, An Indian Drinke. By the wise andmoderate use whereof, health is preserved, sickness diverted, and cured* (1652), preface.

48 William Denton to Sir Ralph Verney, 1 May 1650; M636/10.

49 Willam Denton to Mary Verney, 13 May 1650; M636/10.

50 Sir Ralph Verney to William Denton, 19 May 1650; M636/10.

51 Sir Ralph Verney, 12 May 1650; M636/10.

52 John Cosin, 'Prayers at the point of death', *A Collection of Private Devotions* (1635), 365–6.

53 *Memoirs* I, 475.

54 Sir Ralph Verney to William Denton, 19 June 1650; M636/10.

55 Sir Ralph Verney to Sir Henry Puckering Newton, 11 September 1650; M636/10.
56 Sir Ralph Verney to William Denton, 2 June 1650; M636/10.
57 *Ibid.*
58 *Ibid.*
59 William Denton to Sir Ralph Verney, 20 June 1650; M636/10.
60 Sir Ralph Verney to William Denton, July 1650; M636/10.
61 *Memoirs* I, 477.

Chapter 13

1 James Howell, *Instructions for Forreine Travell* (1642), 105.
2 John Raymond, *An Itinerary containing a Voyage made through Italy* (1648), preface.
3 *Ibid.*
4 *Ibid.*, 249–50.
5 Thomas Raymond, in John Stoye, *English Travellers Abroad, 1604–1667* (1952), 180.
6 Sir Ralph Verney to John Kirton, October 1650; M636/10.
7 *Memoirs* I, 478.
8 Margaret Sherard to Sir Ralph Verney, 15 May 1650; M636/10.
9 *Memoirs* I, 478.
10 Howell, *Instructions for Forreine Travell*, 42.
11 *Memoirs* I, 466–7.
12 *Ibid.*
13 John Clenche, *A Tour in France and Italy, made by an Englishman, 1675* (1676), 19.
14 John Kirton to Sir Ralph Verney, 30 September 1651; M636/11.
15 Anon., 'Directions for such as travel from Paris into Italy'; M636/11. There were twenty sols to the livre.
16 *A Perfect Diurnall*, 7–14 July 1651, 4.
17 *Ibid.*, 14–21 July 1651, 3–4.
18 *Ibid.*, 18–25 August 1651, 2.
19 Sir Roger Burgoyne to Sir Ralph Verney, 11 September 1651; M636/11.
20 *A Perfect Diurnall*, 15–22 June 1651, 12.

21 Anon., 'Directions for such as travel from Paris into Italy'; M636/11.

22 Raymond, *Itinerary*, 252–3.

23 Richard Lassels, *The Voyage of Italy* (1670) I, 64.

24 Raymond, *Itinerary*, 238–9.

25 'Directions'; M636/11.

26 *Ibid.*

27 Raymond, *Itinerary*, 39, 40.

28 Sir Ralph Verney to Mr Banckes, December 1651; M636/11.

29 Mr Banckes to Sir Ralph Verney, December 1651; M636/11.

30 'Directions'; M636/11.

31 Raymond, *Itinerary*, 72.

32 Bray, William (ed.), *The Diary of John Evelyn* (1907), entry for 12 December 1644 but describing Christmas Eve.

33 Lassels, *The Voyage of Italy*, II, 273.

34 Bray, *Diary of John Evelyn*, 11 April 1645.

35 Sir Ralph Verney to Du Val, 12 February 1652; M636/11.

36 *Ibid.*, February 1652; M636/11.

37 Raymond, *Itinerary*, 76; Bray, *Diary of John Evelyn*, 21 February 1645.

38 Raymond, *Itinerary*, 89.

39 Luce Sheppard to Sir Ralph, 3 September 1651; M636/11.

40 Bray, *Diary of John Evelyn*, 11 April 1645.

41 Lassels, *The Voyage of Italy*, II, 413.

42 Raymond, *Itinerary*, 201.

43 Bray, *Diary of John Evelyn*, June 1645.

44 Gideon Harvey, *The Art of Curing Diseases by Expectation* (1689), 153.

45 Sir Ralph Verney to Du Val, February 1652; M636/11.

46 Sir Ralph Verney to William Denton, 25 August 1650; M636/10.

47 *Ibid.*, 23 September 1651; M636/11.

48 *Ibid.*

49 William Denton to Sir Ralph Verney, 22 April 1652; M636/11.

50 'A satisfactory answer of the price as well of the materials as of the workmanship, either for carving or architecture'; M636/11.

51 Note enclosed with Du Val to Sir Ralph Verney, 15 October 1652; M636/11.

52 *Ibid.*

53 John Aris, *The Reconciler, or, a sermon preached before a Communion . . . to which is added a charm for a slanderous tongue, briefly written in a letter to an obstinate offender that way* (1651).

54 *Memoirs* I, 504–5.

55 Sir Ralph Verney to William Denton, 21 September 1652; M636/11.

56 *Memoirs* I, 489.

57 *Ibid.*, 520.

58 Richard Alport to Sir Ralph Verney, 7 February 1651; Sir Ralph Verney to William Denton, August 1651; both M636/11.

59 Articles of agreement between Edward Marshall and Sir Ralph Verney, 2 April 1653; in L. Stone, 'The Verney Tomb at Middle Claydon', *Records of Buckinghamshire*, 16 (1955–6), 80.

60 Prob/11/190.

Chapter 14

1 Robert Herrick, 'A Country-Life: To His Brother, Mr. Tho. Herrick'.

2 Sir Ralph Verney to Will Roades, 23 May 1653; M636/12.

3 *Ibid.* 'Clenge' is a variant of 'cleanse'.

4 By John Broad, *Transforming English Rural Society: The Verneys and the Claydons 1600–1820* (2004), 76.

5 Sir Ralph Verney to Edward Butterfield, 2 October 1654; M636/12.

6 *Memoirs* I, 538.

7 From the title page of the first English translation, published by Robert Pricke as *The Art of Fair Building* in 1670.

8 Sir Francis Bacon, 'Of Gardens', *Essayes and Counsels, Civil and Moral* (1664), 257.

9 *Memoirs* I, 524.

10 Walter Blith, *The English Improver Improved* (1653), Epistle Dedicatory.

11 Sir Hugh Plat, *The Garden of Eden* (1652), 'The Publisher [Charles Bellingham] to the Reader', 10.

12 *Weekly Intelligencer*, 6–13 March 1655, 6.

13   *Mercurius Politicus*, 5–12 July 1655, 16.

14   Sir Ralph Verney to Vere Gawdy, 25 June 1655; M636/13.

15   Doll Leeke to Sir Ralph Verney, 20 June 1655; M636/13.

16   Will Roades to Sir Ralph Verney, 18 June 1655; M636/13.

17   Elizabeth Isham to Sir Ralph Verney, June 1655; M636/13.

18   Tom Verney to Sir Ralph Verney, 16 July 1655; M636/13.

19   Sir Roger Burgoyne to Sir Ralph Verney, 24 June 1655; M636/13.

20   Sir Ralph Verney to John Stewkeley, 25 May 1655; M636/13.

21   Sir Roger Burgoyne to Sir Ralph Verney, 9 July 1655; and Sir Ralph Verney to Sir Roger Burgoyne, 12 July 1655; both M636/13.

22   *Memoirs* II, 15–16.

23   Vere Gawdy to Sir Ralph Verney, 10 October 1655; M636/14.

24   Margaret Sherard to Sir Ralph Verney, 29 October 1655; M636/14.

25   C. H. Firth, 'The Royalists under the Protectorate', *English Historical Review* (October 1937), 641.

26   Sir Gyles Isham (ed.), *The Correspondence of Bishop Brian Duppa and Sir Justinian Isham*, Northamptonshire Record Society, 17 (1955), 115.

27   Sir Ralph Verney to Mun Verney, 4 March 1656; M636/14.

28   *Ibid.*

29   *Memoirs* II, 35.

30   *Ibid.*

31   *The Diary of Thomas Burton* I (1828), 230.

32   Sir Ralph Verney to Mons. Pappin, n.d.; *Memoirs* II, 171.

33   Robert Creighton to Sir Ralph Verney, n.d. [January 1653?]; *Memoirs* I, 505.

34   Robert Creighton to Sir Ralph Verney, 15 July 1653; M636/12.

35   *Ibid.*

36   Sir Ralph Verney to Robert Creighton, 20 March 1654; M636/12.

37   Robert Creighton to Sir Ralph Verney, 15 July 1653; M636/12.

38   *Ibid.*

39   Sir Ralph Verney to Mun Verney, 11 June 1655; M636/13.

40   Sir Richard Hutton, *The Young Clerk's Guide* (1649), title page.

41   Sir Ralph Verney to Robert Creighton, 1653; M636/12.
42   Mun Verney to Thomas Hyde; *Memoirs* II, 49.

Chapter 15

1   *Memoirs* II, 90–91.
2   Jack Verney to Sir Ralph Verney, 31 July 1679; M636/33.
3   Samuel Turberville to Sir Ralph Verney, 30 December 1656; M636/15.
4   *Memoirs* II, 94.
5   Jack Verney to Mun Verney, May 1659; M636/16.
6   Susan Whyman, *Sociability and Power in Late-Stuart England: The Cultural Worlds of the Verneys 1660–1720* (1999), 41.
7   John Earle, *Micro-cosmographie, or, A peece of the world discovered in essayes and characters*, (1628), '9. Younger Brother' (no pagination).
8   *Ibid.*
9   Gerrard Winstanley, *A Declaration from the Poor oppressed People of England* (1649), 4.
10   Sir George Sondes, *A Plain Narrative to the World* (1655), 33.
11   George Saville, Sir Thomas Baines; both in Richard Grassby, *The Business Community of Seventeenth-Century England*, (1995), 40. Grassby's book is essential reading for anyone interested in the subject.
12   *Ibid.*
13   Sir Ralph Verney to an unidentified correspondent, 21 March 1678; M636/31.
14   *Observations and Advices Oeconomical* (1669), 18.
15   Jack Verney to Sir Ralph Verney, May 1659; M636/16.
16   William Wakefield to Sir Ralph Verney, 19 September 1659; M636/16.
17   *Ibid.*
18   Lewis Roberts, *The Treasure of Traffic, or, a Discourse of Foreign Trade* (1641), 54.
19   These examples all come from Stephen R. Smith, 'The London Apprentices as Seventeenth-Century Adolescents', *Past and Present* 61 (November 1973), 152.
20   Jack Verney to Sir Ralph Verney, 14 March 1660; M636/17.
21   William Love to Sir Ralph Verney, 10 September 1661; M636/17.

22   Margaret Sherard to Sir Ralph Verney, 10 June 1656; Will Roades to Sir Ralph Verney, 3 June 1656; both M636/14.
23   *Memoirs* II, 56, 61.
24   *Ibid.*, 138–9.
25   *Ibid.*, 135.
26   William Denton to Sir Ralph Verney, 30 August 1654; M636/13.
27   *Ibid.*, 30 October 1654; M636/13.
28   Cary Gardiner to Sir Ralph Verney, 25 September 1654; M636/13.
29   William Denton to Sir Ralph Verney, 5 October 1654; M636/13.
30   Mall Verney to Sir Ralph Verney, 6 October 1654; M636/13.
31   William Denton to Sir Ralph Verney, 9 October 1654; M636/13.
32   Mall Verney to Sir Ralph Verney, 18 October 1654; M636/13.
33   William Gape to Sir Ralph Verney, 26 October 1654; M636/13.
34   William Denton to Sir Ralph Verney, 9 October 1654; M636/13.
35   Cary Gardiner to Sir Ralph Verney, 15 January 1655; M636/13.
36   *Ibid.*, 30 October 1654; M636/13.
37   William Gape to Sir Ralph Verney, 22 March 1655; M636/13.
38   Pen Denton to Sir Ralph Verney, April 1655; M636/13.
39   Mall Verney to Sir Ralph Verney, 11 April 1655; M636/13.
40   *Ibid.*
41   *Ibid.*, 24 May 1655; M636/13.
42   Sir Ralph Verney to William Gape, 26 November 1655; M636/14.
43   Mall Verney to Sir Ralph Verney, 17 March 1656; M636/14.
44   Robert Kibble to Tom Verney, 31 March 1656; M636/14.
45   Mall Verney to Sir Ralph Verney, 30 September 1656.
46   Sir Ralph Verney to William Gape, 2 March 1657; M636/14.

Chapter 16

1   Tom Verney to Sir Ralph Verney, 11 February 1657; M636/15.
2   Sir Ralph Verney to Mun Verney, 24 June 1656; M636/14.

3 Sir Ralph Verney to Henry Verney, 8 December 1656; M636/15.

4 William Denton to Sir Ralph Verney, 18 December 1656; M636/15.

5 *Ibid.*

6 Sir Ralph Verney to Mun Verney, 8 December 1656; M636/15.

7 Sir Ralph Verney to William Denton, 13 January 1657; M636/15.

8 Mun Verney to Sir Ralph Verney, 25 December 1656; M636/15.

9 *Ibid.*, 14 January 1657; M636/15.

10 Sir Ralph Verney to William Denton, 24 January 1657; M636/15.

11 Sir Ralph Verney to Mun Verney, sent to William Denton, 1 February 1657; M636/15.

12 Mun Verney to Sir Ralph Verney, 29 January 1657; M636/15. The words actually come from Sir Ralph's translation of the letter out of the original French, which he sent to William Denton for comment.

13 William Denton to Sir Ralph Verney, 5 February 1657; M636/15 (my italics).

14 Sir Ralph Verney to Mun Verney, 9 February 1657; M636/15.

15 William Denton to Sir Ralph Verney, 14 February 1657; M636/15.

16 Lady Anne Hobart to Sir Ralph Verney, 5 March 1657; M636/15.

17 Sir Ralph Verney to Mun Verney, 23 February 1657; M636/15.

18 Sir Ralph Verney to Lady Warwick, 10 August 1657; M636/15.

19 Countess of Rochester to Sir Ralph Verney, 29 August 1657; M636/15.

20 Thomas Hyde to Mun Verney, 1 July 1657; M636/15.

21 Sir Ralph Verney to Margaret Sherard, 21 December 1657; M636/15.

22 *Memoirs* II, 69.

23 *Ibid.*, 73.

24 *Ibid.*, 73.

25 *Ibid.*

26 Mun Verney to Margaret Sherard, April 1658; M636/15.

27 Mun Verney to Mary Eure, 12 April 1658; M636/15.

28   *Ibid.*, 7 June 1658; M636/15.

29   Mary Eure to Margaret Sherard, 8 May 1658; M636/15.

30   *Memoirs* II, 83.

31   Henry Verney to Mun Verney, September 1658; M636/165.

32   Edward Butterfield to Sir Ralph Verney, 15 August 1661; M636/17.

33   *Memoirs* II, 175.

34   George Gale to Mary Abell, 7 November 1661; M636/18.

35   Edward Butterfield to Sir Ralph Verney, 16 November 1661; M636/18.

36   *Memoirs* II, 180.

37   Edward Butterfield to Sir Ralph Verney, 16 June 1662; Edward Butterfield to Mun Verney, 16 June 1662; both M636/18.

38   25 December 1661; M636/18.

39   Jack Verney to Sir Ralph Verney, 2 April 1662; M636/18.

40   Jeremy Taylor, *The rule and exercises of holy living. In which are described the means and instruments of obtaining every vertue, and the remedies against every vice, and considerations serving to the resisting all temptations* (1650). There were editions in 1651, 1656 and 1660.

41   Jack Verney to Sir Ralph Verney, 16 January 1662; M636/18.

42   Sir Ralph to Jack Verney, 20 January 1662; M636/18.

43   *Ibid.*

44   Jack Verney to Sir Ralph Verney, 26 March 1662; M636/18.

45   Mun Verney to Mary Abell, 1 May 1662; M636/18.

46   Jack Verney to Sir Ralph Verney, 30 April 1662; M636/18.

47   Mun Verney to Jack Verney, 5 May 1662; M636/18.

Chapter 17

1   *Memoirs* II, 185.

2   Peg Elmes to Sir Ralph Verney, 20 November 1662; M636/18.

3   *Ibid.*, 24 March 1663; M636/19.

4   William Denton to Sir Ralph Verney, 26 March 1663; M636/19.

5   George Savile, Marquis of Halifax, *The Lady's New-Year Gift, or Advice to a Daughter* (1688), 35.

6   *Ibid.*, 37.

7   Lady Anne Hobart to Sir Ralph Verney, 3 April 1663; M636/19.

8   William Denton to Sir Ralph Verney, 6 April 1663; M636/19.

9   Sir Ralph Verney to Mun Verney, 30 March 1663; M636/19.

10   Robert Burton, *The Anatomy of Melancholy* (2001), part I, 147.

11   *Ibid.*, 148.

12   Thomas Willis, *An essay of the pathology of the brain and nervous stock* (1681), 78.

13   Sir Theodore Turquet de Mayerne, *A treatise of the gout* (1676), 80.

14   Burton, *Anatomy of Melancholy*, part 2, 248.

15   Timothy Rogers, *A discourse concerning trouble of mind, and the disease of melancholy* (1691), xi.

16   Burton, *Anatomy of Melancholy*, part 3, 432.

17   Edward Butterfield to Mun Verney, 15 June 1663; M636/19.

18   William Denton to Sir Ralph Verney, 8 October 1663; M636/19.

19   *Ibid.*, 15 October 1663; M636/19.

20   Sir Ralph Verney to Pen Denton, 9 November 1663; M636/19.

21   Tom Verney to Sir Ralph Verney, 11 February 1662; M636/18.

22   *Ibid.*, 12 February 1663; M636/18.

23   *Ibid.*

24   Robert Latham and William Matthews (eds), *The Diary of Samuel Pepys* (1995), IV, 315 (22 September 1663).

25   Tom Verney to William Denton, 3 April 1663; M636/19.

26   Tom Verney to Sir Ralph Verney, 8 October 1663; M636/19.

27   *Ibid.*; M636/19.

28   *Ibid.*; M636/19.

29   *Ibid.*, 12 October 1663; M636/19.

30   *Ibid.*

31   *Ibid.*

32   Thomas Stafford to Sir Ralph Verney, 22 November 1663; M636/19.

33   *Memoirs* II, 197.

34   Edward Butterfield to Mun Verney, 28 December 1663; M636/19.

35   Sir Ralph Verney to Mun Verney, 3 February 1664; M636/19.

36 Doll Leeke to Sir Ralph Verney, 10 February 1664; M636/19.

37 *Ibid.*, 25 February 1664; M636/19.

38 Burton, *Anatomy of Melancholy*, part 3, 286.

39 Lady Anne Hobart to Sir Ralph Verney, 27 March 1664; M636/19.

40 *Ibid.*, 31 March 1664; M636/19.

41 *Ibid.*, 1 April 1664; M636/19.

42 *Ibid.*

43 William Denton to Sir Ralph Verney, 31 March 1664; M636/19.

44 Margaret Elmes to Sir Ralph Verney, 7 April 1664; M636/19.

45 William Denton to Sir Ralph Verney, 7 April 1664; M636/19.

46 *Ibid.*

47 Lady Anne Hobart to Sir Ralph Verney, 13 April 1664; M636/19.

48 Doll Leeke to Sir Ralph Verney, 18 May 1664; M636/19.

Chapter 18

1 Mun Verney to Sir Ralph Verney, 14 April 1664; M636/19.

2 William Denton to Sir Ralph Verney, 14 April 1664; M636/19.

3 *Ibid.*, 7 April 1664; M636/19.

4 *Commentaries on the Laws of England* (1765–9); in Richard Hunter and Ida Macalpine (eds), *Three Hundred Years of Psychiatry, 1535–1860* (1970), 435.

5 James Carkesse, *Lucida Intervalla: containing divers miscellaneous poems, written at Finsbury and Bethlem by the doctor's patient extraordinary* (1679), 9, 15.

6 John Vicars, *A looking-glasse for malignants: or, God's hand against God-haters* (1643), 22.

7 Sir Ralph Verney to Mun Verney, 18 April 1664; M636/19.

8 *Ibid.*

9 William Denton to Sir Ralph Verney, 21 April 1664; M636/19.

10 Lady Anne Hobart to Sir Ralph Verney, 21 April 1664; M636/19.

11 Mun Verney to Sir Ralph Verney, 21 April 1664; M636/19.

12 Sir Ralph Verney to Mun Verney, 25 April 1664; M636/19.

13 BL c.112, f.9.

14 George Trosse, *The life of the Reverend Mr Geo. Trosse, late*

minister of the gospel in the city of Exon . . . (1714); in Hunter and Macalpine, *Three Hundred Years of Psychiatry*, 156–7.

15 Mun Verney to Sir Ralph Verney, 21 April 1664; M636/19.

16 Doll Leeke to Sir Ralph Verney, 27 April 1664; M636/19.

17 Sir Ralph Verney to Mun Verney, 11 April 1664; M636/19.

18 Elizabeth Verney (*née* Kendall) to Sir Ralph Verney, n. d. [1664] ; M636/19.

19 Sir Ralph Verney to Tom Verney, 3 May 1664; M636/19.

20 Vere Gawdy to Sir Ralph Verney, 12 May 1664; M636/19.

21 *Ibid.*, 19 May 1664; M636/19.

22 Draft by Sir Ralph Verney of a letter for Henry Fowkes to send to Tom Verney, 3 May 1663; M636/19.

23 Tom Verney to Sir Ralph Verney, 21 May 1664; M636/19.

24 Sir Ralph Verney to Tom Verney, 11 June 1664; M636/19.

25 Tom Verney to Henry Fowkes, 24 June 1664; M636/19.

26 Tom Verney to Sir Ralph Verney, 10 July 1665; M636/20.

27 William Bray (ed.), *The Diary of John Evelyn* (1907), entry for 9 August 1661.

28 Doll Leeke to Sir Ralph Verney, 18 May 1664; M636/19.

29 Mun Verney to Sir Francis Prujean, 26 May 1664; M636/19.

30 Frances Hobart to Mun Verney, 18 August 1664; M636/19.

31 Frederick Turville to Mun Verney, 24 June 1664; M636/19.

32 Sir Ralph Verney to Mun Verney, 24 August 1664; M636/19.

33 *Ibid.*

34 Mun Verney to George Gale, 26 September 1664; M636/19.

35 Lady Anne Hobart to Mun Verney, 16 September 1664; M636/19.

36 Sir Ralph Verney to Mun Verney, 22 December 1664; M636/20.

37 *Ibid.*, 15 December 1664; M636/20.

38 Mun Verney to Sir Ralph Verney, 9 April 1663; Lady Anne Hobart to Sir Ralph Verney, 27 March 1664; William Denton to Sir Ralph Verney, 7 April 1664; all M636/19.

39 Doll Leeke to Sir Ralph Verney, 26 March 1663; M636/19.

Chapter 19

1 William Bray (ed.), *The Diary of John Evelyn* (1907), entry for 21 October 1644.

2   *Ibid.*

3   Bray, *Diary of John Evelyn*, 19 October 1644.

4   *Ibid.*

5   John Raymond, *An Itinerary containing a Voyage made through Italy* (1648), 19.

6   Bray, *Diary of John Evelyn*, 19 October 1644.

7   Jack Verney to Sir Ralph Verney, 30 June 1662; M636/18.

8   *Ibid.*

9   Montague North to Dudley Foley, Cobbold MSS, Box 17; in Richard Grassby, *The English Gentleman in Trade: The Life and Works of Sir Dudley North, 1641–1691 (1994), 339.*

10 Gwilym Ambrose, 'English Traders at Aleppo (1658–1756)', *Economic History Review* 3, 2 (October 1931), 250fn.

11 *Travels of Peter Mundy*, I, 19.

12 'Diary of Master Thomas Dallam', *Early Voyages and Travels in the Levant* (1893), 32.

13 Ambrose, 'English Traders at Aleppo', 251.

14 Henry Teonge, *The Diary of Henry Teonge . . . Royal Oak* (1927), 140.

15 *Ibid.*

16 *Ibid.*, 161–2.

17 Yasser Tabbaa, 'Circles of Power: Palace, Citadel and City in Ayyubid Aleppo', *Ars Orientalis* 23, (1993), 181–200.

18 Teonge, *Diary of Henry Teonge*, 161.

19 *Ibid.*, 151.

20 Lewis Roberts, *The Marchants Mapp of Commerce* (1638), in *Theatrum Orbis Terrarum* (1974), 134.

21 *Ibid.*, 140.

22 Jack Verney to Sir Ralph Verney, 22 October 1662; M636/18.

23 Mun Verney to Jack Verney, 23 May 1663; M636/19.

24 *Ibid.*

25 *Ibid.*

26 *Ibid.*, 12 June 1663.

27 Jack Verney to Mun Verney, 21 December 1663; M636/19.

28 Jack Verney to Sir Ralph Verney, 20 June 1663; M636/19.

29 Ambrose, 'English Traders at Aleppo', 248.

30 *Ibid.*, 249.

31 *Ibid.*, 254.

32 A. C. Wood, *A History of the Levant Company* (1935), 214.

33   Quoted by Jack Verney to Sir Ralph Verney, 20 June 1663; M636/19.

34   Jack Verney to Sir Ralph Verney, 15 May 1666; M636/20.

35   *Ibid.*, 25 July 1664; M636/19.

36   Sir Ralph Verney to Jack Verney, 16 December 1665; M636/20.

37   *Ibid.*

38   *Ibid.*

39   Jack Verney to Sir Ralph Verney, 10 June 1667; M636/21.

40   *Ibid.*

41   J. B., *The Merchants Avizo* (1616), 64.

42   Henry Maundrell, *A Journal from Aleppo to Jerusalem 1697* (1732), 148.

43   Wood, *History of the Levant Company*, 240–41.

44   Ambrose, 'English Traders at Aleppo', 266.

45   William Lithgow, *The Totall Discourse, of the Rare Adventures, and painefull Perigrinations of long nineteen Years Travayles* (1632), 361.

46   Sieur Dumont, *A New Voyage to the Levant* (1705), 276–7.

47   Robert Halsband (ed.), *The Complete Letters of Lady Mary Wortley Montagu* (1965), I, 368.

48   *Historical Manuscripts Commission Finch* 1 (1913), 406.

49   Lithgow, *Totall Discourse*, 360–61.

50   Dumont, *New Voyage to the Levant*, 262. I'm not sure that 'dull' is the word I'd use.

51   Maundrell, *Journal from Aleppo to Jersalem*, 79.

52   *Ibid.*, 104–5.

53   Jack Verney to Sir Ralph Verney, 1663; received 21 June 1664; M636/19.

54   Mun Verney to Jack Verney, 6 August 1664; M636/19.

55   Jack Verney to Sir Ralph Verney, 2 April 1669; M636/23.

56   *Ibid.*, 25 February 1672; M636/25.

57   *Ibid.*, 6 May 1673; M636/26.

58   *Ibid.*, 25 May 1666; M636/21.

59   *Ibid.*, 9 September 1669; ; M636/23.

Chapter 20

1   *Memoirs* I, 429.

2   Henry Verney to Will Roades, 22 February 1647; M636/8.

3   *Memoirs* I, 404.

4   Mary Verney to Sir Ralph Verney, 18 March 1647; M636/8.

5   *Ibid.*, 7 January 1647; M636/7.

6   *Memoirs* I, 396.

7   William Denton to Sir Ralph Verney, 20 June 1650; M636/10.

8   *Memoirs* I, 520.

9   *A Proclamation . . . prohibiting horse-races in England and Wales for eight months*, 8 April 1658.

10   Anon., *A Timely Advice, or, A Treatise of Play, and Gaming* (1640), 44–5.

11   *Memoirs* II, 30.

12   *Ibid.*, 219.

13   *Ibid.*, 476.

14   *Ibid.*, 222, 223.

15   Robert Almond, *The English Horseman and Complete Farrier* (1673), 41, 42.

16   *Memoirs* II, 223.

17   Pen Denton to Sir Ralph Verney, 2 April 1662; M636/18.

18   Henry Verney to Sir Ralph Verney, 20 August 1671; M636/24.

19   William Denton to Sir Ralph Verney, 28 August 1671; M636/24.

20   Lady Anne Hobart to Sir Ralph Verney, 31 August 1671; M636/24.

21   Sir Ralph Verney to William Denton, 1 September 1671; M636/24.

22   *Memoirs* II, 303.

23   *A Perfect Narrative of the Robbery and Murder Committed . . . upon the person of Mr John Talbot* (1669), 24.

24   Frances Hobart to Sir Ralph Verney, 25 August 1666; M636/21.

25   *Ibid.*

26   Doll Leeke to Sir Ralph Verney, November 1655; M636/14.

27   *Memoirs* II, 350.

28   *Ibid,*, 352.

29   *Ibid.*, 353.

30   Dick Hals to Sir Ralph Verney, 18 February 1671; M636/24.

31   Dick Hals to Mun Verney, 19 February 1671; M636/24.

32   *Ibid.*, 30 April 1672; M636/25.

33   Dick Hals to Sir Ralph Verney, 2 May 1672; M636/25.

34 Dick Hals to Mun Verney, 11 July 1672; M636/25.

35 *Memoirs* II, 356.

36 Dick Hals to Sir Ralph Verney, 8 February 1674; M636/27.

37 Dick Hals to Mun Verney, 26 July 1674; M636/27.

38 Lady Anne Hobart to Sir Ralph Verney, 23 November 1679; M636/33.

39 Dick Hals to Mun Verney, 20 April 1683; M636/37. In 1697 a William Hals was married to a girl in Whitechapel and serving aboard HMS *Lyon*.

40 Dick Hals to Sir Ralph Verney, 27 April 1685; M636/40.

41 *Memoirs* II, 364.

42 *Ibid.*, 353.

43 Anon., *News from Newgate: or, a true Relation of the manner of taking seven persons, very notorious for Highway-men, in the Strand . . .* (1677), 4.

44 Alexander Smith, *History of the most Noted Highway-men, Footpads, House-Breakers, Shop-lifts and Cheats* (1714), II, 286–8.

45 Dick Hals to Sir Ralph Verney, 27 April 1685; M636/40. 'Hanging' Judge Jeffreys was Lord Chief Justice at the time.

46 Touchstone, in Ben Jonson, John Marston and George Chapman, *Eastward Ho!* (1605), IV, ii.

47 Dick Hals to Sir Ralph Verney, 8 February 1674; M636/27.

48 *Ibid.*, June 1676; M636/29.

49 Mun Verney to Jack Verney, 23 May 1663; M636/19.

50 Thomas Shadwell, *Lancashire Witches* (1682), Dramatis Personae.

51 *Ibid.*, Act III.

52 *Ibid.*, Act II.

53 Mun Verney to Sir Ralph Verney, 1680; M636/34.

54 *Ibid.*, 30 July 1679; M636/33.

55 Mun Verney to Jack Verney, 10 December 1679; M636/33.

56 Sir Ralph Verney to Mun Verney, 20 January 1679; M636/34.

57 Mun Verney to Sir Ralph Verney, 16 January 1679; M636/34.

58 A. B. to Sir Ralph Verney, 19 March 1684; M636/38.

59 *Memoirs* II, 279.

60 *Ibid.*

61 *Ibid.*, 251.

62 *Ibid.*, 420.

63 *Ibid.*, 312.

64   Mun Verney to—, 5 September 1685; M636/40.

65   Mun Verney to Munsey Verney, 26 November 1684; M636/39.

66   *Ibid.*, 22 January 1685; M636/39.

67   *Ibid.*, 29 January 1685; M636/39.

68   Sir Ralph Verney to Jack Verney, 8 May 1684; M636/38.

69   *Memoirs* II, 312–13.

Chapter 21

1   Jack Verney, 'Directions to travel from Livorno towards England, through France', n.d. [1674]; M636/27.

2   Sir Andrew Balfour, *Letters Write to a Friend, Containing Excellent Directions and Advices for Traveling through France and Italy* (1700), 52.

3   Jack Verney, 'Directions to travel from Livorno'; M636/27.

4   William Bromley, *Remarks in the Grande Tour of France and Italy* (1692), 22.

5   Anthony Sutcliffe, *Paris: An Architectural History* (1993), 26.

6   Lady Anne Hobart to Sir Ralph Verney, 3 September 1666; M636/21.

7   William Denton to Sir Ralph Verney, September 1666; M636/21.

8   Thomas Vincent, *God's Terrible Voice in the City* (1667), 67.

9   'Theophilus Philalethes', *Great Britain's Glory, or a brief description of the present state, splendor, and magnificence of the Royal Exchange* (1672), 15.

10   Montague North to Dudley Foley, Cobbold MSS, Box 17; in Richard Grassby, The *English Gentleman in Trade: The Life and Works of Sir Dudley North, 1641–1691* (1994), 340.

11   Jack Verney to Sir Ralph Verney, August 1674; M636/27.

12   *Memoirs* II, 271.

13   *Ibid.*

14   Jack Verney to Sir Ralph Verney, 20 August 1674; M636/27.

15   *Ibid.*, 1679; M636/33.

16   Sir Ralph Verney to Jack Verney, 29 September 1679; M636/33.

17   *DNB.*

18   Jack Verney to Elizabeth Palmer, January 1680; M636/34.

19   Jack Verney to Sir Ralph Verney, 6 May 1680; M636/34.

20   Sir Ralph Verney to Jack Verney, 14 April 1680; M636/34.

21   By the beginning of 1680 Sir Ralph was receiving letters addressed to him at 'the Lady Hobart's house next door to ye Black balcony in Holbourne-row, in Lincoln's Inn Fields' (M636/34).

22   Jack Verney to Sir Ralph Verney, 26 April 1680; M636/34.

23   Nancy Nicholas to Sir Ralph Verney, 19 April 1680; M636/34.

24   Jack Verney to Sir Ralph Verney, 26 April 1680; M636/34.

25   Sir Ralph Verney to Jack Verney, 14 June 1680; M636/34.

26   *Ibid.*, 7 June 1680; M636/34.

27   *Memoirs* II, 237.

28   Jack Verney to Elizabeth Verney (*née* Palmer), 24 September 1681; M636/35.

29   Letter addressed from Jane Nicholas to Jack Verney, 11 April 1681; M636/35.

30   Sir Ralph Verney to Jack Verney, 2 May 1681; M636/33.

31   *Ibid.*, 31 March 1684; M636/38.

32   John Lewkenor, *Metellus his dialogues the first part, containing a relation of a journey to Tunbridge-Wells: also a description of the Wells and place* (1693), 47.

33   Elizabeth Verney (*née* Palmer) to Jack Verney, 28 June 1683; M636/37.

34   Jack Verney to Elizabeth Verney (*née* Palmer), 14 February 1685; M636/39.

35   Elizabeth Verney (*née* Palmer) to Jack Verney, 25 June 1683; M636/37.

36   Jack Verney to Elizabeth Verney (*née* Palmer), 24 September 181; M636/35.

37   Jeremy Taylor, *The Rule and Exercises of Holy Dying*, 2–3, 28.

Chapter 22

1   Richard Chandler (ed.), *History and Proceedings of the House of Commons* II: 1680–1695 (1742), 166.

2   *Ibid.*

3   *Memoirs* II, 384.

4   Sir Ralph Verney to Jack Verney, 29 March 1685; M636/39.

5   *Ibid.*, 5 April 1685; M636/39.

6   Mun Verney to Jack Verney, 6 April 1685; M636/39.

7   Sir Richard Temple to Sir Ralph Verney, 17 April 1685; M636/39.

8   *Ibid.*
9   Jack Verney to Sir Ralph Verney, 8 April 1685; M636/39.
10 *DNB.*
11 Sir Ralph Verney to Jack Verney, 2 March 1685; M636/39.
12 *Ibid.*, 9 April 1685; M636/39.
13 *Memoirs* II, 391.
14 *Ibid.*, 392.
15 *An Account of the Ceremonial at the Coronation of Their Most Excellent Majesties King James II and Queen Mary* (1685).
16 *Ibid.*
17 Sir Ralph Verney to Jack Verney, 29 March 1685; M636/39.
18 *Memoirs* II, 394.
19 Jack Verney to Sir Ralph Verney, 5 May 1685; M636/40.
20 Sir Ralph Verney to Jack Verney, 15 May 1685; M636/40.
21 *Ibid.*
22 *Journal of the House of Commons* 9, 18 June 1685.
23 *The Declaration of James Duke of Monmouth, & the noblemen, gentlemen & others, now in arms, for defence and vindication of the Protestant religion . . . (1685)*, 4.
24 Mun Verney to Sir Ralph Verney, 16 July 1685; M636/40.
25 *Memoirs* II, 330.
26 Mun Verney to Sir Ralph Verney, 7 December 1679; M636/33.
27 William Bray (ed.), *The Diary of John Evelyn* (1907), entry for 11 February 1685.
28 *DNB.*
29 J. S. Clarke (ed.), *The life of James II, collected out of memoirs writ of his own hand* (1816), II, 49.
30 Sir Ralph Verney to William Denton, 5 December 1687; M636/42.
31 *Memoirs* II, 456.
32 Sir Ralph Verney to William Denton, June 1688; M636/42.
33 *Memoirs* II, 419.
34 Mun Verney to Betty Phelps, 10 February 1686; M636/40.
35 *Ibid.*, 11 February 86; M636/40.
36 *Ibid.*
37 Mun Verney to Munsey Verney, 15 May 1686; M636/40.
38 *Ibid.*
39 *Ibid.*
40 Mun Verney to Munsey Verney, 21 June 1686; M636/40.

41 Munsey Verney to Mun Verney, 6 June 1686; M636/40.

42 Mun Verney to Munsey Verney, 6 July 1686; M636/40.

43 *Ibid.*, 27 May 1687; M636/41.

44 *Memoirs* II, 408.

45 Cary Gardiner to Sir Ralph Verney, 10 March 1685; M636/39.

46 Sir Ralph Verney to Cary Gardiner, 2 September 1688; M636/43.

47 Sir Ralph Verney to Jack Verney, 4 September 1688; M636/43.

48 Mun Verney to Jack Verney, 3 September 1688; M636/43.

49 Sir Ralph Verney to Jack Verney, 4 September 1688; M636/43.

50 Munsey Verney to Jack Verney, 15 September 1688; M636/43.

51 Cary Gardiner to Sir Ralph Verney, 6 September 1688; M636/43.

52 *Ibid.*, 5 December 1688; M636/43.

53 Bray, *Diary of John Evelyn*, entry for 2 December 1688.

54 Jack Verney to Sir Ralph Verney, 13 December 1688; M636/43.

55 Cary Gardiner to Sir Ralph Verney, 12 December 1688; M636/43.

56 *Journal of the House of Commons* 10, 28 January 1689.

57 Sir Ralph Verney to Jack Verney, 21 February 1690; M636/4.

58 Cary Gardiner to Sir Ralph Verney, 22 February 1690; M636/44.

59 Jack Verney to Sir Ralph Verney, 18 February 1690; M636/44.

Chapter 23

1 Jack Verney to Sir Ralph Verney, 10 December 1691; M636/45.

2 Jack Verney to Tom Verney, 24 August 1694; M636/47.

3 Jack Verney to Sir Ralph Verney, 10 July 1692; M636/46.

4 Ralph Palmer to Jack Verney, 9 April 1692; M636/45.

5 *Memoirs* II, 489.

6 Jack Verney to Sir Ralph Verney, 9 July 1692; M636/46.

7 Cary Gardiner to Sir Ralph Verney, February 1689; M636/43.

8 Sir Ralph Verney to Molly Verney, 9 March 1690; M636/44.

9 Molly Verney to Jack Verney, 16 June 1693; M636/46.

10 *Memoirs* II, 485.

11 Cary Gardiner to Sir Ralph Verney, 20 June 1693; M636/46.

12 Endorsement in Sir Ralph Verney's hand on Cary's letter to him of 20 June 1693; M636/46.

13 Molly Verney to Sir Ralph Verney, 19 July 1693; M636/46.
14 Cary Gardiner to Sir Ralph Verney, 20 June 1693; M636/46.
15 Richard Allestree, *The Ladies' Calling* (1673), 160.
16 N. H., *The Ladies Dictionary* (1694), 342.
17 Cary Stewkeley to Sir Ralph Verney, 10 February 1696; M636/48.
18 *Memoirs* II, 474.
19 Prob/11/427.
20 *Ibid.*
21 *Ibid.*
22 Jack Verney to Sir Ralph Verney, 3 August 1695; M636/48.
23 Sir Ralph Verney to Jack Verney, 5 August 1695; M636/48.
24 Nancy Nicholas to the Countess of Lindsey, August 1695; M636/48.
25 Allestree, *The Ladies' Calling*, 143.
26 N. H., *The Ladies' Dictionary*, 341.
27 John Batchiler, *The Virgins' Pattern* (1661), 8.
28 Jack Verney to William Coleman, 1 April 1685; M636/39.
29 Cary Stewkeley to Jack Verney, 11 August 1696; M636/49.
30 *Ibid.*
31 *Ibid.*
32 Elizabeth Lillie to Jack Verney, 6 September 1696; M636/49.
33 Peg Adams to Jack Verney, 10 September 1696; M636/49.
34 *Ibid.*, 6 September 1696; M636/49.
35 *Ibid.*, 10 September 96; M636/49.
36 Cary Stewkeley to Jack Verney, 13 September 1696; M636/49.
37 Sir Ralph Verney to Jack Verney, 20 September 1696; M636/49.
38 Peg Adams to Jack Verney, 25 September 1696; M636/49.
39 *Ibid.*
40 Sir Ralph Verney's will; prob/11/460.
41 Cary Gardiner to Jack Verney, 27 September 1696; M636/49.
42 *Memoirs* II, 501.
43 Jack Verney to William Coleman, 1 October 1696; M636/49.
44 *Ibid.*, 3 October 1696; M636/49.
45 *Memoirs* II, 501.
46 *Ibid.*, 473.
47 Carey Stewkeley to Jack Verney, 12 October 1696; M636/49.

Bibliography

Abbott, Wilbur Cortez (ed.), *The Writings and Speeches of Oliver Cromwell*, Clarendon Press, 4 vols (1988).

An Account of the Ceremonial at the Coronation of Their Most Excellent Majesties King James II and Queen Mary (1685).

Allestree, Richard, *The Gentlemans Calling* (1660).

Allestree, Richard, *The Ladies Calling* (1673).

Almond, Robert, *The English Horseman and Complete Farrier* (1673).

Ambrose, Gwilym, 'English Traders at Aleppo (1658–1756)', *Economic History Review* 3, 2 (October 1931), 246–67.

Andrews, Jonathan, 'A Respectable Mad-Doctor? Dr Richard Hale, F.R.S. (1670–1728)', *Notes and Records of the Royal Society of London* 44, 2 (July 1990), 169–204.

Angell, James B., 'The Turkish Capitulations', *The American Historical Review* 6, 2 (January 1901), 254–9.

Anon., *A Brief Discourse, declaring the Impiety and Unlawfulness of the new Covenant with the Scots* (1643).

Anon., *A Great Wonder in heaven shewing the late apparitions and prodigious noyses of war and battels seen on Edge-Hill neere Keinton in Northampton-shire* (1642).

Anon., *A Narrative of the Draining of the Great Level of the Fens* (1660).

Anon., *A New Journey to France* (1715).

Anon., *A Perfect Narrative of the Robbery and Murder Committed . . . upon the person of Mr. John Talbot* (1669).

Anon., *Letters from Ireland, relating the several great successes it hath pleased God to give unto the Parliament's Forces there, in the Taking of Drogheda, Trym, Dundalk, Carlingford, and the Nury* (1649).

Anon., *News from Newgate: or, a true Relation of the manner of taking seven persons, very notorious for Highway-men, in the Strand . . .* (1677).

Anon., *The Answer of the Burgesses and other Inhabitants of the Parish of Buckingham, to a late scandalous Pamphlet set forth by Sir Timber Temple* (1679).

Anon., *The Bloudy Persecution of the Protestants in Ireland, being The Contents of severall Letters brought by his Majesties Post from Ireland, November the 21, 1641* (1641).

Anon., *The Last True News from Ireland . . . Wherein is declared many great overthrowes and defeates given to the rebels, likewise the manner how a great castle called Carricke Mayne (within 6 myles of Dublin) was taken by the English* (1642).

Anon., *Two letters one from Dublin in Ireland, and the other from Liverpoole, of a bloody fight in Ireland, at the taking of Drogheda by the Lord Lieutenant Cromwell* (1649).

Anselment, Raymond A., '"The Teares of Nature": Seventeenth-Century Parental Bereavement', *Modern Philology* 91, 1 (August 1993), 26–53.

Aris, John, *The Reconciler, or, a sermon preached before a Communion . . . to which is added a charm for a slanderous tongue, briefly written in a letter to an obstinate offender that way* (1651).

Aston, John, 'Diary', in J. C. Hodgson (ed.), *Six North Country Diaries*, Surtees Society 118 (1910).

Attreed, Lorraine C., 'Preparation for Death in Sixteenth-Century Northern England', *Sixteenth Century Journal* 13, 3 (Autumn 1982), 37–66.

Aubrey, John, *Aubrey's Brief Lives*, ed. Oliver Lawson Dick, Mandarin (1992).

Bacon, Sir Francis, *Essayes and Counsels, Civil and Moral* (1664).

Bagwell, Richard, *Ireland Under the Stuarts*, Longmans, Green & Co., 3 vols (1909–16).

Baillie, Robert, *Letters and Journals: containing an impartial account of public transactions, civil, ecclesiastical, and military, in England and Scotland, from . . . 1637, to . . . 1662*, 2 vols (1775).

Balfour, Andrew, *Letters Write to a Friend, Containing Excellent Directions and Advices for Traveling through France and Italy* (1700).

Barlow, Frank, 'The King's Evil', *English Historical Review* 95, 374 (January 1980), 3–27.

Barriffe, William, *Military Discipline: or, the yong artillery man* (1635).

Batchiler, John, *The Virgins' Pattern* (1661).

Beattie, J. M., 'The Pattern of Crime in England 1660–1800', *Past and Present* 62 (February 1974), 47–95.

Bennett, Martyn, *The Civil Wars in Britain and Ireland 1638–1651*, Blackwell (1997).

Blith, Walter, *The English Improver Improved* (1653).

Bonney, Richard, *The Thirty Years' War 1618–48*, Osprey (2002).

Bourcier, Elisabeth (ed.), *The Diary of Sir Simonds D'Ewes, 1622–1624*, Didier (1974).

Bradford, William, *History of Plymouth Plantation, 1620–1647*, 2 vols (1912).

Bray, William (ed.), *The Diary of John Evelyn*, Dent (1907).

Broad, J., 'Gentry Finances and the Civil War: The Case of the Buckinghamshire Verneys', *Economic History Review*, 2nd Series, 32 (1979), 183–200.

Broad, J., 'The Verneys and the Sequestrators in the Civil Wars, 1642–1656', *Records of Buckinghamshire* 27 (1985), 1–9.

Broad, J., 'Whigs and Deer Stealers in Other Guises', *Past and Present* 119 (1988), 56–72.

Broad, J., 'The Verneys as Enclosing Landlords 1600–1800', in J. Chartres and D. Hey (eds), *English Rural Society 1500–1800* (Cambridge, 1990), 27–53.

Broad, J., *Transforming English Rural Society: The Verneys and the Claydons, 1600–1820*, Cambridge University Press (2004).

Bromley, William, *Remarks in the Grande Tour of France and Italy* (1692).

Brown, Alexander, *The Genesis of the United States*, 2 vols (1897).

Bruce, John (ed.), *Notes of Proceedings in the Long Parliament . . . Taken in the House by Sir Ralph Verney, Knight*, Camden Society, Series 1, 31 (1845).

Bruce, John (ed.), *The Letters and Papers of the Verney Family Down to the End of the Year 1639*, Camden Society, Series 1, 56 (1853).

Brunton, D., and Pennington, D. H., *Members of the Long Parliament*, Allen & Unwin (1954).

Bullock, William, *Virginia Impartially Examined* (1649).

Burges, Cornelius, *The fire of the sanctuarie newly uncovered, or, a compleat tract of zeale* (1625).

Burton, Robert, *The Anatomy of Melancholy*, ed. Holbrook Jackson, New York Review Books (2001).

Calendar of State Papers, Domestic Series, HMSO (1856–1972). *Camden Miscellany* 8, N.S., 31 (1883).

Carkesse, James, *Lucida Intervalla: containing divers miscellaneous poems, written at Finsbury and Bethlem by the doctor's patient extraordinary* (1679).

Carlton, Charles, *Going to the Wars: The Experience of the British Civil Wars 1638–1651*, Routledge (1992).

Carus-Wilson, E. M., 'The Aulnage Accounts: A Criticism', *Economic History Review* 2, 1 (January 1929), 114–23.

Chandler, Richard, *History and Proceedings of the House of Commons*, 13 vols (1742).

Charles I, *His Majesties declaration to all his loving subjects after his late victory against the rebels on Sunday the 23 of October together with a relation of the battell lately fought betweene Keynton and Edge-hill by His Majesties armie and that of the rebels* (1642).

Clarendon, Edward Hyde, Earl of, *The history of the rebellion and civil wars in England begun in the year 1641*, 6 vols (1888).

Clark, G. N., 'The Barbary Corsairs in the Seventeenth Century', *Cambridge Historical Journal* 8, 1 (1944), 22–35.

Clarke, J. S. (ed.), *The life of James II, collected out of memoirs writ of his own hand*, 2 vols (1816).

Claydon House Letters.

Clenche, John, *A Tour in France and Italy, made by an Englishman, 1675* (1676).

Clifton, Robin, 'The Popular Fear of Catholics during the English Revolution', *Past and Present* 52 (August 1971), 23–55.

Coates, Willson H., Young, Anne Steele, and Snow, Vernon F. (eds), *The Private Journals of the Long Parliament: 3 January to 5 March 1642*, Yale University Press (1982).

Colvin, H. M., *The History of the King's Works*, IV, HMSO (1982).

Cornwallis, Sir Charles, *A discourse of the most illustrious prince, Henry late Prince of Wales written Anno 1626* (1641).

Cosins, John, *A Collection of Private Devotions* (1635).

Cottington, R., *A True Historicall discourse of Muley Hamets rising to the three Kingdoms of Moruecos, Fes, and Sus* (1609).

Crashaw, William, *A sermon preached in London before the right honorable the Lord Lawarre, Lord Gouernour and Captaine Generall of Virginea, and others of his Maiesties Counsell for that kingdome, and the rest of the aduenturers in that plantation* (1610).

Culpepper, Nicholas, *Culpeper's astrologicall judgment of diseases* (1655).

D'Alton, John, *History of Drogheda*, Buvinda (1997).

Dallam, Thomas, 'The Diary of Master Thomas Dallam, 1599–1600', in J. Theodore Bent (ed.), *Early Voyages and Travels in the Levant*, Hakluyt Society, 1st Series, 87 (1893).

Dalton, Charles, *The Life and Times of General Sir Edward Cecil*, Sampson Low, Marston, Searle & Rivington, 2 vols (1885).

Davies, G., and Stuart, Bernard, 'The Battle of Edgehill', *English Historical Review* 36, 141 (January 1921), 30–44.

Davies, Godfrey, *The Early Stuarts, 1603–1660*, Oxford University Press (1952).

Davies, Margaret Gay, 'Country Gentry and Payments to London 1650–1714', *Economic History Review*, New Series, 24, 1 (February 1971), 15–36.

Day, Angel, *The English Secretary* (1599).

The Declaration of James Duke of Monmouth, & the noblemen, gentlemen & others, now in arms, for defence and vindication of the Protestant religion . . . (1685).

Denton, William, will of, PRO prob/11/405.

Devey, Joseph (ed.), *The Moral and Historical Works of Lord Bacon* (1852).

Diamond, Sigmund, 'From Organisation to Society: Virginia in the Seventeenth Century', *American Journal of Sociology* 63, 5 (March 1958), 457–75.

Donagan, Barbara, 'Codes and Conduct in the English Civil War', *Past and Present* 118 (February 1988), 65–95.

Drayton, Michael, *Poly-Olbion* (1612).

Dryden, John, *The Works of John Dryden*, University of California Press, 20 vols (1956–89).

Dumont, Jean, baron de Carlscroon, *A New Voyage to the Levant*, 4th edn (1705).

Durston, Christopher, 'The Fall of Cromwell's Major-Generals', *English Historical Review* 113, 450 (February 1998), 18–37.

Earle, John, *Micro-cosmographie, or, A peece of the world discovered in essayes and characters*, 2nd edn (1628).

Edmund Warcupp (trans.), Franciscus Schottus, *Italy, in its original glory, ruine and revival* (1660).

Ettinghausen, Henry, *Prince Charles and the King of Spain's Sister: What the Papers Said*, University of Southampton (1985).

'Eugenius Theodidactus' [John Heydon], *Advice to a Daughter* (1659).

Fermanagh, John Verney, Viscount, will of, PRO prob/11/558.

Ferrier, Richard, 'The Journal of Major Richard Ferrier M.P., while travelling in France in the year 1687', *Camden Miscellany*, N.S., 53, IX (1895).

Fiennes, Nathaniel, *A most true and exact relation of both the battels fought by His Excellency and his forces against the bloudy cavelliers the one on the 23 of October last, neer Keynton below Edge-Hill in Warwickshire, the other at Worcester* (1642).

Firth, C. H., 'Cromwell and the Insurrection of 1655', *English Historical Review* 4, 14 (April 1889), 313–38.

Firth, C. H. (ed.), *The Life of William Cavendish, Duke of Newcastle, to which is added the true relation of my birth breeding and life by Margaret, Duchess of Newcastle* (1890).

Firth, C. H., 'Memoirs of the Verney Family during the Civil War', *English Historical Review* 8, 31 (July 1893), 579–81.

Firth, C. H., 'Cromwell and the Crown', *English Historical Review* 18, 69 (January 1903), 52–80.

Firth, C. H., 'The Royalists under the Protectorate', *English Historical Review* 52, 208 (October 1937), 634–48.

Firth, C. H., *Cromwell's Army: A History of the English Soldier during the Civil Wars, the Commonwealth and the Protectorate*, 3rd edn, Greenhill Books (1992).

Fissel, Mark Charles, *The Bishops' Wars: Charles I's campaigns against Scotland, 1638–1640*, Cambridge University Press (1994).

Forester, H. (trans.), *Memoris of Princess Sophia, Electress of Hanover* (1888).

Fritz, Paul S., 'The Undertaking Trade in England: Its Origins and Early Development, 1660–1830', *Eighteenth-Century Studies* 28, 2 (Winter 1994–1995), 241–53.

Gape, Mary, will of, PRO prob/11/368.

Gape, William, will of, PRO prob/11/348.

Gardiner, S. R., *Prince Charles and the Spanish Marriage: 1617–1623*, 2 vols (1869).

Gardiner, S. R., *History of England from the Accession of James I to the Outbreak of the Civil War, 1603–1642*, Longmans, Green & Co., 10 vols (1895).

Gardiner, S. R. (ed.), *The Constitutional Documents of the Puritan Revolution 1625–1660*, Clarendon Press (1906).

Gataker, Thomas, *A good wife Gods gift and, a wife indeed – two marriage sermons* (1623).

Gilbert, John T. (ed.), *History of the Irish Confederation and the War in Ireland, 1641–1643*, M. H. Gill & Son, 7 vols (1882).

Glow, L., 'The Committee-Men in the Long Parliament, August 1642–December 1643', *Historical Journal* 8 (1965), 1–15.

Gosse, Philip, *The History of Piracy*, Burt Franklin (1968).

Gowing, Laura, 'Secret Births and Infanticide in Seventeenth-Century England', *Past and Present* 156 (August 1997), 87–115.

Gragg, Larry, 'A Vagabond in Paradise – Thomas Verney in Barbados', *History Today* 45, 8 (August 1995), 40–46.

Grassby, Richard, *The English Gentleman in Trade: The Life and Works of Sir Dudley North, 1641–1691*, Clarendon Press (1994).

Grassby, Richard, *The Business Community of Seventeenth-Century England*, Cambridge University Press (1995).

Graunt, John, *Natural and Political Observations . . . upon the Bill of Mortality* (1662).

Green, Mary Anne Everett (ed.), *Calendar of the Committee for Compounding, 1643–1660 General Proceedings*, HMSO (1889).

Greene, Douglas G., 'The Court of the Marshalsea in Late Tudor and Stuart England', *The American Journal of Legal History* 20, 4 (October 1976), 267–81.

Gurr, Ted Robert, 'Historical Trends in Violent Crime: A Critical Review of the Evidence', *Crime and Justice* 3 (1981), 295–353.

Halifax, George Savile, Marquis of, *The Lady's New-Year Gift, or Advice to a Daughter*, 2nd edn (1688).

Hals, Richard, will of, PRO prob/11/456.

Halsband, Robert (ed.), *The Complete Letters of Lady Mary Wortley Montagu*, Clarendon Press, 3 vols (1965–67).

Hamburger, Philip, 'The Development of the Law of Seditious Libel and the Control of the Press', *Stanford Law Review* 37, 3, Historical Perspectives on the Free Press (February 1985), 661–765.

Harvey, Gideon, *The Art of Curing Diseases by Expectation* (1689).

Hearne, Thomas, *Historia Vitae et Regni Richardi II* (1729).

Herrick, Robert, 'A Country-Life: To His Brother, Mr. Tho. Herrick', *The Poems of Robert Herrick*, ed. L. C. Martin, OUP (1965).

Herrup, Cynthia B., 'Law and Morality in Seventeenth-Century England', *Past and Present* 106 (February 1985), 102–23.

Heylyn, Peter, *A full relation of two journeys, the one into the main-land of France, the other into some of the adjacent ilands performed and digested into six books* (1656).

Hibbert, Christopher, *Charles I*, Weidenfeld & Nicolson (1968).

Hill, C. P., *Who's Who in Stuart Britain*, Shepheard-Walwyn (1988).

Hill, Christopher, 'The Correspondence of Bishop Brian Duppa and Sir Justinian Isham, 1650–1660', *English Historical Review* 70, 277 (October 1955), 668–9.

Hill, Thomas, *The Gardeners Labyrinth, or, a new art of gardning* (1651).

'Hillesden Account Book, 1661–67', *Records of Buckinghamshire* 11 (1919), 135–44, 186–98, 244–55.

Howell, James, *Instructions for Forreine Travell* (1642).

Hume, David, *The History of England from the Invasion of Julius Caesar to the Revolution in 1688*, 8 vols (1778).

Hunter, Richard, and Macalpine, Ida, *Three Hundred Years of Psychiatry, 1535–1860*, Oxford University Press (1970).

Hunting, P., 'The Survey of Hatton Garden in 1694 by Abraham Arlidge', *London Topographical Record* 25 (1985), 83–110.

J. A., *An Apology for a Younger Brother* (1641).

J. B., *The Merchants Avizo, or Instructions very necessary for their Sonnes and Servants, when they first send them beyond the Sea* (1640).

J. S., *The Illustrious History of Women* (1686).

[James I] *The Kings Maiesties Speach To the Lord and Commons* (1609).

Jocelin, Elizabeth, *The Mother's Legacy to her Unborn Child* (1624).

Jones, Henry, *A Perfect Relation of the Beginning and Continuation of the Irish-Rebellion* (1641 [1642]).

Jones, Inigo, and Davenant, William, *Britannia Triumphans* (1638).

Journal of the House of Commons, 1–10 (1802).

Kaplan, Lawrence, 'Presbyterians and Independents in 1643', *English Historical Review* 84, 331 (April 1969), 244–56.

Keeler, Mary Frear, *The Long Parliament, 1640–1641: A Biographical Study of its Members*, American Philosophical Society (1954).

Kenyon, J. P., 'The Commission for Ecclesiastical Causes 1686–1688: A Reconsideration', *Historical Journal* 34, 3 (September 1991), 727–36.

Larkin, James F., and Hughes, Paul L. (eds), *Stuart Royal Proclamations*, Clarendon Press, 2 vols (1973–83).

Lassels, Richard, *The Voyage of Italy* (1670).

Lawrence, Edward, *Parents' Groans over their Wicked Children* (1681).

Lewis, Judith, '"'Tis a Misfortune to Be a Great Ladie": Maternal Mortality in the British Aristocracy, 1558–1959', *Journal of British Studies* 37, 1 (January 1998), 26–53.

Lewkenor, John, *Metellus his dialogues the first part, containing a relation of a journey to Tunbridge-Wells: also a description of the Wells and place* (1693).

Lievsay, John L., *Venetian Phoenix: Paolo Sarpi and Some of his English Friends (1606–1700)*, University Press of Kansas, Lawrence (1973).

Lilburne, John, *The Jugglers Discovered, in Two Letters Writ by Lieut. Col. John Lilburne, prerogative prisoner in the Tower of London* (1647).

Lipscomb, G., *The History and Antiquities of the County of Buckingham*, 4 vols (1831–47).

Lipson, E., 'The Elections to the Exclusion Parliaments 1679–1681', *English Historical Review* 28, 109 (January 1913), 59–85.

Lithgow, William, *The Totall Discourse, of the Rare Adventures, and painefull Perigrinations of long nineteen Years Travayles* (1632).

Lloyd, David, *Memoires of the Lives, Actions, Sufferings & Deaths of those noble, reverend, and excellent personages, that suffered . . . for the Protestant Religion* (1668).

Loomie, Albert J. (ed.), *Ceremonies of Charles I: The Note Books of John Finet 1628–1641*, Fordham University Press (1987).

Lough, John, *France Observed in the Seventeenth-Century by British Travellers*, Oriel Press (1984).

Mackerness, E. D., 'Frances Parthenope, Lady Verney (1819–1890)', *Journal of Modern History* 30, 2 (June 1958), 131–6.

Magalotti, Count Lorenzo, *Travels of Cosmo III, Grand Duke of Tuscany* (1821).

Makin, Bathsua, *An Essay to Revive the Antient Education of Gentlewomen* (1673).

Markham, Gervase, *The Complete Jockey* (1695).

Markham, Gervase, *The English House-Wife* (1631).

Marston, Jerrilyn Greene, 'Gentry Honor and Royalism in Early Stuart England', *Journal of British Studies* 13, 1 (November 1973), 21–43.

Matar, N. I., 'The Renegade in English Seventeenth-Century Imagination', *Studies in English Literature, 1500–1900* 33, 3 – Restoration and Eighteenth Century (Summer 1993), 489–505.

Maundrell, H., *A Journal from Aleppo to Jerusalem 1697* (1732).

McClure, Norman E. (ed.), *The Letters of John Chamberlain*, 2 vols (1939).

McElroy, John William, 'Seafaring in Seventeenth-Century New England', *The New England Quarterly* 8, 3 (September 1935), 331–64.

Mendelson, Sara Heller, 'The Weightiest Business: Marriage in an Upper-Gentry Family in Seventeenth-Century England: A Rejoinder', *Past and Present* 85 (November 1979), 126–35.

Mercurius aulicus, communicating the intelligence and affaires of the court to the rest of the kingdome (1643–8).

Mercurius civicus, Londons intelligencer (1643–6).

Mercurius elencticus, Communicating the unparralell'd Proceedings of the Rebels at Westminster, and the Head quarters, discovering their Designes, reproving their Crimes, and advising the Kingdome (1647–51).

Mercurius politicus (1650–61).

Mercurius veridicus, or True informations, of speciall and remarkable passages, from both houses of Parliament, and severall counties of the kingdome (1644–6).

Michael, Emily, and Michael, Fred S., 'Corporeal Ideas in Seventeenth-Century Psychology', *Journal of the History of Ideas* 50, 1 (January–March 1989), 31–48.

Middleton, Thomas, *A Trick to Catch the Old One* (1608).

Mocket, Richard, *God and the King* (1616).

Morgan, Edmund S., 'The First American Boom: Virginia 1618 to 1630', *William and Mary Quarterly*, 3rd Series, 28, 2 (April 1971), 169–98.

Motley, M., 'Educating the English Gentleman Abroad: The Verney Family in Seventeenth-Century France and Holland', *History of Education* 23 (1994), 243–56.

Mundy, Peter, *The Travels of Peter Mundy in Europe and Asia, 1608–1667*: Vol. 1, *Travels in Europe, 1608–1628*, ed. Sir Richard Carnac Temple, Hakluyt Society, 2nd Series 17 (1907).

N. H., *The Ladies' Dictionary* (1694).

Nichols, John, *The Progresses, Processions, and Magnificent Festivities of King James I*, 4 vols (1828).

North, Dudley North, Baron, *Observations and Advices Oeconomical* (1669).

The office of Christian parents shewing how children are to be gouerned throughout all ages and times of their life (1616).

An Ordinance of the Lords and Commons assembled in Parliament; with instructions for the taking of the League and Covenant . . . (1644).

Osborne, Penelope [née Verney], will of, PRO prob/11/427.

Parry, Graham, *The Golden Age Restor'd: The Culture of the Stuart Court, 1603–42*, Manchester University Press (1981).

Pearl, Valerie, 'Oliver St. John and the "Middle Group" in the Long Parliament: August 1643–May 1644', *English Historical Review* 81, 320 (July 1966), 490–519.

A perfect diurnall of some passages in Parliament, and from other parts of this kingdome (1642–9).

A perfect diurnall of some passages of, and in relation to, the armies in England and Ireland (1649–55).

Petrie, Sir Charles (ed.), *The Letters, Speeches and Proclamations of King Charles I*, Cassell (1935).

Plat, Sir Hugh, *The Garden of Eden* (1652).

Playford, John, *A Vade Mecum, or, The Necessary Companion* (1680).

Plumb, J. H., 'The Elections to the Convention Parliament of 1689', *Cambridge Historical Journal* 5, 3 (1937), 235–54.

Pope, Walter, *The Memoires of Monsieur Du Vall* (1670).

Pricke, Robert (trans.), Pierre Le Muet, *The Art of Fair Building* (1670).

[Privy Council] *Whereas it hath pleased God to bless the endeavors of the forces of this Commonwealth, against the Irish rebels and their adherents, in the town of Drogheda which was taken in by storm . . .* (1649).

A Proclamation . . . prohibiting horse-races in England and Wales for eight months, 8 April 1658.

Prynne, William, *Histrio-Matrix* (1633).

Ranson, S., *The Verney Papers Catalogued for the Claydon House Trust* (1994).

Raymond, John, *An Itinerary containing a Voyage made through Italy* (1648).

Reilly, Tom, *Cromwell: An Honourable Enemy*, Phoenix Press (1999).

Roberts, Lewis, *The Marchants Mapp of Commerce* (1638).

Roberts, Lewis, *The Treasure of Traffic, or, A Discourse of Foreign Trade* (1641).

Robinson, Howard, *Britain's Post Office*, Oxford University Press (1953).

Roundell, Reverend Henry, 'Hillesden House in 1644', *Records of Buckinghamshire* II (1863), 93–8.

Royal Commission on Historical Manuscripts, 7th Report (1879).

Rushworth, John, *Historical Collections of Private Passages of State, Weighty Matters, in Law, Remarkable Proceedings in Five Parliaments*, 8 vols (1721).

Russell, Conrad, *The Fall of the British Monarchies 1637–1642*, Clarendon Press (1991).

Rycaut, P., *The Present State of the Ottoman Empire* (1670).

Sandys, George, *A relation of a journey begun An: Dom: 1610* (1615).

Sclater, William, *Papisto-Mastix, or, Deborah's Prayer Against God's Enemies.* (1642).

The Scotish Dove, sent out and returning (1643–6).

Scott, William, and Bliss, James, *The Works of the Most Reverend Father in God, William Laud*, 7 vols (1847–60).

Serjeantson, R. W., 'Nicholas Hill and Edmund Verney in 1606', *Notes and Queries* (June 2005), 224–7.

Shadwell, Thomas, *The Lancashire Witches* (1682).

Sharp, Jane, *The Midwives Book. Or the whole Art of Midwifery Discovered* (1671).

Sharpe, J. A., '"Last Dying Speeches": Religion, Ideology and Public Execution in Seventeenth-Century England', *Past and Present* 107 (May 1985), 144–67.

Slater, M., 'The Weightiest Business: Marriage in an Upper-Gentry Family in Seventeenth-Century England', *Past and Present* 72 (August 1976), 29–54.

Slater, M., 'The Weightiest Business: Marriage in an Upper-Gentry Family in

Seventeenth-Century England: A Rejoinder', *Past and Present* 85 (November 1979), 136–40.

Slater, M., *Family Life in the Seventeenth-Century: The Verneys of Claydon House* Routledge & Kegan Paul (1984).

Smith, Abbot Emerson, 'Indentured Servants: New Light of Some of America's "First" Families', *Journal of Economic History* 2, 1 (May 1942), 40–53.

Smith, Alexander, *History of the most Noted Highway-men, Foot-pads, House-Breakers, Shop-lifts and Cheats*, 2nd edn (1714).

Smith, John, *The General Historie of Virginia, New-England and the Summer Isles . . . from their first beginning An: 1584 to this present 1624* (1624).

Smith, John, *Advertisements for the unexperienced Planters of New-England* (1631).

Smith, Philip, 'Executing Executions: Aesthetics, Identify, and the Problematic Narratives of Capital Punishment Ritual', *Theory and Society* 25, 2 (April 1996), 235–61.

Smith, Stephen R., 'The London Apprentices as Seventeenth-Century Adolescents', *Past and Present* 61 (November 1973), 149–61.

Snow, Vernon F., and Young, Anne Steele (eds), *The Private Journals of the Long Parliament: 7 March to 1 June 1642*, Yale University Press (1987).

Snow, Vernon F., and Young, Anne Steele (eds), *The Private Journals of the Long Parliament: 2 June to 17 September 1642*, Yale University Press (1992).

Sorbière, Samuel, *A Voyage to England, Containing Many Things Relating to the State of Learning, Religion, and other Curiosities of that Kingdom* (1709).

Spalding, Ruth (ed.), *The Diary of Bulstrode Whitelocke 1605–1675*, Records of Social and Economic History, New Series, 13, British Academy (1990).

Sperling, J., 'The International Payments Mechanism in the Seventeenth and Eighteenth Centuries', *Economic History Review*, New Series, 14, 3 (1962), 446–68.

Staves, Susan, 'British Seduced Maidens', *Eighteenth-Century Studies* 14, 2 (Winter 1980–81), 109–34.

Stewkeley, John, will of, PRO prob/11/376.

Stone, L., 'The Verney Tomb at Middle Claydon', *Records of Buckinghamshire* 16 (1955–6), 66–82.

Stoye, John, *English Travellers Abroad, 1604–1667*, Jonathan Cape (1952).

Strong, Roy, *Henry Prince of Wales and England's Lost Renaissance*, Thames & Hudson (1986).

Sutcliffe, Anthony, *Paris: An Architectural History*, Yale University Press (1993).

Tabbaa, Yasser, 'Circles of Power: Palace, Citadel and City in Ayyubid Aleppo', *Ars Orientalis* 23 (1993), 181–200.

Taylor, Jeremy, *The rule and exercises of holy living. In which are described the means and instruments of obtaining every vertue, and the remedies against every vice, and considerations serving to the resisting all temptations* (1650).

Taylor, Jeremy, *The rule and exercises of holy dying in which are described the means and instruments of preparing our selves and others respectively for a blessed death* (1670).

Teonge, Henry, *The Diary of Henry Teonge, Chaplain on Board H. M.'s Ships Assistance, Bristol and Royal Oak*, ed. G. E. Manwaring, Routledge (1927).

'Theophilus Philalethes', *Great Britain's Glory, or a brief description of the present state, splendor, and magnificence of the Royal Exchange* (1672).

Thirsk, Joan, 'Younger Sons in the Seventeenth-Century', *History* 54 (1969), 358–77.

Thorp, Jennifer, 'Dance in Late 17th-Century London: Priestly Muddles', *Early Music* 26, 2 (May 1998), 198–210.

Trosse, George, *The life of the Reverend Mr Geo. Trosse, late minister of the gospel in the city of Exon . . .* (1714).

A true and exact Relation of the Manner of his Majesties setting up his Standard at Nottingham, on Monday the 22. of Aug. 1642; in Larkin, James F., and Hughes, Paul L. (eds), *Stuart Royal Proclamations*, II, Clarendon Press (1983).

Tyacke, Nicholas (ed.), *The History of the University of Oxford*, IV: *Seventeenth-Century Oxford*, Clarendon Press (1997).

Verney, Sir Edmund (d. 1642), will of, PRO prob/11/190.

Verney, Frances Parthenope, and Margaret M., *Memoris of the Verney Family during the Seventeenth Century*, 2nd edn, Longmans, Green & Co., 2 vols (1904).

Verney, Henry, will of, PRO prob/11/337.

Verney, Lady Margaret, will of, PRO prob/11/190.

Verney, Peter, *The Standard Bearer: The Story of Sir Edmund Verney, Knight-Marshal to King Charles I*, Hutchinson (1963).

Verney, Sir Ralph, will of, PRO prob/11/460.

Vicars, John, *A looking-glasse for malignants* (1643).

Vickers, Penelope [*née* Stewkeley], will of, PRO prob/11/706.

Vickers, William, will of, PRO prob/11/433.

Vincent, Thomas, *God's Terrible Voice in the City* (1667).

Vitkus, Daniel J. (ed.), *Piracy, Slavery, and Redemption: Barbary Captive Narratives from Early Modern England*, Columbia University Press (2001).

Wadsworth, James (trans.), *Chocolate: or, An Indian Drinke. By the wise and moderate use whereof, health is preserved, sickness diverted, and cured* (1652).

Webbe, Edward, *The rare and most wonderfull things which Edw. Webbe an Englishman borne, hath seene and passed in his troublesome travailes* (1590). *The weekly account* (1643–50).

Weinreb, Ben, and Hibbert, Christopher (eds), *The London Encyclopaedia*, Macmillan (1995).

Westrup, J. A., 'Domestic Music under the Stuarts', *Proceedings of the Musical Association*, 68th Session (1941–2), 19–53.

Wheeler, James Scott, *The Irish and British Wars 1637–1654*, Routledge (2002).

Whyman, Susan E., *Sociability and Power in Late-Stuart England: The Cultural Worlds of the Verneys 1660–1720*, Oxford University Press (1999).

Wilkinson, Robert, [*The*] *merchant royall a sermon preached at White-Hall before the Kings Maiestie, at the nuptialls of the right Honorable the Lord Hay, and his Ladie, vpon the twelfe [sic] day last, being Ianuar. 6. 1607* (1613).

Willis, John, *The Art of Stenography* (1602).

Willis, Thomas, *Dr Willis's practice of physick* (1684).

Wilson, Arthur, *The history of Great Britain being the life and reign of King James the First* (1653).

Winstanley, Gerrard, *A Declaration from the Poor oppressed People of England* (1649).

Wiseman, Robert, *The Law of Laws: or, the Excellency of the Civil Law* (1656).

Wood, A. C., *A History of the Levant Company*, Oxford University Press (1935).

Wood, William, *Considerations upon the Treaty of Marriage between England and Spain* (1623).

Woodhead, J., *The Rulers of London 1660–1689*, London & Middlesex Archaeological Society (1965).

Wright, Herbert G., 'Boccaccio and English Highwaymen', *The Review of English Studies*, New Series, 1, 1 (January 1950), 17–22.

Young, Peter, *Edgehill 1642: The Campaign and the Battle*, Roundwood Press (1967).

Index